Soviet Union *Kiev* **1975**   895½ feet

U.S. *Tarawa* **(LHA 1) 1976**   820 feet

Britain *Invincible* **1980**   677¾ feet

U.S. *Wasp* **(LHD 1) 1989**   844 feet

Soviet Union *Admiral Flota Sovetskogo Soyuza Kuznetsov* **1991**   894½ feet

France *Charles de Gaulle* **2001**   825 feet

AIRCRAFT CARRIERS

AIRCRAFT CARRIERS

A HISTORY OF CARRIER AVIATION AND ITS INFLUENCE ON WORLD EVENTS

VOLUME II 1946–2006

NORMAN POLMAR

In collaboration with

GENERAL MINORU GENDA
Japanese Air Self-Defense Force
(formerly Captain, Imperial Japanese Navy)

CAPTAIN ERIC M. BROWN
CBE, DSC, AFC, Royal Navy

PROFESSOR ROBERT M. LANGDON
U.S. Naval Academy

COMMANDER PETER B. MERSKY
U.S. Naval Reserve

Silhouette drawings by James M. Caiella

POTOMAC BOOKS, INC.
WASHINGTON, D.C.

Library of Congress Cataloging-in-Publication Data

Polmar, Norman.
Aircraft carriers : a history of carrier aviation and its influence on
world events / Norman Polmar in collaboration with Minoru Genda
... [et al.]. — 2nd ed.
v. cm.
Rev. ed. of: Aircraft carriers : a graphic history of carrier aviation
and its influence on world events. c1969.
Includes bibliographical references and index.
Contents: v. 2. 1946-2006.
ISBN 1-57488-665-8 (hardcover : v. 2 : alk. paper) — ISBN
1-57488-665-8 (pbk. : v. 2 : alk. paper)
1. Aircraft carriers—History. 1. Genda, Minoru 1904-1989. II. Title.
V874.P65 2006
359.9'435—dc22
2005015230

Printed in the United States of America on acid-free paper that meets the American National Standards Institute Z39-48 Standard.

Potomac Books, Inc.
22841 Quicksilver Drive
Dulles, Virginia 20166

Second Edition

10 9 8 7 6 5 4 3 2 1

Frontispiece:
The Cold War era was a period of intensive carrier operations in the overall confrontation between the Soviet Union and the navies of the Western Alliance, and also in numerous small conflicts and confrontations. For much of the era World War II–built *Essex*-class carriers, some extensively modified like the *Shangri-La* (CVA 38), shown here in 1961, formed the backbone of U.S. carrier forces. A4D Skyhawks fly over the ship; on her deck are additional Skyhawks, AD Skyraiders, and F4D Skyrays. (U.S. Navy)

Dedicated to

Shizuo Fukui
Henri Le Mason
Donald Macintyre
A. D. Baker, III

Naval historians, authors, and gentlemen,
who took time from their own important works
to help with this project.

The man who ventures to write contemporary history must expect to be criticized both for everything he has said and everything he has not said.

— Voltaire in a letter to M. Bertin de Rocheret

Volume I Contents

CONTENTS

PERSPECTIVE

It is often recounted that at least since the early 1970s, as world crises arose, in the White House situation room the question would invariably be asked, "Where are the carriers?"

Since the end of World War II, beginning with the American efforts to deter Soviet moves—political and potentially military—into Greece and Turkey, the United States deployed naval forces to most crisis areas. These moves almost always included one or more aircraft carriers. Further, when the 45-year political-military confrontation between the Soviet Union and United States known as the Cold War reached open conflict in part or fully between surrogates, U.S. responses usually involved aircraft carriers, especially in the early stages of the Korean and Vietnam conflicts. But aircraft carriers were also invaluable in non–Cold War crises and conflicts, such as the Anglo-French invasion of Egypt in 1956, the cuban Missile Crises of 1962, British enforcement of the blockade of Rhodesia in 1965–1966, the U.S. air strikes against Libya in 1986, and the landing of U.S. peacekeeping troops in Haiti in 1994.

When, in reaction to attacks by Muslim terrorists on the United States on September 11, 2001, the United States initiated combat operations in Afghanistan in 2001 and Iraq in 2003, aircraft carriers were of particular importance. There were no airfields available to the United States within tactical aircraft range of Afghanistan. Thus, aircraft carriers operating in the Arabian Sea, with their aircraft overflying Pakistan, were the only means of providing tactical air support to U.S. ground forces. The large carrier *Kitty Hawk* was employed in the Arabian Sea as a floating base for Army–Air Force special operations troops and helicopters.

Similarly, the invasion of Iraq in March 2003 saw severe limitations imposed on the American use of airfields in Saudi Arabia (in sharp contrast to the situation in 1991). Thus, carriers were again vital to providing effective close air support for U.S. troops. British and French aircraft carriers also participated in the Persian Gulf operations.

The Soviet Union also recognized the value of aircraft carriers in the Cold War era. Despite leading the West in such naval categories as anti-ship missiles launched from aircraft, surface ships, and submarines, the Soviet Navy initiated an innovative and large carrier construction effort in the late 1950s. This effort produced a series of aviation ships, cumulating in the start of the nuclear-propelled carrier *Ul'yanovsk*; however, that ship was stillborn following the demise of the Soviet Union in December 1991.

Forced to severely reduce its military forces, the new Russia Federation gave up all carriers except for one large ship, the *Admiral Kuznetsov*. But in the post–Cold War era Great Britain is constructing two large conventional carriers (i.e., operated hook/arresting gear aircraft) that will be the largest warships ever constructed in British shipyards. France and India are also acquiring relatively large aircraft carriers. Smaller carriers are operated by several navies: Brazil, Italy, Spain, and Thailand. The carrier issue continues to be examined by China and Japan. The latter is now constructing "air capable" missile destroyers with a significant aviation capability.

In the United States the construction of two types of aircraft carriers continues: First and foremost are large and extremely expensive nuclear-propelled, large deck carriers (CVN). These ships are produced every few years to a basic design that dates to the late-1940s, i.e., to the first super carrier, the *United States*. There are significant improvements to the design, but the latest, the *Gerald R. Ford*, will carry the same number of aircraft, stow the same amount of weapons, and travel at the same speed as previous *Nimitz*-class carriers despite a huge increase in cost. The second carrier type is the "amphibious assault ship" (LHA/LHD), a ship of almost 50,000 tons full load, that operates Vertical/Short Takeoff and Landing (VSTOL) aircraft as well as helicopters. While considered primarily as "L"-type or amphibious ships, the LHA/LHDs have demonstrated considerable versatility. In addition to the amphibious assault role, these ships perform as platforms for mine countermeasure helicopters and for fighter-attack aircraft—today the AV-8B Harrier and in the future Joint Strike Fighter (JSF) or F-35 Lightning.

Indeed, as discussed in Chapter 26, the efficacy of the large deck, nuclear-propelled carrier should be objectively evaluated, not in terms of vulnerability as so often cited by critics, but in terms of efficiency and relative cost. For example, such traditional carrier roles as reconnaissance, anti-submarine warfare, and strike can now be carried out by other naval ships, usually more efficiently and with larger numbers of ships available than possible with the 11 large-deck carriers the U.S. Navy operated when this volume was published.

Thus, while certain carrier issues are debated, new carriers are being constructed and several nations continue to consider carriers vital for providing political-military responses in periods of crisis or conflict. For the foreseeable future, when a crisis erupts, national leaders will ask, "Where are the carriers?"

The first volume of *Aircraft Carriers* describes the development and operations of the world's aircraft carriers from 1909 through September 1945—the end of World War II. This second volume addresses carrier development and operations from 1946 into the early years of the 21st Century.

The term Fleet Air Arm (FAA) is used throughout this volume for British naval aviation. The original FAA was formed in 1924 and was under the Royal Air Force for administration and funding and under Navy control for shipboard operations. The FAA was fully transferred to the Navy in May 1939. The Fleet Air Arm was renamed Naval Aviation in September 1946 but reverted to FAA in May 1953.

Unless otherwise indicated, warship displacements are given in standard tonnage (i.e., ship fully manned and equipped, ready for sea, including all provisions, munitions, and aircraft, but without fuels). U.S. Navy ship displacements are given in long tons, i.e., 2,240 pounds; all other navies use metric tons (*tonnes*), i.e., 1,000 kilograms or 2,204 pounds.

Appendix C of this volume provides the characteristics of aircraft carriers completed from 1917 through 2006.

Aircraft capacities for carriers are the normal maximum number embarked.

Miles are nautical miles (i.e., 1.15 statute miles) unless otherwise indicated, except for aircraft ranges, which are in statute miles (with speed given in miles per hour).

The speed of high-performance aircraft is generally given in terms of a Mach number, related to the speed of sound, which varies with altitude. The speed of sound (Mach 1) is 762 m.p.h. at sea level, 735 m.p.h. at 10,000 feet, 707 m.p.h. at 20,000 feet, 678 m.p.h. at 30,000 feet, and 662 m.p.h. at 40,000 feet. The term Mach is derived from Ernst Mach, an Austrian physicist (1838–1916). Unless otherwise indicated, aircraft maximum speeds are "clean," meaning, without external weapons or fuel tanks.

Acknowledgments

In addition to the comprehensive list of persons, groups, and institutions who assisted in the research, writing, and publishing of this book found in Volume I, the authors would like to thank:

Capt. 1/Rank Sergey Antonov, Assistant Naval Attaché, Russian Embassy, Washington, D.C.

A. D. (Dave) Baker III, naval analyst and writer

James M. Caiella, assistant editor of the Naval Institute *Proceedings* and *Naval History* magazines

John W. Fozard, chief designer of the Harrier aircraft

Wolfgang Legien, Editor-in-Chief of *Naval Forces* magazine

Frank Matthews, son of Secretary of the Navy Francis P. Matthews

James Mulquin, Project Arapaho program manager, Naval Air Systems Command

Dr. William A. Neal, a flight surgeon in the carrier *Constellation* in 1967–1969

Lt. Col. Uri Yarom, Israel Air Force, a pioneer helicopter pilot

Also, Sam Dorrance, Wendy Garner, and Claire Noble of the marketing staff of Potomac Books.

This volume was brought to fruition through the efforts of Michie Shaw and Maryam Rostamian of the production staff of Potomac Books, as well as Richard B. Russell, who is now Director of the Naval Institute Press.

GLOSSARY

Note: The complete list of U.S. Navy ship designations
for aircraft carriers is provided as Appendix B in this volume.

AEW	Airborne Early Warning
AKV	cargo ship—aircraft ferry
AN/	prefix for U.S. electronic equipment (originally Army-Navy)
ASW	Anti-Submarine Warfare
AVT	(1) auxiliary aircraft transport
	(2) auxiliary aircraft landing training ship
bogey	unidentified aircraft
BuAer	Bureau of Aeronautics (U.S. Navy; July 1921 to December 1959)
cal	caliber (1) the diameter of a gun's bore; U.S. naval guns with a diameter of less than one inch (25.4 mm) are measured in "calibers"—fractions of an inch, as .50 calibers—or millimeters (mm)
	(2) the nominal length of the gun's bore expressed in multiples of its bore; thus, a 5-inch/ 38-cal gun has a bore or inner barrel length of 190 inches or approximately $15^7/_8$ feet.
CAP	Combat Air Patrol
CinC	Commander-in-Chief
CNO	Chief of Naval Operations
COD	Carrier On-board Delivery
CV	aircraft carrier
CVA	attack aircraft carrier
CVB	large ("battle") aircraft carrier
CVG	carrier air group
CVE	escort aircraft carrier
CVHG helicopter/ VSTOL	aircraft carrier (with missile armament)
CVL	small ("light") aircraft carrier
CVT	training aircraft carrier
CVW	carrier air wing
deck park	area of flight deck used to park and service aircraft
DMZ	Demilitarized Zone (Vietnam)
ECM	Electronic Countermeasures
ELINT	Electronic Intelligence
FAA	Fleet Air Arm (British; from April 1924)
HMAS	His/Her Majesty's Australian Ship
HMCS	His/Her Majesty's Canadian Ship
HMS	His/Her Majesty's Ship
h.p.	horsepower

JATO	Jet Assisted Takeoff (*rocket* booster)
JCS	Joint Chiefs of Staff (U.S.)
jeep	escort aircraft carrier (U.S. slang)
LAMPS	Light Airborne Multipurpose System (helicopter)
LHA	amphibious assault ship (general purpose)
LHD	amphibious assault ship (multipurpose)
LPH	amphibious assault ship
LST	tank landing ship
MCM	Mine Countermeasures
Mk	Mark (designation)
mm	millimeter
Mod	Modification (designation)
m.p.h.	miles per hour
MSTS	Military Sea Transportation Service (U.S. Navy, 1949–1970)
NASA	National Aeronautics and Space Administration
NATO	North Atlantic Treaty Organization
NHC	Naval Historical Center (U.S.)
n.mile	nautical mile (1.15 statute miles)
PRO	Public Record Office; now British National Archives
radar	*originally* Radio Detecting And Ranging
RAF	Royal Air Force (British; from April 1, 1918)
RCN	Royal Canadian Navy
RIO	Radar Intercept Officer
RN	Royal Navy
SAM	Surface-to-Air Missile
SCS	Sea Control Ship
SIOP	Single Integrated Operational Plan
sonar	*originally* Sound Navigation And Ranging
STOL	Short Takeoff/Landing
STOVL*	Short Takeoff/Vertical Landing
TF	Task Force
TG	Task Group
TU	Task Unit
USN	U.S. Navy
USS	U.S. Ship
VSS	VSTOL Support Ship
VSTOL*	Vertical/Short Takeoff and Landing

* The U.S. Marine Corps used the term VSTOL for the Harrier until early 1995, when the less accurate term STOVL was adopted by Headquarters, Marine Corp. The term VSTOL is used throughout this volume.

1 THE "PEACEFUL" YEARS

Aircraft carriers became an importance influence on the political and military situations in the Mediterranean beginning in 1946. Here the *Midway* steams through a gale east of Sicily. On her flight deck are F4U Corsairs, SB2C Helldivers, and a few special-mission F6F Hellcats. From 1945 to 1955 the *Midway*-class ships were the world's largest carriers. (U.S. Navy)

As the jubilation over the defeat of Germany and Japan subsided, Allied military and naval planners undertook the task of establishing a peacetime military force. The aircraft carrier had proved to be the back-bone of Allied naval power, but no nation—victor or vanquished—possessed a fleet that could challenge U.S. naval might. Further, U.S. possession (and monopoly) of the atomic bomb could be used as a threat to deter other nations from initiating hostilities. And,

the atomic bomb—if and when it was developed by other nations—might be able to destroy an entire carrier task group at a single blow; with an atomic bomb a single plane could deliver the striking power of 20,000 carrier planes or 2,000 B-29s.

Thus, the end of World War II was simultaneously a triumph and potentially the darkest hour for carrier aviation. Indeed, the entire future of navies and naval aviation seemed to be at stake. To many observers, the

1

long-range bomber and the atomic bomb signified the weapons of the future. Even the long-range bomber might soon be replaced by unmanned flying bombs and ballistic missiles—successors to German V-1 and V-2 weapons. Such striking power might alleviate the need for both armies and navies.

Attacks against aircraft carriers began in the United States on November 9, 1945, when Lieutenant General James H. (Jimmy) Doolittle, probably America's best known and most revered airman of the war, told a congressional committee, "Aircraft carriers are going into obsolescence having reached their peak usefulness. Carriers have two attributes: they can move around, and they can be sunk." Doolittle felt that it was necessary for him to rebut statements being made by Admirals Chester W. Nimitz and Marc A. Mitscher about the crucial role of aircraft carriers in winning the Pacific War.[1]

During the next few years the debates over the aircraft carrier in the United States centered on four issues:[2]

1. The internal debate in the Navy from 1945 to 1948 about the future role of the carrier.
2. Problems connected with the unification of the armed forces and the position of the Navy and Air Force in national defense, in the period 1945–1951. These problems concerned the larger question of the armed services' roles and missions, focusing primarily on the possession and use of atomic weapons on one hand and the future of naval aviation on the other.
3. The battle over the role and nature of strategic bombing in future war, which came to a head with the B-36 investigation and the 1949 unification and strategy hearings in Congress. This controversy was sparked by the cancellation of the aircraft carrier *United States* (CVA 58) in April of that year, but its ramifications extended far beyond the carrier-versus-bomber argument.
4. A technological campaign waged by a small group of dedicated naval officers who perfected the means by which nuclear weapons could be fitted to a reasonably effective carrier-based delivery aircraft.

The U.S. and British Navies had long contemplated the postwar political-military environment. Officers in both navies sought to correlate the apparent panacea of nuclear striking power with the lessons of World War II. Among the issues was the fact that U.S. and Japanese carrier-based aircraft *always* defeated land-based aircraft; the outcome was in doubt only when carriers were on both sides of the battle. Even the British carriers, with initially inferior types and numbers of aircraft, continually sailed the Mediterranean Sea and the coastal waters of Europe with relative immunity. Only one of the 25 large/fast carriers lost in World War II, the U.S. *Princeton* (CVL 23), was sunk by land-based aircraft; three of 13 escort carriers sunk during the war were victims of land-based kamikazes. However, many carriers had been severely damaged by conventional air attacks, kamikazes, and submarine-launched torpedoes (see Volume I, pages 529–530).

The success of carrier aviation against land-based aviation was achieved in large part by the carriers' great mobility and versatility, which allowed for surprise and concentration of force that were not possible with land-based aviation. The future role of carrier aviation, and, indeed, of the U.S. Navy, was defined by Fleet Admiral Ernest J. King when, on May 7, 1946, he told a congressional committee that the Navy's functions and capabilities were not restricted to dealing with seaborne objectives and keeping open the overseas supply routes. According to King, the Navy's mission was to deal with "land objectives that can be reached from the sea."

The U.S. Navy began planning a postwar fleet in 1943—at a time when the war was expected to last until perhaps 1947–1948. Over the next few years the Navy staff continuously planned for the future; table 1-1 shows the evolution of the Navy's plans for an active postwar fleet. There was almost a continual decline in total warship, including fast carriers, numbers in successive iterations of the planning, although the number of escort carriers remained relatively constant over the period, a tribute to their versatility.

The immediate postwar cutbacks of the U.S. Fleet were severe. On VJ-day the Navy had some 1,500 combatant ships—carriers, battleships, cruisers, destroyers, destroyer escorts, and submarines—in service. Two years later there were about 270 combatant ships in the active fleet. The reductions were even more severe in the mine, patrol, amphibious, and auxiliary forces. The U.S. Navy had 97 aircraft carriers of all types in commission on VJ-day:

1	CV 3	*Saratoga*
1	CV 4	*Ranger*

1	CV 6	*Enterprise*
17	CV 9	*Essex* class
8	CVL 22	*Independence* class
9	CVE 9	*Bogue* class
4	CVE 26	*Sangamon* class
1	CVE 31	*Prince William*
45	CVE 55	*Casablanca* class
10	CVE 105	*Commencement Bay* class

In addition, there was the pioneer escort carrier *Long Island* (CVE 1), which had been employed as an aircraft transport since August 1942; she had been fully modified for that role in early 1944.

With Japan's capitulation in August 1945, two unfinished *Essex*-class ships and 16 escort carriers were cancelled that month: The 27,100-ton carriers *Reprisal* (CV 35) and *Iwo Jima* (CV 46) had been laid down but not yet launched. The 12,000-ton escort carriers had not been laid down, and only four had been assigned names—the *Bastogne* (CVE 124), *Eniwetok* (CVE 125), *Lingayen* (CVE 126), and *Okinawa* (CVE 127). Even with these last-minute cancellations there were 21 aircraft carriers of four categories on the building ways or fitting out: three large *Midway* CVBs, seven *Essex* CVs, two *Wright* CVLs, and nine *Commencement Bay* CVEs. Work continued on all of these ships except for the *Oriskany* (CV 34); her construction was halted on August 29, 1946, when the ship was 85 percent complete.

Atomic Bomb Targets

With a small active fleet planned for the post-war era the Navy purged 17 tired flattops. The first to go were the venerable *Saratoga* and the light carrier *Independence*. The "Sara" had served in the fleet for 19 years; from her completion in 1927 through August 15, 1945, she recorded 89,195 aircraft landings on her deck. Japanese bombs, torpedoes, and suicide planes had scarred her from stem to stern. The smaller *Independence*, like the "Sara" completed on a cruiser hull, was just 2½ years old but had fought almost continually during the period and had taken a Japanese torpedo during the Tarawa assault. The two ships would now be subjected to the most powerful weapon yet devised by man—the atom bomb.

As early as 1944 the senior officials of the Manhattan Project, which had developed the atomic bombs, had considered the possibility of "testing" an atomic bomb against the Japanese Fleet at Truk during the war. In July 1945 General of the Army Henry H. Arnold, the head of the U.S. Army Air Forces, proposed that the effects of an atomic bomb on a harbor be investigated. A month later the Navy's senior expert on nuclear energy, Rear Admiral Lewis Strauss, proposed that nuclear weapons be tested against surplus warships.

The Navy wanted to know how atomic blasts would affect ships. What of the effects of an air blast in comparison to an underwater blast? How would radiation endanger personnel aboard ship? Could existing ships be modified to survive nuclear attack? Could a single nuclear weapon destroy a task group? A task force? To

---

Table 1-1
PLANNED ACTIVE SHIPS IN THE U.S. POSTWAR FLEET[*]

SHIP TYPE	NOV 1943	MAY 1944	OCT 1945	MAR 1946
Fast carriers	27	21	31	12
Escort carriers	10	22	10	10
Battleships	15	9	5	4
Cruisers	54	42	31	29
Destroyers	162	151	135	126
Destroyer escorts	100	100	36	30
Submarines	150	150	70	80

[*] Adapted from Vincent Davis, *Postwar Defense Policy and the U.S. Navy, 1943–1946* (Chapel Hill, N.C.: University of North Carolina Press, 1962), p. 202.

answer these and many other questions, the use of an atomic bomb against ships was authorized late in 1945, the tests to take place the following May at Bikini atoll in the Marshalls.

Joint Task Force 1 was established to conduct the tests and Vice Admiral William H. P. Blandy was named to command the multiservice experiment that would require the services of more than 200 ships, 42,000 men, and 150 aircraft. Blandy's orders from the Joint Chiefs of Staff stated,

> The general requirements of the test will be to determine the effects of atomic explosives against ships selected to give good representation of construction of modern naval and merchant vessels suitably disposed to give a good gradation of damage from maximum to minimum. . . . Tests should be so arranged as to take advantage of opportunities to obtain the effects of atomic explosives against ground and air targets and to acquire scientific data of general value if this is practicable.[3]

Three atomic detonations were scheduled: "Able" was to be an air burst over ship-filled Bikini lagoon, "Baker" a shallow underwater explosion, and "Charlie" a deepwater shot. The overall project was known as Operation Crossroads. According to Admiral Blandy, "In the face of this new knowledge, these recently discovered truths concerning the atom, so suddenly thrust upon an already chaotic world, not only warfare but civilization itself literally stands at the Crossroads."[4]

The carriers *Saratoga* and *Independence* were among 60 ships and half again as many landing craft that would be used as targets in the tests.[5] While Joint Task Force 1 made ready, the tests were postponed six weeks from May 15, 1946, to July 1, 1946, to allow members of Congress to conclude Washington business and personally observe the Bikini blasts.

At 9:00 A.M. on July 1 a 20-kiloton, Fat Man (plutonium) bomb was released by a B-29 flying more than five miles above the Bikini lagoon. In this first test the *Independence* was placed about one-half mile from the drop point and the *Saratoga* about four miles. The atomic explosion wrecked the *Independence*'s flight deck, ripped away the corner nearest the blast, demolished the carrier's mast and funnels, and ignited fires that gutted the ship. She burned throughout the day and

night but remained afloat without any corrective measures being taken. The light carrier was the most severely damaged ship to remain afloat (a Japanese light cruiser and two U.S. destroyers and two transports were sunk in test Able). The *Saratoga* suffered only superficial damage.[6]

For test Baker another Fat Man bomb was suspended 90 feet beneath an LSM landing ship moored in the lagoon. At 8:35 on the morning of July 25 the bomb was detonated, sending a spectacular column of water 6,000 feet into the air. Then a wall of spray and steam rushed out from the base of the column to envelop the target ships. When the spray and steam dissipated there was no question that the gallant *Saratoga* was dying. She had been moored only 500 feet from the landing ship under which the bomb had been suspended. (For this test the *Independence* had been towed away from the target area.)

The *Saratoga*'s distinctive funnel had collapsed across her flight deck; all tied-down aircraft and equipment on her deck had been swept away; the ship listed heavily to starboard. Tugs were directed to secure lines to her and to beach her if possible. This effort was halted because the carrier and the water around her were too radioactive to permit safe approach. Slowly the "Sara" sank, disappearing beneath the surface of the lagoon 7½ hours after the explosion.[7] The Japanese battleship *Nagato*, a U.S. battle-ship, and three submerged submarines were also sunk in this test.

A massive amount of data was obtained in these tests, so much that test Charlie (the deepwater, 3,000-foot detonation) was postponed and then cancelled. The director of the Los Alamos laboratory, Norris Bradbury, believed that the data from the Baker test made it possible to determine the effects of a deepwater atomic explosion. Also, there were very few atomic bombs in the nation's stockpile—at the time components existed for seven—and hence further expenditure in tests was not considered to be justified.

Although badly damaged and highly radioactive, the *Independence* remained afloat and was towed to Kwajalein in late August. In June 1947 she was towed via Pearl Harbor to San Francisco, where she was used for radiological research until 1951. On January 29 of that year her hulk was towed to sea and sunk in tests of new aerial and underwater weapons.

The carriers *Shangri-La* (CV 38) and *Saidor* (CVE 117) were among the support ships in the Crossroads

Baker Day at Bikini atoll: July 25, 1946. Warships, appearing like toy boats at the base of the explosion, were subjected to two nuclear detonations in the tests of July 1946. Like the "Billy" Mitchell bombing tests two decades earlier, the Navy planned the tests to determine how new weapons would damage ships; like the Mitchell tests, interpretation of the results varied greatly. (U.S. Army Air Forces)

tests. Operating off Roi in the Marshalls, the *Shangri-La* launched pilotless aircraft to fly through the test area and control planes to direct them as well as radio-controlled boats. The *Saidor*, off Bikini, operated primarily photographic aircraft in support of the tests to supplement Army aircraft flying from Kwajalein.

Admiral Blandy gave his view of the lessons of the Bikini tests in a speech in Boston on September 5, 1946:

I believe that if there is atomic warfare in the future, naval war will not be exempt from it. There are those who believe that in future conflicts, great guided missiles will cross the oceans and continents and explode atomic warheads over cities, and that therefore there will be no need for navies. Such weapons may indeed become a reality, but I do not subscribe to the belief that they will eliminate all other kinds of warfare. The ships, weapons, and tactics of sea fighting may change radically, and we should always take the lead in such changes. But I can visualize traffic on the sea for a long time yet, even in war, and therefore fighting on the sea.

Less violent deaths were in store for the uncompleted 27,100-ton carrier *Reprisal*. Her unfinished hull—52.3 percent complete—was launched without ceremony at the New York Navy Yard in 1945. Beginning on April 1, 1948, she was used for underwater explosive tests in Chesapeake Bay. Brief consideration was given in early 1949 to completing the *Reprisal* and her unfinished sister ship *Iwo Jima*, which had been cancelled on August 11, 1945, just over six months after being laid down. But the former ship's hull had been

Two U.S. aircraft carriers were used as target ships in the Bikini A-bomb tests, the *Saratoga* and *Independence*. The "Sara" (top) sank after sailors were unable to board her because of the danger from radiation; her giant funnel has been blown off. The battleship *New York*, also a target, is at right. The "Indy" remained afloat although severely damaged. She then served the Navy for many years as a radiation test ship. (U.S. Navy)

damaged in the weapon tests and the *Iwo Jima* was not far enough along to warrant completion. Both hulls were scrapped.

Of the other carriers disposed of shortly after the war, 11 were scrapped:

CV 4	*Ranger*
CVE 55	*Casablanca*
CVE 65	*Wake Island*
CVE 67	*Solomons*
CVE 68	*Kalinin Bay*
CVE 71	*Kitkun Bay*
CVE 72	*Tulagi*

CVE 93	*Makin Island*
CVE 96	*Salamaua*
CVE 99	*Admiralty Islands*
CVE 103	*Roi*

The escort carriers *Long Island*, *Sangamon* (CVE 26), *Charger* (CVE 30), and *Attu* (CVE 102) were stricken from the Navy list and remodeled for merchant service.

Most of the surviving aircraft carriers—16 CVs, 7 CVLs, and 59 CVEs—were placed in reserve or "mothballed" by the end of 1947. These ships had their interiors sealed to prevent mildew, rot, and corrosion. Fragile external components (such as radar antennas) were removed, remaining topside equipment was covered with preservative (cacooned), devices were installed to prevent underwater deterioration, and the ships were moored in backwaters.

By the end of 1947 the active U.S. Fleet still contained 20 aircraft carriers:

CVB 41	*Midway*
CVB 42	*Franklin D. Roosevelt*
CVB 43	*Coral Sea*
CV 21	*Boxer*
CV 32	*Leyte*
CV 33	*Kearsarge*
CV 36	*Antietam*
CV 37	*Princeton*
CV 40	*Tarawa*
CV 45	*Valley Forge*
CV 47	*Philippine Sea*
CVL 48	*Saipan*
CVL 49	*Wright*
CVE 112	*Siboney*
CVE 114	*Rendova*
CVE 115	*Bairoko*
CVE 116	*Badoeng Strait*
CVE 118	*Sicily*
CVE 120	*Mindoro*
CVE 122	*Palau*

Most of these ships had been completed after the war, the exceptions being the *Boxer*, *Antietam*, *Bairoko*, and *Siboney*, none of which had been in combat. The

The *Midway* was the first of three "battle" carriers to join the U.S. Fleet. The ships were large, heavily armored, and well armed. As built she had long-barrel 5-inch/54-caliber mounts below the flight deck, nine guns to starboard and nine to port. As completed she also had 84 40-mm guns and 28 20-mm guns. In this 1953 view her 5-inch battery has been reduced, 3-inch/50s have replaced 40-mm guns, and all 20-mm mounts have been deleted. (U.S. Navy)

The U.S. Navy's light carrier conversions of World War II were followed by two built-for-the-purpose CVLs—the *Saipan* (above) and *Wright*. These ships were built on hulls identical to the *Baltimore*-class heavy cruisers. Although good ships, they were overshadowed during their brief careers by the availability of larger carriers. Four funnels were angled out aft of the small island structure. (U.S. Navy)

three *Midway*s were the largest war-ships afloat, with a standard displacement of 45,000 tons and an overall length of 968 feet. These were the U.S. Navy's first armored-deck carriers; they had a massive starboard island structure and funnel somewhat reminiscent of the old "Lex" and "Sara." As completed these ships were armed with 18 single 5-inch/54-caliber guns of a new, long-range design (only 14 in the *Coral Sea*) plus 84 40-mm guns, and 28 20-mm guns—the heaviest anti-aircraft battery ever fitted to a carrier.

The *Midway*s were designed to operate up to 144 contemporary aircraft. With an estimated optimum aircraft takeoff and landing interval of some 30 seconds, it would—in perfect circumstances—take more than an hour to launch or recover the air group.[8]

The two light carriers, the *Saipan* and *Wright*, were similar in appearance to their predecessors of the *Independence* class but were larger, displacing 14,500 tons with a length of 683½ feet. Whereas the "Indy" and her sister CVLs were built on *Cleveland*-class light cruiser hulls, the *Saipan* and *Wright* had hulls similar to *Baltimore*-class heavy cruisers. They were designed to mount 40 40-mm guns and 32 20-mm guns, and each could operate some 50 aircraft.

In view of the attitudes of the time and massive reductions in active military forces, the U.S. Navy thus had a relatively large and modern carrier force in the postwar period. By comparison, only one battleship, the *Missouri*, was retained in active service.[9]

Cold War and Cold Ops

At this time Europe received the major share of U.S. interest, and military strength was apportioned accordingly. The communist threat to Europe was considered to be more critical than the communist threat to Asia, although Soviet troops held Manchuria and half of the Korean peninsula, and Mao Zedong's forces had renewed the civil war in China. The U.S. Navy thus maintained a larger active fleet in the Atlantic than in the Pacific. The 20-carrier lineup included six fleet carriers (including the three large *Midway*s), two light carriers, and four escort carriers in the Atlantic Fleet compared to five fleet carriers and three escort carriers in the Pacific Fleet.

As the war ended in Europe the Soviets were in firm control of the eastern European nations, most by military occupation. At the end of the war the communists threatened Turkey and Greece, and Soviet troops moved into Bulgaria and refused to withdraw from Iran.[10] As a countermove, in April 1946, the United States sent the battleship *Missouri*, a light cruiser, and a destroyer into the eastern Mediterranean. Officially the ships were there to return the remains of a Turkish diplomat who had died in the United States in November 1944. American newspaper columnist Walter Lippmann was more to the point when he wrote, "With the *Missouri* treated as a symbol of our power in the Mediterranean we can make it unmistakably clear in Moscow just where we believe the outer limits of their expansion are." From the invasion of southern France in the summer of 1944 until April 1946 light cruisers had been the largest U.S. warships to operate in the Mediterranean Sea.

The *Missouri* and her companions sailed through the Mediterranean, up the Dardanelles, and into the Bosporus, to the Black Sea doorstep of the Soviet Union. The warship visits during April 1946 were warmly received by both Greeks and Turks, and they were strongly criticized by the Soviets.

No aircraft carrier accompanied the *Missouri*. At one stage of planning for the operation the large carriers *Midway* and *Franklin D. Roosevelt* were to have accompanied the dreadnought. However, the carriers were dropped from the operation when the State Department concluded that the Soviets might consider so large a force to be a provocation. But the *Missouri*'s visit initiated the practice of sending major fleet units into the Mediterranean. The *Roosevelt* did operate in the Mediterranean from August 8 to October 4, 1946. On her decks was CVBG-75, a 123-plane "battle carrier air group" consisting of fighter squadron VF-75 with 33 F4U-4 Corsairs, 4 F6F-5P, and 4 F6F-5N Hellcats; fighter-bomber squadron VBF-75 with 32 F4U-4B Corsairs; bomber squadron VB-75 with 24 SB2C-5 Helldivers; and torpedo squadron VT-75 with

another 24 Helldivers and 2 TBM-3E Avengers.[11] *At the time the aircraft on this single carrier possessed more striking power than the combined air forces of all Mediterranean nations.*

During the 1946 cruise the carrier visited Athens to bolster the Greek government in its fight against the communists. During calls at other Mediterranean ports the *Roosevelt* opened her decks to thousands of visitors, starting a custom of "goodwill" visits by U.S. warships. This show of naval force, begun with the *Missouri* visit, was a major milestone in the development of U.S. foreign policy in the postwar era.

The "FDR" was followed into the Mediterranean by the 27,100-ton *Randolph*, which cruised the central sea from November 1 until mid-December, establishing a program of regular U.S. carrier deployments to the Mediterranean. Beginning late in 1947, on a continuous basis, at least one U.S. strike carrier operated in the Mediterranean, and from mid-1951 at least two attack carriers normally operated in that sea until the end of the Cold War.

In March 1947 the United States undertook a major aid program to assist the Greek and Turkish governments in their efforts to resist communism. As part of this program—the Truman Doctrine—U.S. escort

At the end of World War II most of the U.S. Navy aircraft carriers were "mothballed" for possible future requirements. Here the *Essex, Ticonderoga, Yorktown, Lexington,* and *Bunker Hill* are moored at the naval shipyard at Bremerton, Washington. Beyond them is another carrier and several battleships and cruisers. (U.S. Navy)

carriers were pressed into service to deliver aircraft and other material to these nations. U.S. interest in the area continued to increase, and beginning in January 1948 at least one battalion of Marines embarked in a squadron of amphibious ships was maintained in the Mediterranean. Replenishment ships followed, making the carrier and amphibious groups largely independent of land bases in the Mediterranean. With this buildup the U.S. naval forces in the Mediterranean were designated the Sixth Task Fleet on June 1, 1948 (and subsequently the Sixth Fleet on February 12, 1950). This fleet—spearheaded by aircraft carriers—would become a basic instrument of U.S. policy in southern Europe.[12]

The situation in the Western Pacific was somewhat different. Following the Japanese surrender U.S. forces occupied Japan and 47,000 Marines were sent into North China to establish order as the Japanese withdrew and the communists and Chang Kai-shek's Nationalist forces reopened their civil war on a major scale. As the communists advanced, the Marines withdrew, finally abandoning the Chinese mainland in May 1949. Aircraft carriers regularly deployed to the Western Pacific, operating out of ports in Japan and from Tsingtao on the mainland. Naval forces were maintained in the area in support of the U.S. ground and air forces rather than for a purpose of their own.

The communists were victorious in China while U.S. attention continued to focus on Europe. Shortages of trained personnel in the armed services and commitments in Europe steadily drained U.S. forces in the Western Pacific. The last U.S. combat troops departed South Korea in June 1949. That December the last Nationalist forces were forced from the Chinese mainland and took refuge on Formosa, a large island 100 miles from the coast of China. Although U.S. naval forces in the Western Pacific were not reinforced, the importance of the area was recognized, and in August 1949 the afloat naval command was designated as the Seventh Task Fleet (and in February 1950 as the Seventh Fleet).

Most U.S. carrier operations in the immediate postwar years were related to the confrontations with the Soviet Union that would become known as the Cold War. However, several carrier operations were conducted in a considerably colder environment. On March 1, 1946, the large carrier *Midway*, with portions of Carrier Air Group 74 on board, departed Norfolk, Virginia,

with three destroyers, under the command of Rear Admiral John H. Cassady, to conduct cold weather tests in the Davis Strait. Operating off the coast of Labrador and above the Arctic Circle from March 7 to 22, 1946, this evaluation of carrier operations in Arctic waters was called Operation Frostbite. It demonstrated that cold weather carrier operations were feasible, although at a reduced operational tempo. The task force returned to Norfolk on March 22.

Late in 1946 the new carrier *Philippine Sea* was on her shakedown cruise in the Atlantic when she was directed to set course for Norfolk. There six R4D-5L cargo planes were hoisted onto her flight deck on December 31. The twin-engine R4D was the Navy's version of the famed Douglas DC-3, known as the C-47 or Dakota to air forces around the world. With a wingspan of 95 feet and a length of 63¾ feet, the R4Ds would be the largest aircraft yet to fly from a carrier (the PBJ-1H that flew tests from the *Shangri-La* in 1944 had a span of 67½ feet and a length of 51 feet, but was slightly heavier).

The six cargo planes were to be used by Rear Admiral Richard E. Byrd for exploration and logistic support in the U.S. Navy's forthcoming Antarctic expedition, Operation High Jump. Heretofore only austere air support was available for Antarctic explorers. Byrd, in addition to the six R4Ds, would have several light cargo and utility aircraft, and six large PBM Mariner flying boats based on two seaplane tenders. Two OY-1 liaison planes for the Byrd expedition flew aboard the *Philippine Sea* while she was at Norfolk.

The carrier departed Norfolk for Antarctica's Ross Sea on January 2, 1947. En route, the OY-1s were crated for transfer to another ship for direct delivery to the frozen continent. Meanwhile, the R4Ds were fitted with skis. Only three inches of wheel could protrude beneath the skis for takeoff because if more wheel was allowed to show the planes could capsize when they landed on the snow. This, in turn, increased the hazard of takeoff from the carrier.

Only half of the *Philippine Sea*'s flight deck—about 400 feet—could be used for takeoff because of the danger of an R4D wing striking the island structure. An R4D normally required a 2,500-foot runway. To help the planes into the air the carrier would steam into the wind at about 30 knots and each plane would be fitted with four JATO bottles, disposable rocket propulsion tubes resembling large fire extinguishers.[13]

The carrier *Philippine Sea* operated an unusual flight of aircraft in 1947 when she sailed to the Antarctic in support of Rear Admiral Richard E. Byrd's scientific expedition to the frozen continent. Here she passes through the Panama Canal with six R4D-5 (C-47H) transports on her deck. The port-side elevator is swung up for the ship to squeeze through the 110-foot canal locks. (U.S. Navy)

The *Philippine Sea* reached her launch position the third week in January, but bad weather delayed the takeoff until January 29. Finally, there was good weather at the carrier's position and at the U.S. base camp at Little America, 800 miles to the south. On the evening of the 29th—bright daylight in the Antarctic summer—the first two planes were readied for takeoff. If they made

the flight safely the others would follow the next morning. At 10:14 P.M. the *Philippine Sea* was steaming at 30 knots into an 11-knot wind. With Commander William M. Hawkes as pilot and Admiral Byrd as copilot, the first R4D started down the deck. The four JATO bottles fired, and the plane was airborne with a deck run of only 240 feet. Seventeen minutes later the second R4D took off. Early the next morning both planes landed safely at Little America.

Subsequently, the four other R4Ds were launched without incident and touched down on the packed-snow runway. At Little America the planes' wheels were removed and the skis remounted. During Operation High Jump and later Antarctic expeditions these planes provided U.S. explorers with an unprecedented capability for exploration, aerial photography, and supply.

During the R4D takeoffs from the *Philippine Sea* their weights had varied from 25,690 to 26,465 pounds; their takeoff runs varied from 240 feet for the first plane to 171 feet for one of the later R4Ds. The Navy's report on the operation predicted that as many as 11 R4Ds could be launched from a carrier without difficulty and, using JATO, the planes could have had even higher gross weights.

One other U.S. carrier operation of this period was of special interest. After the war both the United States and Soviet Union exploited German missile technology. The German V-2 was the only long-range ballistic missile used in the war and became the progenitor for subsequent ballistic missile development efforts in Britain, China, France, the Soviet Union, and the United States. The Soviets and Americans test fired a large number of V-2s.[14] In September 1947 the carrier *Midway* took on board two operational V 2s (without warheads) and a dummy training missile at Norfolk. Landing craft brought out U.S. and German rocket scientists and engineers who would be aboard for the test firing, among them Wernher von Braun, "father" of the V-2.

The carrier went to sea, and on September 6 one of the V-2s was launched from the carrier's flight deck in Operation Sandy. The 46-foot, 14-ton missile lifted off and immediately began to tilt to starboard, taking off in a 45-degree relative direction—toward the island structure. But within five seconds control vanes returned the missile's attitude to the vertical, and the launch was a success. It was history's only launch of a V-2 missile from a moving "platform."

In a bast of smoke from JATO rocket boosters, an R4D-5 takes off from the *Philippine Sea* en route to the Little America base in Antarctica. The wheels hardly protrude through the skis fitted to the aircraft's landing gear. The ubiquitous aircraft was named Skytrain in U.S. service, but was known worldwide as the Dakota. (U.S. Navy)

The German V-2 rocket was precursor to the postwar development of Intercontinental Ballistic Missiles (ICBM). After World War II the Allies launched 82 surrendered V-2 missiles in tests—3 by British, 11 by Soviets, and 68 by Americans. The last included this test firing of the 13-ton, 46-foot missile from the carrier *Midway* on September 6, 1947. (U.S. Navy)

Although the Navy considered the possibility of improved V-2s as a shipboard weapon, in the event the U.S. Navy—like the U.S. Air Force—initially concentrated on guided/cruise missile technology for the long-range strike role. The report of Operation Sandy noted that a *Midway*-class CVB could transport and launch 80 such missiles, an *Essex*-class CV some 50 missiles, and a CVE an estimated 16 missiles.[15] Proposals were made to complete the unfinished battleship *Kentucky* and battle cruiser *Hawaii* to carry ballistic missiles, but those proposals were soon dropped and both unfinished ships were eventually scrapped.

(Late in World War II both the U.S. Army and Navy developed plans for the mass production of the German V-1 cruise missile—known as the "buzz bomb" for use against the Japanese home islands, to be launched from surface ships, including escort carriers, and from captured offshore islands. The Army Air Forces had production plans to enable 500 JB-2 sorties per day. But the atomic bomb ended the war in the Pacific before the American copies of the V-1 could be used in combat.[16])

One other unusual carrier operation took place in this period. The world's first practical aircraft, the Wright Brothers' 1903 "Flyer," had been on display in England since 1928.[17] The historic aircraft, already disassembled, was packed in three crates and departed England for the United States on board the passenger liner *Mauretania* in late 1948. While at sea, the liner's captain learned of a dockworker strike in New York. Accordingly, the liner stopped at Halifax, Nova Scotia, and the crates were carefully transferred to the escort carrier *Palau*. The CVE then steamed to Bayonne, New Jersey, where the crated aircraft was placed on a truck and brought to Washington, D.C., where, with due ceremony, it was put on display in the Arts and Industries building of the Smithsonian Institution.[18]

The Royal Navy's Nadir

The Royal Navy faced the postwar years with an austere operating fleet as Britain, after almost six years of war, began to rebuild a peacetime economy. The strength and operating efficiency of the Royal Navy declined rapidly, especially in carrier aviation, which, with the aid of U.S. training programs, aircraft, and escort carriers, was a potent force by the end of the war.

The Royal Navy still had no aviators among its senior leaders. At the end of the war the only aviation officer with flag rank was Rear Admiral G. B. Middleton, a naval observer; he was, moreover, a specialist in surface ships and torpedoes. Even the more senior pilots were mostly reserve officers, commissioned and trained during the war and released at the end of hostilities. Not until May 1960 would the Royal Navy have an aviator as First Sea Lord, Sir Caspar John. He had commanded an escort carrier in 1944 and a light fleet carrier in 1945.[19] His appointment came more than 18 years after Admiral Ernest J. King, a pilot, had become Commander-in-Chief U.S. Fleet and Chief of Naval Operations.

The Royal Navy emerged from the war with the six *Illustrious*-class fleet carriers and eight light fleet carriers plus three maintenance carriers available for "peacetime" operations. The surviving prewar veterans *Argus* and *Furious* were stricken in 1946 and 1948, respectively, and scrapped.[20]

Two of the fleet carriers saw no further operational service: The *Formidable*, seriously damaged by German bombs in May 1941 and twice smashed by kamikazes in May 1945, suffered from structural damage and was laid up in November 1946 and sold for scrap in 1953. The *Indefatigable*, struck by a suicider in April 1945, was laid up in December 1946; she was converted to a training and accommodation ship at Portsmouth and was never returned to carrier service. She was sold off for scrap in 1956.

The *Illustrious* was briefly reduced to reserve status in 1947 because of manpower shortages; she was returned to service in September 1948. With the *Indomitable*, *Implacable*, and *Victorious* she would see operational service during the coming years.

The Royal Navy's 35 surviving American-built escort carriers were returned to U.S. control and converted for merchant use or scrapped immediately after the war; one, the *Biter*, went to France. The British-built *Activity* and *Vindex* also became merchant ships, and the *Nairana* was transferred to the Netherlands. Only one escort carrier was retained in service, the *Campania*, which had a brief but active war career.[21] Still flying the White Ensign, in 1949 she served as a floating exhibition hall for the Festival of Britain, and in the fall of 1952 she was flagship and the principal support ship for the first British atomic bomb tests—Operation Hurricane—in the Monte Bello Islands (50 miles off the northwest coast of Australia).[22]

When the *Campania* sailed from England to the Pacific it was assumed by most observers that she carried the components for Britain's first atomic bomb; in fact, the frigate *Plym* that accompanied the *Campania* was the "bomb carrier" with the plutonium for the implosion (Fat Man–type) bomb being flown from Britain to the test site. The bomb was detonated within the *Plym* on October 3, 1952. The frigate was vaporized in the explosion.

The bomb was a prototype for the Blue Danube Mk I, Britain's first nuclear weapon, which would be carried by the Royal Air Force V-bombers—the Valiant, Victor, and Vulcan.[23] At the time the Royal Navy had no potential to achieve a nuclear strike capability: no Navy carrier aircraft existed or was planned that could accommodate such a weapon, and all land-based combat aircraft were operated by the RAF.

Following Operation Hurricane, the *Campania* was laid up in reserve in 1953. Two years later she was towed off to be scrapped. It marked the end of the escort carrier in the Royal Navy.

The postwar Labour government was bent on reducing expenses, a policy that doomed any efforts to quickly complete unfinished carriers or to maintain a large active fleet. By the end of 1947 the Royal Navy had only three aircraft carriers in service: the *Implacable* as a training ship in home waters and the light carriers *Ocean* and *Triumph* in the Mediterranean.

During the remaining years of the decade and into the 1950s the Royal Navy relied upon improved models of World War II–era aircraft and advanced piston-powered planes to fill its few operational carrier squadrons. Of the former, in 1945 the Fleet Air Arm began receiving Seafires powered by the Rolls-Royce Griffon engine, the first being the Seafire XV. Still later model Seafires were introduced into the postwar fleet, some with contrarotating propellers.

Also joining Fleet Air Arm squadrons from late 1945 was the Firebrand, initially proposed as a short-range interceptor, but emerging as a torpedo-carrying fighter. It was a failure. Pilot-historian Eric M. Brown wrote, "as a deck-landing aeroplane it was a disaster and it was incapable of fulfilling competently either the role of torpedo-bomber or that of fighter, but it was built like a battleship—and there were to be those that would say that it flew like one."[24]

Additional fighters joined the FAA in 1947–1948, the Sea Fury and improved versions of the Firefly. The Sea Fury was the last piston-engine fighter produced for the Royal Navy, the fastest piston-engine British naval fighter, and was produced in larger numbers than any other FAA aircraft in the postwar years. Like most of its companions, the Sea Fury was originally designed as a land-based fighter for the RAF (to be named Fury), a lightweight aircraft for use in the Pacific War.

Shortly after the prototype Fury flew on September 1, 1944, the RAF cancelled the Fury program, reflecting RAF interest in jet-propelled aircraft, the imminent Allied victory in Europe, and the availability of U.S. fighter aircraft and existing British fighter aircraft for the final operations against Japan. However, the initial limitations of jet-propelled aircraft aboard carriers and the significant performance improvement of the Sea Fury over the newer Seafires led to additional Sea Fury orders for the Royal Navy.

The British escort carrier *Campania* was the Royal Navy's last CVE, being paid off at Portsmouth on December 15, 1952. Here she is at Freemantle, Australia, earlier that year en route to the Monte Bello Islands to serve as flagship and a support platform for the first British atomic test. (© *Western Australian Newspaper* courtesy FAA Museum)

The advanced, Griffon-engine Seafires began joining FAA squadrons in 1945. The most popular Griffon variant was the Seafire Mk XVII, capable of 387 m.p.h. at 13,500 feet, a climb of 20,000 feet in just over seven minutes, and a ceiling of 35,200 feet. It had two 20-mm cannon, four .303-caliber machine guns, and racks for eight 3-inch rockets. The Seafire Mk 46 (above) had contrarotating propellers and could reach 450 m.p.h. The aircraft had four 20-mm guns and could carry a 500-pound bomb. (*Flight International*)

The prototype Hawker-built Sea Fury flew on February 21, 1945. A total of 668 single-seat Sea Furies and 60 two-seat variants were built for the Royal Navy, and another 354 for Commonwealth and foreign nations. (Fifty-nine of those delivered to the FAA were later refurbished for foreign transfer.) The first production Sea Fury was the Mk X interceptor, which had a maximum speed of 465 m.p.h. The most popular Sea Fury model was the Mk 11 fighter-bomber; 615 of those aircraft were produced. Although their performance was slightly inferior to the interceptor (i.e., 460 m.p.h. maximum), the FB.11 could carry 12 rockets or two 1,000-pound bombs. Both types had four 20-mm cannon.

Postwar versions of the earlier Firefly aircraft included specialized reconnaissance (FR), night-fighter (NF), and anti-submarine (AS) aircraft. The AS.5 variant had a maximum speed of 386 m.p.h. at 14,000 feet and an endurance of 6½ hours. Four cannon were mounted in its wings and 16 rockets or two 1,000-pound bombs could be carried. Those characteristics would enable the plane to establish an excellent record in the ground support and interdiction roles during the Korean War.

Two World War II carrier aircraft did see service in first-line squadrons after 1946. Twelve Barracuda IIIs, a 239-m.p.h. version of the "ugly duckling" torpedo bomber, were in use from 1947 to 1953. The planes briefly operated aboard the *Illustrious*, from November 1948 to January 1949. And, in the 1950s

the FAA took delivery of 180 Grumman/General Motors TBM-3 Avengers modified for ASW operations.

Finally, the Royal Navy flew a number of twin-engine Sea Hornets in the postwar period. The Admiralty had produced a staff requirement for a twin-engine carrier fighter following the successful carrier trials of the twin-engine Mosquito in the spring of 1944. The first of three de Havilland Sea Hornet prototypes flew on April 19, 1945, and the third prototype, the first with folding wings, flew carrier trials from HMS *Ocean* in August 1945.

Three Sea Hornet variants were produced: 78 F.20 fighters, 79 NF.21 night fighters, and 43 PR.22 photo aircraft—with prototypes a total of 200 aircraft. The photo planes were capable of day and night operation. The NF.21, a two-place aircraft, was the standard FAA carrier-based night fighter from 1949 to 1954. The NF.21 could be readily identified by its extended "thimble" nose (which housed ASH radar) and the second cockpit midway along its fuselage. All of these Sea Hornet variants operated from carriers and demonstrated excellent performance—a speed of 430 m.p.h. and a range of 1,500 miles. The fighter variants had four 20-mm cannon and could carry rockets or two 1,000-pound bombs.

Only one night-fighter squadron was formed (No. 809), and it was part of the first British all-weather air group that operated aboard the light carrier *Vengeance* in 1950. The other aircraft in this group were Firefly night-fighter and reconnaissance aircraft. The radar-fitted NF.21s were also employed as leaders for strike aircraft.

The Blackburn Firebrand was in FAA squadron service from 1945 to 1953 as a torpedo-strike fighter. The TF.5 variant had a maximum speed of 350 m.p.h. at 13,000 feet, could climb 2,600 feet per minute, and had a ceiling of 28,500 feet with a torpedo. Armament consisted of four 20-mm cannon and a 1,850-pound torpedo or two 1,000-pound bombs could be carried. (Imperial War Museum)

Probably the most popular FAA piston-fighter in the post-war period was the Hawker Sea Fury. It served in first-line squadrons from 1947 to 1954 (and survived another three years in reserve squadrons). Above is a Mark X fighter-bomber (later changed to FB.10). The aircraft could reach 465 m.p.h. at 18,000 feet, climb to 30,000 feet in less than ten minutes, and had a ceiling of 36,100 feet. Sea Furies were also flown by several other navies and air forces. (Hawker Siddeley Aviation)

The Short-built Sturgeon was a twin-engine reconnaissance-bomber aircraft developed specifically for carrier operation. The aircraft's twin engines had contra-rotating propellers that could push the plane to 370 m.p.h. The first model flew in 1946. However, after a reevaluation of aircraft requirements, all 23 aircraft accepted by the Navy were fitted as target tugs. Some Sturgeons did operate from carriers in that role.

British aircraft carriers in the 1945–1950 period thus operated primarily piston-engine, fighter-type aircraft, mostly the Sea Fury, Seafire, Firefly, and Firebrand. Canada also flew the Sea Fury, Seafire, and Firefly; Australia operated the Sea Fury and Firefly; and the Netherlands flew the Firefly.

The Smaller Navies—Part One

After the French surrender in June 1940 several French warships operated with Allied forces in the Mediterranean, Atlantic, and Pacific, most notably the battleship *Richelieu*, which had been refitted in the United States during 1943. However, there were no French carriers. After spending the first part of the war at Martinique, the carrier *Béarn* was modernized in the United States in 1944–1945, but because of her operational limitations, she was suitable for use only as an aircraft transport. She was supplemented in that role by the American-built escort carrier *Biter*, which was transferred from Britain to France in January 1945 and renamed *Dixmude*.

At the end of the war France still had a large overseas empire that required the support of a fleet. The reoccupation of Indochina in particular caused a heavy demand for French naval and merchant shipping. The French economic situation at the time and the severe damage suffered by French shipyards and heavy industry precluded the construction of large ships although a serious effort was begun to build one or two aircraft carriers that could form task forces with the modern battleships *Jean Bart* and *Richelieu* as well as smaller ships.

The keel of the 18,000-ton aircraft carrier *Joffre*, laid down just before the war began, had been scrapped by the Germans to permit the construction of large cargo ships. However, the machinery for the ship was almost complete and it was hoped to use the equipment in a new carrier. This hope was not realized, and in August 1946 the British light carrier *Colossus* was loaned to the French Navy for five years with the option (subsequently taken up) to purchase the ship outright at the end of this period. Under the French tricolor the carrier was renamed *Arromanches*. The 13,190-ton ship was provided with an air group of British Seafire fighters and American SBD Dauntless dive bombers.

Following the United States, Britain, and France, the next nation to operate an aircraft carrier in the post-war period was the Netherlands, although two British MAC-ships had flown Dutch colors during the war.[25] With considerable overseas territory and the desire to reoccupy the East Indies, the Dutch took loan of the

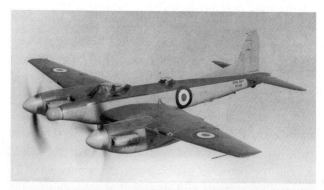

The Sea Hornet was the world's first twin-engine piston aircraft to regularly operate from carriers. Developed from the Mosquito, the de Havilland Sea Hornet NF.21 (above), a two-place variant, had a maximum speed of 430 m.p.h. at 20,000 feet, could climb 4,400 feet per minute, and had a ceiling of 36,500 feet. All variants had four fixed 20-mm guns forward; most marks had provisions for two 1,000-pound bombs or eight 3-inch rockets. The NF aircraft had the ASH radar fitted in a "thimble nose." (*Flight International*)

The Short Sea Sturgeon was a rather ugly, twin-engine aircraft intended for use as a reconnaissance bomber from carriers. Unlike the Sea Mosquito and Sea Hornet, which were developed from RAF aircraft, the Sea Sturgeon was designed specifically for naval service. Two engines with contrarotating propellers could drive the Sea Sturgeon at 370 m.p.h. After the war production of the Sea Sturgeon was halted and the few aircraft completed were used as target tugs. The TT.2 variant shown here had a tail hook, folding wings, and a lengthened nose for cameras. (Crown Copyright)

British-built escort carrier *Nairana*, and renamed the 14,050-ton ship the *Karel Doorman*. She served in the Dutch Navy from 1946 until March 1948, at which time she was replaced by the 13,190-ton light carrier *Venerable*, which was purchased from Great Britain and commissioned in the Royal Netherlands Navy on May 28, 1948, also as the *Karel Doorman*, named for a preeminent Dutch naval hero.[26]

The overseas interests and the maritime traditions of the United States, Britain, France, and the Netherlands made it natural for their navies to acquire aircraft carriers. The next nation to acquire an aircraft carrier set a precedent and established a trend in naval policies. On January 24, 1946, the British light carrier *Warrior* was commissioned in the Royal Canadian Navy. Canada had a long tradition of military aviation. During World War I some 24,000 Canadians served in the Royal Flying Corps, Royal Naval Air Service, and after its formation, the Royal Air Force. In 1920 a Canadian Air Force was organized on an interim basis to provide refresher training for wartime pilots; it became the Royal Canadian Air Force in 1923 and was established on a permanent basis the following year.

The North Atlantic operations of 1942–1943 had shown the need for escort carriers if the Canadian Navy was to continue in its primary role—the defense of North Atlantic convoys. And, if the Canadian Navy was to have a role in the Pacific War, it would almost certainly require aircraft carriers of some sort. The Canadian Navy already operated land-based aircraft.

At the Quebec Conference in August 1943, the Canadian Chief of Naval Staff stated that his problem was "to see that the RCN did not finish the war as a small-ship navy entirely." At that time destroyers were the largest ships in the Canadian Navy. The Chief of Naval Staff expressed the hope that his country's postwar Navy would consist of five cruisers, two light fleet carriers, and three destroyer flotillas.

The decision soon was reached that the Canadian Navy would acquire light cruisers from Britain and would operate escort carriers. Such carriers could be obtained quickly and economically only from the

The French Navy emerged from World War II with two aircraft carriers: the *Béarn*, suitable only for service as an aircraft transport, and the American-built escort carrier renamed *Dixmude*. The *Béarn* is shown at Colombo in October 1945. She has been fitted with cranes; vehicles and landing craft are on her flight deck. (Sub-Lt. G. Hales/ Crown Copyright)

After World War II there was a proliferation of aircraft carriers to the smaller navies, initially to Canada, the Netherlands, and Australia. This is the *Sydney* of the Royal Australian Navy, formerly HMS *Terrible*, with her Sea Fury fighters and Firefly ASW aircraft parked on deck. All carrier transfers were CVL and CVE types. (Royal Australian Navy)

United States. But American law forbade their outright sale to a foreign power, and Canada was reluctant to accept them as Lend-Lease, as Britain had. The best course of action seemed to have Canadian sailors man some of the escort carriers in the Royal Navy, which would help the British with their manning problems and give Canadian sailors experience in carrier operations. This way the Canadian Navy would not have to accept U.S. Lend-Lease. Thus the American-built escort carriers *Nabob* and *Puncher* were largely manned by Canadians, although the ships remained units of the Royal Navy. This solution was not totally satisfactory because of the differences in pay and accommodations between the two navies.

The Canadians continued to look at the possibility of fully acquiring aircraft carriers, with most proposals recommending two light fleet carriers for the Canadian Navy to be used against Japan and be retained after the war. Negotiations were begun in 1944, and although the talks were concluded before the war's end, the first light carrier, the *Warrior*, was not completed and commissioned in the Canadian Navy until January 1946. The British-built *Warrior* served in the Canadian Navy until 1948, when she was replaced by the improved light carrier *Magnificent* (14,000 tons), commissioned on May 21, 1948.

Canada thus inaugurated the practice of operating aircraft carriers among the world's smaller navies, with Argentina, Australia, Brazil, India, Spain, and Thailand following. However, only Australia had an operational carrier before the decade was over. Discussions between Canberra and London led to the British-built *Terrible* (14,000 tons) being commissioned in the Royal

Australian Navy as HMAS *Sydney* on December 16, 1948. She sailed from Britain in mid-April 1949, bound for Australia, her air group consisting of one squadron of Sea Fury Mk 11 fighter-bombers and one of Firefly Mk 6 anti-submarine aircraft. Thus Australia gained an initial carrier force and the only carrier belonging to a Western Pacific nation.

A "non-nation" almost obtained a carrier immediately after the war. In 1947 the United Nations voted to establish both a Jewish state and an Arab state in Palestine, at the time a British mandate. Reportedly, in December 1947 Yehuda Arazi, who was buying arms for the Jewish paramilitary forces in Palestine, conceived a plan to procure an aircraft carrier to transport heavy weapons, combat vehicles, and even aircraft to Jewish-held ports in Palestine. Tactical aircraft might even be catapulted off the carrier.

Accordingly, an American sympathizer, Leonard Weisman, purchased the escort carrier *Attu* (CVE 102) of the *Casablanca* class for $125,000 from a private investor, who had bought it from the government as war surplus. The ship had been "demilitarized"—which included the removal of catapults—and Arazi and Weisman began renovating the ship, which was renamed the *Flying W*, in tribute to Weisman. But there were delays in the renovation and legal problems, and the ship remained in the Norfolk area. Finally, the ship was scrapped in 1948–1949.

Even had the Jewish state—established as Israel on May 14, 1948—received arms shipped aboard the *Attu/Flying W*, it was highly unlikely that the ship would have been placed in service as a carrier. Israel had neither the manpower nor the need for such a ship.

In the late 1940s the world of carrier aviation was changing rapidly, in part because of the arrival on the naval scene of two revolutionary aircraft— turbojets and helicopters—and the development of the atomic bomb.

The USS *Midway* in May 1947 with air group CVBG-1 embarked. The after flight deck is crowded with SB2C-5 Helldivers; forward are F4U-4B Corsairs. They would soon be joined by AD-1 Skyraiders. Visible are part of the carrier's massive battery of 5-inch/54-caliber, dual-purpose guns, and 40-mm and 20-mm anti-aircraft weapons. The 20-mm guns were soon removed while the quad 40-mm mounts were replaced by twin 3-inch/50-caliber mounts. (U.S. Navy)

2 JETS AND WHIRLYBIRDS

The first true jet carrier landing was made by a Vampire I piloted by Lieutenant-Commander Eric M. Brown aboard the British carrier *Ocean* on December 3, 1945. Although the trials were entirely successful, the Vampire did not enter squadron service because of the slow acceleration of its jet engine; according to Brown, "We felt at this stage no jet could be trusted entirely in an emergency requiring a sudden increase of speed. . . . The jet engine's acceleration response was very sluggish." (Charles E. Brown)

Naval officials in Britain and the United States looked on with interest as their air forces developed and flew jet-propelled aircraft. The first jet flight in Britain occurred when a Gloster E.28/39 Pioneer became airborne on May 15, 1941; the first U.S. jet-propelled aircraft, the Bell XP-59A Airacomet, fitted with British engines, flew on October 1, 1942.[1] These were development aircraft. Britain's first jet-propelled combat aircraft was the Gloster Meteor, which first flew on March 5, 1943, and was used to intercept the V-1 jet-propelled bombs being launched against England in 1944.[2]

The U.S. Navy entered the jet era when two 400-m.p.h. YP-59A turbojet aircraft were obtained from the Army Air Forces in November 1943 for flight tests.

The next year the Navy first flew the Ryan XFR-1 Fireball, a combination piston-turbojet aircraft. The Fireball served briefly in Navy fighter squadrons (see Volume I, pp. 499–501).

Credit for the first true jet landing aboard an aircraft carrier unquestionably goes to Lieutenant-Commander Eric M. Brown, who landed a jet-propelled Vampire I fighter on the light carrier *Ocean* on December 3, 1945. The Vampire was Britain's second jet-propelled combat aircraft and introduced the distinctive de Havilland twin-boom design to jet aircraft.[3] Brown, one of Britain's leading naval test pilots, had flown all of the early Allied jets—the original Gloster E.28/39, the Meteor, and the P-59A Airacomet. None of these

Another view of the de Havilland Vampire I trials aboard HMS *Ocean* on December 3, 1945. The *Ocean* was typical of the British CVLs, being larger than their U.S. counterparts of the U.S. *Independence* class and similar to the *Saipan* class. But the British carriers had large-ship island structures compared to the American ships. (Charles E. Brown)

aircraft was considered suitable for carrier trials; the Vampire, which had first flown in 1943, "seemed to be the one for us," according to Brown.

He was "desperately keen to beat the Americans at being the first to operate jets from carriers." The third prototype Vampire I was fitted for the carrier trials, and Brown landed it aboard the *Ocean* in poor weather, having missed a signal indicating that because of the weather the landing trials were cancelled. He made four arrested landings and takeoffs on December 3 and returned to the *Ocean* three days later for 11 more landing cycles. The aircraft carrier had entered the jet age.

The Vampire was produced in a navalized version known as the Sea Vampire F.20. However, the first production F.20 did not fly until October 1948 and only 18 aircraft were built for the Fleet Air Arm. These aircraft were used almost exclusively for trials and training. (In addition, the FAA procured 73 Sea Vampire T.22 training aircraft in the mid-1950s.)

Two later twin-jet Meteors, modified F.3 variants built in 1945, were fitted for carrier operations in 1948, and that spring and summer they were used in a successful series of trials aboard the *Illustrious* and *Implacable*.

A jet fighter for squadron service in the Royal Navy was at last taken in hand with the Attacker, a product of the Supermarine organization that had designed and produced the long line of Spitfire/Seafire fighter aircraft. The Attacker was conceived as a land-based fighter for the Royal Air Force. The prototype flew in

July 1946, but no RAF orders were forthcoming. The second and third prototypes were navalized for carrier operation but without folding wings.

The first of these navalized variants flew on June 17, 1947, and in October of that year underwent carrier trials aboard the *Illustrious*. Production aircraft were not ordered for more than two years, and not until late 1951 did No. 800 Squadron embark in HMS *Eagle* with the Attacker F.1.[4] It was a high-performance and aesthetically attractive aircraft, except for its rudder, which ended several inches short of its tail, giving the rudder a chopped-off look. The FAA took delivery of 149 Attackers of which 84 were FB.2 variants, which could carry two 1,000-pound bombs and four 300-pound rockets on wing pylons. Both the F.1 and FB.2 were armed with four 20-mm cannon.

Lieutenant-Commander Eric M. Brown

By 1954 the Attackers were being replaced in first-line squadrons by Sea Hawk and Sea Venom turbojet fighters.

In contrast to the Royal Navy, the U.S. Navy fostered a major effort in the mid-1940s to develop jet-propelled fighters specifically for carrier operation. Three all-jet prototypes were ordered during the war: the McDonnell XFD-1 Phantom in January 1943 (later redesignated FH-1); the Chance-Vought XF6U-1 Pirate in December of 1944; and the North American XFJ-1 Fury in January 1945. These would be the first carrier-based aircraft produced by McDonnell and North American; Chance-Vought, of course, had a tradition of building outstanding shipboard aircraft.

The twin-engine McDonnell XFD-1 Phantom flew for the first time on January 26, 1945, the world's first pure-jet aircraft designed from the outset for shipboard operation. The plane did not undergo carrier trials until July 21, 1946, seven months and 18 days after the British had flown the jet-propelled Vampire from the carrier *Ocean*. However, whereas the Vampire carrier operation was strictly a test, the XFD-1 Phantom carrier trials were part of U.S. Navy acceptance procedures for a service fighter.

The XFD-1 Phantom was loaded aboard the large carrier *Franklin D. Roosevelt* on the morning of July 19 while the ship was moored at Norfolk. The ship went to sea the following morning. That afternoon the Phantom was brought up from the hangar deck and the ship turned into the wind in preparation for the trials. An electrical failure in the aircraft delayed the trials until the next day.

On the morning of July 21, with Lieutenant Commander James J. Davidson at the controls of the XFD-1 Phantom, the first jet aircraft took off from a U.S. carrier with a deck run of 460 feet. Davidson circled and immediately brought the plane back aboard the ship. In an hour and a half he made five takeoffs and landings; the aircraft was refueled between each cycle to maintain a constant weight. The acceleration of the plane's twin J30 turbojet engines was too slow to permit use of the ship's hydraulic catapults.

Davidson's shortest takeoff run of the day was only 360 feet. The *Roosevelt* trials were successful; the only problem encountered was the relatively slow response of the turbojet engine to sudden throttle movements, an inherent characteristic of early turbojets. On board the "FDR" to observe the trials were two veteran naval aviators: Vice Admiral Arthur W. Radford, who had relieved Marc Mitscher as Deputy Chief of Naval Operations (Air) in January 1946, and Vice Admiral Gerald F. Bogan, Commander, Air Force Atlantic Fleet.

A year after these trials the Phantom, redesignated FH-1, became the first jet aircraft assigned to a U.S. fleet squadron when deliveries to VF-17A began on July 23, 1947.[5] The entire squadron, with 16 Phantoms, qualified for carrier landings aboard the light carrier *Saipan* on May 5–7, 1948. It was the world's first jet squadron to qualify for carrier operation.

Although the FH-1 Phantom would have a brief first-line service life—from 1947 to 1950—it was valuable in introducing jet-propelled fighters to U.S. carrier aviation.[6] It was also flown by the Marine Corps. The FH-1 was the progenitor of the F2H Banshee, flown in the Korean War, the F3H Demon night fighter, and F4H Phantom, the last one of the outstanding fighter-attack aircraft of the Cold War.

The Supermarine Attacker was the first jet aircraft to enter FAA service. The Attacker F.1 fighter had a maximum speed of 590 mph at sea level, could climb to 30,000 feet in 6½ minutes, and had a ceiling of 45,000 feet. Gun armament consisted of four 20-mm wing-mounted cannon; the FB.1 and FB.2 variants were fitted to carry eight 3-inch rockets or two 1,000-pound bombs on wing pylons. Note the streamlined drop tank fitted under the fuselage of this F.1 and the position of the tail fin. (*Flight International*)

The U.S. Navy's first jet aircraft was the McDonnell FH-1 Phantom (initially designated FD-1). At top is the first production FH-1 in flight and, (below) an FH-1 piloted by Lieutenant Commander James J. Davidson taking off from the carrier *Franklin D. Roosevelt* during the first flights of an all-jet aircraft from a U.S. carrier. The FH-1 was rated at a maximum of 479 m.p.h. at sea level, a climb of 4,230 feet per minute, and a ceiling of 41,100 feet. Four .50-caliber machine guns were mounted in the nose. A 295-gallon drop tank could be fitted flush under the fuselage. (U.S. Navy)

The FJ-1 Fury, the second of the U.S. Navy's original three jet fighters to fly, was more promising and became the basis of a highly successful line of Navy fighter-attack aircraft as well as the F-86 Sabre series. The first of three prototype XFJ-1 flew on September 11, 1946. This design was the basis for the Air Force F-86 Sabre. Like the Navy's aircraft, this was to be a straight-wing fighter. But following intense examination of captured German research data, a swept-wing configuration was adopted for the Air Force fighter. The XP-86 flew on October 1, 1947. (More F-86s would be produced than any post–World War II U.S. military aircraft except for the P-80 Shooting Star and its derivatives.)

Meanwhile, the initial, straight-wing FJ-1 series—33 were procured including the three XFJ-1 variants—was followed by the FJ-2 with a 35° swept-back wing, which was identical to the Air Force F-86E Sabre but fitted with carrier launch/arresting hook features.

The F6U Pirate flew late in 1946 and suffered engine failure on its first flight. After additional flight tests, in 1948 one of the three XF6U-1s became the first Navy aircraft fitted with an afterburner. Thirty F6U-1s were then ordered for service, one of which became an F6U-1P photo plane. The planes never entered squadron service being rapidly overtaken by subsequent Navy fighters.

The first U.S. Marine to land a turbojet aircraft on a carrier was Major Marion Carl. A modified P-80A Shooting Star, the Army Air Forces first operational jet, was loaded on the *Roosevelt* by crane, and the carrier went to sea on October 31, 1946. That day Carl made four deck-run takeoffs and two catapult launches; the takeoffs and several arrested landings were made without incident. He made additional landings and takeoffs aboard the *Roosevelt* on November 11. The Navy and Marine Corps subsequently procured 50 single-seat Lockheed P-80s (designated TO-1 by the Navy) and

Lieutenant Commander James J. Davidson discusses landing an XFD-1 Phantom aboard the carrier *Franklin D. Roosevelt* on July 21, 1946, with Vice Admiral Arthur R. Radford (center), the Deputy Chief of Naval Operations (Air), and Vice Admiral Gerald F. Bogan (right), Commander Naval Air Force Atlantic. Radford later served as Commander-in-Chief Pacific then as Chairman of the Joint Chiefs of Staff. (U.S. Navy)

698 two-seat variants (TO-2). The Marines flew a few TO-1s in the land-based fighter role, but most aircraft were flown by the naval services as trainers. None were fitted for carrier operation.[7]

During the immediate postwar years U.S. carrier fighter squadrons mainly operated F8F Bearcats and F4U Corsairs, with some of the latter employed as fighter-bombers. Multipurpose attack squadrons (which replaced the separate torpedo, bombing, and fighter-bombing squadrons in November 1946) flew mostly SB2C Helldivers, and a few had TBM Avengers pending arrival of the potent and versatile AD Skyraider and AM Mauler.

The Hellcat had survived in service after World War II primarily as a night fighter. The F8F-2N night fighter with AN/APS-19 radar was an inferior aircraft because of the drag produced by the radome on its right wing. Thus, the F6F-5N remained in service after the war, although when the Korean War began it had been replaced in carrier air groups by the F4U-5N.[8]

Coming on the scene was the AD Skyraider, unquestionably the best piston-engine attack aircraft ever produced. Its convoluted genesis began with the Douglas SB2D, the prototypes for which were ordered in June 1941 as potential successors to the firm's SBD

Dauntless and to the Curtiss SB2C Helldiver.[9] The first of two XSB2D-1 prototypes, designed by a team led by the brilliant Ed Heinemann, flew in April 1943. It could carry 4,200 pounds of bombs in an internal bay and on wing pylons, or two external torpedoes. Flown by a three-man crew, it had several features not previously found in carrier aircraft: a laminar-flow airfoil, nosewheel landing gear, and two remote-control gun turrets (dorsal and ventral), each mounting two .50-caliber guns; there were also two 20-mm guns in the wings. Maximum speed was 346 m.p.h. Orders were forthcoming.

But in the summer of 1943 the Navy revised its requirements. The heavy defensive armament was no longer needed because U.S. fighters were gaining control of the skies, and the design was extensively revised, resulting in the single-place BTD-1 Destroyer. The twin gun turrets and gunner were removed, and the weight saved was used for additional fuel. The two XBTD-2 prototypes were ordered with their first flight in May 1944.

The Douglas BTD-1 now competed with several other advanced attack aircraft designs: the Curtiss BTC, Kaiser-Fleetwings BTK, and the Martin BTM. Meanwhile, Heinemann's team was also designing an

Table 2-1
EARLY TURBOJET CARRIER AIRCRAFT

AIRCRAFT	FIRST FLIGHT	NUMBER BUILT[*]	GROSS T/O WEIGHT	ENGINES	MAXIMUM SPEED
Sea Vampire F.20	Sep. 20, 1943[**]	18	12,660 lb.	1	526 m.p.h.
FD-1 Phantom	Jan. 26, 1945	61	10,035 lb.	2	479 m.p.h.
Attacker F.1	July 27, 1946[***]	149	12.211 lb.	1	590 m.p.h.
FJ-1 Fury	Sep. 11, 1946	33	15,115 lb.	1	547 m.p.h.
F6U-1 Pirate	Oct. 2, 1946	33	10,741 lb.	1	600 m.p.h.

[*] Only naval procurement.
[**] Flight of prototype Vampire (DH100 Spider Crab).
[***] Flight of the first prototype.

advanced torpedo aircraft, the TB2D Skypirate. This was a very large aircraft—24,111 pounds full load with a 70-foot wingspan: it had a retractable dorsal gun turret, nosewheel landing gear, and a torpedo carried externally. The large R-4360-8 piston engine turned contra-rotating eight-blade propellers.[10] Below about 20,000 feet—without bombs—it could outperform the F4U Corsair. The first of two XTB2D-1 Skypirate prototypes made its first flight on March 18, 1945. While the Navy liked the TB2D for operation from the *Midway*-class carriers, the end of the war led to another reevaluation of aircraft requirements and the cancellation of the 23 TB2D-1s then on order.

Meanwhile, the BTD evolved into the BT2D, initially called the Destroyer II. According to Heinemann, "Compared to any proceeding Douglas plane, the BT2D . . . featured shorter takeoff distance, increased combat radius, better rate of climb, greater load-carrying ability, and improved stability and control."[11] This single-seat aircraft was designed overnight in a room at the Statler Hotel in northwest Washington.[12] The Navy was sufficiently impressed to award Douglas a contract for the final design and production of 15 XBT2D-1 aircraft, soon increased to 25. Although given an *X* prefix, these were production aircraft with some being specialized variants. The first XBT2D-1 took to the skies on March 18, 1945. It was a winner.[13]

The aircraft had a straightforward, uncomplicated design—a low-wing, wide-fuselage, with a large radial-piston engine; weapons were carried on fuselage and wing pylons. Initially three weapon pylons and two 20-

mm cannon (soon increased to four guns) were provided. The aircraft had a remarkable lift capacity with the AD-7 variant having an external payload of more than 8,000 pounds on 15 wing and fuselage stations in addition to the four 20-mm cannon in the wings. In most aircraft the centerline position could carry 3,600 pounds and the two inboard wing positions up to 3,000 pounds each. In May 1953 a standard AD-4B flew at a gross weight of 26,739 pounds—a world record for a single-engine piston aircraft albeit not reflective of a combat load out.

The North American FJ-1 Fury was intended as a production fighter and was the first all-jet fighter to enter squadron service in the U.S. Navy. However, its tenure in the Fleet was brief as the F9F Panther and F2H Banshee entered service, followed by the more-capable, swept-wing FJ variants. Top speed of the FJ-1 was 547 m.p.h. at 9,000 feet, initial climb was 3,300 feet per minute, and ceiling was 32,000 feet. Six .50-caliber guns were mounted around the nose air scoop; all later Navy gun fighters would have 20-mm cannon. (North American Aviation)

Chance-Vought's initial entry into the jet fighter field was the F6U-1 Pirate. Essentially a development aircraft, the F6U pioneered the use of thin sheets of a light material (balsa wood) bonded between thin sheets of metal, the forerunner of "sandwich" aircraft construction. The F6U-1 was rated at 600 m.p.h. at sea level, a climb of 8,480 feet per minute, and a ceiling of 49,000 feet. Four 20-mm cannon were mounted in the nose and wingtip drop tanks were fitted. Note the unusual tail configuration. (U.S. Navy)

In February 1946 the name Skyraider was assigned to the aircraft. On March 11, 1946, the Navy's symbols *B* for Bomber and *T* for Torpedo were dropped from the designation scheme in favor of the all-inclusive *A* for Attack aircraft, and the BT2D became the AD. It was invariably referred to as the "able dog"—the phonetic names for the letters AD. An outstanding aircraft, it was soon nicknamed "Spad," in honor of the outstanding World War I fighter.

The Navy ordered the aircraft into production and deliveries of the production AD-1 began in November 1946 with Attack Squadron 19A the first to fly the aircraft.[14] In 1948 the first specialized variant was delivered, the AD-1Q model. This was a three-place aircraft—pilot, radar operator, countermeasures operator—that could locate, identify, and jam enemy radar and could also serve in the night attack and ASW roles. It was fitted with the AN/APS-19 radar and could carry bombs, albeit less than the straight attack variants. The AD-1Q and subsequent AD-2N quickly replaced the TBM-3E and TBM-3N Avengers aboard carriers in the electronic and night attack roles, respectively. Skyraider variations included six- and 12-place transports, a 2,000-pound-load cargo plane, anti-submarine, utility, drone control, ambulance, airborne early warning, night attack, and nuclear attack configurations.[15]

The AD-4B was the first nuclear-capable Skyraider and the world's first single-engine piston aircraft able to deliver an atomic bomb.

Nuclear Strike

Beginning with the AD-4 variant, the Skyraider could carry the Mk 7 atomic bomb, a 1,630-pound weapon, the first designed to be externally carried by fighter/attack aircraft. While in flight the pilot remotely inserted the ten-pound core of U_{235} or Pu_{239} to arm the weapon. The normal attack profile was to carry a single Mk 7 and two 300-gallon drop tanks, giving the aircraft a radius of some 1,000 miles. Missions were flown at a maximum altitude of 200 feet; often the pilots spent hours at an altitude of only 50 feet to evade hostile radar.[16] Pilots practiced carrier-launched nuclear strike missions in excess of 12 hours.

The Mk 7 bomb became available in January 1952. With a yield of some 20 kilotons, it was slightly more powerful than the atomic bombs dropped on Hiroshima and Nagasaki.[17] The Skyraider could also carry the BOAR, a modified Mk 7 bomb with a rocket booster to give the launching aircraft a limited standoff range. It became available in 1956.[18] Vice Admiral Gerald E. Miller later wrote that in the nuclear strike role,

The U.S. Navy evaluated the Lockheed P-80 Shooting Star fighter for possible service use and Major Marion Carl, a Marine aviator, flew carrier tests of a P-80 from the *Franklin D. Roosevelt* late in 1946. Both the Navy and Marines flew Shooting Stars (designated TO-1) in the late 1940s, but they were not equipped for carrier operation. The Navy later used two-place TO-2/TV-2/T-33 Shooting Stars for training. (U.S. Navy)

The Douglas SB2D was designed as a follow-on to the famed SBD Dauntless. The new plane had two 20-mm wing guns plus two power turrets, each with a single .50-caliber machine gun. However, the total Allied control of the skies over the Pacific in the closing stages of World War II alleviated the requirement for carrier bombers to have a heavy defensive armament. This is one of two XSB2D-1 prototypes, named Dauntless II by Douglas Aircraft. (U.S. Navy)

the propeller-driven [Skyraider] had a high probability of achieving the desired results—better than most. It was a reliable airplane, and it traveled at low level to the target, giving it a high penetration reliability. In addition, the targets to which it was assigned were generally elements of early warning air defense systems such as radars, which were on the periphery of the vast target area.[19]

The Skyraider served as a Navy carrier-based nuclear strike aircraft from 1952 into the early 1960s.[20] It was replaced by more capable jet aircraft and at the time was in great demand for conventional operations in the Vietnam War. A total of 3,180 Skyraiders were delivered through 1957, and the plane served in first-line Navy attack squadrons until 1968 and flew even longer in the U.S. Air Force for rescue combat air patrol in Vietnam.

The Skyraider's only realistic competitor was the Martin AM-1 Mauler, which first flew in the fall of 1945 as the XBTM-1. The Mauler was heavier, 19,200 pounds versus 13,500 pounds gross for the XBT2D-1, and inferior in performance. The Mauler had four 20-mm cannon, and although designed to lift up to three tons, on one occasion a Mauler took off with a 14,179-pound payload including three torpedoes and 12 250-pound bombs. (The record takeoff payload for the Skyraider was 11,944 pounds including three 2,000-pound bombs, six 500-pounders, and six 250-pounders.)

Maulers began joining carrier squadrons in March 1948. Production ended with the 152nd aircraft as the Mauler was edged out by the Skyraider. Also, the Mauler was plagued with material problems, caused mainly by the inexperience of the Martin Company with modern carrier aircraft. The only variant of the AM-1 design was an electronic countermeasures aircraft, the AM-1Q.

As these attack aircraft were going aboard carriers in the late 1940s so were two new fighters, the Grumman F9F Panther and the McDonnell F2H Banshee. The F9F was that firm's first turbojet aircraft, a streamlined, subsonic aircraft that first flew as the XF9F-2 on November 24, 1947.[21] The aircraft was soon ordered into production as a fighter-bomber. Flying from the carrier *Valley Forge*, the F9F would become the U.S. Navy's first jet-propelled aircraft in combat on July 3, 1950. The F9F-2 was credited with a maximum speed of 594 m.p.h. at sea level, an initial climb of 7,700 feet per minute, and a ceiling of more than 40,000 feet. As built this model had an armament of four 20-mm cannon. In service the Navy modified a large number of aircraft to the F9F-2B, with later aircraft being produced in this configuration. The -2B could carry an external payload of 3,000 pounds, including two 1,000-pound bombs plus smaller bombs or 5-inch rockets.

The F2H Banshee was a much-improved successor to the McDonnell FH-1 Phantom. While having some outward resemblance to the earlier aircraft, the

The Douglas BTD-1 Destroyer's sleek lines reveals the aircraft's role as progenitor of the outstanding AD Skyraider. Like the Douglas SB2D and TB2D designs of the same era, the BTD had "bent wings." The letters "FT" on the aircraft's nose indicates the Flight Test division of the Patuxent River Naval Air Test Center in Maryland. (National Air and Space Museum)

An XTB2D-1 Skypirate shows the "bent-wing" and nosewheel configuration of the several Douglas-designed attack aircraft of the period. The large R-4360 radial engine with 3,350 horsepower required contrarotating propellers. Unlike the SB2D Dauntless II, the TB2D had no dorsal or ventral gun turrets. (U.S. Navy)

twin-engine F2H was almost twice the weight of its predecessor. The first XF2H-1 flew on January 11, 1947, and, like the F9F, was quickly placed in production. Both the F9F-2 and F2H-1, the initial variants to enter squadron service, had permanent wingtip fuel tanks. Armament was four 20-mm cannon. The F9F could carry up to 2,000 pounds of bombs and rockets; the F2H could carry 1,000 pounds of bombs. The F2H was one of the highest-flying combat aircraft of its time with a ceiling of some 48,500 feet.

The F2H-1 entered service with fighter squadron VF-171 in March 1949 and the F9F-2 with VF-51 in May 1949. By the summer of 1950 all Navy fighter squadrons had converted to the F9F Panther or F2H Banshee, a very rapid transition from piston to turbojet aircraft.

The Carrier Squeeze

The early jet-propelled fighters and improved piston-engine attack planes for carriers were severely limited by the ships from which they flew. The new jet fighters were as heavy as any carrier bomber imagined when the *Essex* class was designed, and the new attack planes were reaching a gross weight double that of World War II carrier bombers. High landing speeds added to the difficulties of jet operations. The flight decks of the *Essex*-class ships could not take the increased weights, and their aviation fuel capacity was inadequate for the kerosene-gulping jets. Further, the jets could be launched only by catapult and the hydraulic "cats" in the World War II–era carriers were unable to push faster and heavier planes into the air. The *Midway*s were better suited for jet-age operations only by virtue of being

larger, although they had the same catapults and, of course, there were only three of them. The ability of existing aircraft carriers to operate jet aircraft was becoming marginal.

The Royal Aircraft Establishment (RAE) at Farnborough, England, led the search for more effective methods of operating jet-propelled aircraft from carriers. That research and test organization began considering the elimination of wheels from jet aircraft during the war. Unlike piston aircraft with their big, whirling propellers, jet aircraft could—theoretically—land on their fuselage bottom. Eliminating landing gear and related machinery could reduce the weight of the aircraft, allowing for better performance or increased armament (as noted in the Gallery Memorandum). Further, an aircraft without the need to retract the undercarriage could have thinner wings, allowing for additional improvements in the plane's performance.

At an RAE conference in January 1945 several methods of landing and launching aircraft without wheels were discussed. Suggestions included operating wheeless aircraft from soft ground or sand, a sprung deck, flexible material floating on water, wires stretched between towers (a variation of the U.S. Brodie system), a wire net, and a trolley running along tracks. Major F. M. Green, ex–Royal Flying Corps and a leading aeronautical engineer, proposed landing a wheeless jet

The AD Skyraider was the most successful piston attack plane of the post–World War II era, a product of Ed Heinemann's design team at Douglas. The Skyraider was fast, maneuverable, easy to fly, capable of lifting large payloads, and readily modified to special-mission configurations. It would be a first-line naval aircraft for more than two decades, a longevity equalled only by the F4U Corsair. This is a later AD-6 aboard the carrier *Forrestal* in 1956. (Douglas Aircraft Company)

The Skyraider's only competitor was the Martin AM-1 Mauler. The Mauler's performance was slightly inferior to the Skyraider, maximum speed being 367 m.p.h. at 11,600 feet with a climb of 2,780 feet per minute, and a ceiling of 30,500 feet. This AM-1 lifts three torpedoes and a dozen rockets. The torpedoes weighed 6,270 pounds and the rockets 1,674 pounds. (U.S. Navy)

aircraft on a flexible "carpet" suspended by shock absorbers. Such a "runway" coupled with the action of conventional arresting wires could halt the aircraft with a minimum of runout. A carpet 150 feet long and 40 feet wide was proposed for an aircraft weighing about 8,000 pounds. Wear on the rubber surface would be extremely small, especially if the surface were kept wet.

Work on the "undercarriage-less aircraft" project was slow because the RAE was engrossed in testing advanced Allied aircraft and then seeking out and evaluating German aircraft. The flexible deck system was not ready for aircraft landings until late 1947.

Just after noon on December 29, 1947, Lieutenant-Commander Brown in a Sea Vampire with wheels retracted approached a flexible-deck runway at Farnborough. As the twin-boom aircraft approached the carpet area, the plane sank faster than had been anticipated and Brown increased power to check the plane's downward motion. But the slow acceleration response to the throttle (common in early jets) caused the aircraft to keep sinking and strike the ramp at the end of the carpet. The arresting hook bounced up and locked, and the plane's tail booms were damaged, locking the control surfaces. The Sea Vampire bounced twice along the carpet and then hit the ground, badly damaged. Brown was uninjured.

After this inauspicious first effort, changes were made in the landing procedure, and on March 17, 1948, Brown made a perfect flexible deck landing in a Sea

Vampire with wheels retracted. More landings followed at Farnborough, and on November 3, 1948, Brown landed on a flexible carpet installed aboard HMS *Warrior*.

The *Warrior*, recently returned from the Canadian Navy, was provided with a flexible deck of a rubber-like material stretching 190 feet aft from her island structure. From the end of the landing pad to within a few feet of the after flight deck ramp was a metal approach ramp 150 feet long. A single arresting wire was installed near the forward end of the false deck. After a plane caught the wire it was pulled down onto the flexible carpet and slowed to a halt with a runout of only a few feet. A crane then lifted the aircraft onto a trolley; the trolley was winched forward for lowering to the hangar deck by elevator or to the catapult for launching.

The tests on the *Warrior* were conducted from November 1948 to May 1949. More than 200 landings were made by Fleet Air Arm and Royal Air Force pilots and one U.S. Navy test pilot, both ashore and afloat. There were no serious accidents. On occasion a plane would miss the arresting wire, hit the carpet, and actually bounce into the air so that the pilot could fly around for another go.[22]

Evaluation of the tests indicated that the elimination of the undercarriage would represent a 4 to 5 percent saving in aircraft weight. This could lead to improved aircraft designs (e.g., thinner wings) that could further reduce the gross weight by 5 to 6 percent. Translated into performance, for carrier-type aircraft

The Grumman F9F-2 Panther entered U.S. Navy service in large numbers on the eve of the Korean War. The Panther was the world's first carrier-based jet aircraft to enter combat and the first Navy aircraft to down an enemy jet aircraft, i.e., a MiG-15. All production aircraft had fixed wingtip fuel tanks. The Argentine Navy also flew the Panther, with 24 refurbished F9F-2s being based ashore. Those aircrafts were in combat against Chile in 1965. (U.S. Navy)

The McDonnell F2H Banshee—like the F9F—mounted four 20-mm cannon; contemporary Air Force fighters retained .50-caliber machine guns. The F2H-1 entered service with fighter squadron VF-171 in March 1949 and the F9F-2 with VF-51 in May 1949. A short time later all CV-CVB carriers had exclusively jet-propelled fighters. Most F2H-2s and later models also had fixed wintip fuel tanks. (U.S. Navy)

this meant a 45-minute increase in endurance or a 17 to 23 m.p.h. increase in speed.

But the wheelless aircraft would require a flexible deck everywhere it went. It could not land at conventional airfields nor aboard carriers not fitted with a flexible deck. The costs of rigging airfields ashore with flexible decks and of developing a new generation of aircraft to take maximum advantage of the concept were not considered justified for the results gained. The flexible deck concept died, but a closely related project would later revolutionize aircraft carrier design.

The U.S. Navy in 1953 erected a 570-by-80-foot flexible deck at the Patuxent River, Maryland, naval air station. Two modified F9F-7 Cougar turbojet aircraft flew a total of 23 wheels-up landings onto the deck, being piloted by a Grumman test pilot and a Navy pilot. The trials encountered numerous difficulties, and the concept was again abandoned.[23]

During this period test pilot Eric Brown landed a hybrid Meteor Mk 3/4 fighter aboard the carrier *Implacable*. The Gloster meteor was the only Allied jet-propelled aircraft to become operational in World War II. Brown's operations aboard the *Implacable* on June 8, 1948, marked the first by a twin-engine jet aircraft on a British carrier.

The British also conducted tests between October 1945 and February 1946 with the Brodie system, which had been developed in the United States and used operationally at Iwo Jima in 1945. A Piper L-4B observation

A prototype Vampire with its wheels retracted lands on the flexible deck of the carrier *Warrior* during tests of this advanced operating concept. The plane, piloted by Commander Eric Brown, has already caught the single arresting wire and is about to impact on the flexible deck. After each landing the Vampire, which was not fitted for catapulting, took off with a deck run down the 300 feet of clear steel deck forward of the flexible deck. The top of the flexible deck was 2¼ feet above the carrier's steel deck. (Crown Copyright)

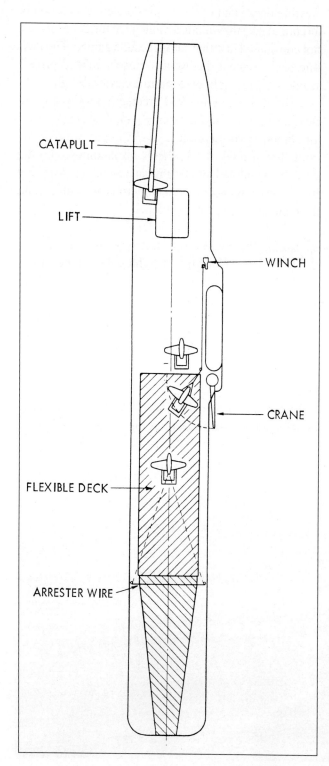

The rubber deck configuration of HMS *Warrior*.

aircraft was used in these trials until February 12, when during a launch the aircraft accelerated too slowly and, when released, crashed, ending the trials. The British were not, however, looking at the Brodie system for shipboard use, but for operations ashore in Malaya.

Whirlybirds Come of Age

Another important although less dramatic development in carrier aviation during the later 1940s was the arrival of helicopters on carrier flight decks. The first recorded instance of a rotary-wing aircraft operating on a carrier was the Pitcairn XOP-1 autogiro trials on the USS *Langley* (CV 1) in 1931.

Autogiros were aircraft that obtained lift with a horizontal propeller—or rotor—that drew energy from the air stream rather than the aircraft's engine. Although the engine could be connected to the rotor during take-off or landing, in flight the engine was geared to a conventional propeller for forward motion. Thus the autogiro could takeoff and land vertically but could not hover.

The XOP-1 underwent a series of landing and take-off trials aboard the *Langley* on September 23, 1931. No further U.S. carrier operations were conducted with the autogiro, but the following June an OP-1 autogiro was sent to Nicaragua for use by the U.S. Marine Corps expeditionary force policing the guerrilla-infested mountain and jungle areas of that country. Although the autogiro operated without difficulty, it lacked the range for worthwhile work and could lift a payload of only 50 pounds.

The Italian heavy cruiser *Fiume* was used for ship-board Cierva C.30A autogiro trials in January 1935, and a short time later, beginning in September 1935, a Cierva autogiro flew from the British carriers *Furious* and *Courageous*. However, there was no serious effort to operate the novelty aircraft from carriers because of the normally short takeoff and landing characteristics of carrier aircraft and the severe performance limitations of autogiros. Ships other than carriers operated floatplanes and flying boats for gunnery observation, scouting, liaison, and utility work.

The Japanese Army imported a Kellett KD-1 autogiro from the United States in 1939 for evaluation of its use as an artillery spotter (it was also evaluated by the U.S. Army as the YG-1). Although the autogiro crashed during the trials, the Kayaba corporation was able to duplicate it as the Ka-1, a useful aircraft for artillery spotting, liaison, and ASW. In the last role it

The Pitcairn XOP-1 autogiro on the USS *Langley* during carrier evaluation on September 23, 1931. The U.S. Navy bought three of these machines, one of which was tested by the Marines in combat during counterguerrilla operations in Nicaragua. The XOP-I could lift only 50-pound payloads with a takeoff run of 200 feet; the Marines' 02U-1 biplanes could lift 200 pounds with the same takeoff run. (U.S. Navy)

was flown from Japanese Army carriers during the war (see Volume I, pp. 261, 263).

During the late 1930s the Germans developed several advanced autogiros and began the transition to "helicopters," aircraft with their engines fully geared to the rotor for horizontal as well as vertical flight. Test landings were conducted on several types of warships, including submarines, and the Flettner Fl 282 *Kolibri* (Humming Bird) was developed specifically for operation from warships.

The Fl 282 had twin two-blade, intermeshing rotors. An official British report noted that the Fl 282 "was the most advanced of the German rotating wing projects and had flown more hours than any other."[24] The analysis continued,

The aircraft was extremely maneuverable and could be flown in very bad weather, in rain, snowstorms and gusty air, and very many tests were made of its autorotational stability, vibration and vibratory stresses. Hundreds of power-off autorotative landings were made. As an endurance test, one aircraft was flown for 95 hours [with landings to refuel and change pilots] without any repairs or replacements being necessary.

During 1942–1943 an Fl 282 made a series of successful flights from a turret of the light cruiser *Köln* in the Baltic Sea. The helicopter was subsequently used in convoy escort operations in the Aegean and

The Italian Navy conducted tests with the La Cierva autogiro, which operated from a wooden deck on the heavy cruiser *Fiume* during January 1935. The tests were conducted with the cruiser at anchor in La Spezia and then underway. Autogiros were flown by several military services into World War II. (Italian Navy)

Mediterranean.[25] A production order for *one thousand* Fl 282s was placed in 1944, but only between 22 and 24 prototypes were completed before the war ended.

There was similar interest in using helicopters for convoy escort in the United States. This interest was first expressed in 1942–1943 by the U.S. Coast Guard, the service being seconded to the Navy and operating a number of escort ships.[26] Early in 1943 the Commandant of the Coast Guard, after witnessing demonstrations of the Sikorsky VS-300 and XR-4 helicopters, urged Admiral Ernest J. King, the Chief of Naval Operations, to obtain helicopters for convoy protection.

Igor Sikorsky's VS-300, which first flew in 1939, was the first successful American helicopter.[27] This vehicle's successor was the VS-316, which, under the military designation XR-4, first flew on January 13, 1942. Admiral King directed the procurement of 23 Sikorsky R-4B helicopters for training (designated HNS-1 by the Navy) and 100 of the advanced R-6A (HOS-1) and 50 R-5A (HO2S-1) helicopters for operational use. Deliveries to the U.S. Navy actually totaled 23 HNS-1, 39 HOS-1, and 2 HO2S-1 helicopters. Another 52 R-4s were supplied to the Royal Air Force and Fleet Air Arm for evaluation, these being known as Hoverfly I in British service; 15 of the R-6 model also went to Britain, these being designated Hoverfly II.

The first shipboard trials by a U.S. helicopter took place aboard the merchant tanker *Bunker Hill* on May 7, 1943, by Army Colonel Frank Gregory flying an XR-4. Later in 1943 Army XR-4 helicopter trials were carried out aboard the British merchant ship *Dagheston*. These trials included her operating a helicopter in the mid-Atlantic while en route to Britain in convoy. However, the trials were severely limited by bad weather. Subsequently, the Coast Guard modified the cutter *Cobb* to a helicopter trials ship, with flights by HNS-1 and HOS-1 helicopters beginning in June 1944. Before the year was over the Army was flying R-4s from aviation repair ships (see Volume I, p. 498).[28]

The greatest strides in helicopter development during World War II were made in the United States and Germany. This was Germany's Flettner Fl 282. Named Kolibri or "Humming Bird," the Fl 282 was specifically intended to operate from ships for convoy protection. The aircraft had two intermeshing rotors atop the fuselage (with no forward or aft props). Two persons could squeeze into the nose cockpit. The Fl 282 was extremely maneuverable and had a maximum speed of 93 m.p.h.; with only a pilot it could remain aloft for more than 2½ hours. (Imperial War Museum)

The U.S. Navy's first helicopter was the HNS-1, a navalized version of Sikorsky's R-4B, which saw limited Army service in Burma before the war ended. Here the Coast Guard tests the rescue capability of an HNS-1 off New York in 1944. The helicopter also flew extensive shipboard trials, those helicopters being fitted with large pontoons that permitted opertions on land, shipboard, and water. (U.S. Navy)

Marines pose for the camera as they land from Piasecki HRP-1 Rescuer helicopters at Quantico, Virginia. The U.S. Marine Corps initiated the development of vertical assault tactics, employing helicopters to land troops behind beach defenses during amphibious operations. The British would be first to use helicopters in a ship-to-shore assault, at Suez in 1956. (U.S. Marine Corps)

Another milestone in helicopter development came in April 1945 when the cutter *Cobb* conducted tests with an HOS-1 fitted with a "dipping" sonar. While the helicopter hovered over the water a sonar transducer was lowered into the sea in an effort to detect a nearby submarine; this was the precursor for helicopter ASW operations.

The U.S. Navy established what was probably the world's first official all-helicopter squadron—Experimental Squadron (VX) 3—on July 1, 1946, to accelerate the evaluation of fleet introduction of helicopters. A year later the squadron began receiving the XHRP-1, which was the first U.S. helicopter developed under military contract. The XHRP-1 had a banana-shape fuselage 48 feet long and was powered by a single engine that drove 41-foot tandem rotors, one mounted atop either end of the fuselage. This helicopter could lift eight passengers in addition to its two-man crew, a significant improvement over the HNS-HOS-HO2S series that carried a pilot and one passenger. A total of 20 XHRP-1/HRP-1 helicopters and six improved HRP-2 (ten-passenger) variants were delivered for Navy/Marine Corps use.

By the end of the 1940s most U.S. aircraft carriers were assigned an HO3S-1 (Sikorsky S-51) for rescue and utility work. This helicopter could fly 364 miles in just over five hours; with three passengers it could go 238 miles in 2½ hours. It had a gross weight of 4,900 pounds with a 1,250-pound payload and could reach a maximum speed of 103 m.p.h. This HO3S-1 is hovering over the carrier *Kearsarge*; F8F Bearcats are parked amidships. (Lt. [jg] C. Daughtry/U.S. Navy)

Marine Helicopter Squadron (HMX) 1 was established on December 1, 1947, to develop tactics, doctrine, training, equipment, and logistics for "vertical envelopment"—amphibious assault by helicopter.[29] In the spring of 1948 the squadron operated five of the new HO3S-1s. Helicopters operated from the escort carrier *Palau* to test the feasibility of carrying troops from ships to beachhead by helicopters. In theory, the five little machines, each with a pilot and two riflemen on board, represented a full helicopter group of 184 HRP-type helicopters lifting a Marine regimental combat team. The experiment was a success, although a ludicrous comparison with later helicopter assault exercises because of the limited number of helicopters available and the small payloads carried.

That same spring, on April 1, 1948, the U.S. Navy disbanded VX-3 and established Helicopter Utility Squadrons (HU) 1 and 2 to provide helicopters for shipboard operation. In June 1948 three of the HU-1's HO3S-1 helicopters and two smaller HTL-2 trainers flew aboard the escort carrier *Bairoko* for support work in Operation Sandstone, a nuclear test in the Pacific.

That summer the HU squadrons began providing two-helicopter detachments to fleet carriers, the first ones being assigned to the *Boxer* and *Princeton*. The helicopters served primarily as plane guards, hovering near the carriers during flight operations to pick up pilots of aircraft that ditched during landing or takeoff. The whirlybirds also performed utility tasks such as transferring personnel, spare parts, mail, and movies between ships. Most of the helicopters assigned to carriers in this period were four-place HO3S-1s. The first HO3S-1 had been delivered in 1947, and 91 were procured for Navy and Marine use.

The ungainly helicopter, along with the jets and the new heavy attack planes, would have a significant place in aircraft carrier operations during the coming decades of "limited" war.

3 ATOMIC BOMBS ABOARD SHIP

A P2V-3C Neptune from composite squadron VC-5 takes off from the *Franklin D. Roosevelt*. The Neptune was the first U.S. Navy aircraft capable of carrying a nuclear weapon. Because existing hydraulic catapults lacked the power to launch the Neptunes, the planes required JATO rocket boosters for deck-run takeoffs. Note the carrier's heavy armament of twin 3-inch/50 and single 5-inch/54 guns. (U.S. Navy)

The U.S. Navy's most significant effort in carrier development in the immediate postwar years was the drive to achieve a nuclear strike capability. When World War II ended the United States had a very limited nuclear capability because of the few atomic bombs available, which could only be delivered to a target some 1,500 miles distance by a limited number of modified B-29 Superfortress bombers. The Navy had no nuclear capability. The atomic bomb had been developed as an Army project with only a few Navy officers involved, albeit in key positions.

The Army Air Forces—which became the U.S. Air Force on September 18, 1947—sought absolute control of the nuclear strike mission and capabilities. Within the U.S. Navy a controversy ensued over what should be the sea service's role—if any—in the delivery of nuclear weapons. As early as July 22, 1946, Assistant Secretary of the Navy for Air John L. Sullivan, as acting

Navy secretary, wrote to President Truman about the mobility and flexibility of aircraft carriers.[1] Sullivan concluded, "I strongly urge that you authorize the Navy to make preparations for possible delivery of atomic bombs in an emergency in order that the capabilities of the Carrier Task Forces may be utilized to the maximum advantage for national defense."[2]

The strongest stand in favor of the Navy developing a nuclear strike capability was made by Rear Admiral Daniel Gallery, the Assistant Chief of Naval Operations for Guided Missiles. In a paper dated December 17, 1947, Gallery urged the Navy to "start an aggressive campaign aimed at proving that the Navy can deliver the Atomic Bomb more effectively than the Air Force can."[3] The report explained the advantages and capabilities of a carrier-based nuclear strike capability as opposed to the use of land-based bombers.

In his lengthy memorandum, Gallery noted that the B-29—with a combat radius of less than 2,000 miles—required overseas bases from which to operate. While the new B-36 "super bomber" would have a greater range, it would need fighter escorts, which, in turn, required overseas bases. The report declared that with overseas air bases there was no need for the long-range B-36.

Next, Gallery addressed the problems and costs of seizing and maintaining overseas air bases. He pointed out that the "enemy" need not possess overseas bases because enemy bombers could fly one-way missions to the United States ending in imprisonment of their crews, "not a very grim prospect" for the enemy fliers. (At this time the U.S. Air Force was also considering "one-way" missions for nuclear bombers striking the Soviet Union, with the planes bombing their targets and then flying on to neutral or friendly countries—if possible.)

Admiral Gallery then made his presentation for an "Atomic Carrier"—CVA:

The carrier can transport the bomber across the ocean and launch it 1,000 miles from its target. Instead of building the transoceanic range into the bomber, and thereby penalizing its performance over enemy territory, we build a transoceanic range into the carrier. We design the airplane for maximum performance on a comparatively short flight.

The importance of an A-Bomb mission is such that we can well afford to expend the airplane that delivers the bomb. But we want to get the crew back. We can do this by stationing submarines at previously designated spots to which the bombers can fly and ditch after delivering the bomb. In this way the carriers are left free to take evasive action as soon as the bomber is launched, making it impossible to follow the bomber back to the carrier.

In describing the proposed carrier, Gallery wrote:

The governing requirement for a CVA (atomic carrier) is to provide the best possible take-off platform for the A-bomber. There should be no island; a new type catapult for launching craft is required; arresting gear is of secondary importance; the Air Group will be on the order of a dozen planes; special high speed submarines for rescue purposes are required.

Gallery depicted the planes to operate from the carrier as

designed for maximum performance for one flight; no landing gear is necessary; take-off will be made from a carriage running along a track on the deck; carriage will be started by catapult or assisted by JATO; planes will be designed for ditching; airplane dimensions can be greatly increased over present sizes now used on carriers. If our A-bomber has a 1,500 nautical mile combat radius it can reach all of Europe and Asia except a few spots in central Siberia. This can be done by launching from carriers on the high seas, excluding the Mediterranean.

Rear Admiral Daniel Gallery (U.S. Navy)

The 1,500 mile bomber will obviously have better performance over enemy territory than a transoceanic bomber. A 1,500 mile bomber designed under the concept above will always have better performance than a 1,500 mile bomber which is forced to take off from land. The principal reason for this is that the take-off distance has an important effect on design, and we always have 30 knots of wind across deck. In addition, the elimination of the landing gear gives us about a 5% advantage in weight. So for a plane of the same size, a carrier plane without landing gear can use the 5% saved in gross weight, and thus get either increased range or higher speed.

Then Admiral Gallery applied the lessons of World War II to operations of his proposed carrier, recalling that a carrier force alleviates the need for airfields on shore, and that a carrier can move 500 miles a day, shifting from the Arctic to the Mediterranean in a week.

His paper noted that "if we start from scratch from the concept outlined above, we will be in a better position than the Air Force to deliver the A-bomb," and concluded,

the major missions of the Navy and Air Force should be as follows:
    Navy: The delivery of an atomic attack on the capitol and industrial centers of the enemy. Secondary mission: Control of the seas.
    Air Force: The defense of the United States against air attack. Secondary mission: The delivery of atomic attacks from overseas bases.

Both Secretary of the Navy Sullivan and the Chief of Naval Operations Admiral Louis E. Denfeld soon disavowed the Gallery Memorandum, declaring "much of his arguments and both of his conclusions are at complete variance with the Navy Department policy and views." Some naval officers supported Navy development of a nuclear striking force. But more believed that the Air Force drive for absolute control of the nation's nuclear strike capability was part of a trend toward accepting nuclear weapons as the only arbitrator of future conflicts. Such a policy would reduce or end the need for a navy and could lead to amalgamation of naval aviation into the Air Force.

This interservice controversy led Secretary of Defense James Forrestal to convene a conference of the service chiefs in the spring of 1948 to discuss the *services* roles and missions. The conference resulted in the Key West Agreement, which recognized the Air Force's sole right to maintain a "strategic air arm" with primary authority over nuclear weapons delivery. However, the agreement acknowledged that the Navy was not to be denied the use of atomic bombs against such naval targets as enemy submarine pens or air bases being used for maritime operations.

Secretary Forrestal, the first "secdef," who had served as Secretary of the Navy from May 1944 to September 1947, endorsed the Navy proposals to build a large carrier and a new "heavy" bomber to operate from the ship. Reportedly, he had "serious misgivings" about such a ship's ability to survive against guided missiles, which were then being developed, but he believed that such weapons would not be perfected for at least five to ten years, a period during which aircraft carriers would remain a valuable element of the nation's arsenal. Significantly, while Forrestal publicly stated that he was against development of a new super-carrier fleet by the Navy, "I felt it was important that one such ship, capable of carrying the weight of a long-range bombing plane, go forward."[4] Privately he favored going ahead with "several such carriers."[5] And Forrestal told the Air Force Chief of Staff "that had we had the A-bomb in 1942 and a plane capable of delivering it from the *Hornet* [CV 8], Doolittle's flight over Japan in April 1942 might have aborted the Japanese war effort."[6]

Carrier-Based Bombers

The earliest known Navy discussion concerning a carrier-based nuclear strike capability took place late in 1945. The subject was discussed in detail by Vice Admiral Marc Mitscher, then Deputy Chief of Naval Operations (Air); Captain William (Deak) Parsons; and Commander John T. (Chic) Hayward. Parsons had played a key role in the development of the atomic bomb and had been the bomb commander on the B-29 *Enola Gay* for the Hiroshima attack. Hayward became involved in the atomic bomb project after working in rocket development.[7]

In 1944–1945 carrier force commanders in the Pacific began calling for attack aircraft with longer ranges than existing planes to provide greater standoff distances from Japanese airfields. In response, the Navy Bureau of Aeronautics held a design competition for a long-range, carrier-based aircraft capable of carrying

A P2V-3C Neptune from VC-5 is loaded aboard the carrier *Coral Sea* at Norfolk, Virginia. Navy pilots practiced carrier landing techniques ashore, but the Navy's leadership refused to permit an actual landing aboard ship. During its reconfiguration to the nuclear strike role all guns were deleted except for the twin .50-caliber machine guns in the tail. (U.S. Navy)

up to 12,000 pounds of conventional bombs, which could be traded off against range. At that time the Navy had no technical data on atomic bombs, not even their dimensions. Soon after the war ended it was known that the Fat Man bomb exploded over Nagasaki had weighed about 10,000 pounds. Commander Frederick Ashworth, who had been bomb commander on the B-29 *Bockscar* that dropped the atomic bomb on Nagasaki, inspected a mock-up of the proposed 12,000-pound-capacity aircraft at the North American plant. Ashworth, on the staff of the Chief of Naval Operations, and Captain Joseph N. Murphy, assigned to the Bureau of Aeronautics, decided that the aircraft design could be modified to carry the Mk III or the new Mk IV atomic bomb.[8]

Commander Ashworth drafted a letter for the Secretary of the Navy to send to the president requesting permission for the Navy to proceed with the aircraft having a nuclear capability. When Forrestal received the draft (he was still Secretary of the Navy), he decided that presidential action was not required and told the Navy to begin work on the project. The Bureau of Aeronautics (BuAer) ordered a *three-engine* attack aircraft from North American Aviation in June 1946. The aircraft was propelled by twin piston engines and an auxiliary J33 turbojet. The first of three XAJ-1 prototypes flew on July 3, 1948. Named Savage, the AJ-1 was intended specifically to operate from the three *Midway*-class carriers as well as future, larger flattops.

But the Savage would not be ready for delivery to fleet squadrons until the fall of 1949, and the Navy was not willing to lose time nor opportunity in the development of a carrier-based nuclear strike capability. The only naval aircraft that could carry a 10,000-pound bomb load and stood any chance of taking off from a carrier deck was the P2V Neptune, a new twin-engine, land-based patrol aircraft. With a wingspan of 100 feet, a length of 78 feet, a height of 28 feet, and a takeoff weight of some 60,000 pounds, the Neptune was considerably larger than the B-25s that had flown from the old *Hornet* (CV 8) and the *Shangri-La*, and the R4Ds that had flown from the *Philippine Sea*.

Extensive tests with the Neptunes were conducted ashore. One of the lead pilots in this project was Commander Thomas D. Davies who, in September 1946, had flown an XP2V-1 Neptune named *Truculent Turtle* from Perth, Australia, to Columbus, Ohio, in 55 hours, 17 minutes. The flight shattered the world's record for distance without refueling, setting a mark of 11,235.6 miles. The Neptune's record stood for almost two decades.[9]

After scores of practice takeoffs from Patuxent River naval air station in Maryland, on April 27, 1948, barges brought two P2V-2 Neptunes alongside the large carrier *Coral Sea*, moored at Norfolk. The planes were lifted to the carrier's deck by crane, looking like giant, prehistoric monsters to the carrier's sailors, who were used to seeing "bombers" with only half the Neptune's wingspan. During the night the *Coral Sea* steamed out into the Atlantic while mechanics tuned and fueled the aircraft.

At 7:16 the next morning the *Coral Sea* was steaming into a four-knot headwind at 28 knots off the Virginia coast. The first Neptune's throttles were pushed to full power by Commander Davies; he released the brakes, and as the plane started forward the eight JATO auxiliary rockets fired, pushing the plane into the air. Minutes later the second Neptune, piloted by Commander John P. Wheatley, started down the *Coral Sea*'s deck, fired its JATO bottles, and lifted into the air.

The Navy now began a program to develop this test into an operational capability. As an interim heavy attack aircraft the Navy ordered 12 Neptunes to be provided with special features for carrier takeoffs and to carry a nuclear weapon, those being designated P2V-3C.[10] The aircraft were provided with special high-altitude engines and tanks for 4,400 gallons of fuel, almost double that of the standard P2V-3. To reduce weight and drag the radome, the dorsal and nose gun mounts and tail skids were removed. Only the twin 20-mm cannon in the tail were retained for defense. The AN/APA-5 bombing system was modified to the AN/APS-31 configuration for high-altitude bombing. The bomb bay was fitted to carry a Little Boy (Hiroshima-type) or later the Mk VIII atomic bomb.[11]

During this period the production of atomic bombs from the relatively limited amounts of fissionable material available as well as the question of service roles and missions caused major interservice arguments. The Navy wanted a portion of the fissionable material allocated to the development of weapons that could be carried by carrier-based aircraft; the Air Force wanted the available material to go into the production of proven bomb designs—that could best be carried by the larger B-29s and follow-on strategic bombers. Approval for the weapons that the Navy wanted was won from the Joint Chiefs of Staff and the crucial Military Liaison Committee of the newly established Atomic Energy Commission through the efforts of Parsons, Arthur W. Radford, and Forrest P. Sherman.[12] Parsons, promoted to rear admiral, was in charge of the Navy's efforts in atomic weapons development. Vice Admiral Radford was Deputy Chief of Naval Operations (Air) from January 1946 to February 1947 and was then Vice Chief of Naval Operations from January 1948 to April 1949. Rear Admiral Sherman was Deputy Chief of Naval Operations (Operations) from December 1945 to January 1948 and became the CNO in November 1949.[13] The Navy's cause was further helped by Commander Hayward, then serving at the Sandia nuclear laboratory in New Mexico, and Commander Ashworth, executive secretary of the Atomic Energy Commission's Military Liaison Committee during the critical years 1947 and 1948.

In anticipation of increased availability of nuclear weapons, the Navy established Composite Squadron (VC) 5 on September 9, 1948, to evaluate heavy attack aircraft and to develop the doctrine and tactics for delivering nuclear weapons from carriers.[14] Captain Hayward took command of VC-5 and Commander

A Neptune from VC-5 blasts off the deck of the carrier *Midway*. A helicopter hovers above the carrier. Neptune operations aboard carriers as well as the initial AJ Savage operations required the carrier's other aircraft to be struck down to the hangar deck or sent ashore. (U.S. Navy)

Ashworth became his executive officer. Additional "heavy attack" squadrons would be formed from this unit as more men were trained and the new AJ Savages became available. (Ashworth would command the second nuclear-strike squadron, VC-6 established on January 6, 1950.)

All 12 of the specially configured P2V-3C Neptunes were delivered to VC-5 by January 1949. After extensive practice takeoffs from land bases, three of the squadron's Neptunes were hoisted aboard the *Coral Sea* on March 4, 1949. Three days later, off the Virginia Capes, the Neptunes took off with the aid of JATO boosters. Captain Hayward was at the controls of the first plane, which weighed 74,100 pounds including a 10,000-pound dummy nuclear weapon.[15] The other Neptunes weighed 65,000 and 55,000 pounds, respectively.

While the second and third bombers flew to a nearby airfield, Captain Hayward's Neptune flew across the country, dropped its "bomb" on the West Coast, and then returned across the United States to land at Patuxent River, Maryland, home base for the squadron. The plane was airborne for nearly 23 hours and flew almost 4,500 miles.

The flight demonstrated that aircraft with a gross weight of 74,000 pounds could be flown from the large *Midway*-class carrier, deliver an atomic bomb on a target as far as 2,200 miles away, and either return to the carrier and ditch nearby or fly off in a different direction after dropping its bomb and come down near a

Captain John T. Hayward (U.S. Navy)

rescue ship or submarine to save the crew. However, the Navy was still far from having a practical carrier-based nuclear strike capability.

The Neptunes made another 20 takeoffs from the *Midway*-class carriers during March, April, May, and June 1949. On September 26, 1949, the Navy gave a sea power demonstration off the Atlantic coast for several senior officials of the Army, Air Force, and the Department of Defense. The climax to the exercise came when Secretary of Defense Louis Johnson; Secretary of the Air Force Stuart W. Symington; General Omar N. Bradley, the Chairman of the Joint Chiefs of Staff; and publisher William Randolph Hearst climbed into a P2V-3C on the deck of the *Midway*. Captain Hayward took the pilot's seat, Secretary Johnson sat in the copilot's seat, and the others took positions aft in the aircraft. Johnson, as will be related, had just ordered the Navy to halt construction of a flush-deck aircraft carrier. Hayward turned to Johnson and said, "If anything happens on this takeoff, we will have a flush-decked carrier, with your approval or not!" Then Hayward took off—with the Neptune's wingtip missing the *Midway*'s island structure by a few feet, but without incident—and returned his distinguished passengers to Washington.

A more meaningful Neptune flight from the *Midway* came on October 5, 1949, when Commander Ashworth took off as the carrier steamed in the Western Atlantic, flew his plane to the Canal Zone, then north to Corpus Christi, Texas, and finally landed at San Diego, California. The flight spanned 4,880 miles in just under 26 hours, a new record for simulated carrier strikes. A still longer flight was made on February 7–9, 1950, when a P2V-3C launched from the *Franklin D. Roosevelt*, operating off Florida, flew to Panama and then on to San Francisco—5,060 miles in 26 hours.

All three of the *Midway*s had their flight decks strengthened to operate the loaded Neptunes and were modified to store and assemble nuclear weapons.[16] The *Coral Sea* was the first to be fitted handle "nukes," the special weapons spaces were installed in the carrier at the Norfolk Naval Shipyard, the work being completed in March 1950.

The ship then moved to the nearby Norfolk naval base, where a crane loaded aboard a P2V-3C. On the night of April 20–21, 1950, a gun-type (uranium) Mk VIII atomic bomb was assembled on board the *Coral Sea*, less certain critical components, and was loaded into the Neptune. At 7:30 A.M. the aircraft took off amid

Jet-Age Carriers

Meanwhile, the U.S. Navy undertook a two-pronged program to bring aircraft carriers into the jet age. One phase was to modernize existing carriers to handle jet aircraft; the other was to construct a new carrier capable of operating current and future heavy attack aircraft.

The first program—Project 27A—involved the modernization of *Essex*-class carriers. The principal changes would be strengthening the flight decks for operating aircraft weighing up to 40,000 pounds (almost double the original capability), installing more powerful hydraulic catapults, removing the twin 5-inch gun mounts to provide more flight deck space, increasing the elevator strength, doubling the aviation fuels storage (with hull blisters that increased their beam from 93 to 102 feet), and providing jet-blast deflectors behind the catapults.

The unfinished carrier *Oriskany* was the first of nine *Essex*-class carriers to be converted under Project 27A. Her construction had been suspended in 1946 when she was 85 percent complete, with most of her island structure, flight deck, and twin 5-inch gun mounts installed. Work resumed on August 8, 1947. First she was partially dismantled—to about 60 percent completion; she was then rebuilt to the 27A configuration and placed in commission on September 25, 1950 (see Appendix D for U.S. carrier modernization programs).

However, even the modernized *Essex*-class carriers would not be able to operate significant numbers of heavy attack planes as could the three *Midway*s and the "atomic carrier" proposed in the Gallery Memorandum. This was 1947—the Neptunes had not yet flown from carriers and the AJ Savage was still being built. The Navy undertook a publicity program to inform the public and the government of the need for a "super carrier" capable of operating nuclear-armed bombers. The campaign met with success when, in 1948, Congress approved funds for construction of a 65,000-ton aircraft carrier. Subsequently named the *United States*, the ship was designated CVA 58, the *A* now signifying "heavy."

The *United States* was probably the first aircraft carrier to be designed from the outset on the basis of aircraft requirements. The Bureau of Ships (BuShips) began design work on the new carrier, initially designated CVB-X. As in previous carrier designs, a variety

An artist's concept of the proposed super carrier *United States*. The design provided four catapults, two on amidships "wings" and two forward; a stern and three deck-edge elevators; and port and starboard horizontal funnels. There were to be periscoping conning towers to starboard. This basic design was employed in all subsequent U.S. super carriers. (U.S. Navy)

of factors were considered. The early BuShips sketches were for a carrier that could accommodate an aircraft the size of a P2V Neptune, about 60,000 pounds gross takeoff weight with a 100-foot wingspan.

As the preliminary design of the ship was under way, the Bureau of Aeronautics initiated planning for a carrier aircraft capable of carrying 8,000 to 12,000 pounds of bombs. The first aircraft that emerged from this effort was the AJ-1 Savage, with a gross weight of 55,000 pounds and a combat radius of 1,000 miles.

BuAer was also looking at a larger aircraft, designated ADR-42, which could operate only from super carriers. The ADR-42 was to weigh some 100,000 pounds at takeoff and was to deliver the same payload as the AJ-1 (up to 12,000 pounds), but at double the range, a combat radius of 2,000 miles. Such an aircraft would be larger than a P2V Neptune and almost twice the gross weight of a wartime B-17 Flying Fortress. This aircraft evolved into the Douglas A3D Skywarrior.

The carrier went through several iterative designs. Early concepts provided for a ship without a hangar deck (because of expected elevator limitations); the large bombers would be maintained and stowed on the flight deck. Forrest Sherman, now a vice admiral and the Deputy CNO (Operations), in the summer of 1946 wrote,

> The Operations Division does not consider that any employment of this strictly offensive type [carrier] will be warranted without far heavier fighter support and CAP [Combat Air Patrol] than could be provided by fighters carried aboard. This ship would always be accompanied by at least two CVs. Accordingly, no sacrifice of primary characteristics is considered to be warranted in order to get fighters on the same bottom.[27]

The approved design was a "flush deck" carrier having a standard displacement of 65,000 tons with a full load displacement calculated at over 80,000 tons. The bridge would be built on an elevator that could be lowered flush with the flight deck to provide an obstruction-free deck. The flight deck design would permit the simultaneous operation of four catapults; four elevators would transfer aircraft between her flight and hangar decks—three deck-edge lifts and one "notched" into the stern.

The largest warship yet constructed, she was to be 1,090 feet overall in length with a waterline beam of

125 feet, making her too large to transit the Panama Canal (the three *Midway*s were also too wide to go through the canal locks). Turbines would drive the carrier at 33 knots. Her unusual features would include funnels projecting from both sides, flush with the flight deck. Details and armament varied through the several designs (Table 3-1 addresses a late design for the *United States* and the subsequent USS *Forrestal* [CVA 59]). Several twin 3-inch/50-caliber and single 5-inch/54-caliber guns, all high-angle anti-aircraft weapons, would be fitted.

The aircraft operating from the *United States* would be long-range bombers and fighters. Preliminary plans had provided for the ship to carry only nuclear strike aircraft, at one point 12 and subsequently 24 of the ADR-42 design. Eventually fighters were added to the proposed CVA air group.

Senior Navy officials projected a need for four carriers of the *United States* design by 1955. They would operate in four task groups, accompanied by *Midway*-class carriers (in three of the groups) and *Essex*-class ships. The smaller carriers would provide escorting fighters and anti-submarine aircraft.

By the fall of 1947 the super carrier was included in the shipbuilding program for fiscal year 1949 (which began on July 1, 1948). A contract for construction of the first super carrier was awarded to the nation's largest shipyard, Newport News Shipbuilding and Dry Dock in Virginia, on August 10, 1948. The Navy began to define the *United States* as an "atomic carrier," both to the public and to Congress. Historian David A. Rosenberg observed, "This emphasis reflected not only the Navy's desire to develop its nuclear capability in the wake of the Bikini tests, but also its apparent belief that the carrier would stand a better chance of getting funded if it were defined in terms of the new technology."[28] But events were taking place in Washington that would have a major impact on the new carrier and the entire U.S. Navy. The Navy and Air Force were engaged in a heated debate over roles and missions, with the place—some would say the survival—of naval aviation a key factor in the debates.[29]

In February 1949 General of the Army Dwight D. Eisenhower, then President of Columbia University, was appointed "principal military adviser and consultant to the Commander-in-Chief [the president] and Secretary of Defense." For the next two months Eisenhower, in effect, served as chairman of the Joint Chiefs of Staff.[30] Next, on March 28, Louis Johnson

Table 3-1
AIRCRAFT CARRIER CHARACTERISTICS

	UNITED STATES (CVA 58)	*FORRESTAL* (CV 59)
Displacement, light ship	61,569 tons	54,600 tons
Displacement, full load	83,200 tons	76,600 tons
Length, overall	1,090 ft	1,039 ft
Length, waterline	1,030 ft	990 ft
Beam, hull	125 ft	$129^{1}/_{3}$ ft
Draft, full load	$34^{1}/_{2}$ ft	$33^{3}/_{4}$ ft
Horsepower	280,000	260,000
Elevators	4 x 100,000 lb	4 x 79,000 lb
Catapults	4 hydraulic	4 hydraulic
Munitions	2,735 tons	2,514 tons
Fuel oil	11,545 tons	8,607 tons
Aviation fuel	1,526 tons	4,679 tons
Manning	4,127 with air group	3,806 with air group

became the Secretary of Defense, replacing James Forrestal, who was in ill health (and would commit suicide on May 22, 1949).

General Eisenhower and Secretary Johnson immediately became involved in planning the next defense budget. Simultaneously, congressional hearings were being held on the current defense budget and President Truman, on April 8, announced the purchase of 39 giant B-36 bombers for the Air Force. The 95 production B-36s already on order would cost more than six million dollars per plane, making them the most expensive aircraft ever procured. On April 15 Johnson asked Eisenhower and the three members of the Joint Chiefs of Staff for their individual views concerning the new carrier.

On April 18 the 15-ton keel plate for the *United States* was laid down at the Newport News yard. Secretary Johnson, anxious to halt construction of the carrier, decided that the *United States* and her aircraft would provide a duplication of the Air Force's strategic bombing mission. He conferred individually with the three service chiefs, and by April 22 he had drafts of all three service chiefs' opinions and had shown them to President Truman. This was the first time that the Joint Chiefs of Staff had been asked for their opinion on construction of the *United States*.

The CNO, Admiral Denfeld, "strongly recommended its construction, pointing out in detail its im-

portance to the evolution of carrier aviation and naval warfare," according to a later statement. The Chief of Staff of the Air Force, General Hoyt Vandenberg, said that he felt the carrier would be used to duplicate the Air Force's mission of strategic bombing and that the ship would cost closer to $500 million rather than the Navy's estimate of $189 million. The Chief of Staff of the Army, General Omar Bradley, supported the Air Force position, declaring (1) the purpose of the new carrier was a primary function of the Air Force; (2) the Soviet Union was not a sea power nor was it dependent upon the sea for obtaining raw materials; (3) the United States and Great Britain already had overwhelming strength at sea; (4) the use of carrier-based aircraft against land targets should be limited to the existing 700-mile combat radius; (5) the initial use of naval air forces in war and as a temporary reinforcement of the Air Force was justified, but naval air should not be considered for sustained operations against enemy territory; and (6) the new carrier would be extremely expensive and would require expensive support and escort ships.

On April 23, 1949, with President Truman's permission, Johnson ordered a halt to construction of the carrier. He took this action without further consultation with Admiral Denfeld—he knew the admiral's views—and without speaking with Secretary of the Navy Sullivan.

The Navy wanted the new carrier to attack targets of *naval* interest—submarine pens, shipyards, naval airfields. This role for carrier-based nuclear strike had been agreed to by Secretary Forrestal and the Joint Chiefs at conferences addressing service roles in Key West, Florida, and Newport, Rhode Island, in 1948. Walter Millis, a leading military historian at the time, described Secretary Johnson's cancellation of the *United States* as "a reckless destruction of the extremely delicate balances which his predecessor [Forrestal] had been at such pains to establish. Secretary Johnson may have felt that he had logic on his side, but military growth and development are not logical processes."[31] Secretary of the Navy Sullivan promptly resigned, noting to Secretary Johnson the importance of the carrier to the Navy and the fact that the president had twice before approved the construction of the ship.

The B-36 Debate

In retaliation for the loss of its new carrier, some naval officers questioned the viability of the B-36 intercontinental bomber and by implication the U.S. military policy of massive retaliation with nuclear weapons. This campaign has been labeled the "revolt of the admirals" as the House Armed Services Committee initiated an investigation of the entire B-36 program.

The B-36 controversy was further colored by rumors that the Soviets were developing a 500-m.p.h. turbojet interceptor that could operate up to 50,000 feet. This was the MiG-15 (later given the NATO code name Fagot[32]). Such an aircraft would make daylight, high-altitude (about 40,000 feet) bombing missions over the Soviet Union extremely costly if not impossible.

To prove its vulnerability, some naval officers asked that a B-36 be made available for aerial intercept tests with the F4U-5 Corsair and the new, twin-jet F2H-1 Banshee. The Corsair could climb 4,230 feet per minute and had a ceiling of 44,100 feet; the Banshee could climb 7,380 feet per minute and could operate at 48,500 feet. Both altitudes were above the ceiling of the B-36. The Navy request was denied. Even if such an experiment were conducted it would have had little practical meaning but, as one Navy historian commented, "It would have made a significant PR splash."[33]

Damning criticism of the B-36 also came from the former head of the Strategic Air Command, General George C. Kenney.[34] Back in December 1946, shortly after the first flight of the XB-36, Kenney had proposed

that the production of B-36s be halted and that those planes almost finished be used as aerial tankers or for anti-submarine warfare. He judged the B-36 was too slow (346 m.p.h. for the XB-36), would fly but 6,500 miles (not 10,000 miles as planned), would be vulnerable to enemy fighters because of the lack of self-sealing fuel tanks, and was, in general, inferior to the advanced B-29 (i.e., the B-50) that did not fly until six months later, in everything but marginal advantages in range and payload.

General Kenney was overruled by the Air Force Chief of Staff and the proponents of the B-36 were somewhat vindicated when in May 1948, the first production aircraft flew 4,000 miles, dropped a 10,000-pound payload, and flew another 4,000 miles before landing. Still, there were some in the Air Force who wanted to skip over the piston-engine B-36 and go directly into jet-powered bombers. The B-36s were produced with some air power advocates believing that they were the best single-weapon answer to the dilemma of limited defense budgets of the late 1940s.

The B-36 was placed on trial in the congressional hearings during the summer of 1949. General Kenney appeared as a witness to declare "the B-36 is a night bomber. I would not use it in the daytime." His successor as head of the Strategic Air Command, Lieutenant General Curtis E. LeMay, disagreed strongly, presenting a case for the B-36 to attack in daylight as well as at night. The cigar-chomping general, who in 1945 had sent B-29s over Tokyo at night at only 5,000 feet in opposition to traditional strategic bombing doctrine, claimed "we can get the B-36 over a target and not have the enemy know it is there until the bombs hit."

Both generals concurred with the decision to cancel the Navy's super carrier which, at the time, symbolized the Navy's challenge to the virtual Air Force monopoly over being able to strike overseas targets with nuclear weapons. The Air Force high command fully supported the B-36—and at the expense of the aircraft carrier. Secretary of the Air Force Stuart Symington declared that the United States should continue to "concentrate on America's greatest asset—quality of product, superior weapons capable of development, and mass production in our system of free economy—weapons like the B-36 with its intercontinental bombing range without refueling, and other modern bombers and planes with their projected intercontinental range with refueling."

Air Force Chief of Staff Vandenberg followed, declaring that he was "in favor of the greatest possible development of carrier aviation to whatever extent carriers and their aircraft are necessary for fulfillment of a strategic plan against the one possible enemy we may have to face [the Soviet Union]. Less than this would be unsound. More than this would be an unjustifiable burden upon the American taxpayer."

General Vandenberg noted that he was "not only willing but insistent that the types of carriers that can help meet the threat of an enemy submarine fleet shall be developed fully and kept in instant readiness. The sea lanes must be kept open. There is no dispute on this matter." But he was quick to add, "I do not believe there is justification for maintaining large carrier task forces during peacetime" and "my opposition to building it [the *United States*], comes from the fact that I can see no necessity for a ship with those capabilities in any strategic plan against the one possible enemy."

To the Air Force the *United States* and carrier striking forces in general represented a duplication of effort and competition for the funding of long-range, land-based bombers. The admirals answered this challenge to Navy policies as the House committee held lengthy hearings in October 1949 to address what became the B-36-versus-carrier controversy.[35] More than 70 Army, Air Force, Navy, and Marine Corps officers testified. The admirals included William Halsey, Thomas C. Kinkaid, Radford, Raymond A. Spruance, Robert B. Carney, and Louis E. Denfeld; statements from Admiral Ernest J. King and Admiral Chester W. Nimitz were read to the committee. The captains who testified included Arleigh A. Burke and John S. Thach.

Among the most articulate witnesses, Admiral Radford, at the time Commander-in-Chief Pacific and Pacific Fleet, said that the issues were broader and more important than simply the B-36 program. Pointing out that an aggressor can choose the time and place to start fighting, Radford made a case for carrier striking power, telling the committee,

> We have in the United States developed mobile air power to such an extent that we can project it anywhere in the world where there is enough water—-and that is quite a large part of the world—and no other country can do that. As I told you, air power is the key to victory in any military operation from now on, all kinds of air

power. The United States has the unique capability to project air power to get control of the air in vital areas of operation. No one else has it. The Navy today must be built not to meet an enemy navy but with the idea, after evaluation, of the need for air power in theaters of war and parts of the world where we can't get air power any other way.[36]

Here were the keys to carrier air power: flexibility and mobility. However, the Navy advanced these features not for their own merit but to maintain and enlarge its own forces, including nuclear strike—part of the perceived panacea.

Behind the scenes there was considerable infighting within the Navy. Newly appointed Secretary of the Navy Francis Matthews had wanted to limit the Navy's testimony to that of its senior admirals, believing that their views would have the most impact on Congress and the public. Vice Admiral Gerald Bogan, recently relieved as Commander Air Force Atlantic Fleet, wrote a letter that such action would effectively "gag" the Navy, and the letter was released to the press. The letter had been endorsed by Denfeld. Secretary Matthews, who had not approved release of the letter, was angry.[37] The Bogan letter and the failure of several flag officers to provide Matthews with copies of their testimony before they appeared before the committee was against regulations in spirit if not in fact. Matthews recalled,

> [W]e had a regular (Navy) Top Policy meeting, and at the conclusion of the meeting they all left. I called Admiral Denfeld back from the door. Without my opening a conversation, he said: "Mr. Secretary, I am sorry that I could not keep my promise to show you my statement, but I was going to give it anyway, no matter what you thought. I thought you would be in a better position if you could tell [Secretary of Defense] Johnson you had not seen it before I delivered it."[38]

Secretary Matthews also tried to bring structure to the Navy's position and to reduce the number of witnesses from the 35 that Denfeld planned to have appear before the committee. In the event, the Air Force made a more structured and, in many respects, more powerful presentation at the House Armed Services Committee hearing. The hearing report concluded,

The Air Force holds the primary responsibility for conducting strategic bombing. It has maintained that the B-36 bomber is its foremost weapon to carry out that mission and that the B-36 can do its job. The committee holds that the nation must rely upon the judgment of its professional leaders in their respective fields in matters of this nature—and that the nation's leaders in respect to weapons of the Air Force are the leaders of the United States Air Force.

The committee deplores the manner of cancellation of the construction of the aircraft carrier USS *United States*, but, because of the pressure of other shipbuilding programs at the present time and the existing budgetary limitations on the Navy Department, will withhold further action—for the present—as regards the construction of this vessel. The committee considers it sound policy, however, for the nation to follow the advice of its professional leaders in regard to this subject in the same manner as has been heretofore done in respect to the B-36 bomber. In the committee's view, the nation's leaders in respect to naval weapons are the leaders of the United States Navy.

The B-36 survived the congressional investigation, and the program was expanded.[39] Admiral Denfeld, whose two-year term as CNO was to end in December 1949, was not reappointed for a second, two-year term. He had failed to effectively organize the Navy's leadership to defend the carrier program and lacked credibility in the debates, having not had aviation commands. (Denfeld had originally told Matthews that he did want to serve a second two-year term. His predecessor, Fleet Admiral Nimitz, had served for only two years as CNO.)

Secretary Matthews learned that Admiral Forrest Sherman, at the time Commander Sixth Task Fleet in the Mediterranean, had been earlier appointed by Secretary Forrestal to work with the Army to draft the unification bill. Matthews recalled, "I read all the statements presented by Sherman and others, and became impressed with his understanding of unification and the implications of the National Security Act and its application to the Navy. I thought: here is the man I ought to have."[40] Sherman, who had shown great political insight while the fleet commander in the troubled Mediterranean area, had commanded the *Wasp* (CV 7)

early in World War II, and had then served in key positions on Nimitz's immediate staff. When Nimitz signed the surrender documents aboard the *Missouri* in Tokyo Bay, he had Fleet Admiral Halsey and then-Rear Admiral Sherman stand beside him. Sherman became the Chief of Naval Operations on November 2, 1949.

Matthew continued to serve as Secretary of the Navy for another 18 months, until July 31, 1951. In accepting his resignation, President Truman wrote, "In doing so I desire to assure you of my appreciation of your able administration of the Department of the Navy during a period of transition and crisis when the demands of the office were many and great."[41]

A Questionable Future

Meanwhile, the Truman–Johnson administration continued to hold close reign on carrier programs. On July 5, 1949, Secretary Johnson set a tentative carrier force level for fiscal year 1951 at only four ships—fewer than the number of carriers then in commission with the Royal Navy. Although in September 1949 Johnson raised the number of planned carriers in active commission to six, the continuing decline of U.S. carrier air power appeared inevitable.

Significantly, funds that had been appropriated for the *United States* were used to modernize existing aircraft carriers, ships that would be ready for war in 1950–1953, and to launch aircraft with conventional weapons. Had the *United States* been built as scheduled she may have been too late to take part in the Korean War and her two dozen nuclear bombers would have been of little practical value in the coming years in view of the massive land-based bomber force being developed by the Air Force.

But the "revolt of the admirals" and the congressional hearings into the B-36 and U.S. defense policy were important. Navy Department historian Jeffrey Barlow wrote,

As a result of these hearings Congress better understood the complementary nature of land- and sea-based air power and the importance of carrier aviation to national defense. This understanding led to congressional support for a resurrection of the Navy's carrier aviation, particularly a new flush-deck aircraft carrier, even before U.S. participation in the Korean War provided the funds to expand the overall [naval] aviation

In the groove: An AJ Savage is about to land aboard the USS *Midway* during Atlantic Fleet exercises in November 1951. The Landing Signal Officer (LSO) is visible at the edge of the flight deck. The plane-guard destroyer steams astern, ready to rescue aviators if their plane comes down at sea. (U.S. Navy)

program. Thus the Navy's development of the *Forrestal*-class super carriers which provided the backbone of the service's power projection capabilities from the mid-1950s onward.[42]

Meanwhile, in China communist forces continued to advance, pushing back the U.S.-supported Nationalist forces of Chang Kaishek, while in Eastern Europe the Soviets consolidated their control of several states, and communist political takeovers were threatened in France and Italy. Threats of nuclear attack did not dissuade the communists; rather, a show of force or the actual application of limited force had more effect. The aircraft carrier excelled in both of the latter operations. The Korean War would mark the rebirth of the aircraft carrier as a mainstay of Allied military might.

4 "THE WRONG WAR"

Carrier-based aircraft had a pivotal role at the start of the Korean War, providing high-performance aircraft that could range over North Korea. Carriers also contributed to strike and close air support operations. These F9F-2B Panthers are being prepared for launch during operations aboard the carrier *Antietam* off the Korean coast in 1952. A plane guard helicopter hovers off the starboard beam. (U.S. Navy)

After almost five years of what was inaccurately termed "peace" and of concentrating political, military, and economic efforts on halting the expansion of communism in Europe, in mid-1950 the United States was fighting communist forces on the mainland of Asia. In reaction to North Korea's military invasion of South Korea two days earlier, on June 27, 1950, President Truman ordered naval and air support of the South Korean republic's efforts against the communist assault. He further instructed the U.S. Seventh Fleet to prevent either a Communist Chinese attack on Formosa (now known as Taiwan) or an assault against main-

land China by the Nationalist troops who had sought refuge on Formosa.

As a result of Secretary of Defense Louis Johnson's "trim the fat" campaign, the U.S. armed forces were lean, far too lean to perform the job at hand. Both of the president's directives placed a heavy burden upon the Navy, which was particularly unprepared for war in the Far East. In June 1950 the Navy had only some 270 combatant ships in commission. The number of aircraft carriers in service stood at 15 with four others in shipyards being modernized. The majority of the active carrier strength was in the Atlantic area.

Of the operational carriers, the four light carriers were engaged in training and experimental duties, with the *Cabot* having been recommissioned in October 1948 for Naval Air Reserve training and the *Bataan* in May 1950 for pilot qualification. The four escort carriers normally operated with anti-submarine squadrons. They would be unable to immediately participate in any other kind of combat. In addition, all of the carriers suffered from severe personnel shortages. The carrier dispositions in June 1950 were:

ATLANTIC		PACIFIC	
CVB	*Midway*	CV	*Boxer*
CVB	*Coral Sea*	CV	*Philippine Sea*
CVB	*F. D. Roosevelt*	CV	*Valley Forge*
CV	*Leyte*	CVE	*Badoeng Strait*
		CVE	*Sicily*
CVL	*Bataan*		
CVL	*Cabot*	BEING MODERNIZED	
CVL	*Saipan*	CV	*Essex*
CVL	*Wright*	CV	*Kearsarge*
		CV	*Oriskany*
CVE	*Mindoro*	CV	*Wasp*
CVE	*Palau*		

The U.S. Navy had two major commands in the Western Pacific: the Seventh Fleet and Naval Forces Japan. The first contained a carrier, a heavy cruiser, eight destroyers, four submarines, and five auxiliary ships plus a few patrol planes. Naval Forces Japan had an anti-aircraft cruiser, four amphibious ships, and a few minesweepers. This assembly was not an impressive force for the largest navy in the world, which was about to embark upon what would be in large measure a sea war and an air war.

The lone Seventh Fleet carrier was the 27,100-ton *Valley Forge*. She had arrived in the Western Pacific in May 1950 and was steaming just north of Hong Kong when the North Koreans struck. In company with two destroyers, she immediately set course for the Philippines to replenish and to be in a better position to support U.S. policy. On her decks was CVG-5, a typical carrier air group of the period, consisting of two fighter squadrons with 30 F9F-2B Panthers; two fighter squadrons with 28 F4U-4B Corsairs; and an attack squadron with 14 AD-4 Skyraiders.

This 4-to-1 ratio of fighters to attack planes in the air group was a continuation of the late World War II trend in carrier loadings wherein fighter-type aircraft increasingly served in the attack role. The F4U-4B variant of the Corsair, like its gull-winged predecessors, was an excellent attack plane and had replaced the unpopular SB2C Helldiver in carrier service. (Many of the early shortcomings in the Helldiver were overcome in the SB2C-3 and later models. The last SB2C squadrons were retired from first-line Navy service in 1949.) The F4U-4B was capable of 446 m.p.h. It had four 20-mm wing guns and could carry eight 5-inch rockets or two 1,000-pound bombs.

The AD Skyraider was superior to both the Corsair and Helldiver in the attack role; however, the F4U was already in quantity production when the AD proved itself and at the time it was more economical to employ Corsair "fighter" squadrons in the attack role than to build large numbers of Skyraiders. The Skyraider would become the outstanding prop-driven attack plane of carrier aviation. The AD-4 version was able to carry up to three 2,000-pound bombs or torpedoes or various combinations of smaller weapons up to 9,000 pounds. "Clean"—without external stores—the AD-4 had a maximum speed of 321 m.p.h. at 18,300 feet. It had four 20-mm cannon for strafing or—if necessary—air-to-air combat.

The F9F-2B Panther was a clean-lined jet fighter armed with four 20-mm cannon in the nose, and its eight wing racks could carry up to 3,000 pounds of bombs and rockets. Fixed 120-gallon wingtip fuel tanks were fitted. Still, the limited endurance of the jet-propelled aircraft made it unprofitable to employ the plane for most attack missions.[1]

Completing the *Valley Forge*'s 86-plane air group CVG-5 were 14 special-mission aircraft: 2 AD-3N night attack, 1 AD-3Q and 3 AD-4Q night/electronic countermeasures, 3 AD-4W airborne early warning, 3 F4U-5N night fighter, and 2 F4U-5P photo planes. The high percentage of special-mission aircraft reveals the complexity of air warfare in 1950 compared to five years earlier when a 100-plane air group had but two photo planes and four night fighters, with the remainder of the group being "straight" fighters and bombers. The air group in the *Valley Forge* was well trained and the leading group in the Pacific Fleet in jet experience.

There was no doubt that the Korean conflict would be an air war. The only question was what kind. When the request was made for U.S. ground troops to be committed on the mainland, an Air Force officer is said to have remarked, "The old man [General Douglas

When the Korean War began the Grumman F9F-2 Panther and the McDonnell F2H-2 Banshee filled U.S. Navy fighter squadrons. These were excellent aircraft, albeit limited in endurance and external payload. These Panthers are from fighter squadron VF-51 flying carrier qualifications aboard the *Boxer* just before the start of the conflict. Two aircraft are on the ship's forward catapults. (U.S. Navy)

MacArthur] must be off his rocker. When the Fifth Air Force gets to work on them, there will not be a North Korean left in North Korea."

But the Air Force's B-29 Superfortress squadrons on Guam were trained for atomic bomb strikes, and President Truman was determined to avoid using nuclear weapons if at all possible. Air Force fighter squadrons in the Western Pacific, based in Japan, Okinawa, and the Philippines, were trained and equipped for air defense operations. Most of these

fighter squadrons flew the F-80C Shooting Star, a 580-m.p.h. jet fighter; the remainder were night-fighter squadrons flying the 460-m.p.h. F-82 Twin Mustang (two F-51 Mustang fuselages joined together with a single wing and stabilizer).

The F-80s had severe limitations. Their firepower consisted of six .50-caliber machine guns, giving them a less potent killing ability than U.S. naval and Soviet cannon-armed aircraft. More significant, the F-80s had a limited range. "Clean" and at altitudes above 15,000 feet, they had an operational radius of approximately 100 miles; with two external fuel tanks these F-80s had a radius of about 225 miles. In June 1950 the Air Force in Japan began fitting F-80s with a locally improvised fuel tank to give the planes a 350-mile radius, but few of the modified fighters were available when war broke out. With standard wing-drop tanks—and hence a reduced speed—the F-80s could operate over South Korea for a maximum of 15 minutes if the planes stayed at their most economic altitude, above 15,000 feet. With no airfields in South Korea capable of handling U.S. jet fighters, "In short, the F-80s were based 150 miles too far from their targets," according to the official U.S. Air Force history of the Korean War.[2]

The fourth Air Force combat plane in the Far East was the B-26 Invader, a twin-engine light bomber of World War II vintage, which would prove most valuable in Korea. However, few B-26s were available in 1950.[3]

When war erupted the Air Force was ordered to send air transports into Seoul and other South Korean cities to fly out American nationals. The primary escorts for this airlift were the piston-engine F-82s because of the limited range of the jet-propelled F-80s.[4] This was acceptable at the time because of the limited quantity and quality of the North Korean Air Force. The North Koreans apparently had 132 combat aircraft at the time—70 Yak-3 (400 m.p.h.) and Yak-7B (360 m.p.h.) fighters, and 62 Il-10 dive-bombers.[5] There were also 22 transports and 8 trainers. All were piston-engine aircraft. (The South Korean "air force" had only a few primary training planes at the time.) The real aerial threats were from Communist China and the Soviet Union, both of which had major air bases within bomber range of all of Korea and U.S. bases in Japan.

Targets in Korea were beyond the effective range of the U.S. B-29 Superfortress bombers based on Guam. All ready B-29s were flown up to Okinawa, where the United States had retained major bases after World War II. While Okinawa was within B-29 range of Korea, the island was also within range of Soviet long-range aircraft flying from China. Still, the island was less vulnerable than the U.S. bases in Japan. The risk was accepted and during the late afternoon of June 28 four B-29s from Okinawa began bombing targets of opportunity along Korean highways and railroad tracks. To again quote the U.S. Air Force official history, "it was a strange employment for the strategic bombers, but

General MacArthur had called for a maximum show of force."[6] It was a beginning—and in the coming three years of war there would be only 26 days that did not record B-29 missions over Korea.

Enter the Carriers

The *Valley Forge* hastily replenished at Subic Bay in the Philippines and departed on June 27, again steaming north. On the 29th she sent 29 Corsairs and Skyraiders winging up the Formosa Strait in a show of force, and early on the 30th she dropped anchor in Buckner Bay, Okinawa. The *Valley Forge* did not sail toward Japan for fear of a Soviet or Red Chinese air strike against the carrier. Further, Okinawa was centrally located between Korea and Formosa, enabling the *Valley Forge* to sortie in either direction, as the situation warranted.

A second aircraft carrier was in the Far East: the British light carrier *Triumph* in Japanese waters.[7] She was part of the British Commonwealth Forces in the area, which also contained two light cruisers, three destroyers (one Australian), and three patrol frigates (one Australian). On the *Triumph*'s decks were 12 Seafire Mk 47 and 12 Firefly Mk I fighters. These were piston-engine aircraft: the Supermarine Seafire Mk 47 was the final variant of that aircraft, a navalized version of the Spitfire Mk 24, which entered FAA service in 1948; the Fairey Firefly Mk I was a two-seat fighter-attack aircraft that entered service in 1943.[8]

The British squadron steamed into Buckner Bay on July 1 and the Allied Striking Force—Task Force (TF) 77—sortied for its first operation of the war. In addition to the *Triumph*, the light cruiser and two of the destroyers were British.

Vice Admiral Arthur D. Struble was Commander Seventh Fleet as well as Commander Task Force 77. He had served most of World War II in Washington but had held high posts in the invasion of Normandy and in some of the later Pacific amphibious operations. Struble was in Washington when the North Koreans invaded the South. He waited for one day while high-level talks were held at the White House and then, assured by the Chief of Naval Operations that U.S. forces would definitely be committed in Korea, departed for the Western Pacific on June 26.

Thus, temporarily the command of the Seventh Fleet and Task Force 77 was in the hands of Rear Admiral John M. Hoskins, commanding Carrier Division 3. Hoskins would retain tactical command of TF 77

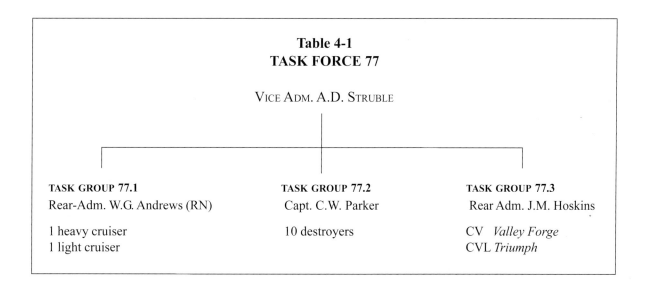

Table 4-1
TASK FORCE 77

Vice Adm. A.D. Struble

TASK GROUP 77.1	TASK GROUP 77.2	TASK GROUP 77.3
Rear-Adm. W.G. Andrews (RN)	Capt. C.W. Parker	Rear Adm. J.M. Hoskins
1 heavy cruiser	10 destroyers	CV *Valley Forge*
1 light cruiser		CVL *Triumph*

after Admiral Struble returned and would direct carrier operations for the first two months of war. This was "Peg-Leg" Hoskins, who had his injured leg amputated during the loss of the CVL *Princeton* in 1944.

Upon his return to the Western Pacific, Admiral Struble conferred in Tokyo with General MacArthur and other senior U.S. commanders. They decided that the Striking Force would attack military targets in the North Korean capital of Pyongyang. Airfields and aircraft would be given first priority and the city's railroad yards and bridges, key links in the transportation of men and material to the front, were assigned secondary priority. Struble then joined Task Force 77. Land-based U.S. aircraft were as yet unable to strike the Pyongyang area.

During the night of July 1–2 and the day and night of July 2 the Anglo-American carrier force steamed northwest, into the Yellow Sea. The carrier pilots knew little of the targets that they would strike. Donald Engen, an F9F pilot, recalled,

> We knew what equipment the North Koreans were supposed to have, but we knew very little about ground or air military units or where they were deployed. We were given civil aviation sectional charts and civil world aeronautical charts with which to plan our attacks. The sectional chart of northeastern Korea had a white blank spot . . . in the eastern mountains of Manchuria. That area was simply annotated on the chart as an area not yet charted and accentuated the strangeness of our situation.[9]

The differences in performance of the aircraft in the two carriers (and even between the piston and jet aircraft of the *Valley Forge*), and the U.S. carrier's ten-knot speed advantage over the British flat-top, presented problems to the commanders, but they were overcome in the shadow of the vital mission at hand. In the pre-dawn darkness of July 3 the carriers reached their launch point some 75 miles off the Korean coast. At 5 A.M. the *Valley Forge* sent off aircraft for anti-submarine and combat air patrols. The threat of North Korean air attack was considered negligible, but the task force was only 100 miles from Red Chinese airfields on the Shantung Peninsula and 220 miles from Soviet airfields at Port Arthur.

Beginning at 5:45 A.M. the *Triumph* flew off 12 Fireflies and nine rocket-armed Seafires to pound the airfield and railway bridges at Haeju, some 125 miles away. Fifteen minutes later the "Happy Valley" sent off her strike against Pyongyang: 16 Corsairs armed with eight 5-inch rockets apiece and 12 Skyraiders, each with two 500-pound bombs and six 100-pounders. After these planes were on their way eight F9F-2 Panthers were catapulted from the *Valley Forge*. Although the jets went last, their higher speed brought them over Pyongyang first to attack North Korean planes on the ground before they could take off to intercept the bombers or flee to safety.

As the 57 carrier planes flew toward their targets the problems of the moment obscured the flight's significance. Here, five years after atomic bombs had devastated Hiroshima and Nagasaki, aircraft carriers were again steaming within range of superior land-based air

The *Essex*-class carrier *Valley Forge* (foreground) was the only U.S. carrier in the Western Pacific when the Korean War began. Here the "Happy Valley" rests at anchor at Sasebo, Japan, in December 1950. Anchored beyond the *Valley Force* are her sister ship *Leyte* and the repair ship *Hector*. Japan provided forward bases for U.S. military forces in the Far East during the conflict. (U.S. Navy)

forces to deliver a strike against land targets. This was an operation that many military leaders—some Navy—believed could not be carried out in the "atomic age." Or, if undertaken, it would merely be redundant to the efforts of long-range, land-based bombers. Fifty-six British and U.S. Navy pilots plus one U.S. Air Force pilot on exchange duty were about to prove the value of aircraft carriers in the atomic age.

The Panthers' cannon blazed as they swept across Pyongyang's principal airfield. The North Koreans were taken by complete surprise. They felt a degree of safety in their capital, which was more than 400 miles from the nearest U.S. airfields (in Japan). Two airborne piston fighters were shot down, the first falling to the guns of F9F-2s piloted by Lieutenant (jg) Leonard H. Plog and Ensign Eldon W. Brown of Fighter Squadron 51, who shared the kill. They were the first Navy jet pilots to down an enemy aircraft. An estimated nine aircraft were destroyed on the ground. The jets then turned their cannon against ground facilities. Moments after the

Panthers arrived the piston-engine Corsairs and Skyraiders came on the scene, spreading more death and destruction. The airfield's tank farm was ignited, all three hangars were demolished, and the runways were cratered. The story was much the same at Haeju, where the British, like the Americans at Pyongyang, encountered no serious opposition. All 57 aircraft returned safely to their carriers.

In the afternoon the two carriers sent strikes against the railroad facilities in their respective target areas. Although the U.S. planes smashed the rail facilities and destroyed 15 locomotives, key bridges were left intact. Again, no carrier planes were lost.

Because of the precarious situation in the Formosa Strait, the carrier strikes had been planned as a one-day operation. But the deteriorating situation in South Korea led to the carriers being directed to continue the attack as long as practical. Railroad facilities supporting the North Korean march into the south were given first priority as targets. On American Independence Day the *Valley Forge* planes returned to the Pyongyang area, attacking the railroads and dropping a span of a vital railroad bridge. This time several Corsairs and Skyraiders were struck by anti-aircraft fire. All made it back to the carrier, but one Skyraider pilot landing on the *Valley Forge* was unable to reduce speed sufficiently, approached too fast and too high, cut his engine, hit the deck, and bounced over the barrier. The AD smashed into the deck park. Next a Corsair's wheel collapsed upon landing; the plane slammed onto the deck. Then the plane-guard HO3S-1 helicopter suffered an engine failure and came down at sea (its crew rescued by a destroyer). Another Skyraider was severely damaged in landing. When the wreckage was sorted out, one Skyraider and two Corsairs were destroyed, six other planes were damaged, and a helicopter was lost. No replacement aircraft were available in the theater. There were no fatalities.

Upon the completion of these strikes Task Force 77 withdrew to Okinawa. The British cruiser and two destroyers were detached to join other Allied surface ships in operations off the Korean coast.

Two days of strikes had again proved the versatility and value of a carrier striking force. In addition to the direct damage inflicted on airfields and railroads, the early appearance of the carrier jets over Korea is believed to have halted Soviet and Chinese plans to provide the North Koreans with large numbers of propeller-driven aircraft. This was the first time that aircraft carriers of any nation had operated jet-propelled aircraft in combat. The results were gratifying. The Panther proved to be an excellent carrier aircraft. Pilots found it comfortable, quiet, dependable, and easy to handle. Later they would also find the F9F capable of absorbing a great deal of punishment and still fly. And, maintenance crews found jets safer to work around than propeller aircraft, cleaner, and generally easier to maintain.

However, the jets burned fuel faster than propeller aircraft, placing some restraints on operations and jet aircraft. Because of this high rate of fuel consumption, they often had to be recovered immediately upon return from a mission and could not be held aloft near the carrier as prop planes could. Also, the Panther was almost seven feet longer than the Corsair, meaning fewer aircraft could be handled aboard ship.

Another problem of carrier operations off Korea was the Navy's relationship with the Air Force. As the war developed the Navy and Air Force argued about communications (ships at sea liked to "keep quiet"), the selection of targets, target priority assignment, and strike coordination. In part, these problems were caused by the Navy's fear of Air Force control over carrier operations.

On the tactical level, the Air Force soon insisted that requests from ground commanders for close air support be approved at a central headquarters where needs would be evaluated against total resources. The

HMS *Triumph* operates off the Philippines in March 1950. On her flight deck are Seafire Mk 47 (forward) and Firefly Mk I fighters. British and Australian light carriers served alongside U.S. flattops throughout the Korean War. The CVLs operated only piston-engine aircraft, but still made a significant contribution to Allied combat capabilities. (U.S. Navy)

Navy and Marine commanders contended that battlefield targets were too fleeting to allow a cumbersome, centralized process to introduce delays; instead, the sea services allocated close air support units directly to subordinate ground commanders, always subject to diversion by higher headquarters when the situation warranted. This difference in philosophy was not resolved until the 1960s, at which time the Navy-Marine procedure was essentially adopted within the defense establishment.

(General MacArthur, as Commander-in-Chief [CinC] Far East, in fact technically controlled the Navy's carriers in the Western Pacific, as would his successor, General Matthew B. Ridgeway. During World War II the Navy had permanently assigned only escort carriers to MacArthur's Seventh Fleet.)

The *Valley Forge* and *Triumph* and their escorts reached Buckner Bay safely on July 6, 1950. Admiral Struble had left Task Force 77 the day before for conferences in Tokyo at which he proposed an immediate resumption of the carrier strikes. However, because of the situation in the Formosa Strait, Task Force 77 remained at Okinawa until the 16th. After the Tokyo meetings Admiral Struble flew to Okinawa and then boarded a destroyer for a high-speed run to Formosa and two days of talks with Generalissimo Chiang Kai-shek, head of the surviving Nationalist forces.

After ten days of unfortunate but in some ways necessary inactivity, Task Force 77 returned to sea on July 16 and set course for the Korea Strait, between Japan and Korea. From a position in the Sea of Japan off Korea's southeastern coast, planes from the carriers covered the unopposed landing of U.S. troops at Pohang, some 65 miles north of the port of Pusan. With a minimum requirement for maintaining air patrols over the Pohang area, TF 77 again ranged its planes against targets in North Korea.

The new carrier strikes had been requested by the commander of the U.S. Air Forces in the Far East. His request indicated target priorities beginning with rail and highway routes and included airfields and petroleum facilities. Such interdiction missions for carrier aircraft were in direct opposition to previously agreed roles and missions for the U.S. armed forces. The interdiction of enemy communications had been considered exclusively as an Air Force domain.

Now, under "coordination control" of the Far East Air Forces command, the *Valley Forge* and *Triumph*

and their consorts steamed some 50 miles off the Korean coast on July 18 and 19, sending off their own ASW and combat air patrols, support aircraft for the Pohang landings, and strikes against highways, railroads, airfields, and industrial plants in the North. A chief target was the North Korean port of Wonsan, where carrier planes destroyed a major petroleum refinery. Air Force B-29s had hit the plant earlier, and although they disrupted operations, the heavy bombers had not scored a single hit on a vital area of the complex. In addition, the carrier strikes destroyed about two dozen enemy aircraft on the ground and damaged the same number. Two carrier planes were lost in these two days of strikes. Both pilots were recovered.

Because of the threat of Soviet submarine and aircraft attack, Task Force 77 avoided operating in the same area for longer than two days, and after the last aircraft were recovered on July 19, the warships moved on, skirting a typhoon in the process. The *Triumph*, with a British destroyer, withdrew from TF 77 for ten days of maintenance in a Japanese shipyard.

Task Force 77—now with one carrier—steamed around the "bottom" of Korea, fueled from a Navy oiler, and on the 22nd, while in the Yellow Sea, flew off strikes against the North and direct support missions for Allied ground troops. However, the planes were unable to make contact with ground controllers and could attack only the more obvious targets. An afternoon effort ended in the same manner.

There was another refueling at sea on the 23rd, and then, because the *Valley Forge* needed to refill her empty bomb and rocket magazines, the carrier made a hasty visit to Sasebo, Japan, on the 24th. The rearming was cut short by the deteriorating situation on the front. On the 25th the carrier was flying off planes throughout the day on direct support and interdiction missions off the eastern coast of Korea. The *Triumph* had returned to sea with the *Valley Forge*, the British light carrier having barely begun her yard work. Again the carrier planes were hampered in their attacks by poor communications with the ground troops and the lack of up-to-date intelligence about the enemy's activities. Then, steaming northeast, Task Force 77 traveled about 150 miles during the night and on July 26 flew relatively successful support strikes from the Sea of Japan. The ships withdrew to refuel at sea on the 27th and then raced around Korea's southern coast to the Yellow Sea to again deliver a series of strikes from off the western coast on July 28–29.

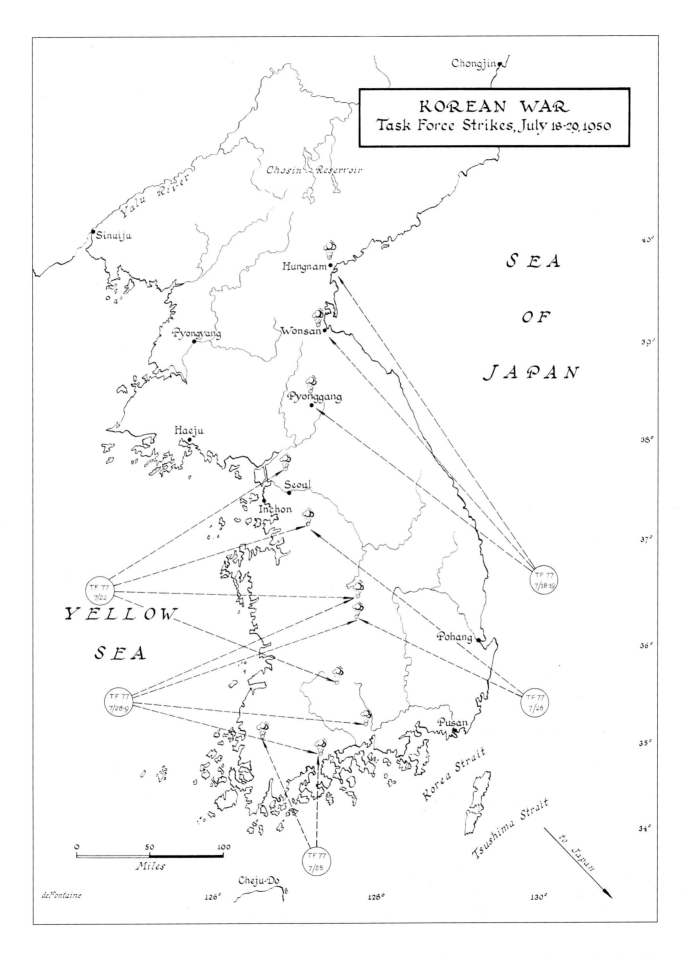

KOREAN WAR
Task Force Strikes, July 18-20, 1950

Chongjin

Chosin Reservoir

Yalu River

Sinuiju

SEA

OF

JAPAN

Hungnam

Wonsan

Pyongyang

Pyonggang

Haeju

Seoul

Inchon

TF 77
7/22

TF 77
7/18-19

YELLOW

SEA

Pohang

TF 77
7/28-9

TF 77
7/26

Pusan

Korea Strait

Tsushima Strait

to Japan

0   50   100
Miles

Cheju-Do

TF 77
7/25

deFontaine

126°   128°   130°

40°

39°

38°

37°

36°

35°

34°

Task Force 77 now withdrew toward Okinawa, in part because of the need to replace lost aircraft and in part because of the continuing threat of a communist assault on Formosa. The *Triumph* was detached to Japan for further assignment to the blockading force that had been established to halt the operation of communist coastal craft in Korean waters.

Operational losses and enemy ground fire had claimed several carrier aircraft, but in most cases the aircrews were recovered. One carrier pilot had been picked up behind enemy lines by an Army helicopter that itself ran out of fuel over communist territory. Both pilots reached friendly lines. One *Triumph* fighter, investigating a radar contact, came too close to an Air Force B-29 and was shot down. A destroyer rescued the carrier pilot.

In 12 days of operations the Task Force 77 carriers had ranged far and wide around the Korean coasts, flying both tactical and strategic missions. If the July 3–4 strikes had proved that carriers could operate in a "modern war," the strikes between July 18 and 28 had proved that mobile and versatile warships were indispensable in Korea.

The *Valley Forge* dropped anchor in Buckner Bay on July 31. The next day she was joined by the carrier *Philippine Sea*. When war erupted in Korea the *Valley Forge* was the only U.S. carrier in the western Pacific. Two *Essex*-carriers were at San Diego on the U.S. West Coast, the *Boxer*, which had just returned from the western Pacific, and the *Philippine Sea*, recently arrived from the Atlantic and scheduled to relieve the *Valley Forge* in October 1950. Their squadrons were not in as high a state of readiness as were those in the *Valley Forge*. Further, the *Boxer* was in need of overhaul after almost six months of continuous service in the Western Pacific.

The escort carrier *Sicily*, also recently arrived from the Atlantic, was at San Diego and her sister ship *Badoeng Strait* was at sea, en route from the West Coast to Pearl Harbor with a Marine F4U fighter squadron, 233 Naval Reserve midshipmen, and five college professors.

The *Sicily*—with a squadron of ASW aircraft embarked—sailed on July 4 for the Western Pacific via Pearl Harbor. Her movement was considered vital in view of the 80 Soviet submarines estimated to be in Asiatic waters. The *Philippine Sea* took aboard needed material from the *Boxer* and cleared San Diego on July 6. The *Philippine Sea*'s air group consisted of two

A bomb-laden AD Skyraider takes off from the carrier *Valley Forge* to strike at enemy troops in Korea. The plane is carrying three 2,000-pound bombs. "501" indicates the first aircraft of the fifth squadron aboard the carrier. The rescue helicopter, ever present during daylight flight operations, hovers to starboard. (U.S. Navy)

fighter squadrons with 28 F9F-2B Panthers, two with 28 F4U-4B Corsairs, an attack squadron with 16 AD-4 Skyraiders, and 14 special-mission Corsairs and Skyraiders. But her air group was not ready for extensive carrier operations, the turbojet Panthers having been just received. To alleviate the situation the carrier had ten days of training in the Hawaiian area and after reaching Okinawa went to sea with the *Valley Forge* for two days of joint operations.

Hastily the *Boxer* was made ready for sea, steamed up to San Francisco Bay, and tied up at the Alameda naval air station to take aboard aircraft needed in the war zone. Beginning on July 8, she loaded 145 F-51 Mustangs and 6 L-5 observation planes for the Air Force, 19 Navy planes, a Marine ground control approach unit with its radar vans and other trucks, a capacity load of fuel and ammunition, and 1,012 passengers. (The F-51s had been recalled from reserve air units to meet the desperate need for these long-range, propeller-driven aircraft over Korea.) Thus loaded, the *Boxer* went to sea on July 14 and crossed the Pacific in a record-breaking 8 days, 16 hours. She unloaded in Japan between July 22 and 27, and then returned to San Diego, arriving on August 4 after breaking her own record with a crossing time of 7 days, 10½ hours.

The fifth U.S. carrier in the Pacific, the "jeep" flattop *Badoeng Strait*, landed her professors at Pearl Harbor, and steamed back to San Diego, to unload her midshipmen and load more Marine fighters. Her decks were crammed with 60 Corsairs (48 F4U-4Bs of two day-fighter squadrons and 12 F4U-5Ns of a night-fighter squadron), 8 OY light observation planes, and 4 HO3S-1 helicopters plus a large number of Marine aviators. She sailed for the Western Pacific on July 14 with several amphibious ships carrying a Marine brigade to Japan.

All five Pacific Fleet carriers were thus committed to the Korean conflict. They were accompanied by a host of cruisers, destroyers, and escort ships flying the colors of the United States, Britain, Australia, and Canada.

And in Washington and London decisions were being made that would bring more carriers to the Pacific from other areas and from the mothball fleets. Meanwhile, the war was fought with the ships in the Pacific at the outbreak of hostilities. The U.S. and British Commonwealth warships closed the Korean peninsula to attack communist coastal traffic and shelled communist troops and installations along the coast. These ships also conducted small-scale "commando" raids, usually to blow up railroad tunnels and other targets immune to air attack. These efforts—primarily by light cruisers, destroyers, and escort ships—were highly successful.

While the fast carriers *Philippine Sea* and *Valley Forge* worked up off Okinawa, the escort carriers went into action. The *Sicily* had raced to Guam with her ASW squadron, but when the submarine threat failed to materialize she unloaded her planes and steamed north to Japan, reaching Yokosuka on July 27. Four days later her sister ship *Badoeng Strait*, transiting with the

F-51 Mustangs are loaded aboard the carrier *Boxer* for a high-speed transit to the war zone. The *Boxer* had just returned from the Western Pacific when the war began. Unable to immediately deploy with an air group, she was pressed into service as a transport to bring out ready-to-fly piston fighters that were needed in the Far East because of the limited endurance of jet aircraft. (U.S. Navy)

amphibious ships, reached Kobe, Japan. The *Badoeng Strait* flew off her 60 Marine-piloted Corsairs for airfields in Japan on August 1–2.

One of the 24-plane F4U squadrons flew aboard the *Sicily* and, in company with a destroyer and a destroyer-minesweeper, the carrier steamed toward Korea.[10] On August 2 she launched Corsairs to fly close support missions for the U.S. and South Korean soldiers in the Pusan perimeter. The *Badoeng Strait* replenished in Japan, embanked another of the Marine F4U squadrons, and with a destroyer and a destroyer-minesweeper, put to sea to rendezvous with the *Sicily* on August 6. The two escort carriers and their four screening ships formed Task Group 96.8 under Rear Admiral Richard W. Ruble in the "Bing-Ding." On the next day the Marine brigade that had crossed the Pacific in the *Badoeng Strait* convoy was landed at Pusan. For six days the "leather-necks" attacked to the west of the perimeter, with Marine-piloted Corsairs from the escort carriers providing close air support. Approximately six F4U-4Bs were always over the Marines during daylight, with each Corsair generally carrying a 500-pound bomb or napalm tank, eight 5-inch rockets, and 800 rounds of 20-mm ammunition for its four guns. Thus began a long, close association of Marine fighters flying from the escort carriers with foot soldiers in Korea. (The 12-plane Marine F4U-5N squadron was based ashore.)

Meanwhile, the larger carriers *Philippine Sea* and *Valley Forge* had sortied from Okinawa, their 80-plus plane air groups bringing to some 250 the number of carrier planes at sea off Korea. A fifth carrier, the British *Triumph*, was on blockade duty.

On the morning of August 5 the two Task Force 77 carriers flew off strikes against targets in southwestern Korea. The *Philippine Sea* planes concentrated on rail and highway bridges that the communists used for transporting supplies; the *Valley Forge* aircraft were assigned to close support missions, the latter operations again hampered by poor air-ground coordination.

During the remainder of the month the four U.S. carriers sent their planes off on primarily close support and interdiction missions, with the two escort carriers remaining off the Pusan perimeter and the two *Essex*-class ships ranging up and down the eastern and western coasts of Korea. While most of the Task Force 77 carrier strikes were flown over South Korea, on the eastern coast the carriers struck as far north as Chongjin,

50 miles from the frontier of Soviet Siberia, and on the western coast carrier planes hit Sinuiju, some 75 miles from the Yalu River and Red China.

There was a comparative lull in the fighting in Korea during the last ten days of August, and the *Philippine Sea* and *Valley Forge* put into Sasebo to replenish from August 21 to 25. On August 25 Rear Admiral Hoskins was relieved after two months as Commander Task Force 77 by Rear Admiral Edward C. Ewen, Commander Carrier Division 1 in the *Philippine Sea*. Ewen commanded TF 77 for only two months before returning the Striking Force to Admiral Hoskins.

The carriers resumed air strikes on the 26th. On occasion their planes made rocket and strafing runs less than 100 yards in front of friendly troops. By the morning of the 27th the carriers were well north of the 38th parallel and flew off strikes against the ports of Wonsan, Songjin, and Chongjin, moving several hundred miles and switching overnight from tactical to strategic strikes.

Task Force 77 then steamed south, around the "bottom" of Korea, and into the Yellow Sea to launch strikes against the western coast between August 29 and September 4. En route the carriers fueled at sea and took aboard replacement aircraft flown out from Japan.

On September 4, 1950, the carrier planes tangled with Soviet aircraft. That day the two fast carriers were between China's Shantung Peninsula and the Korean coast, almost astride the 38th parallel, where the Yellow Sea is only 130 miles wide—a highly restrictive operating area. Strikes were being flown off against targets in the Pyongyang-Chinnampo region. TF 77 steaming off the Korean coast was less than 100 miles from Red China and barely more than that from the Soviet naval and air bases at Port Arthur on Manchuria's Liaotung Peninsula. In the jet age this meant that the carriers, standing off the Korean coast, were operating within ten minutes' flying time of "enemy" air bases.

At 1:29 P.M. on September 4 a destroyer on picket duty 60 miles north of Task Force 77 reported radar detection of an unidentified aircraft approaching from the direction of Port Arthur. Moments later radar on the *Valley Forge* picked up the contact at a range of 60 miles. The "bogey" was approaching at about 200 m.p.h. between 12,000 and 13,000 feet.

Two divisions of F4U Corsairs were airborne to the east of TF 77 on combat air patrol. At 1:35 P.M. one four-plane division was ordered to intercept the approaching aircraft. The radar contact split in two—one aircraft turning back to the north; the other continuing to close on TF 77. Thirty miles from the U.S. ships the Corsairs intercepted the latter plane—a twin-piston-engine Tu-2 attack-bomber with Soviet markings.[11]

On sighting the gull-winged fighters, the bomber nosed down, increased speed, and took evasive action. The bomber now headed east, toward Korea. As the fighters closed, the bomber opened fire on them with its aft-firing machine gun.

This was reported to the carrier and the fighters were immediately authorized to return the fire. The first Corsair missed on its firing run, but the second F4U-4, piloted by Ensign Edward Laney, caught the bomber with its four 20-mm cannon and sent the Soviet aircraft spinning down in flames.

Meanwhile, the carriers began launching additional fighters and the ships of TF 77 stood by to repel enemy aircraft. A destroyer sighted the stricken Tu-2 hitting the water and steamed to the spot. She recovered the body of a Russian flier.[12] No further bogies were picked up on radar screens, and with unfavorable weather over North Korea on September 5, the carriers turned south. The Soviet government denied that any of its aircraft were flying over the Yellow Sea at the time and said that it certainly had none in the vicinity of U.S. carriers.

The Tide Turns

From the first days of the war General MacArthur had hoped to mount an amphibious assault against Inchon, Seoul's seaport on Korea's western coast, outflank the North Korean armies in the south, and destroy them in a giant pincer movement.

By September 1950 the 50-mile Pusan perimeter had been fortified and reinforced. For the northern claw of the pincers General MacArthur had a Marine division and sufficient amphibious ships to mount an assault. The Army opposed the operation; the Navy was hesitant because of a maximum tide of 33 feet at Inchon and other factors that limited an amphibious landing to one of three possible days in the fall of 1950. General MacArthur crushed opposition to his plan, stating, "The amphibious landing is the most powerful tool we have. To employ it properly we must strike hard and deeply into enemy territory." And, in a hushed tone, he declared, "We shall land at Inchon and I shall crush them." General MacArthur chose the earliest possible date for the amphibious assault: September 15.

For this audacious operation 230 ships—from fast carriers to tank landing ships and a rocket support ship—were assembled. The ships were manned by Americans, Britons, New Zealanders, Koreans, Japanese, and Frenchmen. The overall task organization for the assault was Joint Task Force 7 under Vice Admiral Struble, Commander Seventh Fleet. The actual invasion force included the escort carriers *Badoeng Strait* and *Sicily* among its 180-odd ships, along with the cruisers, destroyers, minesweepers, transports, landing ships, and an assortment of miscellaneous ships and craft needed for an assault.

Task Force 77—under Rear Admiral Ewen—numbered three fast carriers, a light cruiser, and 14 destroyers. The fast carriers were the Korean veterans *Philippine Sea* and *Valley Forge,* and the just-arrived *Boxer*. The *Boxer*, after her record-shattering crossings to bring out fighter planes at the start of the war, underwent quick repairs on the U.S. West Coast. She sailed for the battle area on August 24 with a hastily formed air group because a standard air group was not available. Nor were any jet fighters available for her. The *Boxer* thus went into combat with CVG-2 containing four fighter squadrons totaling 64 F4U-4B Corsairs, an attack squadron of 16 Skyraiders, and 14 special-mission aircraft and helicopters. She arrived off Inchon on September 15, the day of the assault. (The *Boxer* was the last CV to deploy with five fighter-attack squadrons; subsequently deployments were with four squadrons, the reduction caused by the increase in aircraft size and the operating tempos.)

The sixth carrier off Korea, HMS *Triumph*, operated off the eastern coast as part of a diversionary operation and then raced around the peninsula to take part in the assault.

For two days Navy planes from the *Philippine Sea* and *Valley Forge* and Marine fighters from the escort carriers joined land-based aircraft in softening up the Inchon-Seoul area before the landing. Then, on the morning of September 15, the first Marines landed under an umbrella of aircraft and behind a carpet of bombardment from cruisers, destroyers, and a rocket ship. Marine Corsairs bombed and rocketed the initial landing beaches at Wolmi Do and then strafed the area seconds before the first landing craft touched ground. It was a perfect example of Marine air-ground coordination and cooperation. The result was never in doubt.

The communists had not believed that the United States could mount a major amphibious assault so soon

Close air support and interdiction of enemy supply routes were vital requirements for aviation in the Korean War. Marine-piloted F4U-4 Corsairs—such as these being readied on the light carrier *Bataan*—were ideal for these tasks. The F4U-4 had six .50-caliber wing guns and the -4B had four 20-mm cannon; both could carry eight 5-inch rockets under their wings and two 1,000-pound bombs on center section wing pylons. (U.S. Navy)

after the war began or that U.S. commanders would risk an assault on Inchon's treacherous beaches. But driven by General MacArthur, the Marines and Navy had led the way. Appraising the landing, MacArthur declared, "The star of the Navy and Marine Corps never shone brighter."

The North Korean forces in the area were soon in full retreat. One hundred fifty miles to the southeast another Allied drive began as U.S. and Korean troops launched an attack from the Pusan perimeter, presenting the communists with a two-front battle. On D-day-plus-two (September 17) Kimpo airfield between Inchon and Seoul was captured, and the next afternoon, with enemy artillery still within firing range, the field was declared ready to receive aircraft. In flew Marine

HO3S-1 helicopters and OY-2 light observation planes, which had been brought to Inchon by a Japanese-manned tank landing ship (LST) and two escort carriers. Next, flying up from Japan, came a Marine night fighter squadron with twin-engine F7F-3N Tigercats (described in Volume I, pp. 497–499). The Allies thus gained use of the best airfield in Korea—and just ten miles from the enemy's lines!

Also on September 17 came the only enemy air reaction to the landings when two Yak-18 piston-engine training aircraft attacked a British and a U.S. cruiser anchored offshore. One plane dropped two 100-pound bombs on the U.S. cruiser *Rochester*, at the time the Seventh Fleet flagship. One projectile hit the ship's aircraft crane, failed to explode, and bounced into the sea; the other detonated close to the cruiser. Next, the planes strafed the British cruiser *Jamaica*, killing one sailor, but her guns shot down one of the Yaks.

At sea the carriers replenished from two oilers, a store ship, and an ammunition ship. With three fast carriers available, two were continually flying off interdiction and support missions while the third ship was replenishing. On September 25 the British light carrier *Triumph* was relieved off Korea by her sister ship *Theseus*, the former ship thus becoming the first carrier to complete a "Korean tour." Whereas the *Triumph* had a squadron of Seafires and Firefly Mk I aircraft, the *Theseus* (and subsequent British carriers sent to Korea) had Sea Furies and Firefly AS.5 aircraft. The Fairey Firefly AS.4 and AS.5 were modified two-seat fighters fitted with ASH surface-search radar and could carry two 1,000-pound bombs or equivalent loads of rockets, depth charges, and (external) sonobuoy dispensers. The four 20-mm cannon of earlier marks were retained. These piston-engine aircraft performed extremely well in the ground-attack and bomber roles. Because U.S. fliers were unfamiliar with these British aircraft, they wore special striped markings reminiscent of D-day markings worn by Allied aircraft in an earlier war.

Seoul fell to U.S. troops on September 27 after bitter fighting, and South Korea was cleared of communist troops by early October 1950. The Allied armies then marched north, into the aggressor's home territory, above the 38th parallel.

General MacArthur had advocated a march north soon after the communist invasion of South Korea. Declaring his intention of destroying the North Korean armed forces and not merely driving them out of South Korea, he declared, "I may have to occupy all of North Korea." But not until the day of the Inchon landing—September 15—was MacArthur instructed that he could plan operations beyond the 38th parallel and then only if Soviet Russia and Communist China showed no signs of entering the war as a consequence of the Allies crossing the parallel. This fear of a wider war led to a policy that only South Korean troops could be employed in operations near the Soviet and Chinese borders and that the bridges over the Yalu River and the port of Rashin (formerly Najin) near the Soviet naval base of Vladivostok could not be bombed.

These limitations were not a severe burden at the time and the Allied armies pushed into North Korea. With the enemy in full retreat General MacArthur decided upon a second amphibious envelopment, this time at Wonsan on Korea's eastern coast, 115 miles north of Seoul and a hundred miles east of the North Korean capital of Pyongyang. This movement would help trap the remnants of the North Korean armies and partially relieve the burden of supply for the advance into North Korea from the country's shattered and inadequate highways and railroads. However, the assault troops were embarked at Inchon, clogging the port for several days and preventing supplies from coming in for the Allied ground forces pushing north.

The Wonsan landing was to be carried out by Admiral Struble's Joint Task Force 7. For this operation the British light carrier *Theseus* remained in the Yellow Sea to strike targets along Korea's western coast. Most of the Allied armada steamed around the peninsula to the eastern coast and began intensive preliminary bombardment of the Wonsan area. There were now U.S. carriers available to Admiral Struble (see Table 4-2).

Table 4-2
SEVENTH FLEET CARRIERS, SEPTEMBER 1950

TASK FORCE 77		TASK GROUP 96.8	
Rear Adm. R.W. Ruble		Rear Adm. E.C. Ewen	
CV	*Boxer*	CVE	*Badoeng Strait*
CV	*Leyte*	CVE	*Sicily*
CV	*Philippine Sea*	6	destroyers
1	battleship		
1	light cruiser		
16	destroyers		

The latest carrier to join TF 77 was the *Leyte*, the 27,100-ton carrier coming from the Mediterranean via Norfolk, the Panama Canal, and Sasebo. She was a welcome addition to the Fast Carrier Force with her air group CVG-3 consisting of one squadron of 16 F9F-2B Panthers, two squadrons with 36 F4U-4B Corsairs, one squadron of 18 AD-4 Skyraiders, and 16 special-mission Corsairs and Skyraiders. Her arrival gave TF 77 almost 350 carrier-based aircraft. In addition there were almost 50 planes in the CVEs of Task Group 96.8. The battleship in TF 77 was the *Missouri*, which had made her Korean War debut as a fire support ship in the Inchon landing.

The Wonsan amphibious operation began with six minesweepers arriving off the port on October 10, 1950, ten days before the scheduled landing. Confronting the sweepers—and unknown to their officers—were 400 square miles of mined water sown with more than 3,000 of the deadly devices. When the extent of the communist minefields became known, the Navy was hard-pressed to clear channels for the landing.

In an effort to clear the mines as quickly and safely as possible, on October 12 the carriers *Leyte* and *Philippine Sea* flew off an "aerial countermining strike." Led by AD Skyraiders equipped with radar and others dropping smoke floats to guide the way, the strike consisted of 31 Skyraiders, each carrying three 1,000-pound bombs and eight F4U Corsairs with one 1,000-pounder each, the bombs fused to detonate 20 feet underwater. Many problems—including total failure of the smoke floats—hampered the unusual effort to detonate the mines by bombing the area. The strike's results are unknown, but they definitely were not significant.

Mines proved to be the war's greatest menace to naval operations. During the Wonsan sweeping operations two 185-foot U.S. minesweepers were sunk, as were a smaller Korean and a Japanese minesweeper. The U.S. Marines finally landed at Wonsan on October 25. There was no opposition to the landing because South Korean troops had occupied the city two weeks earlier.

The fast-moving South Koreans—less encumbered by heavy vehicles and equipment than their U.S. counterparts—had thrust through North Korea in the wake of the retreating enemy and captured Wonsan on the 10th. On the 14th the Marine fighters from Seoul's Kimpo airfield flew up to Wonsan's Kalma Pando airfield. Because the harbor was not sufficiently cleared

of mines to allow cargo ships to enter until October 25, Air Force and Marine planes flew in aviation gasoline (in 55-gallon drums), bombs, rockets, ammunition, maintenance personnel, and everything else needed to support the two Marine fighter squadrons. For 12 days the squadrons were supported entirely by airlift, a remarkable feat, albeit in skies controlled by U.S. aircraft. And, beginning on October 17 the escort carriers *Badoeng Strait* and *Sicily* operated off-shore with their Marine fighter squadrons.

U.S. troops occupied Pyongyang on October 19, but these forces and the South Koreans who were even farther north were suffering from food and supplies shortages, the result of Inchon's limited port facilities, the delay in opening Wonsan, and the poor condition of surface transportation routes. Geography and mines made the clearing of Pyongyang's port of Chinnampo a difficult job, and not until November 20 was a channel opened for deep-draft ships.

As Allied troops moved deeper into North Korea more airfields on the peninsula became available for Allied planes. U.S. aircraft (and a squadron of South African F-51 Mustangs) were based in Korea, and other U.S. aircraft flew long-range missions from Japan with fueling stops in Korea.

Except for the battles with the mines, October was a good month for the Allies: U.S. and other United Nations troops reigned supreme on the ground and in the skies and waters around Korea. Senior Allied commanders expected all organized enemy resistance to cease by Thanksgiving Day in late November. The British light carrier *Theseus*, with no targets to strike, sailed for Japan for onward routing to Hong Kong. On October 22 the fast carriers *Boxer* and *Philippine Sea* departed Korean waters for Japan, the former scheduled to continue on to the U.S. West Coast for her long-delayed overhaul. The *Valley Forge* was to follow soon after. A week later the *Leyte* and *Valley Forge* set course for Japan, leaving only the two U.S. escort carriers off Korea. Even they would not remain long for plans were drawn up to have the *Sicily* and *Badoeng Strait* send their Corsairs ashore and for the *Sicily* to return to Guam and reembark her ASW squadron.

When the *Philippine Sea* departed Korean waters Rear Admiral Ewen was succeeded as Commander Task Force 77 by Rear Admiral Hoskins in the *Valley Forge*. The command change was reversed two weeks later when the *Philippine Sea* returned to battle.

5 "AN ENTIRELY NEW YEAR"

The appearance of the Soviet-built MiG-15 in the skies over North Korea radically changed the air war over the Korean peninsula. Here Soviet personnel on a Manchurian airfield check a MiG-15, given the NATO code-name "Fagot." Photography of MiG-15s in Manchuria was strictly forbidden, hence few images exist. (Yefim Gordon Collection)

October 1950 brought renewed threats from Communist China to enter the Korean War coupled with reports—from sources of widely varying reliability—of Chinese troops already moving into North Korea. Two unidentified aircraft streaked over Seoul's Kimpo airfield and released small bombs on the morning of October 14 and again that night. Four F-51 Mustangs searched for the attackers near Sinuiju airfield on the southern side of the Yalu River and were fired on by Chinese anti-aircraft guns across the river. One F-51 was shot down.

Four days later a reconnaissance RB-29 Superfortress flying along the southern bank of the Yalu counted more than 75 fighters parked on an airfield across the river. The next day the planes were gone,

but the implications were clear. On the morning of November 1, almost within sight of the Yalu, three Yak piston-engine fighters shot down a U.S. observation plane and a light bomber. The ill-fated bomber shot down one of its attackers and Air Force Mustangs hurried to the scene and downed the two other Yaks.

At noon a U.S. reconnaissance plane sighted about 15 Yaks parked at Sinuiju on the North Korean side of the Yalu. F-80 Shooting Star turbojet fighters quickly arrived over the field but they were able to destroy only one plane because the aircraft shelters opened toward the north, requiring effective strafing attacks to be made from the forbidden, Chinese side of the Yalu. Anti-aircraft fire from across the river shot down one of the F-80s. A second strike of F-80s found the Sinuiju field empty.

A still more significant action took place in the skies over North Korea on November 1 when six swept-wing jet fighters streaked across the Yalu from Manchuria and fired on another U.S. light observation plane and a flight of Mustangs. The U.S. planes escaped and returned with the news that Soviet-built MiG-15 fighters—given the NATO code name Fagot—had entered the war.[1]

The MiG-15 at the time was the world's most advanced operational fighter and had entered squadron service in the Soviet Air Forces just a year earlier.[2] With a maximum speed of 680 m.p.h., the MiG-15 was considerably faster than the F-80C Shooting Star (580 m.p.h.) and the F9F-2 Panther (526 m.p.h.); the MiG-15's 51,000-foot ceiling was also superior to the F-80C (43,000 feet) and F9F-2 (44,600 feet). The Red plane was armed with one 37-mm cannon and two 23-mm guns, more powerful weapons but with a slower rate-of-fire than the six .50-caliber guns in contemporary Air Force fighters or the four 20-mm guns in Navy fighters.[3]

The first all-jet air battle in history was fought on November 8 when four MiG-15s engaged four F-80s. These were Soviet-piloted MiG-15s. U.S. records confer the first MiG-15 kill of the war to an F-80 pilot in that encounter. But Soviet records show no MiG losses on that date. Soviet scholars speculate that drop tanks jettisoned by the MiG and the method it used to escape the F-80 might have suggested to U.S. pilots that their prey was hit and falling.[4]

The MiG-15s were rugged aircraft. Describing a later air battle between MiG-15s and U.S. Air Force F-84 turbojet fighters attempting to protect a B-29 strike against the airfield at Namsi near the Yalu border, John R. Bruning wrote of how

> [F-84] gunfire raked the MiG's tail, but complete success again eluded the Thunderjet pilots. Although damaged, the MiG used its superior performance to evade further attack as it escaped.
>
> In reality, the .50-caliber machine gun proved to be an ineffective weapon in the minds of many Soviet pilots. MiGs would frequently come home so full of holes that they looked like cheese graters, yet they had held together and brought their pilots home safely. On occasion, one landed with more than one hundred holes carved out of its wing, tail, and fuselage. Had the U.S. Air Force

adopted the 20-mm cannon as its standard aerial weapon, as the Navy had done some years before, many of those damaged MiGs never would have made it north of the Yalu.[5]

Thus, many MiG-15s shown on U.S. gun camera film to be taking hits and diving toward the ground to evade their antagonists, were listed as kills or probables. But many likely survived the air battle. One Russian-piloted MiG-15 was struck by 150 rounds of .50-caliber ammunition and still landed safely at its base. The MiGs were robust aircraft.

Allied air supremacy over the Korean peninsula was now challenged by hundreds of Soviet-piloted MiG-15s. In August 1950 the Soviet 151st Guards Fighter Aviation Division—with 120 MiG-15 fighters—had arrived at Shenyang in Manchuria to provide air cover for the buildup of the Chinese 13th Army Group.[6] Those aircraft with Soviet pilots engaged U.S. aircraft until early 1951. The Soviet pilots initially wore Chinese-type uniforms, carried no identification, and were given cards with Chinese phrases to be used in radio communications. Of course, in combat they instantly reverted to Russian, which was monitored by U.S. radio intercept stations.[7]

Soviet-piloted MiG-15s fought in the skies over Korea through July 1953. These were air defense units—Protivovozdushnoi Oborony Strany (Air Defense of the Country), known by the abbreviation PVO. One PVO division that fought in Korea included the 587th Naval Fighter Regiment, which flew MiG-15s.[8] Twenty-two Russian fighter pilots received the award Hero of the Soviet Union in the Korean War.

Chinese pilots flew their first combat mission over North Korea on December 28, 1950. One flight of Chinese MiG-15s headed south across the Yalu with two flights of Soviet MiG-15s. Historian Xiaoming Zhang wrote:

> However, the Chinese pilots, who were not proficient in combat flying, became confused as they flew into the combat zone. When the Russian pilots suddenly broke off and dove in search of targets, they left their disconcerted Chinese comrades behind. After failing to spot any enemy aircraft, the Chinese were ordered to return to base. For the next few days the Chinese pilots experienced similar problems.[9]

The Chinese air force had been formally established in November 1949, little more than a year before their first combat missions over Korea. The newly formed People's Liberation Army Air Force took over 113 Nationalist aircraft, most American types. Almost immediately the Soviet Union agreed to provide China with more than 400 aircraft as well as training and support and ground control radars. No jet aircraft were initially provided. But by June 1950 the Soviets were providing the Chinese with the first of hundreds of MiG-15s.

In the skies over North Korea there was little improvement in Chinese pilot proficiency and effectiveness until the fall of 1952. Thus, Soviet PVO pilots carried the burden of the air war over Korea.[10]

On November 9, as U.S. carriers began strikes against Yalu River bridges, Lieutenant Commander William T. Amen flying an F9F-2B shot down the first MiG to fall in battle to a naval aircraft. Although the MiG-15, piloted by Senior Lieutenant Mikhail F. Grachev, was superior in performance, the Navy squadron commander chased the MiG from 4,000 up to 15,000 feet and down again before scoring the kill. Soviet records agree with Amen's claim. Thus, Amen may have scored the first MiG-15 kill of the war.

Commander Amen's victory in a Panther from the *Philippine Sea* was followed by F9Fs from the *Leyte* and *Valley Forge* shooting down two MiG-15s on November 18. No Panthers were lost in these encounters.

The Chinese Assault

On the ground, between October 24 and 28, 1950, South Korean troops were attacked by troops positively identified as Chinese. This action was followed by Chinese assaults against U.S. forces, and on November 3 a U.S. division was forced to retreat some 50 miles to protect its overextended supply lines.

A day later Commander Naval Forces Far East was directed to employ the maximum available naval air power "in close support of ground units and interdiction of enemy communications, assembly areas and troop columns." The following morning Task Force 77 sortied from Japanese ports with the Fast Carrier Force consisting of the carriers *Leyte* and *Valley Forge*, the battleship *Missouri*, and several destroyers. These ships were soon joined by the carrier *Philippine Sea*. The escort carriers *Badoeng Strait* and *Sicily* were also recalled, and the five carriers joined land-based aircraft

in pounding the Chinese armies that were swarming across the Yalu.

General Douglas MacArthur ordered the bombing of bridges across the Yalu in an effort to halt the flow of supplies to the Chinese, but Washington intervened as the State Department reminded President Truman of an agreement between the United States and Britain whereby Manchuria would not be bombed without prior consultation by the two Allied governments. MacArthur was directed to halt the bombing of all targets within five miles of the Yalu until further notice. The general protested and obtained permission to bomb the Korean end of the Yalu spans.

Six major bridges and 11 lesser structures crossed the Yalu, which forms most of the North Korean border with Manchuria. The Japanese had built most of the bridges prior to World War II. Their construction was sound, and the spans were now defended by heavy anti-aircraft batteries and jet fighters. Further, the U.S. planes were restricted from violating Manchurian air space, severely limiting bombing approaches to the bridges across the twisting Yalu. In some places this made attack by level bombers impossible.[11]

At Sinuiju, near the mouth of the Yalu, B-29s were unable to destroy the top-priority railway and highway bridges. Task Force 77 planes undertook a three-day effort against the spans beginning on November 9 and "dropped" the highway bridge. The railroad bridge resisted destruction by Navy planes. Weather slowed the bridge attacks, and even as the B-29s and carrier planes were dropping the spans the Chinese were erecting pontoon bridges across the river. Then, as the river water froze, troops and vehicles moved directly across the river on ice.

The bridge-busting strikes from the carriers usually consisted of 8 AD Skyraiders, each with two 1,000-pound bombs (and on occasion one 2,000-pounder), to drop the spans; 8 to 16 F4U Corsairs with bombs and rockets to strike enemy gun positions along the southern bank of the river; and 8 to 16 F9F Panthers to provide protection against MiGs. Thus, each strike contained up to 40 aircraft. Between November 9 and 21 the carrier planes flew a total of 593 sorties against the Yalu bridges. At the time the carriers were in the Sea of Japan off Korea's eastern coast, forcing the aircraft to make an overland flight of some 225 miles to their targets. Once over the target there was heavy anti-aircraft fire, especially from the river's "safe" northern bank, and the MiGs were awaiting the Navy fliers.

Throughout this period and for the remainder of the war the Chinese concentrations of men, guns, vehicles, aircraft, and supplies on the river's northern bank were immune from Allied attack. General MacArthur repeatedly asked for permission to strike these concentrations in Manchuria as well as certain communication and industrial centers in the country. His pleas were denied as U.S. policy attempted to keep the war within the limitations imposed by the Allied members of the United Nations. Even the right of "hot pursuit" of Chinese across the Yalu was denied to the Allied pilots—at least officially. There were numerous MiG pursuits by F-86s across Yalu as well as periodic reconnaissance sorties.

While the destruction of such Manchurian targets could not conceivably have won the Korean War, such strikes would have undoubtedly (1) slowed the Chinese advance, (2) increased the pressure on the communists to join the Allies at the conference table, and (3) deterred the Chinese from providing substantial assistance to the Viet Minh in Indochina in the early 1950s. However, even had Washington acquiesced to bombing Manchuria, the U.S. Air Force and Task Force 77 were at the time incapable of mounting a major aerial offensive against such targets. Further, such striking power could have been built up in the Korean theater only by severely depleting U.S. strength elsewhere, principally in Europe. In addition to bombers, such

When the Communist Chinese entered the Korean War the Yalu River bridges become a primary target of U.S. bombers. Carrier-based aircraft joined B-29s to attack the bridges, the former being better suited for the bombing techniques required because of political restrictions on the attacks. The bomb craters are on the near (Korean) bank; the untouched installations on the far (Manchurian) side. (U.S. Navy)

operations would require extensive fighter escorts for the B-29s and such operations—at least with conventional bombs—were considered totally impractical for the more vulnerable B-36s.

And, there was the fear of an all-out assault by the powerful Soviet Air Forces. All of Korea and much of Japan lay within range of air bases in Manchuria and Soviet Siberia. Soviet aircraft in the Far East outnumbered the available Allied aircraft in both numbers and in modern types. U.S. strikes against targets in Manchuria and China might have provoked a violent reaction from the "enemies," although, as later ascertained from Soviet documents, certainly not an all-out war.

By late November 1950 there were more than 250,000 Chinese troops in North Korea pushing hard against the 267,000 Allied troops—130,000 U.S. soldiers and Marines, 127,000 South Koreans, and 10,000 men from other United Nations allies. (The North Korean Army had been destroyed by this time.) On November 26, 1950, during an Allied ground offensive, the Chinese launched an all-out ground attack. The Chinese offensive took the Allies by surprise. General MacArthur declared, "we face an entirely new war." After the strikes against the Yalu bridges, the Allied military leaders thought the Communist Chinese—whose numbers were greatly underestimated—had been cut off from their supplies and support. On November 18 the escort carriers had been withdrawn, considered superfluous. The fast carrier *Valley Forge* departed on the 19th, bound for the U.S. West Coast and an overhaul, leaving only the carriers *Leyte* and *Philippine Sea* in Task Force 77.

The Chinese offensive threw Allied forces into a desperate holding action and then retreat. On the 28th the two remaining fast carriers in TF 77 began maximum air operations in support of the hard-pressed Allied forces. On the same day the Allied high command in Japan alerted naval amphibious forces to the possibility of a withdrawal of all ground forces from Korea.

U.S. and other Allied warships throughout the Pacific were alerted, and many immediately set course for Korea. The *Sicily*, which had just arrived in Japan after picking up her AF Guardian ASW aircraft at Guam, sent her planes ashore and again took aboard Marine-piloted F4U Corsairs. Her sister ship *Badoeng Strait*, with her Corsairs still aboard, joined the battle. At Hong Kong the British light carrier *Theseus* hurried preparations to return to the war zone.

The U.S. light carrier *Bataan* had just arrived in Japan, having transported F-84E Thunderjet and F-86A Sabre fighters to the Far East, accompanied by the escort carrier *Bairoko* and a fast tanker. (The swept-wing F-86A, with a top speed of 675 m.p.h., was the first Allied fighter considered the equal of the MiG-15, although the U.S. plane suffered from range and firepower limitations.) The *Bataan* quickly unloaded her Air Force fighters, took aboard a squadron of Marine F4U-4B Corsairs, and reached Korean waters on December 15.

The fast carrier *Valley Forge*, now halfway across the Pacific, was ordered to continue to the United States, exchange her air group for that of the *Boxer*, and return to Korea. In addition, on July 25, 1950, the mothballed *Essex*-class carrier *Princeton* had been ordered activated.[12] The 27,100-ton warship was recommissioned on August 28, 1950, and manned largely by reservists. In late November she departed Pearl Harbor for the Western Pacific and reached Korean waters on December 5.

Accordingly, eight U.S. aircraft carriers of various types plus a British light carrier would be off Korea by the end of 1950. While help was coming, initial Navy share of supporting the withdrawing Allied ground forces in North Korea fell to the *Philippine Sea* and *Leyte*. While Air Force, Navy, and Marine fighters and bombers plastered the advancing Chinese, Air Force and Marine transports parachuted ammunition, medical supplies, water, food, gasoline, and even two-ton bridge sections to the retreating U.S. and South Korean troops. Cargo planes and helicopters darted into open fields to fly out the wounded. The light observation aircraft that traditionally called in air support were assisted by a four-engine Marine transport hastily equipped with additional communications equipment for use as an airborne tactical direction center.

The fighters and bombers strafed and bombed Chinese a mere 50 yards from U.S. troops, with empty shell cases from the planes falling among the friendly troops. The fiery napalm could be used close to friendly forces, in part, because of the 25-degrees-below-zero temperature.

Two carrier planes were lost to enemy action during this period. A Skyraider from the *Leyte* was hit by ground fire and crashed. Its pilot was captured before a helicopter could pick him up. (He was repatriated at the end of hostilities.) The other plane shot down was a Corsair from the *Leyte* piloted by Ensign Jesse Leroy Brown, the U.S. Navy's first black combat pilot.[13] Brown's F4U made a crash landing near the Chosin Reservoir, five miles behind enemy lines. Pilots circling overhead saw that Brown was alive but unable to free himself from the burning wreckage of his plane. Lieutenant (jg) Thomas J. Hudner, Jr., from the same *Leyte* squadron, intentionally crash-landed his plane nearby and ran to help Brown.

"I knew what I had to do," said Hudner. "I was not going to leave him down there for the Chinese. Besides, it was 30 degrees below zero on that slope, and he was a fellow aviator. My association with the Marines had rubbed off on me. They don't leave wounded Marines behind."

Brown's leg was trapped in his plane's wreckage. Hudner packed snow around Brown with his bare hands to keep the flames away from the injured pilot and then returned to his own plane to radio for a helicopter to fly in cutting tools. A whirlybird arrived shortly, but Brown died before he could be freed from the wreckage. For his valiant efforts Lieutenant Hudner became the first Navy man to be awarded the Medal of Honor in the Korean War.

As the retreating U.S. and South Korean troop reached the sea, they were taken off at the ports of Hungnam, Chinnampo, Wonsan, and Inchon and transferred to South Korea. From Hungnam the ships evacuated 105,000 military personnel and 91,000 Korean civilians; another 7,700 personnel were taken out of Chinnampo; 3,800 military and 7,000 civilians were embarked at Wonsan; and almost 69,000 persons were loaded at Inchon. In addition, aircraft flew out thousands more—4,119 from Hungnam in less than four days. And the troops were taken out with their guns, vehicles, and equipment. In most of the evacuations Chinese troops were close behind the withdrawing Allies. Equipment and supplies that could not be evacuated as well as shore installations were destroyed before they could be captured by the communists.

Most of the troops were taken out as fighting units and immediately rejoined the battle to the south (this in contrast to the 338,000 British and French troops evacuated from Dunkirk in the summer of 1940, who took out no heavy weapons, vehicles, or supplies, and in some cases not even individual weapons). Still, the retreat from the Yalu can be considered the largest U.S. military defeat since the fall of Corregidor in May 1942.

The New Line

The Chinese poured south as the Allies withdrew, and plans for the evacuation of all of Korea were made ready. But barely had the New Year begun when the Chinese drive lost momentum. Savage Allied rear guard fighting and the continual pounding of Allied aircraft had made the advance costly. By late January 1951 Allied troops were advancing northward again against only slight resistance. In early February the Chinese high command decided to withdraw to defensive positions just above the 38th parallel.

With the front lines being stabilized, order was imposed upon the carrier forces, which had been hastily built up during December. The *Leyte*, on loan from the Atlantic Fleet, headed back for the U.S. East Coast late in January. Her departure left the fast carriers *Philippine Sea*, *Princeton*, and *Valley Forge* in the Western Pacific. A rotation schedule was drawn up for these Task Force 77 carriers to keep two on the line and a third in Japan for a ten-day rest and replenishment period.

In Task Group 95.1 the light carriers *Bataan* and *Theseus* alternated duty off Korea's western coast, providing support and utility flights for the coastal blockade. The hard-worked escort carriers *Badoeng Strait* and *Sicily* returned to the U.S. West Coast for a needed rest. The escort carrier *Bairoko* remained in the Western Pacific, took aboard an anti-submarine squadron, and, with several destroyers, formed a hunter-killer group (Task Group 96.7) that operated out of Japan. The group was primarily a training unit but was ready for immediate action against hostile submarines.

Allied naval forces in the Western Pacific thus included six aircraft carriers as the war entered another phase. The fast carrier *Boxer* returned to Korean waters in March 1951 after her long-delayed overhaul, relieving the *Valley Forge*. The *Boxer*'s new air group was composed entirely of reserve squadrons recalled to active duty.[14] With the *Boxer* came Rear Admiral William G. Tomlinson, who became Commander Task Force 77. Since the end of 1950 the fast carrier division commanders were alternating in command of TF 77. Rear Admiral Edward C. Ewen had been relieved on Christmas Day 1950 by Rear Admiral Ralph A. Ofstie, skipper of the *Essex* during much of World War II and later a carrier group commander in the Pacific. Ofstie and Ewen alternated command of TF 77 until Tomlinson arrived, with Tomlinson relieving Ofstie

U.S. escort carriers served with valor during the Korean War. The *Sicily* is shown entering San Diego in February 1951 after operations off the Korean coasts. Her crew is spelling out the ship's name on the flight deck—a practice that admirals love and sailors abhor. Two L-5 liaison planes and an HO3S-1 helicopter are parked forward of 11 F4U Corsairs and AD Skyraiders. (U.S. Navy)

after the latter's third turn as Commander TF 77. (In all, 13 rear admirals would command TF 77 during the 37 months of combat of the Korean War, with each admiral averaging four terms at the helm. In addition to those men already mentioned, these division commanders were George R. Henderson, John Perry, Joseph J. (Jocko) Clark, Frederick W. McMahon, Apollo Soucek, Herbert E. Regan, R. F. Hickey, W. D. Johnson, and R. E. Blick. Late in March 1951 Vice Admiral Harold G. Martin relieved Vice Admiral Arthur D. Struble as commander of the Seventh Fleet.

Shortly after Admirals Tomlinson and Martin assumed their respective commands, intelligence reports indicated that the Communist Chinese were about to launch an amphibious invasion of the Nationalist stronghold of Formosa. In a show of force, Task Force 77, with the *Boxer* and *Philippine Sea*, left Korean waters and operated off the coast of China from April 11 to 14. The carrier planes flew aerial parades off the Chinese mainland during this show of force. On the 13th Admiral Martin flew to Formosa for talks with Generalissimo Chiang Kai-shek. While TF 77 carriers were in the East China Sea, the light carriers *Bataan* and *Theseus* operated off the eastern coast of Korea.

The fast carriers then returned to their primary task of interdiction behind the enemy lines in Korea until late April 1951, when the communists launched a

major spring offensive. The flattops then switched to close support operations. All three U.S. fast carriers were kept on the line by daily replenishments at sea, taking on fuel and munitions from late afternoon until midnight. Both light carriers were also kept at sea, with the British light carrier *Theseus* being relieved in late April by her sister ship *Glory*.

During this period carrier-based aircraft made the only aerial torpedo attack of the Korean War—against a dam. The communists controlled the Hwachon reservoir and dam and with it could control the water level on several rivers in Korea. By closing the dam's floodgates the communists could lower the river levels to facilitate their own troop movements; if the Allies attacked, the communists could open the gates, flood the rivers, and impede the Allied advance. U.S. Army Rangers had failed in efforts to capture the dam, and B-29s, using six-ton guided bombs, had failed to destroy the structure.

At 2:40 P.M. on April 30 the Army asked Task Force 77 to have a go at the dam. Eighty minutes after the request was received the *Princeton*'s Carrier Air Group 19 flew off six AD-4 Skyraiders, each carrying two 2,000-pound bombs, with an escort of five F4U-4 Corsairs. The Skyraiders made a divebombing attack on the dam that holed one floodgate. The Army asked the Navy to try again.

An AD-4 Skyraider from attack squadron VA-195 takes off from the carrier *Princeton* for the attack on the Hwachon Dam. The aircraft carries a MK 13 torpedo (with nose guard) and napalm tanks. The Skyraider proved to be an able and versatile aircraft, flying from U.S. and British carriers as well as from land bases. (U.S. Navy)

The *Princeton* made another attempt. A dozen Mk 13 torpedoes had been loaded aboard the carrier when she departed the Bremerton (Washington) Naval Shipyard. Early on May 1 the carrier launched five AD-4 and three AD-4N Skyraiders, plus 12 F4U-4 Corsairs for flak suppression.[15] They were accompanied by F9F-2P photo planes. The eight attack planes each carried a Mk 13 torpedo set for surface run. (The torpedo planes each also carried napalm tanks to be used after the torpedo attack on other targets at the direction of ground controllers.)

The approach for the bombers was difficult because of the hills surrounding the reservoir. One torpedo was a dud and one ran erratic; the six others hit and blasted open the dam's floodgates, destroying communist control of the reservoir's waters. This strike remains the world's only aerial torpedo attack since 1945.

Even before the communist drive ended in mid-May the Allies again went on the offensive, supported by land- and carrier-based aircraft. Also in May a "new" carrier joined Task Force 77, the *Bon Homme Richard*. Recommissioned from the mothball fleet in January 1951, she made her first air strikes of the Korean War on the last day of May. The "Bonnie Dick" took the place of the *Philippine Sea* in TF 77's three-carrier lineup.

The Allies continued on a limited offensive into June 1951, when a Soviet spokesman at the United Nations indicated that there might be some basis for armistice discussions between the Korean belligerents. The armistice talks began in Korea in early July 1951.

The United States abandoned efforts to forcibly unify Korea and began discussions with the purpose of a political rather than military solution to the Korean problem. This "less-than-total-victory" was dictated in large part by U.S. military leaders' opposition to becoming tied down in a "secondary" theater. In testimony before Congress on May 15, 1951, General of the Army Omar Bradley, Chairman of the Joint Chiefs of Staff, declared, "Red China is not the powerful nation seeking to dominate the world. Frankly, in the opinion of the Joint Chiefs of Staff, this strategy [of widening the Korean War] would involve us in the wrong war, at the wrong place, at the wrong time, and with the wrong enemy." Soviet Russia was considered the real enemy, and to quote General Bradley, "taking on Red China is not a decisive move, does not guarantee the end of the war in Korea, and may not bring China to her knees."

Many American political and military leaders accordingly viewed the prospect of "peace talks" most favorably; the politicians could end an unpopular war and the military leaders could concentrate the nation's defenses against Soviet Russia. There was some historic precedent for accepting less than total victory: it had been done several times in the past, notably in the 1798–1800 quasi-war with France and the War of 1812 with Britain. Although there would be two more years of fighting in Korea before a truce was effected, the war had entered still another phase.

While Allied and communist truce delegations talked about an armistice in Korea, the fighting on the ground continued along a relatively fixed front. In the air the fighting raged over much of the Korean peninsula.

In mid-1951 the fast carriers in the Western Pacific were the *Bon Homme Richard*, *Boxer*, and *Princeton*, the last about to be relieved by the *Essex*. While these flattops operated off the eastern coast of Korea in Task Force 77, off the western coast steamed the light carriers *Bataan* and *Glory* and the escort carriers *Bairoko* and *Sicily*, these ships part of TF 95, the Blockading and Escort Force.

The arrival of the *Essex* in Korean waters late in August 1951 marked the first combat deployment of a modernized *Essex*-class carrier. In addition to being better suited for jet operations, she had on board a squadron of F2H Banshees (plus one squadron each of F9F Panthers, F4U Corsairs, and AD Skyraiders, and detachments of special-mission aircraft). McDonnell had developed the twin-engine Banshee in parallel with the Grumman F9F Panther as a carrier-based jet fighter. The F2H-2, which first saw action from the *Essex*, was slightly faster than the Panther, but the new plane's drawbacks included having a wingspan a fraction under 45 feet, seven feet more than the Panther, and being 40 feet long, almost three feet longer than the Panther. Jet aircraft were growing larger and larger. Like the Panther, the Banshee had four 20-mm nose cannon and could carry two 500-pound bombs underwing.

The *Essex* arrived off Korea in the middle of Operation Strangle. Late in May 1951, the U.S. Army high command in Korea proposed severing the battlefield from all communist supplies and reinforcements. Highways were carrying the bulk of the material to communist front lines, and it was proposed that all communist routes be cut in a one-degree strip or "belt" across Korea, from 38° 15' North latitude to 39°

When conventional bombing attacks failed to breach the Hwachon Dam, the Navy employed carrier-based torpedo planes to breach the floodgates, by which the communists were able to control river levels to facilitate their own movements and impede the Allies. Unconventional tactics and weapons were also used in World War II by the Royal Air Force to breach the Ruhr River dams in Germany. (U.S. Navy)

The *Bon Homme Richard* was typical of the *Essex*–class carriers that were hastily reactivated for the Korean War. Although not as well suited to operate jet aircraft as the modernized carriers, these ships provided excellent service in the conflict. The configuration shown here is essentially as the "Bonnie Dick" was completed with improved electronic equipment installed and some guns removed. (U.S. Navy)

15' North. Within this belt Air Force planes would cut roads, drop bridges, and block tunnels on the three westernmost highways; carrier-based aircraft from Task Force 77 would hit the two central routes; and land-based Marine aircraft would take out the three eastern routes. The interdiction effort would be an around-the-clock operation, with roads and potential bottle-necks being hit with regular bombs, delayed action bombs set to explode in from six to 72 hours, napalm, rockets, and gunfire.

Operation Strangle began on June 5, 1951. Hundreds of communist trucks were destroyed in the Air Force–Navy–Marine effort, and bridges and roads were holed and cut. Still, reconnaissance aircraft brought back disappointing news. The number of trucks moving through the belt at night was unchanged. Dirt roads and slave labor made highway repairs simple. Delayed-action bombs were ignored with Oriental fatalism. Operation Strangle continued through September 20, with the *Bon Homme Richard*, *Boxer*, and *Princeton* (replaced by the *Essex* in August) providing the Navy's share of aircraft. Significantly, the rapid buildup of the carrier force necessitated the activation of Naval Air Reserve squadrons to fill their decks. For example, of the 12 fighter and attack squadrons in the three fast carriers off Korea in mid-1951, ten were reserve units. Only air group CVG-19X on the *Princeton* had active squadrons in mid-1951, Fighter Squadron 23 and Attack Squadron 55.[16]

In the midst of the interdiction effort, the newly arrived *Essex* was called upon for another mission, that of providing escort for B-29 Superfortress bombers striking the key communist port city of Rashin

(its Japanese name; "Wojin" is the Korean name of the city). Rashin, only 17 miles from the Soviet frontier, was tied to the Soviet city of Vladivostok by rail, road, and sea. Supplies from Russia were known to pour into Rashin, where they were loaded on trucks for transportation to the Korean battlefields. While Rashin was a key military target, the U.S. State Department urged restraint in bombing the city because it feared that aircraft might stray over or actually bomb Russian territory. B-29s had bombed Rashin by radar, on August 12, 1950, but all of their bombs had missed their targets, most landing in the nearby countryside. Ten days later another B-29 strike was flown. This time bad weather forced the planes to hit other targets in North Korea. After this, at State Department insistence, Rashin was put off-limits to air attack. By the fall of 1951 Rashin was the only city in North Korea that had not been devastated by Allied air power.

The U.S. Joint Chiefs of Staff obtained President Truman's permission to bomb Rashin's railroad yards, and on August 25, 1951, 35 B-29s took off to strike the city. Because the B-29s were forbidden from flying over Soviet territory during their bomb run, they were forced to fly over North Korea en route to the target, giving ample warning to communist fighters and anti-aircraft batteries. As no Allied jet fighters flying from bases in South Korea could escort the bombers so far north, en route to Rashin the B-29s were met by 12 F2H Banshees and 11 F9F Panthers from the *Essex*.

Twenty-nine of the B-29s reached the target and released more than 300 tons of bombs in a visual attack. The marshalling yards were smashed as 97 percent of the bombs struck their target. (One bomber jettisoned a string of bombs at sea, just missing a U.S. cruiser and two destroyers that were standing offshore.) No MiGs attempted to interfere with the B-29s, and the mission went off smoothly. Communists forces no longer had any refuge within North Korea's boundaries.

One of the *Essex* pilots had a lucky escape in this period. On September 3 an F9F-2s from VF-51 were on a low-level flight over North Korea, strafing communist trucks near Wonsan. One plane ran into a cable that sheared six feet off a wing. The pilot managed to reach airfield K-3 in South Korea and, making certain that his plane would come down at sea, safely ejected although his tail bone was cracked. After being picked up by a jeep from the base, he was returned to the *Essex* the next day. The pilot was Ensign Neil A. Armstrong, who would fly 78 combat missions over Korea but would be remembered for another mission—going to the moon in 1969.[17]

The *Essex* was given an unusual mission on October 29, 1951. Allied guerrillas reported that a meeting of Chinese and Korean Communist Party leaders was to take place at Kapsan, 60 miles inland in a mountainous area of North Korea. For this mission the *Essex* flew off 16 strike aircraft: 8 Corsairs from VF-53, each armed with a single 500-pound bomb and 4 250-pounders; and 8 Skyraiders from VF-54, each armed with two 1,000-pound bombs, 8 250-pound bombs, and a 300-gallon napalm bomb.[18] The target area of 3 to 4 acres would be devastated if the attacks were accurate.

Launched 100 miles offshore, the planes flew low over the water and then, when over land, through valleys to evade radar detection. No fighters accompanied the bombers to reduce the chances of detection. At 9:13 A.M.—13 minutes after the delegates were to have taken their seats—the first bombs exploded. All of the bombs fell within the target compound. The aircraft strafed the smoking ruins of the facility.

Guerrillas reported that between 510 and 530 senior communist officials and their staffs were killed in the attack, including the North Korean Army leadership. All party records in North Korea were destroyed. There was no defending anti-aircraft fire, and all of the attacking planes returned safely to their carrier. The Navy pilots were labeled the "Butchers of Kapsan" by the communist radio, which put a price on their heads. (The Navy presented all of the participating pilots with the Distinguished Flying Cross.)

Meanwhile, Operation Strangle continued with unsatisfactory results. Aboard the *Essex* flight opera-

tions were interrupted late on September 16 when one of her Banshees, damaged on a mission over enemy territory, missed the arresting wires, floated over the barrier, and crashed into the deck park forward. Fires flared up and before they were extinguished four planes were destroyed, seven men were dead, and another 27 men were injured. After this accident the *Essex* withdrew to Japan for repairs, not returning to the battle line until October 3.

When the *Essex* again flew off strikes her planes sought out railroad tracks and bridges in North Korea. Previous efforts against the Yalu River bridges and then against highways had not appreciably slowed the flow of material to the communists. Now, with evidence that the Reds were relying more heavily on railways, in October 1951 an effort was begun against this mode of transportation. For this operation Task Force 77 mustered the fast carriers *Antietam* (replacing the *Boxer*), the *Bon Homme Richard* (which would soon be relieved by the *Valley Forge*), and the *Essex*.

Again, it was a multiservice, around-the-clock effort. The night attacks from TF 77 were flown by F4U-5N Corsairs and AD-4N Skyraiders, each fast carrier air group having a detachment of four of each aircraft. The Corsairs' primary mission was night air defense of the carriers, but in the absence of enemy air opposition they joined the AD-4Ns in nocturnal hunts for communist trains, trucks, and repair crews. Striking targets by radar and the light of flares and searchlights, these planes added significantly to their carriers' score of trucks and trains destroyed and road and rail cuts.

The night-flying pilots saw considerable activity on their sorties, this in marked contrast to the nocturnal operations of most World War II carrier fliers. In the 1941–1945 carrier war most of the activity and battles had been in daylight, and most pilots did not like night flying because they rarely saw enemy planes or enemy ships. It was different in Korea; the truck convoys and trains there hid by day and moved at night.

Night operations by carrier aircraft continued from shore bases as well as from TF 77 carriers. Marine night-fighter squadrons VMF(N)-513 and VMF(N)-542 began fighting the nocturnal air war from bases in South Korea in August 1950 with F4U-5N Corsairs and then F7F-3N Tigercats. Shortly after the Inchon landing in October 1950, Marine F7Fs scored two kills of North Korean Po-2 Mule biplanes flying night-harassment flights; a Marine-piloted F4U-5NL from one of the squadrons killed a third Po-2. These

No U.S. aircraft carriers were damaged by enemy action during the Korean War. However, several suffered operational casualties. One of the worst accidents occurred on September 16, 1951, when an F2H Banshee missed the arresting wires on the *Essex*, crashed over a barrier, and smashed into parked aircraft. The resulting explosion and fire killed the plane's pilot and seven other men. (U.S. Navy)

biplanes were known by the troops as "Bed Check Charlie," a term that had been used in World War II in the Pacific.

Subsequently the nocturnal air battles entered the jet era with the arrival of Marine F3D-2 Skyknights in June 1952. About midnight of November 2–3, 1952, an F3D-2 of VMF(N)-513 piloted by Major William T. Stratton Jr. with Master Sergeant Hans C. Hogland as his radar operator, made the world's first nighttime jet-versus-jet aerial kill. Their victim was a North Korean Yak-15 turbojet fighter.

Professional Night Fighters

The Douglas F3D Skyknight was the world's first jet-propelled aircraft developed from the outset as a night fighter to enter squadron service.[18] It was an ungainly, two-turbojet aircraft with a gross weight of 26,850 pounds. The aircraft had side-by-side seating for a pilot and radar operator, was armed with four 20-mm cannon, and had an AN/APQ-35 search and target acquisition radar. Unlike the F4U-5N and F7F-3N, which could carry bombs, the F3D's only armament was four 20-mm cannon.[19]

The XF3D-1 first flew on March 23, 1948, and the F3D-1 entered service in February 1951 with Composite Squadron (VC) 3. Although designed for carrier operation, F3D carrier deployments were few. Navy composite squadron VC-4 put four planes aboard the *Franklin D. Roosevelt* from August 29 to December

19, 1952, for a cruise to the North Atlantic and Mediterranean; one aircraft was lost in the routine operations. In an effort to use F3Ds from VC-4 in the Korean War another detachment of four planes was put aboard the *Lake Champlain* in April 1953 as the carrier headed for the war zone. One of the VC-4 pilots described the experience on the straight-deck carrier:

When we remained at idle for fifteen to twenty minutes, waiting for our turn to be launched, the heat would bake the wood of the flight deck, which had often been previously saturated with oil and fuel spills. Eventually a minor conflagration would start. It wasn't serious, but it was still a "fire on the flight deck" over the public address system, and the whole damn ship would rush to fire quarters. . . . We tried parking the plane with exhausts extending over the deck edge, but we burned up a few fire hoses and life rafts in the catwalks.[20]

In late June 1953 the *Lake Champlain*'s four F3D-2s flew ashore to an airfield known as K-6 near P'yongtaek in Korea to join VMF(N)-513. This ended Skyknight carrier operations. The land-based Marine and Navy F3Ds were successful in night intercepts, proving to be particularly adept at flying escort for B-29s in night bombing raids over North Korea.[21] During the last few months of the war the communists flew night harassment missions over Allied lines with increasing frequency. At the time the Air Force, Navy, and Marine night fighters in Korea were jet-propelled and too fast to cope with the slow, low-flying aircraft. Task Force 77 helped out by sending several F4U-5N Corsairs ashore to operate from an airfield 35 miles south of Seoul. After a week's familiarization with the situation, on the night of June 29–30, 1953, Lieutenant Guy P. Bordelon from the *Princeton* shot down two communist planes. The next night he downed two more, and on the night of July 17 he got his fifth to become the Navy's only air ace of the war with a score of five enemy aircraft.

(Beyond these Navy and Marine night fighters, the Air Force flew a small number of piston-engine F-82 Twin Mustangs and turbojet F-94B Starfire night fighters during the Korean War. A night-flying B-26 Invader also shot down a Po-2.[22])

The train-busting aerial effort continued, with Air Force, Navy, and Marine fliers making thousands of cuts in the 56-inch-wide railways, destroying marshalling yards, dropping bridges, plugging tunnels, and smashing rolling stock. Interdiction of communist road and railway communications continued through the end of the war, but late in June 1952 the emphasis in attacks shifted to transportation centers, manufacturing areas, and supply depots—such as remained—in an effort to force communist concessions at the truce

The Douglas F3D Skyknight was the world's first jet-propelled night fighter built specifically for night operations. This XF3D-1 prototype shows the side-by-side seating for the pilot and radar operator. The definitive F3D-2 had a maximum speed of 490 m.p.h. at 15,000 feet, an initial climb of 2,970 feet per minute, and ceiling of 36,700 feet. (U.S. Navy)

talks. During the 20-month effort to destroy the rail network, planes from Task Force 77 made more than 13,000 rail cuts and destroyed 500 bridges as well as hundreds of locomotives and freight cars, many of them loaded with war matériel.

Command of the Seventh Fleet changed twice during the spring of 1952. Vice Admiral Martin was relieved by Vice Admiral Robert P. Briscoe on March 3, 1952. Briscoe served only until May 20, when he became Commander Naval Forces Far East. Then, Vice Admiral Clark, who had commanded Task Force 77 for almost two months in the fall of 1951, became Commander Seventh Fleet.

In June 1952 the fast carriers in TF 77 launched a major strike against the Suiho Dam, whose hydroelectric plant was the fourth largest in the world and a main source of power for North Korea and Manchuria. Heretofore Suiho had been off-limits to Allied bombers because its location on the Yalu River made an attack without violating Manchurian air space most difficult. Again the B-29s could not hit the dam because their level runs would take them across the river. Adding to the difficulties was the proximity of MiG bases on the Yalu's northern bank.

On June 23 the carriers *Boxer*, *Philippine Sea*, and *Princeton* turned into the wind to fly off aircraft. The three flattops sent off 35 Skyraiders armed with 2,000- and 1,000-pound bombs. When the propeller-driven planes were well on their way the carriers flew off 35 Panthers, 24 of them armed with two 250-pound bombs and the others carrying extra fuel for aerial combat if MiGs appeared on the scene.

The bomb-carrying Panthers streaked down to suppress anti-aircraft fire and the Skyraiders dived on the Suiho power-generating plant. The other Panthers kept high, searching the skies for MiGs. In less than three minutes the carrier planes smashed the power plant with 90 tons of bombs. Every bomb hit the target. A few planes were struck by ground fire, but all but two made it back safely to the carriers. A badly damaged Skyraider and its wingman flew south, the damaged plane making a wheels-up landing at Seoul.

As the Navy planes pulled away from Suiho, Air Force planes arrived to begin a series of follow-up strikes on the complex. During the next few hours 79 F-84 and 45 F-80 fighter-bombers hit the area, followed by 25 F-86 Sabres flying escort for two RF-80 reconnaissance planes.

While bombs rained down on Suiho, carrier- and land-based planes hit 12 other power plants in North Korea; the carriers *Bon Homme Richard*, *Boxer*, *Philippine Sea*, and *Princeton* sent their planes to join Air Force and Marine aircraft in two days of intensive strikes. In this operation the carriers flew 546 attack sorties, the Marines 139, and the Air Force some 400. Eleven of the power plants were knocked out and the near-term use of the two others was questionable.

HMS *Ocean* alternated with the Australian *Sydney* and two other British light carriers in providing a Commonwealth CVL in the Allied naval forces off Korea. Here, in their "invasion" recognition markings, a squadron of Firefly AS.5 and one of Sea Fury FB.11 aircraft are readied aboard the *Ocean*. These aircraft were employed largely in interdiction missions. (Royal Navy)

Two Navy planes were lost in these attacks. Both pilots were rescued.[23]

In an effort to hit well-defended targets with minimum losses in lives and aircraft, the U.S. Navy experimented with "push-button" warfare in Korea from the carrier *Boxer*. F6F-5 Hellcats of World War II vintage were fitted with television-radio guidance systems and loaded with high explosives. With their engines running they were catapulted from the *Boxer*, followed by AD-2Q and -3Q drone-control planes to guide the pilot-less Hellcats to hard-to-hit bridges and crash them into the structures. Between August 28 and September 2 six of these guided missile strikes were flown. Most hit their targets, and only one failed because of faulty control.

A variety of missions kept Task Force 77 carriers busy for the last year of the war. On September 1 the *Boxer*, *Essex*, and *Princeton* sent 144 planes against the oil refinery at Aoji; just four miles from Manchuria and eight miles from Soviet Siberia, another target considered too difficult for B-29s. On October 8 there was another joint Air Force–Navy strike; this time the target was Kowon in eastern Korea, a railroad junction where anti-aircraft batteries had been giving Navy planes a rough time. Ten B-29s, with an escort of 12 Banshees, carpeted the area with 500-pound bombs fused to explode just above the ground. These planes were followed by an 89-plane Navy strike group, which, unopposed by enemy gunfire, bombed and rocketed the rail yards and supply depots. Next the carrier planes turned to hitting communist activities just behind the front lines, beyond the effective range of Allied field artillery.[24]

Throughout this period light and escort carriers performed vital services, normally operating with the United Nations Blockading and Escort Force (TF 95) on both Korea's western and eastern coasts (Task Groups 95.1 and 95.2, respectively). The U.S. carriers that served with this force at various times were the *Badoeng Strait* (which had three war cruises in Korean waters), *Bataan* (three), *Bairoko* (three), *Rendova* (three), and *Sicily* (four). A British Commonwealth light carrier was normally assigned to this force as well.

6 CONCLUDING A WAR

The USS *Essex* was the first modernized ship of her class to participate in the Korean War. Here she lands aircraft while two F2H-2 Banshees from fighter squadron VF-172, with arresting hooks down, wait to come aboard. The Banshees could easily be distinguished from the F9F Panthers by their tail configuration. On the *Essex* an F9F Panther has just landed; AD Skyraiders are parked forward. (U.S. Navy)

The Korean War was a coalition conflict. The British, Australian, Canadian, and New Zealand governments assigned warships to the operational control of the U.S. naval commanders in the war zone. The British light carrier *Triumph* had sent her planes on the first carrier strike of the war in company with the USS *Valley Forge*. The British ship's Seafire and Firefly fighters made a valuable contribution to Allied air strength in the early, desperate days of the conflict.[1]

The British light carrier *Theseus* arrived in the operational area on October 8, 1950, to relieve the *Triumph*. The *Theseus* served until April 1951, when she was relieved by HMS *Glory*. This light carrier served from April to September 1951, and was relieved by the Australian light carrier *Sydney*.

The *Sydney* operated two squadrons of Sea Fury FB.11 fighter-bombers with 22 planes and a squadron of 12 Firefly AS.4 aircraft, essentially the same air group as aboard the British ships. During the fall of 1951 the *Sydney* established a record with 89 sorties in one day and 147 sorties in two days.

The *Glory* returned for a second Korean tour that lasted from early February to late April 1952. On March 17, during strikes against targets on North Korea's western coast, the *Glory* flew off 105 sorties in a single day, a considerable achievement for a CVL of just over 13,000 tons standard displacement. Her No. 804 Squadron flying Sea Fury FB.11 aircraft and No. 812 Squadron with Firefly AS.5 aircraft delivered 68 500-pound bombs and 408 rockets plus 20-mm cannon fire against their targets. The flights lasted 1½ to 2½ hours, with all pilots flying three missions and some a fourth on that day.[2]

The *Glory* was followed into action by the light carrier *Ocean*, which served from early May to early November 1952. The *Ocean*'s Sea Fury FB.11 aircraft of No. 802 Squadron and Firefly AS.5 aircraft of No. 825 Squadron set a new sortie record for aircraft carriers in the Korean War with 123 sorties in a single day on May 17. All aircrews flew four sorties that day and some flew five, a remarkable achievement for 31 aircraft. And, an *Ocean* fighter pilot was the first British pilot to shoot down a MiG-15. The *Ocean*'s aircraft had first encountered MiG-15s on July 27, 1952, when north of Chinnampo on Korea's northwest coast. Several Fireflies were attacked by three MiG-15s (with a total of 12 MiGs sighted in the area). Two Fireflies were damaged, one being forced to ditch and one making a wheels-up beach landing. All four crewmen were rescued. None of the MiGs were damaged.

More encounters with MiG-15s followed and early on the morning of August 9, 1952, four Sea Furies from the *Ocean* led by Lieutenant Peter (Hoagy) Carmichael were attacked by eight MiG-15s north of Chinnampo. In the aerial battle Carmichael scored hits on a MiG-15 that fell to earth and exploded. Two other MiGs might have been damaged. None of the British planes were hit in the dogfight, which lasted four to five minutes.

HMS *Glory* served a third tour in the war zone from November 1952 to May 1953, with the *Ocean* again relieving her for operations during the final days of the conflict.

In addition, the support carrier *Unicorn* served in the Far East throughout the war. Completed in 1943 to a modified CVL design, HMS *Unicorn* was laid up in reserve from January 1946 until 1949, when she was recommissioned for service in the Far East. Arriving on station in October 1949, she was in Singapore, preparing to return to Britain, when the Korean War erupted. For the next three years the *Unicorn* performed valuable service as a troop transport, aircraft ferry, aviation maintenance ship, deck-landing training ship, and operational carrier. In her ferry role she carried Royal Air Force, Australian, and Fleet Air Arm aircraft, transferring naval aircraft to other carriers by crane or, if at sea, by flying them off. She transported U.S. Army as well as British troops between Far Eastern ports. (In the maintenance role she was found to be less efficient than aircraft repair facilities ashore.)

During July 1952, September 1952, and again in July 1953 the *Unicorn* operated in company with the CVL *Ocean* off Korea's west coast, providing a "spare deck" and, with Sea Furies from the *Ocean*'s No. 802 Squadron, providing combat air patrols. And, in a unique action, on September 22, 1951, the *Unicorn* closed with the coast just north of the 38th parallel and used her 4-inch guns to bombard North Korean positions—a unique activity for an aircraft carrier.

In describing the *Unicorn*'s operations in the war, historian David Hobbs noted, "her support for Commonwealth carriers was essential to [the] conduct of their operations."[3]

All aircraft operated by the Commonwealth carriers in the Korean War were propeller-driven planes. The first operational jet squadron of the Royal Navy began receiving jet aircraft in August 1951, but this squadron was a service and tactical trials unit rather than a true first-line combat squadron. Also, experience of that time showed that Allied aircraft carriers were not threatened by high-performance communist aircraft, and hence prop-driven aircraft, with their greater endurance, were in demand for ground support and interdiction missions. Thus, the Attacker, the first operational jet of the Fleet Air Arm, was not used in the Korean War. Although no British-built jet aircraft flew in the Korean War, the power plants for the F-86 Sabre, F9F-2 Panther, and MiG-15 were all based on British engine designs.

The Fast Carriers Triumph

The *Essex*-class ships of Task Force 77 carried the burden of the carrier war in Korea. In all, 11 of these fast carriers saw action: the *Antietam* (one cruise), *Bon Homme Richard* (two), *Boxer* (four), *Leyte* (one), *Philippine Sea* (three), *Princeton* (three), *Valley Forge* (four), *Essex* (two), *Kearsarge* (one), *Lake Champlain* (one), and *Oriskany* (one).[4] The last four carriers were modernized 27A ships, particularly well suited for jet operations. When the *Oriskany* arrived off Korea in late October 1952, her two jet squadrons flew the F9F-5, an improved version of the Panther with a top speed of 579 m.p.h.

The first aerial combat for the new fighters came on November 18, 1952, when four F9F-5 Panthers were on patrol over TF 77, which was supporting a surface bombardment of the extreme northeast Korean coast. The force was about a hundred miles south of the Soviet

The 24th and last *Essex*-class carrier to be completed was the *Oriskany*, commissioned in September 1950. She was especially configured for jet operations, having a reinforced flight deck, increased fuel capacity, and modernized island. Note the absence of guns fore and aft of the island and the AN/SPS-8 height-finding radar installed forward of the pole mast. The "O-boat" and many of her sister ships would be modernized a number of times during the next two decades. (U.S. Navy)

base at Vladivostok. One of the Panthers had fuel pump difficulties and its wingman stayed with it while the two other Panthers climbed to investigate seven aircraft detected by TF 77 shipboard radar.

These bogies had broken off from a larger group of some 16 to 20 aircraft operating north of the task force. The Panthers identified the bogies as seven MiG-15s. The carrier planes were ordered to close with the communist jets. Two and then three of the Panthers fought a brief, fierce battle with the MiGs. Two of the communist planes were shot down, and another was believed damaged; all four Panthers made it back aboard the *Oriskany*, although one was damaged.

This combat debut of the F9F-5 version of the Panther was most successful. The MiGs were superior to the carrier planes in performance and in numbers. But the Americans were unquestionably better fliers. Unfortunately, the U.S. "system" was not up to the Panther pilots' high standards: Task Force 77 radar had not properly reported the incoming raid and was unable to get a "fix" on a pilot who parachuted from one of the downed MiGs, and two other airborne fighter divisions were not vectored into the fight.

For an hour after the aerial battle Task Force 77 radar screens continued to show aircraft to the north, some approaching to within 40 miles of the ships. A slow-flying enemy aircraft in the area suggested a

Soviet rescue plane was searching for survivors. Twice again carrier fighters were vectored out as unidentified aircraft approached; there was one sighting, but the MiGs turned away. By nightfall the radar screens were clear of unidentified aircraft.

When the carrier *Boxer* returned to Korea in May 1953 she had three F9F-5 Panther squadrons plus one of Skyraiders, but she could not effectively operate so many jet aircraft. She traded one Panther squadron to the *Lake Champlain* for a squadron of Corsairs. The latter flattop—with 27A features—was able to handle three squadrons of jets (one F9F and two F2H) plus her AD Skyraider squadron and special-mission aircraft.

Throughout the war the daylight operations of TF 77 carriers were supplemented by their night-flying Corsairs and Skyraiders. These aircraft, as previously related, did an excellent job. However, operating them from the fast carriers was difficult. Major strikes were flown during the day, and the carrier routine for spotting aircraft on deck, preparing ordnance, loading and fueling planes, and so on, was interrupted by launching and recovering the two- and four-plane night missions. The decision was made to operate a carrier with a night air group as had been done in World War II. The carrier would strike communist communication lines and other facilities at night to slow repairs and in general keep the enemy awake. The *Princeton* was

The ubiquitous AD Skyraider was flown in several specialized variants during the Korea War, among them the AD-4N night attack aircraft. This composite squadron VC-35 aircraft—with the squadron's "NR" tail code—was assigned to CVG-5 aboard the *Essex* during her 1951 deployment to the war zone. The aircraft was flown by a pilot and, in a fuselage compartment behind him, a radar operator and Electronics Countermeasures (ECM) operator. An AN/APS-31B radar pod is fitted under the left wing; some 3,000 pounds of bombs and rockets could also be carried. (U.S. Navy)

designated for the project—Operation No Doze—and the night-flying aircraft from the other fast carriers were to be shifted to her decks. However, when she joined TF 77 in March 1953 she was needed in other operations, then required repairs in Japan, and did not see action as a night carrier.

The Navy did score heavily with its night aircraft right up to the end of the war. One of the power plants at the Chosin Reservoir had been a difficult target because of anti-aircraft batteries and MiG interference. Before dawn on May 3, 1953, the *Valley Forge* launched three AD-4N Skyraiders, each with two 1,000-pound bombs. They followed a route that was often taken by Allied reconnaissance aircraft and evoked no enemy fire. By the light of flares, the Skyraiders pummeled the installation.

Fighting in Korea was heavy during the summer of 1953 as the Allies and communists bickered over the truce table. TF 77 carriers were busy flying close-support missions as both sides attempted to profit by last-minute advances. Finally, the armistice document was signed on the morning of July 27, and that night the guns fell silent.

Summing Up

The implications of the Korean War were staggering. The United States had become involved in a war on the Asian mainland, fighting a conventional war against the Chinese, who had manpower resources that were vastly superior to those of the United States. The Soviet Union, beyond providing advisers and arms, had provided 13 air defense divisions—most flying MiG-15s—to fight in the conflict. Never before had the United States engaged in a major conflict under these circumstances.

Further, in an era of international alliances—in which the United States was bound to fight for other countries in the North Atlantic Treaty Organization—the United States had gone to war in aid of a minor nation with which it had no treaty, cultural, or historic ties. If these factors caused a reappraisal by the nation's political leaders, U.S. military leaders also did a great deal of reappraising.

Despite suffering major defeats and almost being driven off of the Korean peninsula in the summer of 1950 and again in the winter of 1950–1951, the United States did not resort to the use of nuclear weapons, although neither President Truman nor President Eisenhower completely ruled out their use. The ground tactics were definitely remnants of World War II as were most of the weapons. Indeed, the more or less continuous front line across Korea near the 38th parallel after the first half year of war, with trenches, bunkers, and patrol actions, was frighteningly similar to the European trench-warfare stalemate of 1915–1918 on the Western Front.

The major difference between the air wars of 1945 and 1950 was the use of jet-propelled aircraft. During the Korean War the United States did not have a clear-cut superiority in either numbers or quality of aircraft. But despite having more fighters in the theater, the Chinese could average only 50 MiG-15 sorties per day on their best days, while the Soviets flew the same number almost every day. The U.S. Air Force could fly up to 900 fighter sorties per day in the war's later stages.[5]

Most significant, U.S. pilots were far superior to the enemy pilots—initially North Korean and then Soviet and Chinese. In aerial combat the U.S. kill-to-loss ratio was reported to have approached 19-to-1 with 147 U.S. planes downed in aerial combat, *according to U.S. data*. The Soviet government later admitted to having lost 345 aircraft while claiming 1,300 American planes shot down, but its claims of U.S. planes includes losses to ground fire.[6] Later Chinese data indicate a claim of 283 jet fighters and 47 other types of aircraft shot down for the loss of only 244 MiG-15s—a kill-to-loss ratio of 1-to-1.35.[7]

As always, combat claims in this conflict were difficult to confirm. Because U.S. fighter pilots fought over enemy territory, gun-camera film was the primary (and often only) means of verifying claims. Often such claims were based on seeing hits on a MiG, not the aircraft going down. But most U.S. aircraft that were shot down crashed in enemy-held areas, where the wreckage could be confirmed.[8]

U.S. Navy carrier-based fighters are credited with shooting down 11 enemy aircraft: Navy F9F Panthers downed two Yak-9 Frank piston fighters and five MiG-15 turbojet fighters; Marine pilots flying F4Us from the carrier *Bataan* downed three Yaks; and Marine Captain Jesse G. Folmar, flying an F4U-4B Corsair from the *Sicily*, downed a MiG-15. On September 10, 1952, Folmar and his wingman encountered eight enemy jets during a strike near Chinnampo, North Korea. Folmar downed a MiG, but his Corsair was damaged in the encounter and he parachuted into the sea, to be rescued by an Air Force amphibian.[9]

As noted previously, U.S. Navy and Marine nightfighter pilots flying from airfields in Korea downed five and ten aircraft, respectively. Navy and Marine pilots on exchange duty with the Fifth Air Force also shot down several enemy aircraft while flying (mostly) F-86 Sabre and F-84 Thunderjet fighters. Navy exchange pilots are credited with four MiG-15s in aerial combat and Marine pilots with 20 MiG-15s. Among the latter, Major John F. Bolt shot down six MiG-15s; he had also shot down six Japanese planes during World War II.[10]

The Navy's casualties in aerial combat were comparatively light, but operational casualties were heavy for carriers during the Korean War. The Navy lost only five aircraft in air-to-air combat. Several hundred were shot down or badly damaged by anti-aircraft fire. There also were scores of operational losses and aircraft destroyed aboard ship. Major losses occurred when, on the morning of August 6, 1952, a fire flared up in the *Boxer*'s hangar deck. The flames ignited gasoline, bombs, ammunition, and planes being readied for the day's operations. Sixty-three men were forced over the side of the ship; all were picked up by lifeboats or helicopters. Seven others were killed in the fire and explosions, and 12 aircraft were destroyed. After hasty repairs in Japan the *Boxer* returned to Korea (to launch the first guided missile attacks of the war).

Further, the United States maintained the aerial initiative, and as Allied aircraft continuously ravaged North Korea's industry, communications, and cities, the enemy carried out only minor air attacks on Allied ground and naval forces in the Korean area and no raids were made against U.S. bases in Japan. On the ground the Allies had been particularly vulnerable to air attack, especially at the port of Pusan, through which most of the war matériel entered Korea and which, in operation around the clock, was a well-lighted and inviting target for air attack.

Although the communists made extensive use of mines in defensive operations, no efforts were made to mine Pusan or the narrow strait between Japan and Korea. Still more significant, no submarine attacks were made against Allied shipping, which was extremely vulnerable. (A single submarine attack would have caused the Allies to establish an active and resource-consuming anti-submarine defense.)

HMS *Glory* was another British CVL that served in the Korean War. Her single port-side catapult is visible; her forward elevator is lowered to the hangar deck; and Fireflys and Sea Furies are ranged on deck. "D-Day" stripes were worn by British naval aircraft so that U.S. pilots did not mistake the unfamiliar British aircraft for communist planes. (FAA Museum)

Military and political leaders who had predicted that future war would be a rapid, catastrophic exchange of nuclear weapons were temporarily silenced. Some civilian and military leaders began to understand the concept of limited war in the nuclear era, of wars of "national liberation"; to some, the events in Greece, Turkey, and Indochina were beginning to form a pattern of aggression that could not be halted by an American threat of nuclear retaliation.

The "big war only" school soon began to argue that the communists had learned in Korea that victory was possible only through nuclear superiority. This argument would soon be given credence by the discovery in the mid-1950s that the Soviets had embarked upon a major program to develop intercontinental ballistic missiles.

A Sea War

Korea was a sea war. Ninety-nine percent of all men, supplies, weapons, and fuels used in Korea reached the Western Pacific by ship. Early in the war the Allies had been pushed into a small perimeter around the port of Pusan. A breakout by land would have been costly and difficult, if not impossible; a breakout via airborne assault was beyond existing capabilities. An amphibious assault (at Inchon) changed the entire course of the war in a few hours. When the entry of Communist Chinese troops threatened to destroy the Allied armies, the Navy safely evacuated the men and their equipment and redeployed them to continue the war. Finally, Allied naval power was responsible for considerable destruction of the enemy by naval guns up to 16 inches in caliber and by carrier-based aircraft.

U.S. carriers regularly operated at night and in bad weather during the Korean War. This snow storm in January 1952 did halt flight operations aboard the *Essex*. Behind the sailors shoveling snow from the flight deck are AD-4NL Skyraiders, F4U-5NL Corsairs, F2H-2 Banshees, and F9F-2 Panthers. The suffix letter "L" indicated "winterized" aircraft. (U.S. Navy)

The U.S. Navy used radio-controlled (drone) F6F-5 Hellcats launched from the carrier *Boxer* to attack targets in North Korea during the Korean War. Here, in June 1953, the carrier *Philippine Sea* is launching a drone F6F-5 from her starboard catapult for use as a target in anti-aircraft fire practice. A second drone Hellcat—with a pilot—is ready to taxi onto the catapult; the pilot will leave the aircraft before it is launched. (U.S. Navy)

Korea had also proved that carrier aviation continued to be a wartime necessity. When the war began Allied jet-propelled aircraft were unable to operate over South Korea for extended periods and could not even reach North Korea from existing land bases. Only carrier-based aircraft were able to range freely over the North. This situation held true until after the amphibious assault at Inchon when the war was three months old. This assault and many other operations during the three-year war were successful to the degree they were largely because of the presence of carrier-based aircraft.

But if sea-based aviation is to share in the credit for Allied successes in the Korean War, it must also share in the failures. A most significant failure was the

Allied effort to sever the communist forces at the front from their supply sources. "The interdiction program was a failure," declared Vice Admiral Jocko Clark, Commander Seventh Fleet. "It did not interdict. The communists got the supplies through; and for the kind of war they were fighting, they not only kept their battle line supplied, but they had enough surplus to spare so that by the end of the war they could even launch an offensive."[11] While limited in its success, the air interdiction effort did raise the war's cost for the communists and, coupled with other aspects of the Allied air operations, enabled the Allied forces to deny the communists their single goal of the war: domination of South Korea.

In the course of the Korean War, 17 U.S. aircraft

carriers flew a total of more than 250,000 operational sorties. To these can be added another 30,000 flown by the one Australian and four British carriers that fought with the U.S. flattops. In all, carriers contributed about one-third of the total air effort in Korea.

The U.S. Director of Naval History, Rear Admiral Ernest M. Eller, has summed up the gigantic naval effort during the Korean War:

The United States and the United Nations stopped aggression (and could have won a clear cut victory) through the sound exercise of control of the sea. This power is, of course, only one facet of national power and itself, alone, could not assure victory in the Korean War, if in any war; yet loss of it would have assured certain defeat.[12]

7 THE COLD WAR NAVY

Nuclear strike was a primary mission of forward-deployed U.S. aircraft carriers during the 1950s and early 1960s. Early in the period, nuclear-capable AJ-1 Savages would come aboard the carriers for exercises. Here the 12 Savages of Heavy Attack Squadron 9 crowd the forward flight deck of the *Coral Sea*. The carrier still has an axial fight deck in this view. (U.S. Navy)

The Korean War had three major effects on the U.S. Navy: (1) the strength of the active fleet was increased, (2) the case for the aircraft carrier in the Cold War era was proved, and (3) the nation embarked upon a major program of warship construction.

Many American leaders viewed the invasion of South Korea as the first step of a worldwide communist attack that might open on the European front at any time. The defense of Europe was unquestionably of more importance than resisting communist aggression on the Korean peninsula. Reinforcements were quickly dispatched to the Sixth Fleet in the Mediterranean Sea. As previously noted, beginning in 1947–1948 the U.S. Sixth Fleet in the Mediterranean had consisted of at least one aircraft carrier with supporting warships and an amphibious squadron with a Marine battalion embarked. In June 1950 the Sixth Fleet contained the 27,100-ton carrier *Leyte*, a heavy cruiser, a light cruiser, and several destroyers.[1]

The 45,000-ton large carrier *Midway* crossed the Atlantic in mid-July 1950, entering the Mediterranean on July 20, 1950. She was joined by her sister ship *Coral Sea*, which arrived in the Mediterranean in September (after which the *Leyte* had departed for Korea). Also in September the escort carrier *Mindoro* joined the Sixth Fleet to strengthen U.S. anti-submarine capabilities in the Mediterranean. With these carriers came additional cruisers and destroyers. Thus the Sixth Fleet became a potent striking force, although at the time without a nuclear strike capability.

After the success of the Inchon invasion and the retreat of the North Korean armies, there was a cutback in the number of ships in the Sixth Fleet. However, the intervention of Communist Chinese troops and Soviet MiG fighters on behalf of the North Koreans

during the winter of 1950–1951 again brought an increase in U.S. naval strength in the Mediterranean. This buildup included a nuclear strike capability when, in early February 1951, six AJ-1 Savage and three P2V-3C Neptune bombers of Composite Squadron 5 arrived at Port Lyautey, Morocco, after a transatlantic flight. The Savages were probably the first carrier-type aircraft to fly across the Atlantic (the planes refueled in the Azores) and marked the first time that the Navy had deployed a nuclear strike force overseas.

Beginning in March the Savages flew from the large carriers *Coral Sea* and *Franklin D. Roosevelt* in the Mediterranean. Both ships had nuclear weapons on board, although the nuclear cores were—at the time— retained in the United States. The Neptunes flew only from shore bases.

The feasibility of carrier operations with the Savage was officially "considered proven," but because of maintenance and operational problems with the AJ-1

An AJ-1 Savage from Composite Squadron 6 on the deck-edge elevator of the carrier *Kearsarge*, about to be lowered to the hangar deck, in July 1952. The carrier deployed to Korean waters the following month—without the heavy attack planes. The *Kearsarge* was a modernized *Essex*-class carrier but did not yet have an angled flight deck. The Savage's wings and tail are folded; wingtip 300-gallon tanks are fitted. (U.S. Navy)

Table 7-1
ACTIVE MAJOR COMBATANT SHIPS, U.S. FLEET

	JUNE 1950	JUNE 1953
Large carriers*	3	3
Fast carriers**	4	13
Light carriers	4	5
Escort carriers	4	17
Battleships	1	4
Heavy cruisers	9	15
Light cruisers	3	1
Anti-aircraft cruisers	1	1
Destroyers	142	245
Destroyer-minecraft	16	16
Escort ships	11	89
Submarines	73	122

In addition, numerous mine, patrol, amphibious, and auxiliary ships were activated.

* *Midway* class.
** *Essex* class.

the decision was made not to keep them aboard ship for extended operations. Instead, they would be held in readiness at advanced bases. If nuclear war appeared "imminent" the Savages would go aboard the carriers, be refueled and armed, and then held ready to strike. The larger Neptunes would, of course, have to be loaded aboard the carriers pier-side by crane. Or, they could fly nuclear strikes from land bases in the Mediterranean area, a possibility that did not please Air Force commanders.

This somewhat awkward arrangement continued for several months until the Savages gained their "sea legs" and were integrated into carrier air groups. Following the initial deployment in February 1951, heavy attack aircraft were continually maintained in the Mediterranean area and at least one *Midway*-class large carrier was always deployed with the Sixth Fleet until the larger *Forrestal*-class ships became available.

On May 25, 1951, three AJ-1 Savages landed aboard the recently completed carrier *Oriskany*, which incorporated the Project 27A improvements in the *Essex*-class design. This was the beginning of a program to provide Pacific Fleet carriers with nuclear strike aircraft. In 1953 a squadron of Savages based at Atsugi, Japan, operated periodically from *Essex*-class ships in the Western Pacific and later three-plane detachments of heavy attack aircraft were assigned to Pacific Fleet

attack carriers on a regular basis. The large Savages were never popular with carrier commanders and initially were sent to nearby land bases when the ships were in forward areas, only occasionally flying from the carriers. (Additional "composite" squadrons flying heavy attack aircraft were activated, and in 1955–1956 the more-accurate designation of "heavy attack" [VAH] was adopted for these squadrons.)

The relatively rapid buildup of U.S. naval forces in the Atlantic, Mediterranean, and Pacific areas during the Korean War was possible through the activation of large numbers of mothballed ships from the reserve fleets. The number of relatively modern major combatant ships (carriers, battleships, cruisers, destroyers, and submarines) and other destroyer-type ships (destroyer minecraft and escort ships) in the active fleet went from some 270 ships in June 1950 to more than 530 ships in these categories three years later.

The large increase in active carrier strength was recognition of the need for these ships in conventional combat in the Cold War era and in an atomic war—the dark cloud that hung over the horizon since the Soviet Union exploded its first nuclear device on August 25, 1949. (The Soviet Union further reduced the U.S. lead by exploding a thermonuclear device in August 1953, only nine months after the first U.S. hydrogen device was exploded.)

The nine fast carriers added to the active fleet in 1950–1953 represented an increase in quality as well as quantity as seven of these carriers were modernized under Project 27A. Two more *Essex*-class carriers were in the yard finishing up their 27A modernization, and six more of these ships had begun or were about to undergo an even more extensive modernization, the so-called Project 27C conversion. Fifteen *Essex*-class carriers would be modernized for jet-age operations, and by 1955 all but two of the 24 ships in this class would be operational. The *Franklin* and *Bunker Hill*, both heavily damaged in World War II and rebuilt, were never reactivated.

Like Project 27A, the 27C conversions provided strengthened flight decks, more flight deck space with the removal of the twin 5-inch gun mounts and streamlined island structures, and increased aviation fuel capacity. The 27C conversions also provided for more powerful arresting gear, steam catapults (a British invention that provided considerably more power and smoother acceleration than hydraulic "cats"), covering over the No. 3 elevator just forward of the arresting wires, installing a deck-edge elevator on the starboard quarter, and enclosing the forward end of the hangar-deck level in a "hurricane" bow to improve seakeeping in rough weather.

Table 7-2
ESSEX-CLASS AIRCRAFT CARRIERS

SHIP		STATUS	MODERNIZATION
CV 9	*Essex*	Recommissioned Jan. 15, 1951	27A 1948–1951
CV 10	*Yorktown*	Recommissioned Jan. 2, 1953	27A 1951–1953
CV 11	*Intrepid*	Recommissioned June 18, 1954	27C 1951–1954
CV 12	*Hornet*	Recommissioned Oct. 1, 1953	27A 1951–1953
CV 13	*Franklin*	Reserve*	—
CV 14	*Ticonderoga*	Recommissioned Dec. 11, 1954	27C 1951–1954
CV 15	*Randolph*	Recommissioned July 1, 1953	27A 1951–1953
CV 16	*Lexington*	Recommissioned Sept. 1, 1955	27C 1951–1955
CV 17	*Bunker Hill*	Reserve*	—
CV 18	*Wasp*	Recommissioned Sept. 10, 1951	27A 1948–1951
CV 19	*Hancock*	Recommissioned Mar. 1, 1954	27C 1951–1954
CV 20	*Bennington*	Recommissioned Nov. 30, 1952	27A 1950–1952
CV 21	*Boxer*	Active when Korean War began	—
CV 31	*Bon Homme Richard*	Recommissioned Jan. 15, 1951	27C 1952–1955
CV 32	*Leyte*	Active when Korean War began	—
CV 33	*Kearsarge*	Recommissioned Feb. 15, 1952	27A 1950–1952
CV 34	*Oriskany*	Commissioned Sept. 25, 1950	Completed as 27A
CV 36	*Antietam*	Recommissioned Jan. 17, 1951	—
CV 37	*Princeton*	Recommissioned Aug. 29, 1950	—
CV 38	*Shangri-La*	Recommissioned May 18, 1951	27C 1952–1955
CV 39	*Lake Champlain*	Recommissioned Sept. 19, 1952	27A 1950–1952
CV 40	*Tarawa*	Recommissioned Feb. 3, 1951	—
CV 45	*Valley Forge*	Active when Korean War began	—
CV 47	*Philippine Sea*	Active when Korean War began	—

* The two ships not reactivated; the *Franklin* and *Bunker Hill* were both severely damaged in 1945 and subsequently rebuilt. They were the only war-built carriers not returned to service after being heavily damaged.

The *Wasp*, after her tragic collision with the high speed minesweeper *Hobson*, late on the night of April 26, 1952. The *Hobson* and other DMS conversions from destroyers retained their ASW weapons, making them useful as carrier escorts. Following the collision—some 700 miles west of the Azores—the *Wasp* returned to the United States and was quickly repaired using the bow of her sister ship *Hornet*. (U.S. Navy)

The *Wasp*, shortly after her modernization, recommissioning, and trials, departed Norfolk en route to the Mediterranean. Just after 10 P.M. on the night of April 26, 1952, she collided with the destroyer-minesweeper *Hobson*, one of the carrier's escorts, some 700 miles west of the Azores. The *Wasp* sliced into the smaller ship, sinking her within minutes. One hundred seventy-six of the *Hobson*'s crew were lost, including her commanding officer; other ships in the force rescued 61 survivors. Apparently the *Hobson*'s captain had misunderstood the carrier's intent as the *Wasp* changed course to land aircraft.

The damaged *Wasp* returned to Bayonne, New Jersey, where she was hastily repaired. The carrier had a 75-foot tear in her bow but little other damage. The bow was cut away from the carrier *Hornet*, being modernized at the nearby New York Naval Shipyard, and barged to Bayonne for installation in the *Wasp*. In late May she again departed for the Mediterranean.

In addition, during the Korean War one light carrier, the *Monterey*, was recommissioned, on September 15, 1950. With the new *Saipan* and *Wright*, and the older cruiser conversions *Bataan* and *Cabot*, there were five CVLs in commission, although only the *Bataan* flew combat sorties.[2] Two other mothballed CVLs were reactivated for transfer to France: the *Langley* in 1951 and the *Belleau Wood* in 1953. They were the first U.S. non-escort carriers to go to other countries. Finally, the four escort carriers in commission in June 1950 were rapidly supplemented by 13 additional CVEs placed in service: eight of the *Commencement Bay* class and five of the older *Casablanca* class. The latter were assigned to the Military Sea Transportation Service and, manned by Navy crews, were employed primarily to transport aircraft for all military services.[3]

Anti-Submarine Warfare

As the Cold War developed in the late 1940s the Western democracies became increasingly concerned about intelligence reports of Soviet submarine developments and construction programs based on advanced German U-boat technologies. The establishment of the North Atlantic Treaty Organization (NATO) in 1949—the first peacetime military alliance in which the United States participated—was motivated in large part by the specter of another Battle of the Atlantic in which Soviet submarines would attempt to sever the shipping lanes between the United States and Canada and Western Europe.

The U.S. Navy undertook several programs to counter the anticipated Soviet submarine forces. These included constructing specialized Anti-Submarine Warfare surface ships and submarines and producing land-based and carrier-based ASW aircraft. From the perspective of aircraft carriers, initially escort and light (small) carriers were expected to operate ASW aircraft. In the late 1940s seven escort carriers of the *Commencement Bay* class were modified to operate ASW aircraft. These ships were sometimes referred to as CVEK, the K indicating hunter-killer ships.[4] All seven were modified by the end of 1949 but were not all available for ASW because of other requirements. In the ASW role, each ship had a composite squadron of 6 TBM-3W and 12 TBM-3S Avengers. The W (warning) planes had the large AN/APS-20 radar for detecting snorkels and periscopes, considered the best search method for open-ocean ASW; the *S* (ASW strike) planes carried rockets, depth bombs, and homing torpedoes.

The AD-3W Skyraider, flown by a crew of three, replaced the TBM-3W Avengers, providing more endurance and capability, although fitted with the same, ubiquitous AN/APS-20 radar. In 1948 the Navy established Carrier Airborne Early Warning Squadrons (VAW) 1 and 2 to provide AD-3W detachments to carriers for both AEW and ASW operations, in daylight and at night.

In 1949 the CVL *Wright* was also employed in ASW operations, although she soon reverted to her primary role of a pilot-training carrier. Shortly after the Korean War the light carriers *Bataan* and *Cabot* were modified for ASW operations and were sometimes referred to as CVLK. From 1952 the CVEK/CVLK carriers operated the more-capable AD-4W and AD-4S Skyraiders in the anti-submarine role. As early as 1949, however, Navy leaders realized the limitations of these ships, especially the escort carriers:

> During operations . . . conducted in North Pacific waters during winter months, jeep carriers proved so unstable as launching and landing

platforms that daytime operating periods were as much as 25 percent under those for [fast] attack carriers, and night operations were deemed so unlikely of success that they weren't even attempted! It is doubted that escort carriers could provide adequate anti-submarine protection to a task group or convoy of ANY speed when operating under those conditions.[5]

The CVLKs experienced similar limitations when operating ASW aircraft. The CVEK/CVLK problems were exacerbated when the AF Guardian began going aboard carriers in early 1954. The Grumman-built Guardian was the world's first specialized ASW aircraft and the largest U.S. single-engine piston aircraft. Originally developed by Grumman as a high-speed torpedo plane designated XTB3F, the Guardian was designed with a piston engine forward and a jet aft of the cockpit to provide bursts of speed up to 356 m.p.h.[6] The prototype XTB3F-1 first flew on December 19, 1946. Development and production of the ASW variants were delayed, in large part because priority was given to Grumman's F9F Panther turbojet fighter. Only one XTB3F-1 was fitted with the jet engine. The jet

---

Table 7-3
ESCORT AIRCRAFT CARRIERS

SHIP		STATUS
T-CVE 58	*Corregidor*	Recommissioned May 18, 1951
T-CVE 64	*Tripoli*	Recommissioned May 1, 1952
T-CVE 86	*Sitkoh Bay*	Recommissioned July 29, 1950
T-CVE 88	*Cape Esperance*	Recommissioned Aug. 5, 1950
T-CVE 92	*Windham Bay*	Recommissioned Oct. 28, 1950
CVE 106	*Block Island*	Recommissioned Apr. 28, 1951
CVE 107	*Gilbert Islands*	Recommissioned Sep. 17, 1951
CVE 108	*Kula Gulf*	Recommissioned Jan. 25, 1951
CVE 110	*Salerno Bay*	Recommissioned June 20, 1951
CVE 112	*Siboney*	Recommissioned Jan. 3, 1951
CVE 114	*Rendova*	Recommissioned Jan. 13, 1951
CVE 115	*Bairoko*	Recommissioned Sep. 12, 1950
CVE 116	*Badoeng Strait*	Active when Korean War began
CVE 118	*Sicily*	Active when Korean War began
CVE 119	*Point Cruz*	Recommissioned July 1, 1951
CVE 120	*Mindoro*	Active when Korean War began
CVE 122	*Palau*	Active when Korean War began

The Grumman Guardian "twins" were the world's first specialized anti-submarine aircraft designed for carrier operation and were the world's largest single-engine piston aircraft. The farther plane is an AF-2S variant for the attack role; the closer is an AF-2W search variant with the AN/APS-20 belly radome. Both have vertical "finlets" on their horizontal tail surfaces. These aircraft are sans squadron/air group markings; the horizontal red stripe was added to the white panels of the U.S. national insignia in 1947. (U.S. Navy)

engine was abandoned, and the plane went into production as the AF-2W, -2S, and -3S. Working in pairs, the AF-2W, with a large belly radome housing the AN/APS-20 radar and flown by a four-man crew, would search at low altitudes for hostile submarine periscopes and snorkels; when a sub was detected the AF-2S or -3S teammate—flown by a three-man crew—would streak in, pinpoint the sub with its smaller AN/APS-30 or -31A radar (and searchlight at night), and attack with rockets, depth charges, or acoustic homing torpedoes. Although a relatively large aircraft—with the AF-2W having a combat weight of 18,630 pounds—the plane flew mainly from escort carriers of the *Commencement Bay* class.

The first of the 387 AF-series aircraft did not join fleet squadrons until October 1950 as a replacement for the outdated TBM Avengers being used for ASW.[7] A total of 11 carrier-based ASW squadrons flew the Guardian.

The Guardian's accident rate was relatively high. It was "definitely underpowered and completely unforgiving when coming aboard ship," recalled Guardian pilot A. Jay Cristol.[8] He continued,

> The R-2800 engine did not have the power to pull you to safety. With CVE operations you

needed 25 knots across the deck for landing. The CVE maximum speed was 19 knots, so if you launched with adequate wind across the deck and returned hours later to a no-wind condition, landing was extremely hazardous. Several planes had their engines break off on arrestment, with the engines tumbling down the flight deck. A fix in the area of the breaks resulted in the fuselage breaking behind the cockpit and the engine and pilot tumbling down the flight deck.

At times Guardians went aboard the larger light carriers and *Essex*-class carriers, but mostly they operated from the CVEs.

The Guardian served in frontline squadrons only until 1954 (and in reserve units until early 1957). Its demise was caused by the S2F Tracker, which, combining both search and attack functions in a single airframe, became the principal U.S. carrier-based ASW aircraft for the next two decades.

New Super Carriers

Even before the outbreak of the Korean War, in 1950, with relatively little debate, Congress approved funds, in the 1951 fiscal year defense budget, for the construction of a large aircraft carrier. The cancellation of the

The AF Guardian was an uncomplicated aircraft to fly but difficult to land aboard escort carriers. Helicopters provided rapid rescue for carrier pilots whose planes ditched while landing or taking off. Here a Piasecki HUP or "hup-mobile" from the escort carrier *Block Island* recovers the pilot of a Guardian that struck the water immediately after taking off in December 1953. (U.S. Navy)

"heavy" carrier *United States* in 1949 had been a blow to the Navy's prestige and to its claim for a major role in the nation's defense structure. Without success, the Navy had at the time argued that the country must not adopt a one-weapon strategy (i.e., massive nuclear strike) or place total reliance on one service (the Air Force). The Navy continued to opt for a mix of weapons with statements such as "we cannot safely place reliance on any single weapon or weapons system, but must carry a relatively 'full bag'—must keep them versatile and adaptable to any situation."

The Navy argued that large, modern carriers were essential for the traditional naval role of "control of the seas." To achieve this control—according to the Navy—the carriers could be called upon to launch nuclear strikes against enemy submarine pens, naval airfields, and other land targets.

The lead ship of this new class of large carriers (CVB) would be named for James Forrestal, the first Secretary of Defense, who, while hospitalized, had committed suicide in 1949.[9] The keel for the *Forrestal* was laid down on July 14, 1952—as the CVB 59—at the Newport News Shipbuilding yard in Virginia. As originally designed she was to be similar to the never-built carrier *United States*, but slightly smaller. The *Forrestal*, as completed to a revised design, would have a standard displacement of 60,000 tons (76,600 tons full load), an overall length of 1,039 feet, and a maximum flight deck width of 252 feet, with geared turbines capable of driving her at about 33 knots.

Originally the *Forrestal* was to have had a retractable bridge, but an early design change provided for an angled flight deck with a fixed structure on the starboard side of her flight deck. Four deck-edge elevators and four steam catapults would speed the handling and launching of her aircraft.

At the time construction of the *Forrestal* began Navy officials said 12 such large carriers—some with nuclear propulsion—would assure U.S. "control" of the seas. Even as the *Forrestal*'s keel was being laid down, Congress authorized the construction of a second large carrier, to be named *Saratoga* (CVA 60). Another large carrier would be funded each year for the next five years.

With this revival in support for aircraft carriers came a redesignation of these ships to reflect their mission rather than their size. The U.S. aircraft carriers designated CVB (three *Midway*s and the unfinished *Forrestal*) and CV (the 24 *Essex*-class ships and the mothballed *Enterprise*) were reclassified as "attack aircraft carriers" with the designation CVA on October 1, 1952.[10]

Based on the success of the *Valley Forge* operating in the ASW role in 1952, on July 8 of that year the classification "anti-submarine warfare support aircraft carrier" (CVS) was established to indicate those ships no longer considered capable of operating the modern jet-propelled fighter and attack aircraft. That summer two operational ships, the *Antietam* and *Leyte* and the three mothballed fast carriers (*Bunker Hill*, *Enterprise*, and *Franklin*) were changed to CVS. Additional *Essex*-class CVAs would become CVS on a regular basis as new attack carriers joined the fleet.

(Subsequently, the *Enterprise*, the U.S. warship that had received the most battle stars for action in World War II, was stricken from the Navy list on October 2, 1956. Despite efforts to preserve her as a memorial/museum ship, she was sold for scrap two years later.)

The New Aircraft

The CVS program emerged as a large, new ASW aircraft was being developed, the Grumman S2F Tracker—always referred to in the fleet as the "Stoof." In the late 1940s carrier-based ASW aircraft had consisted of TBM Avengers, followed by AD Skyraiders or AF Guardians organized into two-plane search and attack teams. These planes were limited by their dependence on a partner aircraft and their single pilot. The Navy sought to combine the search and attack roles

The *Forrestal*—the world's first "super carrier"—under construction in July 1955, after the ship's design was revised to provide an angled-deck configuration with a fixed starboard island structure. There are four deck-edge elevators—three to starboard and one to port (at the forward end of the angled deck). The four catapult tracks are evident in this view. (Newport News Shipbuilding)

in a single aircraft, leading to the Grumman S2F Tracker. Although designed to fly from escort carriers, the Tracker, with its wingspan of almost 70 feet and 42¼-foot length, was more at home aboard larger ships.

The Tracker won out over proposals from 17 other firms. It was a 25,000-pound aircraft with twin reciprocating engines. The weight was only slightly more than that of the single-engine AF Guardian. The first flight took place on December 4, 1952. When delivered to fleet ASW squadrons in February 1954, the Tracker was larger than any other aircraft aboard carriers at the time except the AJ Savage. The Tracker featured an internal bomb bay for homing torpedoes, depth charges, or a nuclear depth bomb; underwing racks for rockets; a retractable AN/APS-38 search ra-

The Grumman S2F Tracker combined elaborate submarine detection and attack capabilities in a single carrier–based aircraft. The Tracker shown here has its Magnetic Anomaly Detection (MAD) boom extended and its fuselage AN/APS-38 radome lowered. There are weapon pylons under the wings as well as a searchlight for night attack, and an internal bomb bay that could hold homing torpedoes or conventional or nuclear depth bombs. The photo at right shows the bomb bay open: it contains a Mk 101 Lulu nuclear depth bomb: there are four lightweight ASW torpedoes on the wing pylons. (U.S. Navy)

A Piasecki HUP-2 helicopter from Helicopter Utility Squadron 2 lowers mail to the heavy cruiser Salem; in the background an oiler refuels the carrier Lake Champlain and a destroyer. During the 1950s the twin-rotor HUP was used primarily as a plane-guard and utility helicopter. In these roles a HUP could carry six persons including pilot and crewman. Some of these helicopters equipped with "dunking" sonar were used for ASW. (U.S. Navy)

dar under its fuselage; a retractable magnetic airborne (submarine) detection antenna in the tail; and a searchlight under its starboard wing. The crew of the Tracker consisted of a pilot, copilot/navigator, radar operator, and MAD—Magnetic Anomaly Detector—operator. Later derivatives of the S2F Tracker were the TF Trader carrier-based cargo plane, TF-1Q electronic countermeasures aircraft, and WF-2 airborne early warning aircraft, the last officially named Tracer, but widely known as the "Willie Fudd."

The WF-2 was technically derived from the TF-1 Trader configuration, replacing the planned WF-1 based on the S2F-1 design. It was a more-capable replacement for the AEW variants of the AD Skyraider. The aerodynamic prototype, a TF-1 with a massive radome above the fuselage, flew on March 1, 1957. A total of 88 WF-2s were produced by Grumman, the first entering service with VAW-12 in November 1959. Four-plane detachments were assigned to attack carriers and, subsequently, they also replaced the AD-5W Skyraiders aboard the ASW carriers.

Beyond the improved radar surveillance provided by the Tracer's AN/APS-82 radar in comparison to the previous AN/APS-20, the four-man crew used advanced Identification Friend or Foe (IFF) to quickly segregate friendly and enemy aircraft, the Bellhop system that could relay its radar presentation to surface ships, and Autocat that relayed communications between widely dispersed surface ships. The WF-2 had on-station time in excess of five hours.

Joining the S2F Trackers in ASW air groups were helicopters especially equipped for hunting submarines. The first helicopter ASW squadron—HS-1—was established on October 3, 1951. The squadron briefly flew the Sikorsky HO4S-1 helicopter but soon received 18 HUP-2 helicopters, a 31½-foot-long whirlybird with a single engine turning tandem 35-foot rotors. However, the manufacturer, Piasecki, could not meet Navy schedules and the squadron did not receive its first helicopter until February 1952 when an HUP-1 was accepted for tests. Two months later HS-1 received the first HUP-2 and that summer the squadron went aboard the escort carrier *Siboney* for carrier qualifications with nine HUP-2 "hup-mobiles." The helicopters were put through their paces aboard ship from June 1 to June 27. One HUP-2 was lost at sea when its engine failed and several others were almost lost. The HUP-2 was not suitable for ASW operations. There were more

carrier tests in August with more problems: three HUP-2S came down at sea but were salvaged.

A larger helicopter was developed specifically for the ASW role: the Bell HSL-1 with a gross weight of 16,800 pounds compared to the HUP-2's 6,000 pounds. This twin-rotor aircraft was not successful, encountering technical problems and being too loud for effective dipping-sonar operations.

Beginning in 1955 all helicopter ASW squadrons received the Sikorsky HSS-1 Seabat, a 12,000-pound helicopter. Flown by a four-man crew, the HSS-1 had dipping sonar and could carry homing torpedoes or a nuclear depth bomb to give it both a search and attack capability. In combination with S2F Trackers, the

A Bell HSL-1 hovers low over the water with a "dipping" sonar dome lowered into the water during ASW exercises. The HSL-1 was specifically designed for ASW operations. Like the HUP and the later H-46 Sea Knight, the HSL featured tandem rotors. The HSL did not enter squadron service because of engineering difficulties. Only 51 HSL-1s were procured by the Navy compared to 249 HUPs and 350 of the later HSS-1 (SH-34) anti-submarine helicopters. (U.S. Navy)

helicopters brought the fleet a potent carrier-based ASW force against diesel-electric submarines. (For a brief period in the mid-1950s some *Essex*-class ASW carriers operated mixed air groups with a squadron of 16 AF Guardians, one of 16 S2F Trackers, and one of about 10 ASW helicopters.)

Formation of these helicopter ASW squadrons in the early 1950s was but one phase of a vast expansion of helicopter operations in naval warfare. Prior to the Korean War the Navy had placed helicopters aboard cruisers and carriers for utility, gun-fire spotting, and rescue work.[11] The Korean War opened new vistas for the whirlybird. The first new application of helicopters in Korea came during the landings at Wonsan in October 1950, when a light cruiser's HO3S-1 was used to spot submerged mines and report them to the minesweepers. The experiment worked so well that helicopters were made a regular part of the minesweeping team, guiding the sweepers to mines and, if the sweepers became trapped, guiding them to safe water. The Navy hastily converted the *LST 799* to a minesweeper tender and helicopter base. She was fitted to accommodate a mine squadron staff and to "mother" small minesweepers and their crews.

Space was made topside and facilities were installed in the *LST 799* to handle up to three helicopters, although only one or two were usually operated. The *LST 799*—the first ship to formally serve as a helicopter carrier in wartime—was sent into Wonsan Harbor late in March 1951. Although communist forces held the city, the U.S. Navy operated freely in the harbor, sweeping mine-free lanes (for bombardment ships) and operating a rescue station where Allied aircraft damaged over North Korea would ditch in the harbor and their crews could be rescued. In addition to performing valuable mine-spotting work, helicopters from the *LST 799* rescued 22 aviators—some from behind enemy lines—and flew them to safety. Helicopters from the battleships and cruisers also helped out in air-sea rescue.

The Marine brigade that reached Korea in early August 1950 had six HO3S-1 helicopters that were used in a variety of roles.[12] In the fall of 1951 a squadron of Marine-piloted HRS-2 helicopters (troop version of the HO4S) was sent to Korea. The helicopters, each able to carry eight troops or an equivalent amount of cargo, were used to lift supplies to isolated combat units, move reconnaissance and rocket units, evacuate wounded, and carry out vertical assault exercises. Occasionally the whirlybirds operated from the escort carriers in Korean waters, the harbinger of a new kind of carrier warfare.

The HRS, the cargo version of the HO4S/Sikorsky S-55, was used by most Marine helicopter squadrons in the 1950s and was flown by the British as the Westland Whirlwind. The HRS could carry eight combat-loaded troops plus the pilots. Here HRS-2 helicopters operate from the escort carrier *Sicily* during a practice assault off South Korea. The ship's elevators bring Marines up to the flight deck to embark in the next "wave" of helicopters. (U.S. Navy)

8 FRENCH AND BRITISH CARRIERS AT WAR

A Curtiss SB2C Helldiver lands aboard the French carrier *Arromanches* operating in the Gulf of Tonkin in late 1953. The French Navy, flying mostly American-built aircraft from former U.S. and British aircraft carriers, made a major contribution to the French air campaign in Indochina. The *Arromanches* has two aircraft barriers rigged forward of the arresting wires as this Helldiver is about to touch down. (U.S. Navy)

As the guns fell silent with the cease-fire agreement in Korea in July 1953, the eyes of the combatants in that conflict turned south to the war in Indochina. There "French Union" troops were battling the Communist Viet Minh.[1] Officially, Indochina was now three quasi-independent nation-states: Laos, Cambodia, and Vietnam. But in the eyes of much of the world—especially in the Orient—the war in Indochina was a

French attempt to retain its prewar colonial empire in Southeast Asia.

In the summer of 1940, with the German victory in France, the French government in Indochina was forced to accede to Japanese demands that the frontier between Indochina and China be closed to the transit of all war matériel. A Japanese control mission was sent into the Tonkin to make certain that the French abided by the agreement. With France defeated and the United States and Britain unable to provide for Indochina's defense, the Japanese were able to press harder and soon demanded bases in Indochina to help pursue the war against China. On September 22, 1940, the Vichy French regime and the Japanese reached an agreement providing for the Japanese occupation of the port of Haiphong and three Japanese air bases to be established in the Tonkin. That same day Japanese troops in southern China moved across the border into the Tonkin and, after brief fighting against the French, occupied two cities. All French military resistance ended by the 25th. The Japanese announced that the attacks in the Tonkin, coupled with minor air attacks, had been made in error and that Japan in fact recognized French sovereignty over Indochina. Still, Rising Sun banners flew over Tonkin's principal cities.

Next, the Japanese puppet state of Siam (now called Thailand) attacked French Indochina in an effort to gain bordering territory in Cambodia. The French inflicted a devastating defeat on the Siamese in the brief fighting in January 1941; however, at "mediation" talks in Japan that spring the French were forced to cede territory to Siam.

The Japanese "invasion" of Indochina continued, with Japanese troops landing at Saigon (now called Ho Chi Minh City) to occupy strategic southern positions in July 1941. These would serve as jumping off points for the invasion of British Malaya in December 1941. While the Japanese controlled the key cities and ports of Indochina during the next four years, French troops remained under arms and French administrators continued to rule the interior. In this situation, anti-colonial nationalist movements prospered in Vietnam. The local communists, with some help from the Chinese, who had long coveted the Tonkin area, grew in power in northern Indochina. Until 1944 the Chinese provided the communists and other Indochinese revolutionaries with funds, military training, and arms. The major revolutionary group was the communist-controlled Viet Minh. By 1944 the Viet Minh had begun military operations against the Japanese and were aiding American pilots downed in Indochina. Soon the United States was providing arms to the Viet Minh.

To further complicate the situation, Free French forces were being infiltrated into Indochina by the Allies. By early 1945 the British and Americans were parachuting men and arms into Indochina on the average of two nights a week. To counter the growing anti-Japanese attitude of the French in Indochina, on March 9, 1945, the Japanese attacked the French garrisons. At some points the French held out for a day or two, but the Japanese coup was too sudden, too strong, and too well planned not to be successful. The Japanese declared the independence of the Empire of Vietnam and set up a puppet government in Hanoi. The communists astutely exploited the popular anti-Japanese feeling; in the Tonkin, where the Japanese had few troops, the Viet Minh proclaimed the Democratic Republic of Vietnam on September 2, 1945.

Thus, when World War II officially ended in the Pacific, the Japanese reigned supreme in the cities of Indochina while most of the Tonkin was in the hands of the Viet Minh. With the end of the war, the Viet Minh occupied Hanoi and took over administration of the Tonkin area.

In the absence of any other major military force, the Japanese remained under arms to maintain order. In mid-September British and Indian troops began arriving in Saigon to take the surrender of the Japanese troops in southern Indochina. As the Commonwealth troops were not sufficient to police the area, Japanese were continued under arms. In the North, Chinese troops arrived to accept the Japanese surrender and recognized the Viet Minh government. The absence of French troops allowed the Viet Minh to solidify their position.

But the nationalistic tendencies in the South were countered by the British, who believed, as one commander declared, "the question of the government of Indochina is exclusively French." The civil war began. French troops in Indochina rearmed, and new French administrators and troops began arriving from Metropolitan France, bringing French rule back to Indochina south of the 16th parallel. The Chinese at first attempted to retain custody of the Tonkin while supporting the local Viet Minh government. This was unacceptable to the French, and as soon as sufficient forces were available, the French moved to retake the North. A French naval squadron, including the old carrier *Béarn*, employed as a transport, embarked French troops near Saigon on February 28, 1946, for movement to the port of Haiphong and the Tonkin. The French squadron approached Haiphong on March 6 and was met by intense gunfire as local Chinese generals opposed the landing. The lead French ship, the light cruiser *Le Triomphant*, was holed 439 times by various caliber shells. Other ships were also hit and the 4,000 troops in the *Béarn* and accompanying ships suffered some

casualties. Still, by the evening of March 8, some 4,000 French troops had landed; 7,000 more went ashore the next day, and another 1,500 on the 10th. More French troops followed and forced the bulk of the Chinese troops to withdraw from Indochina by the summer of 1946. The *Béarn* departed for France on June 10, 1946.[2]

Initially, the French recognized the Viet Minh government in North Vietnam, and arrangements were made for limited and temporary French reoccupation. The French were determined that southern Indochina would remain a French territory; the Viet Minh and many nationalists in the South were equally determined that independence be gained for all of Indochina. These dissidents in the South refused to give up their weapons, and the French began a bloody war of pacification. In April 1946 the communist-controlled Viet Minh government in the North began to unify the scattered resistance groups in the South under communist direction.

There was constant friction in the North between the French and Viet Minh leaders, and open fighting erupted in Haiphong in late November 1946 as the French attempted to halt arms smuggling. The following month French troops occupied Hanoi. France com-

mitted airborne, infantry, armored, air, and naval forces to the conflict. For three years the Viet Minh was pushed back and the areas under French control were extended. Some Viet Minh pockets, mostly in the Tonkin, remained, but the course of the war left little doubt that the French would eventually win. The French fighting forces were well trained and well equipped, and many men were veterans of as many as six years of combat in World War II.

The naval side of the 1946–1949 war in Indochina was primarily made up of small river craft operations. However, France's two operational aircraft carriers, the light carrier *Arromanches* and the escort carrier *Dixmude*, proved to be valuable in the war.

Carriers to Indochina, Part Two

Departing Toulon, France, on January 28, 1947, the *Dixmude* arrived at Saigon on March 3, carrying, in addition to her own SBD Dauntless dive bombers, 29 aircraft for the French Air Force. She subsequently got under way and changed roles, from an aircraft transport to a strike carrier. She launched her first strikes on March 16, 1947, with her aircraft flying support missions along Indochina's central coast (the Annam region), which lay beyond the effective radius of French aircraft based at Hanoi (to the north) and Saigon (to the south). The planes that flew from the *Dixmude* were as obsolescent as their carrier.

These operations were particularly noteworthy as they were the first combat strikes flown by a French aircraft carrier. (The old *Béarn* had not seen combat in World War II, although her squadrons had fought from land bases with distinction in France during the German invasion.) The *Dixmude*'s dive bombers also supported amphibious landings along the Indochina coast and attacked Viet Minh strongholds.

The escort carrier returned to France in April–May 1947 for maintenance. She embarked more aircraft for the French Air Force—a dozen German Ju 52 trimotor transports (built in France) and a dozen Spitfire fighters—and departed for Indochina on September 16. The *Dixmude* was back at Saigon on October 21, 1947, to unload her cargo. She then steamed north into the Tonkin Gulf to operate her SBD dive bombers in Operation Lea, a parachute assault on the Viet Minh headquarters in the Tonkin, some 75 miles north of Hanoi. In the three-week campaign the *Dixmude*'s single air squadron flew more than 200 sorties and

The escort carrier *Dixmude*—the American-built, ex-British CVE *Biter*—was employed on two transport runs from the United States as well as an operational carrier in the Indochina campaign. Here, on her second transport run in September–October 1950, she is carrying 40 F6F Hellcats to Saigon. The *Dixmude* was the second carrier to fly the French tricolor, after the *Béarn*, which never flew aircraft in combat. (U.S. Navy)

Upon her arrival off Indochina the *Arromanches* flew off her planes, which landed at Saigon. The carrier then steamed up the treacherous Saigon River for that city. The carrier, at 13,190 tons and 695 feet overall, was the largest ship ever to navigate the river. There was also the danger of a Viet Minh attack on the ship, and so riflemen stood ready on the flight deck and the ship's anti-aircraft guns were manned and depressed, ready to fire at the "shore"—mostly marshes—along the river.

The ship arrived at Saigon without incident and remained in port for ten days. During this period her SBDs operated from shore bases under Air Force direction. The *Arromanches* returned to sea with her aircraft and operated off the Indochina coast until January 1949. At times the SBDs operated from shore bases, but usually from the carrier, and always performing in the outstanding traditions of the Dauntless that had triumphed at Midway and a dozen other actions in the Pacific War.

However, the SBDs—designed more than a decade earlier—were unfit for further combat operations. Neither the *Arromanches* nor the *Dixmude* was used in Indochina during 1949 and 1950 as the French Navy awaited newer carrier aircraft from the United States. The *Dixmude* was used for training naval pilots, and she embarked in the United States 44 F6F Hellcats and SB2C Helldivers, which she delivered to Bizerta in North Africa in April 1950. She then returned to the United States to pick up 40 F6F Hellcats, which she delivered to Saigon on October 28, 1950, for the French Air Force.

At the time the *Arromanches* was in overhaul and did not return to the combat area until late September 1951. Operating Hellcats and SB2C Helldivers, the *Arromanches* flew 678 sorties during the next quarter in Indochina—an increase of almost 140 percent over the number of combat flights flown during the previous quarter of the war. At times the carrier planes operated from shore bases, and at times they were guided by radar as they flew in the dense clouds and low visibility conditions of the Tonkin. In general, the level of training of French naval fliers and quality of aircraft instruments were superior to those of French Air Force, giving the carrier pilots a decided advantage in the skies over Indochina.

For 7½ months the *Arromanches* operated off the coast, not entering port again until she navigated the winding Saigon River in late April 1952. She departed

dropped 65 tons of bombs. The *Dixmude* again departed Indochina in April 1948.

The *Dixmude*'s "station" off Indochina was not filled until November 29, 1948, when the light carrier *Arromanches* arrived. In addition to being larger than the *Dixmude*, the *Arromanches* could steam at 25 knots compared with *Dixmude*'s 17 knots. This eight-knot difference was of vital importance for operations in the region, where high temperatures and light winds make takeoffs with large combat loads impossible except with long runways or carriers that can create their own wind over deck. The *Arromanches* was on loan from the British, and there was some question of her being used in combat. The decision was finally made, and she departed France on October 30, 1948, carrying material for the French Air Force as well as her own SBD Dauntless dive bombers.

for France and a needed overhaul on May 18. Her time in the yard at Toulon was brief—six weeks—and in August 1952 the *Arromanches* and her Hellcats and Helldivers departed France. She was back in the war zone on September 29. Her air attacks on Viet Minh supply lines proved decisive during the crisis in Thailand in November 1952, forcing the communists to use coolies and bicycles exclusively for logistic support. During that month the ship's two squadrons flew 458 sorties, with her Hellcats flying one-quarter of the total fighter sorties over North Vietnam that month. She again departed Indochina on February 27, 1953.

Her replacement was a "new" carrier, the light carrier *La Fayette*, formerly the USS *Langley*, which had been transferred from the United States on June 2, 1951. Also operating Hellcats and Helldivers, the *La Fayette* was similar in size to the *Arromanches* but could steam at 32 knots. She arrived off Indochina on April 9, 1953, but operated in the war zone only until May 12, when she departed for France.

The availability of improved carriers and aircraft was more than offset from November 1949 when Communist Chinese troops reached the border of Tonkin. The war in Indochina took a new turn shortly thereafter when the first Viet Minh divisions were formed in China. In 1950 these Chinese-trained and equipped troops took the offensive against the French. In this new war the communists soon controlled the mountains and forests while the French Union troops—from France, the overseas territories, and the quasi-independent states of Vietnam, Laos, and Cambodia—dominated the flat country, where the assets of firepower and road and river mobility could be exploited.

When the communists turned to cross the western Tonkin and march toward Laos and Thailand, the French made a massive parachute drop at Dien Bien Phu, a valley astride the communist route into Laos. Dien Bien Phu was to have been an advanced base, totally supported by air, from which French ground forces would seek out and destroy the Viet Minh columns. On November 20, 1953, thousands of parachutes filled the sky over Dien Bien Phu as the first of some 13,000 French, colonial, and Vietnamese troops who would eventually fight in the valley jumped from their transport planes. With them were parachuted munitions and building materials. Cargo aircraft subsequently landed supplies, disassembled 155-mm howitzers and M24 Chaffee tanks, and—reportedly—even prostitutes into the valley fortress during a classic airborne operation.

Even before the first paratrooper landed at Dien Bien Phu, the operation—code name Castor—was

The *Arromanches* showing the lines of her British CVL design. French Navy pilots flying from the *Arromanches*, formerly the British CVL *Colossus*, as well as former U.S. escort and light carriers, were cited by French commanders in Indochina for their aggressive flying in that conflict. French naval aircraft operated from carrier decks and from shore bases in Indochina. (U.S. Navy)

At the time of her combat debut off Indochina in late 1948 the *Arromanches* operated American-built SBD-5 Dauntless dive bombers and British-built Seafire Mk III fighters. These aircraft formed the 1st Flottille (1.F.) and 4th Flottille (4.F.), respectively. (French Navy/E. C. Armées)

doomed to failure. The armistice in Korea had sealed North Vietnam's fate as the Chinese were freed to pour guns, munitions, and technical advisers into the assault on the valley fortress. The French critically underestimated the Viet Minh's ability to move supplies, camouflage their guns, and employ field guns and anti-aircraft artillery. The French overestimated their own ability to provide air support over Dien Bien Phu, some 170 miles from the major French air bases at Hanoi. Napalm bombs, which had turned the tide of earlier battles in Indochina, could not be used effectively against the Viet Minh positions around Dien Bien Phu because rain dampened the dense foliage camouflaging the enemy positions. Further, the spring rainy season hampered air operations over the entire area and requirements to support other operations in Indochina drained the meager air strength available.

During the 5½ months that the French tricolor flew over Dien Bien Phu, the number of planes flying at the peak periods of aircraft availability was fewer than 100 supply aircraft and approximately 150 combat planes. The supply planes were mostly C-47 Dakotas with 29 of the larger and considerably more useful C-119 Flying Boxcars.[3] In addition to conducting parachute drops of munitions and supplies, the C-119s dropped six-ton loads of napalm on Viet Minh positions around the French entrenchment.[4]

The Viet Minh delayed the opening attack on Dien Bien Phu until March 13, 1954. Within hours of its start, the Viet Minh had captured key positions of the French fortifications and were able to bring the single runway under artillery fire. During the 56-day siege of Dien Bien Phu, the transports flew 6,700 sorties and delivered 6,410 tons of supplies and material—an average of 117 tons per day. (As a comparison, during the Soviet siege of Stalingrad, the Luftwaffe flew 6,591 tons of supplies to the besieged German forces in the city—just over 94 tons per day for 76 days.)

There were also numerous light liaison planes and a half-dozen of the invaluable helicopters, the latter Sikorsky S-55/HRS type. Most of the approximately 100 French fighter aircraft supporting Dien Bien Phu were F8F Bearcats flown by Air Force pilots, supplemented by a squadron of Navy F6F Hellcats from the carrier *Arromanches*, which had returned to Indochinese waters on September 29, 1953. The Air Force also flew F8F-2P Bearcats for photo reconnaissance.

About 50 bombers were available to the French, mostly Air Force B-26B Invader light bombers (twin-engine aircraft), a squadron of Navy SB2C Helldivers from the *Arromanches*, and six Navy-manned PB4Y-2 Privateers, large, four-engine patrol bombers used to bomb Viet Minh supply trails. Based at Tan Son Nhut airfield, the Consolidated-built Privateers were the largest aircraft flown by the French in Indochina.[5] From March 13 the Hellcats and Helldivers from the *Arromanches* were based ashore at Cat-Bi (near Haiphong) and Bach-Mai (near Hanoi), reducing their flight time to Dien Bien Phu.

An F6F-5 Hellcat of the French Navy's Flottille 11.F. takes off from the carrier *La Fayette* during operations off Indochina in March 1954. The French Navy operated mainly U.S.-built aircraft in the Indochina War. The French Navy procured 124 F6F-5s and 15 F6F-5N night fighters. The French Air Force took delivery of more than 140 F8F-1 and -1B Bearcats for the war, and most were delivered by U.S. Navy escort carriers. (French Navy/ E. C. Armées)

The combat aircraft flew a total of 3,700 sorties in the 5½ months; Navy planes flew 1,267 of those sorties. Navy pilots won high praise from Dien Bien Phu's defenders. French historian Jules Roy wrote, "At Dien Bien Phu, everybody loved sailors. They fought to help the garrison of the entrenched camp without counting the risk; they went into nose dives over pockets of resistance, whereas the Air Force respected the safety regulations."[6] The Navy suffered severely from the intense anti-aircraft fire, and Navy fliers paid a higher price in lives per sortie than did their Air Force comrades.

To counter French air power the Viet Minh ringed the valley of Dien Bien Phu with a curtain of anti-aircraft fire from hundreds of Russian-made guns. The men who flew over Dien Bien Phu said that the Viet Minh flak "was better than the Nazi flak of World War II" and "was as dense as anything allied pilots had encountered over the Ruhr during World War II."[7] This flak destroyed 48 aircraft over the valley and damaged another 167. Fourteen more planes were destroyed on the ground at Dien Bien Phu by enemy artillery fire. Considering the limited number of aircraft available, these were brutal losses.

Dien Bien Phu quivered under communist artillery pounding and suicide waves of Viet Minh infantry who captured defensive positions. On March 28, 1954, the Dien Bien Phu airstrip was rendered unusable by the heavy shelling. Afterward, only parachute drops could bring reinforcements and munitions to the besieged garrison.

French and U.S. aircraft carriers rushed additional aircraft to Indochina in an effort to turn the tide. On April 18 the U.S. light carrier *Saipan* arrived off Tourane (now Da Nang) and U.S. Marine pilots flew ashore 25 AU-1 Corsairs to be turned over to the French Navy; the carrier then entered the harbor to unload parts and U.S. maintenance personnel. These Corsairs were originally designated F4U-6; they were specifically configured for ground attack, having additional armor plate under the pilot, a single- rather than dual-stage supercharger, and additional racks for a total of 4,000 pounds of bombs and rockets plus four 20-mm cannon.[8]

The AU-1s brought by the *Saipan* were in a poor state, having been hard flown by Marines in Korea. Herculean efforts by U.S. and French mechanics at Tourane made 16 aircraft ready by April 23, when Squadron 14.F flew them to Bach Mai in the Tonkin area. They flew their first strikes against the Viet Minh on the 25th.

Bomb-carrying SB2C-5 Helldivers of the Flottille 3.F. over the Tonkin seek out the enemy. The SB2Cs replaced SBD Dauntlesses previously operated from French carriers. The naval insignia of an anchor superimposed upon the roundels and tail flash is clearly shown on these aircraft. The nearer SB2C is the 16th aircraft of the 3rd Flottille. (French Navy/E. C. Armées)

By this time French officials in Hanoi and Paris and American officials in Washington realized that the only air effort that could affect the battle's outcome was a massive air strike by U.S. planes. President Eisenhower had decided that Indochina must be saved from the communists. He believed that if Indochina fell all of Southeast Asia would come under communist control. As early as January 8, 1954, Admiral Arthur W. Radford, the Chairman of the Joint Chiefs of Staff, suggested U.S. carrier aircraft be used to avert a disaster in Indochina. Radford directed the Commander-in-Chief Pacific to prepare to furnish air support to the French forces. The next day the Chief of Naval Operations (CNO), Admiral Robert B. Carney, advised the Pacific commander that he was considering asking the Joint Chiefs of Staff for permission to base two attack carriers and six destroyers at Subic Bay–Sangley Point in the Philippines for the "ostensible and announced purpose . . . [of] fair weather training."[9]

Admiral Carney set up the tactical organization to command the task force. The Seventh Fleet was being kept in a position to interdict a possible Chinese assault on Taiwan while also standing ready in the event of a resumption of hostilities on the Korean peninsula. Accordingly, Carney directed that a new force—Task Force 70—be established on February 21, 1954, "to conduct training exercises as a cover for possible operations to assist French in Indochina if such operations become necessary."[10] Under the cover name Operation Fair Weather Training, TF 70 was to pre-

pare to intervene with conventional *and nuclear* weapons if so ordered. Vice Admiral William K. Phillips, Commander First Fleet in the Eastern Pacific, was ordered to command the new force, which would operate in the South China Sea from the Philippine bases.

Admiral Phillips organized his force into two task groups: The Attack Carrier Striking Group (Task Group 70.2) under Rear Admiral Robert E. Blick Jr., with the attack carriers *Essex* and *Wasp*, 143 aircraft embarked, and a screen of eight destroyers plus a submarine; and the Logistics Support Group (TG 70.3) under Captain George H. Browne, containing six replenishment ships.[11] The carrier *Boxer* subsequently joined TF 70. Two other attack carriers remained with the Seventh Fleet. The TF 70.2 carriers were provided with special high-frequency radios, apparently for communicating with French forward air controllers.

In Washington, Admiral Radford and General Paul Ely, the chief of the French General Staff, met on March 26. The French proposed a U.S. air strike—given the code name Vulture—to pound the communist positions around Dien Bien Phu in a quick, surprise attack. Proposals for Vulture considered strikes by 60 to 80 B-29s flying from U.S. airfields in the Philippines or by U.S. carrier planes. If the former, carrier fights would escort the B-29s in the event that Chinese fighters intervened in the conflict, as they had in the Korean War.

As the situation in Indochina worsened, U.S. naval strength in the Western Pacific was reinforced. By early April there were eight U.S. aircraft carriers west of Hawaii: the fleet carriers *Oriskany* and *Tarawa* and the light carrier *Saipan* in Japanese waters (the last, with 24 Marine AD Skyraiders normally embarked, was then making ready to carry 25 AU-1 Corsairs from Japan to Indochina); the fleet carrier *Philippine Sea* en route from Hawaii to Japan to relieve the *Oriskany*; the escort carrier *Rendova* at Hong Kong (with an antisubmarine squadron); and the fleet carriers *Boxer*, *Essex*, and *Wasp* in Philippine waters. The last three bore the brunt of the proposed U.S. air intervention in Indochina. Each of the large carriers had three fighter squadrons (with F2H Banshees and F9F Panthers), an attack squadron (with AD Skyraiders), and special-mission aircraft for a total of almost 70 planes per carrier.

Some proponents of a U.S. air strike advocated the use of nuclear weapons, but the weapons were barred because of the difficulty of avoiding casualties to the defenders at Dien Bien Phu while destroying the Viet Minh forces. A nuclear strike, had it been ordered, would probably have been flown by carrier-based aircraft. Composite Squadron 6 in Japan had AJ Savages that could be quickly deployed to the carriers, at least two of which had nuclear weapons on board. At that time nuclear weapons were not stored outside of the United States except in carriers; thus none were available immediately at the B-29 bases on Guam or in the Philippines. Admiral Radford later stated that a strike by carrier planes armed with conventional weapons would probably have been made had the United States intervened.[12]

But the U.S. government was reluctant to make an air strike and then withdraw as the French wanted; complicated communications between the governments, language difficulties, and the rapidity of events worked against a satisfactory understanding. The U.S. government wished to assist the French directly, at least with air and naval forces, but only if given more of a voice in the conduct of the war. There also was the threat of direct Chinese intervention with MiG-15 jet aircraft if U.S. planes attempted to aid Dien Bien Phu's defenders. Indeed, Chinese air intervention was a constant threat, which could have quickly destroyed the French air forces in Indochina—and probably caused direct U.S. intervention.

Finally, the United States did not want to intervene unilaterally, desiring at least British approval of direct participation in the conflict. The British government hesitated and then declared that there should be no Allied action until after the forthcoming international conference at Geneva to discuss Korea's future. Still, President Eisenhower, the Secretary of State, and Admiral Radford strongly supported air intervention. (Of the other members of the Joint Chiefs of Staff, only the head of the Air Force, General Nathan F. Twining, gave limited support to an air strike; the heads of the Army, Navy, and Marine Corps opposed U.S. intervention.) Radford, in March 1954, declared that, to avoid the loss of all Southeast Asia to communist domination, "the U.S. must be prepared to act promptly and in force possibly [in response] to a frantic and belated request by the French for U.S. intervention."[13] And on March 23 he told General Ely that the United States could have 350 carrier aircraft in action over Dien Bien Phu within two days.[14] At the time the carriers *Boxer*, *Essex*, and *Philippine Sea* were operating in the area as TG 70.2.

In support of possible U.S. air intervention, in late March the carriers were operating in the Tonkin Gulf. On March 25 Admiral Phillips was ordered to fly reconnaissance flights over airfields in southern China, and a few days later his planes undertook similar flights over the Dien Bien Phu area. Admiral Phillips flew on one of the latter flights in early April.

The Viet Minh's savage attacks on Dien Bien Phu continued through April and into May 1954. The last French fortified positions fell on May 7. Late on the night of the seventh one of the French Navy Privateers bombing Viet Minh troops along Route 41 was shot down; eight of its crew were killed and two captured, with one of the latter dying in captivity.

Almost 6,000 French and allied troops were killed or missing in the battle for Dien Bien Phu, and another 6,452 were wounded. The Viet Minh captured 6,500 men when the garrison surrendered, many of them wounded.[15] Although the campaign was expensive for

The light carrier *La Fayette*, the former USS *Langley*, operating off the coast of Indochina with American-built aircraft and, near the carrier's island, an HO3S helicopter. The French Navy also received the former U.S. CVL *Belleau Wood*, recommissioned as the French *Bois Belleau*. Along with the British-built CVL *Arromanches*, these ships would form the French carrier force until the early 1960s. (U.S. Navy)

U.S. carriers were dispatched to Southeast Asian waters in 1954, ready for action should the U.S. government decide to intervene in the Dien Bien Phu debacle. Here the carrier *Boxer*, a sister carrier, and their destroyers refuel from fleet oilers in the South China Sea in April 1954. These ships would have launched AJ Savages with nuclear weapons had the decision been made to carry out nuclear strikes. (U.S. Navy)

the French in terms of aircraft, fliers, and logistic support, the garrison at Dien Bien Phu represented only 4 percent of the total French Union forces available in Indochina. For almost half a year these troops had tied down five Viet Minh divisions, or more than one-half of the enemy's main battle force, plus a vast logistic network, including thousands of coolies and laborers. When Dien Bien Phu fell, French military strength in Vietnam was increasing and U.S. military supplies were pouring into the country at an increasing rate.

The French were not defeated in the war but at home and at the conference table in Geneva during the late spring of 1954. In Metropolitan France—which had not fully backed the war in Indochina either materially or psychologically—Pierre Mendés France was elected premier on his vow to secure peace in Indochina within 30 days or resign. Coupled with this attitude were British and U.S. policies: both countries were tired of conflict and apprehensive. Even the old realist Winston Churchill, reelected British prime minister in 1951,

declared in June 1954, "I am of the opinion that we ought to have a try for peaceful coexistence—a real good try for it." Two days later President Eisenhower approved Churchill's views, telling a press conference that the East and West must "find ways of living together."

With this atmosphere prevailing, on July 21, 1954—30 days and a few hours after Mendés France was elected—the Geneva conference brought an armistice to Indochina and put more than half of the country under communist rule. Communist North Vietnam was now a nation of 77,000 square miles (making it almost as large as all of Korea, which had 85,000 square miles) and 12½ million people. After the Geneva agreement was reached, nearly one million people walked, rode, sailed, and swam out of the area given to the communists and sought freedom and refuge in the South.

French carrier operations in the war were overshadowed by the more important ground fighting; U.S. carriers never entered the war. However, the experiences of the Korean War and the near participation of U.S. carriers in the Indochina conflict led to the U.S. national leadership directing that the U.S. Navy to maintain a continuous force of three strike carriers in the Western Pacific (Task Force 77) and two strike carriers in the Mediterranean (Task Force 61). And their ranks would soon be joined by newer and larger ships with more potent aircraft.

As the U.S. carriers stood by in the Far East, aircraft from the *Philippine Sea* were in action, albeit briefly. On July 23, 1954, Communist Chinese fighters shot down a Cathay Airlines DC-4 piston engine passenger plane en route to Hong Kong near Hainan Island, off southern China.[16] Nine people survived and ten people, including three Americans, were killed in the shootdown. A U.S. Air Force amphibian rescued the survivors.

The *Philippine Sea* was in the area and immediately launched AD-4 Skyraiders to search for wreckage and additional survivors. Although the United States recognized a three-mile territorial limit, the planes were ordered to stay more than 12 miles off Hainan, the territorial limit then claimed by China.

The U.S. search flights continued, and on July 26 a large number of "Phil Sea" planes were aloft when two Chinese La-7 piston-engine fighters attacked a flight of Skyraiders from Fighter Squadron 54.[17] Several AD-4 Skyraiders, each armed with four 20-mm cannon, and a single F4U night fighter, took on the La-7s. In the brief mêlée both Chinese aircraft were shot down; the kills were credited to the Skyraiders. There was no damage to the U.S. planes.[18]

At the same time, a Chinese gunboat began firing at the low-flying U.S. planes, but the aircraft were directed not to return fire. No additional survivors were found, and all U.S. planes returned safely to the *Philippine Sea*.

French and British Progress

For the French Navy the war in Indochina ensured the place of aircraft carriers in its future military operations. As already noted, the French Navy's efforts to construct aircraft carriers immediately after World War II were frustrated. In 1947 the French parliament voted to build an 18,500-ton ship, but the project was still being "discussed" in 1948 and was killed in 1949. Even after the light carrier *La Fayette* (ex-USS *Langley*) was accepted on loan in June 1951, and at which time the

Arromanches was purchased outright from Britain, the French government opposed accepting the loan of a second and third U.S. carrier. The events in Indochina proved the fallacy of this outlook, and in September 1953 the U.S. light carrier *Belleau Wood* was transferred to France, becoming the *Bois Belleau* under the tricolor.

During the final stages of French military presence in Indochina the carriers continued to provide air support. The *Bois Belleau* served in the theater from April 1954 to November 1955, the *Dixmude* from August to October 1954, and the *La Fayette* from May to June 1955 and again from February to May 1956.

This rejuvenation—or, perhaps more accurately, the birth—of a French carrier force was crowned in November 1955 when the keel was laid down at Brest for the 22,000-ton carrier *Clemenceau*. She was the largest warship laid down in postwar France and second only to the unfinished *Joffre* as a French ship begun specifically as an aircraft carrier. The *Clemenceau* emerged from her building yard as an excellent and modern warship. Her sister ship *Foch* was laid down in February 1957. And in 1958 the French government approved construction of a 45,000-ton aircraft carrier. Until the new ships were ready, the light carriers *Arromanches*, *Bois Belleau*, and *La Fayette* gave the French Navy a viable albeit limited carrier striking force.

During this same period the Royal Navy was improving its carrier position from the nadir of late 1947, when only one fleet carrier (used for training) and two light carriers were operational. The impetus came, in part, from the continuing requirement for British military forces overseas, particularly in Southeast Asia and Korea. In Southeast Asia the only country where a former colonial power truly succeeded in restoring its control after World War II was Malaya. British rule was resumed with the Japanese capitulation, and the British skillfully acceded to a relatively limited desire for more local autonomy. However, communists, mostly Chinese, threatened the colony, and guerrilla warfare against the British and local nationalistic leaders erupted in 1948.

As in the French struggle against the Viet Minh in Indochina, the British made extensive use of air power in the conflict. The British used primarily land-based Royal Air Force (RAF) units in Malaya, although one squadron of Navy-manned Whirlwind helicopters (S-55/HRS) saw extensive service in transporting troops and evacuating casualties. The light carrier *Triumph* arrived at Singapore in the late summer of 1949 and her Seafires and Fireflies, operating from shore bases, flew a limited number of strikes against communist terrorists.

Of major significance in this campaign were the jet aircraft used against guerrilla-type forces. As the RAF was being reequipped with jet aircraft in the early 1950s, there were considerable questions in some quarters about the new aircraft providing the close air support and armed reconnaissance missions as well as propeller aircraft could. The air officer commanding in Malaya was confident that jet operating techniques could be adapted to meet the requirements of limited-war operations. Proponents of the expanded role for jet aircraft pointed out that the new twin-jet Canberra bomber was designed to bomb from 50,000 feet at almost 600 m.p.h. did not necessarily mean that the Canberra could not be used to bomb accurately from 3,000 feet at 230 m.p.h. Moreover, retaining obsolescent prop-driven aircraft in service would mean keeping two air forces in being because it was necessary to deploy a force of modern, high-performance fighter and bomber aircraft in Malaya to counter the threat of full-scale war in Asia. Air power—and especially the use of a large number of helicopters—was a major factor in the eventual British victory over the communist guerrillas in Malaya.[19]

The first "new" British carrier to be completed after World War II was the *Eagle*, originally the *Audacious* and renamed just prior to being launched in early 1946. Work on the *Eagle* was halted after launching, but as the Cold War intensified, construction was resumed and she was completed on October 1, 1951. With a displacement of 36,800 tons and an overall length of 803¾ feet, the *Eagle* had traditional British carrier lines; her hangar deck was a part of her hull structure, which was topped by an armored flight deck. Her large starboard island structure ran a full quarter of the ship's length. Propulsion machinery consisted of turbines and eight boilers turning four propeller shafts to drive the ship at 31.5 knots. Her defensive armament consisted initially of 16 4.5-inch guns (in twin mounts along the

The sister carriers *Eagle* and *Ark Royal* were the largest British carriers of the 20th Century. This view shows the *Eagle* on sea trials in 1951. Her career with an axial flight deck as shown here would be brief. "J" was the *Eagle*'s code letter, part of a scheme that the U.S. Navy employed briefly after World War II. Her designation was later changed to "E" for *Eagle*. (Royal Navy)

An F9F Panther takes off from the angled deck of the carrier *Antietam* during touch-and-go operations in January 1953. She was the world's first carrier to be converted to an angled-deck configuration. The angled deck provides a landing/takeoff runway while leaving the forward deck available as a deck park or for takeoffs. (U.S. Navy)

flight deck) and 58 40-mm guns, the most powerful anti-aircraft battery ever fitted in a British carrier. So too was her offensive armament, consisting of 80 to 110 aircraft, depending upon type, the most powerful of a British flattop. (Two centerline elevators connected her hangar and flight decks.)

The *Eagle*'s unfinished sister carrier *Ark Royal* (originally named *Irresistible*) was also taken in hand and launched on May 3, 1950. However, while she was being completed, a radical change was made in her flight deck layout with the landing area angled 5½ degrees to port from the ship's centerline.

The concept of an angled or canted landing deck was born in a conference at the Royal Aircraft Establishment (RAE) as the Royal Navy's leading aviators and aeronautical engineers studied the problems of operating wheelless aircraft from carriers, and the compatibility of heavy (at the time 30,000-pound) aircraft with the 800-foot flight decks of the *Ark Royal* and *Eagle*. The chairman of the conference was Captain Dennis R. F. Cambell, at the time Assistant Chief Naval Representative to the Ministry of Aviation (which oversaw all British aviation matters). Cambell, who had flown from the old *Ark Royal* and the ancient *Argus* during his career in naval aviation, proposed a ten-degree offset landing area and showed a rough pencil sketch to the conference. With the angled landing area,

an aircraft that missed the arresting wires could accelerate and take off again rather than crash into a barrier or the aircraft parked at the flight deck's forward end.

The RAE conference was held on August 9, 1951. After further discussions between February 4 and 8, 1952, the light carrier *Triumph* had an angled-deck layout painted on her existing flight deck and certain flight-deck obstructions (e.g., loudspeakers, radio masts) removed.

Aircraft flew touch-and-go landings on the *Triumph*'s angled deck in mid-February. There was a complete and ongoing exchange of carrier information with the U.S. Navy and a short time later similar touch-and-go landings were flown on board the larger U.S. carrier *Midway*, whose deck was also painted with an angled landing area. In both the *Triumph* and *Midway* tests the ships' arresting wires and emergency barriers remained rigged for centerline (axial) landings and consequently were not used. The tests were considered a success.

In September 1952 the 27,100-ton USS *Antietam* entered the New York Naval Shipyard for conversion to the world's first angled-deck carrier. The work was completed in mid-December 1952. Her landing area was angled eight degrees to port with her arresting wires and barriers oriented to the angled deck. She demonstrated the angled-deck concept for U.S. Navy officials and then crossed the Atlantic for similar demonstrations in British waters. The angled-deck concept was immediately accepted in carrier aviation.[20]

During the next few years 15 of the *Essex*-class carriers and the three *Midway*s as well as the *Antietam* were converted to an angled-flight configuration. One of the first to receive the modification was the *Bennington*. On May 26, 1954, she was conducting flight operations off the coast of Rhode Island when, at 6:11 A.M., the hydraulic fluid in one of her catapults exploded, setting off a series of secondary explosions. The carrier suffered 103 crewmen killed and another 201 men injured. The ship was never in danger of sinking and, under her own power, reached port. She was repaired at the New York Naval Shipyard from July 1954 to March 1955, at which time she was provided with an angled flight deck.[21]

The canted or angled deck was the most important development in carrier aviation since the arresting gear. From the earliest days of carrier aviation an aircraft that missed the arresting wires would crash into aircraft parked forward or, from the 1920s, into a barrier erected to protect those aircraft, although many landing aircraft that missed a wire would bounce over the barrier. The angled deck saved numerous pilots, deck crewmen, and aircraft and sped up flight-deck operations.

The completion of the 36,800-ton British carrier *Ark Royal* was delayed to incorporate a 5½-degree angled deck plus two other British devices: her two catapults were steam powered, providing more acceleration for heavy aircraft than the hydraulic catapults then in use, and she had the mirror landing system. The latter innovation—like the angled deck and steam catapult—was needed if carriers were to effectively operate jet-propelled aircraft.

Jet aircraft approached a carrier at speeds that were too high for a landing signal officer or (British) batsman to provide the pilot with adequate warning if he was approaching too high or too low through the use of "paddles" or lighted batons. Lieutenant Commander Nick Goodhart, Captain Cambell's assistant, an engineering officer and test pilot, sought a means of letting the pilot himself determine his approach angle. Initially using his secretary's pocket mirror and the point of her lipstick, he developed the concept of the mirror landing system in 1951. It was flight tested by British and U.S. carrier pilots at Farnborough in 1953 and quickly adopted by both navies. The initial mirror was fabricated of highly polished cast aluminum, formed to a cylindrical concave shape; it was five feet six inches wide and four feet high.

As developed, the device, mounted on the port side of the flight deck, was visible to an approaching pilot. It provided a mirror reflecting a circle of light

HMS *Ark Royal* in May 1957, as completed with a "partial" angled flight deck and a deck-edge lift opposite of the island structure. Her four port-side 4.5-inch gun mounts were deleted. The planes on her flight deck are Gannets, Sea Hawks, Skyraiders, and Wyverns. She has the code letter "O" at her stern, later changed to "R." (Royal Navy)

(leading to the term "meatball") and a datum line of green lights to enable the pilot to see if he was high or low by glancing at the "meatball" relative to the datum line; the mirror was concave so that the pilot could see it as he turned into the angled deck. A pilot could land a high-performance aircraft on a carrier solely by watching the mirror (which was illuminated at night) and the air speed indicator within his cockpit. The air speed was later provided to the pilot by sound pulses in his headphones.

Landings with the mirror system were so accurate that the number of arresting wires (pendants) could be reduced from more than a dozen to as few as four and later to only three. The mirror landing system was succeeded by the improved fresnal lens and subsequent landing devices, all based on Goodhart's concept.

The new *Ark Royal* also introduced the deck-edge elevator to British carriers; coupled with two centerline lifts, it improved the handling of the carrier's 80 to 110 aircraft. (During a refit in 1959, however, the deck-edge lift was removed from the *Ark Royal*.) For close-in defense the ship had 8 4.5-inch guns and 34 40-mm AA weapons. Like her sister ship *Eagle*, the *Ark Royal* was steam-turbine propelled and could reach 31.5 knots. Thus configured, the *Ark Royal* was completed on February 25, 1955, almost 12 years after her keel was laid down. Her first commanding officer was Dennis Cambell, who had conceived the angled flight deck.

Next in size after the *Ark Royal* and *Eagle* in the British carrier fleet was the veteran *Victorious*, originally completed in May 1941. She was rebuilt in 1950–1958, fitted with an angled flight deck, steam catapults, new electronics, and other improvements; her standard displacement was increased to 30,000 tons and her overall length to 781 feet; and her armament changed to 12 3-inch anti-aircraft guns in twin mounts and six 40-mm weapons. (Her sister ships *Illustrious*, *Implacable*, *Indefatigable*, *Indomitable*, and *Formidable* were scrapped in 1953–1957.)

In addition to these fleet carriers the Royal Navy of the mid-1950s had three light carriers of the *Hermes* class: the *Centaur* completed in September 1953, the *Albion* finished in May 1954, and the *Bulwark* ready in November 1954. The nameship *Hermes* herself was not finished until November 1959, and then to a modified design.

The *Albion*, *Bulwark*, and *Centaur* were all completed with a standard displacement of 22,000 tons, were 737¾-foot in length, and were propelled by steam turbines and four boilers turning twin propeller shafts to produce up to 29.5 knots. Each carrier could operate some 45 aircraft, carried between the flight and hangar decks by two centerline elevators. Their design included angled decks and an armament of 26 40-mm guns.[22]

Filling out the Royal Navy's carrier ranks were the smaller light carriers *Glory*, *Ocean*, *Theseus*, *Triumph*, *Vengeance*, and *Warrior*, all 13,190- to 13,350-ton, 695-foot ships with axial decks capable of operating up to 35 piston aircraft. The maintenance carrier *Perseus* remained on the list (until scrapped in 1958) as did the unique *Unicorn*, reclassified as a ferry carrier in June 1953 (and scrapped in 1960).

Thus, in the summer of 1956 the Royal Navy had "on the books" a carrier force numbering three fleet and eight light fleet carriers of various sizes and capabilities. However, the Admiralty had just decided to cease operating jet-propelled aircraft from axial-deck carriers, and most of these ships were in the yard, being fitted with angled decks and steam catapults or were in overhaul.

Four of the British light carriers went to other navies in this period: the *Majestic* to Australia (as the *Melbourne*), the *Powerful* to Canada (as the *Bonaventure*), the *Hercules* to India (as the *Vikrant*), and the *Vengeance* to Australia from early 1953 until August 1955 and then to Brazil in 1957 (as the *Minas Gerais*).

New Aircraft

British and French carriers landed several new aircraft in the decade after World War II. The principal French carrier aircraft was the F4U-7 variant of the venerable Vought Corsair, which had first flown in 1940. The F4U-7 was similar to the AU-1 attack aircraft, and 94 were produced specifically for the French Navy. The last—the last of 15,056 Corsairs—was delivered in December 1952.[23] Corsairs remained in French service, operating ashore (Tunisia) and afloat until October 1964.[24] (In several squadrons they were replaced by another Vought aircraft—the F8U Crusader.) The French Navy also flew Grumman Avengers from their carriers in the 1950s—the TBM-3S and TBM-3W for anti-submarine operations.

The Royal Navy moved rapidly into turbojet fighters. The Supermarine Attacker was quickly succeeded by the Sea Hawk and Sea Venom. The Sea Hawk, the Hawker firm's first turbojet aircraft, was an attractive, straight-wing aircraft that was produced in large numbers for the Fleet Air Arm, as well as for India, West

Germany, and the Netherlands; it was flown from Indian and Dutch as well as British carriers.

The prototype Sea Hawk flew on September 3, 1948, and the first production aircraft was flown three years later. Not until March 1953, was the first Sea Hawk squadron, No. 806, formed, which subsequently embarked in HMS *Eagle*. Production totaled 434 aircraft for the FAA, with the Sea Hawk remaining in frontline squadrons until 1960. The ultimate Sea Hawk variant was designated FGA.6 (for Fighter/ Ground Attack). Eighty-six were produced through 1956 for the FAA.

Soon joining Sea Hawks aboard carriers was the de Havilland Sea Venom, successor to the small number of Sea Vampire fighters previously produced by de Havilland. Also a twin-boom, turbojet aircraft, the Sea Venom was developed as a night fighter, derived from the RAF Venom NF.2. The first naval prototype, modified from a "straight" Venom prototype to the NF.20, carried out trials aboard HMS *Illustrious* in July 1951. The first production Sea Venom, designated FAW.20, flew on March 27, 1953; production aircraft were delivered in March 1954 to No. 890 Squadron. The FAA took delivery of 256 Sea Venoms, which served aboard carriers until late 1960. All carried a pilot and radar operator with side-by-side seating. The final production version, the FAW.22, had four 20-mm cannon and had wing fittings for eight air-to-ground rockets. In 1958 Sea Venoms were fitted with the Firestreak air-to-air missile, the first naval fighter to carry such a weapon. The Sea Venoms FAW.53—built in Australia—flew

from HMAS *Melbourne* for a brief period in the mid-1950s and then, because of a wing defect that could affect catapult launches, were based ashore.

The third major fixed-wing aircraft aboard British carriers in this period was the Westland Wyvern strike aircraft. This was Westland's first aircraft flown by the FAA since the Walrus, an ungalinly, poorly performing, land-based bomber, that had entered naval service in 1921. The Wyvern was designed from the outset for a turboprop power plant, but engine delays caused five prototypes and ten preproduction TF.1 variants to be fitted with advanced piston engines. The first turboprop-powered Wyvern, designated TF.2, flew on January 18, 1949.[25]

Finally, the TF.4, which first flew on May 1951, was ordered into production as a strike aircraft, the S.4, the designation having been changed in 1953. The S.4 entered service with No. 813 Squadron in May 1953 and the following year embarked in HMS *Eagle*. Five Wyvern operational squadrons were formed from the 97 S.4 aircraft—of 124 Wyverns produced—but only one squadron, No. 830 on the *Eagle* saw action, in 1956 at Suez.

The trim-looking aircraft had a massive 4,110-horsepower turboprop engine driving two large, four-blade, contrarotating propellers. It could externally carry a torpedo or three 1,000-pound bombs. Four 20-mm cannon were mounted in the wings.

The aircraft had a brief, five-year career in frontline service. FAA pilot and historian David Hobbs wrote, "What had seemed a good idea in 1945 proved

A flight of Hawker Sea Hawk FGA.4 aircraft from the carrier *Eagle*, at the time assigned the code-letter "J." The ultimate Sea Hawk—the FGA.6 variant—had a top speed of 524 m.p.h. at 10,000 feet with two 100-Imperial gallon drop tanks and two 500-pound bombs. Ten rockets could be carried as alternatives to bombs. Four 20-mm cannon were fitted in the forward fuselage. (*Flight*)

The Sea Venom FAW.22 was the final production version of the aircraft. Several de Havilland jet aircraft featured the twin-boom configuration, in part to minimize the distance from engine intake to exhaust. The FAW.22's top speed was 575 m.p.h. (compared to 630 m.p.h. for the FAW.21); initial climb was 5,900 feet per minute, and ceiling was 40,000 feet. (*Fight*)

extremely difficult to translate into hardware and 3 different engines were tried. The only mark to see service, the S.4, was never a success and its duties were eventually undertaken by jet fighters after 1958."[26]

The French and British navies' new ships and new aircraft would see combat in 1956 in the Suez campaign. Meanwhile, U.S. carriers were engaged in one final "combat" operation in Asian waters in the 1950s. When Chiang Kai-shek's Nationalist forces had fled from China to Formosa, his troops also held on to several islands off the coast of China—Quemoy, Matsu, and the Tachen group, the last about 200 miles northwest of Formosa. Periodically communist artillery on the mainland and ships would attack the islands, which were heavily fortified by Nationalist troops.

In early 1955, however, it appeared the communist troops were massing for an assault on the Tachens and the decision was made to evacuate the 10,000 National

troops, 4,000 guerrillas, and 14,500 civilians to Formosa on U.S. ships. Amphibious ships undertook the massive evacuation while five U.S. carriers and their screening ships stood offshore. Continuous air cover was flown by the carriers with strike groups of four bomb-laden AD Skyraiders kept airborne to ward off communist interference. (The Skyraiders—generally aloft for about four hours per sortie—dumped their ordnance loads into the sea for safety reasons before recovering aboard the carriers.)

There was no interference in the evacuation but one AD-5W Skyraider from the carrier *Wasp* was shot down, being struck by anti-aircraft fire as it strayed over Chinese territory on February 9, 1955. The pilot was able to glide the plane back out to sea, where it ditched. All three crewmen survived and were rescued by National Chinese patrol boats.

Thus ended carrier operations off the Asian mainland—for a few years.

The Westland Wyvern S.4 was the definitive version of this attack aircraft. The aircraft—originally designated TF.4—entered service in May 1953; in service only until March 1958. The S.4 had a maximum speed of 383 m.p.h. at sea level, could initially climb at 2,350 feet per minutes, and had a service ceiling of 28,000 feet—not overly impressive when compared to the F4U Corsair and AD Skyraider. (Royal Navy)

9 THE SUEZ OPERATION

A Sea Venom is catapulted from HMS *Eagle*. Sea Venoms and Sea Hawks—the fighters on board the three British carriers at Suez—with wings folded are in a deck park in the foreground. British carrier aircraft at Suez were painted with "invasion stripes" to facilitate recognition by other aircraft and ground forces. (Royal Navy)

On the evening of July 26, 1956, Gamal Abdel Nasser, the president of Egypt, made a frenzied speech in Alexandria that was climaxed by his declaration: "Egypt will run the Canal. The Suez belongs to us. . . . The Canal will be run by Egyptians! Egyptians! Egyptians!"[1]

With that Nasser and his countrymen seized the Suez Canal. The British and French governments considered the takeover to be a grave threat to their economic and strategic interests. Both countries still had obligations "East of Suez" that could require the rapid transfer of warships and troop ships through the canal, and both nations were dependent upon oil from the Middle East that came through the canal in tankers. Further, France and Britain were the principal shareholders in the Suez Canal Company.

The Egyptians had already demonstrated that they were not above using their previously limited control of the canal to suit their politics, as evidenced by their refusal to permit the passage of Israeli ships or ships of any nation bound for Israeli ports. Both the British

123

and French governments believed that the waterway should not be under the absolute control of any one nation and felt that military action was justified to ensure free transit of the canal by ships of "any" nation (although France and Britain had accepted the ban on Israeli shipping).

But potential Anglo-French military action was hampered by a variety of complicated factors. In the summer of 1956 the French were involved in a violent guerrilla war in Algeria that tied down most of the French Army (three of the five French divisions committed to the North Atlantic Treaty Organization had recently been sent to North Africa). The jet fighters of the French Air Force—with their ground crews, spare parts, fuel, and munitions—were based in France and West Germany, far from the Eastern Mediterranean.

Britain had recently adopted a new defense policy that relied primarily on nuclear weapons rather than conventional fighting forces. The ensuing troop reductions had left barely sufficient men to meet NATO requirements and maintain small garrisons in Cyprus, Malaya, Hong Kong, and a few other scattered possessions. The British Army's single parachute brigade had not jumped in more than a year, was poorly equipped, and could be provided only with obsolescent transport aircraft; most of the Royal Marine brigade was fighting terrorists on Cyprus and had not taken part in an amphibious exercise in more than a year.

The closest British base that could be used as a jumping off point for operations against Egypt was Malta, 935 miles west of Port Saïd (the northern entrance to the Suez Canal). Cyprus was only 225 miles from Port Saïd but had neither the airfields nor ports ready for large-scale operations and, being even closer to Syria, was vulnerable to air attack should other Arab nations come to Egypt's aid.

With this base situation, aircraft carriers would be a vital factor in operations against Egypt's modern air force. In late July 1956, of the 11 British carriers the *Eagle* was the only ship fully operational:

CV *Ark Royal*	Undergoing refit
CV *Eagle*	Operational in Mediterranean
CV *Victorious*	Undergoing modernization
CVL *Albion*	Undergoing refit
CVL *Bulwark*	Flying trials and training
CVL *Centaur*	Undergoing refit
CVL *Triumph*	In reserve; awaiting conversion to cadet training ship
CVL *Ocean*	Officer-recruit training ship
CVL *Theseus*	Officer-recruit training ship
CVL *Glory*	In reserve; future uncertain
CVL *Perseus*	In reserve; future uncertain

To reduce the risk taken in running down the carrier fleet at the peak of the 1950s modernization program, a second carrier, the new light carrier *Bulwark*, was kept available at short notice in home waters. She was employed in trials and training with a reduced complement and had no aircraft assigned. However, additional men and aircraft were ready for embarkation on short notice.

The British government sought to strengthen its military forces to gain leverage in negotiations with the Egyptians and to provide for a solution by force of arms if no other alternative was possible. The armed forces were ordered to prepare for an assault on key points of the Suez Canal. No attempt was made to conceal this buildup and the nature of the military preparations was explained to the British Parliament and the public. The French undertook similar preparations.

The *Bulwark* embarked an air group and sailed for the Mediterranean on August 6, 1956. Her sister ship *Albion* scheduled to complete her overhaul in late October, was hurriedly made ready for sea, and she sailed for the Mediterranean in September. Two older light carriers employed for officer and recruit training at the time of the Egyptian declaration were hastily fitted with several thousand folding camp beds to serve as emergency transports and sailed for the Mediterranean in late July.

British and French military staffs conferred and worked up plans for the assault. On August 11 the commander of British ground forces in the Middle East, General Sir Charles Keightley, was appointed Supreme Allied Commander for the expedition, and Vice-Amiral d'escadre Pierre Barjot, commander of the French Mediterranean Fleet, was named his deputy. Similar Anglo-French commander and deputy commander assignments were made at each echelon of the operation, with Vice-Admiral Manley L. Power given command of the Allied carrier force and Contre-Amiral Yves G. Caron assigned as his deputy.

Ports and airfield facilities on Malta and Cyprus were rehabilitated, and British twin-jet Canberra light bombers were deployed to both islands. Control of the air over the canal zone was not to be the task of land-based fighters from Cyprus and the carrier-based jet fighters controlled the air over the canal zone. Sixty-four Royal Air Force Venoms (600-m.p.h. jet fighters) flew into Cyprus as did 36 French F-84F fighters (American-built aircraft capable of almost 700 m.p.h.). Transport aircraft overflowed the airfields on both islands in preparation for parachuting the spearheads of the 45,000 British and 34,000 French troops into the canal zone to seize key positions.

In the midst of the tumult of these preparations, the light carriers-turned-troop-transports *Ocean* and *Theseus* returned to Britain in the first week of September. Improved troop accommodations were fitted with tiered bunks, installed in their hangars. The *Ocean* was additionally fitted with elaborate medical facilities to serve as a combat hospital ship. Then, on September 26, orders were given for both ships to revert to aircraft carriers.

Stores and equipment loaded aboard a few days earlier were unloaded, and acetylene torches cut out recently installed bunks and other facilities. The *Ocean* and *Theseus* returned to sea on September 31 with aircraft again on their decks. But the aircraft were helicopters: the *Ocean* had a squadron of Navy-manned Whirlwinds—8 HAS.22 and 3 HAR.3 models of No. 845 Squadron; the *Theseus* had 6 Whirlwind HAR.2s and 6 Sycamores of the Army-RAF Joint Experimental Helicopter Unit.[2] The HAS models were American-built by Sikorsky (HO4S-3), the HAR models were British-built by Westland. The HAS models could carry up to ten troops with removal of their AN/AQS-4 dipping sonar; the Bristol Sycamores could lift only *three* troops and their equipment.

The U.S. Marine Corps had experimented with helicopters in "vertical assault" operations since 1948 but had never used them to carry troops ashore in combat. The British military also had studied the question and accepted the feasibility of landing troops from ships by helicopter. During the first two weeks of October the two light carriers practiced helicopter operations. The *Ocean* was then ordered back to her nonflying training duties and the *Theseus* embarked No. 845 Squadron and sailed for Malta. There the Royal Marines first saw the helicopters that would carry them into combat. However, the entire 600-man Marine commando assigned

The Whirlwind helicopter, similar to the American HO4S/HRS (later H-19), was the most capable and the most versatile helicopter in FAA service in the 1950s. Those built by Westland for the Navy (Mks 1–7) had gas turbine engines, which provided faster startup than their American cousins, the Sikorsky-built aircraft (HAR.21 and HAS.22). These Whirlwinds are operating from the deck of HMS *Eagle*. (Royal Navy)

to use the helicopters was unable to exercise with them because of the limited time available. It was most unfortunate that, with the Eastern Mediterranean ready to erupt in flames at any time, the *Ocean* had been returned to training recruits. With the danger signs increasing, belatedly the *Ocean* was again changed from schoolship to warship, embarked the experimental helicopter unit, and sailed for Malta, arriving there on the last day of October.

Five conventional British and French carriers steamed toward the Eastern Mediterranean with 166 aircraft on their decks. These aircraft represented all but one of the first-line carrier planes in the British and French fleets, the missing aircraft being the British anti-submarine Gannet.[3]

On the British carriers were several of the Royal Navy's 50 American-built AD-4W Skyraiders for airborne early warning. Designated AEW.1 in the Fleet Air Arm, the Skyraiders flew in four-plane detachments from British carriers for almost a decade. The AD-4W/ AEW.1 carried a pilot and two radar operators and was the last fixed-wing piston aircraft to operate from British carriers. The FAA acquired 20 new AD-4W Skyraiders from Douglas and 30 from U.S. Navy stocks. They served from November 1951 until November 1960, when they were replaced by the Fairey Gannet AEW.3. The Skyraider AEW aircraft were all assigned to No. 849 Squadron.

The two Avengers in the *Bulwark* were among the last of a group of 100 TBM-3E Avengers provided to the FAA in the 1950s, before the British-built Gannets became available for ASW operations. An eight-plane Gannet squadron was normally embarked in each British strike carrier, but the absence of a submarine threat during the Suez campaign made it possible to replace the Gannets with additional fighter aircraft.

The French carriers employed TBM Avengers for anti-submarine patrol and each flattop had two HUP-2 five-place utility helicopters. Both of these aircraft also were acquired from the United States.

Table 9-1
ALLIED CARRIER FORCE, NOVEMBER 1, 1956

		FIGHTER-STRIKE[*]	SPECIAL-MISSION
CV	*Eagle*	17 Sea Venom FAW.21 24 Sea Hawk FGA.6 9 Wyvern S.4	4 Skyraider AEW.1 2 Whirlwind HAR.3 helicopter (HRS)
CVL	*Albion*	8 Sea Venom FAW.21 19 Sea Hawk FGA.4 and FB.3	2 Skyraider AEW.1 2 Whirlwind HAR.3 helicopter (HRS)
CVL	*Bulwark*	30 Sea Hawk FGA.4, FGA.6, FB.3	2 Avenger AS.5 2 Dragonfly HR.3 helicopter (HO3S)
CVL	*Arromanches*	14 F4U-7 Corsair	5 TBM-3S/W Avenger 2 HUP-2 helicopter
CVL	*La Fayette*	22 F4U-7 Corsair	2 HUP-2 helicopter

* AEW = Airborne Early Warning
  AS   = Anti-Submarine
  FAW = Fighter All-Weather
  FGA = Fighter Ground Attack
  S   = Strike

The Chance Vought F4U-7 variant of the famed Corsair was specifically produced for French naval use in Indochina. Too late for large-scale use in that conflict, it was the mainstay of French carrier aviation at the time of Suez. The F4U-7 was heavily armored for ground support operations, had four 20-mm cannon, and could carry two 2,000-pound bombs or ten 5-inch rockets. Maximum speed was 425 m.p.h. at 23,000 feet. This Corsair is from 12th Flottille. The U.S. Marine Corps flew 110 similar Corsairs designated AU-1. (French Navy)

The Anglo-French carrier planes wore black-and-white invasion stripes, similar to the markings of Allied tactical aircraft for D-Day in June 1944, and by British carrier aircraft in the Korean War, to lessen the recognition problems for warships.

There were two other aircraft carriers in the area: the USS *Coral Sea* and the USS *Randolph*, operating with other surface ships and submarines of the Sixth Fleet, with some U.S. ships steaming off the Egyptian coast. At one point the *Coral Sea* passed through the *Bulwark*'s screen while operating aircraft.

During the subsequent operations, Vice-Admiral D. F. Durford-Slater, a British task force commander, signaled the Admiralty that,

> Sixth Fleet are an embarrassment in my neighborhood. We have already twice intercepted US aircraft and there is constant danger of an incident. Have been continually menaced during the past eight hours by US aircraft approaching low down as close as 4,000 yards and on two occasions flying over ships.[4]

The Anglo-French carriers were also forced to launch aircraft to intercept and identify U.S. carrier aircraft approaching Allied ships. The U.S. ships were in the area ostensively preparing for a possible evacuation of Americans from Egypt. The U.S. Sixth Fleet commander, Vice Admiral Charles R. (Cat) Brown signaled Washington: "Whose side am I on." Admiral Arleigh Burke, the Chief of Naval Operations, responded: "Take no guff from anyone."

Czechoslovakia and the Soviet Union were supplying the Egyptians with modern arms, including MiG-15*bis* and MiG-17F jet fighters and Il-28 Beagle light bombers (to supplement older, British-provided aircraft), as well as heavy tanks and self-propelled guns.[5] For more than a year, Israel had been concerned that the buildup of Egyptian military forces with Soviet-sponsored arms deliveries would lead to another Arab-Israeli conflict. Further, in October 1955 Egypt and Syria established a joint military command, which was expanded in 1956 to include Jordan. At the same time, the Egyptian denial of Israeli shipping through the Suez Canal and Straits of Tiran (from the Gulf of Aqaba) constituted an economic war, and the fedayeen (guerrilla) raids into Israel from Egypt were becoming more frequent and more deadly.

Accordingly, in July 1956 the Israeli government made the secret decision to initiate a war against Egypt, with the primary goal of opening of the Straits of Tiran and defusing any Egyptian military offensive. France—Israel's principal arms supplier—accelerated weapons deliveries and planned a coordinated strategy with the general staffs of the two nations meeting in Paris on October 1.[6] French-supplied jet fighters, tanks, trucks, and half-tracks gave the Israelis an improved (although still inferior) position vis-à-vis Egyptian forces. In addition, a wing of some 50 French F-84 Thunderstreak and Mystére IV fighters was secretly based on Israeli airfields as defense against possible Egyptian

The Fairey Gannet had two turboprop engines with contra-rotating propellers fitted to a single shaft, giving the aircraft a single-engine configuration. Each engine was controlled separately and one was normally shut down for extended, single-engine cruising. Behind the Gannet's pilot, in separate cockpits, sat two ASW equipment operators. An internal bomb bay could hold two homing torpedoes or other weapons; 16 rockets could be mounted on the wings. The Gannet had a top speed of 310 m.p.h. (Royal Navy)

air attacks, especially from the newly acquired Il-28 jet bombers. (The Israelis did not trust the British for such support because of their close ties to several Arab states.)

The War Begins

Without warning, on October 29, Israeli paratroopers dropped deep into the Sinai Peninsula, marking the start of the Israeli invasion of Egyptian territory. The Israeli assault was a complete surprise to the Egyptians—and to the British—for the Israelis had been threatening a move against Jordan.

The Israeli assault gave Britain and France the needed excuse for intervention in the canal zone. At 6 P.M. on the 30th—25 hours after the Israeli assault began—an Anglo-French ultimatum was issued demanding that both belligerents withdraw all armed forces to a distance of ten miles from the Suez Canal (the Israelis were not that close) and "in order to guarantee freedom of transit through the Canal by the ships of all nations and in order to separate the belligerents, [the Egyptian government must] accept the temporary occupation by Anglo-French forces of key positions at Port Saïd, Ismailia and Suez." It took the Israelis four hours to accept the ultimatum (it would cost them nothing) and the Egyptians nine hours to reject it.

The British and French initiated Operation Musketeer at 7 P.M. on the 31st, 15 hours after the ultimatum expired. The delay was caused by reports of U.S. transport planes passing through Cairo while evacuating American civilians from Israel. British Canberra turbojet bombers from both Malta and Cyprus were already airborne when the U.S. planes' location became known in London. Urgent signals were sent from both Malta and Cyprus to recall the bombers; Malta was unable to contact its squadrons, but RAF headquarters on Cyprus made contact with its airborne squadrons, which were able to pass on the message to the Malta-based bombers.

During the delays in mounting the air offensive against Egypt, British politicians had successively reduced the size of bombs that could be used from 1,000-pounders to 500-pounders, and, finally, to 250-pounders, all in the hope of "not overly antagonizing" their former Egyptian allies. And throughout this phase of the campaign, some British politicians hoped that Nasser's will or at least means to fight might be destroyed by air attack alone, alleviating the need for landing Anglo-French troops. According to Randolph Churchill, the politician-journalist son of Sir Winston, "This delectable carrot excited the political appetite of some members of the Cabinet, and made them think that they might achieve their objective [the fall of Nasser] without becoming involved in any land operations."[7]

Finally, on the night of October 31–November 1, British aircraft from Malta and Cyprus began bombing military targets in the canal zone. Allied land-based aircraft would attack targets east of 32° longitude and carriers would strike targets west of 32°. The following morning, coupled with additional land-based air strikes, the five Allied aircraft carriers launched strikes against Egyptian positions.

"Launch Aircraft"

The RAF jet bombers from Malta and Cyprus attacked the runways and hangars of Egyptian airfields. The planes encountered light and inaccurate anti-aircraft fire during their bombing runs. Reportedly, two Egyptian aircraft approached the bombers but were unable to close before the British planes opened their throttles and climbed away. The bomber raids continued through the night. With the dawn came RAF Venom and French F-84 fighters from Cyprus and the carrier-based planes. Neither the Anglo-French carrier aircraft nor the fighters based on Cyprus could match the speed (about 670 m.p.h.), maneuverability, or rate of climb of the MiG-15 or few MiG-17 fighters in Egyptian service. However, the poor morale and training level of the Egyptian Air Force ensured its easy destruction—mostly on the ground—within 36 hours. (When the war began the Egyptian Air Force had approximately 45 operational MiG-15s plus a few two-seat MiG-15UTI trainers, and six improved MiG-17F fighters, the latter given the NATO name Fresco-C.[8])

The first carrier strike on November 1 was launched by the three British carriers consisting of 8 Sea Venoms and 32 Sea Hawks, timed to attack the air bases in the Nile Delta at first light. The Navy pilots found and strafed several MiG fighters and Il-28 Beagle bombers on Egyptian runways. Again, there was little flak and no airborne opposition; all of the planes returned safely to their carriers.

Simultaneously, Sea Hawks provided a combat air patrol over the carriers, and Skyraiders and Avengers fanned out around the carrier force to provide warning of surface or low-level air attacks against the

Carrier striking power in the Mediterranean: the British carriers *Eagle, Bulwark*, and *Albion* steam in formation. These ships—photographed in October 1956—are participating in an exercise off Malta. They formed the British contribution to the Allied carrier striking force in the Mediterranean during the Suez invasion. (Royal Navy)

Anglo-French naval forces. The turboprop Wyverns and piston-engine Corsairs searched for targets of opportunity along the Egyptian coast. The latter sank an Egyptian motor torpedo boat. (On November 4 planes from the British carriers sank two more Egyptian torpedo craft, sparing a third to pick up survivors of the others.) Air operations halted at dusk on the first with the carrier pilots having averaged four sorties each during the day.

Carrier operations on November 2 began with another dawn air strike on the Delta airfields. The Wyverns joined in these attacks when the expected Egyptian fighter opposition failed to appear. Suitable ground targets became scarcer, and by midday it was clear that air supremacy had been won. On this day Egyptian anti-aircraft fire severely damaged a Sea Venom from the *Eagle*. Because his observer was seriously injured and could not bail out, the pilot returned to his carrier and, unable to lower his landing gear, made a wheels-up landing into the flight-deck barrier. A Sea Hawk crashed on landing aboard the *Bulwark* when its arresting hook pulled out; the pilot was lost. The first two days of Operation Musketeer saw no other carrier aircraft losses.

By November 2 the Suez Canal area was wide open for an Allied invasion, but the invasion forces were four days and many hundreds of miles away. As in World War II and the Korean conflict, the assault was of necessity geared to the speed of the troop ships. Although the initial landing at Suez was to be made by parachute troops, the British had the capability of only a single-battalion drop. The French could parachute a larger and better-equipped force and wanted to do so as soon as possible. However, the British hesitated, awaiting the arrival of the seaborne assault forces. (Reportedly, the French fleet—including two aircraft carriers—was in position to support Israeli forces any time after October 26.)

The French troop convoy had left Algiers on October 29 and, steaming at an average of ten knots, could have been off Port Saïd by November 4. The main British assault convoy departed Malta on November 1 and could have arrived off Port Saïd on the 5th. The troop convoy from Cyprus sailed on November 4 and needed only 24 hours to reach Egypt. The helicopter carriers *Ocean* and *Theseus* departed Malta on the evening of November 3, forming the Helicopter Force under Rear-Admiral Guy B. Sayer. Unencumbered by slower merchantmen and landing vessels, these two ships could maintain 20 knots. If just these two ships had been dispatched a day earlier a powerful Anglo-French assault force could have easily landed by parachute, by helicopter, and even by landing craft from the Malta-based transports on November 4 or 5.

But not until November 5 did the British and French paratroopers drop on Port Fouad and Port Saïd, and still another day passed before the seaborne force landed. Vice-Admiral Power, commanding the Allied carriers, offered to speed the capture of Port Saïd by immediately landing the 600 Royal Marines in the *Ocean* and *Theseus* on November 5 to reinforce the paratroopers. The joint Allied Command refused the proposal and instead planned to support the airdrop with a seaborne assault on the sixth. In the interim (on November 5) the Israelis completed their assault, freeing Egyptian forces to oppose the Anglo-French invasion; more important, world opinion had begun to solidify in opposition to Britain and France.

The Anglo-French paratroopers were supported by carrier-based Sea Venoms, Sea Hawks, and Corsairs, whose guns, rockets, and bombs substituted for the tanks and heavy artillery that were not available to the paratroopers. Helicopters from the carriers *Albion* and *Bulwark* flew into the paratroop positions, bringing in cigarettes and beer sent by the two ships' companies and flying out wounded personnel to Allied ships offshore. Later in the morning a French C-47 Dakota transport touched down on a still-contested airfield, disgorged more luxuries, loaded up with wounded, and flew back to Cyprus. The pilot had been seeking information on the possibility of flying French reinforcements into Port Saïd's airfield. Another visitor to the airfield that morning was a Skyraider from the *Albion* with water-filled drop tanks to help quench the thirst of paratroopers who had missed the beer flown in by the helicopters.

Finally, the seaborne assault force approached the coast. For the assault the light carrier *Ocean* had the Joint Experimental Helicopter Unit with six Whirlwind and six Sycamore helicopters, about half of a 600-man Marine commando, and some 600 RAF personnel. The *Theseus* carried ten Whirlwinds of the Navy helicopter squadron, the remainder of the Marine commando, and several hundred support troops, including Army engineers. The landing plan finally adopted provided for two Marine commandos embarked in conventional

transports to first land in assault craft; the commando embarked in the carriers would serve as a mobile reserve to exploit the success of the Marines landed over the beach. Thus, the opportunity for a daring and worthwhile exploitation of the helicopters—under Allied-controlled skies—was lost.

The first amphibious tractors carrying Marines crawled ashore at 6:45 A.M. on November 6. They had been preceded by a brief shore bombardment by three destroyers. Larger warships, including the French battleship *Jean Bart*, had been removed from this mission to minimize possible civilian casualties. The two commandos and a squadron of Army tanks came ashore against light opposition. Overhead British and French carrier fighters flew close support missions.

An hour later the first Whirlwind lifted off the helicopter carriers, the helicopter flying in the commando's commanding officer, his operations officer, and two radiomen. The intended landing zone was covered with smoke and the Whirlwind pilot sought out a clear landing area. He came down in a sports stadium, but no sooner had the Marines jumped clear than it was found that Egyptian soldiers occupied the stadium.

Amid a hail of gunfire the helicopter's passengers clambered back aboard and the machine soared skyward. It was holed by 22 bullets in the fuselage, its rotor blades were nicked, and the pilot was slightly wounded. A safe landing was then made near the port's western breakwater. Ten minutes later six Whirlwinds followed by six Sycamores from the *Ocean* and the remaining *Theseus* Whirlwinds began taking off for the landing zone.

The Army Whirlwinds in the *Ocean* could each carry five fully equipped Marines; the Navy Whirlwinds in the *Theseus* could lift seven men; and the Sycamores could transport three. Each Marine had his own weapon, ammunition, rations, water canteen, gas mask, spare clothing, and ammunition for the crew-served weapons. The Sycamores had their seats and side panels removed to reduce weight; their three passengers sat on the floor, one in the middle with six mortar rounds on his lap and the two others, with their legs dangling over the side, each holding a 106-mm anti-tank round. The center man was also responsible for holding his mates so that they did not fall out. The Whirlwinds were stripped of seats, doors, and windows; their passengers hung on as best they could and a Marine with a submachine gun stood ready in each helicopter to lay down covering fire if the landing was opposed.

Helicopters were used to land troops in combat for the first time on a large scale during the Suez conflict. This painting by Admiralty artist William Herbert Lane shows Royal Marines landing from the carriers *Ocean* and *Theseus* near the de Lesseps statue at Port Saïd. The senior British commanders at Suez were too conservative to properly exploit the capabilities available with helicopter and parachute forces. (Royal Navy)

At three-minute intervals the helicopters came down to hover about a foot above the ground and the Marines jumped clear amid clouds of dust created by the whirling rotor blades. As soon as the passengers were clear, the helicopters pulled away to return to the carriers for another "stick" of troops or cargo. These 22 helicopters landed 100 men in history's first "vertical assault" wave. One Marine was wounded as he landed and was flown back to the carrier. He reached the ship's sick bay just 19 minutes after he had initially left from the flight deck.

In all, 415 Marines and 23 tons of ammunition and equipment were landed in 89 minutes. Only one helicopter was lost during the operation: a Whirlwind from the *Theseus* ran out of fuel and plummeted into the sea near the carrier. A launch from the ship quickly rescued the pilot and three wounded men he was carrying. Marine casualties in the helicopter landings were light. However, in a tragic mistake, one carrier-based Wyvern fired into a concentration of these Marines, killing one and wounding almost a score. The error was made because the carrier pilots and the Joint Fire Support Committee embarked in a ship used different maps; the pilot believed that he was being directed by a fire support team with the troops. The total Marine casualties in the Port Saïd landings were 9 killed and 60 wounded.

Brian Cull, in his excellent *Wings Over Suez*, recorded the British and French carrier operations during the campaign. The carrier force flew several hundred sorties per day. Initially the strike sorties were supplemented by close air support for Marines and paratroopers, photo reconnaissance (by Sea Hawks), combat air patrol, anti-submarine searches, and anti-ship sweeps.

The British helicopter carrier *Theseus* approaches Port Saïd after the city had been captured by Anglo-French forces. On her forward deck are Whirlwind helicopters. HMS *Ocean* and *Theseus* were the first of several dedicated British helicopter assault or "commando" carriers. (Royal Navy)

The initial strikes were flown by turbojet aircraft—Sea Hawks and Sea Venoms—from the British carriers. As there was virtually no air opposition, the French Corsairs and British Wyverns soon ranged over Egypt with bombs and rockets.

And, a Skyraider AEW.1 from HMS *Albion* was pressed into service as a "beer transport." British paratroopers who had landed at Gamil signaled a Skyraider from the No. 849 Squadron flight embarked in the ship that the local water supply was contaminated. In response, the Skyraider was loaded with 1,000 cans of beer—filling every available space, and with one crewmen left behind, the plane safely delivered its needed and precious cargo.

Egyptian MiG pilots lacked the training and experience to challenge British and French aircraft. Many planes were sent to Syria and Saudi Arabia for safety as Nasser sought to preserve his air force for future conflicts with Israel. Most were destroyed on the ground, an estimated 30 MiG-15s being destroyed and five "probables" by carrier aircraft as well as almost 100 other Egyptian planes.

In the air the British carriers lost two Sea Hawks, one Wyvern, and one Whirlwind to anti-aircraft fire. Their pilots were rescued. A second Wyvern, initially thought to have been downed by anti-aircraft fire, was in fact shot down by a MiG-17 *flown by a Soviet pilot*. The Wyvern from the *Eagle*, piloted by Lieutenant Dennis McCarthy, was in a flight of six aircraft attacking the Gamil Bridge, which carried the only road connecting Port Saïd with the interior, early on November 3. (What was thought to be a bridge was actually a causeway for much of its length, requiring 27 bombing sorties to render it impassable.)

As McCarthy was diving on the bridge his Wyvern was struck by what he believed to be anti-aircraft fire. "I got rid of the bombs as quickly as I could and levelled out, heading out to sea. I lost about 200 knots coming out of the dive—it was like hitting a brick wall," he related.[9] Smoke filled the cockpit but he was able to fly his crippled plane some three miles out to sea before successfully ejecting. He inflated his raft and carrier-based Sea Hawks attacked Egyptian gun batteries that fired on McCarthy. Some 75 minutes later he was rescued by a Whirlwind from the *Eagle*.

McCarthy was shot down by one of two MiG-17s on patrol north of Suez. His assailant was Sergey Anatolievich Sincov, a Soviet advisor to the Egyptian Air Force.

The British also suffered the loss of a second Whirlwind that came down at sea. Its pilot and passengers were rescued. Thus, carrier air losses totaled six plus several damaged.

The French carriers suffered one Corsair shot down by anti-aircraft fire, with the pilot being captured and subsequently murdered, and a second plane lost operationally.[10]

Total aircrew losses were one FAA pilot (killed in an accident) and one French Navy pilot. In addition to several deck crashes on the carriers, a Sea Venom aboard the *Eagle* accidentally discharged about 30 rounds of 20-mm ammunition in the hangar; one sailor was killed. (The RAF also lost two aircraft, one to enemy fire and one operationally with a total of five fatalities. Including Army casualties, the total British losses in the six-day campaign was 23 killed; the French dead numbered ten.)

The Egyptian casualties in men as well as equipment were severe, with at least 650 killed and 900 seriously wounded in just the landings at Port Saïd.

The British and French ground forces progressed rapidly and only the cease-fire demanded by the United Nations halted them at midnight of November 6–7. The canal zone was neither captured nor occupied by

Anglo-French forces. The Anglo-French ground war had lasted less than two days. From October 31, when the go-ahead for Operation Musketeer was ordered, until the parachute drop on November 5, the war was fought entirely in the air. Air superiority was won in little more than a day, but neither this war, nor any war, could be won only in the air.

Anglo-French paratroopers and helicopter-landed Royal Marines could have reached Port Saïd on November 3 or 4; British and French seaborne forces could have reached there on November 5. The availability of 143 fighters and bombers from the Allied carriers just over the horizon could have provided the paratroops and Marines with sufficient close air support to ward off Egyptian counterattacks. But the Allies, especially the British, hesitated and the opportunity to establish Anglo-French control of the canal was lost.

The ill-timed and ill-fated Suez campaign again confirmed the role of aircraft carriers in "limited war" and proved the effectiveness of angled-deck carriers (*Albion*, *Bulwark*, *Eagle*) and of helicopter carriers (*Ocean*, *Theseus*). The carriers maintained an excellent sortie rate with a minimum of accidents. Significantly, the Suez debacle led the British government to establish forces capable of rapid intervention in peacetime emergencies in an effort to prevent even limited war. The backbone of these forces would be strike carriers and helicopter carriers.

A Wyvern strike aircraft—its "invasion stripes" removed—sits on a lift aboard HMS *Eagle* in 1957 while a Dragonfly helicopter prepares to land aboard the carrier. Note the contra-rotating propellers of the Wyvern. The Dragonfly, developed by Sikorsky as the S-51/HO3S, was built by Westland, which subsequently produced most FAA helicopters. (Royal Navy)

10 THE SUPER CARRIERS

The first U.S. super carrier to join the fleet was the USS *Forrestal*. Shown here at sea in 1956, she has AD Skyraiders, F2H Banshees, and FJ Furies parked on the forward. Five Savages from heavy attack squadron VAH-7 are on her flight deck. There is a TACAN—Tactical Air Navigation—"pot" atop the foremast; it provided navigation range and bearing data for airborne aircraft. (U.S. Navy)

The USS *Forrestal*—the first U.S. "super carrier"— was commissioned on October 1, 1955. The ship was the world's first aircraft carrier laid down after World War II to be completed and was the largest aircraft carrier built up to that time except for the short-lived Japanese *Shinano*. Significantly, the *Forrestal* was the world's first aircraft carrier built specifically to operate jet-propelled aircraft.

The *Forrestal* had standard displacement of 60,000 tons, was 76,600 tons full load, had an overall length of 1,039 feet, and an extreme hull width of 129$\frac{1}{3}$ feet with a flight deck width of 252 feet. She was too wide to transit the Panama Canal or to enter all but a few of the world's drydocks. This giant flattop was propelled by an eight-boiler, steam-turbine plant capable of driving her at 33 knots.

During construction the *Forrestal* was extensively modified. The original design was based largely on the aborted *United States*. Initial plans for a telescoping bridge were changed to include a neat, squared-off island structure with bridges and funnel, with a mast that hinged down across the flight deck to permit passage under the Brooklyn Bridge en route to the New York Naval Shipyard.[1] Other changes provided an angled landing deck of 10.5 degrees and four steam catapults, both recent British innovations. The catapults—two on the forward flight deck and two on the port-side angled deck—were twice the number installed on previous carrier flight decks (although the three *Midway*-class ships received a third "cat" during their modernizations in the late 1950s). The four steam catapults would permit the *Forrestal* to launch up to eight aircraft every 60 seconds. The high fuel consumption of jet aircraft placed a limit on how many fighters could be kept airborne on combat air patrol, thus there was a requirement to launch up to 32 fighters in four minutes to repel attacking aircraft. The *Forrestal*'s four elevators—one more than in previous carriers—were all deck-edge lifts, three to starboard and one to port, at the forward end of the angled deck. The elevators connected the flight and hangar decks, the latter having a 25-foot overhead compared to the 17½-foot hangar clearances of the *Midway* and *Essex* classes. The *Forrestal*'s size and characteristics would enable the ship to operate up to 100 contemporary jet aircraft (or, as an academic comparison, almost 200 World War II–era carrier aircraft).

Other examples of the increased capabilities available with the *Forrestal* are evident in a comparison with a modernized *Essex*-class carrier:

	MOD. *ESSEX*	*FORRESTAL*	*FORRESTAL* ADVANTAGE
Ship fuel (gallons)	1.5 million	2.5 million	70%
Aviation fuel (gallons)	440,000	1.3 million	300%
Aviation ordnance	650 tons	1,650 tons	154%
Nuclear weapons	130 tons	150 tons	15%

In air operations the *Forrestal*'s design, size, and facilities contributed to rapid aircraft turn-around and the reduction of aircraft accident rates by approximately one-half compared to *Essex*-class carriers. Studies showed that by virtue of her size and design features (e.g., an enclosed, "hurricane" bow), the *Forrestal* could provide a stable base for air operations about 96 percent of the year (345 days) in the adverse sea conditions of the Norwegian Sea and Formosa Strait, as

The *Forrestal*, the first of the super carrier, under construction at Newport News, Virginia. Her deck has a squared-off appearance prior to having the angled-deck markings painted on. The two forward catapults and two waist catapults (opposite the island) are visible, as are the four deck-edge elevators. Eight rapid-fire 5-inch/54-caliber guns are provided, two on each quarter. The forward guns were removed in the 1960s to improve operations in heavy weather. (Newport News Shipbuilding)

compared with 60 percent (220 days) estimated for an *Essex*-class ship. Secretary of the Navy Charles S. Thomas summed up these advantages when speaking at the *Forrestal*'s commissioning; he declared that the carrier "encompasses the greatest amount of the most varied equipment, machinery and lethal weapons ever assembled in one place in man's tumultuous history. . . . she is a dream come true."

The *Forrestal* was especially a dream come true for the Chief of Naval Operations, Admiral Arleigh A. Burke, who had taken that top Navy post six weeks before the carrier was commissioned. A nonaviator, Burke had won fame and his nickname "31-knot Burke" as a destroyer commander in World War II. He served as chief of staff for the Fast Carrier Task Force under Vice Admiral Marc A. Mitscher from March 1944 until late July 1945. As a captain, Burke had been the working-level boss of the "admiral's revolt" in response to the cancellation of the carrier *United States* in 1949. For planning the Navy's attack in the ensuing B-36 investigation, Burke was removed from the flag-officer promotion list by President Harry S. Truman. He subsequently was again selected and approved for flag rank in 1950.[2]

The Korean War and the fear of other Soviet-inspired regional conflicts caused a rehabilitation of the aircraft carrier. When the *Forrestal*'s commission pennant was broken out on October 1, 1955, three sister ships were already under construction: the *Saratoga* (CVA 60), which had been laid down in December 1952, just five months after the *Forrestal*; the *Ranger* (CVA 61), laid down in August 1954; and the *Independence* (CVA 62), laid down in July 1955. The ships were generally similar except that the *Saratoga* and later ships had 1,200-pound-pressure boilers compared to the 600-pound boilers in the *Forrestal*; as a result, the later ships had a higher speed (34 knots) and efficiency, although the *Saratoga* was plagued with engineering problems throughout her career.

A fifth ship of this class had been authorized, and there was talk of "at least" seven additional ships to provide a total of 12 super carriers (for an overall total of 15 modern attack carriers—the 12 *Forrestal*s and 3 *Midway*s). And, there was talk of some of the later *Forrestal*-class ships being propelled by nuclear energy. Under the direction of then-Captain Hyman G. Rickover, the U.S. Navy in August 1951 began studies of nuclear propulsion for surface ships. The Large Ship Reactor (LSR) project was authorized in September 1954, marking the formal start of a large nuclear power plant for large surface warships. (The world's first nuclear-propelled ship, the U.S. submarine *Nautilus*, went to sea in January 1955.)

New Fighters and Missiles

As the *Forrestal* joined the fleet newer and better carrier-based aircraft were entering service. F2H Banshees and F9F Panthers filled most carrier fighter squadrons at the end of the Korean War, with the nuclear-capable F9F-6 Cougar, F7U-3 Cutlass, and later FJ-4B Fury joining the fleet. Composite squadrons (VC) provided detachments of night fighters to carriers—mostly the F2H-4 and the fast-disappearing F4U-5N. In 1954 the Navy designated 16 fighter squadrons—one per carrier—as night and all-weather squadrons, both for the fighter and nuclear strike roles. Most of these squadrons were assigned Banshees with one squadron flying F3D-2 Skyknights.

By late 1954 the Navy had 16 carrier air groups. Their standard composition was four fighter squadrons and one attack squadron, the latter flying the ubiquitous AD Skyraider. Two of the air groups had only three fighter squadrons with two AD squadrons, while another air group had three *fighter* squadrons flying Skyraiders—VF-54, VF-92, and VF-194. Thus there were 62 fighter squadrons in the fleet in December 1954:

SQUADRONS	AIRCRAFT
1	F3D-2 Skyknight
11	F9F-2/5 Panther
23	F9F-6/8 Cougar
16	F2H-2/3 Banshee
1	F2H-4 Banshee
3	FJ-3 Fury
4	F7U-3 Cutlass
3	AD-4/5/6 Skyraider

The F9F-6 Cougar model of the single-jet F9F Panther introduced the swept-wing configuration to operational Navy fighters. The Cougar first flew on September 20, 1951. Used as a day fighter as well as light attack and photo-reconnaissance aircraft, the Cougar series reached the F9F-8 version, which had a maximum speed of 714 m.p.h. Both the Banshee and Cougar had four 20-mm cannon. The latter could also carry up to 4,000 pounds of bombs and rockets. (Camera-configured F2H-2P Banshees also flew from carriers in this period.)

The first U.S. Navy aircraft to deploy overseas with the heat-seeking Sidewinder missile was the F9F-8 Cougar in VA-46 aboard the USS *Randolph* in July 1956. The name Cougar was applied to the swept-wing models of the F9F. The aircraft shown here is carrying four Sidewinders and two 150-gallon drop tanks. The F9F-8B (later AF-9J) could carry a Mk 12 nuclear weapon and one drop tank. (U.S. Navy)

The most radical aircraft to reach the fleet in this period was the Chance-Vought F7U Cutlass, a tailless, single-seat aircraft powered by two jet engines. The plane's wings were swept back 38 degrees, there were no horizontal tail surfaces, and instead of a conventional rudder it had twin rudders halfway between the fuselage and wingtips. On deck the Cutlass sat at a nine-degree angle, which increased to 15 degrees just before the wheels left the deck during takeoff. The first XF7U-1 had flown as early as September 1948, but the plane was underpowered and the production of improved engines was delayed. The plane's radical design also encountered previously unknown aerodynamic problems (the discovery of which allowed technology for later aircraft of radical design to advance).

The F7U-3 Cutlass—powered by twin turbojets—could reach speeds exceeding Mach 1, the speed of sound. The J46 engines provided for single-engine flight for the large, 31,642-pound fighter, even in the critical period after a wave off during a carrier approach. (This was accomplished with the working engine in afterburner, i.e., the auxiliary combustion chamber that provided extra thrust for limited periods.) The F7U-3P photo-reconnaissance and F7U-3M missile-armed variants followed, while the "straight" F7U-3 was configured to carry a nuclear weapon.

Unfortunately, the Cutlass was underpowered, a difficult aircraft to fly, and not popular with pilots, who frequently referred to it as the "Gutless." Still, the plane was an important addition to the Navy's arsenal, especially in the missile version. In March 1956 squadron

VA-83 with F7U-3M Cutlasses, each equipped to carry four Sparrow radar-guided missiles, deployed to the Mediterranean aboard the carrier *Intrepid*. This was the first overseas operation of a Navy missile-armed squadron.[3] Operational accidents were frequent, and the Cutlasses were withdrawn from fleet squadrons in 1957, only three years after the last deliveries.

The first post–Korean War fighter deliveries were improved, swept-wing FJ-2 models of the Fury. In a hasty search for a readily available swept-wing fighter to counter the MiG-15 threat, the Navy sought a navalized version of the Air Force's F-86 Sabre. Ironically, the Sabre (as the XP-86) stemmed from North American Aviation's design for the Navy FJ-1 (see page 24). The prototype XFJ-2 was identical to the swept-wing F-86E except it had an arresting hook, four 20-mm cannon (the Air Force was using six .50-caliber machine guns), and the Navy's dark blue finish. Production FJ-2s, fitted with folding wings, reached the fleet in January 1954. The FJ-3 Fury appeared in time to be the first aircraft to operate from the *Forrestal*. The FJ-3 variant featured a new wing, fuselage, rudder, engine, and landing gear. With six underwing carrying points, instead of two as in the previous model, the FJ-3 added a new dimension to Fury operations, making an excellent platform for the Sidewinder air-to-air missile. By the end of 1956 23 Navy and Marine fighter squadrons flew the FJ-3 and FJ-3M Fury.

The FJ-4 Fury was a complete redesign—in essence an entirely new aircraft, with new fuselage, wing, and control surfaces. It had six wing store points, additional armor, a low-altitude bombing system, and an improved control system for high speed flight at low altitude. North American produced 222 FJ-4B variants through May 1958.

Ten carrier-based Navy attack squadrons flew the FJ-4B Fury, which could lift 4,000 pounds of conventional bombs, or six Sidewinder air-to-air missiles, or five 540-pound Bullpup air-to-surface missiles. The Bullpup was a rocket-propelled, radio-controlled bomb, which accelerated to Mach 2 speeds before striking a target more than three miles from the bomb release point. The initial Bullpup warhead was a 250-pound bomb (performance and payload were improved in later models). The Bullpup missiles were handled as "rounds of ammunition" and required no checks or tests between leaving the factory and loading on an aircraft. The first overseas deployment of Bullpup missiles was with an FJ-4B squadron on the carrier *Lexington*, which joined the Seventh Fleet in the Western Pacific in April 1959. Three Marine attack squadrons flew the FJ-4B; the only other Navy fighter to reach this popularity in attack units was the F9F-8B Cougar, which also served in ten carrier attack squadrons during this period.

And, the FJ-4B variant was the only Fury that could carry a single nuclear bomb—the Mk 7, Mk 12, B28, or B43.

Simultaneous with the introduction of the improved Cougars and Furies in the fleet, the F4D Skyray and F3H Demon all-weather fighters became operational. The F4D—invariably known as the "Ford"—was conceived as a high-performance interceptor with endurance sacrificed for rate of climb and speed. This approach was meant to provide a counter to the threat of high-altitude bomber attacks on carriers that preoccupied many naval planners in the postwar years. However, the F4D was modified during the design to provide a more-balanced capability. The airplane was a single-seat, single-engine design and the Navy's first delta-wing fighter. The first XF4D-1 flew in January 1951. After engine changes and modifications, the Skyray began capturing flight records: On October 3, 1953, an F4D-1 set an official world speed record when it streaked over a three-kilometer course at 752.943 m.p.h. This was the first time that a world speed record was captured by a carrier aircraft. On February 23, 1955, an F4D set an unofficial climb record, reaching 10,000 feet in 56 seconds from a standing start. (This beat out two previous Navy climb records to 10,000 feet set within the month—by an FJ-3 Fury in 73.2 seconds

and an F3H-1N Demon in 71 seconds.) This outstanding performance earned the F4D Skyray a place in Navy and Marine all-weather fighter squadrons with Navy squadron VF(AW)-3 based ashore, at San Diego, being assigned to the North American Air Defense Command, normally composed only of Air Force–manned fighter squadrons.

An improved F4D-2N, later redesignated XF5D-1 Skylancer, was planned, but production was cancelled because of competing high-performance aircraft. A prototype Skylancer reached 1,098 m.p.h. (Mach 1.5) at 10,000 feet and surpassed the Skyray in rate of climb.

The F3H Demon, developed parallel to the Skyray, was intended as a platform for the radar-guided Sparrow air-to-air missile and its AN/APG-51B search and missile guidance radar. The Demon was a swept-wing, single-engine, single-seat fighter that first flew in August 1951. The early models were underpowered, and

One of the most radical aircraft designs was the tailless F7U Cutlass. The Chance Vought F7U-1, which could reach 650 m.p.h., was delivered to training units in early 1952; the production F7U-3 did not reach the Fleet until December 1954. The -3 could reach 700 m.p.h at 40,000 feet and could climb 13,000 feet per minute. Above an F7U-1 assigned to flight test is catapulted from the carrier *Midway* in 1951; below an F7U rides a carrier elevator with its wings folded. (U.S. Navy)

U.S. Navy efforts to quickly develop a swept-wing fighter during the Korean War led to the swept-wing FJ-2 Fury, shown at left in flight next to a straight-wing FJ-1. The North American FJ-2 had a maximum speed of 650 m.p.h. at sea level with a ceiling of 50,000 feet. The FJ-4 was essentially a new, enlarged aircraft, intended specifically to deliver nuclear weapons. At right an FJ-4B (later AF-1E) is carrying three Bullpup air-to-surface missiles, a missile guidance pod, and two 150-gallon drop tanks. (U.S. Navy)

after accidents destroyed six aircraft, the first production models (F3H-1N) were permanently grounded. Of this first batch of 56 aircraft, 29 were modified to F3H-2 standards with installation of the J71 engine. Then production of the most successful Demon, the F3H-3, began. After this inauspicious start the first Demons were delivered to the fleet in March 1956, and the fighter quickly established a fine reputation.

As the Demons were coming off the production line, the Navy announced that all fighters in production would be fitted for in-flight refueling from other carrier aircraft. In-flight fueling allowed for the extension of the range of strike aircraft, the lengthening of combat air patrols, and the refueling of aircraft returning from a mission while clogged flight decks were cleared or other aircraft were landed or launched. The British firm Flight Refueling, Ltd., developed the refueling system adopted for U.S. naval aircraft, in which a tanker aircraft would unreel a flexible, cone-tipped hose so that the pilot of the receiving aircraft could bring his plane below and aft of the tanker, adjust his speed to that of the tanker, and then jockey his plane's probe into the trailing drogue. The probe and drogue would automatically interlock and the fuel would be transferred.

Two other carrier-based fighters that provide an interesting contrast entered U.S. service in the late 1950s: F11F Tiger production ran to only 201 aircraft

while 1,219 F8U Crusaders were built for the U.S. Navy and Marine Corps, plus 42 for the French Navy.

The F11F Tiger had begun life as the F9F-9 but was a new plane rather than an improvement of the F9F Panther/Cougar series. The Tiger was the first airplane to incorporate the so-called area rule concept to reduce drag. This resulted in the plane's fuselage being "pinched in" or indented aft of the wing, so that it somewhat resembled a Coca-Cola bottle. The Tiger's

The Douglas F4D-1 Skyray—this one from VF-213—provided the U.S. Navy with one of the most advanced fighter-interceptors of the 1950s. The F4D-1 could fly more than 700 m.p.h. (Mach 1) above 10,000 feet. Armament normally consisted of four 20-mm cannon in the wings and up to 7,000 pounds of external stores. The Skyray (later F-6A) could carry six fiberglass pods with a total of 42 2.75-inch unguided rockets, four pods with 76 2.75-inch rockets, four Sidewinder missiles, or a mix of Sidewinders and two 300-gallon drop tanks. (U.S. Navy)

swept-back wings were exceptionally thin (so much so that part of the plane's fuel was carried in the rudder structure rather than internal wing tanks).

In July 1954 the first F11F took to the air, and the aircraft soon achieved a maximum speed of 954 m.p.h. at sea level (Mach 0.99) and 730 m.p.h. at 35,000 feet (Mach 1.1), making it the first Navy fighter to exceed the speed of sound in level flight. F11F Tigers first entered Attack Squadron 156 in March 1957, seemingly symbolic of the plane's failure to be accepted as a primary fighter aircraft. Most of the Tigers went to training units, and the few that operated in fleet (carrier) squadrons were soon replaced by other aircraft, notably the F8U Crusader.[4] The F11F's lack of versatility and limited combat radius, coupled with the superiority of the F8U Crusader, are the main reasons for the former aircraft's rapid demise.

The LTV F8U Crusader was developed in response to the Navy's requirement for a supersonic fighter.[5] Faced with the problem of creating a Mach 1+ fighter with good carrier-landing characteristics, LTV designers gave the aircraft a wing that raised up seven degrees during landing and takeoff, thus providing the angle of attack necessary for 130-m.p.h. landing speeds while still permitting the fuselage to be in a near-horizontal attitude for maximum pilot visibility. The first of the single-engine, single-place Crusaders flew in March 1955 (eight months after the first F11F Tiger flight), and Crusaders began reaching the fleet in March 1957 (the same month as the F11F).

The prototype XF8U-1 Crusader exceeded Mach 1 on its first flight; a production F8U-1 set an international speed record of 1,015.428 m.p.h. In June 1957 two Crusaders launched from the carrier *Bon Homme Richard* off the California coast and, after refueling in flight, landed aboard the carrier *Saratoga* off the Florida coast, having spanned the continent in three and a half hours. A month later Marine Major John H. Glenn piloted an F8U-1P reconnaissance variant from California to New York in three hours, 28 minutes, 50 seconds for an average speed of 723.517 m.p.h., a cross-continent record. On three occasions Glenn had to come down from his optimum altitude and slow to 350 m.p.h. to fuel from AJ-2 Savage tankers, but he still maintained an average speed of Mach 1.1 for the flight.[6]

When the Crusader joined the fleet in early 1957, it was armed with four 20-mm cannon, a Sidewinder missile rail on each side of the fuselage, and a rocket pack that opened from the bottom of the fuselage to fire 32 12.75-inch, unguided air-to-air rockets. In later models the fuselage rocket pack was deleted, the missile rails were modified to each launch two Sidewinder air-to-air missiles, and four underwing attachment points were added to carry up to four 1,000-pound bombs or two Bullpup air-to-surface missiles. By 1960 more than half of the Navy's 30 carrier-based fighter squadrons and most of the Marine Corps fighter squadrons flew the Crusader as did the French Navy. F8U-1P Photo Crusaders served in two- and three-plane detachments on all Navy attack carriers and in the three Marine reconnaissance squadrons.

Complementing these new, missile-armed fighters aboard U.S. carriers was a new generation of attack planes. The A3D Skywarrior and the A4D Skyhawk introduced jet propulsion to carrier attack planes. Design of the large Skywarrior had begun in the late 1940s to provide the fleet with a plane capable of launching from large carriers to deliver nuclear weapons over

The McDonnell F3H-2 Demon was used widely as a carrier-based, all-weather fighter. With a maximum speed of 721 m.p.h. at sea level (Mach 0.95) and 648 m.p.h. at 35,000 feet (Mach 0.98), an initial climb of about 12,000 feet per minute, and a ceiling of 48,000 feet, the Demon was superior to many first-line, land-based fighters. Armament consisted of four 20-mm cannon under the cockpit and four heat-seeking Sidewinders or four radar-guided Sparrow missiles. Here a Demon is brought to a halt by an arresting wire aboard the carrier *Franklin D. Roosevelt*. (U.S. Navy)

distances and at speeds comparable to land-based jet bombers. The solution came in the form of the largest carrier aircraft yet developed: the Bureau of Aeronautics (BuAer) had specified a gross weight of about 100,000 pounds. Ed Heinemann, the chief engineer at Douglas Aircraft Company, "whittled away" at a design for the aircraft until a 68,000-pound design, including a 10,000-pound bomb load, was achieved.[7]

When Heinemann showed his preliminary design to Captain Joseph N. Murphy at BuAer the officer exploded. Heinemann recalled,

> "Oh no!" he growled, shaking his head, "not you."
>
> I was wide-eyed, stunned.
>
> "I thought you were an honest engineer, Ed," he said pointedly. "You know good and well you can't produce an airplane of that capability for that weight!"
>
> Not knowing what to say I remained silent, anger building in my own mind.
>
> "I hoped you wouldn't lie about the weight, just to get the business," he said.
>
> Those were fighting words and I was instantly mad as hell. In defense of Murphy I'm sure he was as frustrated about the new bomber and all its ramifications as many of us in the industry were. But if nothing else in my lifetime dealings with the navy, or anyone else for that matter, I have been honest. I was offended but didn't feel that a rejoinder would serve any purpose.
>
> "OK, Murph," I said, gathering up the drawings, "if you're not interested I won't bother you." He knew I wasn't kidding. I could see him hesitating in thought.
>
> "Just leave the drawings here," he muttered hurriedly, "and I'll have them checked over anyway."[8]

The first XA3D-1 flew in October 1952, and production aircraft reached operating squadrons in March 1956. An A3D-2 with improved equipment soon replaced the earlier variants on the production line, and a limited number of photo-reconnaissance (A3D-2P) and electronic countermeasures/reconnaissance (A3D-2Q) aircraft were also produced for carrier operation.

In service the A3D Skywarrior had a normal gross weight of approximately 70,000 pounds (84,000 pounds for the tanker version), a wingspan of 72½ feet, and a length of 73½ feet. The plane's high wings were swept back 36 degrees and folded for carrier storage, as did the plane's 22¾-foot tail fin. Twin jet engines in pods under the wings pushed the Skywarrior to 650 m.p.h. at 10,000 feet (Mach 0.9) and to a ceiling of 41,000 feet.

Seven- to ten-plane A3D heavy attack squadrons (VAH) went aboard carriers of the *Midway* and *Forrestal* classes, providing the fleet with an all-weather, day-night nuclear strike capability. With these larger carriers operating mainly in the Atlantic-Mediterranean areas in the later 1950s, the smaller *Essex*-class attack carriers in the Western Pacific were assigned four-plane A3D detachments, giving the Seventh Fleet a modest heavy attack capability.

The Skywarrior performed well and was held in high regard by Navy fliers. More than ten years after the first fleet deliveries, the carrier-based Skywarrior

The Grumman F11F Tiger initiated the so-called area rule design concept to increase performance; the "pinched-in" fuselage is evident in this 1956 view of an F11F-1. The aircraft could exceed the speed of sound in level flight and one Tiger, fitted with an experimental engine, reached a speed of 1,220 m.p.h. and established an altitude record of 76,939 feet. Normal F11F ceiling was 40,000 feet; the plane could climb some 18,000 feet per minute. Standard armament was four 20-mm cannon and attachment points for Sidewinder missiles, drop tanks, or bombs. (U.S. Navy)

An AJ-2 from heavy attack squadron VAH-16 rigged as an aerial tanker refuels a missile-armed F3H-2M Demon from VF-64 armed with Sidewinder and Sparrow missiles. The heavy attack aircraft—Savages and later Skywarriors and Vikings—made excellent tankers because of their large bomb bays that could be fitted with fuel tanks. Note the Demon's retractable fuel probe. In-flight refueling became a necessity in the jet age because of the high fuel consumption of jet aircraft. (U.S. Navy)

and the land-based Air Force EB-66 Destroyer, derived from the A3D, were performing outstanding service in the air war over North Vietnam in a variety of roles. The last of the 282 A3Ds built for the Navy—an electronics intelligence variant—left a fleet squadron in 1991.[9]

As Skywarriors joined the fleet, they replaced the piston-jet AJ Savages in the heavy attack role. A few Savages were held in the fleet into the early 1960s as aerial tankers and photo planes (the latter AJ-2P). A follow-on A2J Savage, fitted with two turboprop engines turning three-blade, contrarotating propellers, failed because of mechanical troubles with the power transmission. (This same problem killed the follow-on to the AD Skyraider, the turboprop A2D Skyshark.) Also, the development of the pure-jet A3D Skywarrior and the availability of improved catapults for launching all-jet bombers foredoomed the A2J Savage.

The Douglas A4D Skyhawk was in many respects the most remarkable nuclear strike aircraft produced by any nation. In 1950, soon after the Korean War began, the U.S. Navy issued a requirement for an attack plane to deliver nuclear weapons and to perform non-

nuclear interdiction missions; in the latter role it would serve as a possible replacement for the AD Skyraider. At the time the Navy was concerned with the rising size, weight, complexity, maintenance requirements, and cost of aircraft, reflected by the new jet-propelled fighters and the A3D Skywarrior. And, the development of smaller nuclear weapons suitable for fighter-type aircraft had been achieved. The Mk 7 nuclear bomb, the first nuclear weapon intended for carrying externally by fighter/attack aircraft, became available in January 1952 (see page 27). The Mk 7 was the basis for the Betty nuclear depth bomb (1955–1963) and the BOAR (Bureau of Ordnance Atomic Rocket), an unguided, rocket-boosted, nuclear bomb (1956–1963).[10]

In January 1952 aircraft-design genius Ed Heinemann briefed Navy officials on his approach to designing an ultra-lightweight jet interceptor having a gross takeoff weight of about 8,000 pounds. Heinemann was asked if he could apply his methodology to an attack aircraft that, with a nuclear bomb, would gross no more than 12,000 pounds. Employing new concepts in both design and materials, Heinemann's Douglas design team set to work to meet the Navy's specifications,

The most advanced shipboard fighter developed in the 1950s was the F8U Crusader produced by LTV (Ling-Temco-Vought, formerly Chance Vought). These F8U-2NE Crusaders from VF-84 are being launched from the carrier *Independence*. Their wings are pivoted up for takeoff; in flight they will lower flush with the fuselage. The final production Crusader was the F8U-2NE (later F-8E), rated at 1,130 m.p.h. at 35,000 feet (Mach 1.7) and 785 m.p.h at sea level (Mach 1.04). Its time to 57,000 feet was 6½ minutes; that was 1,000 feet less than the plane's operational ceiling. (U.S. Navy)

which included a speed of 500 m.p.h., a combat radius of at least 460 miles, and the ability to carry 1,000-pound bombs. These difficult requirements were met or bettered by Heinemann's team. His efforts led to the signing in June 1952 of a Navy-Douglas contract to provide a plane with an empty weight of 8,136 pounds and a gross weight of 15,000 pounds. Nick-named the "scooter" and "Heinemann's hot rod," the A4D-1 weighed in at 8,400 pounds empty but could lift off at 22,000 pounds including more than 5,000 pounds of weapons. This was a net weight–to–liftoff ratio of 1 to 2.6 compared to the contract's require-ment for 1 to 1.8; the effort to reverse the trend toward larger airframes, increased complexity, and higher costs had been successful.

The single-engine, single-seat YA4D-1 first flew on June 22, 1954, just two years and one day after the contract was signed, almost a record in jet aircraft de-velopment. With a span of 27½ feet, the Skyhawk's wings were small enough that they did not have to fold; it was the first U.S. carrier plane without folding wings since the SBD Dauntless, which had a span of 41½ feet. The diminutive Skyhawk was 39 feet long. In 1955 an A4D-2 set a world speed record of 695.163 m.p.h. over a 500-kilometer course.

In September 1956 fleet squadrons began receiv-ing A4Ds to provide the carrier striking forces with large numbers of aircraft capable of delivering a nuclear weapon. In an effort to hold down weight and com-plexity, the early A4D Skyhawks relied largely on highly

Edward Heinemann

refueling probe was also added to provide in-flight refueling from tanker aircraft or other attack planes carrying "buddy" stores.

The A4D Skyhawk had a remarkable production run, with the last of 3,170 aircraft being delivered in 1979.[11] The Skyhawk served in U.S. Navy and Marine combat squadrons until 1992, and the two-seat TA-4J training and utility variant was in service until 2003.

With the availability of the A4D Skyhawks to deliver nuclear weapons and the relatively limited attack capability of jet-propelled fighters (some being fitted to deliver small nuclear weapons), in the mid-1950s the Navy revised the composition of its carrier

trained pilots for navigation and bomb aiming. The Skyhawk had virtually no electronic or navigation equipment. For routine flights over land areas where electronic instruments were required, the aircraft carried a bomb-shaped electronics pod. For the attack role it had three bomb attachment points, which could hold 5,000 pounds of bombs, rockets, or fuel tanks. Finally, for self-defense and ground attack, there were two 20-mm cannon in the plane's wing roots.

Even before the first production A4D-1 was delivered, the improved A4D-2 was being flown, signaling the beginning of a development program that would see a succession of single- and two-seat designs roll off production lines. Modifications saw the Skyhawk's gross weight increase marginally but gave the aircraft a speed of 685 m.p.h. at sea level (Mach 0.9), electronics, a navigation system, and the ability to lift a greater variety of ordnance including Bullpup missiles, air-to-air missiles and rockets, "iron bombs," and nuclear weapons for a total of 8,200 pounds. A fixed

This Douglas A-4E (formerly A4D-5) from attack squadron VA-212, about to be catapulted from the carrier *Bon Homme Richard* in 1967, shows the trim lines and small size of the Skyhawk. Despite its versatility and effectiveness as a conventional strike aircraft, from the mid-1950s into the 1960s the Skyhawk was considered primarily a nuclear strike aircraft by the U.S. Navy. Forward-deployed aircraft carriers—except those participating in the Vietnam War—usually had two and sometime more Skyhawks armed with nuclear weapons ready to launch in minutes, with their pilots briefed on Soviet or Chinese targets. (U.S. Navy)

The largest aircraft to regularly operate from carriers was the Douglas A3D Skywarrior, a 35-ton nuclear strike aircraft. The plane flew from modernized *Essex*-class carriers as well as from larger ships. The A3D's internal bomb bay could hold four 2,000-pound bombs, 12 1,000-pounders, 24 500-pounders, or a nuclear weapon. The plane was flown by a three-man crew—pilot, bombardier, and navigator-gunner. It was fitted with an elaborate navigation-bombing radar system, and had twin, radar-directed 20-mm guns in the tail. This A3D-2 (later A-3B) is from VAH-3. (U.S. Navy)

A pair of A4D-2 Skyhawks during an in-flight refueling exercise: the A4D at right carries a "buddy store" refueling pod and two 150-gallon drop tanks; the aircraft at left carries a nuclear bomb and two 150-gallon drop tanks. The A4D (later A-4) was the smallest aircraft to carry nuclear weapons. It was also an outstanding conventional attack aircraft. These Skyhawks are from test and evaluation squadron VX-5. (Courtesy Skyhawk Association)

air groups. Since 1942 the Navy had been replacing bombers with fighters on its strike carriers until—during the Korean War era—U.S. carriers had three or four fighter squadrons and one attack squadron (the latter flying AD Skyraiders). However, such fighters as the F6F Hellcat and F4U Corsair possessed excellent attack capabilities.

Because of the new fighters going to sea, which permitted many to be assigned to the attack role, and production of the A4D Skyhawk, the carrier air groups were reorganized. By the early 1960s they were composed of two fighter squadrons, one flying all-weather interceptors (F3H Demons or F4D Skyrays) and one with F8U Crusader day fighters; next, each carrier was provided with two and later three squadrons of jet light attack aircraft (FJ-4B Furies, F9F-8B Cougars, and A4D Skyhawks, with the last supplanting the others by the end of the decade). The larger *Midway* and *Forrestal* ships had a sixth squadron with AJ Savages (being phased out) or A3D Skywarriors to provide a long-range, all-weather strike capability. Thus, the air groups had a 2:3 or 2:4 ratio of fighter to attack aircraft.

Nuclear weapons were loaded in all attack carriers deploying overseas. When in the Western Pacific or Mediterranean, each attack carrier normally kept two light and two heavy strike aircraft fueled and armed with nuclear weapons, with their crews briefed and ready to carry out immediate strikes against specific Soviet or Chinese targets. These four aircraft were assigned to "prime" targets within range of the carrier's position at the time. These prime targets changed almost daily, based on the carrier's position. Similarly, target and route briefings for other pilots were changed as the carrier's position shifted.[12] (Still, during this period of wide availability of nuclear weapons to U.S. air forces, 90 percent of the aircraft ordnance stowage in attack carriers was devoted to conventional weapons.)

Following a trial launch of a Regulus I from the *Princeton* in December 1952, five modernized *Essex*-class ships were provided Regulus missiles in the 1950s: *Hancock, Lexington, Randolph, Shangri-La,* and *Ticonderoga.* In addition, the larger *Franklin D. Roosevelt* and *Saratoga* fired the missile. The Regulus was a pilotless jet-propelled aircraft, 53-feet long, and launched by catapult or a mobile launching platform. The Regulus could fly at almost the speed of sound to deliver a Mk 7 nuclear warhead on a target up to 500 miles from the ship. The missile could be guided by the launching ship, another ship or submarine, or an aircraft, enabling it to maneuver to avoid enemy radar and defenses and to strike moving targets. The Regulus was soon phased out of the carriers but was carried in U.S. submarines until 1965.

The improved, supersonic Regulus II was under development for use aboard cruisers and for 12 nuclear-propelled submarines. There were advocates of a much larger Regulus program. For example, George Fielding Eliot, then dean of American military correspondents, in 1958 published a small volume entitled *Victory Without War, 1958–1961*. The book, published by the semi-official U.S. Naval Institute, advocated the procurement of massive numbers of Regulus II missiles, whose range he wrote could be extended to 2,000 miles, to be placed aboard aircraft carriers:

Let us imagine 20 of these missiles grouped on a *Forrestal*-class carrier, ready to be fired from her four steam catapults—five missiles to each catapult. Each group of five missiles is programmed for a different target. The rate of fire can be as fast as one missile from each catapult every two minutes. . . .

The logistics of the Regulus system is not complicated. We can, during 1958, take three older carriers from the reserve fleet (the *Boxer*, *Franklin*, and *Bunker Hill*) and fit them as missile transports. These ships have the speed, fuel capacity, and sea-keeping qualities to accompany task forces in all weather conditions. Each missile

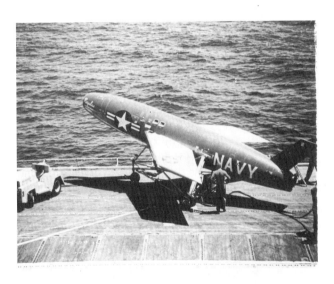 

Several U.S. aircraft carriers, cruisers, and submarines were provided an all-weather strike capability with the Regulus I cruise missile. Essentially an unmanned aircraft, the Chance Vought Regulus I had a near-sonic speed and could deliver a nuclear warhead (Mk 5, later W27) to targets some 500 miles from the launching ship. An improved, supersonic, 1,000-mile Regulus II was cancelled with the development of the longer-range Polaris fleet ballistic missile. (U.S. Navy)

The fleet oiler *Allagash* refuels the *Essex* and accompanying destroyers in the Mediterranean in 1958. The *Essex* demonstrated the mobility of attack carriers when she participated in the U.S. landings in Lebanon and then steamed halfway around the world to join the Seventh Fleet for operations in the Formosa (Taiwan) Strait. Two FJ Fury fighters, with wings folded, are on the *Essex*'s catapults; behind them, tail over the water, is an AJ Savage. (U.S. Navy)

transport could provide stowage for as many as 400 Regulus II missiles. Each [carrier] could operate from her flight deck a number of helicopters which could be used to deliver the missiles to the [attack] carriers as the tactical situation might require. . . .

A further growth factor of sea-based striking power might be gained by fitting the missile transports themselves with one or two steam catapults apiece, which would give them an attack capability of their own.[13]

In the 1950s and 1960s a detachment of three photo-reconnaissance planes (F8U-1P Crusaders) and usually detachments of airborne early warning and electronic countermeasures aircraft (four AD-5W Skyraiders and three AD-5Q Skyraiders, respectively) complemented each attack carrier's fighter and attack squadrons. Some Savages were also assigned to deploying carriers to serve as tankers for their fighter and attack aircraft. Two single-engine, six-place HUP helicopters were carried

on each attack carrier for rescue and utility work as was a twin-engine, 11-place TF Trader Carrier Onboard Delivery (COD) aircraft.

These 70-plus plane air groups and air task groups operated from 15 attack carriers. Fifteen was the "magic number" of attack carriers that the Navy was able to keep in service during most of the two decades after the Korean War. The number sometimes dropped to 14 and on occasion rose to 16 ships. The number 15 was predicated on maintaining two attack carriers with the Sixth Fleet in the Mediterranean and three with the Seventh Fleet in the Western Pacific. Each of the deployed carriers was normally rotated after six months overseas, thus two others were needed to meet overhaul, refit, training, transit, and other operational requirements.

The new, 60,000-ton super carrier *Saratoga* joined the fleet on April 14, 1956, and her sister ship *Ranger* ran up her commission pennant on August 10, 1957. As these new ships entered service, the *Essex*-class carriers least suited for operating modern aircraft were reclassified as anti-submarine warfare carriers to maintain 15 attack carriers in service. Thus by 1958 there were 15 attack carriers in commission (with the *Coral Sea* and *Oriskany* decommissioned for three-year modernizations and conversion to angled-deck configurations; these were the last U.S. carriers to be so modified). The 15 attack carriers in commission were:

CVA 9	*Essex*	Mediterranean
CVA 11	*Intrepid*	U.S. East Coast—operational
CVA 14	*Ticonderoga*	U.S. West Coast—undergoing repairs
CVA 15	*Randolph*	U.S. East Coast—operational
CVA 16	*Lexington*	U.S. West Coast—operational
CVA 19	*Hancock*	Western Pacific
CVA 20	*Bennington*	Eastern Pacific
CVA 31	*Bon Homme Richard*	U.S. West Coast—in overhaul
CVA 33	*Kearsarge*	U.S. West Coast—training
CVA 38	*Shangri-La*	Western Pacific
CVA 41	*Midway*	U.S. West Coast—operational
CVA 42	*F. D. Roosevelt*	Caribbean—training
CVA 59	*Forrestal*	U.S. East Coast—operational
CVA 60	*Saratoga*	Mediterranean Sea
CVA 61	*Ranger*	En route to Pacific via South America

The deployment of the large *Saratoga* and the smaller *Essex* in the Mediterranean was typical of the practice of assigning one large carrier (*Forrestal* or *Midway*) and one of the *Essex* class to the Sixth Fleet. However, the strength of the Seventh Fleet in the Western Pacific was at a low with only two *Essex*-class ships available. In February 1955 the *Midway* had joined the Seventh Fleet after steaming around the Cape of Good Hope from the Atlantic, marking the first time a "large" U.S. carrier had operated in the Pacific. Pending the arrival of the *Ranger* and the completion of the *Coral Sea* modernization (in early 1960), the *Midway* was the only large carrier available in the Pacific.

This was the U.S. Navy's attack carrier lineup on the morning of July 14, 1958, when the president of Lebanon handed the American ambassador in Beirut an urgent request for U.S. military assistance within 48 hours.

Operation Blue Bat

The Eastern Mediterranean had become a hot bed of unrest after Soviet-bloc arms began flowing to several Arab states in the Middle East. In April 1957 the U.S. Sixth Fleet operated in the Eastern Mediterranean as a show of force in support of the Jordanian king, who had just quelled a revolt by pro-Egyptian, communist-inspired elements in his army. Egypt and Syria merged into the short-lived United Arab Republic on February 11, 1958, presenting a major threat to adjacent Jordan and Iraq. In this explosive atmosphere, armed rebellion came to Lebanon in early May 1958, at which time that country's foreign minister suggested that Lebanon might request U.S. military intervention. The United States prepared to intervene, but the Lebanese situation soon improved, although unrest in the area continued. Then, early on July 14, Arab nationalists seized the Iraqi government in a bloody coup, killing the pro-Western king and prime minister.

The president of Lebanon became alarmed. Fearing a sweep of communist-inspired revolution throughout the Middle East, he asked the United States to send troops to Lebanon to preserve order. The Lebanese leader specifically requested American intervention within 48 hours on the mistaken intelligence—derived from newspapers—that most of the Sixth Fleet was off Spain and could not reach Lebanon sooner. He also requested British and French aid within 24 hours. The U.S. government responded immediately to help preserve the recognized Lebanese government, and the intervention was given the code name Blue Bat. (It was soon decided that only American troops would land in Lebanon; the British responded to a Jordanian appeal for aid with 2,000 airborne troops and French warships made a brief appearance off Beirut.)

Despite the smoldering fuse on the Middle East powder keg, the United States was ill prepared for rapid intervention in the area. Two U.S. Army battle groups (about 1,800 men each) were on alert at bases in Germany, but transport aircraft to lift only one battle group were available and even those transports were not ready for immediate operation. Further, the transports would have to fly a circuitous, 2,400-mile route, to avoid communist territory in reaching Adana, Turkey, the nearest Allied airfield to Beirut. U.S. Air Force fighters, light bombers, and reconnaissance aircraft that would support the U.S. landing were based in the United States and would have to fly across the Atlantic and Europe to reach Adana. And their movement would depend on the availability of tanker aircraft for in-flight refueling and cargo planes to carry their support equipment and ground crews. All of these air units would be held in readiness at Adana, 200 miles from Beirut, until the Lebanese capital's airport was secured either by airborne or seaborne assault forces.

Portions of the Sixth Fleet in the Mediterranean were the only U.S. forces capable of immediate intervention. On the morning of July 14 the carrier *Saratoga* and her screening ships were at Cannes, France, some 1,700 miles from Beirut; the attack carrier *Essex* was in Piraeus Bay off Athens, some 650 miles away; and the anti-submarine carrier *Wasp* was at Naples. At that moment the Sixth Fleet included three amphibious squadrons, each with a battalion landing team of some 1,800 Marines. One squadron was south of Cyprus, only 12 hours' steaming from Beirut; a second squadron was north of Crete, and the third squadron was southeast of Italy, steaming toward Gibraltar and return to the United States.

The order was given for the Marine battalion off Cyprus to land at 3 P.M. on the 15th. The landing would coincide with President Eisenhower's announcement of U.S. intervention. The two other amphibious squadrons were to steam east at maximum speed and land their Marines at Beirut on the mornings of the 16th and 18th.

During the night of July 14–15 the carriers *Essex*, *Saratoga*, and *Wasp* recalled their crews from shore liberty, and they weighed anchor early on the 15th, setting course for the Eastern Mediterranean.

At 3:04 P.M. on July 15—just 20 hours after the president of Lebanon had appealed for help—U.S. Marines landed just outside of Beirut. The landing was unopposed except by overzealous Lebanese who flocked to the water's edge to meet the Americans (some to sell refreshments and souvenirs). Moments after the first Marines hit the beach, 11 planes from the *Essex* zoomed overhead—four FJ-3 Furies and seven AD-6 Skyraiders that had flown in to support the Marines after a refueling stop at a British airfield on Cyprus.

The lone Marine battalion would have been hard-pressed had it met military opposition, for the unit was "light" in tanks and artillery. Determined opposition might have pinned down the Marines, preventing them from reaching the Beirut airport (which the Marines secured within an hour of landing), and sparked a coup to depose the pro-Western Lebanese government. But

as one military historian, Colonel Albert Sights, astutely observed, "No opposition appeared, so who can say it was wrong? Politically [the Marine landing] served the purpose. Militarily it was something of a gamble."[14] But it worked.

The U.S. Army and Air Force deferred moving forces until after the initial Navy-Marine landing in Lebanon. The first Army battle group in Germany was not placed on alert until the morning of the 15th and did not begin arriving at Adana, Turkey, until July 17. In the meantime, amphibious ships had landed an additional Marine battalion on the 16th and a third battalion on the 18th. A fourth Marine battalion was hastily flown across the Atlantic in Marine transport planes and landed at Beirut on the 18th. The first Army troops landed at Beirut on the 19th, after having been held at Adana for two days to provide a reserve air assault capability.

On the morning of July 15 the spearhead of the tactical air units being deployed to the Middle East—a 12-plane flight of Air Force F-100 fighter-bombers—took off from a U.S. base on the first leg of the flight to Adana. Of the 12 aircraft launched, one crashed in Canada, seven landed en route, and four made it to Adana after a 12½-hour flight. After this slow beginning the Air Force buildup at Adana gained momentum, although lacking in equipment such as maps, radio facility charts, exposure suits, and other important items. Even when the tactical aircraft buildup at Adana was completed on July 20 (35 fighter-type aircraft, 12 light bombers, and 17 reconnaissance aircraft, all jet-propelled), an Air Force officer reported, "There is considerable doubt as to the conventional combat capability of the F-100 units. Only a few of the F-100 pilots had strafed; none had shot rockets or delivered conventional bombs." The B-57 Canberra light bomber crews were reportedly "incapable of performing efficient conventional weapon delivery."[15]

Navy carriers were in position and their aircraft and pilots were capable of providing almost immediate support for the U.S. landings. Unquestionably, the Marines would have gone ashore without air support. The planes from the *Essex* that were over the beaches moments after the Marines landed ensured that the men could survive against any opposition. (At the time a 2,000-man rebel force was in a section of Beirut less than three miles from the landing beaches, the action the Lebanese Army would take was unknown, and Soviet-equipped Syrian armored troops were three hours by road from Beirut.)

The USS *Saratoga*, the second super carrier, seen in 1959, shows the awesome air strength embarked in these ships. Ranged on her deck (from bow) are 11 A4D/A-4 Skyhawks, 12 F3H/F-3 Banshees, 2 HUP helicopters, 16 AD/A-1 Skyraiders, 12 F8U/ F-8 and 4 F8U-1P/RF-8 Crusaders, and 9 A3D/A-3 Skywarriors; a single TF-1/C-1A Trader cargo aircraft is parked behind the Skyraiders, ready to carry passengers, mail, and spare parts. (U.S. Navy)

After her H-hour support flight of 11 aircraft, the *Essex* kept her planes in the sky over Lebanon almost continually until August 20. The *Saratoga* reached a launch position off Lebanon during the night of July 17–18 to add her air group to the combat air patrol and reconnaissance flights.

During the first days of the Lebanese crisis the attack carriers *Forrestal* and *Randolph* had prepared for sea and then steamed across the Atlantic to reinforce the *Essex* and *Saratoga*. Although the submarine threat to the landing was negligible, the ASW carrier *Wasp* cleared Naples harbor early on July 15 and steamed eastward. Her fixed-wing aircraft and helicopters could have proved useful in reconnaissance and utility roles. (She also carried eight Marine-piloted HRS-3 helicopters to lift troops from the amphibious ships to the beach.) Thus, at the outset of the crisis the Navy was able to place three aircraft carriers and some 200 carrier-based aircraft within striking distance of Lebanon during a three-day period. In just over a week five carriers with 350 aircraft had assembled in the Mediterranean.

Also, the carrier *Antietam*, assigned to training duties at the time, departed the Boston Naval Shipyard on July 15 and, after brief trials, set course for Mayport, Florida. That same day she was ordered into Norfolk, where she loaded Marine aircraft, taking aboard a variety of planes ranging from F9F Cougars to light observation planes and helicopters. She then joined an amphibious squadron for exercises but remained ready for immediate deployment to the Mediterranean.

By late August 1958 the Middle East situation was again relatively stable, although the last of the 6,000 Marines and 8,000 soldiers who had gone into Lebanon were not withdrawn until late October 1958.

In the aftermath of the Middle East crisis, a strange carrier landing occurred. The United States in this period provided Israel with Sikorsky S-58 helicopters, which were designated HSS-1 in U.S. Navy service and HUS-1 in Marine service. In the summer of 1958 a young pilot named Uri Yarom, who had been Israel's first helicopter pilot, took off in an S-58 to pick up a sailor whose eye had been injured on a merchant ship in the Eastern Mediterranean.

The S-58 lacked fuel for the round trip and two 53-gallon fuel drums were carried inside the helicopter. The idea was to raise a drum above the helicopter's fuel tank with the rescue hoist and let the fuel flow by

gravity. "When we tried it [in flight] on the ground it worked O.K.," recalled Yarom. "But when we tried it . . . the wind sucked the remain[ing] fuel from the open tank, and all [of] the cabin was sprayed with fuel mist and we decided to forget the idea."[16]

Frustrated, Yarom spotted several S-58s in U.S. markings flying in formation. He immediately fell in behind them. When the last had landed on the carrier *Wasp*, Yarom hovered his S-58 until he was signaled to land. Brought to the ship's bridge and asked why he landed on a U.S. carrier without permission, Yarom instantly replied, "Sorry, I thought she's one of ours."

The Israeli S-58 was quickly refueled and, given the exact direction and range to the merchant ship, took off to continue the mission. After winching up the injured sailor, the helicopter successfully returned to Israel. (The Israeli government subsequently paid for the fuel provided by the *Wasp*.)

The Offshore Islands

On August 23, 1958, the Communist Chinese guns ringing Amoy Bay on the Chinese mainland opened fire on the so-called offshore islands of Little and Big Quemoy. These islands were Nationalist Chinese strongholds on the doorstep of Red China. The Nationalists had 60,000 troops on the Quemoys; there were another 25,000 men on Matsu Island to the north, which was also subjected to a heavy communist artillery barrage. The Red gunfire was intense, reaching 50,000 rounds per day, and threatened to cut the islands off from receiving supplies and ammunition from Formosa.

At the time of the Lebanese crisis, the U.S. Navy had two *Essex*-class attack carriers in the Western Pacific, the *Hancock* and *Shangri-La*. On July 14 their sister carrier *Lexington* was conducting carrier landing exercises off the California coast. As during the Korean War, the Navy feared that the communists would use American involvement in one part of the world as an opportunity to mount an offensive elsewhere. Accordingly, the CNO, Admiral Burke, ordered the *Lexington* into San Francisco to embark an air group and deploy to the Western Pacific. Within 72 hours of that decision the carrier had loaded the air group, stores, fuel, and munitions, and was under way. After calls at Pearl Harbor and Guam, she joined Task Force 77 on August 7, providing three attack carriers with some 200 aircraft in the Western Pacific.

When the communist guns opened fire on the Quemoys and Matsu on August 23, the *Hancock* was operating east of Formosa, the *Shangri-La* was at Yokosuka, Japan, and the *Lexington* and the ASW carrier *Princeton* were at sea to the east of Japan. The United States had declared previously that it would defend Formosa against a Communist Chinese assault, but the status of the offshore islands vis-à-vis U.S. commitments was nebulous. However, in view of the threat to the islands the U.S. Seventh Fleet was placed on alert and ordered to prepare for major operations against Communist China. The large attack carrier *Midway* had departed the U.S. West Coast on August 16 for a deployment to the Western Pacific. She was at Pearl Harbor on the 23rd and was immediately directed to make best speed to join Task Force 77. Additional cruisers and destroyers were also ordered to the trouble area to bolster the Seventh Fleet's strength.

A sixth carrier joined the Seventh Fleet from an unexpected source: the Sixth Fleet in the Mediterranean. The *Essex* had been on line supporting the Lebanese landings from July 15 to August 20, with only a brief respite at Rhodes in early August. She arrived at Naples for a well-earned rest on August 23; on the morning of August 25 she weighed anchor and set out to join the Seventh Fleet. With an escort of four destroyers, the *Essex* steamed through the Suez Canal and the torrid Red Sea, across the Indian Ocean, and through the East Indies to the South China Sea.

The greatly strengthened Seventh Fleet patrolled the Formosa Strait and escorted Nationalist Chinese supply ships to and from the beleaguered islands, carefully observing the three-mile territorial limit of China while ignoring Red China's announcement that the country had extended its sovereignty to 12 miles offshore. The rapid buildup of the Seventh Fleet and U.S. forces on Formosa, and the obvious U.S. determination to help the Nationalist Chinese hold the islands is credited with convincing the communists of the futility of further aggressive action against the Quemoys and Matsu. The intensive fire against the islands was soon lifted but resumed on an alternate-day-only shelling of considerably less intensity.

Unlike in the Lebanese crisis, the United States had airfields available within tactical striking distance of Amoy Bay. Formosa was 160 miles from the Chinese mainland and the big island's airfields were soon servicing U.S. Air Force and Marine fighters flown in from the Philippines and Japan. Still, the carriers provided highly mobile and potent advanced bases, which the communists could not strike without first flying extensive searches that would, in turn, cost them the element of surprise in initiating offensive actions.

The heroine of the carrier forces in these crises was the veteran *Essex*. What had begun as a routine, six-month deployment with the Sixth Fleet in the Mediterranean ended nine months later after two months in the Seventh Fleet and an around-the-world cruise. During her extended deployment the flattop steamed almost 75,000 miles, almost one-third of the distance the carrier steamed in 2½ years of World War II. (Her intense operations in this period were a major factor in the *Essex* recording her 98,550th arrested landing on June 25, 1960. This surpassed the record set by the old *Saratoga*, which had landed 98,549 aircraft from 1928 to 1946.)

11 NEW CARRIER CONCEPTS

The *Valley Forge* as flagship of ASW Task Group Alfa in November 1958. She steams in formation with six destroyers, most modified with advanced anti-submarine weapons. The large and at times highly advanced Soviet submarine fleet was a major concern of Western political-military leaders throughout the Cold War. Major Western air, surface, and submarine forces—including carriers—were dedicated to the ASW role. (U.S. Navy)

Although there was no immediate threat from hostile submarines in either the Lebanese or Quemoy-Matsu crises, in the 1950s the U.S. Navy was greatly concerned about the Soviet submarine threat as well as the beginnings of a Communist Chinese naval threat, primarily with Soviet-built undersea craft. A large portion of the U.S. Navy's anti-submarine effort and funding went into the operation of ASW support carriers (CVS). These were all *Essex*-class ships that had previously been designated as attack carriers (CVA). When newer attack carriers became available and the CVA force level was maintained at 14 to 16 ships, the older *Essex*-class attack carriers became ASW ships.

At the time of the Lebanese-Quemoy crises 11 ASW carriers were in commission:

Antietam	*Princeton*
Boxer	*Tarawa*
Hornet	*Valley Forge*
Lake Champlain	*Wasp*
Leyte	*Yorktown*
Philippine Sea	

Ten of these ships normally operated with four to six ASW destroyers to form hunter-killer groups. In the ASW role the carriers normally operated a 20-plane

155

squadron of twin-engine S2F Trackers and a smaller squadron of HSS-1 Seabat helicopters. The latter were single-engine, four-place helicopters especially developed for ASW operations. Their "armament" was a dipping sonar transducer, which was lowered into the water while the helicopter hovered a few feet above the water, and two homing torpedoes. The HSS-1 began joining fleet squadrons in the second half of 1955 and was followed by an HSS-1N version capable of day and night instrument flying and automatic hovering. A detachment of radar-equipped AD-5W Skyraiders provided an additional search capability for the hunter-killer group. Periodically, a detachment of fighter aircraft also went aboard the ASW carriers to provide a combat air patrol for the defenseless Trackers and helicopters. F2H Banshees, normally in four-plane detachments, were generally used in this role in the latter 1950s. In 1960 the ASW air groups were reorganized into two ten-plane Tracker squadrons, a 16-plane helicopter squadron, plus the early warning detachment. ASW carriers did not carry fighter detachments from 1960 to 1965.

In response to the increasing Soviet submarine threat and the specter of Soviet nuclear-propelled submarines, the Navy in 1958 established three specialized task groups to develop ASW tactics and to improve fleet readiness. Rear Admiral John S. Thach, a leading fighter pilot of World War II who had conceived the "Thach weave" maneuver, took command of Carrier Division 16 in November 1957 and, strongly endorsed by the Chief of Naval Operations, Admiral Arleigh Burke, formed the first of three ASW groups, Task Group Alfa.[1] Groups Alfa and Bravo were centered on ASW carriers while the third group was composed of surface ASW ships; land-based maritime patrol aircraft supported all three groups. These task groups immediately became the most capable ASW units of any Western Navy.

Meanwhile, the *Antietam*, although classified as an ASW carrier, did not have an air group assigned, and from April 1957 she was used exclusively as a training carrier, operating in the Gulf of Mexico. She served in that role until she was relieved by the *Lexington* in May 1962.[2]

After the hectic year of 1958, the ASW carrier ranks were pruned: the straight-deck carriers were mothballed or converted to amphibious assault ships with the notable exception of the *Lake Champlain*. She survived in the ASW role until mid-1966. The number of ASW carriers in commission (including the training ship) was held at ten or (after 1966) nine ships, with all but the *Lake Champlain* having an angled-deck configuration. In an emergency the training ship could, of course, operate an ASW air group on a limited basis.

The availability of *Essex*-class carriers for ASW

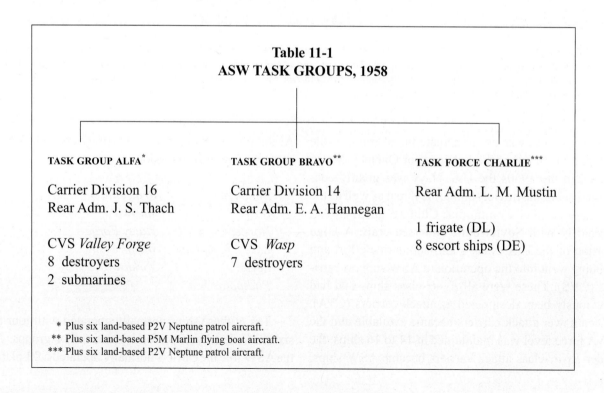

Table 11-1
ASW TASK GROUPS, 1958

TASK GROUP ALFA*	TASK GROUP BRAVO**	TASK FORCE CHARLIE***
Carrier Division 16	Carrier Division 14	Rear Adm. L. M. Mustin
Rear Adm. J. S. Thach	Rear Adm. E. A. Hannegan	
		1 frigate (DL)
CVS *Valley Forge*	CVS *Wasp*	8 escort ships (DE)
8 destroyers	7 destroyers	
2 submarines		

   * Plus six land-based P2V Neptune patrol aircraft.
  ** Plus six land-based P5M Marlin flying boat aircraft.
 *** Plus six land-based P2V Neptune patrol aircraft.

The Sikorsky HSS-1 (later SH-34) Seabat was the ASW helicopter embarked in U.S. carriers from the later 1950s into the 1960s. This HSS-1 from Helicopter ASW Squadron 1 is hovering while lowering its active "dipping" sonar. Normally flown with two pilots and two sonar operators, in the attack mode it was flown by a two-man crew and could carry two ASW homing torpedoes. The improved HSS-1N (SH-34J) could alternatively carry an Mk 101 Lulu nuclear depth bomb. (U.S. Navy)

and training duties ended the need for light and escort carriers in conventional carrier roles. Even before the Korean War, on April 20, 1950, the Navy had authorized the Newport News Shipbuilding Company to undertake a design study for a 25-knot CVE to meet future ASW carrier requirements. Because of the time required for design, authorization, and construction of a new CVE, the Navy also looked into the installation of improved arresting gear and catapults in *Commencement Bay*–class CVEs, and possibly converting the earlier *Casablanca*-class CVEs to helicopter escort ships (CVHE) to accompany convoys.

But it was already clear that the CVEs and even the larger CVLs would not be able to effectively operate the next generation of aircraft. In early 1952 the Commander-in-Chief Pacific, Admiral Arthur W. Radford, observed,

> The CVE is rapidly reaching the obsolescent stage. The ASW plane such as the AF requires a larger and faster carrier for reliable operations. Under light wind conditions operations become dangerous and operational losses increase. Such losses would hardly be acceptable under wartime conditions. The CVE is incapable of covering a fast convoy except under unusually favorable wind conditions. . . . It appears that the *Essex* CVA would be the ideal ASW carrier, having fuel capacity sufficient for the required endurance of itself and escorts, speed to handle modern ASW

planes under any wind conditions, size to handle any type of ASW carrier plane and in sufficient numbers to remain on a Hunter-Killer operation for long operations and to hunt submarines to exhaustion.[3]

That May, Rear Admiral Herbert E. Regan, Commander Carrier Division 17, urged acceleration of the construction of *Forrestal*-class carriers to permit more *Essex*-class ships to be allocated to the ASW role. He noted that the CVEs should be considered useful only as transports and helicopter ships. As a result of his views, in late 1952 the *Valley Forge* (still CVA 45) participated in a hunter-killer exercise off the coast of California. An evaluation read,

> Its advantages were manifold over the CVE/ CVL types. There was ample room for two VS [anti-submarine] squadrons on board. The wide winged AF had sufficient deck space and a carrier that could easily give it safe launch speeds even in a dead calm. All of the advantages of the larger flight and hangar decks, speed, stronger arresting gear and catapults, greater elevator capacity were in marked contrast to . . . the CVE/CVL types.[4]

Some naval officers advocated retaining the CVLs, albeit with a change in their role. Captain Doyle G. Donaho, commanding officer of the *Saipan* while she was operating a squadron of Marine AD Skyraiders, wrote in an evaluation of CVL operations:

It is believed that the embarkation of a single model aircraft of a conventional type [in] a vessel possessing the characteristics of a CVL is wasteful in that the full capabilities of the vessel are not utilized. Under the conditions in which the *Saipan* operated in the Pacific (independent operations with one or two destroyers and with an AD close support air group embarked) the ship could afford itself no air defense protection with fighter type aircraft nor could it provide adequate anti-submarine protection. . . . the CVL[s] should be utilized for the tasks for which they were designed . . . support of fast carrier operations. Operating with a carrier task force with a jet fighter group embarked the CVL is capable of providing all the fighter protection such a force may require . . . and at the same time is able to provide additional striking power against an enemy objective that may be the target force.

Captain Donaho noted that the *Saipan* was capable of embarking and operating 40 F9F-6 type jet aircraft. The CVLs, however, would be unable to operate the next-generation fighter aircraft. Of five CVLs in commission, the two *Saipan*-class ships and three *Independence*-class ships, the last, the USS *Saipan*, was decommissioned in October 3, 1957.

Of the 65 escort carriers on the Navy list on June 12, 1955, 30 were reclassified as helicopter escort carriers (CVHE) and 23 as utility carriers (CVU). The ships designated CVHE were to operate ASW helicopters in the convoy escort role in war-time; the utility carriers would be used to ferry aircraft, troops, and equipment. All of these ships would retain their original CVE hull numbers with the new designations; no material changes were made in any of the mothballed escort carriers. Only 11 of the mothballed *Commencement Bay*–class ships retained a CVE designation.

The older *Windham Bay* carried out an unusual "spy mission" against the Soviet Union shortly before she was decommissioned. During the 1950s the United States carried out reconnaissance missions over the Soviet Union with high-altitude balloons carrying cameras. Launched from bases in western and southern Europe, the balloons drifted over the Soviet Union with transponders aiding their (hoped for) recovery in Japan and at sea in the Pacific.

In the summer of 1958 the Air Force began launching a new series of balloons, known as WS-461L, with the code name Melting Pot.[5] A small number of these balloons were to be launched taking advantage of a newly discovered change in the west-to-east jet stream. Normally, this fast-moving air current stayed at an altitude of 55,000 feet, but during June and July it turned abruptly upward over the Bering Sea, just west of Alaska, climbed to 110,000 feet, and then reversed direction. Deputy Secretary of Defense Donald Quarles stated that using this quirk in the jet stream the balloons' "chance of being detected is rather small and their identification or shootdown practically nil."[6]

The camera balloons were released from the carrier *Windham Bay* operating in the Bering Sea. From July 2 through 14 the Air Force detachment in the ship, with the help of sailors, launched nine balloons. One malfunctioned and came down at sea shortly after launch. The *Windham Bay* then launched several research balloons as a "cover" operation and returned to port. The nine camera-carrying balloons were the last spy craft of that type to be launched by the United States, being succeeded in the overflights by U-2 spyplanes.[7]

Nothing was heard of the *Windham Bay* balloons until July 28, when the Polish government sent a note protesting the overflight of a U.S.-made, camera-carrying balloon that had fallen to earth in central Poland. The loss of these balloons was caused by human error. Each balloon had a timing device that caused it to release the camera and film payload after crossing the target areas. An Air Force technician on the jeep carrier had calculated that the balloons would cross the Eurasian landmass in 400 hours, and thus he adjusted regulators on the balloons to cause automatic descent after a little more than 16 days. When bad weather delayed the launch for three successive days, however, the technician forgot to reset the timing devices. As a result, one balloon payload fell into Poland.

Then the Soviet government declared that the balloons violated Soviet air space. Several months later the Soviets placed the U.S. balloon and photographic equipment on display in Moscow for the world's press. President Eisenhower, angry, declared, "The project is to be discontinued at once and every cent that has been made available as part of any project involving crossing the Iron Curtain is to be impounded and no further expenditures are to be made."[8] The United States never recovered any of the WS-461L balloon payloads.[9]

Carriers continued to launch research balloons. For example, on January 31, 1960, during Operation Skyhook, the *Valley Forge* launched a ten-million-

Carriers were employed in remote areas to launch camera-laden spy balloons as well as instrument-carrying research balloons, as this ten million cubic foot balloon being prepared aboard the *Valley Forge* during Operation Skyhook in 1960. The mobility, open flight decks, and protected hangar decks of carriers made them excellent platforms for a variety of research and test activities. (U.S. Navy)

cubic-foot balloon carrying instruments to measure cosmic rays to an altitude of more than 20 miles.

In 1964–1965 the ex-"jeep" carrier *Croatan* supported another high-altitude research project. Operated by a civilian crew under the aegis of the Navy's Military Sea Transportation Service (MSTS), the ship was "borrowed" by the National Aeronautics and Space Administration (NASA) to serve as a seagoing launch platform for upper-atmospheric sounding rockets. She was extensively modified with an array of antennas, rocket launchers fitted on the flight deck, and telemetry and control vans installed on the flight and hangar decks.

A total of 77 Nike Cajuns, Nike Apaches, and small Arcas meteorological rockets were launched from the *Croatan* as the carrier steamed along the west coast of South America between March 8 and April 22, 1965. The experiments sought to determine the states of the upper atmosphere and ionosphere during solar sunspot minimum, particularly the so-called equatorial electrojet.

All 12 of the *Commencement Bay*–class escort carriers in commission when the Korean War ended were retired by mid-1957, the last "jeep" being the

Badoeng Strait, decommissioned on May 17, 1957. Thus ended the saga of light and escort carriers in the U.S. Navy. Four older "jeep" carriers remained in naval service as cargo ships operated by the Navy's MSTS with the prefix T- added to their utility carrier designation. Soon they, too, were gone, although they were replaced by older, but more sturdy, converted C3 cargo ships reactivated from mothballs and changed to aircraft cargo ships (AKV) in May 1959:

SHIP		DECOMMISSIONED
T-CVU 58	*Corregidor*	Sept. 4, 1958
T-CVU 64	*Tripoli*	Nov. 25, 1958
T-CVU 88	*Cape Esperance*	Jan. 15, 1959
T-CVU 92	*Windham Bay*	Jan. 1959

		TO MSTS SERVICE	
T-CVHE 11	*Card*	July 1, 1958	to AKV 40
T-CVHE 13	*Core*	July 1, 1958	to AKV 41
T-CVHE 23	*Breton*	July 1, 1958	to AKV 42
T-CVHE 25	*Croatan*	June 16, 1958	to AKV 43

The four AKVs were modified for the sealift role: short funnels for their reciprocating (steam) engines were fitted outboard of the flight deck, port and starboard, and two large aircraft/cargo cranes were fitted to their flight deck.

The classifications of 32 mothballed and four active escort carriers designated CVE/CVHE/CVU were changed to cargo ship and aircraft ferry (AKV 8–43) on May 7, 1959.[10] This ended the "escort aircraft carrier" designation in the U.S. Navy. Then, on May 15, 1959, four mothballed ASW support carriers (CVS) and seven mothballed light carriers (CVL) were redesignated auxiliary aircraft transport (AVT 1–11), to remove them from the aircraft carrier roster (see Appendix C). The carrier *Tarawa* followed, being decommissioned in 1960 and changed to AVT 12 in May 1961. These were the first *Essex*-class ships to be dropped from the carrier roles:

SHIP		DESIGNATION
CVS 13	*Franklin*	to AVT 8
CVS 17	*Bunker Hill*	to AVT 9
CVS 32	*Leyte*	to AVT 10
CVS 47	*Philippine Sea*	to AVT 11
CVS 40	*Tarawa*	to AVT 12

(The AVT 1–7 were former CVLs.)

Helicopter Carriers

In the midst of the nuclear-retaliation policies of the early 1950s, an exciting concept in conventional warfare blossomed—vertical envelopment, employing helicopters to land assault troops behind heavily defended beaches or in areas inaccessible to conventional boats or tracked landing craft. The U.S. Marine Corps had initiated experiments in helicopter assault techniques in 1948 and had periodically used light and escort carriers as helicopter-troop ships during exercises. The British light carriers *Ocean* and *Theseus* had operated as helicopter carriers at Suez in 1956, sending a Royal Marine commando and Army and Royal Air Force support personnel ashore in whirlybirds.

The world's first aircraft carrier to be specifically modified for helicopter operations was the USS *Thetis Bay* (CVE 90), one of the 50 *Casablanca*-class escort carriers. Commissioned in April 1944, the 6,700-ton, 512-foot *Thetis Bay* had an uneventful career and was mothballed shortly after the war. She was taken in hand for conversion at the San Francisco Naval Shipyard in June 1955. Berthing and mess spaces were installed for a 1,000-man Marine battalion landing

Technicians from NASA adjust an antenna on a truck aboard the former escort carrier *Croatan* in preparation for the T-AKV being employed to launch upper-atmosphere sounding rockets in 1964–1965. Note the antenna farm on the after portion of the flight deck. Just above the disk antenna is the ship's port-side funnel; funnels on both sides as well as two large cargo cranes were installed for their T-AKV role. (National Aeronautics and Space Administration)

The U.S. Navy's first "dedicated" helicopter assault carrier was the converted escort carrier *Thetis Bay*. Here she stands out to sea in 1956 with her after elevator lowered to the hangar deck. Life rafts adorn the edge of her flight deck. Her initial designation CVHA 1 was soon changed to LPH 6, marking her as an amphibious ("L") ship, and removing her from the carrier category. (U.S. Navy)

team in addition to the ship's Navy complement of 40 officers and 500 enlisted men. (As a CVE the *Thetis Bay* had accommodations for 110 officers and 750 enlisted men.) Cargo elevators and hoists were installed to bring the Marines' ammunition, equipment, and stores from storage compartments to the flight deck. The arresting gear, single catapult, and forward aircraft elevator were removed. The ship's after 45-by-32-foot elevator was retained, but the portion of the flight deck aft of the elevator was cut away. Minor changes were also made in the ship's island structure, and additional command and communications facilities were installed below decks.

Thus refitted, the *Thetis Bay* was recommissioned on July 20, 1956, as a helicopter assault carrier (CVHA 1). In her new role the *Thetis Bay* initially operated 20 HRS helicopters. This single-engine helicopter had been widely used by Marine squadrons in the Korean War and could lift eight to ten troops in addition to its two-man crew.

The escort carrier *Block Island* (CVE 106), a larger *Commencement Bay*–class ship (10,900 tons, 557 feet), began a similar conversion at the Philadelphia Naval Shipyard in 1957. The *Block Island*, first commissioned in December 1944, had served in the Pacific, was station ship at the Naval Academy in Annapolis from 1946 to 1950, and was employed as an aircraft transport during the Korean War. She was reclassified as an amphibious assault ship (LPH 1). For political reasons, the Navy wanted to place these ships in the amphibious/landing ship category rather than the aircraft carriers category to avoid funding conflicts with CV-type carriers. The *Thetis Bay* was redesignated LPH 6 in 1959.[11]

The conversion of the *Block Island* was scheduled for completion in July 1960. However, the Navy was forced to halt work on her because of funding cuts. (As the AKV 38 she was stricken from the Navy list in 1959 and scrapped the following year.)

The Navy next initiated built-for-the-purpose amphibious assault ships with the first, the *Iwo Jima* (LPH 2), being laid down on April 2, 1959, at Puget Sound (Bremerton) Naval Shipyard. But to provide an immediate vertical assault capability in the fleet, three straight-deck *Essex*-class carriers were hastily modified for helicopter operations. The 27,100-ton *Boxer* and *Princeton* were reclassified as amphibious assault ships in January 1959 (LPH 4 and LPH 5, respectively). The *Valley Forge* followed in June 1961 (LPH 8). Their sister ship *Tarawa* briefly operated Marine helicopters in the late 1950s but was not reclassified as an LPH and was mothballed as the CVS 40 in mid-1960.

The *Boxer*, *Princeton*, and *Valley Forge* had served previously as attack and then ASW ships. In this third role they provided the advantages of size, aircraft capacity, and speed over smaller helicopter carriers. As amphibious ships these carriers normally operated half of their eight-boiler, four-turbine power plant to provide a speed of about 25 knots compared to the 19½ knots of the *Thetis Bay* and the 22 knots of the *Iwo Jima* and her sister ships; however, additional engine room personnel could bring the full propulsion plant of the *Essex*es on line to provide up to 33 knots.

In the amphibious assault role each *Essex* could accommodate 1,650 troops and approximately 30 helicopters, the exact number depending upon the type embarked. Each carrier required about 1,000 officers and enlisted men to operate the ship. For a time in the late 1950s these ships had their deck and air departments partially manned by Marines—a total of 10 officers and some 325 enlisted men per ship—because of Navy personnel shortages. This arrangement allowed

The use of *Essex*-class carriers as amphibious warfare ships provided the Navy with a large-scale vertical assault capability. These ships could carry a Marine battalion and supporting units—a total of 1,650 troops—and could operate some 30 helicopters. HUS (later UH-34) Seahorse and HR2S (later CH-37) Mojave helicopters are on the *Boxer*'s flight deck in this photo. Unlike British commando ships, U.S. CVHA/LPH ships did not carry landing craft. (U.S. Navy)

the Navy to save several hundred men and provided Marines with additional training at sea and in helicopter operations. (Platoon-size Marine detachments were normally embarked in U.S. battleships, cruisers, and aircraft carriers to provide internal security, especially for nuclear weapons, and have, on occasion, manned secondary or anti-aircraft gun batteries.)

New helicopters were developed for the new amphibious ships: The large HR2S began reaching the Marines in 1956. This was a twin-engine helicopter with its engines mounted in pods alongside the fuselage and coupled to turn a single main rotor (with 36-foot blades) mounted atop the fuselage. Clamshell nose doors opened to a cargo compartment for 20 troops or 24 litters or three jeep-type vehicles. With a normal takeoff weight of 31,000 pounds and a fuselage length of almost 65 feet, the HR2S was similar to the C-47 Dakota transport in size. Maximum speed for the HR2S was about 130 m.p.h.

In 1957 the Marines began receiving the HUS helicopter, a utility version of the HSS-1 anti-submarine helicopter. The single-engine HUS could lift up to 12 troops or eight litters and had a top speed of 123 m.p.h. Maximum takeoff weight was 13,000 pounds. Nor-

mally, a squadron of 20 to 24 HUS helicopters and a detachment of two HR2S helicopters for heavy lift operated from the *Essex* LPHs.

The world's first built-for-the-purpose helicopter carrier was the USS *Iwo Jima*, commissioned on August 26, 1961. In size she was between an escort and light carrier, having a displacement of 13,465 tons and an overall length of 592 feet. However, she "looked heavier" by virtue of her flight deck being supported by her hull structure in the manner of British and later U.S. fleet carriers. The ship had a small island on the starboard side of her flight deck, combining bridges with a small funnel. There were two 3-inch twin gun mounts immediately forward of the island and two 3-inch mounts at the after end of the flight deck.

The flight and hangar decks were connected by two deck-edge elevators, one to port opposite the island and one to starboard aft of the island. The hangar, with a 20-foot overhead, could accommodate nine HR2S-type helicopters or 20 smaller HUS/HSS-1 type. Normally ships of this class operated 20 to 24 medium troop helicopters, 4 heavy lift helicopters, and 4 small observation helicopters.

Improved berthing and mess arrangements were

provided in the *Iwo Jima* class for a Marine staff and landing force of 230 officers and 1,900 enlisted men plus the ship's company of 50 officers and 500 enlisted men—a total of almost 2,700 personnel. There were excellent command and communication facilities for the time, and a large hospital to handle combat casualties flown aboard by helicopters returning from the assault. Propulsion consisted of a two-boiler steam turbine plant turning a single propeller shaft to drive the ship at a sustained speed of 20 knots; maximum speed was about 22 knots.

Following the *Iwo Jima* into the fleet were six sister ships: *Okinawa* (LPH 3) commissioned in 1962; *Guadalcanal* (LPH 7) in 1963; *Guam* (LPH 9) in 1965;

Tripoli (LPH 10) in 1966; *New Orleans* (LPH 11) in 1968; and *Inchon* (LPH 12) in 1969.

Another Controversy

The beginnings of the rejuvenation of the U.S. Navy's amphibious assault capabilities—exemplified in the helicopter carrier program—came at a time when the nation's strategic policy was still based on nuclear retaliation. Any communist encroachment on "free world" territory would be met with swift, deadly retaliation by U.S. nuclear bombers. This was the official U.S. and North Atlantic Treaty Organization (NATO) policy despite the fact that conventional military forces and economic aid had stopped communism in Western

Flight deck operation on an *Essex*-class LPH: An HUS Seahorse, the troop version of the HSS-1 Seabat, prepares to land cargo while another HUS (lower left) and HR2S-1 Mojave are maintained on the flight deck. The Marine Corps took delivery of 549 HUS variants from 1957 to 1968; the Navy bought 385 HSS variants from 1954 to 1966. Several other nations flew these helicopters. (U.S. Navy)

A Marine "mule" utility vehicle with a 106-mm recoilless rifle drives out of the "bow doors" of an HR2S-1 Mojave helicopter during an exercise. The HR2S was the first twin-engine helicopter to be used in amphibious assault operations. The Navy evaluated an HR2S-1W variant for the AEW role; it was fitted with the AN/APS-20E search radar. (U.S. Marine Corps)

Europe, Greece, Turkey, Lebanon, Malaya, the Philippines, and Korea. Even the Quemoy-Matsu crisis of 1958 could be included in this list, for while the United States was prepared to employ nuclear striking forces,

Communist China at the time had no nuclear weapons and the U.S. and Nationalist Chinese air and sea forces could unquestionably have held off communist assaults against the islands without using nuclear weapons.

The *Forrestal*-class attack carriers, each operating some 50 nuclear-capable attack aircraft, was a component of the U.S. nuclear striking force. The U.S. Congress voted funds to construct one super carrier each year from fiscal 1952 through 1958; the *Forrestal*, *Saratoga*, *Ranger*, *Independence*, *Kitty Hawk*, *Constellation*, and *Enterprise*. The first six ships were basically *Forrestal*-class ships, each with newer features and each slightly larger than her predecessor. The *Kitty Hawk* (CVA 63) and *Constellation* (CVA 64) differed from the others in several ways: they had a modified flight deck and island structure arrangement. Their portside elevator was moved farther aft, reducing the possibility of damage from heavy seas and being stuck in the down position, which would affect angled-deck operations. On the starboard side the island was moved aft, with two deck-edge elevators forward and one aft of the island. These two ships also introduced guided missiles to carrier defensive armaments, each having a twin Terrier surface-to-air missile launcher on each

The helicopter carriers *Iwo Jima* and *Okinawa* (above) were the world's first purpose-built helicopter ships. Note the starboard and port deck-edge elevators, boxlike island structure, two 3-inch/50-caliber twin gun mounts forward of the island, and two more cut into the after flight deck. These LPHs could carry more than 2,100 troops. One later ship did have davits for four LCVP landing craft. (U.S. Navy)

quarter in lieu of the 5-inch guns found on earlier ships. The Terrier was a 27-foot, 1,100-pound, radar-guided missile with a range of about 20 miles.[12]

The *Enterprise* (CVAN 65) went a step farther in shipboard armament: as completed she had none, relying instead on her interceptors and the guns and missiles of escorting ships for defense. But of considerably more significance, the *Enterprise* was built with a nuclear propulsion plant that gave her a range measured in years rather than miles.

No attack carrier was authorized in fiscal year 1959, which began on July 1, 1958—the year of the Lebanese and Quemoy-Matsu crises—nor was a carrier approved in the following year. Opponents of attack carriers were many, and with the coming of intercontinental ballistic missiles and the rising costs of warship construction, the opposition gained strength. Clarence Cannon, chairman of the powerful House Appropriations Committee, declared that the billions of dollars spent by the United States on aircraft carriers were utterly wasted, adding that the carrier-building program is "the most colossal national debacle in all military history." With the Navy simultaneously developing the submarine-launched Polaris ballistic missile, one U.S. senator expressed a typical layman's view when he asked the Secretary of the Navy: "Why do you need a new carrier if the Polaris missile is so good?"

Still another attack leveled at the carriers was based on their apparent vulnerability to supersonic aircraft and missiles. The verbal blows against aircraft carriers were countered by an "admirals' revolt," somewhat akin to that of the late 1940s when the Secretary of Defense cancelled the super carrier *United States* and the Navy, in turn, opened fire on the B-36 program. One fleet commander, Vice Admiral William R. Smedberg, declared, "In our recent exercises with the Air Force we picked up the planes—I can't say just how far away because it is classified, well over 200 miles away— and we started shooting them down at 180 miles and we had practically all of them splashed before they got within 70 to 100 miles of our carriers."

Secretary of the Navy Charles S. Thomas summed up the Navy's view on carrier survivability in a 1956 statement:[13]

Locating the *Forrestal*-type carrier in the vast ocean wastes will be an exceedingly difficult problem. First of all, a ship well out to sea and cruising at top speed is hard to find, even with the most advanced search aircraft. The patrol planes searching for it will have to literally cover thousands of square miles of ocean. Even if the general location of the carrier is known at one moment, this information would be of little value a few hours later. In six hours, a carrier could be anywhere in a 100,000 square-mile circle of ocean. In another six hours, the mobile airbase could be lost anywhere within nearly a half-million square mile circle of ocean. If a patrol plane strays only one degree off its course searching for a ship 500 miles at sea, he would miss the target by many miles.

Another aspect of the very difficult problem of searching a large ocean or sea for one particular type of ship is the "spoof" or "ghost" problem— the problem of "mistaken identity." At any given hour, night or day, 2500 ships are somewhere in the Atlantic Ocean. At any given hour, night or day, 700 ships are in the Mediterranean. Even the finest, fastest, best-equipped jet reconnaissance planes, equipped with the most powerful and discriminating radar, must, after locating a target on their radar, determine what it is. Even a lowly tramp steamer reflects a radar signal; even a small island (and there are hundreds of islands in the Mediterranean) can look like a carrier. Even experienced aviators have made many mistakes in identifying real ships, let alone radar echoes. Submarines, freighters, even whales have been reported as "carriers." And in these days of electronic magic, simple devices are available which can mislead the most experienced radar operator.

Thus, the problem is not simply finding a carrier, but identifying it as well.

And even if the search plane is successful in his search, and if he confirms the presence of a carrier task force, he will probably have been intercepted by the carrier's own fighters and shot down.

Searching for the mobile airbase at sea will cause the enemy to use many of his planes. If he ever finds it, the enemy will also use much of his air potential, both offensive and defensive, to defend against the lethal threat the mobile airbases poses, and to use part of his airpower to try and neutralize it.

In other words, our carriers force an enemy to dilute his offense, to spread and divert his

The first four ships of the *Forrestal* design were built with eight 5-inch/54-caliber single rapid-fire gun mounts; the next three ships, the *Kitty Hawk*, *Constellation* (above), and *America* were instead armed with two twin launchers for the Terrier surface-to-air missile. This weapon had a range of some 20 miles and the Terrier BTN variant was fitted with the W43 nuclear warhead. (U.S. Navy)

defense. Carriers bleed off a significant portion of his air power which might otherwise be used against our homeland. And in modern war, the more of the fighting that can be done over, under, and on the sea, the less will be the risk to our own country. But let us assume that an enemy search plane has located, has identified the mobile airbase, and has survived to warn his bases. The enemy now faces the dangerous assignment of attacking the mobile airbase task force. . . . First, he has to fight through the outer screen of guided missile ships. That screen will probably be operating many miles from the carrier itself; our new missiles, available and operational now, have very substantial ranges. . . .

In addition to missile defenses, enemy aircraft will have to fight through the carrier's own fighter cover. . . .

In my opinion, an objective and impartial analysis will prove that the *Forrestal* mobile airbase is the best protected and least vulnerable weapons system that we have.

Secretary Thomas and the admirals were equally adamant in their defense of aircraft carriers vis-à-vis the Soviet submarine threat. In discounting the threat of ballistic missiles the carrier proponents were quick

to point out that ballistic missiles must be aimed at a specific target before they are launched, and their direction cannot be altered in flight to take into account a carrier's movement between the time her position is reported, the time the missile is fired, and the time the missile reaches its impact area. In contrast, noted the admirals, the exact location of every U.S. air base at home and abroad was well known to the Soviets.

The more logical of the opponents of carriers called attention to the development of standoff guided weapons, which could be launched by aircraft remaining out of ship-to-air missile range and guide the aerial missiles to the target; these opponents also noted that carriers spent a significant portion of their time in port, presenting an opportune target for more conventional forms of air and missile attack.

However, the increasing cost of carrier construction was probably the major factor in ending the one-per-year carrier program. The Navy provided these estimates of carrier costs to Congress in April 1959:

PROGRAM	SHIP		COST
Fiscal 1952	CVA 59	*Forrestal*	$189,463,000
Fiscal 1953	CVA 60	*Saratoga*	$214,387,000
Fiscal 1954	CVA 61	*Ranger*	$182,162,000
Fiscal 1955	CVA 62	*Independence*	$222,796,000

Fiscal 1956   CVA 63 *Kitty Hawk* $217,963,000
Fiscal 1957   CVA 64 *Constellation* $247,620,000
Fiscal 1958 CVAN 65 *Enterprise* $393,167,000 *

* The total construction cost of the *Enterprise* would be $445 million, making her the most costly warship built to that time.

Thus, in the summer of 1958, when aircraft carriers were rushed to the Eastern Mediterranean and then to the Western Pacific in response to communist threats, Congress did not approve funds for additional carriers. Meanwhile, the Navy called for continued carrier construction. A landmark report sponsored by CNO Admiral Burke described the national military problems to which the future Navy must respond:

> *First*, the United States must have a guaranteed ability to deter all-out war. This means above all that we must have nuclear retaliatory forces which cannot be knocked out by surprise attack.
>
> *Second*, the more certainly we can deter all-out war, the more certain the threat of limited aggression will become. We must be able to defeat limited aggression on whatever scale the Soviet bloc is able to wage it, and that is now a very large scale. We must be able to this without provoking all-out war.[14]

The Navy report called for a force of 12 modern attack carriers—six with nuclear propulsion—as well as nine ASW carriers and three "large training carri-

ers." This meant that five more CVANs would have to be built during the next decade.[15]

In 1959 the Navy's request for funds to build an attack carrier was again opposed. Probably the most powerful congressional opponent of carriers was Representative Cannon, still the outspoken head of the House Appropriations Committee. A longtime foe of carriers (i.e., pre-B-36 controversy), Cannon made a scathing attack on the Navy during hearings held in the summer of 1959:

> We stand today exactly where Chamberlain stood when he met Hitler at Munich [1938]. Hitler had the planes. England was deficient in airpower. Today [Nikita] Khrushchev has the missiles and the submarines. We are deficient in both. We have frittered away on carriers the time and attention and money we should have devoted to the missile and the submarine. . . . Russia has been too wise to build a single carrier. They have copied every weapon we have devised except the carrier. That has been . . . the only difference in the military programs of the two nations. And as a result America has dropped every year in relative military power and Russia has risen every year. . . . There can be no other explanation. It is as simple as that. It is the carrier.

Cannon could muster enough backing for the House to drop the carrier from the defense budget; however,

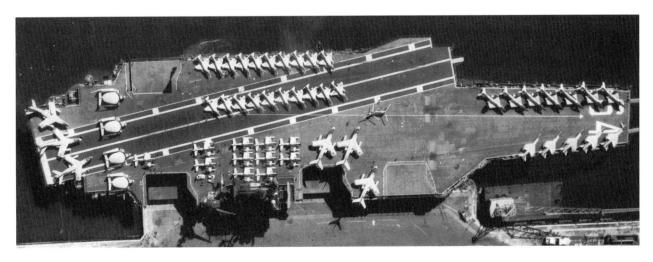

The *Constellation* at Mayport, Florida, shows the improved flight deck arrangement for the *Forrestal* design: two starboard deck-edge elevators forward of the island and the port-side elevator aft of the angled flight deck. The ship has F3H (later F-3) Demon and F8U (F-8) Crusaders forward; A3D (A-3) Skywarriors amidships and aft; A4D (A-4) Skyhawks and AD (A-1) Skyraiders in the waist, and four WF (E-1) Tracer AEW aircraft aft; at the time the ship operated part of air group CVG-5. (U.S. Navy)

the Senate, traditionally more sympathetic to the Navy, instead approved the $260 million that the president had requested for the new carrier and added $100 million to provide nuclear propulsion in the ship. The issue was compromised with only $35 million being approved to begin work on a nuclear-propelled carrier. But President Eisenhower, opposing the additional expense of nuclear propulsion, refused to allow the Navy to spend the funds.

Nuclear propulsion was becoming a major point of contention within the greater controversy of aircraft carriers. The official Navy policy at the time declared that the additional cost of providing a carrier with nuclear propulsion—$130 million above the price of an oil-burning carrier—was not worth the advantages gained. The director of the Navy's nuclear propulsion program, Vice Admiral H. G. Rickover, told Congress that it would be "darned . . . well stupid" to vote funds for a conventional carrier rather than a nuclear ship. Making it clear that he was speaking for himself and not for the Navy, Rickover said putting money into an oil-burning carrier would be buying obsolescence, the same "as if you bought diesel submarines today." (All U.S. combat submarines laid down after 1956 had nuclear propulsion.)

For the fiscal year 1961 (which began in July 1960) Congress and the president at last agreed on the construction of another attack carrier—the eighth since World War II—to be conventionally powered. At the time the U.S. Navy had an operating force of 14 attack carriers: four *Forrestal*s, three *Midway*s, and seven *Essex*-class ships. These carriers were supported by nine *Essex*-class ASW ships with a tenth serving as a training carrier.

The attack carrier operations vividly reflected U.S. reaction to international crises. In August 1960, in response to "missile rattling" by Soviet Premier Nikita Khrushchev, caused in part by United States and United Nations intervention in the Congo strife, the U.S. Navy moved quickly to boost the striking power of the Sixth Fleet in the Mediterranean and the Seventh Fleet in the Western Pacific.

The large attack carrier *Independence* and the smaller CVA *Intrepid* entered the Mediterranean late in August on a normal six-month deployment. In early September the carrier *Saratoga* arrived in the Mediterranean. Simultaneously, three attack carriers were maintained in the Seventh Fleet, the *Hancock*, *Oriskany*, and *Ticonderoga*. The striking power of the carrier forces was further increased during the fall of 1960 when two attack carriers in each fleet flew ashore a squadron of fighters and embarked an additional squadron of light attack aircraft. The fighters were kept ready at Rota, Spain, and Atsugi, Japan, for rapid return to their carriers should they be needed.

With only 14 attack carriers in service at the time, the overseas deployment of six CVAs placed a considerable strain on the Navy. To maintain a normal rotation policy with six carriers continually deployed, the Navy required a force of 18 CVAs. The attack carrier ranks were increased briefly to 16 ships in 1961 as new attack carriers were completed and the assignment of older *Essex*es to the ASW role was delayed.

During the 1960 crisis period ASW carriers were assigned to the Sixth and Seventh Fleets (the *Valley Forge* and *Hornet*, respectively). When the newly independent Congo erupted in civil war in mid-1960 the ASW carrier *Wasp* rushed to Accra, Ghana, to unload

The *Valley Forge* was the U.S. Navy's last straight-deck ASW carrier, serving in that role until mid-1961, when she became an amphibious assault ship (LPH 8). In this 1959 photo the "Happy Valley" has 14 S2F Tracker ASW aircraft on her flight deck; two ASW helicopters are also visible. The ship retained her original 5-inch/38-caliber twin gun mounts fore and aft of the island and single mounts on the port side of the flight deck. (U.S. Navy)

225,000 gallons of aviation gasoline to relieve a critical shortage of fuel for transport aircraft flying United Nations troops and supplies into the strifetorn country. The carrier had on board six twin-engine C-1 Trader cargo aircraft and eight Marine helicopters to aid in evacuating civilians from the interior of the Congo, if required to do so.

Beyond the need for increased U.S. naval strength in the Mediterranean and Western Pacific, events forced the Navy to deploy carriers to the Caribbean. In mid-April 1961 several U.S. warships, including carriers, stood off Cuba during the ill-fated Bay of Pigs invasion by 1,700 U.S.-trained troops, mostly Cuban exiles (see Chapter 14), and carriers steamed off southern Hispaniola in late June 1961 and again in November 1961, when uprisings seemed imminent as a result of the assassination of Dominican dictator Rafael Trujillo in late May of that year. In November 1961 carriers patrolled off Guatemala and Nicaragua when their governments requested U.S. assistance in preventing a communistled invasion of those nations.

And on January 6, 1961, the continued communist-inspired crises around the globe were brought into focus by Premier Khrushchev when he declared,

> There will be liberation wars as long as imperialism exists, as long as colonialism exists. Wars of this kind are revolutionary wars. Such wars are not only justified, they are inevitable. . . . The peoples win freedom and independence only through struggle, including armed struggle. . . . We recognize such wars. We have helped and shall continue to help people fighting for their freedom.[16]

After World War II the United States failed in its efforts to eliminate "limited" or "brush-fire" wars with the threat of massive nuclear retaliation. The United States, which had for more than a decade given overwhelming priority to the establishment of forces to fight nuclear wars, was faced with the specter of continued conventional warfare in the nuclear era.

12 CARRIER PROLIFERATION

In several respects the Royal Navy led in the development of aircraft carrier technology in the post–World War II era despite being resource limited. The light carrier *Hermes* was redesigned during construction. She is shown here in 1960 with Sea Vixen all-weather fighters. The large 3-D radar antenna atop of island structure is the Type 984. It was also fitted in the larger *Ark Royal*, *Eagle*, and *Victorious*. (Royal Navy)

After World War II there was a proliferation of aircraft carriers in the smaller navies of the world. Whereas in the prewar years only Great Britain, the United States, Japan, and France possessed carriers, two decades after the war ten navies operated these ships. The United States and Britain finished the war with large carrier fleets and the lone French carrier *Béarn* was succeeded by newer ships, at first foreign built and then of indigenous construction.

The first of the smaller navies to operate an aircraft

carrier was Canada. Canadian naval squadrons operated from American-built, British-manned escort carriers during World War II and several Canadian pilots flew in Fleet Air Arm squadrons. After the war, from early 1946 until early 1948, the Canadian Navy operated the British-built light carrier *Warrior* on loan. She was replaced by the larger, 14,000-ton light carrier *Magnificent*, which was commissioned on loan in the Canadian Navy in April 1948. Like her predecessor, the *Magnificent* initially operated British-built aircraft, Sea Fury FB.11 fighter-bombers and Firefly AS.4 anti-submarine aircraft. The ASW aircraft were replaced by American TBM-3E Avengers.

With the advent of the angled deck and jet-propelled aircraft, in 1952 the Canadian Navy purchased outright the unfinished British light carrier *Powerful*. The *Powerful*, which had been launched in February 1945, was later converted to an angled-deck configuration and was fitted with the latest carrier equipment including a steam catapult. Although of the same class as the *Magnificent*, the new ship thus had superior operating capabilities. The ex-*Powerful* was commissioned as HMCS *Bonaventure* in early 1957.

The Canadian Navy turned entirely to the United States for aircraft for the *Bonaventure*, acquiring a squadron of jet-propelled McDonnell F2H-3 Banshee fighters to give her a limited, all-weather air defense capability; a squadron of twin-engine Grumman Tracker

ASW aircraft; and a detachment of Sikorsky HO4S-3 ASW helicopters. The Trackers were produced under license in Canada as the CS2F-1 and, with improved equipment, as the CS2F-2. The HO4S-3 helicopters were replaced in the early 1960s by the American HSS-2 Sea King, initially delivered "off the shelf" from its American manufacturer with later helicopters assembled in Canada.

The *Bonaventure*'s Banshees were phased out in September 1962 as they approached the end of their service life. Additional trackers took their place aboard ship, limiting the ship exclusively to surveillance and ASW operations. With the use of U.S. aircraft the Canadian Navy relied on U.S. naval training facilities, and when the *Bonaventure* was in overhaul, her aircraft flew from U.S. ASW carriers.

Australia soon followed Canada into carrier operations, commissioning the British-built light carrier *Terrible* as HMAS *Sydney* in December 1948. With her Sea Fury FB.11 fighter-bombers and Firefly AS.4 aircraft, the *Sydney* made a significant contribution in the Korean War. Delivery of a second British-built carrier was delayed, and from 1952 to 1955 the Australian Navy additionally operated the British light carrier *Vengeance* on loan as a training ship.

The British light carrier *Majestic*, on which all work had halted at the end of World War II, was completed as an angled-deck configuration and commissioned as

The Canadian carrier *Bonaventure* refuels from the replenishment ship *Provider*; a destroyer refuels simultaneously from the *Provider*'s starboard side while two others await their turn. In this period most small-carrier Navy operated British-built light carriers but flew American as well as British fixed-wing aircraft and American helicopters. (Royal Canadian Navy)

HMAS *Melbourne* in November 1955. She arrived in Australia the following May and initially operated one squadron of Sea Venom FAW.53 jet fighters and two squadrons of Gannet AS.4 turboprop ASW aircraft.

After studies of the Navy's missions and the increasing costs and operating expenses of a naval air arm, the Australian Ministry of Defence announced in December 1959 that ASW capabilities would be stressed and that carrier operations would cease in 1963, when the existing Sea Venoms and Gannets reached the end of their service life. However, in late 1960 the Australian government decided to purchase British-built Wessex helicopters, an export version of the U.S. Navy's HSS-1, to enable the *Melbourne* to continue to operate in an ASW role.

An Australian ASW helicopter squadron was formed in July 1963 with the delivery of the first 10 of 27 Wessexes on order. At the same time, the increasing Communist Chinese threat in Southeast Asia and the growing militancy of Indonesia led to a reappraisal of Australian defense plans. The *Melbourne*'s Sea Venoms and Gannets were extended in service to provide the Australian Navy with a viable carrier force until newer aircraft could be delivered. During 1967 the replacements arrived: American-built A4D-5 Skyhawks to replace the Sea Venoms in the fighter-bomber role and S2F-3 Trackers to join the Wessex helicopters in replacing the Gannets.

With acquisition of the *Melbourne*, the slightly older but well-worn light carrier *Sydney* had been relegated to training status in April 1955. After a period of uncertainty concerning her future, in 1962–1963 the *Sydney* was modified to serve as a fast transport. Her catapults, arresting wires, and other equipment were removed, and troop accommodations were fitted. In her new role she served partially as a naval training ship, but primarily as a transport for Army troops, vehicles, and equipment. In that role she provided support for the Australian troops participating in the Vietnam War.

The *Melbourne* collided with the Australian destroyer *Voyager* off the Australian coast on February 10, 1964, slicing the smaller ship in half. Eighty-two men from the *Voyager* were lost in Australia's worst peacetime maritime disaster. The carrier was quickly repaired.

But the *Melbourne* collided with another destroyer on the early morning of June 3, 1969. This time the victim was the USS *Frank E. Evans* as the two ships were operating in the South China Sea. Sliced in two,

The Dutch carrier *Karel Doorman* was also a former British CVL. The ship was modernized with an angled flight deck, steam catapult, and advanced electronics, with two LW-01/SGR-114 air search radars dominating the island structure. The LW-01 was a highly efficient, long-range, S-band radar; the antennas were approximately 36 feet wide and 16 feet high. S2F Trackers are being prepared for launch. (Royal Netherlands Navy)

the forward third of the destroyer sank immediately, taking the lives of 74 Americans. Another 38 men were thrown into the sea, with several rescued by Wessex helicopters that were airborne at the time; ships saved the others. The after section of the *Evans* remained afloat with additional survivors.

The Netherlands Navy operated the British-built escort carrier *Nairana* from 1946 to 1948 and then purchased the light carrier *Venerable*, commissioning the latter ship in March 1948. Both of these ships were renamed *Karel Doorman*. The CVL *Karel Doorman* initially operated British Sea Fury FB.11 fighter-bombers and Firefly AS. 4 and 5 ASW aircraft. Later, 23 Sea Fury FB.51s were built in Holland under license.

From 1955 to 1958 the *Karel Doorman* was modernized in a Dutch shipyard, receiving an angled flight deck, a steam catapult, and an elaborate electronics suite. She returned to service with a squadron of British-built Sea Hawk FGA.6 jet fighter-bombers and one of American-built TBM-3S and 3W Avengers. These

The carrier *Karel Doorman* operated the Hawker Sea Hawk FGA.6, the only turbojet fighter to be flown by the Royal Netherlands Navy. In this 1959 photo the Sea Hawks are armed with Sidewinder air-to-air missiles. The aircraft are inscribed with Kon[inklijke] Marine. (Royal Netherlands Navy)

aircraft were in turn replaced by S2F-1 Trackers and by HO4S-3 and then HSS-1 ASW helicopters. (Canada provided some of the Trackers, as CS2F-1, and the United States supplied the remainder as well as the helicopters.)

The Trackers were nuclear-capable, fitted to carry a U.S. B57 multipurpose nuclear bomb that could be used in the ASW role. The casings were stored aboard the *Karel Doorman*, with the cores—kept ashore in Britain under American control—to be transferred at pier side or flown aboard when needed.

Smaller Navies[1]

The Canadian, Australian, and Dutch navies operated aircraft carriers as a logical extension of their convoy escort forces and, in the case of the Netherlands, the naval forces necessary to support overseas possessions. There was little criticism of these three navies investing time, effort, personnel, and finances in carriers and their aircraft. However, the three other small navies that developed carrier aviation in the 1950s and 1960s might have better invested their resources in destroyer-type ASW ships, land-based naval aviation, and possibly other forces, from both economic and military viewpoints. The operation of aircraft carriers by Argentina, Brazil, and India has been expensive for the returns. Possession of an aircraft carrier by these navies is, in part, a matter of prestige. Much the same as several lesser navies, each possessed a single battleship or two before World War II. However, the relative costs of operating a carrier and her aircraft squadrons is considerably more than operating battleships, and former two-battleship nations, such as Argentina and Brazil, operated but one carrier. Similarly, the former "one-battleship navies" of Chile and Turkey were unable to afford an aircraft carrier.

Brazil became the first South American nation to acquire a carrier when it purchased the British-built light carrier *Vengeance* in December 1956. The ship had been completed in 1945 and had served under Australian colors from early 1953 until August 1955. After being purchased by Brazil, from mid-1957 until December 1960, she underwent extensive modernization in a Dutch shipyard, receiving an angled flight deck, steam catapult, and advanced electronics. The ship was commissioned in the Brazilian Navy as the *Minas Gerais* at Rotterdam on December 6, 1960. In mid-January 1961 she departed for Brazil's politically stormy waters.

The long Brazilian coastline had fostered an early interest in naval aviation and the Brazilian naval air arm with the purchase of a seaplane in 1913. This purchase was followed by the establishment of an army air arm, and the two flying services operated side by side until a 1946 law created the Brazilian Air Force. This legislation forbade other services from flying aircraft.

When Brazil purchased the carrier, the Brazilian Air Force was given the task of establishing a carrier air group of six S2F-1 Tracker ASW aircraft and six S-58 type (HSS-1) ASW helicopters. Despite opposition from Brazil's Air Force and president, in mid-1963 the Brazilian Navy formed a separate *Fôrça Aéra Naval*. By the end of the year this naval air arm had obtained 38 fixed-wing aircraft and helicopters of various types, the largest component being 12 American T-28C piston-engine trainers suitable for carrier operation. Most of the planes were purchased abroad—the T-28s in France—in the names of private citizens and smuggled into Brazil. The Navy conducted its own flying school at a closely guarded base that was forbidden to Brazilian Air Force planes. This situation, worthy of a comic operetta by Messrs. Gilbert and Sullivan, often forced the *Minas Gerais* to go to sea without aircraft or with those of one service or the other, but with no cooperation or coordination between the two air arms. Allegedly, the Air Force shot down a Navy helicopter during this impasse; after that incident the air minister resigned.

Table 12-1
AIRCRAFT CARRIERS IN THE SMALLER NAVIES, 1968

NATION	SHIP	FORMERLY	STANDARD DISPLACEMENT	PRIMARY AIRCRAFT
Argentina	*Independencia*	HMS *Warrior*	14,000 tons	S2F-1 Tracker HSS-1 (utility)
Australia	*Melbourne*	HMS *Majestic*	16,000 tons	A4D-5 Skyhawk S2F-3 Tracker Wessex (ASW)
Australia	*Sydney*	HMS *Terrible*	14,380 tons	none; employed as transport
Brazil	*Minas Gerais*	HMS *Vengeance*	15,890 tons	S2F-1 Tracker HSS-1 (ASW)
Canada	*Bonaventure*	HMS *Powerful*	16,000 tons	CS2F-2 Tracker CHSS-2 (ASW)
India	*Vikrant*	HMS *Hercules*	16,000 tons	Sea Hawk FGA.6 Alizé (ASW)
Netherlands	*Karel Doorman*	HMS *Venerable*	15,892 tons	S2F-1 Tracker HSS-1 (ASW)
Spain	*Dédalo*	USS *Cabot*	11,000 tons	SH-3D (ASW)

respectively, these light carriers and the *Arromanches* provided the French with a viable carrier force during the 1950s. (The escort carrier *Dixmude* was redesignated an aviation transport in 1951.) These carriers flew F4U-7 and AU-1 Corsair fighter-bombers, and TBM-3 Avenger ASW aircraft provided by the United States.[5]

Interestingly, the French delay in initiating the construction of aircraft carriers after World War II made it possible to incorporate the angled flight deck, steam catapult, and other innovations in the design of the new ships. These features, coupled with the French Navy's lack of experience in carrier design and construction, provided an unusual situation for French engineers and naval architects. The results were the long, clean lines of the carrier *Clemenceau*, laid down in November 1955, and her sister ship *Foch*, laid down in February 1957.

On a standard displacement of 22,000 tons, these ships had an overall length of 869 feet, with this dimension also being the length of their flight decks. This is an exceptional displacement-to-length ratio as evidenced in comparison with the British *Hermes* of 18,600 tons and 737³/₄ feet or the modernized U.S. carriers of the *Essex* class, which displaced about 33,100 tons and were almost 900 feet overall (ratios of 1000:38, 1000:32, and 1000:27, respectively). Thus, the French carriers had more deck operating space per ton of displacement than did their contemporaries. The French ships were each provided with a large hangar and two elevators. The lifts were laid out to avoid interference with landing operations or with use of the two steam catapults (one forward and one on the angled deck). There is an elevator slightly to starboard of the ship's centerline forward of the island structure and a starboard deck-edge lift aft of the island.

The first attack carriers built outside of the United States since World War II were the French *Clemenceau* (above) and *Foch*. The ships' excellent design includes two elevators and two steam catapults (one forward and one on the angled deck). Alouette ASW aircraft are on the *Clemencea*'s flight deck in this view. She was intended from the outset to operate jet aircraft. (French Navy/ E. C. Armées)

The island structure combines the bridge control spaces, electronic antennas, and funnel with a protective fiberglass sphere enclosing the aircraft approach radar housed at the after end of the island. Eight rapid-fire 3.9-inch guns provided the original close-in defense for each ship. Also significant, the *Clemenceau* and *Foch* were provided with a twin-propeller-shaft power plant of an advanced design that could provide a sustained speed of 32 knots. The power rating per shaft of the French carriers was surpassed only by that of the U.S. super carriers. Previous two-shaft carriers, among them the British "light" carriers through the *Centaur-Hermes* class, had a maximum speed of 28 knots, 4 knots less than the sustained speed of the French ships. (The U.S. light carriers, with four-shaft cruiser propulsion plants, were capable of 32 or 33 knots.)

The *Clemenceau* was completed in November 1961, and the *Foch* in July 1963. A new generation of French carrier aircraft was developed to operate from the ships, each of which could operate more than 40 aircraft (e.g., two 12-plane jet squadrons, a 12-plane ASW squadron, and 6 helicopters). The first jet-propelled aircraft operated by the French Navy—the French-built versions of the Sea Venom FAW.20—flew from these carriers; in French service these fighters were named Aquilon.

The leading French aircraft firm of Générale Aéronautique Marcel Dassault produced the Étendard IV fighter for the new aircraft carriers. Originally designed to a French Air Force requirement, the Étendard IV was a single-seat, transonic interceptor and ground support aircraft. Sixty-nine Étendard IV-M interceptor/ground attack aircraft were produced for the French Navy. Each had two 30-mm cannon and four underwing pylons for up to 3,000 pounds of bombs, rockets, missiles (including the U.S. Sidewinder), or fuel tanks. However, one cannon and its 125-round magazine were normally removed to permit the installation of radio navigation equipment. In addition to the Étendard IV-M, a photographic reconnaissance/tanker variant known as the IV-P was produced for carrier service. The 21 aircraft built to this specification had five nose and ventral camera positions, a fixed refueling probe mounted immediately above the nose, and could carry external "buddy" refueling packs and fuel tanks for refueling other carrier aircraft. (The refueling probe in the IV-M aircraft retracts when not in use.) The prototype Étendard (designated IV-01) first flew on July 24, 1956; the first navalized IV-M (for *Marine*) flew on May 21, 1958; the first production IV-M entered service with the 15th Flottille in June 1962 (replacing the unit's F4U-7 Corsairs).

These aircraft were complemented on the *Clemenceau* and *Foch* by Crusaders purchased from the United States. Forty-two aircraft, designated F8U-2NE(FN) and later F-8E(FN), were provided to the French Navy. The principal difference between the standard U.S. Navy F8U-2NE/F-8E Crusaders and the French aircraft was wing modification to reduce their landing speed by 17 m.p.h. The 1,120-m.p.h. (Mach 1.7) French Cru-

saders were armed with four 20-mm cannon and could launch four Sidewinders or the French Matra R-530 air-to-air missiles. These aircraft were delivered to France in 1964.

The third fixed-wing aircraft aboard the *Clemenceau* and *Foch* was the Alizé (Tradewind). This anti-submarine aircraft was powered by a turboprop engine and had a combined hunter-killer capability. Radar and other submarine detection equipment were carried in the Alizé, and the plane's weapons bay could hold a torpedo or three 353-pound depth bombs. Underwing pylons could hold two additional depth bombs plus six 5-inch rockets or two air-to-surface guided missiles. The plane's maximum speed was 292 m.p.h., and it had a normal endurance of five hours, which, with an auxiliary fuel tank, could be extended to seven hours, 40 minutes. A three-man crew flew the Alizé: the pilot and radar operator were in side-by-side seats and an ASW systems operator was in a side-facing seat behind them. The Indian Navy also flew the Alizé, from the carrier *Vikrant*.

With the completion of the *Clemenceau* and *Foch* the French Navy returned the *Belleau Wood* (in 1960) and the *Langley* (in 1963) to the United States, both of which were scrapped. The British-built light carrier *Arromanches* was retained by France, modernized in 1957–1958 to provide a limited angled deck and was employed as a combination training-ASW ship, normally

The only supersonic shipboard fighters to be developed outside of the United States were French and Soviet. The French Étendard IV (right) was a single-engine aircraft with a maximum speed of 673 m.p.h. at 36,000 feet (Mach 1.02), a ceiling of 50,850 feet, and an initial climb of almost 20,000 feet per minute. In this view an Étendard IV-P reconnaissance/tanker aircraft refuels an IV-M variant. (Général Aéronautique Marcel Dassault)

A pair of Étendard IV-P reconnaissance/tanker aircraft fly formation. These aircraft carry five cameras; they are unarmed. They are distinguished by a fixed refueling probe; the IV-M variant's probe retracts. The IV-P first flew on November 19, 1960. Beginning in 1982 these aircraft flew combat missions over Lebanon, the Persian Gulf, and former Yugoslav territory. (French Navy/E. C. Armées)

operating Alizé fixed-wing aircraft and French-built versions of the HSS-1 helicopter. The HSS-1 helicopters were used in the ASW and vertical assault roles. The larger, triple-turbine, 27-passenger Super Frelon was the main helicopter used by the French Navy in amphibious operations.

By the mid-1960s France was able to put to sea the world's fourth most powerful navy (after the United States, Britain, and the Soviet Union). The modern, highly efficient carriers *Clemenceau* and *Foch* were the backbone of this revitalized French sea power.

The French Air Force—the *Armée de l'Air*—flew ex-U.S. Navy AD Skyraiders from land bases in this era. In 1959 the Air Force had acquired 93 ex-U.S. Navy AD-4N and -4NA aircraft for use in the war in Algeria. They replaced P-47D Thunderbolts of World War II vintage. The French flew the Skyraiders for a short period, and several were subsequently transferred to Cambodia, Chad, and the Central African Republic.

(The French and Italian Navies also built several helicopter-carrying cruisers in this period. The French *Jeanne d'Arc*, a 13,000-ton ship completed in 1964, had a larger helicopter deck aft, a light armament, and accommodations for 700 troops. Eight large helicopters could be embarked on the flight and hangar decks. She was employed primarily as a training ship.

(The Italian Navy, forbidden at the time to operate fixed-wing aircraft, built several helicopter-carrying cruisers. The two ships of the *Andrea Doria* class, 5,000 tons standard, completed in 1964, were armed with the Terrier surface-to-air missile and could embark four AB 204 light ASW helicopters. The third ship of this type was the *Vittorio Veneto*. This 7,500-ton ship, completed in 1969, also had a Terrier missile system and could operate six large SH-3 Sea King or nine smaller AB 212 ASW helicopters.)

Fleet Air Arm Progress

Following the Suez debacle in the fall of 1956 the British government reviewed its defense policy and the subsequent spring published a Defence White Paper promulgating a defense policy for the next five years. The new program gave priority to the continued development of a British nuclear force to serve as a deterrent to Soviet aggression; the same White Paper also announced a planned increase of conventional naval

In addition to the Étendard, the French carriers *Clemenceau* and *Foch* operated American F8U-2NE (F-8E) Crusaders. Built by the LTV corporation, these could carry the MATRA R530 as well as Sidewinder air-to-air missiles and four 20-mm cannon. The prototype, shown here, first flew on February 27, 1964; a nose probe was fitted for flight tests. Forty-two Crusaders were built for France. (Ling-Temco-Vought)

strength in the seas East of Suez to provide rapid-reaction conventional forces to deal with "Peacetime emergencies" before they could escalate to open warfare.

The lessons of Suez were evident: (1) aircraft carriers were important to provide control of the air and ground support for ground forces in operations beyond the limited range of land-based tactical air power and (2) small units of well-trained and well-equipped infantry units, with air support, must be maintained within rapid striking distance of potential trouble areas.

With regard to aircraft carriers, post-Suez British planning generally provided for four strike carriers in service at any given time. Leading the carrier lineup was the 36,800-ton *Ark Royal*, completed in early 1955. The veteran *Victorious* was completely rebuilt and recommissioned in 1958 (with a standard displacement of 30,350 tons). Beyond the new flight deck arrangement, steam catapults, mirror landing gear, and a rejuvenated propulsion plant, the *Victorious* was the first British carrier without hammocks—she had bunks for all of her ratings. And, she was the first carrier to be fitted with the massive Type 984 three-dimension (3-D) radar to provide long-range, all-weather detection of aircraft.[6] The Type 984 had a "searchlight" array approximately 15 feet in diameter that housed a series of electronic lenses that produced two beams, one relatively wide that scanned at low angles and one a pencil beam that scanned vertically as the antenna rotated. (The carriers *Ark Royal*, *Eagle* and *Hermes* were also fitted with the Type 984 during their modernizations.)

Because of the limited number of aircraft carriers available in the post–World War II era, British fleet carriers had to operate aircraft for both the attack and ASW roles. This is the two-level hangar of HMS *Eagle* with, clockwise from upper left, Gannet AEW, Wessex HAS, Scimitar, and (lower level) Buccaneer aircraft. The tail dive brakes of Buccaneer "09" on the lower level are extended. (Royal Navy)

The *Victorious* was the only British carrier that saw extensive operations in World War II to see significant post-war service. She underwent several modernizations during her 26-year career, which came to an end in 1967. She is shown here in 1958 refueling from the tanker *Tideflow*. Her flight deck is angled nine degrees, her island is topped by the Type 984 radar antenna, and there is a lattice mast aft of her island. Sea Venom fighters are parked forward. (Royal Navy)

When the *Victorious* joined the fleet the large *Eagle* began a five-year modernization, the 44,100-ton ship emerging from the yard in 1964. Next, the 22,000-ton light carrier *Centaur*, which had been launched in 1947, was redesigned to incorporate many large-carrier features and was completed in 1953. She would stand in as a strike carrier until the *Eagle* finished modernization. The fifth carrier was the *Hermes* (23,000 tons), also begun as a light carrier of the war program and commissioned in 1959. She, too, was extensively redesigned and completed with an angled deck, a deck-edge elevator to port and a second lift on the centerline aft, two steam catapults, and a highly advanced electronics system. About the only characteristics in common with her former sister ships *Albion*, *Bulwark*, and *Centaur* was her limited aircraft capacity—about two dozen contemporary aircraft—and speed of 28 knots.

HMS *Albion* flew the only major combat missions by British carriers between the Suez assault of 1956 and the Balkans upheavals in the 1990s. As strife continued on Cyprus between Greek and Turkish factions, Sea Venom FAW.21s from No. 809 Squadron in the *Albion* flew strikes against terrorist hideouts in the Troodos Mountains. The August 1958 operations, using unguided rockets, involved the only known use of British fighter-attack aircraft during the Cyprus Emergency.

After the Cyprus crisis, armed trainers, Auster liaison aircraft, and helicopters flew support missions there. The Army Auster AOP.9 aircraft flew on and off carriers on several occasions in the 1960s. For example, the *Hermes* landed aboard three Austers off Cyprus during August 1962 to test operational liaison between ground troops and the Navy. Other carriers on which Austers are known to have operated are HMS *Albion* and *Centaur*.[7] (The indomitable Eric Brown, in 1946 while a test pilot, had flown a German Fi 156 *Storch* [Stork] liasion aircraft—also sans hook—from the light carrier *Triumph*.)

A new generation of aircraft joined the Fleet Air Arm to fly from these carriers. The first of these was the Sea Vixen all-weather fighter, the replacement for the Sea Venom. Both aircraft had the twin-boom configuration common to de Havilland jet aircraft, but that is where their similarities ended. The Sea Vixen was much larger than its predecessor (about 35,000 pounds at takeoff compared to 15,800 pounds for the Sea Venom), the newer aircraft had two jet engines instead of one, and the new fighter had a superior performance. The first FAA fighter with missiles in place of guns, the Sea Vixen had two retractable rocket pods, each housing 14 unguided 2-inch rockets, and carried four Firestreak infrared homing missiles. In the strike role the Sea Vixen could carry two 1,000-pound bombs or four 500-pounders or two Bullpup air-to-surface missiles. The Sea Vixen was flown by a pilot housed in a cockpit offset to the left side of the fuselage with the navigator sitting beside the pilot but lower, within the fuselage. The aircraft's advanced radar was linked directly to the Type 984 3-D radar to enhance long-range interception of approaching aircraft. The first flight of the Sea Vixen occurred on September 26, 1951, but squadron deliveries did not commence until No. 892 Squadron began receiving aircraft in July 1959. The FAW.2 variant began reaching the Fleet in 1963. The principal difference between the variants was provision for the improved Red Top infrared air-to-air missile and deletion of the retractable fuselage rocket pods. A total of 114 Sea Vixens was produced.

For the Navy's day-fighter/strike requirement the Scimitar was developed by the Supermarine firm. This single-place, twin-engine aircraft was the first British carrier aircraft capable of supersonic flight, achieved in a shallow dive. Taking off at approximately 34,000 pounds, the Scimitar provided a heavy lift capacity: up to 1,000 pounds of weapons could be attached to each of four underwing pylons. Typical loads in the strike role were two 1,000-pound bombs and two 100-Imperial gallon drop tanks or 24 3-inch rockets or four Bullpup missiles. Four 30-mm cannon were fitted in the Scimitar for its fighter role and Sidewinder missiles could be carried. A camera package could be installed in the aircraft for reconnaissance missions.

The Scimitar, which entered squadron service in 1958 with No. 803 Squadron, was the first British carrier aircraft to have a nuclear strike capability, being fitted to carry a Red Beard tactical weapon. The weapon weighed 1,750 pounds and had an explosive force of 15 kilotons, i.e., about the size of the Hiroshima and Nagasaki bombs.

Seventy-six Scimitars were built, and they were in service from 1958 to 1966, when they were replaced by one of the world's most advanced tactical strike aircraft, the Buccaneer. Several innovative aerodynamic features were incorporated in the Blackburn design for the Buccaneer to provide the required performance—low-level, in excess of Mach 0.9—and withstand the severe "metal fatigue" encountered when flying in that flight profile.[8] These features included bleeding compressed air from the engines over the wings and control surfaces and employing the "area rule" or pinched fuselage-concept used in the earlier Grumman F11F Tiger.

The Buccaneer was capable of flying at sea level, below enemy radar and missile defenses, at speeds above 700 m.p.h. to deliver nuclear weapons. The aircraft's great range was demonstrated when a Buccaneer launched from a carrier in the Irish Sea and carried out a simulated low-level attack on Gibraltar and returned to the carrier, an unrefueled, nonstop flight of

Light observation-type aircraft have regularly operated from aircraft carriers, among them the Fieseler Fi 156 *Storch* (Stork), landing on the carrier *Triumph* in 1946 (above), and a Taylorcraft Auster AOP.9 coming aboard the *Hermes* in 1962 (below). The latter ship has a Whirwind helicopter hovering nearby. Operations with light aircraft demonstrated carrier flexibility. (Royal Navy)

The twin-boom de Havilland Sea Vixen was the FAA all-weather fighter of the 1960s. The Sea Vixen FAW.1 had a maximum speed of 690 m.p.h. at 10,000 feet (Mach 0.9), an initial climb of over 10,000 feet per minute, and a ceiling of 48,000 feet. The pilot's cockpit was offset to the left side with the navigator's position in the right side of the fuselage. Note the twin exhaust openings of the FAW.2 aircraft parked on the *Ark Royal*'s flight deck. The aircraft also had an attack capability. (Royal Navy)

more than 2,300 miles, which, to quote a Hawker Siddeley spokesman, "is by no means the limit of the aircraft's unrefueled range." (The Buccaneer was fitted for in-flight refueling.)

A two-seat, twin-engine aircraft, the Buccaneer was laden with electronic equipment to assist in the evasion of enemy defenses and allow it to navigate and strike targets in any weather. Up to 4,000 pounds of conventional weapons or a Red Beard tactical nuclear weapon could be carried internally on a rotating bomb door; alternatively a camera pack could be fitted for reconnaissance missions. In addition, four underwing attachment points each could hold a 1,000-pound bomb or Bullpup missile or smaller weapons.[9] The Buccaneer was one of the largest aircraft to operate on British carriers, being matched in weight but not dimensions only by the F-4K Phantom in the later 1960s.[10] Gross weight of the Buccaneer S.1 was approximately 45,000 pounds (a weight equaled by the FAW.2 variant of the Sea Vixen; the later Buccaneer S.2 had a gross operating weight of about 51,000 pounds). In addition to folding wings, which reduced its wingspan to 20 feet, the Buccaneer's nose folded back and its tail-cone dive brakes opened to reduce its length to 50 feet, 7 inches, acceptable dimensions for British carrier lifts.

The first Buccaneer flew on April 30, 1958, following an initial contract for 20 preproduction aircraft for tests and evaluation. In October 1959 the Royal Navy ordered the Buccaneer S.1 into production. The first operational squadron—No. 801—was formed in July 1962 for service aboard the *Ark Royal*.

Even as the first frontline Buccaneer squadron was forming, the Royal Navy ordered production of the Buccaneer S.2 with more-powerful engines and greater range. Hawker Siddeley proposed several improved Buccaneer variants, one a supersonic aircraft. And, Buccaneers were proposed for RAF land-based operation but were rejected, the RAF claiming that the aircraft's range was inadequate for its requirements. (The RAF preferred instead to proceed with the TSR.2 nuclear strike aircraft; after cancellation of that aircraft in 1965 the RAF again rejected the Buccaneer, opting instead for the American F-111K. Procurement of the F-111K was cancelled in 1968, and in July of that year the RAF very belatedly ordered the Buccaneer. The end of the British conventional carrier program in 1978 led to transfer of naval Buccaneers to the RAF for land operation; an additional 45 were produced for that service.)

With Scimitars aboard strike carriers in squadron strength at the turn of the decade and the Buccaneers on the way, late in 1960 the Royal Navy could load nuclear weapons in aircraft carriers for delivery by aircraft. In addition to being able to carry out strikes with conventional or nuclear weapons, the Scimitar and Buccaneer (as well as Sea Vixen) could serve as aerial tankers by carrying refueling stores. The Scimitar, with its heavy lift capability, was employed primarily in the aerial tanker role in support of the Sea Vixens and Buccaneers until it was phased out of service in late 1966.

Supplementing the Sea Vixens, Scimitars, and Buccaneers aboard British carriers in this period were Gannet airborne early warning aircraft and Wessex anti-submarine helicopters. The Gannet AEW.3 was a development of the Gannet AS-series and successor to the AD-4W/AEW.1 Skyraiders that flew in the Royal Navy from 1953 to December 1960. With its double turboprop engine providing an endurance of about five hours, the Gannet made an excellent airborne radar picket. On search missions, the Gannet normally cruised on one of its turboprop engines, with the power being changed to the alternate engine every half hour.

The prototype Fairey Gannet AEW.3 first took to the air on August 20, 1958. This aircraft featured the same basic wings and engines of the ASW variant but had an entirely new fuselage and rudder. The AEW version carried a three-man crew: a pilot in a bubble cockpit and two radar observers seated side-by-side behind and below the pilot. The American-developed AN/APS-20 search radar antenna was housed in a "guppy" projection below the fuselage and electronic countermeasures devices were carried internally and on two wing store stations. Four-plane flights of the Gannet AEW aircraft were assigned to each operational strike carrier to fulfill the roles of aircraft detection, strike direction, electronic countermeasures, detection of surfaced or snorkeling submarines, and surface search.[11]

Faced with the problems of limited carrier deck space and too few carriers for specialized roles further complicated by the increasing size of anti-submarine aircraft, the Royal Navy decided to assign ASW aircraft to strike carriers and to use only helicopters for carrier-based ASW. The most practical course in ob-

The Vickers–Supermarine Scimitar was a strike fighter flown from British carriers in the ground support, strike, and tanker roles. Maximum speed of the Scimitar F.1 was 635 m.p.h. at 36,000 feet (Mach 0.95) with a 12,000-feet-per-minute climb, and a ceiling of 48,000 feet. Scimitars were first delivered to FAA squadrons in June 1958, four years after the Scimitar's first flight. (Royal Navy)

taining an ASW helicopter appeared to be adoption of the Sikorsky S-55, already in wide service with the U.S. Navy as the HO4S-3 and the U.S. Marine Corps as the HRS (as well as the Army as the H-19). The United States had already supplied 25 of these helicopters to the Royal Navy. The ASW version was designated the Whirlwind HAS.22 and the transport the Whirlwind HAR.21.

The first Whirlwind produced in Britain under license was the HAR.1 transport and rescue version, which first flew on August 15, 1953. Several Whirlwind HAR variants followed and the HAS.7, the British-built ASW version, first flew in late 1956. The Whirlwind HAS.7 carried a three-man crew, had dipping sonar, and could lift a homing torpedo for a total loaded weight of 7,800 pounds; top speed was 110 m.p.h. with a maximum range of more than 300 miles.

In response to the demands for more potent ASW weapon systems, the Fleet Air Arm turned to the improved Sikorsky S-58 after procuring the HAS.7

Table 12-2
FLEET AIR ARM FIGHTER-ATTACK AIRCRAFT

AIRCRAFT	OPERATIONAL	GROSS T/O WEIGHT	WINGSPAN	LENGTH
Scimitar F.1	1958	34,200 lb	37 ft 2 in	55 ft 4 in
Sea Vixen FAW.1	1959	35,000 lb	51 ft	55 ft 7 in
Buccaneer S.1	1962	40,000 lb	42 ft 6 in	62 ft 4 in
Phantom F-4K	1969	56,000 lb	38 ft 5 in	57 ft 7 in

The most advanced carrier aircraft produced by Britain since World War II was the Hawker Siddeley Buccaneer strike aircraft. The S.2 variant had a speed of some 620 m.p.h. at 30,000 feet (Mach 0.92) and 645 m.p.h. at 200 feet (Mach 0.85); it could climb about 15,000 feet per minute. The plane's bomb bay doors rotated to release bombs—four 1,000 pounders—or to expose a six-camera reconnaissance package. Up to 12,000 pounds of bombs or four Bullpup air-to-surface missiles could be carried on four wing pylons. These views show a Buccaneer S.1 streaking over the carrier *Eagle* and an S.2 variant carrying two Bullpup missiles and two MATRA rocket pods. Note the open and closed positions of the plane's tail dive brakes. (Royal Navy; Hawker Siddeley Aviation)

Whirlwinds. Again, the basic S-58 was already in U.S. Navy service as the HSS-1, in the Marine Corps as the HUS (and with the Army and Air Force as the H-34). Known in the FAA as the Wessex, the principal difference between the HSS-1 and the Wessex HAS.1 was that the British helicopter had a gas turbine engine in place of the piston engine of the American version. Although slightly less powerful, the British engine was considerably lighter than the piston unit and gave the Wessex a much improved performance. Despite the high fuel consumption, the gas turbine engine was found almost ideal for helicopters because its smooth operation reduced the vibration present in all rotary-wing aircraft. Other advantages include simplified controls and the ability to be airborne only 45 seconds after a cold start (compared to an average of 15 minutes for the HSS-1 on a reasonably cold day). Finally, the adoption of the gas turbine Wessex HAS.1 simplified the aviation fuel problems in British carriers as the gas turbine burned the same fuel (essentially kerosene) as the turboprop Gannets and "straight-jet" fighters and attack aircraft.

The first frontline Wessex HAS.1 squadron, No. 815, embarked in the *Ark Royal* in September 1961. The Wessex HAS.1 had better night/all-weather capabilities than its American cousin, the HSS-1N. With a loaded weight of 12,600 pounds, the British helicopter had a maximum speed of 138 m.p.h. and a range of 340 miles. The helicopter's submarine detection system consisted of dipping sonar, and it could carry up to four homing torpedoes (with a reduction in fuel load). The helicopter was flown by a pilot, copilot, observer, and sonar operator.

The Commando Ships

The second stage of the post-Suez revision of British military policy—providing small, well-equipped, and well-trained combat units to deal with "peacekeeping" requirements in the Indian Ocean–Southeast Asia areas—was spelled out in the annual Defence White Paper issued at the beginning of 1958. The policy statement stressed the vastness of the area, the need for rapid intervention, and the versatility of sea power. These factors led to the decision to maintain a force of Royal Marines and helicopters embarked in a commando carrier East of Suez at all times.

The commando carrier would be similar to the U.S. Navy's amphibious assault ships (LPH). However,

whereas the U.S. ships normally operated as part of an amphibious squadron with a variety of other amphibious ships, the British commando carriers would generally operate independent of other amphibious ships. Thus, the British ship would have more extensive command and control facilities, carry a more balanced landing force, and have landing craft in addition to helicopters with which to put troops and equipment ashore.

The Royal Navy found it expedient and feasible to convert existing aircraft carriers to commando ships. The 22,000-ton light carrier *Bulwark* returned from her last commission as a fixed-wing carrier in late 1958 and entered the yard for conversion to a helicopter ship. Although the *Bulwark*'s flight deck had earlier been arranged for angled-deck operations, no structural changes had been made. Accordingly, helicopter spots were marked on her flight deck, her arresting gear and catapults were removed, and accommodations were initially provided for some 600 troops in addition to a ship's company of some 1,000 officers and enlisted men. Extensive air conditioning was installed to allow sustained operations in tropic areas and four assault landing craft were fitted on amidships davits. The *Bulwark*'s armament was reduced to 18 40-mm anti-aircraft guns (later reduced to eight guns in twin mounts).

While the *Bulwark* was undergoing conversion, the Admiralty announced that her sister ship *Albion* would also be fitted as a helicopter carrier after the *Bulwark* was ready for operations. Two ships of this type would ensure at least one always on station East of Suez while

A Fairey Gannet AEW.3 lands on the U.S. carrier *Forrestal*. This aircraft, developed from the Gannet ASW aircraft, had two radar operators seated within the fuselage, behind the pilot. Contrarotating propellers are turned by the plane's twin turboprop engines. The "guppy" radome houses the AN/APS-20 search radar. The "H" on the tail fin indicated that the plane was assigned to HMS *Hermes*. (U.S. Navy)

The British version of the Sikorsky S-58/HUS/HSS-1 helicopter was the Westland Wessex. The HAS.1 had a gas turbine vice reciprocating engine (note exhausts below cockpit) and carried active "dipping" sonar and two homing torpedoes. With ASW gear removed, up to 16 troops could be embarked, with some No. 845 Squadron helicopters being redesignated HAR.1 for service in North Borneo. The Wessex Mk I served in FAA squadrons until 1979. (Westland Aircraft)

the other was undergoing overhaul or was in transit. With the conversion of the *Albion* and *Bulwark* the Royal Navy had only five carriers capable of operating fixed-wing aircraft, the *Eagle*, *Ark Royal*, *Victorious*, *Centaur*, and *Hermes*. The older light carriers *Glory*, *Ocean*, *Perseus*, and *Theseus* were scrapped between 1958 and 1962; the light carrier *Triumph* was taken in hand for conversion to a repair ship in 1958; the *Majestic*, which had served in the Canadian Navy from 1946 to 1957, was scrapped in 1963; and the unfinished *Leviathan* was broken up in 1968.

The *Bulwark* was recommissioned as the Royal Navy's first commando carrier on January 19, 1960. A 600-man Marine commando was embarked with weapons and about 50 vehicles. To lift the Marines the carrier was assigned a Navy squadron flying 16 Whirlwind HAR helicopters, the British transport version of the HRS/HO4S series, plus five spare Whirlwinds. The Whirlwind, capable of lifting only 1,000 pounds—four or five men and their battle equipment—was of limited value in the transport role. However, no other helicopter was available at the time, in part because the British aviation industry was concentrating on nuclear strike forces.

After a brief period of work-up and trials in British waters, the *Bulwark*, her commando, and helicopters sailed for East of Suez. A short time later the British amphibious squadron, consisting of a headquarters ship, three tank landing ships (LSTs), and three tank landing craft (LCTs), departed the Mediterranean for a new base at Aden on the southernmost tip of the Arabian peninsula. The arrival of this squadron at Aden provided a valuable heavy-lift capacity for Army tanks and artillery to supplement the *Bulwark*'s Marines, but the LSTs and LCTs suffered from the chronic slow speed of amphibious ships (13 knots maximum compared to 28 knots for the *Bulwark*).

British naval strength East of Suez was thus one strike carrier with her attendant cruisers and destroyers, one commando carrier, and the amphibious warfare squadron. A balanced, but small naval force for an area that stretched more than 5,000 miles from Aden to Hong Kong, about twice the length of the Mediterranean. When the first test of British ability to intervene quickly with the forces came, the commando carrier was within reasonable steaming distance of the trouble spot; the strike carrier East of Suez was almost as far away as was possible.

This test came in the summer of 1961. Late in June, Abdul Karim Kassem, the fiery and intemperate dictator of Iraq, laid claim to the oil-rich territory of Kuwait in the Persian Gulf. The Iraq armed forces almost outnumbered Kuwait's entire population and the Iraqis were armed with modern Soviet weapons, including MiG-19 fighters. Much of Iraq's armed forces were concentrated to the north to cope with Kurdish discontent. However, an infantry division remained in the south with an armored brigade near Basra, a 50-mile drive along a good road from Kuwait. To oppose an invasion, Kuwait could muster only a single, well-armed battalion group of some 1,500 men. This force would be unable to halt an Iraqi assault.

Iraq's seizure of Kuwait would alter the balance of power in the Middle East and possibly deprive the noncommunist world of a prime source of petroleum. If Kuwait, a former British protected state, fell, so could other, poorer Arab countries, and Iran and Turkey might then be outflanked by procommunist forces. Britain and several Arab countries offered to aid Kuwait in resisting Iraqi aggression. The sheik of Kuwait hesitated in accepting these offers, fearing that Kassem might react to such aid with an immediate invasion that would overwhelm the small oil sheikdom before help could arrive. Allied forces would have to arrive in Kuwait as soon as news of such intervention reached Baghdad. Troop mobilizations or movements in nearby Arab countries or a reinforcement of British positions in the Middle East were likely to spark an Iraqi invasion or, at the least, be used by Kassem to foment anti-Western and anti-colonial passions. Only naval forces could allow the major buildup within striking distance of Kuwait without warning Kassem.

Realizing the limitations of the slow amphibious ships, the British had kept an LST loaded with tanks in the Persian Gulf since the amphibious warfare squadron shifted to Aden. These tanks and their crews were periodically rotated, and in late June 1961, in addition to the Navy LST, a civilian-manned LST with the relief tank force was also in the gulf.

The *Bulwark* was at Karachi when the crisis began, having entered the port on a courtesy call and to refuel prior to conducting hot weather trials off the eastern coast of Arabia. The commando carrier weighed anchor on June 29 and steamed toward the Persian Gulf. The lone British strike carrier East of Suez, the *Victorious*, was in the South China Sea at the time and was immediately ordered to set course for the Persian Gulf.

Until June 29, Kassem seemed content to watch world reaction to his claim on Kuwait without taking further action. On that day Western intelligence reports began to indicate Iraqi reinforcements, especially armored units, were moving south. The next day the sheik of Kuwait formally asked his allies for military assistance. The British and Saudi Arabian governments announced they would help Kuwait resist Iraqi aggression. The *Bulwark* steamed up the Persian Gulf at high speed. She was ordered to land her commando the following day, July 1. The commando carrier arrived off Kuwait the morning of the first to join the headquarters ship, an LST of the amphibious squadron, and a British frigate. In addition to threat of attack by the MiG-19s of the Iraqi Air Force was the threat of attack by 12 Russian-manned torpedo boats reported at nearby Iraqi port of Basra. The frigate and the *Bulwark*'s own guns could provide little defense against an attack by MiG-19s or the torpedo boats. There were no friendly fighters within combat radius of Kuwait, and the *Victorious* was too far away to send off her planes. As with the U.S. Marine landing in Lebanon three years earlier, this landing would be a calculated risk, pinning much on the value of surprise. The British did not hesitate; they had learned the costs of such delays

at Suez. A stroke of luck came when a sandstorm blew up, reducing visibility to about a mile and effectively concealing the British ships. The sandstorm also lowered temperatures, enabling the *Bulwark*'s helicopters to work more efficiently than would have been possible in the normal temperatures of the area.

One after another the *Bulwark*'s 16 helicopters lifted from her deck carrying Marines and their equipment. About one-half of the helicopters had taken off empty and hovered nearby while the others loaded troops and took off. Then the empty Whirlwinds overhead touched down to load their "sticks" of Marines.

The first British carrier to be fully adopted for the helicopter assault role was the *Bulwark*, shown here at Singapore. She has Marine vehicles and artillery parked aft; two Whirlwind helicopters are forward. The vehicles are normally stowed on the hangar deck. The smaller vehicles can be slung under helicopters and flown ashore; the larger ones are transported in four landing craft carried on davits. (Royal Navy)

A Kuwaiti helicopter sent to guide the Whirlwinds ashore became lost itself, and the *Bulwark*'s radar guided the helicopters to Kuwait's airport. The helicopters landed the Marines at the airport to prevent an Iraqi air-landing assault on the capital and to hold open the runways to fly in British reinforcements. Kuwait's single battalion group was already deployed to the north of the capital across the expected invasion route.

As the Marines took up defensive positions on the airfield, a squadron of RAF Hunter fighters began arriving from the British base at Bahrain, 250 miles away, to provide ground support and limited air defense capabilities. The subsonic Hunters were not considered capable of opposing the MiG-19s, especially without the aid of radar warning and direction installations. Also, the LST landed her tanks to reinforce the Marines.

During the night of July 1–2 the *Bulwark*'s four landing craft brought in the commando's trucks and trailers. This last operation was difficult because of the darkness and prevailing wind. The proximity of torpedo boats at Basra made it an uneasy night for the *Bulwark*'s captain. For the remainder of the crisis the *Bulwark* spent the nights maneuvering in the gulf.

Meanwhile, the Marine commando began moving up to defensive positions north of the city, employing the *Bulwark*'s helicopters, military vehicles, and hired local vehicles. With the airfield secured additional British troops were flown in and two squadrons of Canberra jet bombers arrived along with a second squadron of Hunter fighters. This air traffic thoroughly congested the airfield, which could handle the arriving aircraft at intervals of only about 20 minutes. Not until the *Victorious* arrived off Kuwait on July 9 was a realistic air defense provided for the forces ashore and offshore. The *Victorious*, with her Type 984 radar, also provided control of the crowded skies over Kuwait, a task that the operations people in the *Bulwark* had been hard-pressed to carry out with their limited equipment. A second strike carrier became available when the *Centaur* passed through the Suez Canal during the night of July 5–6 and then stood by off Aden awaiting further developments.

After additional Marines and soldiers were flown in, the *Bulwark*'s commando returned to the vicinity of the airport to form a mobile reserve that could be rushed to reinforce other troops. An attempt was made to base the *Bulwark*'s helicopters ashore with the Marines to improve reaction time. However, the aircraft and pilots both suffered, and it was decided that with the good communications available the helicopters should be based aboard ship.

On July 8, with it obvious that the British would defend Kuwait against any manner of attack, Kassem explained that his earlier statements were meant only to establish a formal claim on Kuwait and that he would not enforce that claim with aggression. With the immediate threat over, the *Bulwark* began taking aboard 200 Marines and soldiers each day for baths, good meals, beer, and rest in air-conditioned spaces. Exactly three weeks after the landing the *Bulwark* reembarked her own commando and its vehicles and the next day set course for Singapore. Other British troops remained in Kuwait until a 2,500-man force from the Arab League began arriving in Kuwait on September 19 to ensure the sheikdom's independence.

Bushfires from Aden to Zanzibar

HMS *Albion* was recommissioned on August 1, 1962, as the Royal Navy's second commando ship; the term "carrier" was deleted in the Royal Navy as it had been in the U.S. Navy to avoid confusion with fixed-wing carriers.[12] Outwardly *Albion* was similar to her sister ship *Bulwark*, but her commando and helicopters were different. The Royal Marines had no field artillery, and to provide fire support four 105-mm howitzers manned by 60 Royal Artillerymen were attached to the *Albion*'s commando.

In lieu of the all-Whirlwind helicopter squadrons in the *Bulwark*, the *Albion* initially was provided with 8 Whirlwinds and 12 of the newer Wessex Mk I helicopters. The latter, with a greater range and speed than the Whirlwinds, could each carry 12 loaded troops versus five in the older helicopters. The Wessex could alternatively carry up to 4,000 pounds of cargo, including artillery and small trucks slung externally. Further, the Wessex helicopters had four weapon stations and could be armed with combinations of machine guns, pods of 2-inch rockets, and SS.11 wire-guided, anti-tank missiles. Later the improved Wessex Mk 5 would become available. Similar helicopters were later assigned to the *Bulwark*.

The commando ship *Albion* sailed for duty East of Suez in November 1962. While steaming across the Indian Ocean en route to Singapore, she received orders to make all speed possible. Trouble had started in Borneo on December 8, 1962, with a small and not too significant rebellion in the Sultanate of Brunei, a

Royal Marines rush to board Wessex HAR.5 helicopters of No. 848 Squadron on the commando ship *Albion* during an amphibious exercise. Each of the nine helicopters on her deck could lift some 12 troops and their equipment, meaning more than 100 men could be simultaneously landed at the objective. Such vertical assault tactics made traditional over-the-beach assaults obsolete. (Royal Navy)

British protectorate lying within the then-British colony of Sarawak. The rebellion itself was quickly suppressed by British troops brought in by air and sea at the request of the sultan. Order was restored, and the rebel leader fled to the Philippines.

Many of the rebels had taken refuge in the jungle, and some had crossed the border into Indonesia. These rebels were rearmed and trained by the Indonesians and, with Indonesian soldiers, returned across the border into Sarawak. Thus, the British were faced with the problem of guerrilla infiltration along hundreds of miles of jungle border.

Upon her arrival at Singapore, the *Albion* embarked additional troops and set course for Borneo, where she arrived on December 15. The *Albion*'s 18 helicopters were immediately committed to support of the British forces ashore. The helicopters made it possible for the troops to reach areas otherwise inaccessible and to patrol areas more rapidly and with fewer men than possible with surface transportation. The *Albion*'s eight Whirlwinds were based ashore while the longer-legged Wessex helicopters operated from both the ship and shore bases. Some of the advanced bases in Borneo were nothing more than clearings in the jungle stocked with a few cans of fuel. Maintaining the helicopters ashore—and indeed just surviving—was a considerable challenge to the helicopter pilots and maintenance personnel. According to one account, the enlisted mechanics

> were called upon to maintain the aircraft in weather that was either very hot or very wet; seldom anything between. Camp beds and mosquito nets were the order of the day and the accommodations more usually a hastily erected *basha* [Bamboo hut]. The food was usually Campo Rations augmented by whatever could be acquired from . . . the native tribes.[13]

For the next three years British and Malaysian forces were engaged in a difficult campaign—termed a "confrontation"—against Indonesian regulars and guerrillas. The Royal Navy's main task was to guard the Malaysian coastlines against enemy landings, generally from sampans and sometimes from Indonesian motor torpedo boats, the latter again provided by the Soviets. The British problem was complicated by the traditional barter trade between the Indonesian islands and the thousands of fishermen in the narrow Malacca

and Singapore Straits. The brunt of this patrol effort fell on the small ships, but the larger ships, including the commando ships, regularly fueled, provisioned, and otherwise supported the smaller ships. More important, either the *Albion* or *Bulwark* was normally in the area to ferry troops, vehicles, helicopters, and light fixed-wing aircraft to and from the operational area. The commando ships' own helicopters as well as their Marines were often ashore. When operating in support of ground forces these Navy helicopters—many flown by Marines—came under RAF operational control. This cooperation and the participation of Australian and New Zealand forces made the campaign one of the most integrated in British military history. This confrontation with Indonesia continued until the abortive communist coup d'etat in Indonesia and the subsequent military takeover in the fall of 1965.

During 1963 the Royal Navy adopted a policy of keeping at least two strike carriers in addition to one commando ship East of Suez. One Marine commando was aboard the on-station commando ship, one additional commando and a Marine brigade headquarters was maintained at Singapore, and a third commando was based at Aden. The commando ships could squeeze aboard two commandos for brief periods; thus the Royal Navy had a potent amphibious striking force available in Indian Ocean–Southeast Asia areas during this period.

While the British were heavily involved in the confrontation with Indonesia, civil war erupted in Yemen creating a requirement for land and air forces to patrol the frontiers of Aden and the South Arabian Federation. Land-based forces, essentially dependent upon seaborne logistics, carried out this work for the most part. Then a third crisis erupted: Late in January 1964, following the revolution on the East African island of Zanzibar, army units of nearby Tanganyika mutinied. More trouble was believed to be brewing in adjacent Kenya and Uganda. All of these new states were at the time members of the British Commonwealth. In Kenya and Uganda the loyal government forces had control of the principal airfields making it possible to fly in British troops from Aden and the United Kingdom. However, in Tanganyika the rebels had seized the airfields and the capital city of Dar-es-Salaam and its docks.

At the time the only commando ship East of Suez, the *Albion*, was off Borneo. Fortunately, the strike carrier *Centaur*, formerly a sister ship to the *Albion* and

Bulwark, had just arrived in Aden after transiting the Suez Canal and Red Sea. The *Centaur* quickly embarked the 600-man Royal Marine commando at Aden, its trucks and 70 tons of ammunition and supplies, and five Army armored scout cars. Two large RAF Belvedere twin-turbine, 19-passenger helicopters were brought aboard at Aden and the carrier's own aircraft were stowed on the hangar and flight decks, leaving only enough deck space free to operate three of the ship's Wessex helicopters. The six Wessex HAS.1 helicopters in the *Centaur* were stripped of their sonar gear to enable each to carry eight troops.

The commando and its equipment were loaded aboard in less than half a day, and just after midnight on the night of January 20–21 the *Centaur* departed Aden for the East African coast. En route Marine, helicopter, and ship officers worked out landing plans. The six Wessexes and two Belvederes would fly in the troops in eight- and 16-man "sticks," respectively; the larger helicopters would also fly in the larger vehicles as required. Two older Whirlwind helicopters aboard the ship for rescue work would be held in reserve. Men and equipment needed to be sorted out, but the tremendous amount of material on board the 22,000-ton warship prevented the Navy's normal standards of order.

The situation was further complicated by such problems as the Marines having brought on board 130 cans of gasoline for their vehicles—a serious fire hazard; the Belvedere rotors not folding, thus preventing them from being lowered to the hangar deck; and camp beds for Marines and supplies of every description being crammed into almost every square foot of space below decks. In the event that the *Centaur* had to operate her fixed-wing aircraft, plans were made for each Marine to pick up his weapon, equipment, bed, and bedding and be squeezed into corners to free additional operating space. This evolution, known as "Sardine Stations," was never ordered.

On the night of January 24–25, 1964, the *Centaur* closed Dar-es-Salaam and took aboard the former commanding officer of the Tanganyika Rifles, who had been in hiding since the mutiny. A regular British officer, he would be in overall command of the operations ashore. The first assignment of the Marines was to disarm the mutinous troops in barracks to the north of the city.

Two open areas were available for a helicopter landing: one a mile or two south of the barracks and the other a sports field only 50 yards from the nearest barracks. If the helicopters came down at the more distant clearing, the mutineers might have time to organize a

Aircraft carriers have continually displayed their characteristics of mobility and flexibility in "brush-fire" operations, such as the military mutinies in East Africa in 1964. During those events the light fleet carrier *Centuar* hastily embarked some 600 Royal Marines, their vehicles, and stores. Using her ASW helicopters for transport, the *Centaur* served as a combination strike/commando ship with excellent results. (Royal Navy)

determined resistance before the Marines could reach the barracks; if the Marines were landed close-in a few mutineers with automatic weapons could conceivably wreak havoc among the vulnerable helicopters as they came down. It was decided to land close to the barracks because it required the simpler plan, increased the chances of surprise, and would put the Marines inside the minimum range of the mutineers' mortars. To be on the safe side, an alternate landing strip was designated some distance away.

The *Centaur* steamed close to shore to reduce the helicopter turn-around time, and at 6:10 A.M. the first wave of helicopters took off; five minutes later the Marines were scrambling out of the helicopters as they hovered a few inches above the ground alongside the barracks.

Suddenly the early morning sky exploded. A British destroyer offshore fired airbursts from her 4.5-inch guns over the barracks; the Marine company that had just landed added to the display by firing its anti-tank rocket launchers off to the sides of the camp. While the Marines had achieved complete surprise, the mutineers soon began a light return fire. The Marines worked closer to the resistance under cover of rifle and light machine-gun fire. When the mutineers refused a call by their former commanding officer to surrender, the Marines fired a rocket into the roof of the guardroom. The mutineers immediately gave up.

It took only 70 minutes to land the three rifle companies of the commando and two hours to search out the area and round up most of the mutineers. A few escaped into the brush. (The commando's support company was temporarily held aboard the *Centaur*.) According to the commanding officer of the commando:

> In retrospect the operation was easy; at the moment of landing, with so few helicopters on a vulnerable LS [landing site] and the inevitable political restrictions on suppressive fire, we wondered at our own rashness. Perhaps the very suddenness and violence of the first 40 minutes prevented serious fighting and casualties at Colito [the barracks] and after.[14]

With trucks flown in by the Belvederes and others taken from the Tanganyika Rifles, the Marines set out for the airfield (ten miles away) and Dar-es-Salaam. Marines in helicopters went first to reconnoiter as armed men were reported in both places. The armed men left the airport just as the Marines arrived by helicopter. The Marines then moved on Dar-es-Salaam from the airport (to the south) and barracks (to the north). There was no opposition in the city, only a warm welcome.

Next, the Marines were asked to deal with another rebellious battalion of the Tanganyika Rifles at Tabora, 340 miles up country. The commando's support company was brought ashore to patrol Dar-es-Salaam, and the remainder of the commando made preparations to move up to Tabora. Since the town was beyond the effective range of the helicopters in an assault role, the RAF made preparations to fly transports into Dar-es-Salaam to move the Marines to Tabora. However, while waiting for the RAF planes a commercial four-engine transport was made available and some three score Marines flew up to Tabora. In the meantime, the *Centaur* had cleared off the last of her guests and was back in the fixed-wing aircraft business. She flew off a flight of Sea Vixen fighters that arrived over Tabora just before the transport.

As the transport was approaching the runway another aircraft was seen coming down on the same strip from the opposite direction. With sharp words over the radio and sharp maneuvering the other plane won out, and the Marines touched down a minute or two later. The second plane was an RAF transport from Nairobi carrying RAF troops who were also coming to secure the airfield.

The mutineers at Tabora had returned their arms to the armory, and the Marines were directed to stand by. During the remainder of the afternoon two full Marine companies were flown into Tabora. The native battalion was then assembled and the leaders of the mutiny arrested. This was less than 24 hours after the original landing outside Dar-es-Salaam.

The commando was then told to stand by for another operation. One company was left at Tabora and the other flew back to Dar-es-Salaam. This final operation was at Natchingwea, 220 miles south of Dar-es-Salaam, where a company from the Tabora battalion had mutinied. The circumstances were similar; the troops had handed in their arms, but the proximity of the barracks to the airfield made it imperative that loyal troops be sent in. Again the *Centaur*'s Sea Vixens provided cover while RAF transports flew in a company of Marines. The rebel leaders were quickly apprehended and the arms secured.

On January 30 another Marine commando was flown into Tanganyika from Britain. The Marines landed from the *Centaur* were loaded aboard the strike carrier *Victorious* for further transfer to the commando ship *Albion*. On February 25, five weeks after the Marines had set out on their odyssey, the commando was returned by helicopters to its base at Aden.

The operation had been an excellent example of an aircraft carrier's flexibility. Without the *Centaur*, landing troops in Tanganyika would have been risky if not impossible. The mutineers had controlled the airfields and docks when the operation began and, as evidenced by the reaction to the initial helicopter landing, were ready to use their weapons. A parachute drop based on airfields in Kenya or Uganda would have involved delays and the risks inherent in parachute operations, particularly the vulnerability of the paratroopers while descending and assembling on the ground in the face of hostile ground fire. Further, the *Centaur* was able to provide tactical aircraft to cover the landings in the event major resistance was encountered.

In her combined roles of commando ship and strike carrier the *Centaur* was a busy ship and in a six-month period steamed some 50,000 miles, a mark comparable with "hot war" operations.

British carriers in the post-Suez period demonstrated their continuing value and simultaneously their increasing age. The Washington Treaty–era 20-year "rule" of warship obsolescence went by the books as the *Victorious*, first completed in 1941, and the later carriers of the war programs continued to operate the newer jet-propelled aircraft. Still, the increasing size, landing speeds, and complexity of the newer aircraft imposed severe restrictions on the carriers. The large *Ark Royal* and *Eagle*, each designed to operate up to 100 aircraft, in the early 1960s could operate less than half that number including eight ASW helicopters. The *Victorious* could operate 25 fixed-wing aircraft and eight helicopters and the two other British strike carriers, the *Centaur* and *Hermes*, could operate about 20 fixed-wing aircraft plus eight helicopters in the early 1960s. The five British carriers thus had an aggregate capacity of about 145 fixed-wing aircraft and 40 helicopters. Newer aircraft carriers were sorely needed.

The light fleet carrier *Hermes* was extensively redesigned during construction and was completed with many advanced features. The Type 984 radar antenna dominates her island structure. The *Hermes* is shown here in 1966 with Sea Vixen all-weather fighters and Buccaneer strike aircraft. In company with the larger *Ark Royal*, *Eagle*, and *Victorious*, she served as a first-line carrier despite her smaller size and slower speed. (Royal Navy)

With the Navy Estimates for 1962–1963 it was at last announced: "There is no need to order a new carrier yet but the necessary design work has been put in hand."

The Next Generation[15]

On July 30, 1963, the British government announced a new aircraft carrier to replace both the *Ark Royal* and *Victorious*. With the *Centaur* due to be phased out of service in the mid-1960s, the new carrier together with the extensively modernized *Eagle* (44,100 tons) and *Hermes* (23,000 tons) would provide for a force of three strike carriers until at least 1980. In his announcement, Peter Thorneycroft, then–Minister of Defence, stated that the new carrier would have a standard displacement of about 50,000 tons and would be designed specifically for Vertical Takeoff and Landing (VTOL) as well as conventional aircraft operations. On the subject of ship propulsion, Thorneycroft said that a nuclear power plant had been considered but rejected, noting "there may well be a future for nuclear propulsion for surface ships, but to embark on what would be largely an experimental venture in the case of a capital ship like an aircraft carrier would be to take a very considerable gamble."

The Defence White Paper of 1964 spelled out more details of the new ship: "When the new aircraft carrier joins the Fleet in the early 1970s she will incorporate the results of advances in scientific and technical invention over the last twenty years which will make her a great deal more formidable even than the modernised *Eagle*, though her size will be only marginally greater." Designated the CVA.01 for planning purposes, the new carrier design would be approximately 900 feet overall in length with a displacement of 53,000 tons. This was larger than any previous British carrier and put the new ship in the same class as the U.S. *Midway* (45,000 tons) and cancelled British *Gibraltar* (45,300 tons).[16]

To hold down displacement, growth of the flight deck arrangement provided for few aircraft to be carried beyond those that could be stowed in the hangar, and there would be no armor, not even for magazines. The parallel-lane flight deck was the most unusual feature of the CVA.01 and was considered the next generation in aircraft carrier design after the angled flight deck. The flight deck provided for a landing and take-off lane and a separate parking lane. This layout offered two major advantages over the angled deck: Upon landing during periods of low visibility or through a

The Royal Navy, which conceived the angled flight deck, proposed the parallel deck concept for its next generation of aircraft carriers. The first carrier was the CVA.01, to be named *Queen Elizabeth II*. Note the position of the island to permit aircraft to taxi along the starboard side, the inboard elevator forward of the island, the deck-edge lift aft, and the slight angle (3½ degrees) of the landing lane. (Royal Navy)

low cloud ceiling the carrier pilot's first view of the flight deck occurs very late. For the pilot of a high-speed aircraft this leaves little or no time to make corrections in lining up with the angled flight deck. Invariably, the first indication of the carrier to a pilot landing under these conditions is the ship's wake, especially at night as the ship creates a bioluminescent trail. However, the wake indicates the axis of the ship, which differs several degrees from the center of the angled deck. With the parallel deck the landing lane is only 3½ degrees off the ship's axis. While perfectly parallel deck lanes were desired, this angle, about half that of other modern carriers, was imposed because an extreme flight deck width of 184 feet was required to provide passage through certain canals and entry into drydocks.

Also, the angled deck divided the remainder of a carrier's flight deck into a major area on the starboard side forward and a minor area on the port side aft. The latter could not be used during flight operations and is essentially wasted space. With the parallel deck concept, after landing the aircraft turns right out of the arresting wires and taxis aft on the inboard side of the island structure to refueling and rearming points or to the after elevator. After being serviced, the aircraft, with wings now folded, taxis forward on the outboard side of the island to the catapult position forward.

The elevator arrangement of the CVA.01 would be similar to that of the French carriers *Clemenceau* and *Foch*, with the no. 1 lift forward of the island and slightly to starboard of the centerline; U.S. carrier experience in heavy seas led the British to place this forward elevator inboard. The no. 2 lift would be at the edge of the flight deck aft of the island. The other CVA.01 aviation features included a steam catapult on the forward flight deck and one on the landing lane, and landing aircraft would engage wires of a water-spray arresting gear that would engage aircraft at higher landing speeds than possible with contemporary equipment. A unique feature of the device was its ability to halt all aircraft, regardless of weight and landing speed, in the same runout distance, thus simplifying flight deck operations. The water-spray arresting gear would be about one-third the weight and one-half the cost of existing arresting equipment. The carrier's island structure would be large, in the traditional British design, stretching 200 feet or almost a quarter of the ship's length. The island would be only 18 feet wide and placed inboard 34 feet to allow aircraft to taxi around both sides without interfering with aircraft landing operations.

These features would enable the CVA.01 to operate about 70 aircraft—Buccaneer S.2 strike aircraft, SH-3D ASW helicopters, and F-4K Phantom fighters, the last produced in the United States. Close-in defense for the ship would be provided by a twin Seadart anti-aircraft missile launcher on the carrier's fantail. This after missile position placed the flight deck ramp just forward of the quarterdeck, meaning that an aircraft falling short on landing could make a "nasty mess" on top of the Seadart missile launcher. However, extensive analysis of accidents revealed that since the introduction of the mirror landing system, and with the four arresting wires positioned well up the flight deck, there had been no case of a stern crash as a result of an aircraft falling short of the flight deck on a British carrier.

To propel the CVA.01 the Royal Navy accepted an oil-burning, steam turbine power plant with three propeller shafts. Three shafts offered a better margin for battle damage than would two and required considerably less space and man-power than a four-shaft plant. Designed sustained speed was 28 knots.

With construction scheduled to begin in 1966, the CVA.01 would enter for service in 1972 with the name expected to be *Queen Elizabeth II*. The British carrier fleet would be reduced to three ships upon completion of the CVA.01, but the new ship would provide a major qualitative improvement in the Royal Navy; and, there was already talk of the CVA.02 and possibly a CVA.03. The future of British and French carrier aviation, as well as that of several other countries, seemed assured.

13 NEW SHIPS AND PLANES

Nuclear propulsion and piston-engines converged for a brief period aboard the USS *Enterprise* as AD-6/A-1H Skyraiders of attack squadron VA-65 are armed and readied on the flight deck. This October 1962 photo shows the "billboard" antennas of the AN/SPS-32 and AN/SPS-33 radars. Each Skyraider has 12 500-pound bombs on wing pylons plus a centerline bomb and two 300-gallon drop tanks. (U.S. Navy)

The *Enterprise* introduced nuclear propulsion to aircraft carriers. She has the improved *Forrestal* deck arrangement coupled with a unique island structure. In this 1962 photo all four of her elevators are at the hangar-deck level. Although the *Enterprise* could operate for several years on a single uranium "fueling," she must regularly replenish because of the fuel and munition consumption of her aircraft and the needs of her crew and air wing of more than 5,000 men. Alongside is the ammunition ship *Shasta.* (U.S. Navy)

The 1960s began with the U.S. Navy commissioning three super carriers within a single year. The *Kitty Hawk* hoisted her commission pennant on April 29, 1961, and the *Constellation* joined the Fleet on October 27, 1961. Both ships were behind their construction schedules, the *Kitty Hawk* because of poor workmanship at the New York Shipbuilding Corporation yard, where she was built, and the *Constellation* because of a severe fire while under construction at the New York Naval Shipyard (in which 50 yard workers were killed and 323 were injured). The new *Enterprise* was placed in commission on November 25, 1961.

As noted earlier, the *Kitty Hawk* and *Constellation* were improved versions of the *Forrestal* design. So was the "Big E," which carried the name of the most famous World War II–era U.S. carrier, which, despite efforts to save her as a memorial, was stricken from the Navy Register on October 2, 1956, and scrapped. The new *Enterprise* was the largest warship yet built, with a standard displacement of 75,700 tons and an overall length of 1,123 feet. Her deck arrangement was similar to that of the *Kitty Hawk* and *Constellation*, but the *Enterprise*'s nuclear power plant required no funnel and her island structure was a boxlike affair mounting massive fixed radar antennas—"billboards"—that formed the side panels and a dome studded with electronic countermeasures antennas. The fixed radars, four

AN/SPS-32 for long-range search and AN/SPS-33 for height finding, provided rapid detection and computation of targets.[1]

The *Enterprise* had eight nuclear reactors that provided steam to turn four turbines and four propeller shafts to drive her in excess of 30 knots—a speed officially described only as making the *Enterprise* faster than any other carrier in history. But the speed of the *Enterprise* was not as significant as her ability to accelerate or decelerate rapidly without having to turn up additional boilers or to have additional personnel man the engineering spaces. This allowed the *Enterprise* to turn into the wind to launch or recover aircraft and then rejoin the main force or return to course faster than conventionally powered carriers. The most impressive capability of the *Enterprise*'s propulsion plant was range—measured in years rather than miles. Eight nuclear reactors in the *Enterprise* drove the ship more than 200,000 miles in three years on the first loading of uranium fuel rods; the second set of uranium cores—installed in early 1965—had about 25 percent greater life, and cores subsequently developed could drive the ship for almost 15 years on a single fueling. The newer cores were more expensive than those first installed, but their cost per mile was less.

Although the world's largest warship at the time, the *Enterprise* initially had no armament other than her aircraft. In an effort to hold down her construction cost (to $445 million) no guns or missiles were installed, although space was reserved for a Terrier surface-to-air missile system. She was subsequently provided with a point-defense missile system consisting of eight-rail launchers for the Sparrow III air-to-air missile. This system, dubbed "Sea Sparrow," was a close-in or "terminal" defense with target acquisition by radar or visual means although the missiles themselves were radar guided. The Sparrow III missile had a range of about ten miles.

As these three super carriers were being completed, the Kennedy administration, which took office in January 1961, was facing its first international crisis. Soviet pressure on the Western enclave in Berlin increased, reaching a climax on August 12–13 when the border between East and West Berlin was closed and the Berlin Wall was erected. President Kennedy's reaction was to increase the readiness of the armed forces. For the Navy this included retaining the carrier *Lexington* in an attack status to increase the number of operational attack carriers from 14 to 15. Other ships were reactivated from the mothball fleet, approval was given to increase the size of the active Army, 250,000 reservists of all services were called to active duty, and Air Force bombers scheduled for disposal were retained in service.

The noted U.S. Army historian S. L. A. Marshall tied the 1961 increase in U.S. combat forces to the completion of the three super carriers in the same year. Discussing aircraft carriers in the nuclear era, he wrote,

> Risks have to be run in determining force and armament levels. There is never any such thing as perfect, all-around balance. When we attempt to be safe everywhere, we are safe nowhere, for the bill would wreck the economy. So it is simply idle to speculate about whether one super carrier would have more influence on operations, come war, than an additional army corps, which could be organized, equipped and paid for one year for a roughly equivalent sum. Enough to sum up then my view that the super carrier afloat today has more restraining value on the USSR, and a more positive deterrent to thermo-nuclear war, than the 1961 call-up of two Army divisions kept in the United States.[2]

Such sentiments concerning super carriers were not necessarily shared by the administration. Congress had authorized funds for another super carrier (the eighth) to be started in fiscal year 1961, and designated CVA 66, she was laid down on January 9, 1961.[3] The budget for the fiscal year 1962 (beginning July 1, 1961) did not include a new carrier. Funds for a ninth super carrier (CVA 67) were authorized the following year, but the administration delayed awarding a contract for the ship as controversy raged over her propulsion plant.

New Planes

New aircraft, designed primarily for operation from super carriers, went aboard U.S. carriers in the early 1960s. The new fighter was the McDonnell F4H-1 Phantom, a twin-engine, two-place, multipurpose aircraft. McDonnell initially designed the aircraft as a single-place, fighter-attack aircraft, at one point designated AH-1. During the plane's development the Navy requirements changed to include a long-range, high-altitude interceptor. The four 20-mm cannon originally planned were deleted, and sophisticated electronics and

A McDonnell F4H-1/F-4B Phantom from fighter squadron VF-114 shows the graceful but angular lines of this outstanding aircraft. An infrared sensor protrudes under the streamlined nose, which contained the AN/APQ-72 air intercept radar. The F-4B had a maximum speed of 1,450 m.p.h. at 48,000 feet (Mach 2.2) with four Sparrow missiles and 915 m.p.h. at sea level (Mach 1.2); its initial rate of climb was 28,000 feet per minute with four missiles; ceiling was 62,000 feet. The Phantom could fly safely with one of its two engines shut down. (U.S. Navy)

An improved F-4J Phantom with six Sparrow III air-to-air missiles and three drop tanks shows the aircraft's planform. The F-4J was the last production version of the Phantom. Phantoms were flown by the U.S. Navy, Marine Corps, and Air Force; the Royal Navy flew the F-4K variant from carriers while 11 other nations flew the Phantom from land bases. U.S. Navy and Marine F-4s had no internal gun armament. (U.S. Navy)

an all-missile armament were provided. A radar operator was seated behind the pilot to aid in operating the complex electronics system.

The first XF4H-1 flew on May 27, 1958, and it soon became apparent that the aircraft was a "winner." On November 22, 1961, an F4H-1 Phantom reached a speed of 1,606.324 m.p.h.—a new world record. More records fell to the Phantom: sustained level flight at 66,443.8 feet; an altitude of 98,558.5 feet (Phantoms subsequently reached more than 100,000 feet); and streaking from Los Angeles to New York in 2 hours, 47 minutes, 18 seconds, an average of 869.7 m.p.h. with the aircraft carrying a 600-gallon drop tank and missiles. The aircraft was refueled in flight three times. In all, F4Hs established 15 world records for speed, altitude, and climb. As an example of the Phantom's initial climb without stores—50,000 feet-per-minute— if a brick were dropped from 40,000 feet at the same moment that a Phantom was launched from a carrier deck, the fighter could reach 40,000 feet before the brick struck the water.

The competitor to the F4H-1 as the Navy's advanced fighter was the Chance Vought F8U-3 Crusader III, the latest model in that successful fighter line.[4] The F8U-3 Crusader was significantly larger and had a more powerful engine—hence better performance—than the earlier Crusaders. The first flight on an XF8U-3 occurred on June 2, 1958, and the aircraft subsequently achieved a speed of Mach 2.39. Heat limitations of the plexiglass windshield prevented further acceleration; it was estimated that the F8U-3 had the potential of achieving Mach 2.9 (approximately 1,950 m.p.h.) at 35,000 feet.

Although faster and more maneuverable, the Crusader still represented a single-engine, single-place, specialized interceptor compared to the two-engine, two-man, multimission F4H-1. The Navy selected the F4H-1, which was ordered into production as the Phantom II, or just "Phantom" to newcomers to naval aviation who had not known the FH-1 Phantom, the U.S. Navy's first operational jet aircraft.[5]

The Phantom was the U.S. Navy's first operational fighter without guns, and it relied on an air-to-air armament of six Sparrow radar-homing missiles or four Sparrows and four Sidewinder infrared missiles for intercept missions. In the attack role a Phantom could carry a payload of almost six tons, including such combinations as 11 1,000-pound bombs or 18 750-pounders or 11 napalm tanks or 4 Bullpup air-to-surface missiles. Four Sparrows could be carried with any of these attack loads. (There were four semi-recessed Sparrow bays under the fuselage plus four underwing and one centerline pylon.) Maximum overload weight for the F-4B was 54,800 pounds with 13,320 pounds of weapons.

The Phantom was unquestionably the most versatile and best-performing fighter aircraft of its time. The

The F8U-3 Crusader III lost in competition to the F-4 Phantom II to become the U.S. Navy's all-weather, missile-armed fighter. Shown here carrying two Sparrow III missiles, the F8U-3 did not have an internal gun. The aircraft had large ventral fins aft that were rotated to horizontal during low-speed flight and turned vertical to provide stability during high-speed (Mach 2+) flight. Note the air-intake configuration. (U.S. Navy)

plane began reaching fleet squadrons in early 1962. Phantoms provided a single aircraft for all fighter functions, ending the assignment of separate day and night fighter squadrons to carriers, a practice that had begun in 1954.

Because of its size and complexity, the Phantom was not embarked in *Essex*-class carriers, although trials aboard the *Intrepid* demonstrated that these smaller ships could safely operate the aircraft. By the mid-1960s attack carriers of the *Midway* and larger classes each operated two Phantom squadrons, while the *Essex*es remaining in the attack role (five ships in 1968) each carried two squadrons of Crusaders. (These and all other naval aircraft were redesignated in 1962, the F4H becoming the F-4 and the F8U the F-8; see table 13-1.)

The U.S. Marine Corps employed Phantoms for its land-based fighter-attack (VMFA) squadrons and flew the RF-4B in the photo-reconnaissance role. The Phantom also made history when the U.S. Air Force adopted it as its standard all-weather fighter (F-4C) and photo-reconnaissance aircraft (RF-4C), making the Phantom the first shipboard fighter to be accepted in large numbers by a land-based air force—albeit at the direction of Kennedy's Secretary of Defense, Robert S. McNamara.

Significantly, while all U.S. Air Force Phantoms— RF-4s as well as "straight" F-4s—could deliver a variety of nuclear weapons, no Navy or Marine Corps Phantoms in fleet squadrons were wired for nuclear weapons. Rather, the number and variety of carrier-based attack aircraft were deemed sufficient for the nuclear strike role. (Earlier carrier fighters—variants of the F9F Panther, F2H Banshee, F3H Demon, FJ Fury, and F7U Cutlass—could carry nuclear weapons.)

The Phantom was also flown by the Royal Navy in the F-4K variant as successor to the Sea Vixen, and the F-4M was flown by the Royal Air Force. The use of British-made engines and air-frame modifications in the F-4K permitted lower landing speeds necessary for use on the Royal Navy's smaller carriers.[6] In all, McDonnell Douglas built 5,050 Phantoms (and another 124 aircraft were produced in Japan).[7] This was the third largest production run of a combat aircraft in the West, after the F-86 Sabre/FJ Fury and F-80/T-33/TO programs.

A third U.S. carrier-based fighter under development during this period was a subsonic aircraft. This aircraft was to have been a launching platform for the long-range, air-to-air Eagle missile. Development of the missile began in the late 1950s, and on July 21, 1961, Douglas Aircraft received a contract to design an aircraft to launch the missile. Known as the F6D-1 Missileer, the fighter was to have had the capability of remaining aloft for several hours, orbiting a task force with eight Eagle missiles on wing pylons. Endurance was obtained at the expense of speed with the twin-jet aircraft being subsonic. Gross weight would be about 50,000 pounds. However, the project was cancelled on April 25, 1961, in favor of pursuing conventional fighter concepts.

Table 13-1
U.S. CARRIER-BASED AIRCRAFT DESIGNATIONS

Example: RF-4B (formerly F4H-1P)

R = modified mission (Reconnaissance)
F = basic mission (Fighter)
4 = design in mission aircraft series (4th)
B = series in design (2nd)

PRE-1962	NAME	NEW
AD	Skyraider	A-1
AJ	Savage	A-2
A3D	Skywarrior	A-3
A4D	Skyhawk	A-4
A3J	Vigilante	A-5
A2F	Intruder	A-6
FJ	Fury	F-1
F2H	Banshee	F-2
F3H	Demon	F-3
F4H	Phantom	F-4
F4D	Skyray	F-6
F8U	Crusader	F-8
F9F	Panther/Cougar	F-9
F3D	Skyknight	F-10
S2F	Tracker	S-2
WF	Tracer	E-1
W2F	Hawkeye	E-2
HSS-2	Sea King	H-3
HRS	—	H-19
HO4S	—	H-19
HUP	—	H-25
HSS-1	Seabat	H-34
HUS	Seabat	H-34
HR2S	—	H-37
HRB	Sea Knight	H-46

The Missileer was proposed as an air defense fighter, to fly Combat Air Patrol (CAP) with six Eagle long-range, air-to-air missiles. Douglas was selected in July 1961 to develop the aircraft, designated F6D. With a strong resemblance to the F3D Skyknight, it was to have twin engines and fly with a crew of three—pilot, copilot, and missile control operator. In overload condition two additional missiles could be carried under the fuselage. The subsonic, single-mission aircraft was abandoned within a year of the contract award. (Douglas Aircraft)

The world's only supersonic carrier-based attack air craft was the North American A3J Vigilante, developed during this period to meet the U.S. Navy's requirements for an all-weather, high- or low-level nuclear strike aircraft. Planned as a successor to the A3D/A-3 Skywarrior, the Vigilante was smaller (normal gross weight was about 55,000 pounds with a maximum of 62,000 pounds in the A3J-1); however, the Vigilante's performance was far superior to that of the subsonic Skywarrior, with a top speed of 1,320 m.p.h.

The first Vigilante flew as the YA3J-1 on August 31, 1958, and was ordered into production as the A3J-1 (subsequently A-5A). This aircraft, which first entered fleet service in January 1962, had a revolutionary "linear" bomb bay to facilitate high-speed weapons delivery. The internal tunnellike bomb bay was between the aircraft's two jet engines with the payload being ejected through an opening below the fin with the end of the tunnel being capped by a jettisonable fairing to reduce drag en route to the target. The B27 nuclear bomb was located at the forward end of the bomb bay, rigidly interconnected to two 275-gallon fuel tanks.[8] These tanks were emptied en route to the target, and in the attack the bomb-tank package was ejected rearward along rails with the empty fuel tanks serving to stabilize the weapon as the package was ejected at supersonic speeds. Two underwing pylons could each carry a nuclear weapon or a 1,000-pound bomb or a 400-gallon drop tank.[9] A two-man crew flew the plane and operated its elaborate electronics, navigation, and bombing systems. For self-defense the Vigilante relied upon high speed and maneuverability.

Fifty-seven A-5A and two improved A-5B Vigilante strike aircraft had been produced when the decision was made in 1963 to halt procurement because of the availability of ballistic missiles in the U.S. nuclear arsenal; this reduced the requirement for carrier-based strategic strike aircraft. Although the Vigilante was a formidable and successful strike aircraft, difficulties were encountered with its linear bomb bay and the package payload provided little weapons flexibility.

There was a requirement for the reconnaissance version of the Vigilante, the RA-5C, which had first flown in June 1962. This aircraft, with a gross weight approaching 70,000 pounds, was fitted with radar, infrared, electromagnetic, and television sensors, several cameras, and high-intensity strobe flashers for night photography. All systems could be operated regardless of aircraft speed with no loss of quality.

Twelve aircraft ordered as A-5B and 79 ordered as RA-5C were built to the recce configuration. Also, 52 earlier A-5A and A-5B aircraft were remanufactured to the RA-5C standard to meet Vietnam War requirements. (Total YA3J/A3J/A-5 production was 156 aircraft.) Although the RA-5C originally retained the linear bomb bay and had four underwing weapon pylons, the aircraft was not employed in the attack role. The Vigilante proved extremely successful in the reconnaissance role. RA-5Cs were assigned to six-plane squadrons on the larger carriers with the first squadron—Reconnaissance Heavy Attack Squadron (RVAH) 5—deploying aboard the *Ranger* in June 1964.[10]

All reconnaissance information collected by an RA-5C was instantaneously recorded on magnetic tapes that, together with exposed photographic films, were fed into the carrier's Integrated Operational Intelligence Center (IOIC) as soon as the plane landed aboard ship. The IOIC immediately processed the large amount of data obtained by the aircraft and then produced integrated presentations for the force commander and his staff. The key values of the RA-5C/IOIC system were the vast volume of data that could be handled and the speed with which it could be processed. This IOIC "read out" could also be provided to other ships equipped with data transmitting systems compatible with those of the carrier. (On the smaller *Essex*-class carriers the reconnaissance mission was performed in the 1960s and 1970s by three-plane detachments of RF-8A/G Crusaders.)

The line of heavy attack aircraft—AJ/A-2 Savage, A3D/A-3 Skywarrior, and A3J/A-5 Vigilante—were complemented in carrier air wings by the A4D/A-4 Skyhawk as a nuclear strike and light attack aircraft. But there was a need to both replace the AD/A-1 Skyraider as a tactical heavy-lift attack aircraft and to provide a true all-weather attack aircraft.

These requirements led to the Grumman A-6 Intruder (originally A2F), the first aircraft in history designed specifically to strike targets obscured by bad weather or darkness. And, the Intruder would carry out these strikes at very low level. Requirements for the aircraft, drawing extensively on Korean War operations of the night-flying Corsairs and Skyraiders, were formulated in 1956. The Intruder, like the British Buccaneer, was a twin-engine, two-place aircraft, but in the British aircraft the crewmen were seated in tandem while they were side-by-side in the U.S. plane. The early Intruders had a normal loaded weight of 43,000 pounds and a maximum of 54,000 pounds. They had a maximum speed of 635 m.p.h. at sea level with five 1,000-pound bombs. Conventional or nuclear weapons could be carried on five pylons for a maximum of 15,000 pounds, a lift capability exceeding the celebrated Skyraider series. No guns were fitted.

A vital feature of the early Intruders was the Digital Integrated Attack Navigation Equipment (DIANE) that combined search and track radars; navigation, communications, and identification equipment; a cockpit display system; and a high-speed digital computer. With DIANE the pilot could preselect a target, guide the aircraft, release the weapons, and leave the target area automatically. Thus the pilot could fly an entire strike mission without visual references from the time the aircraft was catapulted from a flight deck until it entered the final approach for a carrier landing. The ultimate A-6E variant was provided with improved avionics and the Target Recognition Attack Multisensor

(TRAM), Forward-Looking Infrared (FLIR), a combination laser designator/range finder, and a laser designation receiver, making the Intruder one of the most capable strike aircraft in existence.

A prototype A2F-1 Intruder flew on April 19, 1960, and deliveries to the fleet began in February 1963. While the Intruder was actually a new type of carrier-based attack plane, it was the numerical replacement for the propeller-driven A-1 Skyraider aboard carriers. Although all attack carriers were intended to receive an Intruder squadron, production schedules and attrition in the Vietnam War enabled only a few *Essex*-class CVAs to operate the aircraft. By the 1970s all U.S. carrier air wings had an Intruder squadron (along with two light attack squadrons and two fighter squadrons plus special-mission aircraft). The standard Intruder unit had ten A-6s and four KA-6D tankers. Carrier Air Wing 3 was reorganized in 1983 to evaluate an all A-6E attack capability, with the carrier *John F. Kennedy* (CV 67) embarking two F-14 fighter squadrons and two A-6E squadrons (with 25 Intruders) with no light attack aircraft. The cancellation of follow-on Intruder variants ended this wing concept in 1989.

For day attack missions the carriers received newer models of the diminutive but powerful Skyhawk during the 1960s: the A-4C (formerly A4D-2N), which first flew in 1959, had terrain-avoidance radar and a limited all-weather capability. The first A-4E (A4D-5) flew in mid-1961, introducing two additional weapons pylons (for a total of five) and multiple bomb racks enabling the plane to lift a wide variety of bombs and missiles (totaling 8,200 pounds). Improved engines give the A-4E a top speed of 685 m.p.h. (Mach 0.9) at sea level when "clean" and 576 m.p.h. (Mach 0.8) with bombs and missiles.

To counter the threat against U.S. naval forces from high-speed aircraft and long-range, air-launched guided missiles, a new Airborne Early Warning (AEW) aircraft

A North American A3J-3P/RA-5C Vigilante of reconnaissance heavy attack squadron RVAH-5 from the carrier *Constellation* over the South China Sea. The aircraft is fitted with the camera/sensor "canoe" under the fuselage. Although recon variants retained a strike capability, they were never used in the attack role in combat. (U.S. Navy)

An A3J-1/A-5A Vigilante attack aircraft on the deck of the carrier *Enterprise*. The Vigilante was designed to provide carriers with a long-range, supersonic strike capability. The aircraft was rated at 1,385 m.p.h. at 40,000 feet (Mach 2.1) and 685 m.p.h. at sea level (Mach 0.9). Service ceiling was 64,000 feet. A Vigilante set a world record by lifting a 2,204-pound payload to 91,450.8 feet. The wingtips (and nose section) folded upward for carrier stowage. (North American Aviation)

was developed for carrier operation. The existing carrier AEW aircraft, the E-1B Tracer (formerly WF-2), developed from the S2F Tracker, could not accommodate the latest electronic and computing equipment required for air warfare in the Mach 2 spectrum. Developed by Grumman as the W2F-1 and changed to the E-2A, the new AEW aircraft was the world's first aircraft developed specifically for that role. The E-2 Hawkeye was easily distinguished by its 24-foot, disc-shaped "rotodome," which housed a rotating AN/APS-96 radar antenna. The rotodome revolves in flight at the rate of six times per minute; when aboard ship it can be lowered two feet to facilitate hangar stowage. Installed in the plane was an Airborne Tactical Data System (ATDS), which automatically sent data to a carrier or other warships with compatible equipment; or, the E-2A could serve as an autonomous detection and command/control system to provide warning of enemy attacks, direct friendly interceptors, detect and jam enemy electronics, or coordinate friendly air strikes and other air operations, all with the carrier remaining electronically silent if desired.

The equipment to carry out these missions, including six digital computers, accounted for some 10,000 pounds of the aircraft's gross takeoff weight of 49,500 pounds. Twin turboprop engines powered the E-2.

The first Hawkeye took to the air on October 21, 1960, and the first fully equipped aircraft flew the following April. Fleet introduction began in January 1964 while the aircraft was still undergoing Navy evaluation. An early warning squadron VAW-11 detachment took the Hawkeye into combat aboard the *Kitty Hawk* in 1966. Although initial Navy requirements directed that the E-2 be capable of operating from modernized

Essex-class ships, the cost as well as size of the aircraft prohibited it being used aboard the smaller carriers. Thus the *Essex* CVA as well as CVS carriers continued to use the E-1B Tracer (better known as the "Willie Fudd" from its earlier WF designation). The E-1B had a wingspan of 72 feet 4 inches and a length of 45 feet 4 inches; the E-2's wingspan is 80 feet 7 inches and length is 56 feet 4 inches.

With the introduction of these new aircraft the attack carrier air groups (CVG) were redesignated as wings (CVW) on December 23, 1963, to better equate them with Air Force tactical air wings.[11] But because of the naval aviators' mood of defiance, carrier wing commanders continued to be called CAG for Comman-

The Grumman A2F/A-6 Intruder was developed to provide an all-weather, day/night strike capabilities. The plane could lift weapon loads in excess to those carried by the A-1 Skyraider and had a relatively long endurance/range. Here an A-6A is about to be catapulted from the carrier *Independence* shortly before the carrier steamed for Vietnam to enter combat with the first Intruder squadron, VA-75. Note the refueling probe in front of the cockpit; three 300-gallon drop tanks and practice bombs are mounted on the plane's five pylons. (R. C. Lister, U.S. Navy)

Grumman developed specialized AEW aircraft for carrier operation, the most advanced aircraft of their type when they became operational. The WF-2/E-1B Tracer (left) was derived from the S2F/S-2 Tracker design; the improved W2F-1/E-2A Hawkeye was a new design aircraft. Behind the pilot and copilot positions is a three-man radar console compartment. The plane was used extensively to control U.S. air operations over North Vietnam. (U.S. Navy)

der Air Group. By the mid 1960s air wings of forward-deployed attack carriers consisted of some 75 aircraft, except for the nuclear-propelled *Enterprise* (which carried about 100 aircraft) (see table 15-1).

Four-Engine Aircraft

Several odd aircraft came to rest on U.S. carriers during the 1960s. Among them were two large aircraft: the widely flown, four-engine C-130 Hercules and the experimental, four-engine XC-142 Vertical/Short Takeoff and Landing (VSTOL) transport. In the late 1930s the Royal Navy had developed two four-engine reconnaissance aircraft for carrier operation, the Airspeed AS 39 and General Aircraft Limited GAL 38, but neither went aboard ship (see Volume I, pages 69–70).

A KC-130F, a four-engine turboprop aircraft, conducted a series of carrier evaluation flights on the *Forrestal* in the fall of 1963.[12] The Lockheed Hercules made 44 approaches to the *Forrestal* on October 30, 1963, with 16 resulting in touch-and-go landings. The remainder were intentional wave offs, made to determine the aircraft's response during a carrier approach. A week after the test flights, the KC-130F, piloted by Lieutenant James H. Flatley III, made three touch-and-go and four full-stop landings on the *Forrestal*. The maximum aircraft weight during this phase of the tests was 92,000 pounds. No carrier arresting gear was employed, and the aircraft rollout was as little as 270 feet. To accomplish this, Flatley had reversed the engines just before touchdown and applied the brakes as soon as the plane touched the deck. After each of the four full-stop landings, the KC-130F took off with deck runs

as short as 330 feet. The final series of tests aboard the *Forrestal* were held on November 21–22, when the KC-130F made seven touch-and-go and 17 full-stop landings. In these tests gross aircraft weight reached a maximum of 120,000 pounds. The aircraft's 132½-foot wingspan and 92-foot length made the Hercules the largest aircraft ever flown aboard a carrier.[13]

Although the demonstration flights went extremely well, "Herk" operations from a large carrier were not practical. First, Flatley was one of the Navy's top pilots. Second, the flights were undertaken in daylight with relatively calm seas. Third, after landing the aircraft—too large for the elevators—tied up a large amount of the flight deck. And, if the aircraft had suffered a mechanical problem and could not launch, that deck space would be lost until spare parts and possibly technicians could be flown out to the ship. The question of operating C-130s from ships was again raised in 2004–2005 as the U.S. Navy developed the concept of "sea basing" with large, maritime prepositioning ships. Then, too, it was found impractical.

The first American-built VSTOL aircraft to operate from a carrier was the Hiller-Ryan XC-142A, a tactical transport powered by four turboprop engines.[14] The XC-142A had a tilt-wing that could rotate up to 100 degrees from the horizontal position to deflect its slipstream, thus achieving vertical flight. During May 1966 an XC-142A made 50 landings and takeoffs aboard the carrier *Bennington*; 44 were shortrun landings and six were in the vertical mode. The aircraft's most dramatic maneuver was making a vertical takeoff, hovering above the flight deck for a few moments, then changing wing

The largest aircraft ever to land and take off from an aircraft carrier was this KC-130F Hercules, piloted by Lieutenant James H. Flatley, III. The Lockheed "Herk"—the most widely flown tactical transport of its time—is a conventional transport that has excellent short-run take-off and landing characteristics. Despite the success of these 1963 trials aboard the *Forrestal*, regular operations of such large aircraft is not practical. (U.S. Navy)

angle, and speeding away in forward conventional flight. With a gross weight of about 30,000 pounds, the XC-142A had a speed range from 35 m.p.h. *backward* to 400 m.p.h. in forward flight. In addition to the *Bennington*, the XC-142 also flew from a Navy docking well amphibious ship.

While the U.S. Navy had no plans for the regular use of either the C-130 Hercules or C-142 VSTOL transports from carriers, the feasibility of operating aircraft with their troop and cargo capabilities from carriers provided an attractive possibility for contingency planning. Launched from land bases with extra fuel, these aircraft could be flown aboard carriers operating in remote areas and loaded with troops, and could fly assault forces ashore without relying on land bases or even refueling facilities within thousands of miles of

the objective area. Further, the C-142 provided the capability of landing troops in remote areas where airfields were not available; the C-130 could operate from rough-ground airstrips.

The C-130F had a ferry range of 5,000 miles, a tactical radius of 1,200 miles, and could lift either 92 troops or 30,000 pounds of cargo. The C-142 had a ferry range of 3,000 miles, a tactical radius of 470 miles, and a cargo capacity of 32 troops or 8,000 pounds. A pair of dividers marking off these distances on a globe will show an impressive range of operations open to the imaginative military planner who has these aircraft and large carriers available to him.

One other four-engine aircraft flew from a U.S. carrier: the Quiet Short-Haul Research Aircraft (QSRA), a Short Takeoff/Landing (STOL) aircraft being evaluated by the National Aeronautics and Space Administration (NASA) and the Army. The QSRA was a de Havilland of Canada Buffalo that had been extensively rebuilt with four turbofan engines, an upper-wing blowing system, and T-tail configuration. The aircraft had an empty weight of 36,800 pounds and maximum takeoff weight of 50,000 pounds.

On July 10, 1980, off the coast of San Diego, the QSRA flew trials from the large carrier *Kitty Hawk*. Flown by a team of one Navy and two NASA pilots, the QSRA flew 37 touch-and-go landings and 16 full-stop landings and takeoffs. Again, the aircraft's slow landing speed—75 m.p.h.—alleviated the need for arresting gear.

Improved combat aircraft were deployed on the U.S. Navy's anti-submarine carriers during the 1960s. The earlier twin-engine S-2 Trackers (formerly S2F) were replaced by improved S-2D (S2F-3) and S-2E (S2F-3S) models with greater range and improved submarine detection equipment.

The HSS-1N (redesignated SH-34J in 1962) in helicopter ASW squadrons was replaced by the HSS-2 Sea King (changed to SH-3). This helicopter was a large, 17,800-pound, twin-turbine "whirlybird" with much improved capabilities over its predecessor. Still, the SH-3 was designed to operate from escort carriers as well as larger ships. The helicopter's normal length of 72½ feet (with rotors in operating position) could be reduced to 46½ feet by folding the main rotor blades and the tail rotor pylon.

The SH-3A reached 210 m.p.h. during tests, although its normal maximum speed at sea level was 153 m.p.h. with two Mk 44 torpedoes. An SH-3A set a world distance record when it flew nonstop from the carrier *Hornet* off the Pacific coast to the carrier *Franklin D. Roosevelt* off the Atlantic coast, a distance of 2,116 miles, flown in 15 hours, 51 minutes. An advantage of the SH-3A over other helicopters was its boat-shaped hull and stabilization floats (which housed the retractable landing gear) to permit emergency water operations. A pilot, copilot, and two sonar operators flew the helicopter. Equipment for automatic hovering and all-weather flight and advanced dipping sonar made the Sea King a potent search aircraft. For attack the SH-3A could carry four "lightweight" ASW homing torpedoes or a Mk 101 Lulu nuclear depth bomb.[15] With these aircraft the ASW carrier air group of the mid-1960s numbered 20 S-2D or S-2E Trackers and 16 SH-3A Sea Kings plus three E-1B Tracer radar aircraft.

The hostility of North Korean and, subsequently, Indonesia and North Vietnam, all of which possessed

Another four-engine aircraft evaluated aboard carriers was the Quiet Short-Haul Research Aircraft (QSRA), a NASA-sponsored hybrid aircraft that had four turbofan engines. A converted de Havilland of Canada Buffalo, the QSRA had excellent Short-Takeoff/Landing (STOL) characteristics, which were demonstrated on the carrier *Kitty Hawk* in 1980. This was the only four-engine "propellerless" aircraft to fly from a carrier. (NASA)

The Ling-Temco-Vought XC-142A was powered by four turboprop engines that could rotate to the vertical position for vertical flight, providing excellent VSTOL characteristics. The aircraft, shown here during trials aboard the carrier *Bennington* in 1966, was a precursor to the Bell-Boeing V-22 Osprey "tiltrotor" VSTOL aircraft. Although evaluated in a triservice program, there was no production of the C-142 as a military transport. (U.S. Navy)

MiG-type aircraft, threatened U.S. anti-submarine patrols in Southeast Asian waters during this period while Soviet land-based reconnaissance aircraft had begun overflying U.S. carriers (see below). To counter these threats, beginning in 1954 the Navy assigned fighter-type aircraft to ASW carriers.

The first detachment was from composite squadron VC-4, flying F4U-5N Corsairs from the carrier *Antietam* for various periods in 1954–1955. The initial assignment of Corsairs to CVS-type carriers was followed by detachments of F9F-5 Panthers, F9F-8 Cougars, and F2H Banshees. The *Essex*-class ASW carriers could not operate the newer, larger, more capable fighters that joined the Fleet because of limited deck space and the ships' hydraulic catapults. The last fighter-type aircraft deployed with ASW carriers through May 1959. The Douglas A4D Skyhawk resolved this problem. The fast, nimble, and small Skyhawk was the perfect ASW fighter. The Skyhawks were armed with two 20-mm cannon and could carry two Sidewinder missiles and a centerline 150-gallon fuel tank.

Attack Squadron 64 provided the first A4D-2 Skyhawks to the carrier *Wasp* for a North Atlantic deployment from February to June 1962.[16] Subsequently Skyhawk detachments deployed aboard ASW carriers through 1973. Several deployments aboard carriers were made by detachments of Marine-piloted Skyhawks. On July 1, 1965, the Navy established ASW Fighter Squadron (VSF) 1 to provide four-plane Skyhawk detachments to Atlantic Fleet carriers. To support Pacific Fleet ASW carriers a VSF-1 detachment was set up at Alameda, California, in July 1966; that unit became VSF-3 in March 1967.

VSF-1's Skyhawks made a squadron deployment with 14 A-4B aircraft on the ASW carrier *Shangri-La* to the Mediterranean from October 1966 to May 1977. The squadron also deployed aboard the attack carrier *Independence* in the Mediterranean from May 1968 through January 1969. Skyhawks from other squadrons made additional CVS deployments, and detachments aboard ships off Vietnam also flew strike missions.

Proposals for a specialized CVS-based interceptor were rejected. The shortage of attack aircraft in the Vietnam War and the lack of a viable air threat led to Skyhawks being removed from ASW carriers and assigned to attack units. VSF-1 and VSF-3 were deactivated in 1968–1969.[17]

The *Essex*-class carriers that operated ASW air groups were periodically replaced by newer ships: as new large carriers joined the CVA ranks the oldest *Essex* attack carrier was reclassified as a CVS. The large and at times highly advanced Soviet submarine fleet was a major concern for Western political and

A Sikorsky HSS-2/SH-3A Sea King hovers over a submarine during Seventh Fleet maneuvers in 1966. The turbine-powered Sea King could seek out submarines with dipping sonar or a towed magnetic detector, and could attack with homing torpedoes. In the Vietnam War these helicopters periodically shed their ASW equipment and, fitted with machine guns and rescue hoists, flew search-and-rescue missions. (U.S. Navy)

The ubiquitous A4D/A-4 Skyhawk was the perfect VSF "fighter" for operations from ASW carriers. This A-4C Skyhawk stands ready to take off in defense of the carrier *Hornet*. It is armed with Sidewinder missiles and two internal 20-mm cannon. A U.S. A-4C shot down a MiG-17 with Zuni unguided rockets; Israeli Skyhawks also shot down MiGs. (U.S. Navy)

military leaders throughout the Cold War. Major Western air, surface, and submarine forces—including aircraft carriers—were dedicated to the ASW role.

In this period ten *Essex*-class ships were designated CVS:

ATLANTIC	PACIFIC
Antietam	*Bennington*
Essex	*Hornet*
Intrepid	*Kearsarge*
Lake Champlain	*Yorktown*
Wasp	*Randolph*

The eight angled-deck ASW carriers in service by the late 1960s had been modernized in the so-called FRAM (Fleet Rehabilitation And Modernization) program from 1961 to 1967. In addition to an extensive updating, these carriers were fitted with an AN/SQS-23 sonar for submarine detection. (Experiments with sonar in the CVL *Wright* some years earlier had shown the value of this equipment in ASW carriers; the *Wright* is believed to have been the first U.S. aircraft carrier fitted with sonar.)

The eight angled-deck, FRAM-modernized ships plus the straight-deck *Lake Champlain* carried ASW air groups. The *Lake Champlain* had been slated to receive an angled deck in 1957, but it was not provided. The *Antietam*, the pioneer angled-deck carrier, in April 1957 had relieved the CVL *Saipan* as the Navy's training carrier for student pilots. The *Antietam* served in the training role (designated CVS) until October 1962. Twice in 1961 the carrier took time from pilot training to rush medical personnel, supplies, and helicopters to hurricane-devastated areas in Texas and British Honduras.

The CVA *Lexington* was to become the training carrier and was changed from CVA to CVS on October 1, 1962, but the Cuban Missile Crisis kept her in service as an attack carrier and she did not take up training duties until December 1963. (The *Lexington*'s designation was changed to CVT 16 on January 1, 1969, to better denote her role.)

Crises continued to flare up around the world as new super carriers and new aircraft were joining the U.S. Fleet. The crisis over Berlin in mid-1961 was followed by communist forces in Laos violating a cease-fire in May 1962. The Seventh Fleet's amphibious force—including the assault ship *Valley Forge*—was ordered to land its 1,800 Marines to ensure the independence of neighboring Thailand and to support U.S. diplomatic efforts to save the independence of Laos. These troops were put ashore in Thailand on May 16, 1962, without opposition.

Closer to the United States, in April 1961 came the debacle of the Bay of Pigs, named for the landing area of a disastrous attempt to invade Cuba and overthrow Fidel Castro, whose guerrilla forces had seized control of the country on January 1, 1959. And, the stage was being set for the Cuban Missile Crisis, the closest that the super powers came to nuclear conflict during the 45-year Cold War.

14 CARRIERS TO CUBAN WATERS

The crews of three Atlantic Fleet carriers—the *Independence*, *Saratoga*, and *Intrepid*—spell out a commemoration of U.S. Naval Aviation's 50th anniversary during 1961. Two of the carriers, the *Independence* and *Saratoga*, were involved in the 1961–1962 crises in the Caribbean. Aircraft carriers were important for U.S. operations against the island nation despite the proximity of Cuba to the United States. (U.S. Navy)

The island of Cuba lies 90 miles south of Key West, Florida. The United States had a dominating interest in the island—both political and economic—until January 1, 1959, when revolutionary Fidel Castro overthrew the existing dictatorship. Cuban-American relations soon deteriorated as Castro adopted communism and, rebuffed by the United States, sought aid from the Soviet Union.

In response to this situation, the U.S. Central Intelligence Agency (CIA) recruited and trained a military force of some 1,400 Cuban exiles in Central America. This force was intended to invade Cuba in the spring of 1961 to trigger a counterrevolution against Castro.[1] The force would land on beaches on the southeastern side of Cuba, an area known as the Bay of Pigs. Only Cuban exiles were to participate in the actual invasion.

President Kennedy directed that no U.S. forces would provide direct assistance and cancelled earlier plans for U.S. aircraft to support the landing. The commanders of the invasion force were so informed. However, two U.S. aircraft carriers were ordered to the area, the CVA *Independence* and the CVS *Essex*, the latter having recently converted from the attack to the ASW role. This potential Navy participation was given the code name Bumpy Road.

On April 3, 1961, the *Essex* departed Norfolk, Virginia, with her ASW air group. Also embarked was Commander Carrier Division 18, Rear Admiral John A. Clark as Commander Special Task Group 81.8. The U.S. Navy force comprised of the *Essex* and five destroyers. At Norfolk, Clark had been personally briefed by Admiral Robert L. Dennison, Commander-in-Chief of all U.S. forces in the Atlantic. On being told his mission, Clark responded, "You mean I'm to go down there armed to the teeth, but I'm supposed to do nothing?"

Once at sea the *Essex*'s engineers hastily converted some of her aviation gasoline tanks to store jet fuel (JP-5). The following day, April 4, one of her two 12-plane squadrons of S2F Trackers was flown off. As those planes departed, 12 A4D-2 Skyhawk light attack aircraft of Attack Squadron 34 flew aboard.[2] Simultaneously, a flock of some 15 TF-1 Trader COD aircraft flew on and off the *Essex*, taking off the Tracker ground crews and bringing aboard those of the Skyhawks plus their support equipment. The *Essex* retained a second 12-plane S2F squadron, a squadron of 16 HSS-1 Seabat helicopters, and four AD-5W Skyraider radar aircraft.

The Skyhawks of VA-34 embarked in the *Essex* had been on two hours' alert at their Florida base for a secret deployment since mid-March. Aboard ship the Skyhawks' U.S. markings were painted out and their pilots removed all personal identification items. Their mission: to *possibly* provide air cover for the counter-Castro invasion on the day of the landings. But the VA-34 pilots were not trained in air-to-air combat, and while their planes were armed with two 20-mm cannon, they were not fitted for air-to-air missiles. (Also in the area was a U.S. amphibious task force with a Marine battalion landing team embarked with helicopters and landing craft to put them ashore.)

The Bay of Pigs assault, after several delays, was set for April 17. Briefings to the *Essex* A4D and S2F pilots were given by Admiral Clark and two officers from the CIA. The planes flew surveillance for the rebel invasion ships, which were coming from Nicaragua. Communications with Washington were maintained

The *Essex* was present for the Bay of Pigs fiasco in 1961 and for the Cuban Missile Crisis in 1962. This view shows the carrier about to launch a TF-1/C-1A Trader cargo aircraft; A-1 Skyraiders are clustered around her island structure. Shortly after this photo was taken the *Essex* transitioned in March 1960 from a CVA to a CVS. In that role she flew A4D-2/A-4B Skyhawks during the Bay of Pigs invasion. (U.S. Navy)

continuously as the Kennedy administration placed increased restrictions on the U.S. forces: the *Essex* was to come no closer than 50 miles to Cuba, aircraft were to operate no closer than 15 miles, and no more than four aircraft were to be on station at one time.

Meanwhile, on the morning of April 15, nine B-26 Invaders flown by rebel and CIA contract pilots took off from Nicaragua. Eight bombed air bases in Cuba and returned to Nicaragua; the ninth flew to Miami, where the pilot landed, showed faked bullet holes in his aircraft, and said that he had defected from the Cuban Air Force. At the United Nations U.S. Ambassador Adlai Stevenson, who did not know that the pilot was lying, used the Cuban's story to explain charges that the United States had mounted an air attack on Cuba. A second air strike by rebel B-26s had been scheduled for the 16th, as the invasion force neared the shore. President Kennedy, concerned about U.S. credibility, cancelled the strike.

The first landing at the Bay of Pigs occurred shortly after 1 A.M. on April 17. Cuban Sea Fury piston-engine fighters quickly shot down two of the Nicaguran-based rebel B-26s and sank the invasion ship carrying most of the ammunition and radios for the assualt.[3] A troop transport was hit and ran aground. Kennedy authorized B-26 night attacks on Cuban air bases, but they were ineffective.

At the time the invading force had thought that it was under attack by Cuban MiG-15 fighters and T-33 Shooting Star armed training aircraft.[4] There were no MiGs in Cuba at the time.

On the beach, the invaders soon came under heavy fire from Castro's tanks, artillery, and infantry. Within a few hours it was obvious that the invasion was a failure. On the 18th the U.S carriers were directed to send unmarked aircraft to within 15 miles of the beach to ascertain the situation. While the *Essex*'s A4Ds had their markings painted out, the several AD Skyraiders launched by the *Independence* did not. Soon the planes were allowed to fly over the beaches, but only to carry out reconnaissance and not to engage Cuban air or ground forces.

Hemmed in by superior Cuban ground forces, supported by ex-British Sea Furies, B-26s, and armed T-33 jet trainers, the rebels on the landing beaches were decimated. The invasion was a disaster. Admiral Arleigh A. Burke, the Chief of Naval Operations, joined other officials in a midnight meeting at the White House on the night of April 18–19 to discuss whether or not to permit carrier planes to gain control of the air over the beach. At first the president authorized one hour of air cover the morning of April 19: the invader's B-26s would support the remnants of the landing force while cargo planes would drop them ammunition and supplies with air cover would be flown by six unmarked Skyhawks from the *Essex*. Then that authorization was withdrawn. (During the night two C-54s had dropped supplies to the invasion force and a C-46 had landed on an airstrip in the invaders' hands to unload supplies.)

Reportedly, Admiral Burke pleaded, "Let me take two jets and shoot down the enemy aircraft."[5] President Kennedy responded, "No." He said he had repeated "over and over again" that he would not commit U.S. forces to the invasion. Burke responded that unmarked carrier aircraft be permitted, with orders not to fire, to fly low over the beaches as a show of force. Again Kennedy refused. Burke suggested sending in a destroyer to provide fire support, especially to knock out Castro's tanks.

> The President got angry. "Burke, I don't want the United States involved in this," he said sharply.
>
> Burke, feeling he had "never been so distressed," raised his voice. He wanted to be "as forceful as I could be in talking to the President." He said, "Hell, Mr. President, but we *are* involved!"[6]

The carriers did not send their aircraft over the beach to aid the rebels. The surveillance missions by A4Ds continued as below them the Castro forces destroyed the invading rebels. Two HSS-1 helicopters on

Admiral Arleigh A. Burke (U.S. Navy)

the *Essex* had their ASW gear removed and were loaded with food, water, and medicine to be flown—at night—to rebel pockets that were holding out. That mission was cancelled.

On April 23 the *Essex* sent her remaining S2F Tracker squadron to the U.S. base at Guantanamo Bay, presumably to clear her deck for additional attack planes from the *Independence*. Only a few ADs from the "Indy" refueled on the *Essex* and carried out surveillance missions over the Bay of Pigs during the next few days. The Trackers returned to the *Essex* on the evening of April 26. The *Essex*-launched attack planes ceased their penetrations of Cuban air space at that time, and the invasion fiasco came to a close.

Hemmed in by superior numbers of Cuban troops who were supported by aircraft, only a few of the rebels made it to the temporary safety of the mountains. Some were taken off by U.S. Navy landing craft that stood off of the beaches. The fighting on the beach killed about 1,650 of Castro's men and 114 of the invaders. Castro's forces took 1,189 rebel prisoners. There was no anti-Castro uprising; anyone who might have joined in a rebellion was in jail.

The Bay of Pigs invasion could not have succeeded without direct U.S. military participation. Certainly carrier-based air would have been a key factor in the success of an invasion, but the White House had already changed the location of the invasion, from an area near mountains that could have provided a base for the rebels, to the untenable Bay of Pigs. The Kennedy administration's cancellation of air strikes, restrictions on U.S. participation, and changes in the invasion plan doomed the operation to failure before it began.

Two significant results of the ill-fated invasion of Cuba were President Kennedy's decisions to approve Operation Mongoose, a CIA-led program of sabotage and guerrilla attacks against Cuba, and develop plans for a full-scale U.S. invasion of Cuba. On May 1, 1961, Secretary of Defense Robert S. McNamara and Admiral Burke met with President Kennedy to discuss the latter operation. The initial plan was for 60,000 troops, heavily supported by air and naval forces, to invade Cuba. "It was estimated that complete control of the island could be obtained within 8 days, although it was recognized that guerrilla forces could continue to operate beyond the 8th day in the Escambray Mountains and Oriente Province."[7] The plan underwent several changes, and after Soviet defensive arms were observed being shipped to Cuba, the U.S. force was greatly enlarged. Subsequently, a tentative invasion date was set for November 1962.

The next crisis over Cuba—and *the* most dangerous U.S.-Soviet confrontation of the entire Cold War—came on October 22, 1962, when President Kennedy publicly revealed a Soviet strategic missile buildup in Cuba. High-altitude U-2 spyplanes had flown over Cuba since October 27, 1960. These were CIA aircraft and their initial flights had been personally approved by President Eisenhower. With indications of Soviet military activity in Cuba, beginning on the night of October 13–14, 1962, Air Force pilots began making the Cuban overflights. Film from the two U-2C flights that night revealed the presence of Soviet offensive, nuclear-capable missiles being emplaced on the Caribbean island.

Additional U-2 flights were flown on the 17th, and two days later, on the basis of their photographs, President Kennedy ordered a national military alert. Plans were prepared for a blockade of the island to halt the further shipment of offensive weapons, for an invasion, and for "surgical" bombing strikes. The Strategic Air Command placed some 65 B-52 bombers on airborne alert and brought its other bombers and land-based strategic missiles to a high state of readiness. From ports along the East Coast warships and support ships went to sea.

On the night of October 22, President Kennedy went on television to tell the world that "unmistakable evidence" showed that the Soviets were preparing offensive missile sites in Cuba. "The purpose of those bases can be none other than to provide a nuclear strike capability against the Western hemisphere." Kennedy ordered a naval and air "quarantine" on the shipment of further offensive weapons to the island; if that failed, the United States would launch a full-scale invasion of Cuba.

At the time of his speech Task Force 135—centered on the carriers *Enterprise* and *Independence*—had been on station for more than 48 hours and was maintaining a dawn-to-dusk fighter patrol over the U.S. base at Guantanamo Bay. The task force had additional fighters ready to launch and more than 100 attack aircraft within three hours of being launched. (En route to the Caribbean the *Enterprise* flew off her squadron of A3J-1 Vigilante nuclear-strike aircraft and landed aboard a squadron of 20 Marine A4D Skyhawks to provide an increased tactical strike capability. The shift was carried out while the ship was under way, with COD aircraft transferring the non-flying personnel and equipment required for the exchange.) Of course, the early deployment of carriers attracted far less press attention and speculation than did the massive recalls of Air Force and Army personnel to bases throughout the country.

The Kennedy administration now wanted low-level, detailed photos of the missile sites. Six Navy F8U-1P/RF-8A Crusader photo planes, flying from Key West, Florida, undertook the first U.S. low-level overflights of Cuba on October 23, 1962—Operation Blue Moon. As they began their photo runs over Cuba, the planes flew at speeds 400 m.p.h. at altitudes of about 400 feet.[8]

Returning to Cecil Field near Jacksonville, Florida, the planes' exposed film was quickly removed and rushed into the adjacent Navy photo laboratory. Led by Commander William B. Ecker, commanding officer of Light Photographic Squadron 62, Navy and Marine pilots continued to fly low-level RF-8A missions, carrying out more than 80 sorties during the crisis. The RF-8As were joined from October 26 by Air Force RF-101 Voodoo photo planes.[9] The low-level photo missions also had a harassment value, as the Soviet officials could have no doubt that the Americans knew precisely what was happening and that the photo planes could be followed by strike aircraft.

High-flying U-2s also continued their overflights. One was shot down on October 27 by an SA-2 surface-to-air missile and its Air Force pilot was killed. That weapon had been launched by a Soviet local air defense commander—without authorization. The Kennedy administration had previously decided that if a U-2 was downed a retaliatory strike would be launched to destroy a missile site. But the president choose to wait. Suspecting that the Soviets were delaying while more strategic weapons were made ready, plans for a comprehensive air strike against *ballistic* missile sites were discussed with new urgency. The carrier-based attack aircraft were ready to go, but for reasons that remain obscure the Air Force required 48 hours before it could launch a similar strike. Interestingly, Secretary of Defense McNamara had placed four Tactical Air Command squadrons on alert to launch such an attack on the 21st. A week later those squadrons needed 48 hours to launch an attack; possibly the squadrons had been recycled by the Air Force to prepare for a nuclear strike (as were Tactical Air Force units in Europe and the Far East) and the time was needed to change weapons and brief new targets.

Also on the 27th, Fidel Castro ordered his own anti-aircraft guns to fire at the low-flying photo planes. (At least one other U-2 was fired on by a Soviet-manned SA-2 missile battery.)

At sea the quarantine forces initially consisted of the ASW carrier *Essex*, cruisers, destroyers, and land-based reconnaissance and patrol aircraft. To counter a possible Cuban assault on the U.S. naval base at Guantanamo Bay at Cuba's southeastern end, Marine reinforcements were flown into the base. Air support for the defenders would come from the base's own airfield, air bases in Florida, and aircraft from the attack carriers *Enterprise* and *Independence*, which were steaming within striking distance of Cuba.

Subsequently, additional carriers joined the growing armada (table 14-1). Thus a total of six aircraft carriers

The RF-8 Crusader performed outstanding low-level photo reconnaissance over Cuba and over Southeast Asia in the 1960s. This RF-8A is from the light photograph squadron VFP-62 detachment aboard the carrier *Forrestal*. President Kennedy personally awarded a unit citation to the squadron for its role in the Cuban Missile Crisis. The plane's camera ports are readily evident; the "recce birds" were unarmed. (U.S. Navy)

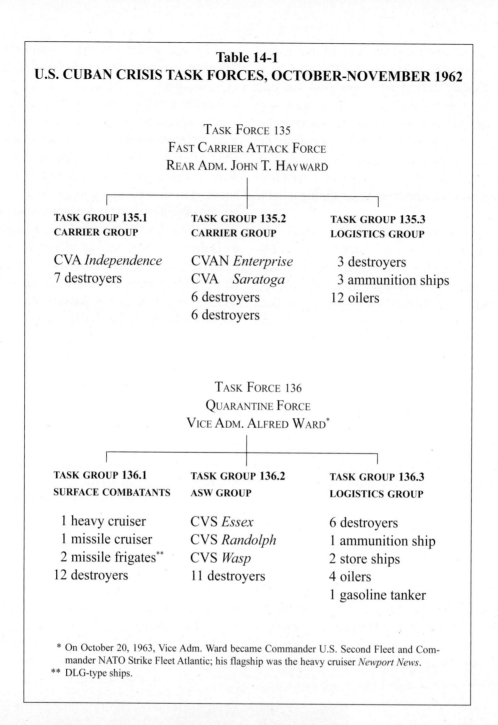

Table 14-1
U.S. CUBAN CRISIS TASK FORCES, OCTOBER-NOVEMBER 1962

TASK FORCE 135
FAST CARRIER ATTACK FORCE
REAR ADM. JOHN T. HAYWARD

TASK GROUP 135.1 CARRIER GROUP	TASK GROUP 135.2 CARRIER GROUP	TASK GROUP 135.3 LOGISTICS GROUP
CVA *Independence* 7 destroyers	CVAN *Enterprise* CVA *Saratoga* 6 destroyers 6 destroyers	3 destroyers 3 ammunition ships 12 oilers

TASK FORCE 136
QUARANTINE FORCE
VICE ADM. ALFRED WARD*

TASK GROUP 136.1 SURFACE COMBATANTS	TASK GROUP 136.2 ASW GROUP	TASK GROUP 136.3 LOGISTICS GROUP
1 heavy cruiser 1 missile cruiser 2 missile frigates** 12 destroyers	CVS *Essex* CVS *Randolph* CVS *Wasp* 11 destroyers	6 destroyers 1 ammunition ship 2 store ships 4 oilers 1 gasoline tanker

* On October 20, 1963, Vice Adm. Ward became Commander U.S. Second Fleet and Commander NATO Strike Fleet Atlantic; his flagship was the heavy cruiser *Newport News*.
** DLG-type ships.

took part in the quarantine and related operations during the crisis. In addition, in preparation of an amphibious assault on Cuba, 42 amphibious ships of the Atlantic Fleet and 22 "amphibs" from the Pacific Fleet were at sea, the latter having passed through the Panama Canal. These ships included three Atlantic Fleet helicopter carriers—the *Boxer*, *Okinawa*, and *Thetis Bay*—and the *Iwo Jima* from the Pacific. All were laden with Marines, their helicopters, weapons, and vehicles.

At sea the Soviets turned back merchant ships that obviously were carrying missiles from crossing the quarantine line. Several Soviet diesel-electric submarines were detected, tracked, and eventually forced to the surface for visual identification by U.S. ASW forces. There were tense negotiations during the confrontation. Then, in the words of Secretary of State Dean Rusk, "We're eyeball to eyeball and I think the other fellow just blinked." The Soviet government agreed to withdraw the ballistic missiles and, subsequently, the Il-28 Beagle bombers from Cuba.[10] In return the U.S. government agreed not to invade Cuba and to remove (highly vulnerable) Jupiter ballistic missiles from Turkey.

Unknown at the time to U.S. intelligence agencies, the Soviets had already landed in Cuba 128 nuclear warheads for tactical and strategic missiles, as well as six bombs for Il-28 bombers. Another 24 missile warheads were in a ship moored offshore.[11]

During the Cuban crisis the U.S. Navy armada was supplemented by several ships from Central and South American navies, and by squadrons of land-based Navy patrol planes and by an Air Force contingent of 16 piston-engine KC-97 tankers and five photo-reconnaissance variants of the B-47 Stratojet bomber. Still, the immediate availability of carriers greatly simplified drawing tight the quarantine net around Cuba and provided a potent fighter and attack force in place at the beginning of the crisis. And, in a letter to Commander Ecker, President Kennedy praised the role of the Crusader photo planes during the crisis:

> I would . . . reaffirm my thanks to you for your hard work during those weeks. As I said at our meeting in Boca Chica [Florida], the reconnaissance flights which enabled us to determine with precision the offensive build-up in Cuba contributed directly to the security of the United States in the most important and significant way.

The Lockheed U-2 spyplanes that belatedly brought the initial, critical photographs of the Soviet military buildup in Cuba had overflown the Soviet Union 24 times from July 4, 1956, to May 1, 1960. The overflights—flown by U.S. and British pilots—ceased abruptly when the 24th overflight, a U-2C flown by CIA pilot Francis Gary Powers, was shot down by an SA-2 missile on May 1, 1960. The spyplanes continued to fly missions over many other parts of the world, including China with Taiwanese pilots at the controls. However, even with a maximum U-2 range of some 3,000 miles some areas of interest to the U.S. intelligence community could not be reached by U-2s flying from "safe" land bases. Accordingly, in mid-1963 the CIA initiated Project Whale Tale to adapt U-2s for carrier operation.

The U-2's glider configuration enabled it to take off unassisted from a carrier with a high wind over deck. Its slow approach speed made arrested landings relatively easy when the arresting gear was set at its lowest setting. The carrier provided 30 knots of wind over the deck resulting in a U-2 closing speed of just 50 knots. The plane had plenty of power for wave off during landing.

The first carrier flight tests occurred in August 1963. In the dead of night a U-2C was loaded by crane onto the *Kitty Hawk* at the North Island naval air station in San Diego. The next morning, as the ship steamed off the California coast, Lockheed test pilot Bob Schumacher took off and made a number of practice approaches and then tried to land on the ship. According to a CIA report, "Although the takeoff was very successful, the attempted landing was not. The aircraft bounced, hit hard on one wing tip, and then just barely managed to become airborne again before reaching the end of the deck."[12]

Three U-2A aircraft were provided with strengthened landing gear, an arresting hook, and "spoilers" on the wings to cancel aerodynamic lift once the aircraft

The helicopter carrier *Okinawa* at speed; Marine HUS-1/UH-34D Seahorse helicopters are parked on her flight deck. Four LPHs and 60 other amphibious ships were readied for the planned invasion of Cuba in the fall of 1962. That was the largest assembly of amphibious ships at any time since the end of World War II. The *Okinawa*'s starboard deck-edge elevator is lowered to the hangar deck. (A. L. Smith, U.S. Navy)

With flaps, wheels, and arresting hook (behind flaps) lowered, a wide-wing U-2R lands aboard the carrier *America* in November 1969. Earlier a U-2G flew an operational mission from the carrier *Ranger* in the Pacific. U-2 operations from carriers proved to be completely feasible and some U-2 variants were built with special features for carrier flights. (Lockheed)

was over the flight deck. These aircraft were designated U-2G and painted with N-series civilian serials and Office of Naval Research markings. In preparation for further carrier operations, Schumacher and other CIA pilots made practice landings in T-2A Buckeye jet trainers on the *Lexington*.

The first carrier landing of a U-2G took place on March 2, 1964. Although the CIA has not released details of these trials, there are indications that they took place aboard the *Kitty Hawk* and possibly the *Enterprise*. In the first landing the hook engaged but the rear of the U-2 tipped up and the nose dug into the deck, breaking the pitot tube. After hasty repairs the U-2 was easily flown off. A few days later Schumacher and other CIA pilots made several successful landings and takeoffs.

The only operational U-2 carrier mission—Operation Seeker—occurred in May 1964 when the *Ranger* launched one or possibly two U-2G spyplanes to monitor the French nuclear tests at Murora Atoll in French Polynesia. The U-2G photographs indicated that the French would be ready for full-scale production of nuclear weapons within a year.

Two larger and heavier U-2R aircraft flew trials aboard the carrier *America* off the coast of Virginia on November 21–23, 1969. These two aircraft also had N-serials. The U-2R variant, which had entered service in 1967, was significantly larger than the earlier U-2 with double the range and four times the sensor payload. It was designed to be fitted with a carrier hook if required. Senior Lockheed test pilot Bill Park, a former Air Force fighter pilot, flew the *America* trials after an abbreviated carrier training course. Reporting on the *America*/U-2R trials, he observed,

> The airplane demonstrated good waveoff characteristics and I felt at the time that landings could be made without a hook. We required very little special handling and even took the airplane down to the hangar deck. The outer 70 inches of the wings fold and by careful placement on the elevator we could get in [the hangar] with no problem.[13]

The official CIA history states that there were no further U-2 missions from aircraft carriers:

> Aircraft carriers are enormously expensive to operate and require an entire flotilla of vessels to protect and service them. The movement of large numbers of big ships is difficult to conceal and cannot be hastily accomplished, while the deployment of a solitary U-2 to a remote airfield can take place overnight.[14]

New Challenges

The year 1963 brought two new challenges to aircraft carriers: Soviet overflights and Secretary McNamara's cost-effectiveness studies.

Earlier Soviet reconnaissance aircraft had made occasional overflights of U.S. carriers (leading to the assignment of A-4B Skyhawk "fighters" to ASW carriers deploying to the Western Pacific). Beginning late in January 1963 the Soviets initiated a series of overflights of U.S. carriers, mostly by Tu-20 long-range reconnaissance aircraft, designated Bear-D by NATO.[15] Between January 27 and February 27 Soviet planes flew over the carriers *Constellation*, *Enterprise*, *Forrestal*, *Kitty Hawk*, and *Princeton*. The overflights occurred in both the Atlantic and the Pacific—the *Constellation* was looked over by Soviet planes some 600 miles south of Midway Island; the *Forrestal* just southwest of the Azores. In all cases the carriers were in international waters. Shipboard radar detected the snoopers some 200 miles out, and in the case of the attack carriers, Phantom and Crusader fighters "escorted" the Soviet planes while they were in the vicinity of the American ships. In some instances U.S. Air Force fighters also escorted the Soviet planes on their overflights when they passed near U.S. air bases in Iceland and elsewhere.

Secretary McNamara revealed the overflights to the press on February 28, 1963, stating that he saw no cause for alarm and noting that any nation had the right to photograph ships in international waters. Navy officials were quick to point out that the carriers were steaming on normal sailing routes with their schedules published and had made no effort to keep radio silence. Vice Admiral William A. Schoech, the Deputy Chief of Naval Operations (Air) at the height of the overflights in 1963, declared that the purpose of the Soviets was twofold:

to undermine the American public's confidence in the carrier as a striking force and to convince the Russian people that carriers were obsolescent as justification for the Soviet Navy's lack of such ships. Undoubtedly the overflights were also being made to provide realistic training for Soviet naval aviators.

In June 1963 the *Ranger* became the sixth U.S. carrier to be overflown by Soviet aircraft in that year. Six Tu-16 Badger turbojet bombers flew near the ship as she steamed about 330 miles east of Japan. In all, there were 14 overflights of U.S. carriers in 1963. The number dropped to four in 1964 as the Soviets returned to the more mundane practice of sending electronics-laden intelligence ships or destroyers to trail U.S. aircraft carriers during fleet exercises. Still, Soviet planes periodically returned to streak over the carriers.

On May 25, 1968, a Tu-16R Badger streaked over the *Essex* during operations in the Norwegian Sea.[16] One of the Badger's wings touched water as it turned, and the plane crashed and exploded. There were no survivors from its crew of six or seven commanded by Major Pliev. The *Essex* suffered no damage. Periodic Soviet overflights continued. In May 1979 two Il-38 May reconnaissance aircraft flew so close to the carrier *Midway*, which was operating in the Arabian Sea, that aircraft in the ship's landing pattern had to take evasive action.

Reviewing the Soviet overflights, Vice Admiral Gerald E. Miller later observed,

The overflights by Soviet Bear and Badger aircraft were of great concern to U.S. naval

A U-2R at rest on the flight deck of the carrier *America*. Folding outer wing panels made it feasible to take the aircraft down to the hangar deck by elevator. The large, two round objects in the center of the carrier's island structure are AN/SPG-55 directors for the ship's Terrier surface-to-air missiles. U-2s have tandem landing gear and rest on downturned wingtips after landing. (Lockheed)

A Soviet Tupolev Tu-16 Badger overflies the USS *Kitty Hawk* in the North Pacific in January 1963. Soviet naval aircraft regularly overflew U.S. carriers in the early 1960s. Usually—but not always—they were detected in time to launch "escorting" fighters, as these F-4 Phantoms from VF-114. Carrier critics cited these overflights as evidence of carrier vulnerability. (U.S. Navy)

aviation, *not* because they posed a threat to the carriers but because they provided ammunition to the U.S. Air Force for use in their traditional contention that the carriers were vulnerable to air attack and therefore a waste of the U.S. taxpayer money. It was a case of U.S. interservice rivalry. Consequently, any carrier commanding officer or embarked admiral, transiting the Atlantic or operating in the Mediterranean or Western Pacific, was enjoined to take special precautions to avoid the overflights. Many tactics were employed to counter the event, including high transit speed, longer ocean routes, and electronic silence.[17]

Badgers and Bears flew from bases in the Soviet Union and, from March 1968, Badgers flew from the Cairo West airfield in Egypt, observing U.S. and British ships in the Mediterranean. Initially a unit of six Tu-16R aircraft was based in Egypt; the aircraft had Egyptian markings and their Soviet crews had Egyptian insignia on their flight suits. The unit was later joined by Tu-16SPS electronic jamming aircraft (NATO Badger-J).

Overflights continued on a periodic basis. In the fall of 2000 Russian Su-24 Fencer and Su-27 Flanker aircraft overflew the *Kitty Hawk* in the Sea of Japan. Subsequently photos of the ship's flight deck were e-mailed by the Russians to the carrier's commanding officer.

A more serious challenge to aircraft carriers came from Secretary McNamara. No new attack carrier was proposed for the fiscal 1964 budget, which began on July 1, 1963. In presenting the defense budget to Congress on January 30, 1963, Mr. McNamara stated, "Tentatively, one new attack carrier, conventionally powered, will be started every second year. The last carrier [the CVA 67] was included in the fiscal year 1963 shipbuilding program and, tentatively, the next carrier will be started in fiscal year 1965, and another in fiscal year 1967."

Then, on February 22, 1963, Mr. McNamara directed the Navy to justify its operation of 15 attack carriers as well as requests for new construction. This analysis would be considered against land-based tactical air power on a cost-effectiveness basis. The attack carriers were no longer considered of prime importance to the U.S. strategic offensive forces because of the increase in the nation's long-range missile forces. By mid-1963 more than 400 nuclear-tipped ballistic missiles would be operational, including 144 aboard nine Polaris submarines. By the end of the year almost 600 strategic missiles would be available.

Vice Admiral Schoech was appointed director of the carrier studies and Rear Admiral Turner F. Caldwell, Jr., was chosen as head of the main Sea-Based Air Strike Study that would attempt to justify the requirement for 15 (or more) aircraft carriers; Rear Admiral John B. Colwell chaired the panel studying nuclear propulsion for surface ships, especially aircraft carriers.

When the carrier for fiscal year 1963 (the CVA 67) was proposed in early 1962, both the Secretary of the Navy and the Chief of Naval Operations had asked for a ship with conventional propulsion since, at the time, it was estimated that a nuclear-propelled carrier would cost one-third to one-half more than an oil-burning ship. Also, they felt that more time was needed to evaluate performance of the first two nuclear surface ships (the carrier *Enterprise* and the cruiser *Long Beach*, both completed in late 1961). Based on operating experience with these ships, by early 1963 the Navy was asking that the CVA 67 as well as all future combat ships over 8,000 tons standard displacement have nuclear propulsion.

The nuclear propulsion study for aircraft carriers was presented to Secretary McNamara on April 20, 1963. It was promptly rejected. McNamara described it as "intuitive rather than quantitative." He told the Navy that the report failed to tell the magnitude of the increase in effectiveness or the possible reduction in existing forces that could be achieved with nuclear-propelled ships. McNamara's rejection of the study directed the Navy to assemble detailed data for mixes of conventional and nuclear-propelled carriers and escorts and for varying deployments and intensity of operations in hypothetical situations. The Navy would have to demonstrate a worthwhile increase in combat effectiveness or a smaller force of ships to justify the added costs of nuclear propulsion.

The Navy's second effort at the nuclear power study was reported to Secretary McNamara on August 12, 1963; it too was sent back for additional work. While awaiting further revision of the study, on October 9 the Secretary of Defense informed the Navy that he had decided against nuclear propulsion for the already authorized CVA 67 and ordered that the ship be built with conventional propulsion. McNamara explained that with this action he hoped to avoid further delays in building the ship and that he would not prejudge the issue of nuclear propulsion in subsequent surface warships.

Secretary McNamara's decision caused an explosion of protest from the Navy and Congress. Secretary of the Navy Fred Korth resigned, an action reminiscent of Secretary of the Navy John Sullivan's resignation when the first U.S. super carrier, the *United States* (CVA 58), was cancelled in 1949. The later resignation was equally ineffective. The Joint Congressional Committee on Atomic Energy held hearings on the controversy. In announcing the hearings, Senator John O. Pastore, the outspoken committee chairman, declared,

Testimony received by the Joint Committee in the past and in hearings held aboard the nuclear carrier USS *Enterprise* on March 31, 1962, indicate that the military performance of a nuclear carrier is far superior to conventional ships. If only economic factors were the basis for deciding the types of ships the Navy will have, then it would not have converted from sail to coal burning and then from coal burning to oil.

The committee listened to a parade of witnesses from the Atomic Energy Commission, led by AEC Chairman Glenn Seaborg and Vice Admiral H. G. Rickover; from the Navy, led by Secretary Korth and Chief of Naval Operations David L. McDonald; and from the Department of Defense, led by Secretary McNamara and Dr. Harold Brown, Director of Defense Research and Engineering.

During the hearings Secretary McNamara put the cost of a nuclear-propelled carrier at about one-third more than a conventional ship:

Construction of nuclear-powered carrier	$371.0 million
Initial nuclear cores	32.0 million
Additional light attack (A-4) squadron	37.4 million
Total	440.4 million
Construction of CVA 67	277.2 million
Difference	$163.2 million

Proponents of nuclear propulsion were quick to point out that the oil for operating the conventional carrier was not taken into account while the nuclear cores, which would provide "fuel" for seven years, were included. Also, the cost of the additional aircraft squadron was questioned when included as part of the ship construction and operating costs.

In explaining his position, Secretary McNamara told the committee,

> The nuclear carrier has characteristics that the conventional-powered one does not. In that sense the nuclear-powered is superior to the conventional-powered carrier. But in my opinion, and one shared by others, the substitution of a nuclear-powered carrier for the conventional would not strengthen us vis-a-vis the Soviets.

Asked by Senator Pastore if the new carrier was needed at all, Secretary McNamara responded, "I put it fairly low." He expanded his statement to note, "I am inclined to believe we need [the CVA 67] but not as much as we need many other things. I don't believe we need the additional performance in this carrier that nuclear power would bring."

The committee issued a scathing report on December 21, 1963, that called McNamara's cost-effectiveness arguments in support of an oil-burning carrier "misleading," "misinformed," and "incorrect." The committee stated that the total lifetime (30-year) cost of a nuclear-propelled carrier was only about 3 percent more than the lifetime costs of a conventional carrier and its aircraft. The committee recommended

1. That the decision to install conventional propulsion in the new aircraft carrier, the CVA 67, should be set aside and plans made to install nuclear propulsion in this ship;
2. That the United States adopt the policy of using nuclear propulsion in all future major surface warships; and
3. That a vigorous research and development program for surface warship nuclear propulsion be continued.

At Secretary McNamara's direction, the CVA 67 was ordered on April 30, 1964, with a conventional power plant. The ship's keel was laid down on October 22, 1964, and would be named *John F. Kennedy* for the martyred president.

Of more importance than the issue of propulsion for aircraft carriers was the question of whether the ships themselves would be built. Some of McNamara's advisers advocated halting all further attack carrier construction and allowing the CVA ranks to diminish after completion of the CVA 67 in 1969. Without additional construction the attack carrier force would shrink to nine ships by 1979:

	1968	1969	1971	1977	1978	1979
Essex class	4	2	—	—	—	—
Midway class	3	3	3	2	1	—
Forrestal class	7	8	8	8	8	8
Enterprise	1	1	1	1	1	1
	15	14	12	11	10	9

However, the Navy's Sea-Based Air Strike Study was creating a creditable attitude toward attack carriers within the Department of Defense. Still, no attack carrier was requested by the Kennedy or Johnson administrations, nor was one authorized by Congress in the fiscal 1963, 1964, or 1965 budgets.

Fifteen attack carriers were in service at the time, but Secretary McNamara gave strong indications that he would reduce this force in the early 1970s. On February 18, 1965, he explained to Congress,

> We plan in the 1970s to make some reduction in the number of attack carriers. My review of this issue during the past few months confirms my judgment that the introduction of the far more effective *Forrestal* class carriers, the moderni-zation of the *Midway* and the *FDR*, the intro-duction of the A-7A, the A-6A and the F-111B, the release of the carriers from the strategic mission, as well as the overall increase in the quantity, range and effectiveness of land-based tactical air power generally, justify the planned reduction. We are continuing to program tentatively the construction of a new attack carrier in [Fiscal Year] 1967.

Secretary McNamara thus proposed to reduce attack carrier strength to 13 ships in the early 1970s: the three *Midway*s, the eight *Forrestal*-class ships, the *Enterprise*, and—possibly—one new ship (CVA 68). But for the time being the Navy had 15 attack carriers and one of those was nuclear propelled. The *Enterprise*

The first all-nuclear-propelled naval force—Task Force 1—circumnavigated the world in 1964 in a dramatic demonstration of the potential for nuclear power. Here the carrier *Enterprise*, missile cruiser *Long Beach* (center), and missile frigate/large destroyer *Bainbridge* cruise the Mediterranean prior to beginning Operation Sea Orbit. (U.S. Navy)

deployed to the Mediterranean from August to October 1962 and again from February to September 1963. She entered that ancient sea once more in February 1964. That May she was joined by the nuclear-propelled missile cruiser *Long Beach* and the nuclear-propelled missile frigate *Bainbridge* (7,850 tons, completed in late 1962). These three ships formed the world's first all-nuclear task group.

The three nuclear ships steamed past Gibraltar and out into the Atlantic on July 31, 1964, beginning a much-rumored, around-the-world cruise, Operation Sea Orbit. Commanded by Rear Admiral Bernard M. Strean and designated Task Force 1, the nuclear ships set out on a dramatic demonstration of their capabilities. The ships steamed around Africa, through the Indian Ocean, across the Pacific, around South America, and returned to the U.S. East Coast in early October 1964. This was only the third time in history that a U.S. aircraft carrier had operated in the Indian Ocean, the first having been the old *Saratoga* (CV 3) during World War II and the second the *Bon Homme Richard*. A few months before the *Enterprise* cruise, during April–May 1964, the "Bonnie Dick" with three destroyers and an oiler—known as the Concord Squadron—spent six weeks making goodwill visits to Indian Ocean ports.

The Task Force 1 circumnavigation was made in 64 days with visits to ports in Pakistan, Australia, New Zealand, and Brazil. In addition, "underway visits" were conducted off several other countries as the carrier's four C-1A Trader COD aircraft flew aboard up to 32 dignitaries at a time for a day of visits and demonstrations while the ships were at sea.

During the 30,500-mile cruise the ships were under way 57 days, averaging 22 knots. The voyage could have been cut to 42 or 43 days with higher speeds. Task Force 1 demonstrated the ability of a nuclear task group to operate anywhere in the world on short notice, totally independent of land bases and logistic support ships. The only "supplies" taken on board were a round of cheese from an Australian destroyer, a pound of coffee from the president of Brazil, and special food for a kangaroo the task group acquired in Australia. Yet, the 6,057 officers and enlisted men in the three nuclear ships ate a quantity and quality of food beyond the imagination of Magellan's sailors in their circumnavigation (of 1519–1522) and even the men of the 16 U.S. battleships that steamed around the world in 1907–1909.

The New Role

The controversies over the construction of additional attack carriers and their power plants overshadowed the change in the attack carrier's role. Beginning with the deployment of AJ-1 Savages and P2V-3C Neptunes to the Mediterranean area in February 1951, the Navy had steadily built up a carrier-based nuclear strike force.

By the early 1960s this force had 14 or 15 ships capable of operating a total of 700 attack aircraft that could be armed with nuclear weapons. For a brief period even their fighter aircraft were being fitted to deliver nuclear weapons. However, at any given time only five carriers (with about 250 attack aircraft) were within striking distance of the Eurasian land mass, and periodically two or three of those ships were in port with a reduced ability for immediate nuclear retaliatory strikes. Still, this role in the U.S. nuclear deterrent force was a major consideration in maintaining the 14 or 15 attack carriers in commission during the later 1950s and early 1960s.

The transition of the attack carrier from the category of "strategic offensive forces" to "general purpose forces" was in large part a psychological change. Although supporting the attack carrier as a nuclear strike weapon enabled it to survive in the era of "nuclear retaliation," the Navy generally emphasized the attack carrier's non-nuclear capabilities. One of the early statements in recognition of this carrier role by a senior officer came during the B-36 hearings of 1949 when Admiral Arthur W. Radford declared, "The Navy today must be built not to meet an enemy navy but with the idea, after evaluation, of the need for air power in theaters of war and parts of the world where we can't get air power any other way."

Admiral Harry D. Felt succinctly expressed this thought in October 1957 when, as Vice Chief of Naval Operations, he told a Navy Day audience,

> There is a tendency to associate the *Forrestal*-class carriers and the nuclear-powered carrier [*Enterprise*] exclusively with nuclear general war retaliation. Actually, attack carriers are an economical and ready means of applying U.S. tactical air power to limited war situations. They can be moved quickly on the seas around the peripheral trouble spots. They avoid the thorny and involved problems of bases on foreign soil.

But while the Navy recognized the role of the attack carrier in non-nuclear conflict, the carrier was not widely accepted except as a source of "catch-words." Politics and glamour were on the side of the high-speed, long-range nuclear strike forces—strategic bombers. Thus carrier-based aircraft of the 1960s and their assignment still reflected the nuclear deterrent policies

A carrier-based A-7A Corsair attack plane takes to the air with air-to-air and air-to-ground guided missiles. It could lift a maximum of about 15,000 pounds of ordnance. Early A-7 aircraft were fitted with two 20-mm cannon; however, on the basis of experience in the air war over Vietnam these guns were superseded by a single 20-mm M61 "Gatling gun" capable of firing at a rate of 6,000 rounds per minute. The single-seat, single-engine aircraft has a maximum speed (clean) of 679 m.p.h. at 5,000 feet (Mach 0.9). (U.S. Navy)

of the 1950s and not the limited-war capabilities of the Kennedy-McNamara strategy. The partial exceptions were the Skyhawks and Skyraiders. Modifications to the A4D/A-4 series made the Skyhawk a good, all-purpose attack aircraft even though it had been designed to deliver a single nuclear weapon under visual flight conditions. Unquestionably, the AD/A-1 series was the outstanding piston-engine attack aircraft of the post–World War II era. But while the Skyraider could provide limited-war quality, by the mid-1960s the numbers were few. In the Korean War attack carriers operated a 14-plane Skyraider squadron plus 28 prop-driven F4U Corsairs. By 1967 only the 5 carrier squadrons had Skyraiders (of 50 attack squadrons assigned to carrier air groups). Interestingly, the U.S. Air Force belatedly recognized the need for non-supersonic attack planes in 1963 and acquired some 60 discarded Navy AD-5/A-1E Skyraiders for its newly created air commando squadrons.

The high percentage of fighter aircraft aboard attack carriers also belied their limited-war capability. The fighter-to-attack ratio of approximately 5:8 seemed overly defensive when the fighters were Mach 1.7 Crusaders and Mach 2.4 Phantoms, armed with Sparrow and Sidewinder missiles, and directed by elaborate shipboard and airborne control systems. Crusaders and, especially, Phantoms could serve in the attack role, but on such missions they proved considerably more expensive to operate than attack planes. Conversely, the Skyhawks and even the prop-driven Skyraiders had some success in the fighter role.

The first jet-age carrier aircraft designed specifically for limited-war conflicts was a result of the Sea-Based Air Strike Study conducted in 1963. The Navy's requirement called for an aircraft with a primary mission of ground support to replace the A-4 Skyhawk on attack carriers. In an effort to provide the fleet with an operational aircraft as soon as practical, the Navy looked at proposals to adapt four existing aircraft: the Douglas A-4 Skyhawk, the North American F-1 Fury, the Grumman A-6 Intruder, and the Ling-Temco-Vought (formerly Chance Vought) F-8 Crusader.

LTV won the competition and was awarded an initial contract on March 19, 1964, for development of the A-7A light attack aircraft. Essentially a shortened, subsonic variant of the F-8 Crusader, the A-7A had a greater combat radius, a more versatile weapons capability, and could lift a heavier payload than the A-4E Skyhawk.

The A-7A had 60 percent more endurance than the A-4E. It had six wing pylons plus two fuselage points (for air-to-air missiles or rockets) in place of the five pylons on the A-4E, and the A-7A could lift about 15,000 pounds of ordnance compared to less than 12,000 pounds for the Skyhawk. The A-7 could carry nuclear weapons. As with all attack aircraft, the A-7 could carry "buddy" stores for fueling other aircraft

The ASW carrier *Hornet* launches S-2D Trackers from Carrier Anti-Submarine Air Group (CVSG) 57 for patrol over the South China Sea. In the 1960s the ASW carriers normally used their Trackers for five-hour patrols; the planes usually carried an anti-submarine torpedo in their bomb bay and two pods of 2.75-inch rockets on wing pylons. (U.S. Navy)

and was equipped for in-flight refueling. Of major significance, the A-7 had an improved flight time-to-maintenance ratio over earlier turbojet aircraft.

The A-7A, assigned the popular name Corsair, first flew on September 27, 1965, only two years after the aircraft was first proposed. The first deliveries to Navy attack squadrons took place in 1967. The Air Force—at congressional direction—reluctantly procured the aircraft in large numbers, but the Marine Corps did not fly the A-7.

The carrier air wings developed during the 1950s and early 1960s would be challenged in the 1960s in the longest and most controversial conflict in American history when carrier aviation returned to Indochina.

15 WINGS OVER SOUTHEAST ASIA . . . AGAIN

Crewmen on the carrier *Ticonderoga* load Sidewinder air-to-air missiles on an F-8E Crusader of fighter squadron VF-53 during the Tonkin Gulf crisis of August 1964. The Seventh Fleet's carriers enabled the United States to strike targets in North Vietnam without entering into "third-party" talks to use foreign bases. The "Tico"—a veteran of World War II—was the first carrier to see combat in the Vietnam War. (U.S. Navy)

With the fall of Dien Bien Phu on May 7, 1954, the French effort in Indochina suffered a strategic and political defeat. Public clamor at home forced the French government to actively seek a peace with the triumphant Viet Minh. The Geneva agreements of 1954 partitioned Vietnam into North and South Vietnam, with a Demilitarized Zone (DMZ) along the 17th parallel. But peace did not come to the region. The communists began guerrilla warfare in the south. They also began infiltrating neighboring Laos to aid the rebel Pathet Lao forces seeking to overthrow the government of Prince Souvanna Phouma as well as that of Prince Norodom Sihanouk in Cambodia.

Throughout the late 1950s and early 1960s, U.S. aircraft carriers maintained a presence in the South China Sea as the turbulence continued.[1] The *Midway* steamed off Vietnam in February 1961 when the trouble in Laos threatened to boil over into a larger conflict. The United States provided six outdated T-6 trainers to the royalist forces, to be used as fighter-bombers against the insurgents, to counter Soviet arms provided to the Pathet Lao. When the Vietnamese communists (now referred to as Viet Cong—a derogatory South Vietnamese term for Vietnamese communists) sent troops to aid the Pathet Lao, the whole of Southeast Asia appeared ready to ignite. However, a coalition government, including both Pathet Lao and royalist interests, was finally agreed upon, and for the moment the trouble ceased.

In this environment, the U.S. government decided to provide South Vietnam with increased aid, including military advisers, communication equipment, weapons, and aircraft. Beginning in September 1960 the South Vietnamese were provided with AD-6/A-1H Skyraiders from U.S. Navy surplus stocks. The situation seemed to be coming under control to the point that Secretary of Defense Robert S. McNamara declared in 1961 that American aid was beginning to work against the communists. However, the South Vietnamese Army, trained in the American model for open, set-piece battles, was neither prepared nor psychologically ready to fight a counter-guerrilla campaign. The lessons learned in blood by the French armed forces less than a decade before were ignored. And from a political viewpoint the repressive regime of Ngo Dinh Diem, president of South Vietnam since 1954, made the country ripe for increased Viet Cong activity.

On November 1, 1963, a military coup, supported by the U.S. government, overthrew the dictator and his family. Diem was murdered on the way to the headquarters of those generals who remained loyal. A new government was installed with General Duong Van Minh at its head, but by January 30, 1964, Minh had been overthrown by General Nguyen Van Thieu. In turn, Thieu found himself facing daily demonstrations by disgruntled Buddhists clamoring for a greater voice in the government. Khanh called for a more aggressive stance against the North and urged his countrymen to invade North Vietnam. He was supported by the personable head of South Vietnam's air force, General Nguyen Cao Ky, who was becoming an embarrassment to the United States. As a peace offering, President Lyndon Johnson, who had assumed the presidency after John F. Kennedy's assassination in November 1963—three weeks after Diem's death—allowed contingency planning for air attacks on the North.

U.S. Seventh Fleet warships, including aircraft carriers, patrolled off South Vietnam. Unarmed reconnaissance flights over the area were now being conducted on a regular basis from the carriers. During late May 1964 the attack carrier *Kitty Hawk*, steaming in the South China Sea off the coast of Vietnam, launched reconnaissance missions over Pathet Lao territory in an effort to aid the Laotian neutralist regime. The RF-8A Crusaders crisscrossed the communist areas of the country. Occasionally light anti-aircraft guns, provided to the Pathet Lao either by China or the Soviet Union, fired at the aircraft. One of these first recce flights— flown by Lieutenant Charles F. Klusmann on May 21— was hit by ground fire. The Crusader burned in the air for 20 minutes en route back to the *Kitty Hawk*. It landed safely aboard the ship.

On June 6 ground fire again hit Lieutenant Klusmann's RF-8A over Laos. This time the damage was severe, and he ejected from the crippled jet, parachuting safely to the ground. When a *Kitty Hawk* helicopter attempted to pick him up he waved the whirlybird away. Nearby communist troops fired on the helicopter, and despite some damage it returned to the carrier. Klusmann was captured. (Almost three months later he escaped from his captors and reached safety.)

The ground fire encountered by the reconnaissance flights led to their being "escorted" by carrier fighters. One of these Crusader escorts was shot down on June 7. The pilot, Commander Doyle Whynn, parachuted from the plane and was rescued after spending a night in the jungle. The loss of two high-performance aircraft in as many days to communist gunners concerned U.S. authorities as the portent of heavy losses to conventional anti-aircraft fire over Southeast Asia. The gunners who claimed the Crusaders on June 6 and 7 were probably North Vietnamese rather than Pathet Lao troops.

Although the U.S. government announced that reconnaissance flights from carriers would continue as necessary, the flights' significance was forgotten with escalation of the war in South Vietnam, which regularly spilled over into Laos as U.S. and Laotian aircraft began bombing communist supply lines into South Vietnam. Subsequently, Air Force RF-101 Voodoo photo planes based in Thailand, escorted by F-100 Super Sabre fighters, provided aerial reconnaissance for the anti-communist forces in Laos.

The increase of Viet Cong operations in South Vietnam led the United States to send more advisers into the country, and on December 11, 1961, the aircraft transport (ex-escort carrier) *Core* arrived at the South Vietnamese capital and principal port of Saigon with 32 H-21 Shawnee helicopters and 400 men of two U.S. Army transportation companies. The H-21s were flown ashore to support South Vietnamese troops. As a senior U.S. Army officer later observed, "This event had a two-fold significance: it was the first major symbol of United States combat power in Vietnam; and, it was the beginning of a new era of airmobility in the United States Army."[2] Twelve days after the *Core* arrived in Saigon, the helicopters—representing several times the capability that had been available to the French forces in Indochina—carried out the first "airmobile" operation in Vietnam. In Operation Chopper the H-21s lifted 1,000 Vietnamese troops to attack a suspected Viet Cong headquarters.[3]

These H-21s were the first of several thousand helicopters and light aircraft that were transported to South Vietnam by various types of aircraft carriers during the 1960s. Helicopters gave the anti-communist forces in

Vietnam a battlefield and logistic support mobility unequaled in military history. And, when properly employed, the helicopter could negate some the most successful communist tactics that had been used against the French—the road ambush and isolation of small outposts.

On April 15, 1962, the helicopter carrier *Princeton* flew off a squadron of Marine helicopters—24 UH-34D Seahorse—and three Cessna OE-1B light observation aircraft (one of which developed engine trouble in flight and returned to the *Princeton* to make a successful landing even though the "Bird Dog" was not fitted with a tail hook). The helicopters and two other OE-1s flew into Soc Trang, about 85 miles south of Saigon in the Viet Cong–infested delta region. This Marine helicopter squadron—the deployment was called Operation Shufly—was the first U.S. combat unit sent into Vietnam. These Marines were the first of some 525,000 U.S. ground, air, and naval forces deployed to Vietnam within the next few years.

Coupled with this initial deployment of U.S. helicopters in South Vietnam, other U.S. forces were moving into Southeast Asia to provide an improved

The USS *Princeton*—a Korean War veteran—while serving as a helicopter carrier in the Western Pacific. Marine UH-34D Seahorse helicopters are on her flight deck as the ship conducts an underway refueling. The LPHs converted from *Essex*-class carriers were replaced by purpose-built *Iwo Jima* class LPHs beginning in 1961. There are empty 40-mm gun positions on her bow. (U.S. Navy)

capability for direct military intervention. Some 50 B-57B Canberra jet bombers of the U.S. Air Force were sent to the Philippines (there was still no airfield available between Adana, Turkey, and Clark Field in the Philippines that could immediately support U.S. warplanes).

U.S. Seventh Fleet warships continued to cruise the South China Sea. Destroyers began sorties into the Gulf of Tonkin, bordered by North Vietnam, China, and Chinese-controlled Hainan Island. The destroyer operations—given the code name DeSoto—gathered Electronic Intelligence (ELINT), collecting data on North Vietnamese radars and communications.

In January 1964, about the time the DeSoto patrols began, the U.S. National Security Council authorized the highly secret Plan 34A MAROPS (Maritime Operations), allowing the Central Intelligence Agency to support covert South Vietnamese operations against North Vietnam. The plan had two parts: the infiltration of South Vietnamese agents into North Vietnam by aircraft and boat and hit-and-run attacks against North Vietnamese shore installations by high-speed craft manned by South Vietnamese or mercenaries hired by the CIA.

"Although some individuals knew of both 34A operations and DeSoto patrols, the approval process for each was compartmentalized, and few, if any, senior officials either planned or followed in detail the operational schedules of both," Secretary McNamara later wrote in his memoirs. "We should have."[4]

On the night of August 3, 1964, South Vietnamese small craft participating in 34A MAROPS attacked two North Vietnamese islands in the Tonkin Gulf. The U.S. destroyer *Maddox* had commenced a DeSoto patrol on July 31. On the morning of August 4, shortly after the South Vietnamese attack, the *Maddox* steamed into the northern end of the gulf.

The Gulf of Tonkin

The *Maddox* was passing off the coast of Hon Me Island, 30 miles south of the North Vietnamese PT boat base at Loc Chao, which South Vietnamese commandos had raided in the night. The *Maddox*'s radar detected the approach of three unidentified high-speed craft, obviously North Vietnamese motor torpedo boats.

The onrushing MTBs headed straight for the *Maddox*. Three 5-inch rounds fired by the *Maddox* failed to deter them. At a range of nearly three miles, two of the communist boats launched an 18-inch torpedo. Both

missed the *Maddox*, which was taking evasive action. The MTBs launched all six of their torpedoes. The U.S. destroyer returned fire and the crew believed that the third North Vietnamese MTB was hit.

While this engagement was in progress, a flight of four F-8E Crusaders, launched earlier from USS *Ticonderoga* on a training mission under Commander James B. Stockdale, was vectored to the area. Establishing radio contact with the *Maddox* and the embarked destroyer division commander, the Crusaders were ordered to attack the torpedo boats as they retired to the North. Armed with 20-mm cannon and Zuni unguided rockets, the fighters swung in over the North Vietnamese craft and made several attacks. The pilots reported sinking the third, already damaged torpedo boat. The U.S. participants estimated that one MTB was sunk and two others were heavily damaged. In fact, two were damaged, none sunk; all were returned to service.

By presidential order, the *Maddox* was joined by the destroyer *Turner Joy*. The carrier *Constellation* was also routed from Hong Kong to the Tonkin Gulf, some 400 miles away. Meanwhile, the planes from *Ticonderoga* maintained a daylight watch. During the night the destroyers retired to about 100 miles offshore to reduce the danger of night torpedo-boat attack. But on the night of August 4–5 the *Maddox* picked up five high-speed radar contacts, again identified as North Vietnamese torpedo boats. With bad weather covering the area, the U.S. destroyers never had visual contact with the enemy PT-boats. There were radar contacts and then sonar contacts identified torpedoes in the water.

The *Ticonderoga* launched two A-1 Skyraiders, followed by a flight of F-8E Crusaders, again led by Stockdale, to provide air cover.[5] By midnight the torpedo boats had vanished from the radar screens. The destroyers had fired several hundred rounds of 5-inch and 3-inch ammunition at the unseen assailants.

The senior officer embarked in the destroyers urged caution on senior U.S. commanders in Hawaii and Washington: "Freak weather effects on radar and overeager sonar men may have accounted for many reports. No actual visual sightings by the *Maddox*. Suggest complete evaluation before any further action taken."[6] The North Vietnamese did not attack on the night of August 4–5; no North Vietnamese MTBs were at sea.[7]

Still, with reports of two unprovoked attacks on American men-of-war in international waters, the time for retaliatory action had come. President Johnson went on television to announce the actions he intended to take. He had planned the American response carefully. Johnson said, "Our response for the present will be limited and fitting. . . . We will seek no wider war." His remarks had been in coordination with the ongoing attack half a world away. "That reply is given as I speak to you tonight. Air action is now in execution against gunboats and certain supporting facilities in North Vietnam which have been used in these hostile operations."

An hour before the president spoke, the *Constellation* and *Ticonderoga* began launching a strike of 64 aircraft:

CONSTELLATION	TICONDEROGA
5 F-4B Phantoms	16 F-8E Crusaders
15 A-4E Skyhawks	16 A-4C Skyhawks
8 A-1H Skyraiders	4 A-1H Skyraiders

In addition, both carriers kept fighters aloft to ensure control of the air should North Vietnamese fighters attempt to interfere with the strike.

Four torpedo-boat bases were the principal targets. The area of coverage ranged from a small base at Quang Khe, 50 miles north of the demarcation line between North and South Vietnam, to the large base at Hon Gai in the North. A heavy overcast hampered the carrier planes, which began attacking their targets at about 1 P.M. local time. Over Hon Gay anti-aircraft fire downed an A-4E from the *Constellation* flown by 26-year-old Lieutenant (jg) Everett Alvarez. He ejected from the aircraft and was captured by the North Vietnamese, making him the first Prisoner of War (POW) of the conflict. (He was released in 1973, after eight and a half years in prison.)

Farther south, heavy flak over the MTB base at Loc Chao hit two Skyraiders from the *Constellation*; one crashed, its pilot killed; the second A-1H returned safely to the carrier.

The largest target was the naval base at Phuc Loi and the nearby oil storage facilities at Vinh, which were struck by *Ticonderoga* planes. Twelve of the 14 oil storage tanks—10 percent of the country's storage capacity—were destroyed. In response to heavy fire from guns at Vinh, planes attacked gun positions. A Crusader was hit by ground fire but was able to limp south to land at Danang, South Vietnam. The southernmost target was a small base at Quang Khe.

The attacking planes damaged facilities and at all four bases and destroyed or damaged an estimated 25 MTBs and gunboats, more than half of the North Vietnamese naval force. The cost had been two aircraft shot down and two others damaged with one pilot dead and one captured.

For the six months after the Tonkin Gulf Incident the men, ships, and planes of Task Force 77 stood ready, prepared to make any additional attacks ordered. The North Vietnamese MTB attacks again brought into focus the value of carrier aviation. The aircraft on the carriers *Ticonderoga* and *Constellation* were immediately available for retaliatory strikes; their use required no negotiations with a third country for using bases and no delay for permission to overfly a third country to carry out the attack mission. The United States acted entirely on its own, with no need to consult other nations.

The attack carrier *Ranger* and the ASW carrier *Kearsarge* were directed to steam toward the Tonkin Gulf, the *Ranger* to provide additional attack capability and the *Kearsarge* to guard against interference by Chinese submarines. This would give TF 77 a striking force of three attack carriers and one ASW carrier. The Chinese shifted a few fighter units into North Vietnamese bases but otherwise made no overt moves to counter the U.S. carrier force. The United States, in turn, brought several Air Force squadrons, as well as support personnel and equipment, into South Vietnam. The Vietnam buildup had begun.[8]

Immediately after the Gulf of Tonkin incident, the Marine reconnaissance squadron in Japan—Marine Composite Squadron 1—was alerted for deployment. Two Marine RF-8As flew from Japan to the Philippines and then flew aboard the *Constellation*.[9] The Laotian government had requested reconnaissance flights of its borders and of the Plain of Jars. Shortly after their arrival, however, the Marines were transferred to the smaller attack carrier *Bon Homme Richard* as the "Connie" was leaving the line.

A second RF-8A detachment rotated aboard the *Bon Homme Richard* in September 1964. This second detachment was transferred from the "Bonnie Dick" to the *Ticonderoga* on October 9 and transferred back to the "Connie" on October 29. The Marine photo planes remained on the "Connie" until another Marine detachment replaced them and sent them back to the Philippines on November 10. These detachments consisted of 2 pilots and 15 enlisted men. The Marine pilots flew a large number of missions, with Navy pilots from the ships' RF-8 detachments flying some of the easier photo missions.

The United States had not been involved in a large-scale shooting war for almost 12 years. The experiences of Korea were beginning to fade, and the prospect of American soldiers fighting and dying once again in a far-off Asian country was unsettling to most citizens listening to the president that midsummer's evening in August. But after the initial furor of the Tonkin Gulf Incident, the country heard little about the war. There were occasional newspaper reports of terrorist activities in Saigon and outlying countryside hamlets, and sometimes a news item telling about an aircraft carrier off the coast. But things were relatively quiet as far as the United States was concerned until February 1965.

By that time dissatisfaction with General Thieu's government had prompted street demonstrations in Saigon and other South Vietnamese cities. The United States sent an advisory team under National Security Adviser McGeorge Bundy to observe the situation and recommend appropriate action. On February 7, 1965,

shortly before Bundy's team was to leave South Vietnam, the U.S. military compound at Pleiku airfield and nearby Camp Holloway in the Central Highlands were attacked by Viet Cong guerrillas. Eight Americans were killed and more than 100 were injured. American officials saw little choice but to make another strike in retaliation for this new attack.

President Johnson authorized a carrier strike in concert with the South Vietnamese Air Force against the military barracks and staging area at Dong Hoi, just north of the 17th parallel, in other words, the DMZ. The strike—given the somewhat evocative name Flaming Dart I—was delayed by the bad weather characteristic of the South China Sea at that time of year. However, the South Vietnamese contingent, led by no less a personage than General Ky, the air force commander, in his personal A-1H Skyraider, struck a secondary target at Vinh.

By noon the carriers had received orders to launch their aircraft, and the newly arrived *Coral Sea* and *Han-*

Early in 1965 the carriers of the Seventh Fleet began sustained air strikes against North Vietnam and communist forces in South Vietnam. These A-4C Skyhawks are being serviced aboard the carrier *Ranger*; in the distance are the carriers *Coral Sea* and *Hancock* with screening destroyers. Beyond the Skyhawks are an F-4B Phantom and an RA-5C Vigilante. (U.S. Navy)

cock launched 49 aircraft against the barracks at Dong Hoi, while the *Ranger* sent a 34-plane force 15 miles inland against the barracks at Vit Thu Lu. The *Ranger's* planes were unable to hit their target because of the weather, but the strike at Dong Hoi by the *Coral Sea* and *Hancock* destroyed much of the facility. One A-4E from the *Coral Sea* was lost, its pilot, Lieutenant E. A. Dickson, ejecting over the water. He was never found.

Assessing the results of the strike at Dong Hoi and its effect on the political situation, American officials expected another response from the communists. They had not long to wait. On February 10 the Viet Cong blasted an old hotel, being used as an enlisted men's quarters, in Qui Nhon, killing 23 American soldiers and wounding 21 others. Operation Flaming Dart II began the next day. The three aircraft carriers flew off another strike aimed at the Chanh Hoa barracks, 35 miles north of the DMZ. The 99 aircraft in the strike force faced the same weather as the strike on February 7—a 500-foot ceiling and less than one-mile visibility.

The northeast monsoon, as this system of rain and fog was called, plagued the carrier fleet for much of the war. Only the advent of more technically capable aircraft, able to fly right through the scud and bomb accurately with little or no visual reference, could overcome the tremendous problems posed by the weather. The northeast monsoon is born with the surface winds that spread inland from the South China Sea from November through April. When the warmer air meets the cooler outbreaks of polar air pushing southward from Siberia and China, the system begins a clockwise swirl that produces northeasterly surface winds that reach from the South China Sea to continental Asia. The mountainous terrain of North Vietnam also contributes to the formation of this system of rain and clouds, which was known as the *Crachin* to the Vietnamese and the sailors who plied the waters off Vietnam.

The formidable monsoon seemed to be at its height during the early strikes of February 1965. The Flaming Dart II strike of February 11 met with limited success as the aircraft from *Ranger*, *Coral Sea*, and *Hancock* attacked the Chanh Hoa barracks. The North Vietnamese responded with heavy anti-aircraft fire, shooting down three U.S. planes and damaging others. Two of the carrier pilots were rescued, but the third was captured after ejecting from his crippled F-8. These raids were the first of the so-called Alpha Strikes, which included various elements of the carrier air wing in a coordinated effort against the target—fighters, attack

Arrows: Communist Infiltration Routes after U.S. Involvement

planes, airborne early warning aircraft, tankers, and helicopters (for rescue).

The carriers' fighters also flew various Combat Air Patrol (CAP) stations over TF 77 ships and the target area in the event North Vietnamese or Chinese aircraft appeared. After the Gulf of Tonkin incident of August 1964, a DeSoto Patrol CAP was also flown when U.S. destroyers were operating in the gulf area on surveillance missions. Some fighter squadrons had F-8Cs while others flew F-8Es. The E models had a heavier, reinforced wing with hardpoints for carrying bombs. The C variants carried only Sidewinders on fuselage racks. Thus, the F-8Cs usually were allocated the CAP role, flying at higher altitudes, while the F-8Es were used to attack ground targets and provide low-level fighter escort if needed.

The results of the Flaming Dart raids, especially the second strike, were inconclusive. The Viet Cong was unimpressed by U.S. actions and continued periodic attacks against American installations. It was becoming evident that a program of mere response to communist acts was not going to have much impact.

President Johnson was advised and gradually pressured to allow an ongoing program of interdictive strikes to begin.

Of note, the *Oriskany* arrived on the Dixie Station in early April 1965 to support U.S. operations in South Vietnam. In addition to one Navy squadron of F-8E Crusaders, two of A-4E Skyhawks, and one of A-1H/J Skyraiders plus detachments, Carrier Air Wing 16 aboard the "O boat" included Marine all-weather fighter squadron VMF(AW)-212 flying F-8D Crusaders. This marked the first time since the Korean War that a Marine squadron was deployed aboard a fleet carrier. Only two other Marine squadrons would fly from carriers during the Vietnam conflict—VMA(AW)-224 with A-6A Intruders from the *Coral Sea* in 1971–1972 and VMFA-333 with F-4J Phantoms from the *America* in 1972–1973. In addition, the Marines provided detachments of EA-6B, RF-4B, and RF-8A aircraft to several carriers.

Against the North

Under the code name Rolling Thunder, the U.S. Air Force and Navy were tasked with bombing attacks that were to progress from just north of the DMZ to the outskirts of Hanoi. Rolling Thunder provided for the bomb line to be moved nearer to the North Vietnamese capital, causing the communists to sue for peace when their capital was threatened. Interference from Washington largely negated whatever promise Rolling Thunder held. To the consternation of most senior U.S. military commanders, severe restrictions were imposed on the missions. No air strike was to be flown without prior and specification approval. No prestrike photography was permitted.

Navy reconnaissance aircraft, the RF-8 Crusaders and the more sophisticated RA-5C Vigilantes, were either to accompany the strike force into the target area or fly immediately after the attack planes for bomb damage assessment. The reconnaissance community was concerned with this particular restriction. Many reconnaissance fliers, along with their valuable aircraft and photography, were lost or captured because North Vietnamese defenses were, of course, alerted by the time the main strike force had passed over the target, leaving the gun and missile batteries ready and waiting for the lone RF-8 or RA-5C that would come behind the strike.

Another restriction placed on the Rolling Thunder missions was that no follow up secondary strike could be flown, thus eliminating the "one-two punch" that was necessary to ensure the destruction of certain targets. Unexpended ordnance could not be used on a target of opportunity but had to be dropped into the sea prior to returning to the carrier. With respect to air to air combat, the rule was that enemy aircraft had to be positively identified before engaging—more easily said than done when closing speeds were on the order of 1,000 miles per hour. And, should weather or operational considerations force cancellation of the mission for a particular day, the entire process of authorization had to be repeated before rescheduling.

To coordinate the initial Rolling Thunder strikes a system of times over the target was assigned to Navy and Air Force aircraft. But this was difficult to coordinate and a system was adopted whereby North Vietnam was divided into geographic areas called "route packages." This permitted each service to specialize in a specific area, getting to know the enemy targets and defenses there. Further, a geographic point in the Gulf of Tonkin was selected as the locus of Task Force 77's operations against North Vietnam and was given the code name Yankee Station.

(At a later date, Dixie Station was created at the request of General William Westmoreland, Commander U.S. Military Assistance Command Vietnam. Westmoreland was so impressed by the Navy's carrier support of infantry operations that he asked for a permanent carrier presence off South Vietnam. This presence was all the more necessary because the United States lacked proper land bases from which ground-support aircraft could operate. While Westmoreland's request was a feather in the cap of naval aviation, it also put a further burden on the carrier forces requiring ships to stay at sea, servicing both stations, much longer than the normal line period. Dixie Station also evolved into a sort of "warming up" area for newly arrived carrier air wings. In the relatively "peaceful" atmosphere of the southern war zone, where communist air defense was at a minimum, green air crews could get used to dropping bombs, rocket and strafing attacks, and the unrelenting pressure of daily combat operations before going north into the "real" world of anti-aircraft guns and missiles, MiGs, and the threat of capture.)

The first Navy strike of Rolling Thunder took place on March 18, 1965, when aircraft from the *Coral Sea* and *Hancock* bombed supply buildings at Phu Van and Vinh Son; all of the aircraft returned, some with light damage. Subsequent attacks brought increased casual-

An A-4E Skyhawk from the *Independence* starts to pull up after attacking a train at Van Hoi, North Vietnam. Carrier-based aircraft were used in "strategic" as well as tactical roles in the air war over Vietnam; ironically, the large B-52 strategic bombers were initially denied the opportunity to strike North Vietnamese targets because of the military and psychological advantages to be gained by the communists if a B-52 were to fall in North Vietnam. (U.S. Navy)

ties, aircraft losses, and pilot capture. The attacks moved up and down the North Vietnamese coast, coming within 70 miles of Hanoi. While the strikes seemed to have some strategic value, the main result was that the communists stopped traveling and resupplying their units during the day. They shifted to small, camouflaged activity at night along what was to become known as the Ho Chi Minh Trail, which eventually stretched from North Vietnam to Laos. Bearers became one of the basic means of transporting supplies, along with trucks and bicycles. Because of a restriction against the bombing of villages, the Viet Cong parked its vehicles in the open during daylight in villages, where they could be seen clearly and, therefore, be safe from attack.

On March 29, 1965, the detachment from heavy attack squadron VAH-2 on the *Ranger* became the first A-3B Skywarriors to drop bombs in combat when six planes flew a strike against Bach Long Vi Island in the Gulf of Tonkin. Although heavy haze prevented visual sighting of the targets, the crews of VAH-2 dropped 12 tons of bombs with radar bombing. Throughout the summer of 1965 detachments of Skywarriors on each attack carrier demonstrated their versatility as bombers, aerial tankers, and reconnaissance aircraft.

In addition to the February and March 1965 air strikes of Flaming Dart and Rolling Thunder, the U.S. naval forces began other important operations. In February, a maritime surveillance program was begun in which air and surface units of the U.S. Navy and Vietnamese forces patrolled the various rivers for waterborne communist supply efforts. In company with the surface craft, land-based patrol squadrons—under Operation Market Time—ranged from southern Cambodia up to the 17th parallel.

Another important operation during this period was the landing of U.S. Marines at Da Nang on March 8. A Marine brigade of some 3,500 troops landed to reinforce the anti-communist forces in the city. It was a prelude to other Marine operations, such as the June landing at Chu Lai (see below).

With the gathering momentum of Rolling Thunder and the increasing frequency of American air strikes, it was only a matter of time before the North Vietnamese took stronger defensive measures. On April 5 an RF-8A from the *Coral Sea* brought back photographs of the first Surface-to-Air-Missile (SAM) site to be positively identified. Discovery of the SA-2 site, 15 miles southeast of Hanoi, was of such great importance that the Task Force 77 commander flew to Saigon to discuss the photos with the Seventh Air Force commander. Both men agreed that immediate action was required to meet this new and dangerous threat to American flight crews. A plan was forwarded up the chain of command for a joint Navy–Air Force strike at the missile site. Permission to mount such an attack was refused. A second site appeared a month later, and by July 1965 several SAM sites were in evidence with the first becoming operational.[10]

Not until several U.S. planes had been shot down—the first Navy losses were A-4 Skyhawks from the *Midway* in August 1965—did Washington sanction anti-SAM missions. The first operation, given the code name Iron Hand, began on August 12. Although considerable effort was expended in hunting missile sites, the first actual strike against a SAM site was not carried out until the morning of October 17. Four A-4E Sky-hawks from the *Independence*, with an A-6 Intruder as pathfinder, found a site near Kep airfield, north of Hanoi, and destroyed it with iron bombs.

The introduction of SAMs and radar-directed anti-aircraft guns gave rise to a unique and sometimes costly little war within a war: electronic countermeasures. The SA-2 Guideline missiles used throughout the Vietnam War were described by the pilots fortunate enough to see them and return as "flying telephone poles." A 35-foot-long, two-stage missile with a 349-pound, high-explosive warhead, and a ceiling of approximately 70,000 feet, the SA-2 demanded new countermeasures by U.S. aircraft.

The U.S. Air Force and Navy–Marine Corps developed separate counters to the concentrations of missiles along the various route packages flown by their planes. An early practice was to fly toward the target at low level and high speed until a preplanned point of identification, usually a prominent landmark or bend in a river, was reached. At that time, the pilot altered course to another preplanned point, pulled his plane into a climb, and then dived toward the target and released his weapons. This "pop-up" procedure brought the bombers down to the range of small-arms fire, and there was enormous pressure on the pilot to quickly identify his several landmarks and target accurately at high speed.

Other anti-SAM measures included use of chaff, the dispensing of countless strips of aluminum foil to jam enemy radar. This oldest of ECM tactics, dating back to the Battle of Britain in 1940, was adequate, but the aircraft releasing the chaff had to fly tight formations at low levels to sew a proper pattern. Thus, they needed their own armed escorts and became vulnerable to anti-aircraft fire.

Air launched missiles were also used against SAMs: The AGM-45A Shrike could detect P-12 or Spoon Rest-A target acquisition radar and follow the radar's emission or beam down to impact. The Shrike's fragmentation warhead could shred the antenna and possibly the adjacent radar van. Although the Shrike was initially highly successful, the North Vietnamese countered it by alternatively turning their radars on and off, reducing the time that the signal was available for the Shrike to home on.

The Navy employed the EA-3B Skywarrior, and the Marines flew the EF-10B Skyknight—both long-serving aircraft—to seek out enemy radars for attack by other aircraft. The land-based Skyknights, which saw combat as F3D night fighters in Korea, flew in the ECM role until 1969. They were later replaced in Marine aviation by the EA-6A Intruder, also based ashore.

The First Air Battles

Surface-to-air missiles were not the only threat to U.S. air attacks against North Vietnam. Additional early warning radar sites were installed, and a large infusion of fighter aircraft, especially MiG-17s, was observed as the months progressed. The MiG-17, assigned the North Atlantic Treaty Organization name Fresco, was a development of the MiG-15 fighter. Although at Mach 0.95 it was significantly slower than the supersonic F-4 Phantoms of the U.S. Navy and Air Force, the MiG-17 had greater maneuverability and its two 23-mm and one 37-mm cannon plus air-to-air missiles posed a major threat to American aircraft.

It was only a matter of time before air-to-air combat was joined. The MiGs had made their first appearance during a 50-plane U.S. raid south of Hanoi on April 3, 1965. North Vietnamese fighters made one firing pass at the strike force and kept going. The next day, however, the MiGs' attention was more concentrated, and the first two U.S. aircraft lost to enemy fighters were Air Force F-105 Thunderchief attack planes.[11] Additional encounters occurred in the following weeks.

The first Navy aircraft shot down by MiGs was an F-4B Phantom from Fighter Squadron 96 aboard the *Ranger*. On April 9 the ship began launching two Phantoms for combat air patrol over the northern Tonkin Gulf. The first aircraft suffered an engine failure as it was being catapulted; the crew ejected and was rescued but the plane was lost. An ominous start to the mission.

A standby Phantom took the downed aircraft's place and the two fighters streaked northward. They were intercepted by four *Chinese* MiG-17s. The two Phantoms being relieved also joined the mêlée. The aerial battle took place at high altitude near Hainan Island. One of the MiG-17s exploded as the U.S. aircraft loosed Sparrow missiles at their antagonists. When the battle ended one of the Phantoms was missing.

The U.S. aircraft was thought to have been downed by a MiG although a Chinese newspaper later claimed that a Phantom-launched Sparrow had killed the aircraft. The downed MiG-17 was thought to have been destroyed by Lieutenant (jg) Terence Murphy and his back-seater, Ensign Ronald Fegan, whose Phantom had disappeared. But no one was given credit for the MiG-17 because of the sensitivity of engaging Chinese aircraft. Chinese MiGs downed five Navy aircraft and two Air Force aircraft during the Vietnam War.[12]

On June 17 Secretary of the Navy Paul H. Nitze was aboard the *Midway* as part of a tour of the fighting area. To the delight of the ship's crew, he had the opportunity to announce over the public address system that two F-4B Phantoms had scored the first MiG kills of the war. The executive officer of VF-21, Commander Louis C. Page, his Radar Intercept Officer (RIO), Lieutenant Jack E. D. Batson, and Lieutenant John C. Smith, Jr., and his RIO, Lieutenant Commander R. B. Doremus, had tangled with four MiG-17s south of Hanoi. As the two flights closed on each other at nearly 1,000 miles per hour, the two Phantoms fired Sparrow missiles. Two of the MiGs burst into flames and went down.

On June 20 a MiG-17 was brought down by prop-driven Skyraiders from the *Midway*. Two MiG-17s jumped four A-1Hs on a bombing strike over North Vietnam. The MiGs fired two missiles at the Skyraiders, both of which missed. The MiGs chased the Skyraiders, and in the ensuing aerial battle Lieutenant Clinton B. Johnson and Lieutenant (jg) Charles W. Hartman III each received "half" credit for shooting down a MiG-17 with 20-mm gunfire. Pilot skill and the Skyraider's outstanding maneuverability led to the victories.[13] (*Midway* aircraft would also score the final MiG kill of the war some eight long years later.)

Meanwhile, carrier-type aircraft began operating ashore. U.S. Marines had been heavily engaged in combat since coming ashore at Da Nang on March 8, 1965. Subsequently, providing organic air support was given

The A-3 Skywarrior was the most versatile carrier-based aircraft of the Vietnam War. It was flown in the bomber, photo-reconnaissance, tanker, and electronic countermeasures roles. This Skywarrior from airborne early warning squadron VAW-13 is one of 34 converted to the EKA-3B configuration combination tanker/ECM aircraft. Note the electronic blisters and aerials on and beneath the fuselage, and the "bobtail" antenna. (Paul R. Derby, U.S. Navy)

a high priority, and on May 7, 1,400 Marines and Navy Seabees waded ashore at Chu Lai, some 50 miles south of Da Nang, to build an airfield for ground-support operations. Brigadier General Marion Carl, World War II fighter ace and test pilot, led this landing. On June 1 the Chu Lai airstrip was operational as Marine A-4E Skyhawks flew their first missions against the Viet Cong. Chu Lai, which would also serve as a main base of operations for Marine helicopters, became an immediate target of the Viet Cong (see below).

And, the U.S. Air Force began operating A-1E Skyraiders from bases in South Vietnam in June 1964. The Air Force had earlier evaluated the Skyraider but rejected it, primarily because of interservice politics. The South Vietnamese had been flying Skyraiders since 1961. Now the U.S. Air Force acquired about 150 surplus Navy A-1E aircraft, which they modified (including compatible radios and dual controls for a two-man crew). These "Spads" were invaluable for close air support and, especially, as protection for helicopter rescue operations because of their large bomb loads, long endurance at low altitudes, and ability to take battle damage and keep flying.[14] (All surviving Air Force A-1s were given to the South Vietnamese in November 1972 when U.S. forces ended combat operations in Vietnam. At one point the South Vietnamese had more than 300 Skyraiders in service.)

A major new aircraft entered the combat arena in June 1965, as the carrier *Independence*, on loan from the Atlantic Fleet, steamed into the Gulf of Tonkin with Attack Squadron 75 on board flying the A-6A Intruder. The Korean War had demonstrated the need for a true all-weather aircraft capable of flying long distances, day or night, and delivering a large bomb load. The A-6A (originally A2F-1) made its first flight in 1960 and VA-75 Intruders first launched from the *Independence* against targets in North Vietnam on July 1, 1965. That first mission took the new aircraft to targets south of Hanoi, those targets being located entirely by radar. In the following weeks the "Indy" Intruders struck bridges, power plants, barracks, ammunition depots, and railway installations in a continuous pounding of North Vietnamese territory, in every type of weather, fair or foul, day or night.

November 1965 saw the arrival of the *Kitty Hawk* with the second A-6 squadron, VA-85. These Intruders in this squadron also took on difficult targets in difficult weather conditions. A measure of the effectiveness of the new aircraft was established when, during a Radio Hanoi broadcast on April 20, 1966, the North Vietnamese hotly claimed that the Americans were using B-52 heavy bombers against the country's population centers. The proof, according to the communist broadcaster, was the use of B-52s against the Uong Bi power plant two days before. In reality the strike against this important facility was flown by two Intruders from the *Kitty Hawk* (as discussed below).

The *Kitty Hawk* brought another new aircraft to the hostilities in November 1965, the E-2A Hawkeye from Grumman, the same company that produced the Intruder. The Hawkeye was a radar-picket or AEW aircraft, distinguished by the large, rotating radar dome ("rotodome") mounted atop its fuselage. The twin turboprop aircraft succeeded the Grumman E-1B Tracer, providing considerably more AEW capability and endurance. The E-2A could provide warning of approaching aircraft, vector defensive fighters, guide strike aircraft to and from targets on the ground, and radio messages from a strike force over its target back to the carrier task force. Other uses were general surveillance, coordination of airborne refueling, vectoring aircraft in need of fuel to a waiting tanker, and search and rescue control. With a crew of two pilots and three controllers, the E-2A became the fleet's aerial nerve center.

The nuclear-propelled carrier *Enterprise*—with 102 aircraft of Carrier Air Wing 9 embarked—arrived on Yankee Station on December 2, 1965. Nuclear propulsion had come to the Vietnam War. The largest warship built to that time, the "Big E" brought a combination of the newest technology and its own imposing physical presence to the Tonkin Gulf. After an initial workup on Dixie Station, the nuclear carrier moved up to Yankee Station and on December 17 launched her first strike against targets in the North. By the end of her first week of combat operations the *Enterprise* had set a record of 165 combat sorties in one day, surpassing *Kitty Hawk*'s 131. The *Enterprise*'s commanding officer, Captain James L. Holloway III, commented, "The tons of bombs that have flown off this ship would stagger you."

Not said by Holloway—or by other Navy or Air Force spokesmen—was the reality of the bombing effort: each service was simply generating sorties, to put more planes over targets so that they could rack up ever higher totals, responding to Secretary of Defense McNamara's calls for quantitative data to impress Congress and President Johnson. In many instances it became almost irrelevant which targets "Big E" planes

Table 15-1
NOMINAL CARRIER AIR WINGS, 1965

	ESSEX CLASS	*MIDWAY* CLASS	*FORRESTAL* CLASS	*ENTERPRISE*[#]
Fighter	24 F-8E	24 F-4B[*]	24 F-4B	24 F-4B
Attack	28 A-4E	28 A-4C/E	28 A-4C/E	56 A-4C
	12 A-1H/J	12 A-1H/J	9 A-1H/J[**]	
Heavy attack	—	9 A-3B	—	3 A-3B
Reconnaissance	3 RF-8G	2 RF-8A	6 RA-5C[***]	3 RA-3B
	6 RA-5C			
AEW	4 E-1B	4 E-1B	4 E-1B or E-2A	4 E-1B
ECM	—	—	3 EA-1F	3 EA-3B
Helicopter	2 UH-2	2 UH-2	3 UH-2	3 UH-2

  * 12 F-4B and 12 F-8D on the *Coral Sea*.
 ** Alternatively 9 A-6A in some ships.
*** Alternatively 3 RF-8G in some ships.
  # On her first deployment the *Enterprise* additionally carried six EA-3B and RA-3B Skywarriors.

The carrie
Seasprite
and four l
(R.W. Lew

Canal, th
lantic, re
around-tl

Amp
enth Flee
the helic
tion Starl
success i
ning to d
after it w
commun
on all sid
detected
from the
sion was
made a jo

struck or how much damage was inflicted or, on occasion, whether the bombs were jettisoned at sea because a target was obscured by clouds or smoke.

The three carriers on Yankee station at the close of 1965—*Enterprise*, *Kitty Hawk*, and *Ticonderoga*—ended the year with one of the largest strikes yet flown against North Vietnam. On December 22 they sent 100 planes against the thermal power plant at Uong Bi—the first time that an industrial target as opposed to military bases and support installations was struck. The large plant, a source of national pride for North Vietnam, was approached from the north by the planes from the *Enterprise*, while the *Kitty Hawk* and *Ticonderoga* force attacked from the south. By 4 P.M., when the last wave of aircraft left the target, some 15 miles northeast of the harbor city of Haiphong, the plant was billowing forth oily smoke; all sections of the complex had been hit. Two *Enterprise* Skyhawks were lost to the intense flak.

By the time a Christmas truce began on December 24, 1965, ten carriers had participated in combat action against the communists since August 1964. In this first full year of the war nearly 57,000 combat sorties had been flown from the carriers, with more than 100 aircraft lost. Eighty-two Navy fliers were killed, captured, or missing; 46 others had been rescued, most by Navy or Air Force helicopters, sometimes under fire.

However, communist leaders were not deterred in the least. Indeed, they were escalating the war. Rolling Thunder, the bombing program of intimidation aimed at bringing the North to the conference table, was failing. The Viet Cong showed no signs of wanting to talk. The Christmas truce of 1965 and the accompanying halt in bombing operations by the U.S. forces lasted for 37 days. Washington waited in hope that the communists would begin peace talks; instead the North Vietnamese used the time to reconstruct bridges and facilities damaged in previous strikes and to augment their growing air defense network. Reconnaissance flights during the period gave ample evidence of the industry of the enemy. Additional anti-aircraft gun emplacements were detected between Hanoi and the Chinese border. Petroleum and storage facilities were being constructed underground to escape future air strikes.

The Johnson administration had to face the sobering fact that the previous year's bombing efforts had been in vain. Rolling Thunder I had been a dismal failure in its main objective of forcing the communists to negotiate. The men and aircraft lost during the 1965 strikes had been largely wasted.

Admiral U. S. Grant Sharp, the Commander in Chief U.S. Pacific Command, pressed for resumed bombing operations against North Vietnam, declaring "a properly oriented bombing effort could either bring the enemy to the conference table or cause the insurgency

An A-6A Intruder is catapulted from a waist catapult of the carrier *Independence* while an A-4 Skyhawk is readied for launching. The "Indy" flew the first combat missions with Intruders of attack squadron VA-75. The new aircraft had a remarkable capability for night and bad-weather bombing operations. (R.C. Lister, U.S. Navy)

close-in protection by seven U.S. Army UH-1E gunship helicopters.

In three days of fighting, followed by several days of mopping up, the Marines devastated the enemy force, killing 645 by body count. Later intelligence reports put the enemy losses at more than 1,000 dead plus wounded. Marine casualties were 45 dead and 203 wounded. Several helicopters and one observation plane were shot down by enemy gunfire. However, all but one UH-34 were recovered, repaired, and returned to service.

The first U.S. amphibious assault of the war, which involved the first use of helicopters to land U.S. troops directly into battle, provided the first major U.S. ground victory in Vietnam. As the war progressed an amphibious task group, including a helicopter carrier, remained in the South China Sea, ready to land Marines by helicopter, landing craft, and amphibious tractor as the ground situation demanded.

An anti-submarine carrier also continually operated in the Vietnam area. The ship's S-2E Trackers, armed with ASW torpedoes and air-to-surface rockets, patrolled the area, keeping vigil for potentially hostile submarines and assisting in the blockade against arms being smuggled along the Vietnamese coast. SH-3A Sea

King helicopters regularly had their sonar equipment removed and were temporarily assigned to attack carriers to supplement the rescue helicopters in those ships. For the rescue role the SH-3s were fitted with removable armor and hand-fired machine guns. A CVS detachment of AD-5W Skyraiders often operated from the CVAs to perform a variety of missions with their AN/APS-20 search radar. The four-plane A-4 "ASW fighter" detachments on the ASW carriers also flew from the attack carriers on occasion to fly strike missions, generally over South Vietnam.

The ASW carrier *Intrepid* appeared off Vietnam in 1966 as a "limited attack carrier" with a unique air wing. Arriving on Dixie Station on May 1, 1966, the *Intrepid* was deployed in response to General Westmoreland's request for a carrier to support ground operations in South Vietnam. Previously an Atlantic Fleet CVS, the *Intrepid* had been designated as a "limited CVA" in October 1965. She exchanged her ASW aircraft for four attack squadrons with 28 A-4B Skyhawks and 24 A-1H Skyraiders, plus UH-2 Seasprite rescue helicopters. (The *Intrepid* made three deployments of about eight months each to Vietnam in 1966–1969. Her embarked aircraft varied on those cruises; see Table 15-2.)

An *Intrepid* Skyraider scored the second kill of a

		Table 15-2	
		USS *INTREPID* AIR WINGS	

	APR–NOV 1966	MAY–DEC 1967	JUNE 1968–FEB 1969
Fighter	—	—	6 F-8C
Attack	24 A-1H/J	14 A-4B	46 A-4C/F
	28 A-4B/C	24 A-1H/J	28 A-4B/C/E
AEW	—	3 E-1B	3 E-1B
ECM	—	3 EA-1F	3 EA-1F
Reconnaissance	—	—	1 RF-8G
Helicopter	3 UH-2A/B	3 UH-2A/B	3 UH-2A/B

MiG by propdriven aircraft during the Vietnam War. Lieutenant (jg) William T. Patton used his A-1H Skyraider's 20-mm cannon to kill the MiG-17 on October 9, 1966.

A Long, Hard War

As 1966 began it was obvious that the air war would be long, difficult, and costly. The U.S. commander-in-chief in the Pacific, Admiral Sharp, would recall,

It was not until the last day of January that air strike operations against North Vietnam were in fact begun again. At that time Rolling Thunder 48 was executed, consisting only of armed reconnaissance strikes south of twenty-one degrees north and, as usual, prohibiting air operations in the vital Hanoi/Haiphong area and the northeast sector. Further, SAM suppression operations were now to be restricted to this armed reconnaissance area. We were starting 1966 with heavier restrictions [than] we had in late 1965![19]

North Vietnam's air defense system was proving to be a deadly threat. In January 1966 six carrier aircraft and five crewmen were lost during raids; in February ten planes and ten men went down. Flak seemed to be the greatest danger. SAMs, although in abundance, took a lesser toll. In October 1966 figures were published that indicated that, of the 397 aircraft that had been lost, only 22 could be attributed to missiles. Such figures were of little comfort to the fliers who had to eject from their crippled planes after taking a hit from a SAM, especially those pilots who were captured by communist forces.

The LPH *Boxer* at Mayport, Florida, about to depart for Vietnam with a full load of 1,200 troops, 205 helicopters, and 6 OV-1 Mohawk fixed-wing aircraft of the Army's 1st Cavalry Division (Air Mobile). The aircraft have been coated to protect them from salt and spay during their high-speed transit. The *Boxer*—then a fleet carrier—had made a similar aircraft lift during the Korean War. (U.S. Army)

Pilots discovered that avoidance of SAMs took courage, skill, and physical stamina. But the missile could be beaten. The tactic was devised wherein the pilot, upon sighting the missile, would time himself and at the appropriate time would execute a high-G turn counter to the missile's flight path. The missile's guidance would supposedly lose the target, breaking lock, and would eventually blow up without damage to its intended victim. The plan worked on a number of occasions, but it took iron nerve and resolve for a pilot to hold his plane steady until he pulled the stick hard over.

The Air Force and Navy established special procedures and teams to rescue downed fliers, generally involving helicopters standing at the ready at remote bases ashore or on ships in the northern Gulf of Tonkin. Combat aircraft were readied for dispatch to provide fire cover rescues, with supporting AEW aircraft and tankers prepared to participate. Special E&E—Escape and Evasion—courses were given to air crewmen, and their equipment included handheld radios to contact would-be rescuers after they reached the ground.

Many downed fliers were rescued and many were not. The communists sometimes spread parachutes on the ground and used captured survival radios to lure rescuers into traps. Very few men escaped from capture. One of the most remarkable episodes of the war began on February 1, 1966, when German-born Lieutenant (jg) Dieter Dengler launched from the *Ranger* in an A-1H Skyraider as part of an interdiction mission near the Laotian border. Ground fire severely damaged his plane, and Dengler was forced to crash-land in Laos. After initially evading capture through the night, he was finally caught by Pathet Lao troops, who tortured the American as they force-marched him through several villages.

Arriving at a jungle camp, Dengler was thrown together with other prisoners, some of whom had been held for more than two years. From March through late June the prisoners survived the continuous harassment, planning eventual escape should an opportunity present itself. On June 29, after learning of a plan to kill the prisoners, Dengler and his fellow captives made their escape in a hail of gunfire in which six of their communist guards were killed. Wandering in the dense jungle, Dengler, severely ill with jaundice, lived on fruits, berries, and some rice he had managed to save during his captivity.

The escapees floated down a river on a raft they constructed. Dengler became separated from the group after it was attacked by villagers. Twenty-two days after his escape, frightened, and on the edge of despair, Dengler found a clearing, formed the letters S-O-S with some rocks, and waited to be rescued or die. Later that morning an Air Force A-1E spotted the signal and directed a helicopter to pick up Dengler.

Dengler's rescue and story of survival and determination electrified the country. Eventually he was returned to flying status. Much of what he had learned

The former escort carrier *Core*, converted to an aircraft cargo ship, was one of several AKVs employed to deliver aircraft to Vietnam. Several AKVs had twin funnels installed amidships, and cranes fitted forward and aft, port and starboard, respectively. The *Core* has three A-1 Skyraiders (two with protective coatings) and 15 UH-1 Huey helicopters on her flight deck. (U.S. Navy)

The Vietnam War took a heavy toll of U.S. aircraft and airmen. However, elaborate search-and-rescue efforts saved many pilots and air crewmen. Lieutenant Jack A. Terhune of VF-154 ejected from his damaged F-8D Crusader some 20 miles short of the carrier *Coral Sea*. Eighty seconds after parachuting into the water he was picked up by a helicopter from the ship. An escorting fighter observes the ejection; Terhune's cockpit canopy is above the second Crusader. (U.S. Navy)

about survival was incorporated into the curriculum at various military survival schools.

Losses of air crews and aircraft led Congress and the press to ask questions about the efficacy of the air war. In a front page story on October 9, 1966, *The New York Times* pinpointed several areas of concern in the air war. Aircraft production was not keeping pace with combat attrition, even though Secretary McNamara had authorized increased production; the combat and operational loss rates were escalating. As far as flight personnel were concerned, the paper quoted Representative Otis G. Pike, the Democratic chairman of a House Armed Services subcommittee on aircraft production and requirements, as saying that the Department of Defense had wasted too much time studying the problem. The proper solutions were increased production and training. Another source told of shortages of 1,660 Navy and 650 Marine pilots. Competition from the commercial market, especially from the lucrative airlines, and frustration over government restrictions on the fighting were cited as the causes for the shortages in the cockpits.

A Department of Defense investigation showed that pilots were flying an average of between 16 and 22 combat missions per month over the North, with some pilots making as many as 28. In this high rate of exposure the chance of being shot down increased tremendously. Although the Defense Department attempted to cut back the rate of pilot deployments, by the end of the war in 1973 a few individuals had flown some 300 missions. The input for pilot training was increased, but it would be 18 months before improvement would be seen. To ease the immediate pilot shortage, some shore assignments for pilots were eliminated, and input to such assignments as postgraduate school was reduced.

As pilot training was increasing, so was the production of bombs, rockets, and ammunition. The remaining stockpiles of World War II bombs were funneled into the pipeline. Meanwhile, the air war over Vietnam was escalating.

16 ESCALATION TO ESCALATION

The USS *Enterprise*—the world's first nuclear-propelled aircraft carrier—arrived off Vietnam in December 1965. Beyond making seven deployments to the war zone, the "Big E" also participated in the meaningless assembly of U.S. warships in the Sea of Japan following the North Korean seizure of the U.S. spy ship *Pueblo* and the shooting down of a U.S. Navy EC-121 surveillance aircraft. (R.D. Moeser, U.S. Navy)

The air war over Vietnam escalated when the first MiG-21 fighters were sighted in December 1965. The MiG-21 Fishbed was a delta-wing, Mach 2 aircraft that, like its predecessors from the Mikoyan-Gurevich design bureau, was noted for simplicity and maneuverability. The MiG-21 was a specialized air-superiority fighter. Aviation expert William Green wrote that its appearance over Vietnam in 1966

> served to underline the dangers of ignoring such simple combat aircraft, for the Russian fighter

possessed much the same speed performance as the Phantom II . . . coupled with superior manoeuvrability affording it a distinct advantage under conditions of close-in fighting, and its manufacturing cost is less than a quarter of that of the infinitely more sophisticated American fighter. . . .

It is universally praised on the score of handling ease, performance, servicing and maintenance simplicity, and ability to operate from relatively poor surfaces and short runways.[1]

249

The MiG-21 (NATO code-name Fishbed) was the most potent Soviet-produced fighter of the 1960s. In many respects an outstanding combat aircraft, MiG-21s still had an unfavorable air-to-air combat exchange with U.S. fighters, in large part because of superior American pilot training. U.S. Navy carrier-based F-8 Crusaders downed 3 MiG-21s and F-4 Phantoms downed 13. (U.S. Department of Defense)

The MiG-21s initially kept their distance from U.S. aircraft. However, on April 26, 1966, two MiG-21s attacked three Air Force F-4C Phantoms escorting two RB-66 reconnaissance aircraft. One of the Phantom pilots fired two Sidewinder missiles at one of the MiGs, at least one striking its target. The Vietnamese pilot was seen to eject from his stricken plane.[2]

Several MiG-17s had been shot down prior to the April 26 clash, but this victory over the more advanced MiG-21—called Fishbed by NATO—by the larger, supposedly less agile F-4 Phantom showed that in the hands of well trained pilots the Phantom could hold its own. This was history's first engagement of supersonic aircraft in which one was shot down.

The U.S. Navy had not scored a MiG kill since October 1965. The four MiGs so far credited to the Navy were shot down by three Phantoms and one A-1 Skyraider. The Navy's other carrier-based fighter, the F-8 Crusader, had been in action since the very beginning of the war but had yet to score. On June 12, 1966, Commander Hal Marr, commanding Fighter Squadron 211 on the *Hancock*, gained the first MiG kill by a Crusader. Flying escort for a force of A-4s, Marr and three other F-8E pilots from VF-211 saw four MiG-17s commencing low-level attack runs from below the 3,500

foot clouds that covered much of the attack route. Turning toward the oncoming MiGs, Marr fired a Sidewinder, which missed, but a second missile blew a MiG apart at an altitude of only 50 feet. Marr then turned his fighter toward another MiG and fired his 20-mm cannon until his 576 rounds of ammunition were expended. He was credited with a probable second kill.

Nine days later, on June 21, Commander Marr's wingman on the 12th, Lieutenant (jg) Philip V. Vampatella, shot down another MiG-17 in one of the most dramatic MiG encounters of the war. Vampatella was in a flight of Crusaders called in to cover a rescue attempt of an RF-8 pilot shot down earlier. Orbiting the area in low clouds and well within the envelope of North Vietnamese defenses, the four fighters waited for the arrival of a rescue helicopter.

Vampatella felt his plane shudder as he took a hit from anti-aircraft fire. He continued with his flight but shortly thereafter he and his section leader, being the lowest on fuel of the flight, prepared to detach to find a tanker and refuel. The two F-8Es had barely set course for the tanker when they heard a "Tallyho, MiGs!" The remaining two fighters had sighted MiG-17s approaching and were maneuvering to meet the enemy fighters. Vampatella and his section leader turned back to join their comrades, but Vampatella found that his aircraft could not keep up with his leader; it had evidently sustained more damage than he had originally thought.

The other Crusaders and MiGs had already joined the battle when he arrived, some 30 seconds behind his leader. Vampatella saw a MiG-17 closing on an F-8. Not knowing who was in the threatened American plane, Vampatella broadcast a frantic call for all Crusaders to break right. However, the call was not in time, and the Crusader was hit and went down.

Angry and frustrated, Vampatella spotted another MiG-17 closing on him from the rear. Wrapping his plane into a tight, diving turn, Vampatella headed for the ground, his damaged aircraft bucking and yawing. Skimming the trees at almost 700 m.p.h., he pulled up, apparently having lost the chasing MiG. He looked around and saw his would be attacker behind him, evidently headed for home. Deciding to delay finding a tanker to replenish his fuel supply, which was approaching a critical state, Vampatella went after the MiG. He closed rapidly on his retreating prey, fired a Sidewinder, and watched the North Vietnamese plane disappear in a large cloud of smoke.

The elated Navy pilot immediately set course for the coast, hoping that he could locate a tanker before his engine flamed out from lack of fuel. With about eight minutes of fuel remaining he found a tanker and, after some initial difficulty, plugged in. However, the tanker could give him only enough to gain a few more minutes of flight. The *Hancock* was some 60 miles away, and with damage to his horizontal stabilizer inhibiting control of the aircraft, Vampatella was not sure he could make it back to the ship.

He did land aboard safely. He found that his tail had taken a direct hit from a 37-mm cannon burst, with about 80 smaller holes from shrapnel dotting his Crusader's surfaces. Because Vampatella chose to go after the MiG instead back to his ship, with low fuel and flak damage, the young fighter pilot was a bona fide hero. He was awarded the Navy Cross, second only to the Medal of Honor for heroism in combat.

A second VF-211 kill was scored on the 21st when Lieutenant Gene Chancy, with only 20-mm cannon fire, downed a MiG-17. (During the Vietnam War Navy planes shot down only four MiGs with only cannon fire, two by F-8 Crusaders and two by A-1 Skyraiders. The Air Force scored several MiG kills with cannon fire.)

The carriers' prime mission was still attack, and A-4 Skyhawk squadrons continuously harassed the Viet Cong truck convoys that ranged up and down the Ho Chi Minh Trail. The hunt was particularly successful at night, when the trucks took advantage of the darkness to move in large numbers. The A-4s from the *Coral Sea* were becoming specialists in this type of work. The Skyhawks would work in pairs, one A-4 carrying flares to light up suspected target areas. With the trucks lit up for a few seconds, the second A-4 would zoom in and drop its bombs. The method was quite successful, and many trucks were caught and destroyed.

Bridges were tempting but deceptive targets. Of obvious strategic importance, the spans across the various rivers and waterways of North Vietnam, particularly those that carried rail traffic and linked North Vietnam with China's supply lines, received a good deal of attention from the A-6 Intruders. The bridges were heavily defended, and missions against them were among the most dangerous undertaken by U.S. planes during the war.

On August 12, 1966, the Hai Duong Bridge between Hanoi and Haiphong was dropped by one A-6 Intruder. Flying at night, the plane put five 2,000-pound bombs on target and got away before the surprised North Vietnamese could fire a single shot. However, many bridges in North Vietnam were dropped only at a significant cost of planes and crews. Further, the bridges could be rapidly repaired, while floating bridges (some floating just below the surface) were hastily erected at the site of damaged bridges or on alternative routes.

On June 29, 1966, Secretary of Defense Robert S. McNamara faced a gathering of media reporters. He opened with the news that Navy and Air Force bombers had "inflicted heavy damage on three of North Vietnam's petroleum facilities." There had been one loss, an Air Force F-105, during the attacks that struck at Haiphong, Hanoi, and Dosan. With the attacks on communist oil storage complexes, the war had taken a new, meaningful, and obviously dangerous step. From the outset, U.S. military commanders had pressed for permission to strike at the very heart of the North's war machine, the Petroleum-Oil-Lubricant (POL) infrastructure and heavy industry areas in the Northeast.

However, President Johnson was reluctant to escalate the war by allowing strikes into those heavily populated areas. The North Vietnamese were more practical and in late 1965 had begun building underground storage facilities and increasing the defenses of existing ones in anticipation of increased American attacks.

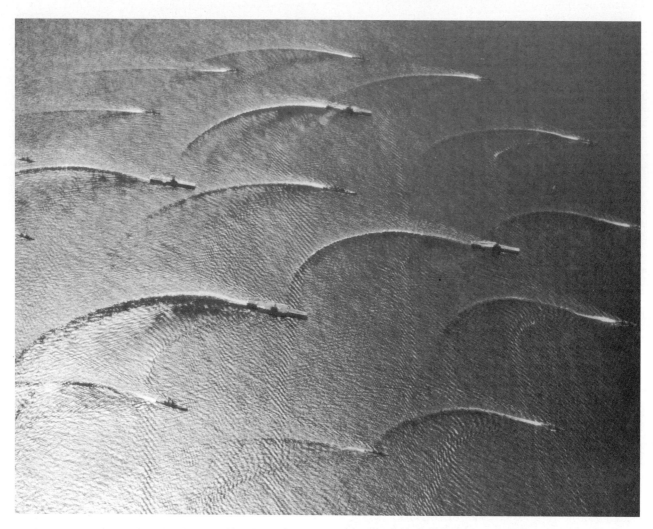

Reminiscent of World War II, Task Force 77 with the attack carriers *Coral Sea*, *Hancock*, and *Ranger*, and the ASW carrier *Yorktown* maneuvers in the South China Sea. Their supporting ships include a guided missile cruiser, a cruiser-size frigate, and 11 destroyers. At the height of the conflict the Navy generally operated up to three carriers on Yankee station in the Gulf of Tonkin and one carrier on Dixie station, off South Vietnam. (U.S. Navy)

U.S. aerial photos provided increasing evidence that the communists were also bent on escalating the supply flow to their troops in the South. Finally the president and Secretary of Defense gave approval in April 1966 for the planning of POL and industry strikes.

Permission to execute the attacks was withheld, however, mainly because the administration continued to be afraid of harming civilians within the targeted areas. Only after two months of repeated discussions and assurances, during which Air Force and Navy commanders agreed to limit their bombing to specific areas and refrain from bombing third country ships or personnel, did Washington allow the operation, known as Rolling Thunder 50, to commence.

On June 29, 1966, aircraft from the carrier *Ranger* struck the Haiphong POL complex. With F-4s flying

protective cover, the A-4s dropped 19 tons of bombs and 5-inch Zuni rockets, all within eight minutes. An RA-5C reconnaissance pilot flying behind the bombers later said, "It looked as if we had wiped out the entire world's supply of oil."

Meanwhile, some 70 Air Force planes had taken off from bases in Thailand to strike at Hanoi's petroleum depot, North Vietnam's second largest POL facility. By the time *Ranger* had recovered her aircraft, word had been flashed to an anxious president that the entire strike force had returned safely.

In his June 29 news conference, Secretary McNamara stated that Washington had given permission to launch the attacks in order "to counter a mounting reliance by North Vietnam on the use of trucks and powered junks to facilitate the infiltration of men and equipment from North Vietnam to South Vietnam." McNamara was evasive in answering questions about possible reactions from other countries, whether any ships besides the North Vietnamese ones were in the harbors, and whether other nations had been notified about the attacks.

As the air attacks against the North's industrial complexes and POL facilities continued, the North Vietnamese tried once more to carry out a torpedo boat attack against American warships. On July 1, F-4 Phantom crews from the *Constellation* sighted three P-4 MTBs as they began an attack against the U.S. destroyers *Coontz* and *Rogers*, some 55 miles southeast of Haiphong. While the destroyers tracked the attackers on radar, F-4s and then A-4s from the "Connie" and *Hancock* strafed the hapless MTBs. Some torpedoes were fired at the forlorn range of 12 miles. All three MTBs were sunk. Among the 19 MTB crewmen rescued by the *Coontz* was Senior-Lieutenant Tran Van Bao, who had commanded the same three MTBs in their attack against the *Maddox* in 1964!

For the Navy, air-to-air combat was sporadic after the initial flurries earlier in the year, even though MiG activity was increasing. North Vietnamese pilots and their commanders were more aggressive, obviously learning from experience and their victories over American planes.

The next Navy MiG kill after Vampatella's score in June came on October 9, 1966. Commander Richard Bellinger, flying an F-8E Crusader from the *Oriskany*, gained the Navy's first victory over a MiG-21. The kill was especially satisfying for the 42-year-old pilot because he had been forced to eject from his aircraft on July 17, when a MiG-17 got on his tail during a swirling dogfight and shot up his Crusader. He was able to regain control of the damaged fighter, but after rendezvousing with a tanker Bellinger was unable to extend his in-flight refueling probe because of damage. His fuel gone, Bellinger ejected 40 miles from Da Nang.

Three months later, on October 9, Bellinger, commanding Fighter Squadron 162, was looking for revenge. Flying escort for a strike group from the *Intrepid*, Bellinger and three other F-8Es, acting on vectors from an E-1B Tracer to intercept the MiGs. Bellinger selected a single MiG-21 going after the strike force. The MiG pilot, apparently spotting the onrushing Crusader, broke off his attack.

As the MiG-21 rolled inverted, split-essing toward the ground, Bellinger followed and fired two Sidewinders. The stricken MiG smashed into the rice paddies. Back aboard the *Oriskany*, Bellinger said, "I've waited 20 years for something like this. It was a tremendous feeling." Having flown B-17s and B-25s in World War II as an Army pilot, Dick Bellinger had traded his silver wings for Navy gold and had flown 77 combat missions in F2H Banshees in Korea. In his third war he had finally scored an air-to-air kill.

(The Air Force had its hands full during this time as MiGs were in the air over Hanoi constantly from September to December 1966; the Air Force downed six MiGs from July to September.)

Carriers in Flames

Two-and-a-half weeks after Commander Bellinger's aerial victory, the *Oriskany* fell victim to a threat that stalks all carriers—the volatility of their munitions, fuels, and aircraft. On October 26, 1966, the weather over North Vietnam forced cancellation of the morning strikes. The aircraft were disarmed and munitions were returned to the magazines. Among the munitions were a large number of magnesium parachute flares.

Two seamen handling the flares accidentally set one off. In panic they slammed the flaming flare into a locker containing almost 700 flares. (One Washington columnist later wrote that sources he talked to claimed that the two young sailors were "playing catch" with the flare when it ignited.) The resulting conflagration spread into the nearby hangar bay, touching off other ordnance. The flames burned through four deck levels, reaching the officer staterooms. Many of the pilots who had just stood down or returned from the mission were killed, unable to escape the fire. Firefighters fought the fames while other crewmen jettisoned bombs over the side, some engulfed in flames as they rolled the ammunition over the side. A total of 343 bombs up to 2,000 pounds were thrown overboard.

Forty-four men died on the *Oriskany*, including the commander of Air Wing 16; many others were injured. Two helicopters were destroyed, and four A-4s were damaged. The *Oriskany* made her way to the Philippines for minor repairs and then headed across the Pacific to the San Francisco Naval Shipyard for major repairs. The *Oriskany* was the first of three U.S. carriers to be racked by major fires and explosions.

The next carrier to fall victim was the *Forrestal*, on loan from the Atlantic Fleet. On June 6, 1967, the

Smoke pours from the carrier *Oriskany*, in flames in the Tonkin Gulf. No U.S. carrier was damaged by enemy action during the Vietnam War, but three were devastated by accidents. All U.S. airfields in South Vietnam came under attack by enemy sappers, rockets, or mortars during the conflict with the loss of several hundred light aircraft and helicopters. (U.S. Navy)

super carrier departed Norfolk, Virginia, for her first combat deployment. The *Forrestal* arrived on Yankee Station on July 25 and immediately began combat operations. The ship's aircraft flew 150 sorties during the next four days, without the loss of a single aircraft.

Just before 11 A.M., on July 29, the second launch of the day was being readied when a 5-inch Zuni rocket accidentally launched from an F-4B Phantom on the after end of the flight deck. It stuck a drop tank mounted beneath an A-4E Skyhawk piloted by Lieutenant Commander Fred White.[3] The 400-gallon drop tank erupted in a ball of flame. The flames spread rapidly.

Wind spread the flames, engulfing the after end of the stricken ship. The 4½ acre flight deck, hot from the flames, was littered with smashed aircraft with crewmen struggling to clear away bombs and ammunition, throwing the ordnance over the side. A chief petty officer spotted a bomb already surrounded by flames and, with only a hand fire extinguisher, started toward the danger. The bomb exploded as he approached it, killing him. Ordnance was pulled off aircraft and thrown over the side. One 130-pound lieutenant found the strength to heave a 250-pound bomb overboard. The ship's two trained firefighting teams were devastated, most of the sailors killed in the explosions.

A 1,000-pound bomb dropped onto the deck from Lieutenant Commander John S. McCain's A-4. Flames exploded the bomb. McCain climbed from his cockpit and out over the plane's fixed-refueling probe before dropping to the flight deck as flames encircled his aircraft. Other pilots fled their planes as the flames spread and a total of seven bombs detonated on the flight deck. Berthing spaces immediately below the flight deck became death traps for 50 sailors as burning aviation fuel spread below decks. Other crewmen were blown overboard by explosions.

Nearby ships hastened to *Forrestal*'s aid. The *Oriskany*, herself a victim of a tragic fire less than a year earlier and rebuilt, stood by to provide fire fighting and medical aid to the larger carrier. Destroyers came alongside to spray water onto the burning *Forrestal*. Within an hour the fire on the flight deck was under control. But secondary fires below deck took another 12 hours to contain. The damage was catastrophic.

By the time the fires were finally brought under control, 134 men had lost their lives, another 60 were seriously injured; 21 aircraft were destroyed, and 41 others damaged. The *Forrestal* made her way to the Philippines and then home, arriving at Norfolk on September 14. It would require seven months and cost $72 million to repair the carrier.[4] The carrier never made another Vietnam deployment.[5]

(Commander McCain and several other pilots volunteered to remain in the war zone and transferred to other carriers; McCain went to the *Oriskany*. His A-4 was shot down on his 23rd combat mission over North Vietnam on October 26, 1967. He became a prisoner of war.[6])

The nuclear-propelled *Enterprise* was the third carrier to be stricken by fire and explosions in this period. On January 14, 1969, the "Big E" was steaming off Hawaii on an exercise prior to returning to Vietnam. A Zuni rocket on an F-4 was accidentally ignited, and within minutes the blaze had reached major proportions. For three hours flames and explosions racked the flight deck. This time 28 men died and 15 aircraft were destroyed.

Repairs to the nuclear carrier, costing an estimated $56 million, were made at Pearl Harbor. The *Enterprise* returned to the war zone, arriving on Yankee Station on October 8.

None of the three stricken carriers was ever in danger of sinking. Still, flames and explosions had rendered them incapable of operation and sent them in to port for major repairs. (The *Forrestal* repairs at San Francisco and other Vietnam-related work at the yard delayed modernization of the carrier *Midway*, which had entered the yard in February 1966. The *Midway* did not return to service until January 1970. That delay forced *Coral Sea*'s modernization to be cancelled.)

The campaign against North Vietnam's POL structure continued for the remainder of 1966 and into 1967. Large strikes in July and August 1966 took out major portions of the communist facilities, as well as rolling rail stock, trucks, and river and canal barges used to transport men and supplies south. In Washington, aerial photographs shown during press conferences and released to newspapers and magazines showed huge columns of dense black smoke billowing up from burning depots, some clouds as high as 35,000 feet.

Still, by the end of 1966, General William Westmoreland could say only, "There is no lessening of enemy determination." American newspapers were aware of the lack of progress in slowing down communist supply lines and the mounting losses of men and aircraft that were making the air strikes costly. Secretary McNamara was quoted as expecting to lose 580 aircraft by year's end, at a cost of more than $1 billion. Questioned by one senator, the secretary declared that, yes, the North had very little industry but that the strikes were actually directed "principally against the lines of communication over which they are moving men and equipment into South Vietnam."

The skepticism of the media was obvious. A *Washington Post* column of September 20, 1966, asked "How Many Bridges Were There?" in response to the large number of bridges being attacked and reported as downed during the summer strikes. The same bridges were being attacked because the North Vietnamese were adept at rebuilding the spans in a short time.

The carrier *Forrestal* in flames in the Gulf of Tonkin on July 29, 1967. The destroyer *Rupertus*, off the carrier's port side, provides fire-fighting assistance. The *Forrestal* was the most heavily damaged and suffered the most casualties of the three aircraft carriers that suffered major fires during the Vietnam War. (J. Nikas, U.S. Navy)

The USS *Enterprise*, the world's largest warship, was stricken by fire on January 14, 1969, during an exercise off Hawaii. All three carriers stricken by fire and explosions during this period survived, in large part due to the excellent fire-fighting and damage-control proce-dures developed by the Navy during World War II. Unfortunately, safety failures caused all three disasters. (U.S. Navy; S.A. Osterbauer, U.S. Navy)

Although the papers admitted that the strikes had indeed destroyed much of the above-ground POL areas, the columnists were quick to point out that the missions were extremely costly. For instance, "it took 11 missions with a total of 40 airplanes last week to destroy a 50-car freight train near Hanoi." And the pilots were facing flak as thick, or thicker, than that encountered by crews over Germany in 1945. A letter published in the magazine *Aviation Week & Space Technology* and succeeding correspondence, written first by an Air Force F-4 pilot, then answered by a Navy Phantom pilot, produced several hard-hitting questions and facts. Why, the initial letter asked, was the Air Force risking two highly trained, very expensive pilots in one F-4? Why did these multimillion dollar aircraft fly with a minimal bomb load?

"There is nothing more demoralizing than the sight of an F-4 taxiing out with nothing but a pair of 81s or 82s (250- and 500-pound bombs, respectively) nestled among its ejector racks," said one of the letters. Sortie numbers seemed to be more important than results. The amount of aircraft a squadron or wing commander could point to as arriving over a target was evidently more important than, say, the number of barges and oil tanks destroyed.

The Navy F-4 pilot, whose letter was printed in a succeeding issue, confirmed the frustrated Air Force pilot's views, while a young Marine second lieutenant completely rebuffed his fellow pilots. The letter writing and the cynicism of the newspaper columnists only contributed to the administration's previous reluctance to go after the enemy's resources in even greater efforts. While the strikes did continue, they were not enough, and the Soviets and Chinese kept pouring supplies, guns, and aircraft across the borders and into North Vietnamese ports. In September 1966, U.S. officials claimed that the USSR had doubled the size of North Vietnam's MiG-21 force and sent some 800 Soviet advisors and instructors.

As U.S. military leaders clamored for increased action, the Johnson administration seemed to be working counter to the general prosecution of the war. Admiral Ulysses G. Sharp, Commander-in-Chief Pacific and an outspoken, increasingly critical senior officer, called for greater interdiction efforts. Citing the need to hinder Chinese and Soviet assistance to North Vietnam, to stop the flow of supplies south to the Viet Cong, and to destroy the North Vietnamese capacity to make war, Sharp noted the necessity of destroying six basic

areas or "systems" in the North: electric power, war industries, transportation, military bases, oil storage, and air defense. All needed to be hit harder and more often.

The initial "safe" zone around Hanoi, in which no bombs could be dropped, was another sore point. Most U.S. military commanders agreed that, even with strikes on important industrial areas outside the city, until major civilian population centers were affected, the communists would stick it out and not negotiate.

Admiral Sharp proposed in January 1967 that targets within his list of six so-called systems be approved as packages rather than on a piecemeal basis.[7] He claimed that he would then be allowed greater flexibility concerning weather and intelligence factors. While Sharp pressed for more strikes, Secretary McNamara had difficulty at Washington news conferences explaining war policies and the high aircraft losses. On February 15, when asked if he was indicating that the previous year's strikes had failed, McNamara gave a lengthy dissertation on the bombing program's prior objectives: to raise South Vietnamese morale, reduce the flow of supplies to the South, and make the North understand the futility of any attempt to subjugate South Vietnam.

The next question dealt with what the reporter termed "rather confusing figures" on aircraft losses. In response, McNamara ran the historical gauntlet from World War II onward, dividing aircraft into fixed-wing, transport, reconnaissance, and other types. Somewhere in all of the explanations was an answer. McNamara was desperately trying to reassure a doubting Congress that aircraft production was well ahead of combat losses in Vietnam.

Still, columnists such as Carl Rowan, in an article in the May 25 issue of the *Chicago Daily News*, questioned the economics of "raining millions of dollars worth of explosives" on North Vietnam's industrial areas without seeing a definite effect. Indeed, Rowan wrote, "the Pentagon estimates there are now 50,000 North Vietnamese soldiers in the South, as against 11,000 two years ago." Referring to the loss of 544 fixed-wing combat airplanes up to that time, Rowan wondered whether the loss of 200 airmen and $1.1 billion in planes was a fair exchange for what seemed to be very little reduction, if any, of the North's insurgent activities. Other reports told of increased air defense systems as well as truck convoys moving along the Ho Chi Minh Trail with near impunity.

Beneath all the wartime bravado, in Washington many Johnson administration and defense leaders were

A massive tonnage of bombs was dropped by carrier aircraft during the Vietnam War, but the efficiency of carrier attacks with "iron bombs" was very limited. Here sailors with attack squadron VA-72 aboard the *Franklin D. Roosevelt* prepare folding-fin bombs for another attack on North Vietnam. (J.D. Goss, U.S. Navy)

painfully coming to the terrible realization that the North Vietnamese could probably fight indefinitely, taking strike after strike, accepting cuts in supply routes, industrial ruin, and whatever else the American attacks brought. Significantly, Secretary McNamara realized the conflict's futility—almost from its start.[8]

Most U.S. military commanders believed that as long as North Vietnamese population centers, port facilities, major airports, and agricultural facilities remained largely untouched, there could be no hope of bringing the communists to the negotiation table. However, in spite of pleas by Admiral Sharp and other senior commanders, Washington continued to dole out targets. On May 23, 1967, the administration drew a ten-mile circle around Hanoi. No bombs could be dropped inside of the circle. This was a direct rebuff to the contention that only with direct attacks on the civilian population could the war proceed to a conclusion.

Other restrictions continued to be imposed. The port of Cam Pha, an important North Vietnamese coal depot, could not be attacked when foreign ships were in the harbor. The North took advantage of this situation, and it was a rare day when a foreign ship was not tied up to a pier at Cam Pha. (Upon seeing the massive pile of coal in plain view at Cam Pha, one *Coral Sea* F-4 pilot recommended that defused napalm be dropped on the pile, followed shortly by bombs to ignite the doused mountain of coal. The result, he said, would be much like a huge barbecue fire started with lighter fluid. Although this proposal sparked some official interest initially, the plan never progressed beyond air wing level.)

Nevertheless, in June 1967 the Soviets claimed that a merchant ship at Cam Pha had been attacked, resulting in the death of a crewman. Although an investigation was launched immediately, Washington could not prove that the ship had been attacked, even when Premier Alexi Kosygin presented President Johnson an expended 20-mm shell at a subsequent summit meeting.

From August 1964 through the end of 1966, 12 attack carriers and the limited-CVA *Intrepid* made 25 deployments to Vietnamese waters, with some of the carriers making two and three combat cruises.[9] These carriers had launched thousands of combat sorties. The almost daily strikes against the North had diverted civilians, who would otherwise have been employed in activities against the South, to air defense duties in the North. Supply lines into the South were affected, and the cost of operations in the South to the Hanoi government was increasingly more expensive. But the communists continued the war with absolutely no indication that they wished to negotiate an end to the conflict.

The air war over Indochina continued into 1967. And it continued to be an air war minutely managed from Washington. As far as the Air Force was concerned, the new year of 1967 started off with a bang. An elaborate operation code-named Bolo was planned because of the heavy attacks on Air Force bomber strikes by MiGs that, after attacking, ran for the safety of airfields that they knew to be off limits to the Americans. (This situation was not unlike that in Korea 15 years earlier when communist fighters retreated north across the Yalu River where U.S. pilots were officially forbidden to go.)

In Operation Bolo—what was called the first "pure fighter sweep" of the Vietnam War—several fighter wings under the command of Colonel Robin Olds, a 24-victory ace of World War II, shot down seven MiG-21s on January 2, 1967, depleting North Vietnam's inventory of those advanced fighters by nearly half. The Air Force had duped the North Vietnamese air controllers into believing that F-4 Phantoms were an F-105 strike group heading for targets in North Vietnam.

Two more MiG kills on January 6 seemed to cause a temporary standdown in the communist camp, and little MiG activity was seen until March 1967. However, by March the MiGs were up in force again, and it was clear—even to those in Washington—that the airfields could no longer remain off-limits.

Thus, on April 24 aircraft from the *Kitty Hawk* struck the major MiG base, built by the Japanese during World War II, at Kep, 37 miles northeast of Hanoi. The carrier planes inflicted damage to the 7,000-foot main runway and support buildings. Two MiG-17s that tried to take off were shot down by Navy F-4s. Aircraft from the *Bon Homme Richard* also hit Kep, damaging several MiGs on the ground as well as downing two MiGs in the air.

The Air Force also struck North Vietnamese airfields. April and May became periods of ferocious air combat, as the MiGs rose to do battle with the strike groups to defend their bases. May 13 was a particularly successful day for the Air Force, as seven MiG-17s were downed by two Phantoms and five F-105s. The Air Force, in the six-month period of January to June, accounted for 46 MiGs, a number that caused Lieutenant General William Momyer, commander of the Seventh Air Force, to declare to a Senate committee, "We have driven the MiGs out of the sky for all practical purposes."

But the American success was short lived. Resupplied by the Soviets and Chinese and with new tactics, North Vietnamese MiGs reappeared in strength in August, shooting down several U.S. aircraft during a strike against the Yen Vien railroad yards.

The Navy shot down its share of MiGs during this frantic period. Aircraft from Carrier Air Wing 21 on the *Bon Homme Richard* made all of the scores except for the two initial kills on April 24 when Kep was hit for the first time. One of two MiG-17s brought down on May 1 fell to a Skyhawk pilot who had joined the landing pattern above the North Vietnamese airfield. Lieutenant Commander Ted R. Swartz in an A-4C was firing Zuni unguided rockets at aircraft on the ground when his wingman told him there was a MiG on his tail. Taking advantage of the Skyhawk's excellent role rate, Swartz pulled above and behind his pursuer and fired Zunis. The rockets slammed into the MiG-17, sending it crashing into the ground.[10]

The Navy scored six MiG-17 kills in May, five by F-8 Crusaders plus Swartz's A-4 victory. Navy fighters claimed five more MiGs during 1967, bringing the total for the year to 17. The disparity between Air Force and Navy kill totals was not easy to explain, but the Navy was sufficiently disturbed by it to have Captain Frank W. Ault, who had commanded the carrier *Coral Sea* during a seven-month deployment to Vietnam, lead a study of the situation. The "Ault Report," published in 1968, recommended several improvements, among them increased missile reliability (another study showed that during that period some 50 air-to-air missiles had been fired in combat without downing one enemy aircraft), more training in air-combat techniques, and the establishment of a school with the primary function of providing advanced training in these techniques.

Initially called the U.S. Navy Postgraduate Course in Fighter Weapons Tactics and Doctrine, this school became known as "Topgun" and was established at Miramar, California, northeast of San Diego. The first class, with special emphasis placed on what one pilot called "old fashioned dogfighting with new-fashioned weapons," convened in March 1969. Carrier fighter pilots and radar intercept officers attending Topgun flew their own airplanes against the instructors, usually recently returned Vietnam veterans, who flew small, highly maneuverable F-5 and A-4 aircraft, painted in camouflage schemes of communist fighter aircraft. The F-5s and A-4s provided a good approximation of the smaller communist fighters, such as the MiG-17 and MiG-21. In part thanks to Topgun, the Navy's kill score improved in air-to-air combat. In 1968 the ratio of Navy kills to planes lost was about two to one. By 1972, when the action heated up again and several classes of Topgun graduates had reached the fleet, the ratio had jumped to 12 to 1.[11]

March 1967 saw the monsoon abate slightly, and the hard pressed crews of the strike groups welcomed the clearer weather. This time also saw an interesting, if oddball, experiment in camouflage. Half of the *Kitty Hawk*'s aircraft were repainted in a green camouflage scheme, to render the planes less visible from above. The Air Force had begun painting its planes in camouflage some months before.

Accordingly, some squadrons of Carrier Air Wing 11 were repainted in camouflage for the remainder of the cruise, into June, but the results were negative. During night operations the dark green made the planes more difficult to see, and carrier operations at night, especially from a dark, rainswept flight deck, were dangerous at best, requiring the most visibility available. The Navy decided upon the *Kitty Hawk*'s return to the States in June 1966 to eliminate the camouflage.

The improving weather in March and April 1967 brought increased missions and increased loss rates. April was the most costly month to date, with 21 carrier aircraft and 15 crewmen lost. On April 18, two A-6A Intruders struck the Uong Bi thermal power plant for the second time. Since the first large strike on December 22, 1965, the power plant had been repaired. The complex supplied one third of the power for Hanoi and almost all for Haiphong. The two Intruders, each armed with 13 1,000-pound bombs, were launched from *Kitty Hawk* before midnight.[12] The two planes made their way to their target, flying at low level to avoid radar detection. The two Intruders made their landfall as scheduled and attacked the target separately, within seconds of each other. The strike was so perfectly co-

ordinated and executed that the North Vietnamese defenses were caught flatfooted. The Intruders sped away before the guns on the ground opened fire. The 26 half-ton bombs all hit the target, decimating the important complex. As mentioned before, the communists were enraged and claimed that the Americans were using giant B-52 bombers against helpless civilian population centers.[13]

A diplomatic incident occurred the next day, April 19, when 24 aircraft from the *Kitty Hawk* struck the harbor town of Cam Pha, 35 miles south of the Chinese border. The master of a Polish merchant ship in the harbor claimed to have been nearly struck by a bomb. Messages flew between Washington and the Seventh Fleet regarding the incident. Striking so close to China's borders was considered politically dangerous. The Chinese government began claiming numerous violations of their airspace by "United States imperialists." On April 12, a KA-3B tanker had been declared overdue from a flight from the Philippines to the *Kitty Hawk* in the Gulf of Tonkin. Shortly afterward, the Chinese claimed the destruction of the aircraft after it overflew Chinese territory. The State Department lodged protests, but the Chinese maintained that the plane was attacking Chinese fishermen on the high seas in the Gulf of Tonkin.

The KA-3B tankers were unarmed but retained their weapons bay, and the United States never denied that the Skywarrior was armed. This was not the first time such a situation had occurred. From time to time, there were claims and counterclaims of shootdowns and harassment. (American pilots in hot pursuit of escaping MiGs might have inadvertently—or perhaps intentionally—chased their quarry into Chinese air space.)

During April 1967 a major change in battle orders that divided up North Vietnam target areas was instituted. The Navy was given the responsibility of keeping the coastal area, especially Haiphong, under attack, while the inland targets, Hanoi and the area west of the capital, were put under Air Force cognizance. This delegating of responsibility made a certain familiarity possible for pilots who flew over the same area regularly. Therefore slight but possibly important changes in enemy reactions, forces, and deployments could be noticed more readily. Another related bonus was a reduction of losses as the same crews flew the same routes, getting to know the various defenses and the best ways to avoid them.

The *Ranger*'s A-7s flew strikes against coastal defense sites and truck convoys and in support of Marine ground operations soon after arrival. But time and the weather were against much of the effort, and only the A-6 Intruders flew on a regular basis. The worsening weather allowed the North Vietnamese to repair many bridges that had been damaged by the strikes. This naturally prompted additional strikes by Navy aircraft.

MiG activity was constant, although not at the peak level of the summer months. Navy fighters downed only three MiGs in the last three months of 1967. However, a Marine was able to chalk up that service's first MiG kill, albeit by an exchange pilot flying an F-4D Phantom with the Air Force who bagged a MiG-17 on December 17. This was the only Marine air-to-air kill until 1972, when another Marine exchange pilot flying an Air Force Phantom shot down a MiG-21. (Marine aviation's fixed-wing aircraft mission in Vietnam was primarily flying support for ground units, giving Marine fliers little opportunity to fly over North Vietnam.)

By the end of 1967 the Navy and Air Force had accumulated massive numbers of sorties flown, bombs dropped, and MiGs shot down, but the hard fact remained that the North Vietnamese had no desire to negotiate. As the Christmas 1967 truce approached, it was obvious that the enemy was going to use the stand down, as he always did, to move men and supplies south without fear of hindrance from air strikes. Thousands of vehicles clogged the trails and waterways leading into South Vietnam, waiting for the truce period to begin. Navy and Air Force reconnaissance pilots and their ground crews worked feverishly over the Christmas holiday, flying many sorties over the supply trails; each mission brought back ample evidence of communist activity. It was clear that the North Vietnamese were planning one or more major actions.

Hardly had the New Year's truce ended when strikes were launched. F-8 Crusaders from *Oriskany* used Sidewinder missiles, intended for aerial combat, against communist rail traffic. The Sidewinder, a heat-seeking missile that homed on heat from exhaust emissions, was found to be very effective against locomotives. Crusader pilots from Fighter Squadron 162 were credited with several engines destroyed. Activity was especially heavy during the period January 2–11, 1968, as aircraft from *Oriskany*, *Coral Sea*, and *Ranger* struck the bridges around Hanoi and Haiphong, SAM sites, and storage depots.

A Helicopter War

"In country" the Vietnam War became a "helicopter war" as the U.S. Army and Marine Corps flew thousands

Marines, laden with packs and weapons, climb up the rear ramp of a CH-46 Sea Knight of helicopter squadron HMM-261 on the deck of the helicopter carrier *Iwo Jima* during an exercise in the Mediterranean. The CH-46 and CH-53 Sea Stallion helicopters provided a major improvement in Marine-Navy amphibious assault capabilities. (M. T. Snyder, U.S. Navy)

of choppers and the Navy flew a small number.[16] In 1964 the more-capable Boeing CH-46 Sea Knight replaced the UH-34 (formerly HUS) troop carriers in Marine service.

The H-46 series—similar in concept to the Boeing CH-47 Chinook—was a tandem-rotor, twin-turboshaft helicopter. Developed under the pre-1962 designation HRB-1, the Sea Knight had a tricycle landing gear and small, wheel housing sponsons aft (easily distinguishing it from the CH-47 Chinook). There was a rear ramp for the rapid loading and unloading of cargo, including small vehicles. Cargo capacity of the CH-46A, the first production model, was 6,600 pounds internal or up to 25 troops could be carried. Later models, with more powerful turboshaft engines, had a greater payload, for example, 9,000 pounds for the CH-46E.

The YHC-1A Sea Knight prototype flew on April 22, 1958, and Marine medium-helicopter squadron HMM-265 took the first CH-46A deliveries in June 1964.[17] The Navy took delivery of 264 Sea Knights and the Marine Corps received 360 helicopters from 1961 to 1977. (Several other countries also flew the Sea Knight, with the Swedish Hkp-4 variant fitted for antisubmarine warfare.)

The Marines gained another new helicopter early in 1967 when four giant CH-53A Sea Stallions arrived at the Marble Mountain facility in January. These four aircraft represented a quantum leap in helicopter airlift capability. The Sikorsky-built CH-53A, powered by twin turboshaft engines, could lift 38 troops or 8,000 pounds of cargo internally with a rear ramp permitting vehicles to be carried and troops to rapidly unload. Alternatively, 13,000 pounds of cargo could be carried by sling. By the end of the year CH-53s had retrieved 120 damaged UH-34s and CH-46s from combat areas and had lifted uncounted troops and tons of supplies. The CH-53A was first flown on October 14, 1964, and the helicopter entered Marine service in 1966 with HMH-463.[18]

As noted earlier, the Marines also flew "outdated" aircraft from bases in South Vietnam: The Douglas EF-10B Skyknight was flown in the electronic countermeasures role until the Grumman EA-6A Intruder replaced it in 1969. Marines also flew the Grumman TF-9J Cougar, another Korean War–era aircraft, primarily in the forward air control role. Marines flew this swept-wing plane until 1969, when the two-seat A-4F and TA-4J Skyhawks replaced it.[19] The missions

A CH-53 Sea Stallion from helicopter squadron HMH-361 lifts cargo from the deck of a helicopter carrier. Like the smaller CH-46, this helicopter has a rear ramp to facilitate the loading of troops and small vehicles. The later CH-53E Super Stallion variant had three engines (versus two in earlier models) and remains the most powerful helicopter in the West. (E. L. Goligoski, U.S. Navy)

flown by these two-seat "Scooters" included gunfire spotting for Navy warships, among them the battleship *New Jersey* during her single deployment to Vietnamese waters in 1968.

The *Pueblo* Incident[20]

While aircraft of TF 77 flew daily strikes against the Viet Cong, an event occurred in the Sea of Japan that momentarily diverted American attention from Vietnam. On January 22, 1968, the U.S. intelligence collection ship *Pueblo*, operating in international waters off the eastern coast of North Korea, was surrounded by North Korean patrol boats and, after a brief fusillade of fire, was boarded and taken into Wonsan Harbor.[21] The *Pueblo* was the first U.S. naval ship to surrender at sea since the War of 1812. One of her 83-man crew was wounded by gunfire and died during imprisonment.

In response, Task Force 71, based on the carrier *Enterprise*, at the time steaming toward her third combat cruise off Vietnam, was created. It appeared that the nuclear-propelled carrier might launch its aircraft in a retaliatory strike against North Korean targets, but that idea was abandoned when the *Pueblo* arrived in Wonsan Harbor six hours after being boarded and darkness fell.

The few U.S. Air Force and Marine combat aircraft available in South Korea and Japan were not on alert, and the latter would have had to refuel at South Korean bases to operate over the eastern coast of North Korea. It was questionable if a handful of U.S. aircraft could have had any impact on the situation, even if they could reach the ship at sea before nightfall. The Johnson administration quickly rejected proposals for air strikes, a commando raid from a submarine, and other U.S. military actions. Indeed, a U.S. congressional investigation concluded, "The Navy had no contingency plans whatsoever to provide for going to the rescue of the USS *Pueblo* in an emergency."[22]

The carrier task force, designated Operation Formation Star, remained in the Sea of Japan awaiting orders. Five additional carriers joined TF 71 during the next few weeks—the attack carriers *Coral Sea*, *Ranger*, and *Ticonderoga*, and the ASW carriers *Kearsarge* and *Yorktown*, plus additional cruisers and destroyers.

The crisis evolved into a waiting game, with the North Koreans holding the American crew as hostages against air strikes. After an American apology, the 82 surviving crewmen were released on December 23, 1968.

Relieved by the *Kitty Hawk* in the Sea of Japan on February 6, the *Enterprise* steamed south, arriving on Yankee Station on February 21. By the time of her arrival major battles in South Vietnam had begun, heralding the long-awaited communist invasion of the South.

Communist forces struck on January 30, 1968, at various points in South Vietnam—Nha Trang, Pleiku, Da Nang, and Qui Nhon. The attacks were begun a day before the Vietnamese holiday of Tet, the lunar new year, on the 31st. The communists, in an elaborately planned ruse, had indicated a willingness to talk peace and had kept the Americans off-balance during this period while they moved supplies and men south. Viet Cong guerrillas even penetrated the American Embassy in Saigon on the 31st, but after initially blasting holes in the protective walls, they were repulsed by American and South Vietnamese guards. All of the attackers were killed.

Primarily a land battle, with little or no naval or air activity, the 1968 Tet Offensive was part of an overall communist assault. Although the Viet Cong pressed the attacks, within two weeks, communists losses were 32,000 dead and 5,800 captured. The communists had gained no sizeable territory, and even more important, they had failed to rally the South Vietnamese populace to their side. But, in the United States, newspapers and television screamed that a massive U.S.–South Vietnamese defeat was in the making.

While the major news from Vietnam during early 1968 revolved around the communist offensive during Tet and the battle for Khe Sanh, major changes of an operational and political nature had occurred by April. Foremost was President Johnson's imposition of a so-called partial bombing halt that prohibited attacks north of the 20th parallel. This area, covering all but the southern section of North Vietnam, was designated in an effort to motivate the communists to participate in negotiations. President Johnson had been under considerable pressure from those who wanted the United States to disengage from Vietnam and also from those who wished a sizeable reinforcement of American troops as a result of the Viet Cong attacks during Tet. And there was the upcoming presidential election to consider. Johnson had announced that he would not seek reelection in November.

President Johnson was finally convinced that further reinforcements were not the answer and that only a dialogue between the communists, the South

This EA-1F Skyraider from airborne early warning squadron VAW-33's detachment aboard the carrier *America* shows the final configuration of the "Spad" flown by U.S. carrier air wings. This Electronic Countermeasures (ECM) variant, flown by a crew of four with side-by-side seating, was one of 54 aircraft converted from AD-5N models for the ECM role. (U.S. Navy)

Vietnamese, and the Americans could resolve the conflict. In a misguided gesture of good faith, he initiated the bombing halt, which relieved pressure on Hanoi and Haiphong—much to the relief of the North Vietnamese. (The situation could be compared, in some respects, with the Battle of Britain in 1940. Just at the moment when Luftwaffe bombing strikes and fighter sweeps appeared to be on the verge of bringing about the total collapse of the Royal Air Force Fighter Command, the Germans halted daylight operations over England, switching to night attacks, and postponing indefinitely their projected assault on Britain. The British were able to take advantage of the breathing space this "bombing halt" afforded them and reinforce their air defenses. The Germans had held the advantage and given it up.)

Changes were also made in the U.S. Navy's carrier air wings. There were more A-7 Corsairs, which were proving to be highly capable attack aircraft. On April 10, 1968, the last Douglas A-1 Skyraider attack air-craft was retired from fleet service. The last carrier squadron to operate the "Spad" in the attack role was VA-25 on the *Coral Sea*. In a career spanning 23 years, the prop-driven Skyraider had flown in Korea as the major carrier attack aircraft and had served with Navy, Air Force, and South Vietnamese squadrons in the Vietnam War. Beyond strike, close air support, and rescue support operations, a pair of Skyraiders from the *Midway*'s VA-25 shot down a MiG-17 in aerial combat while a second fell to the 20-mm cannon of a single A-1 from VA-176 aboard the *Intrepid*. The distinction should be made that VA-25 retired the last *attack* Skyraiders. Detachments of EA-1F electronic countermeasures aircraft continued to serve aboard carriers in Southeast Asia until February 1969, the last on the *Ticonderoga*. The last EA-1F Skyraider cruise on a carrier was a detachment's eight-month deployment to the Mediterranean in the *John F. Kennedy*'s air wing in late 1969.[23]

Various Skyraider models had also flown from British, Canadian, and French aircraft carriers.

During the summer of 1968, with the partial bombing halt restricting attacks against North Vietnam, the A-7 Corsair squadrons on the *Constellation* and *America* were busy flying missions in the southern panhandle region of North Vietnam and Laos. In late September all four A-7 squadrons hit targets near Vinh—bridges, barges, and storage depots, as well as radar sites. The anti-aircraft fire was intense, and several Corsairs were hit; one, damaged and seeking an alternate landing field, crashed as it approached the U.S. airfield at Da Nang.

The *Ticonderoga* brought two more Corsair squadrons to the war. These were the first A-7B variants to enter combat and demonstrated the aircraft's ability to operate from the *Hancock*-class (modernized *Essex*) carriers.

17 A WAR LOST

An F-4B Phantom from fighter squadron VF-154 is towed toward a catapult aboard the carrier *Ranger* operating in the Tonkin Gulf. A trio of Phantoms streaks overhead. The Phantom was a first-line fighter and attack aircraft that was flown by the U.S. Navy, Marine Corps, and Air Force as well as by several other nations. The Royal Navy flew the F-4K variant of the Phantom from carriers. (U.S. Navy)

The air war over Vietnam began to change dramatically in the spring of 1968. With the imposition of the partial halt on U.S. bombing of North Vietnam on March 31, 1968, the hunting ground for MiGs was considerably reduced. Sometimes U.S. shipboard and Airborne Early Warning (AEW) aircraft radar would track MiGs on their way south toward the Vinh area, the northernmost point to which American strikes could go. The MiGs would attempt to entice U.S. fighters into violating prohibited airspace, but the American pilots, under strict radar control and hindered by rules of engagement, would not play the game. In fact, the Air Force was able to rack up only eight MiG kills during 1968, all in the January–February period, i.e., prior to the bombing halt.

The Navy did no better: the year's first Navy kill did not occur until June 26, when an F-8E Crusader from the *Bon Homme Richard* shot down a MiG-21 while returning from an escort mission. Three kills were made in July, while August and September each saw one MiG downed. Most of the Navy's kills in 1968 were achieved by Crusaders flying from the *Hancock*-class 27C carriers—the *Oriskany*, *Bon Homme Richard*, and *Hancock*. The large-deck carriers had F-4 Phantoms in their fighter squadrons. One of those F-4 squadrons scored the first kill credited to an Atlantic Fleet unit on July 10, 1968, when an F-4J from the *America* killed a MiG-21.

A MiG-21 kill on September 19, 1968, was of some significance, as it was the last confirmed score of the Vietnam War by a Crusader. The F-8C fighter was from the fighter detachment on the limited-CVA *Intrepid*. A pair of the ship's Crusaders mixed it up with a pair of MiG-21s, shooting down one with a Sidewinder missile. Although the second MiG-21 then took on the two Americans and both Crusaders fired missiles, that plane escaped. Labeled as "MiG Master" by public affairs officers, Crusaders officially shot down 18 MiG-17s and MiG-21s. A *Hancock*-based fighter scored a 19th in May 1972; however, this unusual kill occurred because the MiG pilot ejected before the Crusader that was pursuing him came within firing range. This kill was not credited to the Crusader pilot.

The need for aerial reconnaissance was most strongly felt during the Christmas truce periods, especially that of 1967–1968 before the Tet Offensive and after the November 1, 1968, bombing halt. While most of the American forces enjoyed a holiday stand-down, the photo detachments worked hard. As has been noted, recce flights were the earliest form of American activity over Indochina in the early 1960s. The RF-8A and later RF-8G Crusaders comprised the "light" photographic units (designated VFP) while the "heavy" units flew the RA-3B Skywarrior (VAP) or RA-5C Vigilante (RVAH). The various restrictions on reconnaissance missions as well as strike missions, coupled with North Vietnamese knowledge that bomb-damage assessment flights would always follow the attack, led to a very high loss rate among photo planes.

The carrier *Ranger* brought the first RA-5C squadron to Vietnamese waters in August 1964. The size of the "Vigi" and its associated Integrated Operational Intelligence Center (IOIC) limited its use to the large-deck carriers. The RA-5C, both its airframe and engines and its reconnaissance systems, demanded a very high level of maintenance support, but the "system" provided excellent intelligence.

The RF-8 flew throughout the Vietnam conflict, and the last photo Crusaders were retired from active squadrons in June 1982. The faster, more-capable RA-5C largely replaced the RA-3B Skywarrior. The RA-5C itself survived in the fleet until November 1979. Motion-picture reconnaissance was explored with cameras installed in the RA-5C and A-4 Skyhawk. The latter aircraft had much greater success because the RA-5C movie camera was an improvised affair while the A-4's camera, installed on the centerline, provided a forward view of the aircraft's flight path and was comparatively easy to maintain.

These Navy reconnaissance aircraft as well as land-based Air Force and Marine photo planes flew tactical reconnaissance missions. Strategic photoreconnaissance of Indochina was flown in 1967–1968 by the A-12 Oxcart, the Mach 3 precursor to the SR-71 Blackbird, which took over that role in 1968. Unmanned reconnaissance aircraft (drones) were also flown over North Vietnam; most were modified variants of target drones.

On April 14, 1969, the North Koreans again challenged American resolve. In the first major international crisis of the Nixon administration, North Korean fighters shot down an unarmed U.S. Navy EC-121 electronic surveillance aircraft over international waters. The entire 31-man crew was killed.

Task Force 71 of *Pueblo* fame was reactivated, again with the *Enterprise* as flagship, and steamed toward North Korean waters. But the *Enterprise*, coming out of a Japanese shipyard, had almost empty magazines, having earlier transferred her munitions to carriers operating in the Tonkin Gulf. Other carriers were ordered to the area.

U.S. land-based patrol planes found debris of the downed EC-121, and destroyers recovered several bodies. President Nixon ordered resumption of reconnaissance flights over the Sea of Japan soon after the incident. By the end of April, after another a meaningless show of force, the *Enterprise* task force had been reduced to eight ships from the high point on April 21 of 29 ships, including four carriers—the "Big E," the CVAs *Ranger* and *Ticonderoga*, and the CVS *Hornet*.

Despite the partial halt in U.S. air strikes, communist forces continued to press the attack in South Vietnam. In an effort to silence criticism at home and to further encourage the communists to negotiate, President Johnson, in his last major decision of the war, instituted a complete halt to the bombing of North Vietnam, to commence on November 1, 1968. The last mission north of the Demilitarized Zone (DMZ) was credited to planes from the *Constellation*, which flew a final bridge-busting mission.

President Nixon returned the Republicans to the White House in January 1969. His election to the presidency came after several years of intense U.S. involvement in Vietnam. There were massive American ground troops in South Vietnam, with massive U.S. naval and air forces supporting them in Thailand, the Philippines, and Guam and the U.S. Seventh Fleet was offshore. But vocal and sometimes violent outcry in the United States over the war and the failure of Secretary of Defense Robert S. McNamara and the military leaders to effectively prosecute the war prevented the Johnson administration from achieving a military solution to the conflict. With the North Vietnamese seemingly unafraid of the American military power arrayed against them resulting in a stalemate, the incoming Nixon administration had few alternatives. Large-scale withdrawal was the path chosen.

Throughout the first half of 1969 U.S. air operations concentrated on communist forces in South Vietnam in observance of the bombing halt of the North imposed the preceding November. However, June 5 saw strikes into North Vietnam in retaliation for the shooting down of an RF-8 photo Crusader. To safely conduct reconnaissance missions, armed escorts and anti-SAM aircraft as well as Navy and Marine supporting aircraft were tasked with protecting the photo birds.

The Pacific Fleet's light-photo squadron—VFP-63— was given its own F-8H fighters to provide mixed fighter-photo detachments. But this teaming was not successful, and the regular fighter squadrons continued to provide escort for the photo Crusaders.

As the war continued in the South, with minor U.S. aerial incursions into the North, American policy began a new tack when President Nixon announced on June 8, during a meeting with South Vietnamese President Nguyen Van Thieu, that he was ordering a phased withdrawal of American troops. Twenty-five thousand U.S. troops were withdrawn from South Vietnam by the end of August. Over the next year more than 100,000 troops were pulled out of South Vietnam while the several hundred riverine and coastal patrol craft were transferred from the U.S. Navy and Coast Guard to the South Vietnamese.

The carriers remained on station. In July 1,025 sorties were flown by carrier aircraft in the northern area of South Vietnam. In September F-8s from the *Hancock* flew missions in support of the 1st Marine Division, southwest of Da Nang.

After a 16-month interlude, an American aircraft downed a MiG when an F-4J from the *Constellation* shot down a MiG-21 on March 28, 1970. This was the only American aerial kill for the next two years. Navy pilots had speculated on the MiGs' reluctance to appear after the bombing halt, especially when the U.S. fighters involved were Crusaders. More likely, the North Vietnamese were concentrating their resources against Air Force raids. Attempts by F-8 pilots to entice MiGs over the South were not successful, even when the lure was the B-52 Arc Light raids; elaborate "pincer" movements set up by the frustrated Crusader pilots went untested.

The new year saw the war continue in much the same vein as in the previous 12 months, but the phased-withdrawal program was becoming a hard fact for the ground forces. Marine aviation was also reduced as several fighter and attack squadrons returned to Japan and the United States. Marines even evacuated the important airfield at Chu Lai, which they turned over to the U.S. Army in October.

A significant operation occurred off the coast of North Vietnam early on November 21, 1970, when U.S. special forces raided the prison compound at Son Tay, 23 miles northwest of Hanoi. No Navy planes had dropped bombs over North Vietnam in more than two years. On the night of November 20–21, as part of the elaborate cover for the raid, planes from the *Hancock*, *Oriskany*, and *Ranger* flew a "strike" over Haiphong—dropping flares to distract the Vietnamese from the Son Tay operation. With precision, the commandos assaulted the prison—to find it empty of captured American pilots. The 61 prisoners had been removed to another camp four months earlier.

The veteran carrier *Bon Homme Richard*, after completing a record sixth combat deployment to Southeast Asia in November 1970, was scheduled for decommissioning by mid-1971, leaving the *Oriskany* and *Hancock* as the only 27C carriers in combat. Both of these "27-Charlies" continued to deploy to Vietnam. They operated F-8J Crusaders, making the *Hancock* the last U.S. carrier to operate Skyhawks—three squadrons of the A-4F variant. The *Hancock* completed the last deployment with Skyhawks and Crusaders in

October 1975, ending the combat career of those aircraft in the U.S. Navy.[1] Skyhawks, some operating from aircraft carriers, continued in service with other nations' air arms into the 21st Century. The small, highly specialized Skyhawk had become one of history's most widely used and versatile attack aircraft.

The F-8J survived in U.S. service only until 1975, when it was replaced in Navy and Marine fighter squadrons by the more-versatile F-4 Phantom and in Navy squadrons by the more-capable F-14 Tomcat.[2] There had always been rivalry between F-8 and F-4 squadrons, which argued about the single-versus-two-seat advantages of each aircraft, as well as the fixed-gun armament of the F-8 as opposed to the all-missile configuration of the Phantom. The F-14 was also a two-seat aircraft. The subsequent generation of fighter-attack aircraft was the F/A-18 Hornet, which came in both single- and two-seat variants.

At-sea, underway replenishment enabled U.S. carriers and their supporting ships to remain on station for sustained periods during the Vietnam War. Here the large replenishment ship *Sacramento* transfers fuel to the carrier *Hancock* while the supply ship's UH-46 Sea Knight helicopters transfer bombs and other ordnance to the carrier. (U. F. Falk, U.S. Navy)

A KA-6D Intruder tanker refuels an EA-6B Prowler electronic counter-measures aircraft. Grumman converted 90 earlier Intruders to the tanker variant. Note the drop tanks and the hose-drogue housing under the tanker's fuselage. The Prowler was developed from the Intruder. Both aircraft have ungainly fixed refueling probes in front of their cockpit. (U.S. Navy)

Corsair operations entered a new phase in April 1970 when the first A-7Es deployed in *America* with attack squadron VA-147, which had been the first squadron to fly the A-7A in combat, and VA-146. The E model featured greater weapons-delivery accuracy and the more-powerful Rolls Royce Allison turbofan engine. The first combat missions were flown on May 23, 1970. The A-7E, fitted with a Head Up Display (HUD) that enabled the pilot to concentrate on his mission without diverting his eyes downward to his instruments, was particularly active at night along the Ho Chi Minh Trail.

The *America* also brought two new models of the Intruder, the A-6C and the KA-6D tanker, to the combat zone. The A-6C featured a system called TRIM—for Trails, Roads, Interdiction Multisensor—that incorporated large wing-mounted pods with electro-optical sensors. The A-6C employed a video that indicated targets along ground routes. The night-flying Intruder thus gained another attack capability.

The KA-6D was a dedicated tanker, representing a new generation of carrier refueling aircraft. Converted from earlier variants the KA-6D tankers had avionics deleted from the after fuselage to provide space for a reel and drogue; up to five 300-gallon drop tanks could be carried for the transfer of about 2,300 gallons when loitering 150 n. miles from the carrier or about 800 gallons when 450 n. miles from the carrier.

The continuing communist infiltration and encampments in Cambodia finally forced the Cambodian government to seek American aid, especially after a March 18 coup that deposed Prince Sihanouk while he was in Moscow trying to get the Soviets to reduce their activity in his country. General Lon Nol, upon taking over the government, asked for American help, and by April 29, 1970, a full-scale invasion of Cambodia was under way, with allied forces spearheaded by South Vietnamese units. The campaign, which brought storms of protest from anti-war groups in the United States, was unable to stem the communist incursions in Cambodia, and the communists continued to use the country as a base of operations against South Vietnam.

And, it was clear by the November 1, 1968, bombing halt that Rolling Thunder was a failure. Its intention had been to hinder communist aggression and eventually bring the North Vietnamese to negotiations. However, with the bombing halt in the North, U.S. air operations did not cease. In fact, the bombing did not stop or even diminish. It was merely transferred across the Annamite Mountains to focus on the infiltration corridors running through Laos. The network of routes that made up the Ho Chi Minh Trail had always been prime target for both day and night operations. Much effort had been made to cope with the special problems caused by the twisting, heavily camouflaged jungle trails and roads by which the Viet Cong moved their arms and supplies to the southern areas. With the end of the Rolling Thunder campaign, the Defense Department recommended that concentrated operations begin against this supply network as it filtered through Laos.

By early 1971 intelligence indicated a forthcoming North Vietnamese invasion of Cambodia and/or Laos and South Vietnam. It was clear that American forces would be needed to counter this threat. Accordingly, plans were drawn up and given the code name Lam Son 719, commemorating a Vietnamese victory over the Chinese in the 15th Century. South Vietnamese Army units jumped off from Quang Tri Province in northern South Vietnam and made their way to Tchepone, just over the Laotian border, on February 8, 1971. Under an umbrella of U.S. aircraft, South Vietnamese forces crossed into Laos, enabling American officials to cite the program of Vietnamization of the war and its own phased withdrawal of troops from the combat zone.

The North Vietnamese put up strong opposition, and the South Vietnamese forces finally had to call for helicopter evacuations in several areas, at times under heavy fire. By March 25 the last of the South Vietnamese forces had left Laos, with Hanoi and Saigon both claiming victory. Although the Saigon government claimed disruption of the supply routes, within a week reconnaissance pilots reported traffic again on the trails and moving southward.

The carrier *Hancock*, still flying A-4 Skyhawks, operated in support of Lam Son 719. The A-4s were largely responsible for anti-truck attacks along the Ho Chi Minh Trail through Laos. There were also the occasional retaliatory raids into southern North Vietnam by U.S. aircraft. Working in conjunction with Air Force forward air controllers, the *Hancock*'s A-4s operated mainly in the passes—Mu Gia, Ban Karai, and Ban Raving—on the Laos-Vietnam border, and sometimes they went into the Laotian panhandle. Strikes were flown both night and day against vehicle traffic.

The Skyhawks were also responsible for Iron Hand anti-SAM missions in which two aircraft armed with radar-homing Shrike missiles were sent against SAM sites posing a threat to the larger strike force. Sometimes the hunters became the hunted, as on the mission of April 28, 1971. Four A-4s launched from the *Hancock* to escort a photo plane toward a supposedly unoccupied SAM site. Soon after crossing the coast, warning lights in the cockpits of the A-4s indicated that they were being tracked by SAM-related radars. With the radar warning warble droning in their ears, the pilots saw a brilliant orange flash in the west as an SA-2 rose toward them. With training instilled since the earliest days of flight indoctrination, the leader called for the

flight to break right. But the Soviet-made missile was too close and seemed to have a good lock on the A-4s as it matched their evasive maneuvers.

One of the pilots broke into the missile's flight path and executed a steep dive, which the missile could not immediately follow. Watching the SA-2, the A-4 pilot pulled out of his dive and then into a hard left roll and steep climb. The missile passed some 800 feet below the flight. A second missile approached the group, but similar action evaded this threat too and the photo plane successfully shot the "unoccupied" SAM site.

The failure of the Laotian trail campaign to halt or even appreciably slow the flow of supplies to the South seemed to set the stage for a major action by the North Vietnamese. As the New Year began, U.S. air activity was stepped up. The communists were known to be bringing increasing numbers of SAM launchers toward the Demilitarized Zone. In the last three weeks of 1971 ten U.S. aircraft were lost over North Vietnam and Laos to a variety of weapons.

In the first three months of 1972, 90 protective reaction raids were flown by Navy and Air Force planes against the SAM and anti-aircraft sites, compared with 108 strikes during all of 1971.

Off the coast, only the *Coral Sea* and *Constellation* patrolled their beat, both ships on their sixth combat cruise. The *Hancock* joined them in early February 1972.

The year 1972 was pivotal for the American forces in this long, frustrating conflict, especially in the air. The battle between the MiGs and American fighters was again joined on January 19, 1972, when an F-4J from Fighter Squadron 96 on the *Constellation* shot down the tenth MiG-21 brought down by Navy fighters. Sighting a pair of MiG-21s during a photo escort mission, the F-4J crew flew right up behind the lead MiG and shot a Sidewinder missile at him at an altitude of only 600 feet. The missile missed, and the two MiGs began to run. In the twisting pursuit the F-4J fired a second missile that found its mark and blew the tail section off the North Vietnamese fighter. The elated pilot, Lieutenant Randy (Duke) Cunningham, and his Radar Intercept Officer (RIO), Lieutenant (jg) William (Irish) Driscoll, flew back to the *Constellation*. It would be four months until their next kill.

An F-4B off the *Coral Sea* made the Navy's next MiG kill on March 28. Two Phantoms were vectored toward MiG-17s during a photo-escort mission. A tighter-turning North Vietnamese MiG-17 was able to get behind the lead American fighter. After a series of turns, the F-4B regained the advantage and fired a Sidewinder missile. The MiG-17 pilot wrapped his plane up into a tight turn, escaping the missile. The flight leader called for his wingman to try his luck, and the second F-4B pulled behind the MiG and fired another Sidewinder. This one brought down the MiG.

Not until May did Navy aircraft score another kill, but that was the most productive month of the entire war for carrier fighters: 16 MiGs were downed as well as a MiG-17 that ventured too far out toward the cruiser *Chicago* in the Gulf of Tonkin and was shot down by a Talos surface-to-air missile. Four of these MiG kills went to a Phantom flown by Lieutenants Cunningham and Driscoll of VF-96 aboard the *Constellation*. They scored their second kill, a MiG-17, as well as a *truck* that they shot with a Sidewinder on May 8. Two days later, taking part in a large attack on the rail yards of Hai Duong, between Hanoi and Haiphong, they were in a section of seven F-4Js assigned to flak suppression. The "Connie" A-6s and A-7s went after the rail yards while the F-4Js broke off to engage the estimated 22 MiGs that attempted to intercept the strike force. Dodging SAMs and flak, the Phantoms dropped their bombs on a large storage building and climbed back to engage the MiG force. In fierce aerial combat, Cunningham and Driscoll downed a MiG-21 and a MiG-17.

Heading for the coast, Cunningham sighted a low-flying MiG-17 that was apparently flown by a leading North Vietnamese ace, who was credited by communist sources with up to 13 American kills. Cunningham and Driscoll engaged the camouflaged MiG-17 in a swirling dogfight with both aircraft trading advantages. Finally, the MiG pilot disengaged and headed away, probably because he was low on fuel, placing himself at an ultimately fatal disadvantage. The F-4J was now above and behind the fleeing MiG, and Cunningham fired another Sidewinder. The missile flew straight to the MiG and detonated, sending pieces flying off the North Vietnamese fighter. Cunningham was not sure he had killed the MiG and fired his last Sidewinder just as the MiG exploded in front of him. Thus, Cunningham and Driscoll became the first U.S. aces of the Vietnam War and the Navy's first jet aces.

With their Sidewinders gone—they still had two Sparrows—and their fuel low, Cunningham and Driscoll turned toward the coast and the *Constellation*. More MiGs were sighted. Their F-4J was headed toward Nam Dinh, a hotbed of SA-2 sites, but there was no indication of enemy radar emissions and Cunningham pushed on. Suddenly a SAM detonated nearby, severely damaging the Phantom.[3] The two Navy fliers tried to nurse the crippled Phantom back to the "Connie" but were forced to eject. They came down at sea, close to the coast. Intense fire from communist guns on shore and approaching North Vietnamese small craft hampered rescue operations. Protected by A-7 attack planes, the two men finally were picked up by a Marine CH-46 helicopter and returned to the *Constellation*.

May 10, 1972, was the heaviest day of aerial fighting in the war with eight MiGs destroyed by Navy

The U.S. Navy's first jet aces were Lieutenant Randall Cunningham (left) and Lieutenant (jg) William P. Driscoll, shown here in June 1972 with Secretary of the Navy John W. Warner and Chief of Naval Operations Admiral Elmo R. Zumwalt. Warner subsequently became a U.S. senator and Cunningham a member of the House of Representatives. (Billy Mason, U.S. Navy)

The Soviet intelligence collection ship *Gidrofon* keeps watch on U.S. carrier operations in the Gulf of Tonkin in November 1969. Beyond the *Gidrofon* the carrier *Coral Sea* and her escorts refuel from a Navy fleet oiler. Soviet intelligence ships—called AGIs by NATO—observed U.S. carrier activities, possibly reporting strike launches to North Vietnamese command centers. (H. H. Thomas, U.S. Navy)

pilots for the loss of two Phantoms, one flown by Cunningham and Driscoll. The second F-4J was downed by anti-aircraft fire. (Both crewmen ejected and were captured; the pilot died in captivity.) Air Force planes destroyed three more MiGs, and two Air Force planes were downed in air-to-air combat while two were downed by ground fire.

As May continued Navy pilots and their RIOs in two F-4s downed two MiG-19s on May 18 and on the 23rd an F-4B from the *Midway* scored a double MiG-17 kill. June was not as intense as May, with only three MiGs shot down by carrier fighters, but the action was

constant. A *Saratoga* F-4 scored the first MiG-21 kill by an Atlantic Fleet carrier on June 21.

A major factor in the success of the carrier fighters was the radar controllers on cruisers and destroyers in TF 77 ships operating in the northern Gulf of Tonkin. These ships used their long-range air-search radars to seek out aircraft over North Vietnam and warn U.S. pilots of approaching communist aircraft and vectoring fighters. (The E-1B Tracer and E-2 Hawkeye AEW aircraft generally flew only during U.S. strike operations.) One controller, Chief Radarman Larry H. Nowell, in the cruiser *Chicago*, was cited for participating in intercepts that resulted in the downing of an estimated 12 MiGs.

The increased MiG activity in 1972 also enabled the Air Force to acquire its first aces—three months after the Navy. The Marines were finally able to chalk up their first kill with an all-Marine crew flying a Marine aircraft. Marine aircraft began flying from Navy carriers in 1971, the first time Marine fixed-wing aircraft had flown from Navy ships in a decade. A Marine A-6A Intruder—VMA(AW)—224 squadron flew from the *Coral Sea* to support South Vietnamese troops and also participated in aerial mining operations.

Subsequently the *America*'s air wing included Marine F-4J squadron, and one of these Phantoms from VMFA-333 scored a kill on September 11, 1972. Major Lee Lasseter and his RIO, Captain John Cummings, and their wingman engaged two MiG-21s some three miles north of Hanoi. In a running, low-level mêlée, Lasseter and Cummings fired four Sparrow and two Sidewinder missiles at one MiG without effect. The MiG-21 then turned on the Phantom, and Lasseter shot it down with another Sidewinder.[4] On the dash back to the coast the Marines fired their last Sidewinder at another MiG-21 and were credited with a partial kill. A SAM then hit the Phantom. Their wingman's F-4J was also damaged. Both crews ejected over the sea, south of Haiphong, where rescue helicopters picked them up.

The intense air-to-air combat of 1972 gave a good indication of the value of the Topgun training program. Cunningham, Driscoll, and several of the other victors of air-to-air engagements were Topgun graduates (see pages 259–260).

The Easter Invasion

MiG activity was increased primarily to cover North Vietnam's buildup in material. On March 30, 1972, the Thursday before Good Friday, three North Vietnamese divisions pushed through the DMZ. Eventually, 120,000 troops, forming 12 of Hanoi's 13 regular combat divisions, were sent into South Vietnam. The border town of An Loc was besieged as the South's troops fell back against the communist onslaught. The North was using tanks in force for the first time in the war. One North Vietnamese division headed toward Hue, rolling over former American bases at Khe Sanh, Con Thien, and Camp Carroll in Quang Tri Province. Troops and hundreds of Soviet tanks faced the South's defenders, primarily green, untried troops.

Operation Arc Light—B-52 strategic bomber strikes—was almost immediately expanded as the bombers were called in from Guam to strike enemy troop concentrations at An Loc from April through May, giving the South Vietnamese forces breathing space and time to regroup to counter the communist invasion. May 1 saw a reorganized defense of Hue begin, with reinforced southern divisions finally wresting control of the besieged area from the communists. The South had made good use of anti-tank weapons, slowing the advance of the North's armored forces, while the B-52 raids and Navy offshore fire support held the North Vietnamese down.

Beyond ordering a step-up in B-52 operations, an order for the Marines to return to Vietnam sent several squadrons of aircraft scrambling back from their bases in Japan and the United States. Only about 500 Marines remained in Vietnam by mid-1972. In response to the Easter assault, on April 5 two Marine F-4 squadrons were ordered to return. Flying from Da Nang, the squadrons began combat operations on April 9. They were joined by a third F-4 squadron, flown in from Hawaii, as well as the Marine A-6 squadron from the *Coral Sea*. In addition, A-4 Skyhawks returned to South Vietnam, with two Marine squadrons flying into Bien Hoa. Operations from Bien Hoa began on May 19, with the main effort concentrating along the Cambodian and Laotian border invasion points.

The Marine air effort was extended into northern Thailand when two F-4J squadrons were sent to the partially completed field at Nam Phong, 300 miles from Da Nang and about the same distance from Hanoi. Begun five years earlier as a support facility, Nam Phong had never been finished. Navy Seabees were rushed in, and the 10,000-foot runway was hastily completed. The two F-4J squadrons along with an A-6 squadron began operations on June 24. The Marines who lived and flew from Nam Phong called the austere facility the "Rose Garden."

The Easter invasion had caught the Navy with only two carriers, the *Coral Sea* and *Hancock*, in the Gulf of Tonkin. The *Constellation*, at Hong Kong, was immediately recalled, as was the *Kitty Hawk*. Meanwhile, the nuclear-propelled *Enterprise* was in the Indian Ocean, having been sent there at the outbreak of the Indo-Pakistani War. She, too, returned to the gulf. They were soon joined by the carrier *Midway*. Thus, by July 1972 there were six U.S. carriers in the gulf, the largest number of the war. All were flying strikes in support of the efforts to resist the massive North Vietnamese invasion.

The Easter invasion led to the dispatch of the Atlantic Fleet's *Saratoga* to the war. Orders came for the ship, at Mayport, Florida, to load aircraft, fuel, provisions, and other material on April 8. Within 60 hours the big carrier was underway. After a month-long transit, the *Saratoga* arrived on Yankee Station on June 2. The *Saratoga*'s aircraft flew hundreds of missions supporting South Vietnamese troops, hitting gun and mortar sites, bunkers, and supply areas near An Loc, where the communists posed the strongest threat, as well as strikes in the Mekong Delta and near Saigon. The "Sara" planes also ranged farther north, to Haiphong, to strike railway yards and bridges around the port city.

The ship's fighters, besides escorting the large A-6 and A-7 bomber forces, also contributed to the strike effort with the use of laser-guided bombs as well as conventional iron bombs. On June 21 a "Sara" F-4J scored the ship's first MiG kill; a second MiG was destroyed in the early evening of August 10. Both kills were MiG-21s.

The Mining Offensive—At Last

In the midst of North Vietnam's all out invasion, Washington sought to show some restraint. For more than two years the president's national security advisor, Dr. Henry Kissinger, had been holding secret and public meetings with North Vietnam's Le Duc Tho in Paris, trying to arrive at a cease-fire agreement. The North Vietnamese played for time, alternatively agreeing, then disagreeing with the American representatives.

Finally, on May 2, five days after the North had unleashed what Kissinger called "the heaviest artillery barrage of the war and large numbers of tanks," he confronted Tho. In a frustrating exchange, the wily Tho tried to intimidate Kissinger with wide-ranging references to American unrest at home and dissatisfaction with the war, intimating that the North Vietnamese now held the upper hand and were convinced of their ultimate victory in the South. Kissinger could do little but report back to President Nixon that, once more, the Vietnamese had proved intransigent.

In what Kissinger referred to as "one of the finest hours of Nixon's presidency," the president, for the first time in the war, ordered the aerial mining of Haiphong and other major North Vietnamese harbors to curb the flow of war supplies. With a strategic summit meeting between Nixon and Soviet President Leonid Brezhnev in the final planning stages, the strong possibility of intensified public outcry at home, and the imminent collapse of South Vietnam facing him, Nixon had decided to gamble and shut off the flow of Soviet supplies at their source. Kissinger wrote, "In an election year, he [Nixon] risked his political future on a course most of his Cabinet colleagues questioned."[5]

At the time that the mining decision was made the U.S. intelligence community estimated that Hanoi received 2.1 million tons of supplies per year through Haiphong harbor, including all of its oil, according to Kissinger. Railways at the time carried only 300,000 tons, or one-seventh of the Haiphong total. To shift the bulk of the supplies from sea to rail transport would be more expensive, would take time, and would involve agreements between the Chinese and Soviets, who were increasingly distrustful of each other.

The Navy had planned for the mining operation for several years. On May 8 A-6 Intruders and A-7 Corsairs from three carriers sowed mines in North Vietnamese harbors—Haiphong, Hon Gay, and Cam Pha—and several lesser ports. The carrier fliers encountered heavy anti-aircraft fire and SAMs, but the mines were dropped. Within two weeks the mining operation had closed North Vietnam's ports; in succeeding months the carrier planes "reseeded" the Haiphong approaches. The carrier planes laid a total of 7,996 mines off 12 ports.[6]

Numerous communist-bloc merchant ships that were en route to North Vietnam were diverted elsewhere. The 27 merchant ships caught in North Vietnam's ports remained there as no attempt was made to clear the mines. Vice Admiral William P. Mack, then Commander Seventh Fleet, later wrote, "What happened was that all traffic into Vietnam, except across the Chinese border, stopped. Within 10 days there was not a missile or a shell being fired at us from the beach. The North Vietnamese ran out of ammunition, just as we always said they would." (Long expecting the United States to mine the harbors, the communists had gradually shifted most of the weapon deliveries from the Soviet Union to rail carriage through China.)

This new U.S. aerial offensive was given the code name Linebacker. Originally, the initial strikes had been called Freedom Train; the new name was given to include the aerial-mining operation. Along with the mining, the bombing strikes against the North were escalated to the most intense level of the war. The Rolling Thunder strikes of the first three years of the war paled in comparison to Linebacker's impact in the first four months of the resumed bombings of 1972. In addition to stopping supplies from moving south, the U.S. air strikes were responsible for the North Vietnamese ground forces' failure to take and hold areas. As the South Vietnamese regrouped and reengaged the enemy under heavy U.S. air cover, the communists fell back from Kontum, Pleiku, An Loc, and Quang Tri. Their plans for conquest had been thwarted because of the strangling of their supply lines, a step that U.S. military commanders had long believed would bring about a North Vietnamese surrender, or at least make them more amenable at the negotiation table. Under constant attack from carrier-based aircraft and Air Force fighter bombers as well as B-52s, the Hanoi government began to show signs of a willingness to proceed more directly with the peace talks.

The B-52s had made their first raids on Hanoi and Haiphong on April 17. The raids stirred a storm of controversy about major escalation of the war by the United States, but the B-52s continued their strikes on the North Vietnamese capital until October 23, when it seemed that the communists were about to ask for a cease-fire.

In the meantime, the six carriers on station in July—*America*, *Hancock*, *Kitty Hawk*, *Midway*, *Oriskany*, and *Saratoga*—continued sending waves of planes over the North and over contested areas of South Vietnam. A four-ship task unit steamed off Haiphong to shell the port city in August, while planes from the *Midway* attacked the harbor.

Weather proved to be a major problem during Linebacker, especially for missions over North Vietnam. Clouds, fog, and rain hung off the northern coast, often making the bombing of specific targets impossible. In the South, even if the weather did not cooperate, strikes could still be flown using a bombing method whereby the A-7s could release their bombs on an appropriate radar fix from a ground station.

The *Oriskany* did not have an easy time of it during this last combat cruise. A faulty screw swung the carrier into the ammunition ship *Nitro* during a night replenishment; this resulted in the loss of the *Oriskany*'s deck-edge aircraft elevator. The ship continued operations. But during this same period the ship lost a propeller and then had to retire to Yokosuka, Japan, for major repairs.

The Final Strikes

The hope of October 1972 that the peace talks in Paris would produce a cease-fire quickly evaporated. After President Nixon had halted bombing attacks north of the 20th parallel, the North Vietnamese refused to deal in earnest. They again used the respite to repair damaged facilities and build up stocks of weapons. Further, the North Vietnamese delegation walked out of the talks on December 13. At the same time, South Vietnamese President Thieu, furious at Nixon for seeking what he considered a separate peace with the North, plagued Kissinger and his team with 69 major changes to the initial treaty draft.

With very few options left to him, President Nixon ordered a maximum bombing effort aimed at Hanoi and Haiphong. December 18, 1972, saw the first strikes of Linebacker II as waves of B-52s and F-111 strike aircraft attacked Hanoi and nearby airfields and missile sites. A defensive curtain of flak, SAMs, and MiGs met the attackers; three of the giant B-52s were shot down on the first night. The tail-gunner of a B-52D claimed the first fighter kill ever by a U.S. strategic bomber, a MiG-21 destroyed by the plane's quad .50-caliber gun turret. Another B-52 gunner destroyed a second MiG on December 24 as the massive bombing attacks against the North continued.

President Nixon's decision to unleash the bombers against Hanoi met with angry words in the American press and questions in Congress. *Time* magazine, which had recently selected both Nixon and Kissinger as its Men of the Year, declared that "Nixon seemed determined to bomb Hanoi into a settlement that he is willing to accept." Confounded by the long years of endless conflict, Congress gave consideration to cutting funds for the war or simply halting all expenditures.

Radio Hanoi announced that American bombs had fallen in a POW camp and that several prisoners had been wounded. North Vietnamese magazine articles told of Pham Tuan, a MiG-21 pilot, who shot down a B-52 on December 27, a claim the U.S. Air Force denied.[7] (One MiG-21 pilot was credited with shooting down 14 U.S. aircraft as the North Vietnamese attempted to publicize the massive losses being suffered by U.S. aircraft.)

The Linebacker II attacks continued through December 24, Christmas Eve, when a 36-hour stand-down over the holiday commenced. On the night of December 26–27 an elaborately planned strike hit Hanoi and

The EA-6B Prowler resembles the A-6 Intruder, from which it was derived. Grumman produced 170 of these electronic countermeasure aircraft. The four-place EA-6B could easily be distinguished by the electronics pod atop the vertical fin. Up to four jamming pods can be carried on wing pylons as can HARM anti-radar missiles. Numerous upgrades have enabled these aircraft to serve effectively into the 21st Century. (John Leenhouts, U.S. Navy)

Haiphong in a stream of planes that proved to be the peak of the 11-day Linebacker II operation. Within a 15-minute period a force of 120 B-52s struck the cities from three different directions, overtaxing and confusing the North Vietnamese defenses. The Air Force, Navy, and Marine Corps flew 113 aircraft in support of the B-52s. Two more B-52s were shot down that night.

In all, Linebacker II cost 15 B-52s lost to SA-2 missiles in a period of 11 days as well as several Air Force and Navy support aircraft, mostly F-111s and A-6s that were attacking SAM sites.[8] Prior to the B-52s' arrival Navy planes flew airfield suppressions strikes, especially against Kep, the main MiG base in the Hanoi region, as well as other airfields. And during these intensive B-52 strikes Marine EA-6A Intruders, flying from South Vietnam, and carrier-based Navy EA-6B Prowlers were employed to detect and jam enemy radars to assist the B-52s in penetrating to their targets. The EA-6A was a two-place modification of the Intruder. The EA-6B Prowler was an enlarged aircraft, with three electronic countermeasures operators in addition to the pilot; it was the most capable tactical electronic warfare aircraft of its time. (The EA-6B had entered Navy service in January 1971; the first Prowler deployment was a four-plane detachment aboard the *America* in June 1972.)

During Linebacker II the EA-6A and EA-6B jammers flew three and four missions per day. Initially the Prowlers were forbidden from flying over land to prevent their advanced electronics gear from falling into

communist hands should one be shot down. Their services were invaluable in detecting and jamming those radars associated with the SA-2 missiles and anti-aircraft guns.

Navy aircraft shot down only one MiG in December 1972, the only kill by a naval aviator since the Marine score in September. An *Enterprise* based F-4J shot down a MiG-21 on December 28. In addition to the two MiG kills by B-52s in December, the Air Force claimed three MiGs in December, all downed by Phantoms.

The Navy also suffered its last aircraft loss to a MiG on December 28, 1972, when an RA-5C Vigilante from the "Big E" was shot down by a MiG-21 firing an Atoll air-to-air missile despite the efforts of an accompanying Phantom. The "Vigi" pilot ejected and became a prisoner; the naval flight officer died in the incident.[9]

The B-52 raids continued until December 29, when the North Vietnamese indicated that they might resume negotiations.[10] The entire Linebacker II operation—the mining of harbors as well as the intensive strikes on Hanoi and Haiphong—had brought the North Vietnamese back to the negotiations, at least for the moment. Admiral Thomas H. Moorer, then Chairman of the Joint Chiefs of Staff, said, "I am convinced that Linebacker II served as a catalyst for the negotiations." Accordingly, President Nixon halted the bombings. With the culmination of Linebacker II, U.S. air operations in Vietnam declined rapidly.

A Doubtful Ending

The American public, having given President Nixon a mandate in the election of November 1972, demanded quick results. Le Duc Tho, the chief communist negotiator, was evidently under the same pressure from his government. The talks resumed while U.S. aircraft flew bombing strikes against North Vietnam below the 20th parallel starting on January 3, 1973.

The U.S. Defense Department on January 9 issued permission for fighters to pursue MiGs that attacked the bombers, right up through the North Vietnamese panhandle if necessary. Three days later the last MiG shot down during the war fell over the northern part of the Gulf of Tonkin by an F-4J from the *Midway* using a Sidewinder missile. Fighters from the *Midway* had shot down the first and the last MiGs destroyed in the Vietnam War.[11]

Navy and Marine fighter and attack aircraft had accounted for 58 MiGs confirmed in air-to-air combat as well as two An-2 biplane transports; a Marine F-4J from the carrier *America* also bagged another MiG-21.[12] Two Marine pilots on exchange duty with the Air Force had each killed one MiG. (The U.S. Air Force was credited with 137 MiGs downed during the war, including two shot down by B-52 tail-guns.)

Most of the Navy's MiG kills were obtained with Sidewinder and Sparrow missiles. Only one of the 18 confirmed MiG kills by F-8 Crusaders was obtained solely by gunfire; the others were by Sidewinders or a combination of missiles and cannon fire. But all 37 of the Navy kills by the "gunless" F-4 Phantoms were by missile. The two MiG-17s destroyed by A-1H Skyraiders were also shot down with gunfire while the MiG-17 downed by an A-4C Skyhawk was the victim of unguided Zuni rockets. The single MiG kill by Marines flying an F-4J from a carrier was made with a Sidewinder.

The MiG-versus-U.S. exchange rates in air-to-air combat, based on U.S. data, were

Navy F-8	6.00:1
Navy F-4	5.42:1
Air Force F-4	3.07:1
Air Force F-105	1.37:1

The combined F-4 exchange rate with MiGs was 3.38:1.

North Korean pilots flew some of the North Vietnamese MiGs. The Korean pilots were not successful: at least 14 were shot down within a two-month period in 1967. Because of those losses the Korean pilots were "sent . . . packing."[13]

Although Russians manned portions of the North Vietnamese air defense system and trained Vietnamese pilots, Russians did not fly combat missions as they had in the Korean War. Still, North Vietnamese records indicate that U.S. fighters did down a MiG-21U "Mongol" two-seat trainer on November 11, 1972, piloted by a Russian. Reportedly, a Russian instructor and his Vietnamese student, flying their unarmed trainer, were approached by four U.S. Phantoms. Already low on fuel, the MiG fled the Americans, guided in the escape effort by ground-control radars. The MiG evaded several Sidewinder missiles. Then, as their engine stopped for lack of fuel, the Russian and his student ejected. Moments later a Sidewinder destroyed their abandoned aircraft. However, U.S. records show no kill being claimed by Air Force or Navy pilots that day.[14]

Finally, on January 23, 1973, a cease-fire was announced. The U.S. and North Vietnamese negotiators in Paris had agreed to end the fighting, return the POWs, and clear the harbors of mines. American newspapers carried the administration's declaration of "peace with honor." On January 27, Commander Dennis Weichman brought his A-7E Corsair back to the *Oriskany*, completing his 625th combat mission, the most of any naval aviator.

That same day saw the last combat loss of a U.S. carrier aircraft over Southeast Asia when an F-4J Phantom from the *Enterprise* was shot down by anti-aircraft fire near Quang Tri on January 27, 1973. Three more carrier aircraft were lost operationally during the next two days: an A-7E from the *Constellation* disappeared on a night training flight and two F-4J Phantoms collided in flight.

The mining of North Vietnamese harbors in May 1972 now required clearing the mined areas. The mines had timers, which would deactivate them after a specific period, or they would become inert when their batteries were exhausted. Still, for practical and political reasons there had to be a sweep effort. Navy and Marine CH-53 Sea Stallion helicopters were rigged with mine countermeasures gear. Operating from the helicopter carriers *Inchon*, *New Orleans*, and *Tripoli*, and from other amphibious ships, the Sea Stallions conducted sweeps of Haiphong and other harbors during January 1973. Several surface minesweepers also participated in the operation, given the code name End Sweep. The operation ended on July 27.[15]

America's longest and most frustrating war had come to an end. The last American troops "in country" were flown out, all facilities and equipment that remained were turned over to South Vietnamese forces, and most of the ships of Task Force 77 steamed over the horizon. South Vietnam had been saved.

The signing of the cease-fire agreement in Paris did not mean the end of combat in Southeast Asia. Forces in Cambodia and Laos continued to fight against communist insurgents who had been operating in those countries as long as their compatriots had in Vietnam. As American withdrawals from Vietnam continued and the POWs returned home, Air Force and Navy aircraft flew strikes into Laos.

In Cambodia, the situation was desperate. The capital of Phnom Penh, encircled by communist forces, was virtually cut off from the world and faced imminent

A Marine CH-53A/RH-53A Sea Stallion configured for the Mine Counter-measures (MCM) role tows mine-sweeping gear through Haiphong Harbor, North Vietnam, during the 1973 operation. These helicopters were assigned to Navy MCM squadron HM-12 operating from the helicopter carrier *New Orleans*. The view from the helicopter's rear ramp shows the MCM "sled" being towed at high speed. (U.S. Navy)

starvation. Its only lifelines to the outside world were the convoys of small craft that ran the communist gauntlet up the Mekong River. Although supported by American aircraft, these craft suffered heavy losses from the communist troops along the banks. The convoy of April 5 reached Phnom Penh with only eight of the original 18 craft. Aircraft from the *Enterprise* as well as Air

Force planes based in Thailand conducted strikes against the enemy. The communists protested the American strikes as a major violation of the Paris accord. (In response, the United States halted Operation End Sweep activities on April 19.)

However, by June 1973 all sides had agreed to improve cease-fire enforcement, and by August 15 all

American Embassy strikes against Cambodia and Laos were halted. The Laotians had accepted a coalition government, and the Cambodians were essentially left to fend for themselves. It was obvious that Dr. Kissinger had not achieved "peace with honor" and that, in effect, the United States had been taken in. The only positive result of the Paris talks had been the release of 566 U.S. prisoners of war.

The final communist assaults were not long in coming. Cambodia fell first, with elements of the communist Khmer Rouge and thousands of North Vietnamese and Viet Cong troops putting a stranglehold on Phnom Penh, closing the Mekong to all river traffic. Rocket and artillery fire struck the airfields and major towns.

The South Vietnamese Army and Air Force, operating for the first time without American support, were not able to stem the tide. It was clear that a communist takeover would happen within days. Thus, Operation Eagle Pull was initiated, and the evacuation of the Americans in Saigon was begun on April 12, 1975, with Marine, Air Force, and CIA helicopters providing the transport. The *Midway* and *Enterprise* had been recalled to the South China Sea to cover the evacuation. The *Enterprise* was on her first deployment with a new fighter aircraft—the F-14A Tomcat.

As the communist troops swept southward toward Saigon, the two squadrons of F-14s provided fighter cover during Operation Frequent Wind, the evacuation of Saigon. The older carriers *Coral Sea* and *Han-*

cock provided additional support. The *Midway* left much of her air wing in the Philippines and embarked ten Air Force CH-53 and HH-53 Sea Stallion helicopters for the evacuation. The State Department advised the carrier to prepare for 1,500 American and Vietnamese evacuees. Preparations were made to feed and berth 3,000 persons. For possible "crowd control" two M60 machine guns were set up on the island structure to cover the fight deck, armed Marines were posted at key positions on the flight and hangar decks, and Navy officers handling the operation were issued .45-caliber pistols.[16]

By April 25 the communists had swept up Hue, Da Nang, Nha Trang, and other South Vietnamese cities and were approaching Saigon. Planes from the four carriers offshore swept over the city, providing escort for the helicopters from the *Midway* that had begun picking up American and specific South Vietnamese officials and their families leaving Saigon.

South Vietnamese aircraft also tried to cover the evacuation—F-5s and A-37s overflew the operation. However, some of these aircraft were piloted by South Vietnamese defectors who had, perhaps prudently, decided to switch sides. There was one report of an F-5 wingman turning on his leader in an apparent effort to shoot him down. Many South Vietnamese pilots continued to fight for the falling government, covering evacuation operations until the morning of April 30. Others escaped with their aircraft, flying their F-5s and A-37s to Thailand; still others flew helicopters out

A Marine lieutenant assists a Vietnamese woman from a Marine CH-46D Sea Knight of squadron HMM-165. Sixty-one Marine CH-46 and CH-53 embarked in carriers made 556 flights from Saigon to U.S. ships some 80 miles offshore; the ten Air Force CH-53 and MH-53 helicopters made 82 evacuation flights. (U.S. Navy)

In addition to U.S. military helicopters, some 20 helicopters flown by Air America—a CIA front company—and South Vietnamese Air Force helicopters flew refugees out to U.S. ships offshore. These helicopters were generally pushed into the sea to keep flight decks clear; here a South Vietnamese UH-1 Huey is pushed from the command ship *Blue Ridge* after being unloaded. (U.S. Navy)

to the U.S. ships offshore, jumping from their aircraft, hoping to be rescued by the Americans. One South Vietnamese Air Force major, carrying his wife and five children in an O-1 Bird Dog, managed to land his plane on the *Midway* after repeated passes and dropping a note requesting permission to land. The deck eventually was cleared, and he landed his propeller-driven observation plane on the carrier. Several Vietnamese UH-1 Hueys and one CH-47 Chinook also landed on the *Midway*. One Huey had 52 people, mostly elderly and children, on board; it flew so low that when over the water it flew in ground effects, hardly gaining enough altitude (as fuel burned off) to clear the *Midway*'s flight deck.

The U.S. and Vietnamese helicopters brought out 1,400 Americans and 5,600 South Vietnamese from Saigon to the *Midway* and the amphibious ships standing offshore. The carrier took aboard 3,500 Vietnamese. In the evacuation, one Marine CH-53 carried more than 80 men, women, and children on a flight; Marine CH-46 Sea Knights carried some 60 persons. Two Marine helicopter pilots were lost in the operation when a CH-46 helicopter crashed at sea.

But hundreds of Vietnamese who had worked for the U.S. government and intelligence agencies were left on the U.S. embassy grounds and at other points around the city. On April 30, 1975, North Vietnamese tanks rolled into Saigon and through the gates of the Presidential Palace. South Vietnam fell to the communists.

The *Midway* was the last of 17 U.S. attack carriers to participate in the conflict. Each flattop made from one to ten deployments to Southeast Asian waters from 1964 to 1975:[17]

America (3)	*Intrepid* (3)
B. H. Richard (6)	*Kitty Hawk* (9)
Constellation (8)	*Midway* (9)
Coral Sea (8)	*Oriskany* (10)
Enterprise (7)	*Ranger* (8)
F. D. Roosevelt (1)	*Saratoga* (1)
Forrestal (1)	*Shangri-La* (1)
Hancock (9)	*Ticonderoga* (7)
Independence (1)	

The *Shangri-La*, rated as a CVS since June 30, 1969, deployed to Vietnam in 1970 as a "limited CVA," as did the *Intrepid*. Carrying two F-8H squadrons and three A-4C/E squadrons, the *Shangri-La* operated on Yankee Station from March to December 1970. The *Ticonderoga* made five deployments as a CVA; another two, in 1971 and 1972, were as a CVS with an antisubmarine air group embarked. Four other ASW carriers participated in the conflict:

Bennington (4)	*Kearsarge* (4)
Hornet (3)	*Yorktown* (3)

Several ex-U.S. escort carriers configured as aircraft cargo ships (AKV), operated by civilian crews of the Military Sea Transportation Service, carried aircraft and troops to South Vietnam as did one foreign carrier. HMAS *Sydney*, modified to serve as a fast transport, made 21 trips to South Vietnam during the war, carrying troops, helicopters, vehicles, and equipment for the Australian contingent fighting against communist forces.

The *Mayaguez* Incident

Shortly after the collapse of South Vietnam, American resolve was put to one final test in Southeast Asia. In a move reminiscent of the North Korean seizure of the *Pueblo* in 1968, Cambodian gunboats seized the American merchant ship *Mayaguez* on May 12, 1975. The *Mayaguez* was steaming in international waters, heading for Thailand, when she was stopped by a small gunboat, boarded, and her 40 crewmen captured by the new communist government of Cambodia. Coming fast on the heels of the humiliating fall of Saigon, this brazen act was too much for the U.S. government.[18]

President Gerald R. Ford, who had taken over the government from President Nixon less than a year before, felt that he had to move quickly. The disaster of the Watergate scandal, in the midst of which Nixon became the only U.S. president to resign from office, the communist takeover of South Vietnam, and the general feeling across the country of frustration made strong, positive action mandatory.

At the U.S. National Security Council (NSC) meeting on May 12, Secretary of State Henry Kissinger asked, "What do we have in the neighborhood of the incident?"[19] It was the question asked since the 1960s whenever the United States faced a crisis: "Where are the carriers?"

At the time the carrier *Coral Sea* was en route to Australia for the Coral Sea Battle commemoration while the smaller *Hancock* was at Subic Bay in the Philippines. In addition, there were numerous U.S. aircraft—from B-52 strategic bombers to U-2 reconnaissance aircraft—at bases in Thailand. Vice President Nelson Rockefeller observed at the NSC meeting,

> I think this will be seen as a test case. I think it will be judged in South Korea. I remember the *Pueblo* case. I think we need something strong soon. Getting out a message and getting people ready will not do it.
>
> I think a violent response is in order. The world should know that we will act and that we will act quickly. We should have an immediate response in terms of action. I do not know if we have any targets that we can strike, but we should certainly consider this. If they get any hostages, this can go on forever.[20]

Rockefeller reiterated that simply moving the carriers "is not action." And, fearing a delay would allow Congress to become involved and the "doves would start talking," he declared, "But, unless the Cambodians are hurt, this patter will not be broken."

A force of 288 U.S. Marines was quickly assembled at the U.S. air base at Utapao, Thailand. One helicopter crashed killing all 23 on board as the troops were

The ASW carrier *Intrepid* underway as a limited-CVA with her flight deck showing A-4 Skyhawks and A-1 Skyraiders. The ship's shift from the ASW to limited-attack role during the Vietnam conflict demonstrated the flexibility inherent in aircraft carriers. Note the ship's starboard deck-edge elevator and the shape of her forward elevator. The after centerline elevator was deleted in modernized *Essex*-class carriers. (F. M. Horvath, U.S. Navy)

being assembled. Using Air Force CH-53 Sea Stallion helicopters, the Marines assaulted Koh Tang Island off the Cambodian coast at dawn on May 15 in the belief that the *Mayaguez* crew was being held on the island.

In fact the location of the *Mayaguez*'s crew was not known; there were unsubstantiated reports that the crewmen had been released in small boats in the Gulf of Siam to await rescue. The Sea Stallions landed their troops on Koh Tang and were met with intense small-arms fire from the large force of Cambodian defenders, who were expecting a Vietnamese attack. Two helicopters were shot down as they attempted either to land or, after unloading troops, to take off. The remaining CH-53s of the initial assault force managed to get back to Utapao, leaving the Marines pinned down under heavy fire.

Simultaneously, three Air Force helicopters lowered Marines onto to the U.S. frigate *Harold E. Holt* to form a boarding party to storm the *Mayaguez*. They then stormed the merchant ship, supported by carrier aircraft, to find that the ship had been abandoned. That left the hard-pressed Marines on Koh Tang. Throughout the day U.S. Navy and Air Force planes struck the Cambodian mainland to stop a Cambodian attempt at reinforcing its contingent on the island. The surviving Marines on the ground were airlifted out by nightfall, still under heavy gunfire. Total U.S. military casual-ties were 18 men killed, 3 missing, and 50 wounded, in addition to the 23 killed in the helicopter accident in Thailand.

Meanwhile, the Cambodians had released the *Mayaguez* crew, sending them back to their ship in a fishing boat. The strong U.S. reaction to the seizure of the *Mayaguez*, which the Cambodian government had not authorized, apparently secured the crewmen's release. The storming of Koh Tang, the use of American aircraft once more, and the eventual return of the merchant sailors dispelled a little of the frustration that most Americans had felt with the fall of South Vietnam. The captain of the *Mayaguez* visited the *Coral Sea* soon after his release to thank the men on the ship for coming to his crew's aid. He said, "If it hadn't been for *Coral Sea* and the destroyers [*Henry B.*] *Wilson* and *Holt*, we probably would be in a Cambodian prison camp today."

With the conclusion of the *Mayaguez* incident, American presence in Southeast Asia dwindled. Combat involvement had ended as it had begun nearly 11 years before. An American ship had been attacked on the high seas and elements of the Navy's carrier force had been pressed into service. The United States still maintains carrier patrols in the Western Pacific, but for all intents and purposes, after a presence of 30 years, U.S. carrier aviation in the South China Sea had come to an end.

HMAS *Sydney* at sea in 1964 as a fast transport, employed during the Vietnam War to support Australian troops fighting in South Vietnam. Cranes are installed forward and aft of the island structure to lift heavy equipment; all aviation gear has been deleted from the ship. Built as the British CVL *Terrible*, she was commissioned in the Royal Australian Navy in December 1948. (Royal Australian Navy)

The shadow of an RF-8A Crusader reconnaissance aircraft passes over a burning North Vietnamese motor torpedo boat in the Song Giang River in 1965. This photo mission, launched from the carrier *Midway*, was one of thousands flown over North and South Vietnam, Cambodia, and Laos by Navy and Marine RF-8s and Navy RA-5C Vigilantes operating from aircraft carriers. These excellent aircraft were later replaced by the Tactical Air Reconnaissance Pods System (TARPS) carried on F-14 Tomcats and, subsequently, by the Shared Reconnaissance Pod System (SHARPS) mounted on F/A-18 Hornets. These pod-mounted reconnaissance systems were not as effective in relative terms as the dedicated "recce" aircraft, and their fighter pilots lacked the specialized training and mission experience of the pilots from VFP, VAP, and RVAH squadrons. (U.S. Navy)

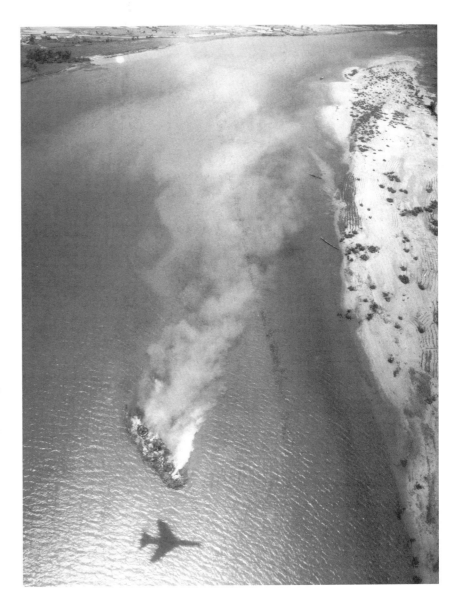

18 CARRIER CONTROVERSIES

Secretary of Defense McNamara approved the construction of three nuclear-propelled carriers (CVAN 68–70) based on their importance in the Vietnam War. The *Nimitz*, shown here on sea trials in 1975, was a refinement of the *Forrestal* design. The ship's small island structure and the arrangement of deck-edge elevators are evident; the blast shields for the two waist catapults are raised (just forward of the port-side elevator). (Harold Phillips, U.S. Navy)

The availability and effectiveness of carrier-based tactical air power in the Vietnam conflict led Secretary of Defense Robert S. McNamara to a new appreciation for the aircraft carrier. U.S. carrier operations during 1965 caused Pentagon analysts to reevaluate the carrier program. As a result, McNamara proposed the construction of additional super carriers, explaining, "Although the investment to procure these ships is substantial, our experience in Vietnam and recent study results indicate that total costs to procure, support, and defend overseas land-based tactical air forces are comparable to total costs of carrier task forces of equal capability."[1]

Mr. McNamara's statement to the Congress on February 23, 1966, announced a new policy and construction program for aircraft carriers:

> In my appearance here last year . . . I discussed a plan which would have reduced the

attack carrier forces to 13 ships and 13 air wings by the early 1970s. A reduction of this order was considered appropriate for several reasons: the introduction of far more effective ships and aircraft into the fleet, the release of the attack carriers from the strategic [nuclear] alert mission, and the overall increase in quantity, range, and effectiveness of land-based tactical air power generally. Since that time a plan has been developed for the attack carrier forces which I believe is superior to the one discussed last year. Under the new plan, the number of ships would be held at 15 but the number of air wings would be reduced to 12—an increase of 2 ships and a reduction of 1 air wing compared with the previous plan. Significantly more useable combat power could be obtained from a force of 15 carriers and 12 air wings than from a force of 13 carriers and 13 air wings, and at no increase in cost.

The Navy's attack carrier strength briefly reached 16 ships when the *America* (CVA 66) was commissioned on January 23, 1965; however, the *Midway* was decommissioned early in 1966, when she began an extensive modernization, returning the attack carrier force to 15 ships plus the limited-CVA *Intrepid*. In Secretary McNamara's revised 15-carrier force would be four nuclear-propelled ships, the *Enterprise* and three later ships; the eight carriers of the *Forrestal* type;[2] and the three extensively modernized *Midway*-class carriers.

The first of the new nuclear-propelled carriers was funded in the fiscal year 1967 (beginning on July 1, 1966). Congress had originally provided $35 million in the fiscal 1960 budget for long-lead nuclear components for a second aircraft carrier of the *Enterprise* design. The Eisenhower administration, however, deferred the project, shifting the funds to the Polaris missile program. Thus, not until Secretary McNamara's belated recognition of the value of carriers was the CVAN 68 authorized. The ship would be slightly larger than the *Enterprise* and would cost an estimated $544 million. Technological advances would give the new nuclear carrier improved endurance and performance characteristics with a two-reactor steam plant. This ship—designated CVAN 68 and later named *Nimitz*—was scheduled for completion in 1971. The two other nuclear carriers planned in the 15-carrier force would be built at two-year intervals with the CVAN 69 planned for completion in 1973 and the CVAN 70 in 1975. These ships, with an estimated 30-year service life, would be in service into the 21st Century.

When the *Nimitz* was commissioned in 1975 she was the largest and most expensive warship yet constructed. With a standard displacement of 81,600 tons, the ship was more than 93,000 tons at full load. Two large A4W reactors replaced the eight reactors in the *Enterprise* to provide 280,000-shaft horsepower to drive the ship at more than 30 knots. The ship's basic configuration, however, was similar to the *Forrestal* series: it had an angled flight deck, four deck-edge elevators, and four catapults with a hull design that dated to the cancelled carrier *United States*.[3]

The similar CVAN 69 was laid down in 1970 and the CVN 70 in 1975. The *Nimitz* had cost $635 million; the CVAN 69 cost almost $800 million, and the CVN 70 was the first carrier to cost more than $1 *billion*.

To increase the availability of carriers in forward areas, the decision was made to homeport ships overseas. The first U.S. capital ship ever based overseas was the *Midway*, which arrived at Yokosuka, Japan, on October 5, 1973. Her air wing was stationed ashore at Atsugi, Japan. This forward-basing eliminated the trans-Pacific transits for the ship, increasing carrier availability in the Western Pacific and Indian Ocean. A second carrier was to be homeported at Athens, Greece, but because of political changes in that country in the early 1970s the plan was aborted.

As U.S. aircraft carriers fought the air war over the Indochina peninsula, other U.S. carriers as well as other nations' carriers were heavily engaged in "peacetime" deployments and crisis response. While the U.S. Navy kept up to five attack carriers plus anti-submarine and helicopter carriers deployed to Southeast Asia, it also sustained two attack carriers in the Mediterranean and, at times, carriers operated in other areas.

In 1967 a major conflict again erupted between Israel and Arab states. The immediate cause of this war was the Egyptian blockade of the Strait of Tiran, Israel's outlet to the Red Sea, on May 22, 1967. Two weeks later, on June 5, Israeli aircraft streaked over Egypt, Iraq, and Syria, destroying their air forces, which consisted mainly of Soviet-supplied jet fighters and bombers. Jordan's small, primarily British-equipped air force was also devastated. In all, the Israelis, flying French-built jet fighters and attack planes, struck 20 enemy airfields in the first three hours of the war. The Israelis claimed the destruction of 451 Arab aircraft on the ground and in the air—among them 145 MiG-21s—in the first two and a half days of what became known as the Six Day War.[4] Most of the remaining Arab air strength was destroyed in the next couple of days. The Israel Air Force lost 40 aircraft, approximately 20 percent of its combat aircraft, in the conflict.

The speed and effectiveness of the Israeli strikes, coupled with such tactics as flying out over the Mediterranean and then circling toward Egypt from the sea at low levels to avoid radar detection, led the Egyptians to believe that U.S. and British carrier-based aircraft were participating in the attack. There were still vivid memories of the British and French carrier attacks in November 1956 during the previous Arab-Israeli conflict. Thus Egypt's President Gamal Abdel Nasser, with the agreement of Jordan's King Hussein, declared that U.S. and British carrier aircraft were attacking the Arab nations in conjunction with the Israeli strikes. (King Hussein later acknowledged that no U.S. or British warplanes had been sighted over Jordan.)

At the time the U.S. Sixth Fleet was operating in the eastern half of the Mediterranean and included the large attack carriers *America* and *Saratoga* and the ASW carrier *Essex*. (On the eve of the war the limited CVA *Intrepid* had passed through the Suez Canal and into the Red Sea en route to her second Vietnam deployment.) The British carrier dispositions in the area at the time were the *Victorious*, which had just transited through the Suez Canal, at Malta and the *Hermes* at Aden. Both were too far from the fighting to have flown combat strikes.

The United States was in a position to prove that the U.S. carriers in the Mediterranean had not participated in the war by virtue of a Soviet naval squadron operating in the same area as the Sixth Fleet. Soviet warships were continually passing through the U.S. formations and were in an excellent position to observe the launch of bomb-laden aircraft.

The U.S. warships went to an increased state of readiness on the morning of June 5 when word was received of the outbreak of full-scale war in the Middle East. The carriers continued to fly routine air patrol and reconnaissance missions until the early afternoon of June 8 when word was received that unidentified aircraft off the coast of Sinai were attacking the U.S. electronic surveillance ship *Liberty*.[5] Vice Admiral William I. Martin, Commander Sixth Fleet, ordered his two carriers to immediately launch protective aircraft for the *Liberty*. Four *conventionally* armed A-4 Skyhawks and four A-1 Skyraiders were launched from the *Saratoga* with an escort of four F-4B Phantoms to drive off the attackers—although the identity of those attackers was not yet known. Another four A-4s were launched with buddy stores to serve as tankers. The 16 aircraft were launched in ten minutes with eight minutes' notice.

At the time the *America* was engaged in a nuclear weapons loading exercise. Her commanding officer, Captain Donald D. Engen, immediately halted the exercise but would not launch aircraft armed with conventional weapons until the "nukes" had been lowered to their magazines and properly stored.[6]

Several popular accounts assert that the U.S. carriers launched aircraft with nuclear weapons, especially F-4B Phantoms.[7] However, Navy Phantoms were not wired to carry nuclear weapons nor were their crews trained in nuclear weapons delivery, and it was "unthink-

able" for a carrier's captain to launch nuclear-armed aircraft without specific direction from Washington or the theater commander-in-chief.[8] Subsequently, the *America* did launch four armed A-4C Skyhawks with an F-4B Phantom escort—none carrying nuclear weapons. The orders from the Sixth Fleet commander to the carriers stated, "You are authorized to use force including destruction as necessary to control the situation. Do not use more force than required. Do not pursue any unit towards land for reprisal purposes. Purpose of counterattack is to protect *Liberty* only."[9]

Some popular accounts continue to contend that the "Sixth Fleet's immediate response was to launch aircraft against Egypt, the initial suspect for the attack on board the Sixth Fleet flagship. . . . Sixth Fleet aircraft were recalled just in time, heading toward Egypt."[10] This statement is also totally false. Sending off four light attack aircraft escorted by four fighters to strike (multiple) Egyptian airfields in the midst of a war is too ridiculous contemplate.

Before the carrier planes reached the stricken *Liberty* the Israeli government had contacted Washington to admit that its planes had made the attack in error. Secretary McNamara ordered the carrier planes recalled. The Skyhawks, Skyraiders, and Phantoms were recalled, and helicopters from the carriers flew to the *Liberty* to bring in medical personnel and to take off wounded. (The battered U.S. spy ship suffered 34 dead and 171 wounded.)

Significantly, the Skyhawks carrying Bullpup missiles with highly volatile fuel could not land back aboard the carriers with those weapons. Instead, those planes landed at the NATO airfield at Souda Bay, Crete. They unloaded the missiles and returned to the carriers; the missiles were later brought back to the ship.

The Middle East war ended without the United States becoming directly involved. An important result of the 1967 conflict was the change in French policy, France having been Israel's principal arms supplier from 1956 to 1967. After the 1967 conflict the United States became the main supplier of arms to Israel, including large numbers of two U.S. carrier aircraft—Phantoms and Skyhawks—as well as several E-2 Hawkeyes.

In addition to CVA deployments, during the 1960s ASW carriers were carrying out exercises against the increasing force of Soviet nuclear-propelled submarines. And, the ASW carriers were employed in a new role—as space recovery ships—which they shared with

Aircraft carriers have often been called upon to support scientific endeavors (e.g., Antarctic exploration, research balloon and missile launchings). During the 1960s and 1970s carriers were the prime recovery ships for most U.S.-manned space launches. At left, a Marine UH-34D Sea horse lowers the Mercury capsule of Astronaut Alan B. Shepard, Jr., to the carrier *Lake Champlain*. Below, the ASW carrier *Wasp* approaches the Gemini capsule of Astronauts Eugene A. Cernan and Thomas P. Stafford after their three-day space mission; frogmen have attached flotation collars to the capsule.(U.S. Navy; National Aeronautics and Space Administration)

helicopter carriers (LPH) as the ships were available. On May 5, 1961, Lieutenant Commander Alan B. Shepard, Jr., became the first American in space when he reached an altitude of 116½ miles in the Mercury capsule *Freedom 7* in a suborbital flight launched from Cape Canaveral, Florida. Shepard, in his capsule, was picked up in the Atlantic Ocean, 302 miles down range, by a helicopter from the carrier *Lake Champlain*.

Helicopters from carriers recovered the astronauts in all subsequent U.S.-manned space flights of the Mercury (one-man), Gemini (two-man), Apollo (three-man), and Skylab series with two exceptions:[11] On July 21, 1961, Air Force Captain Virgil I. Grissom made a 15-minute suborbital flight from Cape Canaveral, Florida, in the Mercury capsule *Liberty Bell 7*. The craft successfully parachuted down to the sea, but a premature blowoff of the hatch cover led to the capsule flooding and the helicopter from the *Randolph*, unable to lift the additional weight, jettisoned the capsule (which was salvaged from the ocean floor in 1999). And, on February 20, 1962, Marine Lieutenant Colonel John H. Glenn, the first American to orbit the earth, and his spacecraft were recovered by a destroyer and were subsequently transferred to the carrier *Randolph*.

While man rocketed away from Earth, war erupted again in the ancient lands of the Middle East. The fighting began on October 6, 1973, with a surprise crossing of the Suez Canal by Egyptian forces to assault Israeli positions in the Sinai. The conflict was called the Yom Kippur War because the Arab states attacked Israel on the holiest day for Jews, the day of atonement. At the time the U.S. Sixth Fleet in the Mediterranean included the attack carriers *Franklin D. Roosevelt* and *Independence*. The CVA *John F. Kennedy*, in the North Sea, and the helicopter carrier *Iwo Jima*, in the Atlantic, were ordered to join them.

Unlike the fighting in 1956 and 1967, which ended in quick Israeli victories, this conflict dragged on. The Soviets began a rapid buildup of their forces in the Mediterranean as ships streamed southward through the Turkish Straits, while Soviet cargo aircraft began a massive airlift of arms and material into Syria and Egypt. Some evidence indicated that the Soviets had flown nuclear weapons into Egypt, to be used (by Soviet troops) to prevent a total Israeli conquest of Egypt.

The U.S. government responded with an airlift of weapons to Israel, and on October 19, U.S. Navy pilots begin ferrying A-4 Skyhawk attack aircraft from the United States to Israel. The aircraft staged through the Azores and refueled on the carrier *Roosevelt*, steaming south of Sicily, as most NATO nations denied use of their air bases for the planes en route to Israel.

On the afternoon of the 22nd both Israel and Egypt accepted a cease-fire sponsored by the United States and the Soviet Union. By that time Israeli forces had pushed back the Syrian and Egyptian forces and destroyed or encircled most of the Egyptian Army. The Soviet naval buildup continued; by the 24th there were 80 Soviet naval units in the Mediterranean: 16 submarines; 26 surface combatants, including the helicopter carrier-missile cruiser *Moskva*; and 38 amphibious and support ships.[12] This was the largest Soviet force yet assembled in the Mediterranean. By October 31 there would be 96 Soviet units, including 23 submarines and 34 surface combat ships.

The Commander Sixth Fleet, Vice Admiral Daniel Murphy, later wrote,

> The U.S. Sixth Fleet and the Soviet Mediterranean Fleet were, in effect, sitting in a pond in close proximity and the stage for the hitherto unlikely "war at sea" scenario was set. This situation prevailed for several days. Both fleets were obviously in a high readiness posture for whatever might come next, although it appeared that neither fleet knew exactly what to expect.[13]

The U.S. Sixth Fleet, with submarines and surface combatants, was outnumbered by the Soviet buildup. The Soviets were far superior in numbers of anti-ship missiles and torpedoes. Still, the three U.S. aircraft carriers and their embarked air wings unquestionably tilted the "balance" in favor of the United States.

(Meanwhile, the U.S. 82nd Airborne Division at Fort Bragg, North Carolina, and transport aircraft were placed on alert for deployment to the Middle East, as were the two battalions of Marines embarked in ships in the Mediterranean. The Strategic Air Command's B-52s and their tankers were placed on a higher level of alert.)

On October 30 major U.S. warships began to move westward. On November 3 the Soviet forces began to disperse. The Yom Kippur War had again focused U.S. attention on the Middle East, including the Persian Gulf. In the aftermath of the 1973 war, the carrier *Hancock* and escorts were sent to the northwest Indian

By the 1970s Soviet warships were operating regularly in the spheres of U.S. carrier operations. These were for both intelligence collection and for training for potential attacks when a conflict began. Here, in 1971, a Soviet Kashin-class guided missile destroyer comes alongside the carrier *Franklin D. Roosevelt* in the Mediterranean. (U.S. Navy)

Ocean; they were followed by the *Oriskany*. The logistics support of these ships—the nearest U.S. naval base was Subic Bay in the Philippines—led to the development of long-range support procedures.

These deployments caused Secretary of Defense James Schlesinger to express interest in a continuous carrier deployment to the area. But such a deployment would have placed an unacceptable strain on the remainder of the fleet with ongoing U.S. commitments to keep two carriers in the Mediterranean and at least two in the Western Pacific. Nevertheless, Schlesinger's interest in the region persuaded him to keep the *Hancock* and *Oriskany* in commission for another two years, maintaining a force of 15 attack carriers. That number, beginning in 1974, would decline to 12 carriers. It was believed that 12 could still permit the continuous deployment of two ships to the Mediterranean and two or three to the Pacific–Indian Ocean by homeporting two ships abroad. In the event only the

Midway was based overseas, in Japan.

Meanwhile, new carriers were joining the fleet. The second nuclear-propelled carrier, the *Nimitz* (CVAN 68), was commissioned in 1975.

New Kinds of Carriers

In the post-Vietnam drawdown of naval forces, the attack carriers *Hancock* and *Oriskany* were retired. The *Hancock* had served in World War II and Vietnam; laid up in mothballs in 1946, she had been converted to an angled-deck carrier in 1951–1954 and thus missed the Korean War. She was decommissioned on January 30, 1976, and scrapped. The *Oriskany*, the last *Essex*-class ship to be completed (1950), also served in two wars, Korea and Vietnam. Her commissioning pennant was hauled down on September 30, 1976, and she was later sunk as an artificial reef. She was the last of her class in service except for the pilot training carrier *Lexington*, which served in that role from 1963 until 1990.[14]

On June 30, 1975, the *Nimitz* and the still-building CVAN 69 were redesignated as multi-mission aircraft carriers (CVN); all other attack carriers were changed to CV/CVN in 1973–1975. The CV designation meant that their fighter, attack, and special-mission aircraft would share flight decks with ASW aircraft. This was a return to the pre-1952 situation, when a single carrier could perform all fleet missions.[15]

By 1975 the *Essex/Hancock*-class carriers serving in the ASW role (designated CVS) were worn out and had been decommissioned. The last CVS was the *Intrepid*, which hauled down her commission pennant on March 15, 1974. Their rehabilitation would have been costly, especially if they were to operate the Lockheed S-3A Viking, a turbojet replacement for the long-serving S-2 Tracker. In the post-Vietnam period funds were not available to operate specialized ASW carriers while at the same time the increasing Soviet submarine threat demanded more anti-submarine forces.

From December 1969 to June 1970 the *Forrestal* deployed to the Mediterranean with eight SH-3D Sea King ASW helicopters in her air wing; from July to December 1970 the *Independence* deployed to the Med with another eight SH-3D helicopters. The "Indy" operation was reported as "eminently successful in providing close-in ASW defense for the CVA task group. The SH-3 is effective in producing timely datums at extended distance from the force."

Admiral Elmo R. Zumwalt, who became Chief of Naval Operations in July 1970, endorsed the CV concept. He later observed,

> Of course, modifying carriers in such a way dissatisfied some people. They pointed out (correctly) that making a carrier capable of two dissimilar missions made it less capable than it had been of either one. They also pointed out (again correctly) that on the record of recent wars and crises a carrier was more likely to be called on for projection [of strikes] than for sea control.[16]

The *Saratoga*, undergoing minor modifications before she deployed to the Mediterranean in June 1971, became the first "CV." An ASW analysis center was installed as was stowage for 50 Mk 46 torpedoes and 2,500 expendable sonobuoys, and shops were set up to support ASW electronic systems. A minor problem was configuring the ship for aviation gas (for S-2 Track-ers), as all other embarked aircraft used JP-5 jet fuel.

The ship embarked half of an ASW air group. To make space for these aircraft the "Sara" left ashore four F-4J Phantoms, four A-7A Corsairs, and four RA-5C Vigilantes. Her embarked Carrier Air Wing 3 thus consisted of

20	F-4J	Phantoms
20	A-7A	Corsairs
9	A-6A/B	Intruders
4	KA-6D	Intruders (tankers)
4	EA-6A	Prowlers (electronic countermeasures)
4	E-2B	Hawkeyes (airborne early warning)
10	S-2E	Trackers (ASW)
8	SH-3D	Sea Kings (ASW)

During her five-month deployment to the Mediterranean the *Saratoga* flew off her ASW aircraft to bases at Sigonella, Sicily, and Souda Bay, Crete, to test the ability to rapidly reconfigure to a strike role. And, en route back to the United States in late October, she embarked an additional 12 S-2E and 8 SH-3D aircraft to conduct intensive ASW exercises.[17] Twenty-two attack aircraft and the four EA-6As were sent ashore to make space. The deployment was considered a success, although it was not without difficulties.

Accordingly, the decision was made to modify the *Forrestal* and all later carriers to accommodate mixed air wings. The three *Midway*s were too small to handle the additional aircraft ASW control center and support facilities. Two more carriers, the *Independence* in the Atlantic and the *Kitty Hawk* in the Pacific, deployed with S-2 Trackers and SH-3 Sea Kings before the S-3A Viking became available. The S-3, which first flew on January 21, 1972, became operational in early 1974. It was designed to the approximate dimensions of the Tracker but was faster and carried more advanced ASW equipment. The internal weapons bay, sized to hold four lightweight ASW torpedoes or a nuclear depth bomb, had a capacity of 2,400 pounds. There were also two wing pylons (which in the later S-3B could carry the Harpoon anti-ship missiles). A crew of four flew the aircraft.

The carriers modified to carry the S-3 Vikings were provided with an ASW tactical command center, storage for ASW weapons and sonobuoys, and test and maintenance facilities. The *Kennedy*, sailing for the Mediterranean in late June 1975, became the first ship

The Lockheed S-3 Viking was the ultimate carrier-based ASW aircraft. This S-3B aircraft, carrying two Harpoon air-to-surface missiles, shows the under-fuselage sonobuoy chutes; the tail Magnetic Anomaly Detection (MAD) boom is retracted. The S-3 was designed to be within the approximate dimensions of the piston-engine Tracker, but was faster and carried more advanced ASW sensors. The internal weapons bay, sized to hold four lightweight ASW torpedoes, could carry 2,400 pounds of weapons or auxiliary fuel tanks. Maximum speed was 500 m.p.h. at sea level; patrol range was approximately 2,650 miles. (Lockheed)

to deploy in the CV configuration with S-3s on board. As Rear Admiral Staser Holcomb later observed, "While there had been little doubt that the 'CV concept' was workable, the upheavel it caused—both physical and philosophical—was a healthy reminder of the inherent flexibility of the aircraft carrier."[18]

Another type of aircraft carrier—the Sea Control Ship (SCS)—was developed during Admiral Zumwalt's tenure as Chief of Naval Operations. The SCS was to be primarily an ASW ship to escort convoys, amphibious groups, and underway replenishment groups in situations when a larger CV/CVN was not available. A surface warfare officer, Zumwalt followed three naval aviators as CNO.[19] He sought to increase the striking power of surface ships—mainly with Tomahawk and Harpoon cruise missiles—and to enhance the Navy's anti-submarine effectiveness against a rapidly improving Soviet submarine force. Indeed, the Harpoon anti-ship missile was developed specifically for use by ASW aircraft against surfaced Soviet cruise missile submarines.

Zumwalt's sea control ship was initiated under the rubric "air capable ship" for the ASW role. Preliminary studies looked at an enlarged destroyer-type ship accommodating several helicopters. The design evolved into a small aircraft carrier and, in 1973–1974, was enlarged into a ship of 17,000 tons full load displacement with a length of 670 feet and a speed of 25 knots. This enlarged SCS was to operate 16 ASW helicopters and 5 Harrier-type Vertical/Short Takeoff and Landing (VSTOL) aircraft, the latter to provide a limited air defense capability. (Table 18-1 shows the original SCS design features; the Harrier program is described in Chapter 19.)

The SCS could handle only helicopters and VSTOL aircraft as it had no arresting gear or catapults, features that drove up the size and hence cost of a conventional carrier. The ship would have a hangar deck, to house most of the aircraft, and two elevators. The construction cost was to be "capped" at $100 million per ship (with eight ships planned) or about one-tenth the cost of a *Nimitz*. Obviously, their roles were very different and no further comparisons should be made.

Admiral Zumwalt wrote of the SCS:

> Her principal peacetime purpose was to show the flag in dangerous waters, especially the Mediterranean and the western Pacific where the Sixth and Seventh Fleets operate, so that the big carriers that are the Navy's most important ships could withdraw from the front lines and deploy out of reach of an enemy first strike, thus putting themselves in a favorable position to respond to such a strike—and therefore deter it. To use the undoubted vulnerability of carriers to Soviet cruise missiles as an argument for getting rid of carriers, as some Defense critics do, seems to me a classic example of throwing out baby with the bath water.[20]

To evaluate the SCS concept, Admiral Zumwalt established an interim sea control ship program employing the LPH *Guam*. The 10,700-ton helicopter carrier embarked a squadron of SH-3G (later SH-3H) Sea Kings and also operated a small number of AV-8A Harriers during the tests, which were conducted in the North Atlantic from January 1972 to April 1974.[21] Zumwalt considered the tests successful, and Secretary Schlesinger endorsed the SCS program.

In January 1973, based on early phases of the tests, two shipyards were awarded contracts for detailed design of the ship. Funds were provided in the fiscal 1974 budget for long-lead components for the program. However, the cost of the ship was increasing—to $130,300,000 for the lead ship—and there were criticisms of the ship, especially in a General Accounting Office (GAO) report:

> Based on the tempo of operations observed, it is questionable whether the helicopters planned for the SCS can meet the 15-day mission requirement of maintaining two sonobuoy ASW barriers while also providing a surveillance aircraft 50 percent of the time.

> The AV-8A is restricted to daylight rear hemisphere engagement and is not capable of effectively intercepting a missile or attacking ships considered to be the 1980 threat.[22]

The critics of the SCS program, led mainly by Admiral H. G. Rickover, head of Navy nuclear propulsion, objected to the ship for numerous reasons, both valid and spurious. Zumwalt stepped down as CNO on July 1, 1974, and his successor, Admiral James L. Holloway III, a naval aviator who was Rickover trained, quickly halted the SCS effort despite his earlier commitment to VSTOL aviation. Congress—mainly on the basis of the GAO study—delayed and then withheld funding for the SCS. (The Spanish Navy subsequently constructed a ship of similar design, the *Principe de Asturias*, completed in 1988, and one for the Thai Navy, the *Chakri Nareubet*, completed in 1997.)

A VSTOL warship was almost built—the air-capable destroyer (designated DDH). The Litton/Ingalls shipyard in Pascagoula, Mississippi, sponsored a series of studies in the mid-1970s into operating VSTOL aircraft from modified destroyers.[23] At the time the yard was constructing 30 *Spruance*-class ASW destroyers.[24]

The DDH would displace 12,300 tons full load with a length of 563 feet. Carrying a limited gun, missile, and ASW armament, the ship would have a ski-ramp forward, a large hangar-superstructure amidships, and a landing area aft. It was to operate eight Harriers or six ASW helicopters.

Congress authorized two *Spruance* DDHs in fiscal year 1978 and funded one ship, with the proviso that, in the wording of the Senate Committee on Armed

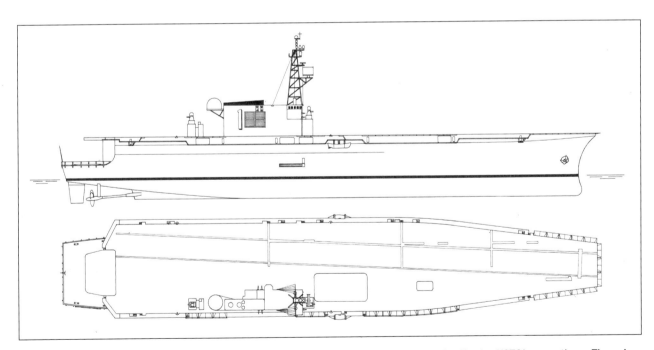

The Sea Control Ship—this is a late SCS design—was to have an angled flight deck for Harrier VSTOL operations. There is a centerline elevator offset just forward of the island structure and a stern elevator. Congress refused to authorize such ships because of their limited capability and strong opposition from advocates of large carriers. Modified versions of the SCS were built in Spain for the Spanish and Thai Navies. (U.S. Navy)

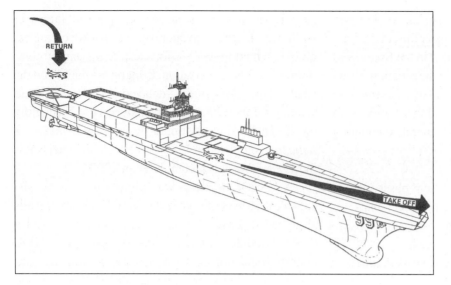

The DDH was a proposal for a modified *Spruance*-class ASW destroyer, reconfigured with a vertical landing deck aft, a large amidships hangar, and a takeoff deck forward, shown as a ski-ramp in some iterations. There was a small island structure and gun on the port side, forward. The DDH variant would have a slightly greater beam and fin stabilizers. An ASW "air group" could consist of nine AV-8B Harriers and two light helicopters. (Litton Shipbuilding)

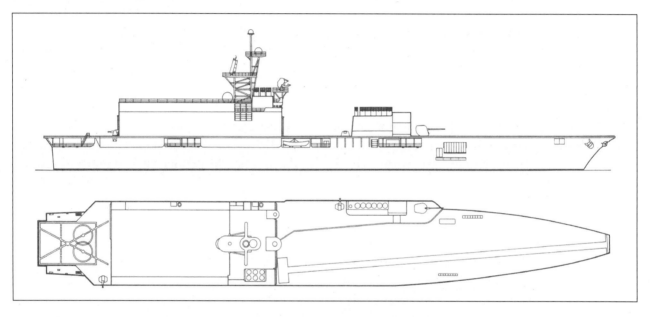

Services, "The committee does not intend for these funds to be used for acquisition of two standard [*Spruance*] class destroyers; rather, it is the committee's intention that these ships be the first element in a new technology approach to the problems of designing surface escorts. The standard [*Spruance*] class design should be modified to substantially increase the number of helicopter aircraft carried." This feature could permit the eventual modification of the ships to also operate Harrier-type VSTOL aircraft. However, the Navy chose to build the ship as a standard *Spruance*, with the ship being ordered in September 1979 (the USS *Hayler* [DD 997]). The ship was initially listed as DDH 997 in Navy working papers. No additional DDHs were funded by Congress.

The VSTOL Carriers

Still another relatively small, hermaphrodite carrier was considered in this period. A highly controversial aspect of nuclear-propelled carriers was their escorting ships. The U.S. Navy's first nuclear-propelled surface ship was the missile cruiser *Long Beach*, commissioned in 1961. A large ship of 14,200 tons standard displacement, she was intended primarily for anti-air warfare. The *Long Beach* was not duplicated. Instead, the Navy built a small number of nuclear destroyer-type ships, designated DLGN as well as large numbers of conventional ships, including destroyers (DD), guided missile destroyers (DDG), and guided missile frigates (DLG), to escort carriers as well as for other duties.[25]

From 1962 to 1980 the Navy commissioned eight DLGN-type ships as well as 70 conventional destroyer-type ships. The reason for this ratio was cost: nuclear propulsion had a major impact on ship construction costs. Congress rarely considered the long-term advantages of nuclear propulsion (e.g., no fuel oil, fewer support ships) and long-term disadvantages (e.g., manning costs, disposal problems) in funding warships except for submarines.

In the early 1960s the Navy was forced to cancel a new class of DLGNs fitted with the Typhon advanced anti-air missile system because of costs and technical difficulties. A successor anti-air warfare ship, the so-called strike cruiser (CSGN), was proposed in the early 1970s to carry a more-advanced anti-air radar/fire-control system called Aegis. The strike cruiser proposed for the fiscal year 1976 program was to displace 15,900 tons standard and 17,210 tons full load, be almost 710 feet long, and be driven by twin nuclear reactors at about 30 knots. The CSGN would be primarily an anti-air warfare ship but would carry a large number of anti-ship missiles, have limited ASW capability, and mount a single advanced 8-inch gun for shore bombardment. The estimated cost of the lead CSGN was almost $1.4 *billion* dollars. At the time nuclear carriers were costing about $2 *billion*. Thus, even in series production, two CSGNs would probably cost more than the carrier that they were escorting, in addition to the costs of two to four conventional destroyers per carrier group.

Admiral Hollway and, of course, Admiral Rickover strongly supported the nuclear CSGN. Indeed, Rickover's efforts had led Congress to pass legislation in 1974 requiring that "major combat vessels for the strike forces"—certainly including Aegis ships—be nuclear propelled.[26] The head of the Aegis program, Rear Admiral Wayne E. Meyer, proposed that the Aegis system be "shoehorned" into the *Spruance* destroyer design; those 7,800-ton ships were already on the building ways.[27]

Admirals Holloway and Rickover persisted with significant support from Congress, although it became increasingly obvious that the strike cruiser program was unaffordable. Finally, in January 1975, Secretary Schlesinger decided against requesting funds for any Aegis ships. Only when President Ford advised Congress that conventionally propelled Aegis ships were required in the national interest, and Admiral Holloway reversed his position, was the Aegis/*Spruance* program approved.[28]

Some advocates of the strike cruiser persisted, and the Naval Sea Systems Command (successor to the Bureau of Ships) proposed a strike cruiser "Mark II"—with a flight deck. Retaining most of the CSGN armament, the Mark II would have an angled flight deck (with an 8-inch gun and missile launcher forward) and an elongated island structure with hangars to house six Harrier VSTOL aircraft plus three ASW helicopters. Initially the Mark II cruiser was to have neither a hangar deck nor elevators. A further modification did consider those features, which would increase the ship's full load displacement to about 18,000 tons. The Mark II concept strongly resembled the Soviet *Kiev*-class VSTOL carriers, which were getting considerable attention at the time (see Chapter 23).

The strike cruiser—in any variant—was never built. The last nuclear-propelled DLGN-type ship was authorized in fiscal year 1975 and was completed in 1980. By 1998 all nuclear screening ships had been discarded; they were expensive to operate and lacked the Aegis and advanced ASW systems of oil-burning warships.[29]

A final U.S. carrier concept of this period was the VSTOL Support Ship (VSS). Increasingly, many in the Department of Defense, Congress, and even the Navy believed that the sea control role required an aviation ship less costly than the *Nimitz* design. Among its congressional supporters was Senator John C. Stennis, chairman of the powerful Senate Armed Services Committee, who declared, "It is time to augment our fleet of 12 large-deck carriers with a new class of several smaller carriers embodying modern technology as to both carrier and aircraft design."[30] Still, Congress had rejected the SCS in large part because of its small size and limited aircraft capacity, although several members of Congress rejected the "small" carrier concept at the urgings of Admiral Rickover, who considered such ships a threat to the future construction of nuclear-propelled super carriers.

Navy studies in the mid 1970s indicated that more-capable VSTOL aircraft would be forthcoming. Accordingly, the VSS carrier concept was developed in order to, according to Secretary of Defense Donald Rumsfeld, "permit a more flexible employment of sea-based tactical air in a wider range of low threat situations and also would have an anti-submarine capability."[31] Admiral Holloway, who had commanded the nuclear carrier *Enterprise* and had become Chief of Naval Operations in July 1974, sponsored the VSTOL stud-

The strike cruiser (CSGN) Mk II was an effort to imitate the Soviet cruiser-carrier designs of the *Kiev* class, combining an Aegis missile cruiser with a VSTOL carrier. However, the U.S. design had neither a hangar deck nor elevators; rather, the aircraft were hangared in the massive island structure. There are 5-inch guns and Mk 26 missile launchers forward and aft; 24 Harpoon anti-ship missiles are in canisters atop the island, which has the four "faces" of the AN/SPY-1 phased-array radar. (U.S. Navy)

ies and had publicly supported their findings, which proposed smaller carriers, referred to as air-capable ships. Holloway wrote, "VSTOL aircraft will increase aviation mission performance by our air-capable ships and will enormously increase the flexibility of aircraft carrier design."[32]

The VSTOL ships, possibly with a limited arresting gear and catapult capability (primarily for the E-2 Hawkeye), would have a full load displacement of at least 29,000 tons. The fiscal 1978 budget included token funding for the first ship, planned for authorization the following year with a second VSS in fiscal 1981. Cost of the VSS was estimated at about $1.28 *billion* compared to a minimum of $2.2 *billion* for a fourth *Nimitz*-class carrier.

Then, Admiral Holloway again reversed his position and would not support the ship or VSTOL aircraft in the face of Admiral Rickover's opposition. Thus the VSS program also died. The construction of *Nimitz*-class carriers continued. The CVN 71—fourth ship of the class—was authorized in fiscal 1980 by an enthusiastic Congress that overrode a presidential veto by Jimmy Carter, who opposed building such an expensive warship. The Carter administration, which entered office in January 1977, resurrected and enlarged the VSS concept, now labeled CVV, as an alternative to another *Nimitz*-class ship. Carter's Secretary of Defense, Harold Brown (who had been Secretary of the Air Force in the 1960s), argued for the CVV:

Construction of this new carrier would mark an essential and important step in reversing the trend of the last decade toward ever larger, more expensive ships. This Administration is fully committed to reversing this trend.

The CVV as currently designed will be equivalent in size and a far more capable ship than the one it replaces—the USS *Midway*. With respect to the most likely threat—the Soviet Union—it will also be much more capable than any carrier projected to be built outside of the United States. The CVV will have improved aviation characteristics, the CV/CVN habitability standards and a capability to operate all of the Navy's current aircraft. The USS *Midway* cannot now support the S-3, F-14, or E-2C operations. The hangar height [24½ feet] permits full flexibility for all aircraft maintenance functions; and elevators, catapults, and other aviation features will be capable of supporting all existing Navy carrier-based aircraft. . . . The CVV's normal operating airwing is expected to include about 60–65 modern aircraft, compared with about 90 for existing *Forrestal/Nimitz* CV/CVNs.[33]

Obviously the CVV would be an oil-burning carrier. The cost savings between a CVV and a larger *Kennedy*- or *Nimitz*-type ship would be $80 million to

Table 18-1
CARRIER DESIGN CHARACTERISTICS

	SCS DESIGN*	VSS DESIGN**	CVV DESIGN
Displacement			
light	9,770 tons	20,115 tons	45,200 tons
full load	13,735 tons	29,130 tons	59,800 tons
Length (overall)	610 feet	717 feet	912 feet
Beam	80 feet	87 feet	126 feet
Draft	$21^{1}/_2$ feet	$25^{1}/_3$ feet	$34^{1}/_2$ feet
Propulsion	2 gas turbines	4 gas turbines	2 steam turbines***
horsepower	45,000	90,000	140,000
shafts	1	2	2
Speed			
maximum	26 knots	30 knots	27.8 knots
sustained	23–25 knots	28 knots	—
Range/20 knots	7,500 n.miles	7,500 n.miles	—
Manning#	approx. 700	1,600	4,025
Aircraft	3 AV-8B Harrier 17 SH-3 Sea King	4 AV-8B Harrier 6 SH-2 LAMPS## 16 SH-3D Sea King	60–65 conventional aircraft

    *   Basic design.
   **   Final design VSS III.
 ***   6 boilers (1,200 pounds-per-square inch).
    #   Includes air wing.
  ##   Light Airborne Multi-Purpose System (helicopter).

$180 million. In addition, it was calculated that the 30-year life cycle costs of the larger carriers would be $5 *billion* to $6 *billion* greater than for the CVV, primarily because accountants included the costs of fuel and ships to supply it to the carrier. Some of the arguments were similar to those advanced by Secretary McNamara more than a decade earlier when he opposed nuclear-propelled carriers. (Of course, such debates did not factor in the increased costs of the personnel that operated nuclear plants, the costs of handling nuclear fuels and waste material, and later disposing of the nuclear plants.)

The Carter administration—and many naval officers—were truly concerned about the increasing size and costs of warships. Regardless, no alternative carrier could be considered in the face of the congressional "old guard," ably encouraged by Admiral Rickover. Construction of the *Nimitz* class continued. Indeed,

carriers of the basic *Nimitz* design would be constructed for a longer period than any other warship class in history, from the keel laying of the *Nimitz* in 1968 well into the 21st Century.

A Carrier Reject

One other aircraft of this period that warrants discussion is the General Dynamics F-111, which gained notoriety as the TFX—Tactical Fighter Experimental. It was the most controversial aircraft to ever touch down (albeit briefly) on a carrier deck.

The Air Force initiated the F-111 program to provide a successor the F-105 Thunderchief, a long-range, tactical nuclear strike aircraft. Secretary McNamara redirected the program in 1961—and relabeled it TFX— to provide a single aircraft design for tactical strike, close air support, fleet air defense, and battlefield interdiction. He envisioned the Air Force, Navy,

The prototype of the General Dynamics F-111B during a test flight with wings swept back. The TFX program sought to provide a single aircraft for multiple roles in the Air Force, Navy, and Marine Corps. The F-111B was to carry 6,000 pounds of weapons in an internal bay plus bombs, missiles, and drop tanks on wing pylons. Maximum speed without external stores was to be 910 m.p.h. at sea level and 1,450 m.p.h. at 40,000 feet. The aircraft had an escape capsule containing the entire cockpit rather than ejection seats. (U.S. Navy)

and Marine Corps all procuring TFX variants. Although the Air Force and Navy had differing requirements for a tactical aircraft, Admiral George W. Anderson, the Chief of Naval Operations (an aviator), and General Curtis E. LeMay, the Air Force Chief of Staff, publicly announced their endorsement of the new aircraft program on September 1, 1961.

After a convoluted selection process, Secretary McNamara on July 1, 1962, ordered a runoff between Boeing and General Dynamics designs on the basis of performance, cost, and commonality. The Air Force selection board and the Air Force Council approved the Boeing proposal. But on November 24, 1962, McNamara announced in favor of the General Dynamics design.

Less than a month later the Air Force began to procure 23 aircraft from General Dynamics for research, development, test, and evaluation—18 F-111A models for the Air Force and 7 F-111B models for the Navy. The F-111A was a large aircraft. With twin TF30 turbofan engines, it weighed 46,172 pounds empty with a maximum (runway) takeoff weight in excess of 91,000 pounds. The most prominent feature of the F-111 was its variable-sweep or "swing-wing" configuration. The wings extended for landing, takeoff, and economical cruise flight; they retracted or "tucked back" for high-speed (Mach 2+) flight.[34]

The principal difference in the two F-111 models was the larger wing for the F-111B, which had a span of 70 feet in the fully extended (16-degree sweep) setting—seven feet greater than the F-111A. This increased wingspan provided a lower landing speed for the Navy model, considered a critical factor for carrier landings. The F-111B also had the advanced AN/AWG-9 radar-fire control system and long-range Phoenix missiles to defend carriers from Soviet long-range bombers.

The first F-111A flight occurred in December 1964, and the first F-111B took to the skies on May 18, 1965. Production contracts for the Air Force followed. The early F-111As suffered a variety of problems, numerous aircraft were lost in accidents, and they were grounded on several occasions.

Meanwhile, the Navy's leadership unanimously opposed procurement of the F-111B, even before it flew carrier trials. The naval aircraft was heavier than specified, probably would not meet performance requirements, and was behind schedule. Still, publicly—and to Congress—the Navy officially held out hope for the aircraft. In May 1967 the Chief of Naval Operations, Admiral David L. McDonald (an aviator), told a congressional committee that he had reason, "I think, to believe that we are getting a carrier-suitable airplane in spite of the weight and one that will do a job for us." But a disillusioned Congress was not buying the "party line," and funding for F-111Bs was limited.

Finally, with congressional support, the Navy withdrew from the F-111 program in May 1968, contending that the aircraft was severely overweight and unsuitable for carrier operation. On July 19, 1968, a stop-work order was issued, and 28 aircraft on order for the Navy were cancelled, although seven F-111B models were delivered to the Navy through February 1969. In July 1968 an F-111B flew carrier trials aboard the *Coral Sea*.[35]

(Air Force F-111A aircraft were used in strikes against North Vietnam from a base in Thailand in 1968 and 1972–1973. These were single-plane missions, flown at night, to demonstrate the aircraft's night/

low-level strike profile. Having suffered initial teething problems and several losses, F-111s were successful during the latter deployment, as they were in the Gulf War of 1991.

(In an effort to support the F-111 program and to keep production lines alive, Secretary McNamara also ordered the aircraft into production as a *strategic bomber* and 76 FB-111A models were eventually built. In all, the Air Force bought 531 F-111s. The last to see Air Force service were converted electric jamming variants, the EF-111A Ravens, which served until May 1998, when their role was taken over by Navy-Marine EA-6B Prowlers.

(A planned procurement of the F-111K by the Royal Air Force was cancelled—the aircraft was too expensive. But the Royal Australian Air Force purchased 24 F-111C models. Those "down under" aircraft are expected to fly until 2020—long after the Navy's succes-

sor to the F-111B, the F-14 Tomcat, had been retired.)

The F-111 trials aboard the *Coral Sea* were not the only "unusual" carrier operation in this period. On April 21, 1972, two twin-engine B-25 Mitchell bombers took off from the *Ranger* steaming off San Diego. The flights, by privately owned B-25s, marked the 30th anniversary of the Doolittle raid on Japan and were witnessed by several hundred guests aboard the carrier.

Following cancellation of the F-111B the Navy initiated a new fighter to take advantage of the AN/AWG-9 and the Phoenix missile. This was the F-14 Tomcat, developed by Grumman, the Navy's long-time favorite for fighter aircraft. The F-14 was a variable-sweep-wing fighter with the wings extending for cruise, landing, and takeoff, and sweeping back for high-speed flight. The wing sweep changed automatically as the pilot maneuvered the aircraft. A two-place fighter, the F-14 was from the outset intended for the attack role as

A Grumman F-14A Tomcat from fighter squadron VF-1 lands aboard the carrier *Enterprise* while an F-14A from VF-101 flies with wings extended; the latter has low-visibility markings. The F-14 was an outstanding fighter and the last of a long line of Grumman carrier fighters that dated back to the FF-1 of 1931. The two-place F-14A had a maximum speed of 1,585 m.p.h. at 40,000 feet and a ceiling of 68,900 feet. Built as a fleet air defense fighter, upgrades eventually enabled the Tomcat—dubbed "Bobcat"—to carry a variety of air-to-ground guided bombs and missiles. (U.S. Navy; Peter B. Mersky collection)

well, but the upgrades were not immediately provided when the aircraft entered service in January 1973. Up to 14,500 pounds of external stores could be carried: originally there were four fuselage missile positions (4 Sparrow or 4 Phoenix) and two wing positions (4 Sidewinder or 2 Sparrow or 2 Phoenix); alternatively fuel tanks or a TARPS reconnaissance pod could be carried with a reduced missile load.[36] Subsequently, the F-14B/D were fitted with racks for "iron bombs" and laser-guided bombs; the F-14D also had pylon adapters for air-to-surface missiles. An internal 20-mm Vulcan "Gatling gun" was fitted.

By the mid-1970s major changes in the direction of carrier aviation were in the offing. A most significant change occurred in 1976 when the carriers were removed from the Single Integrated Operational Plan (SIOP), the U.S. nuclear strike plan. At that time the

United States had more than 8,000 strategic nuclear warheads on intercontinental ballistic missiles, ballistic missile submarines, strategic bombers, and forward-based strike aircraft.

The carrier-based nuclear strike aircraft, which had been primary players since the SIOP was developed in late 1960, now became a nuclear "reserve force." The carriers retained nuclear weapons on board, and pilots were trained in their delivery. But no longer were the ships required to be within certain distances of launch points and the pilots were no longer briefed (and rebriefed) on specific targets in the Soviet Union, China, and other communist counties. Rather, should the "balloon go up," the carriers would be ordered to conduct nuclear strikes against targets within range of their operating area.

One participant in the SIOP observed, "Freedom from the restrictive aspects of the SIOP was a welcome relief" for carrier operations.[37]

Table 18-2
U.S. CARRIER-BASED NUCLEAR STRIKE AIRCRAFT

PRE-1962	1962	NAME	NUCLEAR VARIANTS
AD	A-1	Skyraider	A-1D,-1E,-1G,-1H,-1J
A2D	—	Skyshark	cancelled
A3D	A-3	Skywarrior	A-3A,-3B
A4D	A-4	Skyhawk	A-4A,-4B,-4C,-4E,-4F,-4L,-4M
A2F	A-6	Intruder	A-6A,-6B,-6C,-6E
AJ	A-2	Savage	A-2A,-2B
A2J	—	Savage	cancelled
A3J	A-5	Vigilante	A-5A,-5B,-5C, RA-5C (A3J-1P)
—	A-7	Corsair	A-7A,-7B,-7E
F9F-8B	F-9	Cougar	AF-9J
F2H	F-2	Banshee	F-2B,-2C,-2D
F3H	F-3	Demon	F-3A,-3B,-3C
FJ	F-1	Fury	F-1C, AF-1E (FJ-4B)
F7U	—	Cutlass	F7U-3
—	F/A-18	Hornet	early models
S2F	S-2	Tracker	S-2A,-2B,-2C,-2D,-2E
—	S-3	Viking	S-3A,-3B
HSS-1	SH-34	Seabat	SH-34J
HSS-2	SH-3	Sea King	various models
—	SH-60	Seahawk	SH-60B,-60F

19 NEW DIRECTIONS

Even as the British government announced plans to phase out the Royal Navy's aircraft carriers, a carrier was operating off of the African cost to provide a close watch on merchant shipping, a mission that could not be effectively carried out by land-based aircraft. This is the *Eagle* on the Beira patrol; her crew enjoys the sun during a break in flight operations. At left are Sea Vixen all-weather fighters and Gannet AEW aircraft. (Royal Navy)

During the 1960s British carriers were being forward deployed in support of Whitehall's foreign policy. On November 11, 1965, the white minority government of Rhodesia in eastern Africa declared its independence from Great Britain. British Prime Minister Harold Wilson declared the action "illegal" and "treasonable." In an effort to bring down the rebellious Rhodesian government the British sought an economic blockade of the new nation. The most critical commodity that the British sought to bar was oil, which normally reached land-locked Rhodesia through the port of Beira in Portuguese-controlled Mozambique.

A British frigate attempted to "persuade" a Greek tanker against entering Beira, but failed. The frigate's captain was not authorized to use force. A short time later the United Nations Security Council approved an economic sanction against Rhodesia and the British imposed an oil blockade of Beira. HMS *Ark Royal* took up the "Beira patrol" beginning in July 1965 while assigned to the Far East Fleet. She was relieved in January 1966 by HMS *Eagle* as the carriers and other warships sought to interdict military supplies en route to Rhodesia. The *Eagle* returned to Singapore on May 10, 1966, having been at sea for 71 days during which time she flew 1,880 sorties and steamed 30,000 miles.

This was a record for British ships in the 20th Century exceeded only by the oiler *Tidepool*, one of the auxiliaries that replenished the carriers at sea, which had remained at sea for 80 consecutive days. The carriers averaged more than 20 sorties per day with their Scimitar, Sea Vixen, and Gannet fixed-wing aircraft and Wessex helicopters; the *Eagle* also operated a squadron of Buccaneer strike aircraft.

In contrast, after difficult discussions, Britain gained permission for land-based reconnaissance aircraft to operate from the Malagasy island republic, formerly the French colony of Madagascar. The island's government, still associated with France, initially hesitated in granting permission. Beginning in mid-March 1965 the British were able to operate three Royal Air Force (RAF) Shackleton patrol aircraft from the island. The Shackletons were limited to daylight flights because of the airport's lack of night-flying equipment, and they averaged one multi-hour sortie per day.

While the Beira patrol was operating, on February 22, 1966, the British government released its Defence White Paper—officially the Statement on the Defence Estimates 1966—presented by the Secretary of State for Defence, Denis W. Healey. It cancelled construction of the CVA.01, the first post–World War II British carrier, which was to have entered the fleet in 1972. The White Paper explained that

> Experience and study have shown that only one type of operation exists for which carriers and carrier-borne aircraft would be indispensable: that is the landing, or withdrawal, of troops against sophisticated opposition outside the range of land-based air power. It is only realistic to recognise that we, unaided by our allies, could not expect to undertake operations of this character in the 1970s—even if we could afford a larger carrier force.

The document went on to elucidate:

> Our plan is that, in the future, aircraft operating from land bases should take over the strike-reconnaissance and air-defence functions of the carrier. . . . Airborne early-warning aircraft will . . . [subsequently] operate from land bases.

The White Paper called for the acquisition of 50 American-built F-111K land-based strike aircraft, which, with a force of long-range V-bombers, would allow Britain to exert influence East of Suez.[1] Eric Grove, an

Underway replenishment at sea permitted British carriers to remain on station for sustained periods while supporting British foreign policy. Here the *Ark Royal* refuels from the replenishment ship *Tidesurge*, which is also refueling the destroyer *Troubridge*, in the Beira Straits in 1966. HMS *Ark Royal* and *Eagle* were Britain's largest warships of the post–World War II period except for the battleship *Vanguard*, completed in 1946. (Royal Navy)

insightful British naval historian, wrote, "The decision to abandon CVA.01 was perhaps the most traumatic shock to the Royal Navy of the entire postwar period. The fleet carrier had been central to the Royal Navy's plans and self-image for the last quarter century."[2]

The White Paper's statements on the employment of land-based air power vis-à-vis carrier aviation seemed completely opposite to the studies and experience that Secretary of Defense Robert S. McNamara had used to justify the increased American investment in carrier aviation, which he requested the day after the British White Paper was published. Indeed, British experience gave lie to the White Paper. In the East African revolts the British were faced with less than "sophisticated opposition" and the troubled areas were within the range of land-based aircraft. Still, strike carriers had an important role. The expectation that major operations would not be undertaken in the 1970s and beyond "unaided by our allies" ignored the reality that Britain's only ally with major naval forces was the United States. Yet, Britain in 1966 was obligated by treaty to the defense of 17 Asian and Pacific nations and still had several overseas possessions, among them the Falkland Islands in the South Atlantic.

Even the White Paper noted,

The aircraft carrier is the most important element of the Fleet for offensive action against an enemy at sea or ashore and makes a large contribution to the defence of our seaborne forces. It can also play an important part in operations where local air superiority has to be gained and maintained and offensive support of ground forces is required.

This clear, concise statement appeared in the same White Paper as the declaration that carrier aviation was indispensable only in "the landing, or withdrawal, of troops against sophisticated opposition outside the range of land-based air power."

From a cost viewpoint the 50 F-111K aircraft were priced at $300 million. The CVA.01 was to have cost $200 million plus about $100 million for the ship's aircraft. Even though a single carrier would be fully operational for only some eight months per year, the argument could be made that in the real world of politics and base and overflight rights, the carrier made far more sense.

Almost simultaneously, the government announced that the major Royal Air Force base at strategically located Aden would be reduced to a "transit field" by 1968, removing the possibility of operating the F-111Ks from there. (In July 1967 the British government announced that it would "withdraw altogether" from bases in Singapore and Malaysia by the mid-1970s, leaving only the possibility of Darwin and the yet-to-be-built Gan airfield in the Maldive Islands on which to base the F-111Ks.)

Appalled at the decision to cancel the CVA.01 the Minister of Defence for the Royal Navy, Christopher P. Mayhew, and the First Sea Lord, Admiral Sir David Luce, both resigned their offices. The public outcry led to a debate in Parliament, in which Mr. Healey declared,

Those who are saying, for whatever reason, that the phasing out of the carrier force in up to ten years' time means the end of the Royal Navy, are doing the Fleet a grave disservice. The fact is that the United States is the only country in the world which plans to maintain a viable carrier force around the world through the 1970s. Neither the Soviet Union nor China has carriers or plans to have them, nor does any of the countries with whom our commitments might have engaged us in hostilities over the last twenty years.

Mr. Healey was technically correct. But there had been no enemy carriers when Britain fought Germany and Italy, or when it halted aggression by Iraq against Kuwait and by Indonesia against Malaysia, or when it put down rebellions in Tanganyika, or when it attempted to seize the Suez Canal. Britain had carriers in each of those situations and could not have done as well as it did without them.

The cancellation of the CVA.01 marked a victory for the Air Ministry and the RAF, which had long argued at all levels of government and in the press that carriers were vulnerable and that land-based aircraft could perform all CVA missions. Also, the CVA was a costly weapon system.

The Royal Navy initiated a series of studies to determine the missions and composition of the fleet without large carriers. When the CVA.01 was cancelled it was envisioned that commando (helicopter) carriers, destroyers, frigates, and submarines would become the backbone of the fleet and hence of Britain's overseas military power. At the time the Navy had four carriers and two commando ships in service, plus the *Centaur* laid up in reserve (from December 1965) and being used as an accommodation ship. All four active fleet carriers had been extensively modernized.

The first carrier to be discarded was the veteran *Victorious*. It was announced on November 23, 1966, that she was to be stricken. The grand old lady of the fleet was stripped, her hulk was formally decommissioned on March 13, 1967, and she was scrapped. The *Hermes* completed her last commission as a fixed-wing carrier in June 1970 and began conversion to a commando ship. (The *Hermes* rejoined the Fleet in that role in 1973, at which time the *Albion* was discarded.)

The *Ark Royal*, modernized from October 1966 to February 1970, and the *Eagle* carried on, participating in national and North Atlantic Treaty Organization exercises. Further, crises and counter-guerrilla operations required the continued presence of the fleet carriers and commando ships East of Suez. This led to the government decision to retain two fleet carriers into the 1970s. (The training of Fleet Air Arm pilots for fixed-wing aircraft had stopped in 1966.)

The *Eagle* completed her last commission in January 1972—20 years after she was completed—and she was cannibalized for parts to support the single remaining British fleet carrier, the *Ark Royal*. At the time the "Ark" carried 38 aircraft, about one-half the air wing of a U.S. carrier.

12 Phantom FG.1
15 Buccaneer S.2
 4 Gannet AEW.3
 7 Sea King HAS.1

The *Ark Royal* sailed on. The government announced that after 1976 no British warships would be regularly deployed to the Mediterranean, although some would be sent for periodic exercises. (The British left its last bases on Malta by 1979.) In related moves the *Bulwark* was taken out of service in 1976 and laid up in reserve, and the *Hermes* was refitted from March 1971 to August 1973 as an ASW carrier for assignment to NATO operations in the North Atlantic. Thus ended the career of specialized commando ships (i.e., helicopter assault carriers). Upon rejoining the fleet the

The carrier *Hermes* in one of her many configurations. Begun as a CVL during World War II, she was not completed until 1959, after which she operated as a fleet carrier. This shows the *Hermes* in 1974, shortly after her conversion to a commando ship. She has a single Sea King helicopter parked aft on her flight deck. Less than a decade later she would serve in combat as a VSTOL carrier. (Royal Navy)

TABLE 19-1
ROYAL NAVY CARRIERS, 1966

SHIP	DISPLACEMENT*	COMPLETED	FIXED-WING AIRCRAFT +HELICOPTERS
Victorious	30,530/35,500 tons	1941	23 + 8
Eagle	43,000/50,000 tons	1951	34 + 10
Albion	23,300/27,300 tons	1954	— 16
Bulwark	23,300/27,300 tons	1954	— 16
Ark Royal	43,080/50,390 tons	1955	40 + 8
Hermes	23,000/27,800 tons	1959	22 + 8

* Standard/full load displacement.

Hermes carried both Wessex troop helicopters and Sea King ASW helicopters, and participated in both commando and anti-submarine exercises.

Operating in the North and South Atlantic and the Mediterranean, the *Ark Royal* also flew trials with RAF Kestrel Vertical/Short Takeoff and Landing (VSTOL) aircraft in February 1963 and the Harrier VSTOL aircraft in May 1971—harbingers of the future. The carrier finally was decommissioned in December 1978.

The *Hermes* continued as an ASW helicopter ship, and in March 1978, the *Bulwark* was taken in hand for operational service as an ASW helicopter ship. She was recommissioned in February 1979, embarking Sea King troop and ASW helicopters. These two helicopter ships were being retained on an interim basis until new aviation ships could join the fleet.

The Odd Ships

Although aircraft carriers were the capital ships of the U.S. and British navies during the Cold War, a few carriers performed important service in ancillary roles. The British light carrier *Triumph* of 13,350 tons was converted to a heavy repair ship between January 1958 and January 1965. Although in the yard for seven years, the actual conversion took about two and a half years as work periodically was halted because of higher priority projects. As a repair ship the *Triumph* had structures built on her flight deck to house a wood store, acetylene and cement plants, and work spaces. Forward there was a helicopter repair area with a landing space. All but two of the ship's 19 small boats were carried on the former flight deck. The *Triumph*'s hangar deck was converted to an elaborate shop area. She could provide ships alongside with steam, water, electric power, and other services so that they could shut down their own machinery for maintenance or repairs.

In addition to her normal complement of 500 officers and ratings, the *Triumph* could accommodate four fleet maintenance units totaling 285 men and, if required, about 400 additional personnel from ships under repair could be berthed and fed without undue strain. To facilitate maneuvering the ship, a centerline conning position was installed on the flight deck, just aft of the helicopter platform. An armament of four single 40-mm guns was provided.

The *Triumph* arrived at Singapore in late February 1965 for duty as an escort maintenance ship. In that role much of the ship's heavy repair equipment was in a state of preservation. The *Triumph* served with the Far East Fleet from 1965 until that force was disbanded in early 1972, at which time she returned to Portsmouth. She underwent a refit in 1972–1975 but was then laid up until towed off for scrapping in 1981.

The first U.S. aircraft carrier to be fully converted to a specialized role was the USS *Wright*, a 14,500-ton light carrier. The *Wright* and her sister ship *Saipan* had been completed in 1946–1947 and, following operational and training duties, were mothballed in the later 1950s; subsequently reclassified as aircraft transports (AVT). The *Wright* entered the Puget Sound (Washington) Naval Shipyard in May 1962 and was recommissioned as a command ship (CC 2) on May 11, 1963. As such, she and the converted cruiser *Northampton* served as emergency national command posts.[3] Both

The CVL *Triumph*, as converted to a heavy repair ship, supporting four destroyers and frigates at Singapore in 1965. She could provide maintenance for almost all aspects of modern surface warships. Note the deck structures inboard of her island and amidships. A helicopter landing spot is marked on her forward deck. Four heavy-capacity cranes are mounted on the former flight deck. (Royal Navy)

were based on the U.S. East Coast and equipped to provide elaborate command and control facilities to high-ranking commanders, including the President of the United States, in the event of a crisis or conflict.

In her new role the *Wright* was easily identified by five fiberglass masts, 33 to 83 feet tall, that supported electronic antennas, the tallest of which was 114 feet, on her former flight deck. The after portion of the deck was available for helicopters to fly senior officers and their staffs aboard. Below decks were war rooms, conference rooms, special communications spaces, and accommodations for senior officers and their staffs. As a command ship the *Wright* had a ship's company of about 700 officers and enlisted men plus 1,000 men to operate her command and control facilities.

At least on an experimental basis, the *Wright* carried an "unmanned" or drone helicopter, a Kaman QH-43 Huskey used to raise a 10,000-foot-long wire antenna into a vertical position for Very-Low Frequency (VLF) communications from the ship to submarines. The QH-43 drone did carry a qualified pilot, whose function was to monitor the instruments and be ready to release the antenna and land the helicopter in the event of a failure of the antenna winch system. A controller aboard the *Wright* "flew" the helicopter. A UH-2A Seasprite helicopter for utility use was also

embarked. For the remainder of the 1960s either the *Wright* or *Northampton* was usually at sea for two weeks at a time off the Atlantic coast.

The *Saipan* began a similar conversion (to become CC 3) in February 1963, but work was halted a year later when she was about 65 percent complete. Her conversion was cancelled when the Department of Defense decided to operate only two afloat national command posts, and the *Saipan* was completed as a communications relay ship.

The first aircraft carrier to be converted to a communications relay ship was the *Gilbert Islands*, a 10,900-ton escort carrier. The CVE entered the yard in August 1962 and was recommissioned as the USS *Annapolis* (AGMR 1), on March 7, 1964. In that role the ship was a sea-going communications relay station, capable of operating for prolonged periods while under way or at a remote base. Her facilities could augment existing communications systems, replace communications lost to disaster or enemy action, or provide communications for a special operation in a remote area. These services were essentially relay, that is, she provided communications for a commander embarked in another ship or ashore; the AGMRs, unlike the *Wright* and *Northampton*, had no command facilities.

Multiple forms of communications—visual, facsimile, radio-teletype, carrier wave (code), and voice—were installed in the *Annapolis*. In all, the ship had approximately 30 transmitters to provide a frequency coverage from low frequency to ultra-high frequency; power outputs for these transmitters ranged from ten watts to 10,000 watts. There were 60 receivers. Most of the transmitters and receivers were installed on the former hangar deck. The ship's flight deck sprouted five large antenna towers, which, through a system of multicouplers, allowed several transmitters and receivers to share a given antenna. Space was provided for helicopter operations. The *Annapolis* had a crew of about 700 officers and enlisted men, approximately one-third of whom were communications or electronics specialists. As an AGMR she mounted eight 3-inch guns in twin mounts.

With the cancellation of the *Saipan*'s conversion to a command ship the CVL was selected in September 1964 for completion as a communications relay ship. She was recommissioned as the USS *Arlington* (AGMR 2) on August 27, 1966. The *Arlington* was similar in configuration to the *Annapolis* but shared the 30-plus-knot speed of the *Wright* compared to the 19-knot speed of the *Annapolis*. Both of the former light carriers mounted eight 40-mm guns in twin mounts.

Another U.S. carrier employed in a specialized role was the former escort carrier *Croatan*. Since 1958 she had served as a Navy civilian-manned cargo ship and aircraft ferry (T-AKV 43). For three months in early 1965 she operated as a rocket base for the National Aeronautics and Space Administration. (See pages 159–160.) Plans were made to convert the 27,100-ton fleet carrier *Bunker Hill* into an electronics test ship as part of Project Southern Cross, an advanced shipboard communications program. The carrier, severely damaged off Okinawa by kamikazes in May 1945, had been rebuilt and then laid up in mothballs after World War II. In May 1965 she was towed to San Francisco, where her conversion began. However, funding cuts caused a major reduction in the project's scope. As a limited electronics test ship, the *Bunker Hill* was moored in San Diego harbor until 1973 and then scrapped.[4]

During this period consideration was also given to converting an aircraft carrier to a helicopter maintenance ship for the Army. The large number of helicopters operated overseas in the 1960s led to the requirement for a floating repair base. Experience with helicopters in the Korean War and South Vietnam showed that effectiveness and efficiency of repair units were lowered when aircraft maintenance was performed in mud, rain, heat, wind, or blowing sand. Requirements such as guard and mess duties further reduced maintenance unit effectiveness. There was also the problem

The command ship *Wright*, converted from a light carrier, steams off the coast of southern California. The ship was employed as a National Emergency Command Post Afloat (NECPA), complementing airborne command posts to serve the president and senior defense leaders in a national emergency. The ex-cruiser *Northampton* served in this role while conversion of the CVL *Saipan* was begun. (H. I. Bottorff, U.S. Navy)

The communications relay ship *Arlington*, the converted CVL *Saipan*, at sea off Guantanamo Bay, Cuba, in 1967. In the post–World War II era CVLs had a limited role as fleet carriers in the U.S. Navy, but served effectively in the French and Spanish Navies, with two ships providing platforms for the specialized CC/NECPA and AGMR roles. (U.S. Navy)

of maintaining adequate living quarters for personnel, spare parts storage, fresh water, and provisions in overseas areas.

Studies looked at 17 ship types and concluded that an *Essex*-class carrier would best suit the Army's needs. Escort carriers were also considered, and at one point there was strong support for employing the light carrier *Langley*, which the French had just returned, as a helicopter maintenance ship. The final analysis determined that a seaplane tender was the most economically feasible ship, although an aircraft carrier would provide better working, living, and storage spaces. The

The CVE *Gilbert Islands*, seen shortly after her conversion to a communications relay ship and renamed *Annapolis*. She and the AGMR *Arlington* (ex-CVL *Saipan*) were named for the sites of major U.S. Navy radio stations. The AGMR configurations further demonstrated the versatility of aircraft carriers. Unlike the NECPA ships, the AGMRs did not have command and control facilities. (U.S. Navy)

9,090-ton seaplane tender *Albemarle* was plucked from the mothball fleet, and in 1964 she was converted to a helicopter repair ship and placed in service as the *Corpus Christi Bay* (T-ARVH 1). With a civilian operating crew and a 300-man Army maintenance unit, she was assigned to support U.S. Army aviation in the Vietnam conflict.[5]

Straight Up and Down

In May 1961 the British Admiralty proposed a new major fleet unit to the Ministry of Defence—the "escort cruiser."[6] The proposed ship was to (1) operate ASW helicopters, enabling fleet carriers to operate more fixed-wing aircraft in their place, (2) carry surface-to-air missiles for fleet defense, and (3) provide major command facilities, replacing light cruisers that were being retired. Initially a class of four escort cruisers was proposed with a standard displacement of some 13,500 tons. Each ship was to operate up to nine Sea King helicopters and would carry the Seaslug air-defense missile. Manning was estimated at about 900 men per ship. The four ships were to join the fleet in 1968–1969.

Then, as too often occurred, budget considerations forced a reduction in ship size and capabilities. The design was reduced to a standard displacement of 10,000 tons; each ship would carry only four helicopters, with a smaller missile system and reduced crew. And the completion period was stretched out to 1969–1971. The escort cruiser program survived the CVA.01's cancellation in 1966, but the loss of the large carrier meant that the cruiser's design had to be recast in 1967 to provide a greater helicopter capability. A 12,500-ton design—still to operate nine Sea Kings—was developed, but the ship now began to look like a carrier, with a full hangar deck, two elevators, and a large, starboard-side island structure. The standard displacement of some design options increased to 17,500 tons, the size of a light carrier (CVL). Studies continued. A major develop-ment in this non-carrier program occurred in 1969 when the Minister for the Navy, Dr. David Owen, publicly mentioned the possibility of RAF Harriers operating from both commando ships and the new cruisers.[7]

After World War II the British and U.S. Navies explored Vertical Takeoff and Landing (VTOL) aircraft for use aboard small ships. In the spring of 1946 the Fairey company began investigation of VTOL fighters, leading to the delta-wing Fairey Delta, a turbojet aircraft. Scale models and then, beginning in 1951, a manned prototype flew. In the United States, the Convair XFY-1 and Lockheed XFV-1, both turboprop-powered "tail sitters," flew in 1954 as prototypes for shipboard VTOL aircraft. None of these aircraft entered production.

One other naval VSTOL fighter was attempted in the United States, the North American/Rockwell XFV-12A.[8] This was a thrust-augmented-wing prototype of a supersonic fighter/attack aircraft. The aircraft had a single turbojet engine for Mach 2 performance. Ground testing began in July 1977 and suspended tether trials the following year. But the latter trials and wind tunnel tests demonstrated that the concept was impractical and the project was abandoned without the single prototype having flown.

Meanwhile, in Britain the Hawker firm produced the P.1127 Vertical/Short Takeoff and Landing (VSTOL) aircraft for the Royal Air Force, which designated it the Kestrel FGA.1. The aircraft was based on a French engine concept and was funded by both Britain and the United States. The first P.1127 flew on October 21, 1960, and limited carrier trials of the aircraft were conducted on the *Ark Royal* in February 1963. Twelve landings and takeoffs were made while the ship was under way; half of the flights were made in the vertical takeoff mode.

Although these tests as well as operations aboard the *Bulwark* in 1966 proved that the Kestrel could operate from carriers, the Royal Navy did not feel that VSTOL aircraft had been developed to the point that they offered significant advantages over conventional, fixed-wing aircraft. Catapults would still be required to launch the VSTOL aircraft because takeoff with a combat load would not be possible in the vertical mode; also, the downward vector of the exhausts would cause thermal problems during catapult launches and other operations. The RAF accepted the Kestrel as a ground-support fighter, but production of an improved P.1154 VSTOL fighter—a proposed Mach 1.5 aircraft in response to a NATO requirement—was cancelled in 1965.

Nine Kestrel GR.1s were built, and following British evaluation, six were shipped to the United States in early 1966 and assigned the U.S. designation XV-6A.[9] Flown by U.S. pilots, they made a series of landings and takeoffs on the carrier *Independence* in May 1966. Trials also were conducted aboard the amphibious ship *Raleigh*. While the flights were successful, the U.S. armed services did not recommend adoption of the

A Hawker P.1127—given the military designation Kestrel FGA.1—lands aboard the carrier *Ark Royal* during shipboard trials in February 1963. A planeguard Whirlwind helicopter hovers nearby. The Kestrel was also evaluated by the U.S. military services with the designation XV-6A, with shipboard trials on the carrier *Independence*. The Kestrel was the forerunner to the highly successful Harrier series of VSTOL aircraft. (Royal Navy)

The *Invincible*-class VSTOL carriers had a lengthy and complex development period. But they emerged as true aircraft carriers, albeit small, with a full-length flight deck and a hangar deck, connected by two centerline elevators. Their massive island structure features two large funnels for their gas turbine exhaust. A Sea Dart surface-to-air missile launcher is "notched" into the forward flight deck. The deck letter "N" is assigned to the *Invincible*. (Imperial War Museum)

VSTOL fighter because of inferior performance in comparison with conventional aircraft, the ability of existing carrier aircraft to operate from small airfields ashore fitted with catapults and arresting gear, and the development of heavily armed helicopters for operations in remote areas.

The RAF initiated procurement of the Harrier GR.1, a P.1127 derivative with a level-flight speed of Mach 0.98. The GR.1 could be fitted with two 30-mm gun pods or up to five 1,000-pound bombs or equivalent loads of drop tanks and rockets in the short takeoff mode. The first RAF Harrier flew on August 31, 1966, six months after cancellation of the CVA.01; the RAF took delivery of its first Harrier GR.1 in April 1969.

Dr. Owen's statement that RAF Harriers might operate from the new ASW cruiser led Hawker Siddeley to immediately propose a naval variant of the Harrier—the Sea Harrier. This proposal was not taken up at the time. However, by 1970–1971 the cruiser-carrier studies had evolved into a ship of 18,750 tons standard displacement. Because of the decision to employ gas turbines (i.e., turbojet engines) rather than steam

turbines in the ship, considerable space was lost to air intakes and exhausts, providing space for only ten helicopters in a CVL-size ship. The ships were referred to in this period as "through-deck cruisers," as the Admiralty eschewed the term "carrier" for political reasons. Some journalists promptly dubbed the concept the "Harrier carrier."

The lead ship—to be named *Invincible*—was ordered from the Vickers yard at Barrow-in-Furness on April 17, 1973. By that time the Admiralty had established a requirement for ship-based Harriers, but procurement could not be pursued because of the economic crisis that followed the Yom Kippur War (October 1973) when Arab states raised oil prices. The Sea Harrier, distinguished by a raised cockpit and corrosion-resistant structure, flew for the first time on August 20, 1978, and deliveries to the FAA began in June 1979. Thirty-four FRS.1 aircraft were ordered, enough for a transition-conversion unit and three fleet squadrons.[10] At the time there was significant debate over whether the RAF also should provide Harriers for the carriers or control all Harriers, whether flown by RAF or Navy pilots.[11]

Without the Sea Harrier the FAA would have become an all-helicopter force, hence, in the words of historian Owen Thetford, the aircraft "was of paramount historical importance." The Sea Harrier FRS.1, shown here in flight with outrigger wheels raised, and on a ski-jump at the Royal Aircraft Establishment with landing gear lowered, was a remarkable aircraft. Maximum speed was 737 m.p.h. with a radius of 290 miles in the strike role and 460 miles in the interceptor role. Two 30-mm detachable cannon pods were fitted under the fuselage with a maximum weapons load of 8,000 pounds of guns, bombs, and missiles being carried, albeit to shorter ranges. The aircraft's wings did not fold; note the tail radar warning housing. (British Aerospace)

The *Invincible* was commissioned as an "ASW carrier" on July 11, 1980, a year and a half after the last fleet carrier, HMS *Ark Royal*, was paid off. By that time two similar ASW carriers were on order from Swan Hunter at Wallsend-on-Tyne. The *Invincible* had a standard displacement of 16,000 tons and was 19,500 tons fully loaded with an overall length of 677¾ feet. Propulsion was provided by four gas turbines that gave the ship a maximum speed of 28 knots. Armament, as built, consisted of a twin-rail Sea Dart surface-to-air launcher—no guns. (Later rapid-fire guns were installed for defense against cruise missiles.)

Early studies had indicated that a catapult would be necessary to launch a loaded Sea Harrier. But the ship was too small and the lack of steam propulsion made such a device too difficult. Instead, the ship would have a seven-degree "ski-jump" at the bow. The ski-jump was conceived in 1969 by Lieutenant Commander Douglas R. Taylor and, independently, by Ralph Hooper at Hawker Siddeley. The firm and, subsequently, the Ministry of Defence supported the idea, and flying trials at the Royal Aircraft Establishment Bedford began in 1977. The trials began with a ramp angle of six degrees, which eventually increased to 20 degrees. The trials demonstrated that at all angles a loaded Harrier could launch in a much shorter distance than a deck run and achieve altitude faster. Further, the ski-jump permitted launches without wind over the deck.[12]

The *Invincible* was completed with a seven-degree ramp; her two sister ships would be provided ski-jumps of nine degrees. The older *Hermes* was taken into the yard and provided with a 12-degree ski-jump.

By mid-1982 the *Invincible* was ready for commissioning and the second ship, the *Illustrious*, had been launched. Again faced with budget problems, the government decided that only two VSTOL carriers would be retained. The *Hermes*, modified to operate Sea Harriers as well as helicopters, would be sold. The new *Invincible* would be sold to Australia, leaving the two later ASW carriers in the Royal Navy. (The older ASW-commando carrier *Bulwark* had been taken out of service in 1981.)

These plans became irrelevant on April 2, 1982, when Argentine troops stormed ashore in the Falkland Islands in the South Atlantic.

20 CARRIER WAR IN THE SOUTH ATLANTIC

Two small VSTOL carriers—the veteran HMS *Hermes* and the brand-new HMS *Invincible*—enabled British forces to recapture the Falkland and South Georgia Islands. When the Falklands conflict began the British government was in the process of reducing its carrier force in favor of land-based aviation. But the Royal Air Force was unable to provide effective air operations in the conflict. Here the *Hermes* has Sea King helicopters parked forward, adjacent to the ship's ski-jump; a U.S. Navy SH-2 LAMPS I helicopter hovers over the ship. (Royal Navy)

The Falkland Islands have long been claimed by Argentina, whose officials refer to the islands as the Malvinas. The Falklands lay some 350 n.miles east of Argentina and almost 7,000 n.miles southwest of Britain.[1] Ownership of the island of South Georgia, almost 700 n.miles east of the Falklands, also was disputed. In late 1981 the Argentine government made the decision to recover the Malvinas, which had a polulation of about 3,000.

Dr. Robert Scheina, an authority on South American armed forces, wrote,

The underlying factor was the frustration of decades of fruitless negotiations with the British.

The more immediate factors were the need of the junta to defuse domestic pressures caused by a poor economy; [Admiral] Jorge Anaya's desire to be the individual responsible for the recovery of the islands; and the desire of the military junta to leave a legacy.[2]

The naval ice patrol-intelligence ship *Endurance*, which embarked two light helicopters and a detachment of Royal Marines, "defended" these British possessions.[3] As tension between Britain and Argentina increased in late March 1982, two British nuclear-propelled attack submarines (SSN) were deployed to the South Atlantic.

The Argentine Navy at the time could muster an aircraft carrier, a light cruiser, seven destroyers (some armed with Exocet anti-ship missiles), three frigates (with Exocet), and a variety of lesser ships, plus two new, German-built Type 209 submarines and a war-built U.S. submarine of the GUPPY configuration.[4]

The carrier was the *25 de Mayo*, the last of the Royal Navy *Colossus*-class CVLs. Completed as HMS *Venerable* in 1945, she had served in the Netherlands Navy as the *Karel Doorman* from 1948 to 1968. She was heavily damaged by an engine room fire in April 1968 during a refit and was placed in reserve pending disposal. Instead, she was sold to Argentina in October and repaired in Rotterdam, where she was fitted with the boilers and turbines from the unfinished British CVL *Leviathan*. After the extensive refit, in 1969 she was commissioned in the Argentine Navy as the *25 de Mayo*.[5]

In early 1982 she was assigned 20 aircraft:

  5 Super Étendard fighter-bombers
10 A-4Q Skyhawk fighter-bombers
  5 S-2A Tracker ASW aircraft

The Super Étendards, however, could not operate from the carrier because of the limitations of her single catapult and the ship's maximum speed of 20 knots. In the coming conflict the Super Étendards operated from the Rio Grande airfield at Tierra del Fuego at the bottom of the South American continent.

The French-built Super Étendards had entered service with the 2nd Naval Air Fighter-Attack Squadron late in 1981, and five of an order for 14 aircraft were operational. Their pilots had limited flight time in the aircraft, which were fitted to carry the French-produced Exocet anti-ship missile. When the war began, only five air-launched missiles had been delivered with the full consignment due to be delivered by September 1982.[6] The French-developed Exocet missile had a range of some 25 miles when fired from a ship and more than 30 miles when launched from an aircraft. It was a sea-skimming missile with a 364-pound high-explosive warhead. Immediately the Argentine government sought to acquire additional Exocet missiles, both overtly and covertly.[7]

The Argentine naval air arm also had two overage SP-2E Neptune reconnaissance aircraft and a variety of trainers, transports, and helicopters. The Argentine Air Force had another 46 A-4B/C Skyhawk fighter-bombers plus 11 Mirage III fighters, 34 Daggers (the Israel-built derivatives of the Mirage V), 6 Canberra Mk 62 light bombers, 25 Pucará ground attack aircraft, a large force of transports and training aircraft, and—significantly—two KC-130 Hercules tankers.[8] The combined air forces thus possessed a potent capability. However, the high-performance fighter aircraft were severely limited by flying from mainland bases. For example, the Dagger was a Mach 2 aircraft but needed drop tanks to operate over the Falklands and could not achieve Mach 1 because of their drag.

British naval historian Eric Grove observed,

> The stage was being set for the most remarkable and unexpected naval event of the postwar era, the Falklands Island War of 1982. In this conflict the Royal Navy would suffer its worst warship losses of the post-1945 period and score its greatest success in projecting power over thousands of miles to the other side of the world.[9]

On April 2, 1982, several hundred Argentine marines and commandos came ashore at several points near Port Stanley, capital of the Falklands, from an offshore task force, including the carrier *25 de Mayo* with 1,500 soldiers embarked. The Argentine troops were carried ashore by helicopters, landing craft, and amphibious tractors. The 69 Royal Marines and 11 Navy personnel at Port Stanley, after initially resisting the invasion, were ordered by the governor to surrender to halt further bloodshed.

The next day there was a major Argentine troop landing on South Georgia Island, 780 miles to the east of the Falklands. There the situation was more complex.

On March 19, 1982, Argentina had landed 42 scrap metal salvagers on South Georgia Island who raised the Argentine flag. The next day, HMS *Endurance* was dispatched from Stanley with her 14-man Royal Marine detachment plus nine marines from the Stanley garrison. These 23 troops were landed on South Georgia on March 23. Three days later 100 Argentine troops arrived by ship, purportedly to protect the salvagers.

Following the large-scale landings in the Falklands, additional Argentine forces were landed on South Georgia on April 3. The small Royal Marine detachment put up a brief but fierce resistance. They inflicted several casualties on the enemy, shot down a Puma helicopter carrying Argentine troops, damaged another helicopter, and inflicted major casualties on a corvette with anti-tank weapons, machine guns, and sniper fire. Then they, too, surrendered.

While diplomatic efforts were undertaken by the British government to expel the Argentines, on April 12 the British imposed a maritime exclusion zone 200 miles around the Falklands against Argentine naval ships. On the 23rd the British warned that any approach by Argentine forces that could threaten to interfere with the mission of British forces in the South Atlantic would be "dealt with appropriately."

British Options

The closest base available to the British for South Atlantic operations was the spartan airfield—a single 3,000-foot runway—on Ascension Island, just south of the African "bulge," 3,700 n.miles from Britain and just over 3,000 n.miles from the Falklands. Two British nuclear-propelled attack submarines were immediately dispatched to the Falklands. On April 2, the day of the Falklands invasion, Rear Admiral John (Sandy) Woodward led a force south from Gibraltar, consisting of five destroyers and two frigates. In Portsmouth, the carriers *Hermes* and *Invincible* were hastily made ready for war.

Rear Admiral Woodward, a submarine specialist, proved an excellent choice to command Operation Corporate, the code name for retaking the Falklands. A few weeks earlier, in an exercise in the Arabian Sea, Woodward had commanded a destroyer, three frigates, and three replenishment ships that were to make a simulated attack against a U.S. carrier battle group. The "starting distance" was 200 n.miles from the USS *Coral Sea*. The carrier's aircraft sighted Woodward's ships as the exercise began. Still, the audacious admiral was

able to close to within *11 miles* of the carrier in a destroyer to simulate firing four Exocet missiles. Woodward wrote of two lessons he learned from the exercise:

> The first was to beware of becoming overengrossed in one area of operations at the risk of ignoring another. The second was that, in a limited war, in perfect weather, under the cover of darkness, one fairly old destroyer or cruiser, or whatever, *is* capable of getting right up to within eleven miles of a modern strike carrier in a full battle group.[10]

In mid-1982 the Royal Navy had three Vertical/Short Takeoff and Landing (VSTOL) carriers: The venerable *Hermes* (completed in 1959), the *Invincible* (1980), and the new *Illustrious* (1982).[11] Another VSTOL carrier, the *Ark Royal*, was under construction. In February 1982 the British and Australian governments had agreed to sale of the *Invincible* to replace HMAS *Melbourne* and the *Hermes* was scheduled for disposal.

The *Hermes* and *Invincible* sailed from Portsmouth on April 5, with 1,500 Royal Marines embarked in addition to their aircraft. In "peacetime" the two VSTOL carriers normally embarked 5 Sea Harriers and 10 Sea King ASW helicopters. As they put to sea the *Hermes* carried 12 Sea Harriers and 9 Sea Kings; the *Invincible* had 8 Sea Harriers and 11 Sea Kings—a total of 20 fixed-wing aircraft and 20 helicopters—Britain's entire carrier-based air arm.[12]

The Royal Air Force was directed to augment the carrier force with a squadron of Harrier GR.3 aircraft, to be transported south on the container ship *Atlantic Conveyor*. However, the need for Harrier modifications and training caused the RAF aircraft to miss the sailing date. The GR.3 did not have anti-corrosion features or provisions for Sidewinder missiles, and its inertial platform (for leveling and direction) was not suitable for alignment on a moving flight deck.[13]

Ten of these RAF aircraft made a 4,600-mile flight from Britain to Ascension Island with several in-flight refuelings from tanker aircraft. Six FAA Sea Harriers made the flight to Ascension later in the month and four more RAF Harriers made the flight in early June (see table 20-1).

As the two carriers steamed south, the French sent aircraft to overfly the task force carrying Exocet missiles to enable the British ships to practice detecting radar emissions from the launching aircraft and the missile. More British ships, including the large liners *Queen Elizabeth II* and *Canberra* pressed into service as troop ships, were dispatched as they became available. En route to the Falklands the carriers and accompanying amphibious and auxiliary ships transferred men and equipment, using the Sea King and Wessex helicopters embarked in the carriers and other ships. Eventually 110 British ships were involved in retaking the Falklands: 5 nuclear and 1 diesel-electric submarine, 2 VSTOL carriers, 36 other warships, 22 naval fleet auxiliaries, and 45 merchant ships with all-volunteer civilian crews.

As the ships steamed south and once in the operational area, men and equipment were frequently shuffled between the ships. Disaster struck on May 19 when Sea Kings were transferring Special Air Service (SAS)

commandos from the *Hermes* to the amphibious ship *Intrepid*. A large sea bird was sucked into a Sea King's engines and the overloaded helicopter plunged into the water. Nine survivors were pulled from the water in various stages of shock and hypothermia; 22 other men died—2 aircrew, 18 from the SAS, a soldier from Royal Signals, and an RAF officer.

The first assault of the British campaign was against remote South Georgia, too far from Argentina for land-based aircraft to give support to the small Argentine garrison. The first action took place off South Georgia on April 25 when helicopters from frigates attacked the Argentine GUPPY submarine *Santa Fé* on the surface, damaging her and forcing her to seek refuge in Grytviken Harbor, where she sank.[14] The same day Royal Marines and special forces recaptured South

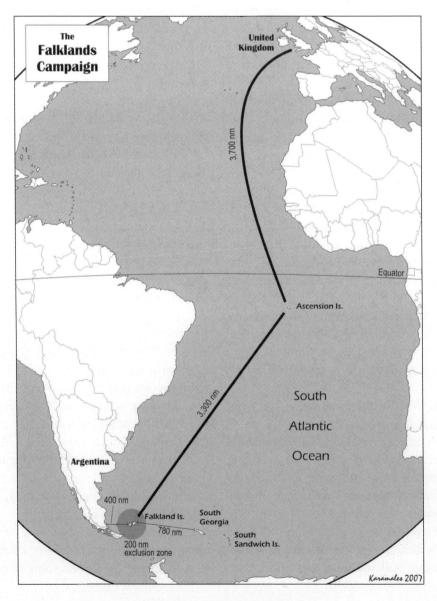

Georgia. The island provided a forward anchorage for repair and support ships.

The air war began on May 1 when a single RAF Vulcan bomber flying from Ascension Island (with five in-flight refuelings en route) attacked the airstrip at Port Stanley before dawn. The plane released 21 1,000-pound bombs, only one of which struck the runway.[15] A raid by carrier-based Sea Harriers followed the Vulcan. Nine Sea Harriers struck the runway at Port Stanley, and three struck a small strip at Goose Green at dawn. Cluster bombs destroyed three Argentine Pucara light attack aircraft at the latter field. This was the first combat for Harrier-type aircraft.

Later in the day three British warships closed with the main island to carry out shore bombardment. Sea Harriers chased away a light attack aircraft that threatened the ships. These air and surface strikes were intended to give the impression of an attempted landing to draw out the Argentine Navy and Air Force.

The Argentine plane that approached the British ships flew from a Falklands airstrip. From bases in Argentina a flight of Air Force Dagger fighters approached but refused to engage the Sea Harriers at low altitude, where the slower VSTOL aircraft had an advantage in maneuverability and, because of the Dagger drop tanks, similar maximum speeds. There was a second approach in the afternoon. Attack aircraft also came out from the Argentine mainland and succeeded in damaging a British frigate with cannon fire. In re-turn, shipboard controllers directed Sea Harriers in shooting down two Daggers and a Canberra bomber; another Dagger was damaged and, when landing at Port Stanley, was shot down by *Argentine* anti-aircraft fire.

The Argentines realized their vulnerability to the Sea Harrier. Significantly, they failed to base their high-performance aircraft at Port Stanley, in part because of the threat of carrier air strikes, thus reducing the effectiveness and time over target as their planes flew a round-trip of approximately 800 miles from their mainland bases.

Meanwhile, by April 27 the Argentine Navy had formed its surface forces into four task groups to counter British assaults against either the Falklands or the Argentina mainland. The major groups were TG 79.3, consisting of the 6-inch gun cruiser *General Belgrano* (ex-USS *Phoenix*) and two ex-U.S. destroyers, the latter armed with Exocets, and TG 79.4, comprised of the carrier *25 de Mayo* and two modern, British-built missile destroyers. Believing that the British shore bombardment was the harbinger of an immediate landing at Port Stanley, the *25 de Mayo* group closed and prepared for an air attack. The morning of May 2 dawned clear and calm and the wind-over-deck was insufficient for the carrier to launch bomb-laden Skyhawks. The carrier withdrew. Also that morning, an attack by two of the Argentine Navy's Super Étendards carrying Exocet missiles—flying from the Rio Grande naval air base in Tierra del Fuego—was aborted when they

The VSTOL carrier *Hermes* departed from Portsmouth for the South Atlantic on April 5, 1982. The smaller *Invincible* sailed with her. At the time they were the Royal Navy's only operational aircraft carriers. Troops and much of her crew are assembled on the *Hermes*'s flight deck. Crowds of well-wishers lined the jetty as the ships departed on their odyssey to the South Atlantic. (Imperial War Museum)

missed their in-flight refueling rendezvous with an Air Force KC-130 Hercules tanker.

Less fortunate was the cruiser *Belgrano*. On the 30th the British nuclear submarine *Conqueror* had detected the *Belgrano* group refueling from a tanker. The SSN trailed the cruiser, and with approval from Rear Admiral Woodward, on the afternoon of May 2 the *Conqueror* closed for an attack. Woodward, in view of his success against the USS *Coral Sea*, understood fully the threat of surface ships armed with Exocet missiles. The *Conqueror* fired a spread of three torpedoes at the cruiser. Two scored hits, and the 44-year-old ship quickly rolled over and sank. The third torpedo struck a nearby destroyer but failed to explode. One of the destroyers ineffectively dropped depth charges and then both fled the area. Of the *Belgrano*'s crew of some 1,200 men, 321 were lost in the sinking and during the one to two days that some of the survivors were in rafts in the wintry water.

Sinking the *General Belgrano* caused the Argentine Navy to recall its other surface warships, including the *25 de Mayo* task force, to coastal waters.[16] The submarine threat remained, and the diesel-electric submarine *San Luis* still threatened the British forces. Destroyer and frigate helicopters, occasionally joined by carrier-based Sea Kings, pursued the submarine relentlessly. The submarine commander claimed to have had an opportunity to attack a British carrier, but faulty wiring in his fire control panel made his torpedoes ineffective. The British expended scores of ASW torpedoes and depth charges, also without effect.

Rather, the principal threats to British forces were aircraft and, especially, the five air-launched Exocet missiles. On the morning of May 4 the carriers were steaming some 100 miles off Port Stanley. An Argentine Navy SP-2E Neptune intercepted the radar emissions of three British destroyers on radar picket stations. In response, two of the Navy's Super Étendard aircraft, armed with Exocets were scrambled from Rio Grande airfield to attack, their principal target being the two British carriers. The Étendards approached the warships at low level to avoid radar detection, popping up to 120 feet to gain radar lock-on of the targets and launch missiles. Still, a destroyer was able to detect the aircraft's radar emissions and briefly "painted" the aircraft with her radar. Chaff was fired to distract the two approaching missiles. Another destroyer, the 3,500-ton *Sheffield*, with her electronic detection system degraded because she was using her satellite communications, was struck on the starboard side by an Exocet. The missile penetrated into the ship's engineering spaces. The 364-pound warhead failed to detonate, but the ensuing fire was fed by unburnt missile propellant and flammable material within the ship. The flames were quickly out of control. The second Exocet narrowly missed a frigate and, decoyed by chaff, crashed into the sea.

The *Sheffield*, burning out of control, was abandoned because of the fears of a magazine explosion and of submarine attack. She lost 20 men with a further 24 injured. (Later her burnt-out hulk was taken in tow, but she sank in heavy seas on May 10.)

The cross-decking of men, arms, and supplies was a continuous activity in the British task force during Operation Corporate. Here Sea King helicopters move supplies between an amphibious ship and the carrier *Hermes*. Almost 200 FAA, RAF, and Army helicopters participated in the British effort to capture the Falklands. (Imperial War Museum)

Admiral Woodward knew that if an Exocet missile hit and put out of action one of his two carriers the entire plan to retake the Falklands would have to be postponed indefinitely. Accordingly, he had his ships stand farther offshore, limiting the Sea Harriers to relatively ineffective high-level bombing, as the more effective, low-level strikes burned too much fuel. His destroyers and frigates closed with the Falklands at night to bombard the Argentines with their 4.5-inch guns. And, Sea Kings periodically landed special forces on the islands for reconnaissance and sabotage operations.

The Sea Harriers continued their attacks against Argentine positions in the Falklands. On May 4 a second RAF Vulcan mission was flown from Ascension; the aircraft required in-flight refueling multiple times to complete the mission. This plane launched a single Shrike anti-radar missile at the large AN/TPS-43 radar at Port Stanley airfield. The missile damaged the radar's antenna but did not destroy it. Flying from Ascension Island, the RAF undertook a total of five strike missions by Vulcan strategic bomber aircraft: three single-plane sorties with each Vulcan carrying 21 1,000-pound bombs attacked Port Stanley airfield and two single plane sorties with anti-radar missiles attacked Argentine radar installations.[17] According to the official U.S. Navy report on the lessons of the Falklands, the Vulcan missions "had virtually no impact on either the Argentine surveillance radars or on Port Stanley Airfield. Both the airfield and surveillance radar installation remained operating until the last day of the war."[18]

On the ninth Sea Harriers attacked the Argentine intelligence ship *Narwal*. One crewman was killed, and 25 were taken prisoner by British surface ships before she sank.

Meanwhile, Whitehall struggled with the Exocet problem, the situation being exacerbated after the devastation of the *Sheffield*. In several European capitals British operatives ensured that the Argentines could not purchase additional missiles, either overtly or covertly.

Proposals to destroy the five Super Étendards and three remaining air-launched Exocets included bombing with RAF Vulcans or carrier-launched Harriers or a major commando raid by the SAS in a combined air-submarine operation or a landing by C-130 Hercules on the Rio Grande runway in an assault inspired by the Israeli raid on Entebbe, Uganda, in 1976.[19] Finally, the decision was made to fly in an SAS team in a Sea King

HC.4 flying at near maximum range from the carrier *Invincible*.

This was Operation Mikado: The Royal Navy helicopter from No. 846 Squadron would drop the SAS team near Rio Grande, then fly into nearby Chile and intentionally crash land. The three-man crew would then claim that they had become lost through a navigation error. The nine-man SAS team would destroy the Argentine aircraft or missiles or actually kill the pilots in an attack on the officers' mess at meal time. Then they, too, would cross into neutral Chile.

On May 17 the *Invincible*, escorted by the missile frigate *Brilliant*, made a high-speed run toward Tierra del Fuego and launched the heavily laden Sea King HC.4 late that night. As the helicopter approved the objective its radar warning receiver detected a lock-on by hostile radar. Then a flare was observed some distance away. The helicopter touched down, and as the SAS gear was being unloaded, another flare was sighted. The SAS captain in charge made the decision to abort the mission.

The Sea King had insufficient fuel to fly the 500 miles back to the *Invincible*. Accordingly, the Sea King flew into nearby Chile, unloaded the commandos in a remote area, and then flew on to carry out the pre-planned crash. All 12 men aboard the helicopter survived the operation.

Almost immediately another effort was initiated to carry out Operation Mikado. This time two C-130 Hercules transports would carry an SAS raiding party to attack Rio Grande. But that effort was scrubbed as events, including the sighting of an Argentine destroyer apparently on radar picket duty off the coast of Tierra del Fuego, rapidly occurred in the South Atlantic.

In a more successful SAS operation, on the night of May 14–15, under cover of a naval bombardment, Sea King helicopters from the carrier *Hermes* landed 48 SAS commandos on Pebble Island in the Falklands. Three nights earlier an SAS recon squad had gone ashore by helicopter to identify targets. The SAS raiders now destroyed 11 Argentine aircraft, an ammunition dump, and a radar installation. All departed safely by helicopter after the attack.

Land the Landing Force

The British finally assembled sufficient troops—two full brigades were shipped from Britain—and amphibious shipping to undertake the recapture of the Falklands. On May 20 British troops landed at four points around

San Carlos, on Falkland Sound, which separates the main Falkland islands. Troops were landed in small craft and helicopters carried their heavy weapons and supplies as Sea Harriers maintained combat air patrol over the large assault force. The landing took the Argentine high command by surprise as they had expected an assault on Port Stanley, the capital and principal city, on the other side of East Falkland Island.

The next day, May 21, waves of Argentine aircraft began attacking the invasion force. Anti-aircraft gunfire and missiles filled the skies as the Argentine Skyhawks swooped down to mast height in their attacks. Indeed, some bombs were released too low to arm and embedded themselves in the destroyer *Antrim* and frigate *Argonaut*. Bombs sank the frigate *Ardent*. Other ships were damaged. Gunfire and Sea Harriers shot down 15 Argentine aircraft. The British foothold on the main island was secure.

The attacks continued. On the 23rd another frigate was damaged and an unexploded bomb penetrated the frigate *Antelope*. The following day as demolition experts attempted to disarm the bomb it detonated and the ship sank. In return, six Daggers and one Skyhawk were shot down.

The scene of the air attacks shifted offshore on May 25. Two Super Étendards launched Exocets at a radar target that their pilots believed was a British carrier. While the warships were able to launch chaff to decoy the missile, the large target ship—the container ship *Atlantic Conveyor*—had neither electronic countermeasures nor chaff. She had arrived near the carrier force in mid-May carrying 8 Sea Harriers, 6 RAF Harrier GR.3s, 4 large Chinook cargo helicopters, and 8 other helicopters plus considerable matériel. The 14 Harriers were flown off to the carriers, and one Chinook and one Wessex were flown ashore.

Both Exocets struck the *Atlantic Conveyor*, igniting massive fires and sinking the ship. The loss of the three Chinooks as well as six Wessex helicopters and a Lynx with the ship would be critical to the ground forces as the helicopters were considered vital to the advance of the British troops.[20] After the loss the carriers *Hermes* and *Invincible* each embarked a Lynx helicopter that, when an air attack was imminent, took off carrying decoys to lure Exocet missiles away from the carriers.

On the 28th two Sea Harriers shot down an Argentine C-130 Hercules employed in the surveillance role. Other C-130s and Electra transports flying from the mainland managed to sneak into the Port Stanley airfield delivering munitions until the British captured the airfield.

Again, on May 30, two Super Étendards and four A-4C Skyhawks sought out the British carrier force, one of the former carrying the fifth and last air-launched Exocet missile. Despite the claims of surviving pilots the British ships suffered no damage. Two Skyhawks were shot down. Another Exocet fired from a land launcher struck a British destroyer, inflicting major damage.[21] Thus the launch of seven Exocets—five from aircraft and two from land—sank a destroyer and a large cargo ship/aircraft transport, and damaged another destroyer. It was a high launch-to-kill ratio.

Table 20-1
HARRIER DEPLOYMENTS TO THE FALKLANDS

TRANSIT METHOD	SEA HARRIER	HARRIER GR.3
Embarked in HMS *Hermes*	12	—
Embarked in HMS *Invincible*	8	—
Flown from Britain to Ascension Island		
directly to carriers	—	4
via *Atlantic Conveyor* to 52°S and flown to carriers	8	6
via *Contender Bezant* to 52°S and flown to Port Stanley	—	4
Totals	28	14

The VSTOL carrier *Hermes*, looking weathered, in the South Atlantic during the Falklands conflict. Her flight deck is crowded with Sea Harriers of No. 800 and No. 899 Squadrons, and Harrier GR.3s of RAF No. 1 Squadron. The Lynx helicopter at her stern is ready to become airborne to provide electronic countermeasures in the event of a missile attack. A replenishment ship steams nearby. (Imperial War Museum)

On June 7 Royal Marines captured Mount Low, which overlooked the Stanley airfield. That day, as British troops neared Port Stanley, Skyhawks and Daggers again attacked the landing ships. Two landing ships were hit and set on fire; one had to be scuttled. There was heavy loss of life. The final British assault, against Port Stanley, began on June 14. That evening the Argentine commander in the Falklands surrendered.

Carriers Triumphant . . . Again

The availability of two VSTOL carriers enabled the British to mount Operation Corporate. Without those ships the British had absolutely no possibility of retaking the islands. Naval Harriers and RAF Harrier GR.3 aircraft flown from Ascension and carried out in the merchant ships *Atlantic Conveyor* and *Contender Bezant* replenished the carriers' small complements of Sea Harriers. In all, 28 Sea Harriers and 14 RAF Harriers were eventually deployed to the South Atlantic.

The four RAF Harriers that flew to the carriers directly from Ascension had a nine-hour flight with multiple in-flight refuelings. The naval Sea Harriers flew more than 1,100 combat air patrol missions and 90 attack missions; the RAF planes flew 125 ground-attack and tactical reconnaissance missions (with camera pods) from carriers and from airstrips ashore. The official British record states, "These aircraft were a major success, showing themselves to be flexible, robust, reliable and effective. . . . There was 95% availability at the beginning of each day and 99% of all planned missions were flown."[22]

In the ground-attack and anti-shipping role the two types of Harriers delivered fewer than 200 "iron" bombs (up to three 1,000-pound bombs per sortie) and four laser-guided bombs. These inflicted relatively little damage but had a great psychological impact on both Argentine and, after their landings, British troops.

The Sea Harrier demonstrated that it was a match for Argentine aircraft, scoring 20 confirmed and 3 probable kills against fixed-wing aircraft. Of those, 16 kills and 1 probable were with AIM-9L Sidewinder missiles; the others with 30-mm cannon fire.

Six Sea Harriers were lost: two to enemy action—one to ground fire and one to a Roland surface-to-air missile—four were lost operationally as one aircraft

FAA and RAF Harriers were, in many respect, the heroes of the Falklands War. The container ship *Atlantic Conveyor* conveyed Harriers and helicopters to the British task force. As the ship approached the war zone a Sea Harrier (forward) was kept armed, manned, and ready to take off should the ship be approached by Argentine aircraft. RAF Harriers were maintained mostly by naval personnel, as this GR.3, armed with laser-guided bombs, on the *Hermes*. (British Aerospace; Imperial War Museum)

slid off a flight deck, one struck the sea after takeoff, and two simply disappeared, probably colliding in flight. Four pilots were lost, but only one, Lieutenant-Commander Nick Taylor, to enemy fire. No Harriers were lost in air-to-air combat. Three RAF GR.3 aircraft were lost to Argentine ground fire, including one to a Blowpipe missile; their pilots survived. Thus, a total of six Sea Harriers and three RAF Harriers were lost in the six-week conflict. In view of the number of missions flown, these aircraft had a truly remarkably low loss rate.

In addition to the ten helicopters lost in the *Atlantic Conveyor*, three helicopters were destroyed when warships were sunk or damaged; another four were lost to enemy action, including one shot down by an Argentine Pucara light attack aircraft; and six were lost operationally, including the Sea King that was intentionally destroyed after the aborted raid on Rio Grande airfield. Finally, a Sea Dart missile from a British destroyer shot down a Gazelle light helicopter at a range of more than 11 n.miles; the helicopter was apparently out of the speed/altitude parameters set for friendly helicopters in the task force area. Thus, a total of 22 helicopters were lost in the conflict of almost 200 helicopters of different types that were embarked in the British ships.[23]

The *Hermes* and *Invincible* were operating in the storm-swept South Atlantic, in winter. A British Aérospace report noted,

> The flight decks of the carriers were moving vertically at times through 90 feet and the weather produced cloud bases typically 200 feet and often down to 100 feet during flying operations. Visibility was typically ½ nautical mile and often much less. One Harrier recovered to the deck of *Hermes* in horizontal visibility of 200 feet on one notable occasion.[24]

Operations on the relatively small carriers were never cancelled because of the sea state. Conventional fixed-wing carrier aircraft would have been unable to operate in those weather conditions, not even from large-deck carriers.

The carrier crews and Navy-RAF maintenance personnel worked day and night to prepare, launch, and recover their Harriers and Sea Kings. For example, on May 1 the *Hermes* launched 12 Sea Harriers for the attack on Port Stanley and Goose Green. One hour after they (all) returned to the ship, six of the aircraft were airborne on combat air patrol to defend against an expected counterattack and the six others were ready

A Harrier takes off from the *Hermes*'s ski-jump while crewmen prepare bombs and air-to-air missiles for subsequent operations. Three Sea King helicopters are parked forward. The crews of the two VSTOL carriers performed remarkably in the South Atlantic conflict, achieving record high availability rates for their Harriers as well as helicopters during the winter season. (Imperial War Museum)

for launch. Indeed, at the start of a flying day the *Hermes* regularly had 13 out of 14 aircraft serviceable, of which ten would be available at the end of the day after some 45 sorties had been flown.

The most critical shortfall in the fleet was the total lack of Airborne Early Warning (AEW) aircraft. The official British report noted,

the absence of AEW was a severe handicap against Argentine air attacks mounted at very low level, especially at San Carlos where [shipboard] radars deployed suffered considerable interference from surrounding high land. The lack of AEW also proved an important limitation in the task force's ability to deal with the threat from Exocet by intercepting the aircraft carrying it before the missile could be launched.[25]

The British White Paper of 1966 led to the belief in some circles that RAF land-based AEW aircraft (i.e.,

the turbojet Nimrod) could provide radar coverage for naval forces at sea. The Falklands again demonstrated the fallacy of employing land-based aircraft to support distant naval operations. This severe limitation was partly overcome shortly after the Falklands War when HMS *Illustrious*, the second new VSTOL carrier, arrived with two Sea King helicopters fitted with the Searchwater surveillance radar. (The *Illustrious* remained in the Falklands area until October 21, 1982, when the first RAF Phantoms arrived to be based ashore to enhance British defenses in the islands.)

Argentine losses were considerable: a submarine, a cruiser, a patrol craft, an intelligence trawler, and two cargo ships were sunk. Sea Harriers shot down 20 aircraft plus 3 probables. British warships shot down another 28 aircraft (plus 2 probables) with surface-to-air missiles and 7 (plus 1 probable) with gunfire. Once ashore British soldiers and Marines shot down 24 Argentine planes (plus 8 probables) while special forces, naval gunfire, and bombs destroyed another 31 Argen-

Another highly innovative carrier project was the British fitting of the Thorn-EMI Searchwater radar to Sea King helicopters to compensate for the lack of carrier- and land-based AEW aircraft. Here a Sea King AEW.2 flies with its radar lowered and another, also from No. 849 Squadron, sits on the flight deck of the USS *George Washington* with the radar in the stowed position. These aircraft had a mission duration of up to 4½ hours. (Westland; Joseph Strevel, U.S. Navy)

Homecoming: The VSTOL carrier *Invincible* returns to Portsmouth amidst jubilation in September 1982. The Falklands marked the first major naval conflict since World War II, involving air, surface, and submarine forces. Turbojet aircraft and anti-ship and anti-aircraft missiles were major factors in the Falklands campaign; all had their debut in World War II. (Royal Navy)

tine aircraft on Falklands airstrips—a total of 110 aircraft destroyed plus 14 probables.

The Falklands was a major victory for British military forces and, most especially, for the carriers and their VSTOL aircraft and helicopters. Britain would retain all three of the *Invincible*-class VSTOL carriers and pursue further Harrier development and procurement.

There were nuclear weapon implications in the Falklands conflict. The WE177 kiloton-range weapon, which had entered the British inventory in the 1960s, was embarked in the carriers for the strike role by Sea Harriers, and in carriers and surface combatants for use as ASW weapons by Sea King helicopters. While the British government has not revealed numbers, the *Hermes* carried 40 percent of the entire British stockpile of WE177C nuclear depth bombs while and the *Invincible* carried 25 percent.[26] In addition, two Type 22 frigates each had probably two WE177C nuclear depth bombs on board. These totaled about 30 nuclear weapons of a total stockpile of "around 40" tactical nuclear weapons available to the Royal Navy and for use on RAF Nimrod maritime patrol aircraft.

When the War Cabinet was informed that "nukes" were in ships heading for the Falklands, the decision was made to remove them before the ships entered combat. There was concern that a nuclear-armed ship could be damaged or sunk, and treaty obligations forbade taking nuclear weapons in some South Atlantic areas. Concern was even voiced for a nuclear-armed ship being sunk in shallow water and salvaged by the Argentines.

But the Chief of Defence Staff, Admiral of the Fleet Sir Terence Lewin, wanted the weapons retained in the warships in the event that Soviet submarines became involved in the conflict in support of Argentina.[27] According to the official report on nuclear weapons,

It was possible that, at the same time as the Falklands, operation, a state of tension with the Soviet Union might develop. The removal of the weapons would make the re-deployment of the ships for NATO tasks dependent on first re-embarking their nuclear weapons. This could cause a delay in their deployment and necessitate a return to a [United Kingdom] port unless we were prepared to re-embark the weapons at sea. To take the latter course in tension would be highly visible to the Soviets who could be expected to be marking [trailing] our ships.[28]

(The Soviets are believed to have provided the Argentines with some satellite-derived intelligence during the conflict.)

The decision was made to remove the nuclear weapons from the warships. The two frigates, the *Brilliant* and *Broadsword*, transferred their nuclear weapons to replenishment ships on April 16 and 20, respectively. But the replenishment ships in turn transferred the nuclear weapons to the two carriers in May when they were required in the combat area.

One-half of the *Invincible*'s nuclear weapons were transferred to the replenishment ship *Fort Austin* on June 2, with the remaining weapons sent over on the following day. The *Hermes* retained her weapons until June 26, when they were shifted to the replenishment ship *Resource* for return to Britain. The weapons from the two frigates as well as the transfers between the carriers and replenishment ships were accomplished by jackstay (i.e., underway replenishment gear).[29]

The WE177 remained in the British inventory for RAF and FAA aircraft until March 1998, when the last were withdrawn from service.[30] At that time the only remaining British nuclear weapons were Trident strategic missiles launched from submarines. But the carriers would still be invaluable in supporting British interests in far-flung areas.

21 LESSONS AND FINANCES

An Argentine Super Étendard fighter-attack aircraft practices touch-and-go landings on the USS *Ronald Reagan* (CVN 76) in the South Pacific in June 2004. Although Argentina no longer has an aircraft carrier, its naval air arm periodically practices carrier operations when a Brazilian or U.S. flattop is available. *Étendard* means "standard," as in a battle flag. (Konstandinos Goumenidis, U.S. Navy)

While the Falklands conflict again demonstrated the effectiveness of aircraft carriers, the relatively high costs of constructing and maintaining the ships, and the increasing costs of aircraft meant that fewer navies could afford to operate aircraft carriers. By the end of the century several navies had ceased to operate the ships.[1]

Argentina, operating the former British CVL *War-* *rior* as the carrier *Independencia*, in 1968 acquired the former Dutch CVL *Karel Doorman*. Built as HMS *Venerable* and like the *Warrior* a unit of the *Colossus* class, the ship was purchased on October 15, 1968, and completed refitting and modernization in August 1969. She was renamed *25 de Mayo* and sailed for Argentina on September 1. Accordingly, the *Independencia* was withdrawn from service in 1971 and scrapped.

329

The *25 de Mayo* was operated for more than a decade, although by the time of the Falklands conflict in 1982 she was experiencing propulsion and catapult problems. After a long period of inactivity she was formally discarded in 1997 and scrapped, ending carrier activity in the Argentine Navy. (After 1993 Argentina's Super Étendard and Tracker pilots practiced touch-and-go landings on the Brazilian *Minas Gerais* and U.S. aircraft carriers to maintain a level of carrier qualification.)

The only other South American Navy to operate aircraft carriers is Brazil, which operated the modernized *Minas Gerais* (ex-HMS *Vengeance*) until 2001, when she was decommissioned and scrapped. Her replacement was the former French carrier *Foch*, placed in commission as the *São Paulo* on November 15, 2000. The *São Paulo* arrived in Brazil in late February 2001. With a full load displacement of 32,780 tons, she is the largest warship to have ever sailed in a South American navy. In Brazilian service her initial air group consisted of only 14 A-4 Skyhawks and a half-dozen helicopters of various types.

The French Experience

The French Navy operated the carriers *Clemenceau* (completed 1961) and *Foch* (1963) in support of national political-military interests for almost four decades. They operated a succession of advanced aircraft produced by the highly competent French aviation industry—with one notable exception when the French Navy selected an American aircraft.

From the 1960s the *Clemenceau* and *Foch* operated Étendard and F-8E(FN) Crusader fighter-attack aircraft, and Alizé ASW aircraft plus helicopters. In the summer of 1977 several Crusaders from Flotille 14.F participated in training missions over Djibouti. On May 7 two Crusaders were airborne for an exercise against French Air Force F-100 Super Sabres based at Djibouti. The Crusader leader intercepted two fighters, which he assumed to be F-100s. The "bogies" were actually two Yemenite MiG-21 fighters, each armed with four air-to-air missiles. The two Crusaders prepared to engage, but there was no fight.

Seventeen crusaders were upgraded in the 1990s to F-8EP variants. Crusaders were in French service until October 1999.

Dassault followed the Étendard with the Super Étendard, an improved fighter-attack aircraft of similar configuration. Three Étendard IV-M aircraft were

modified for development of the new aircraft. The first "new" Super Étendard flew on November 24, 1977, and deliveries to the fleet of 71 aircraft began the following year.[2] The Argentine Navy ordered another 14 Super Étendards for operation from its carrier *25 de Mayo*. (Five had been delivered by the start of the Falklands War of 1982.) In 1983 five French Super Étendards were leased to Iraq.[3]

The Super Étendard was armed with two 30-mm cannon and could carry up to 4,600 pounds of stores, including the Exocet anti-ship missile and the AMSP nuclear missile. (The 30-mm cannon are removed when carrying either of these missiles). In 1988 the carriers *Clemenceau* and *Foch* embarked the ASMP—*Air-Sol Moyenne Porté*—the only nuclear weapon to be embarked in French carriers. The ASMP was a Mach 2+ missile carrying a TN81 300-kiloton warhead for attacking land targets. The missile was credited with a range of some 185 miles when launched from high altitude and 50 miles when launched from low altitude. An improved ASMP-A land-attack missile is now in French naval service.

The two French carriers also embarked the Alizé ASW aircraft. Three prototypes and two pre-production aircraft were followed by 75 delivered to the French Navy for shipboard and land use. Another 12 Alizé were produced for the Indian Navy for carrier operation.

One other French naval aircraft of particular note was the Aérospatiale SA 321 Super Frelon (Hornet), which operated from carriers as well as amphibious ships in this period. This large helicopter, powered by three turboshaft engines, flew in a number of roles—anti-ship (with Exocet guided missiles), ASW, and transport. In the last role the Super Frelon on occasion flew from carriers. In the ASW role—with 24 of the SA 321G anti-submarine variants built for the French Navy—the Super Frelon carried up to four "short" torpedoes or depth charges and could be armed with machine guns.[4] In the transport role it can accommodate 28 troops or 8,000 pounds of cargo. The helicopter can also be configured for minelaying and minesweeping.

The Super Frelon, which first flew in 1959, was also flown by the Chinese Navy and the air forces of Iraq, Israel, Libya, South Africa, and Syria. And, it was employed in civilian service.[7]

Most impressive has been the French Navy's construction of a nuclear-propelled aircraft carrier, the *Charles de Gaulle*.[5] The carrier was a replacement

Troops board an SA 321G Super Frelon on the flight deck of the carrier *Foch* in June 1977. This variant was con-vertible from the ASW to the troop carrier role. The Super Frelon is the largest helicopter currently in naval service other than the U.S. Navy-Marine H-53 series. The Aérospatiale-built helicopter is also flown by the Chinese and other armed forces, with some aircraft produced in China. (French Navy)

for the fleet carriers *Clemenceau*, discarded in September 1997, and *Foch*, discarded in November 2000. The latter ship was transferred immediately to Brazil.

The French government in September 1980 approved the acquisition of two nuclear-propelled aircraft carriers as replacements for the two earlier ships. The subsequent shipbuilding plan called for construction of the first CVN to begin in 1986 and for the ship to join the fleet in 1996. The second CVN was to be started in 1991 and completed within ten years. The keel for the *Charles de Gaulle* was laid down at the navy yard in Brest in April 1989, making France the second nation to initiate the construction of nuclear carriers.[6]

The *Charles de Gaulle* began sea trials in January 1999, and major problems were immediately encountered. Severe vibrations were experienced, requiring replacement of the ship's two propellers; there were electrical problems; and it was determined that the angled deck was too short to land the American E-2C Hawkeye aircraft being acquired by France. Those aircraft were ordered after the ship was designed. The angled deck was lengthened 14½ feet. The ship finally entered service in April 2001.

The *Charles de Gaulle* has a standard displacement of 37,085 tons and at full load is 40,600 tons with an overall length of 857 ¾ feet. Two pressurized-reactors provide steam for twin turbines to drive the ship at 25 knots—some seven knots slower than the *Clemenceau* class. Two steam catapults were fitted and two starboard deck-edge elevators connected the hangar and

flight decks. Some 40 aircraft were embarked, including Rafale-M and Super Étendard fighter-attack aircraft, E-2C Hawkeye AEW aircraft, and helicopters.

The Rafale M (for *marine*) is the carrier-based variant of an advanced multi-role aircraft developed by Dassault as successor to the F-8 Crusader and Super Étendard in the fighter-attack, reconnaissance, and "buddy" tanker roles. The single-seat Rafale M and the similar, two-seat Rafale N can carry a variety of air-to-surface weapons including the AMSP nuclear missile. The Rafale ("squall") is a twin-engine aircraft that features low observability (stealth) characteristics that include reduced radar and infrared signatures. The aircraft has an integrated countermeasures system, electro-optical sensors, and an electronically scanned array radar. A reconnaissance pod can be fitted and some sub-variants will support a "buddy" refueling system.

The Rafale has a built in, rapid-fire 30-mm gun. A variety of air-to-air and air-to-surface missiles can be carried, including the Exocet anti-ship missile, as well as laser-guided bombs. The aircraft has five fuselage attachment points, three pylons under each wing, and two wingtip missile launch rails. Almost 21,000 pounds of weapons and fuel can be carried externally.

The first flight of the prototype Rafale A took place on July 4, 1986. The Navy's Rafale M achieved initial operational capability with Flottille 12.F in 2002, the squadron being assigned to the carrier *Charles de Gaulle*. These aircraft began flying combat missions in May 2006 during operations in support of

The *Charles de Gaulle* was the only nuclear-propelled aircraft carrier to be completed outside of the United States. Shown here with Super Étendard fighter-attack aircraft parked aft of the island structure, and a Grumman-built E-2C Hawkeye AEW aircraft (wings folded) forward of the island. The ship has a most unusual island structure, inundated with radomes. (DCN)

multinational forces in Afghanistan. In March 2007, three improved Rafale Ms fitted to launch laser-guided bombs began operations from the carrier over Afghanistan. (The first French Air Force squadron with Rafales became operational in 2006; in March 2007, the French Air Force made its first Rafale deployment with three aircraft to Dushanbe, Tajikistan, in support of operations in Afghanistan.)

The carrier-capable Rafale N is a two-seat combat aircraft, similar to the Rafale M. The French Navy plans to acquire 60 Rafale M/N aircraft to provide fighter-attack squadrons to two carriers, plus training and replacement aircraft.

The *Charles de Gaulle* mounts 32. Aster surface-to-air missiles in vertical launchers and two Sadral point-defense missile systems are fitted. Eight rapid-fire 20-mm guns are also fitted.

The construction of the second nuclear carrier—possibly to be have been named *Richelieu*—was continually delayed, primarily because of fiscal constraints. The decision subsequently was made to procure the second carrier with conventional propulsion. The decision was then made to have some form of collaboration with Britain in the CVF program (see Chapter 26). It is important that the new carrier become operational

by 2015, when the *Charles de Gaulle* is scheduled for a lengthy refueling and overhaul.

The Canadian carrier *Bonaventure* ended fixed-wing aircraft operations in December 1969. She then operated briefly as a troop transport and, with six Sea King helicopters embarked, as a replenishment ship. She was paid off in 1970 and scrapped.

The Netherlands similarly ended carrier operations in 1968 when the *Karel Doorman* was decommissioned and almost immediately sold to Argentina.

Italy, which had belatedly initiated an aircraft carrier program during World War II, finally placed a carrier in commission in 1985, the *Giuseppe Garibaldi*, the name honoring the 19th Century patriot who founded modern Italy. The *Garibaldi* was built as a small ASW helicopter ship, 13,850 tons full load and 591 feet in length. The ship was placed in commission in September 1985. She could accommodate up to 18 Sea Kings, with 12 of them stowed in the hangar deck. As an ASW ship she mounted a DE-1160 sonar as well as torpedo tubes.

The ship was completed with a 6.5-degree ski-ramp, at the time said to be for protection of the flight deck from excessive spray. This feature meant that the ship could embark fixed-wing aircraft although an Italian law of 1937 forbade the Italian Navy from operating aircraft. Helicopters were acceptable because they did not exist at the time that the 1937 law was enacted during the Mussolini fascist regime.

Finally, in January 1989 the Italian parliament passed a law permitting the Navy to fly fixed-wing aircraft. The Italian Navy had evaluated both the Sea Harrier and the American-produced AV-8B variant. Initial orders for the latter, some to be assembled by an Italian firm, were placed in 1989. From 1994 the Italian Navy took delivery of 16 AV-8B and 2 TAV-8B aircraft. The first landing on the *Garibaldi* was in November 1994. Either 10 Sea Harriers or 16 SH-3D Sea King ASW helicopters or a mix of aircraft can be embarked in the ship.

In January 1995 the ship and her Harriers were in combat providing support for United Nations troops evacuating Somalia. That was a half century after the first Italian efforts to develop aircraft carriers.

In 1998 the Italian government provided funds for the construction of a second, multipurpose carrier, the *Cavour*.[7] The ship, laid down in 2001, will be a 26,500-ton warship with a length of $768^5/_6$ feet. Also fitted with sonar and ASW torpedo tubes, her air group will consist of 8 AV-8B Harriers and 12 Merlin helicopters. A docking well will accommodate four LCM(6) landing craft or one U.S. air cushion landing craft. The ship was to be completed in about 2008.

The Merlin is the successor to the SH-3 Sea King in several navies and air forces. Developed as the EH.101, the helicopter was produced by the merged consortium of Agusta and Westland.[8] After a lengthy development program, the first flight of an EH.101 occurred on October 9, 1987. The first military delivery was ten years later, when the Royal Navy accepted its first delivery of the Merlin MH.1 in December 1998, and sea trials aboard the VSTOL carrier *Ark Royal* were completed in February 2002.[9] The Fleet Air Arm procured 44 HM.1 variants.

The Merlin is larger than the Sea King and has three turboshaft engines. For the ASW role the Merlin has dipping sonar and sonobuoys; also fitted are radar and electronic warfare systems. It can carry up to four homing torpedoes or depth charges or anti-ship missiles.

The *Giuseppe Garibaldi* was Italy's first aircraft carrier, the fruition of efforts that began before World War II. Here the *Garibaldi* steams at high speed in preparation for launching the five Harriers VSTOL aircraft on her flight deck; two Sea King helicopters are parked aft. The ship's shallow-angle ski-ramp is evident in this view. [*no credit*]

Spain built an even smaller carrier, the *Principe de Asturias*, a 15,912-ton ship with a length of 640 feet and a 12-degree ski-ramp. Her design was based on the U.S. Sea Control Ship (SCS) of the Zumwalt era (see Chapter 18). Constructed at the Bazán shipyard (later Izar) in Ferrol, she was commissioned in May 1988 as a replacement for the helicopter carrier *Dédalo*, the former U.S. CVL *Cabot*. She was in Spanish service from 1967 to 1989 and in August 1972 a Hawker Siddeley pilot demonstrated a Harrier GR.3 aboard the *Dídalo*. Although the Spanish were impressed with the demonstration, political problems prevented them from acquiring the aircraft directly from Britain. Thus, the Spanish aircraft—named Matador—were acquired via the U.S. Marine Corps. These aircraft, single-seat AV-8S (British Mk 55) and two-seat TAV-8S (Mk 58), were followed by the American-built EAV-8B Harrier beginning in 1987. The *Principe de Asturias* can operate up to 24 aircraft—EAV-8B Matador VSTOL aircraft and helicopters, the latter including SH-3D/G Sea Kings and SH-60B Seahawks.[10] Normally six to eight Matadors and up to 16 helicopters are embarked. Additionally, Spain has began the construction of a 27,000-ton amphibious helicopter ship in 2005. She was scheduled to be completed in about 2009.

Asian Navies

India, the first Asian nation to operate an aircraft carrier after World War II, sailed the *Vikrant* (ex-*Hercules*) until early 1997, when she was retired after almost 37 years of service. The former HMS *Hermes* of 28,700 tons full load was placed in commission as the *Viraat* in early 1989.[11] Thus the Indian Navy operated two carriers for eight years, bringing to fruition the plan for a two-carrier fleet first espoused in 1947.

India was the only export customer for the Sea Harrier; Hawker Siddeley's VSTOL demonstrator flew from the *Vikrant* in July 1972. But not until January 1983 were the first Sea Harrier FR.51 VSTOL aircraft, forming No. 300 squadron, delivered for the carrier to replace the Indian Navy's outdated Sea Hawk fighters.[12] The *Viraat* now operates up to 12 Sea Harrier fighter-attack aircraft and more than a dozen helicopters of various types. But the *Viraat* is severely limited by her age—she was launched in 1953 and completed in 1959—hard service, and several casualties including engine room flooding in 1993 and a major fire in 1994.

The Indian government, which is responsible for the defense of several islands in the Indian Ocean and which believes that aircraft carriers are needed to protect the surface fleet, has embarked on a major carrier program.[13] The Soviet Union, which in the mid-1960s had replaced Great Britain as the primary source of Indian military equipment, had long sought to provide India with an aircraft carrier. But not until the demise of the Soviet Union was such a transfer negotiated. The conventional carrier *Gorshkov* entered service with the Soviet Navy in late 1987 but ceased operations in 1991. The ship was the subject of negotiations with India beginning in 1994.[14] As part of the sale agree-

Spain's *Principe de Asturias*—the name given to the heir apparent to the Spanish throne—was built to the U.S. Navy's Sea Control Ship (SCS) design. The Spanish Navy previously operated a former U.S. Navy CVL as a helicopter carrier. The *Principe de Asturias* in this 1996 photo has only helicopters on her flight deck. The ship also operates Harrier/Matador VSTOL aircraft.

The former HMS *Hermes* in what is probably her final configuration, serving as the Indian Navy's *Viraat*. The Indian Navy, originally dependent upon Britain for its warships, subsequently turned primarily to the Soviet Union for such ships. The *Viraat* is shown here at Bombay in February 1997. She is scheduled to be replaced by an indigenously built carrier. (NAVPIC-Holland)

ment the Soviet Union agreed to extensive modifications of the ship at the Sevmash shipyard at an estimated cost of US$675 to 700 million in addition to the estimated purchase cost of US$1.5 *billion*.[15] The modifications include enlarging the flight deck, providing a 14.3-degree ski-ramp, updating electronic systems, and deleting the 12 P-500 Bazalt (NATO SSN-N-12 Sandbox) anti-ship missiles. With an expected full load displacement of some 45,000 tons, the ex-*Gorshkov*—to be renamed *Vikramaditya*—will be the world's largest aircraft carrier outside of the U.S. and Russian Navies.[16]

The ex-Soviet ship was scheduled to enter Indian service in about 2013. The air group of some 30 aircraft will consist of MiG-29K Fulcrum-D fighter-bombers, Ka-27 Helix ASW helicopters, and the Ka-27RLD/Ka-31 variant of the Helix fitted for the airborne early warning role.[17]

Beyond the ex-*Gorshkov*, a carrier to replace the *Viraat* is being constructed in India. Euphemistically designated an "air defense ship," the new carrier will probably have the name *Vikrant* when she is completed about 2012. The ship was laid down in April 2005 at the Cochin shipyard in Kochi. She will have a full load displacement of some 40,000 tons on a length of approximately 827½ feet. Gas turbines will give her a speed of some 28 knots. The new ship's air group is planned to consist of 16 of the new Light Combat Air-

craft (LCA) or MiG-29K fighters plus 20 helicopters for ASW, AEW, and other roles.

Thailand became the second Asian nation to operate a carrier after World War II when the Spanish shipyard Bazán at Ferrol, which built the *Principe de*

The new configuration of the Indian carrier *Vikramaditya*, formerly the Soviet carrier *Admiral Flota Sovetskogo Soyuza Gorshkov*, is shown in this artist's concept. The ship's flight deck and island structure will have been significantly changed before the *Vikramaditya* becomes operational in the Indian Navy about 2013. Another mid-size carrier is under construction in India, labeled as an "air defense ship." (*Naval Forces*)

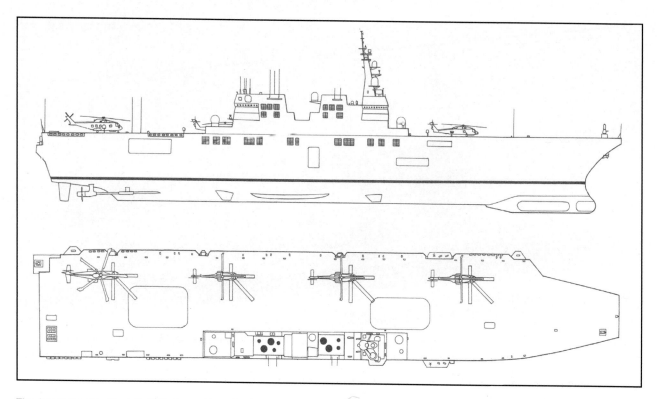

The Japanese Maritime-Self Defense Force is planning a class of 13,500-ton "destroyers" that would normally operate three SH-60J Seahawk and one MH-53E Sea Dragon helicopters. Such a ship must be considered the harbinger of a true aircraft carrier. As indicated in this sketch, the design has two elevators connecting the flight and hangar decks. (*Ships of the World*)

Asturias, constructed the *Chakri Nareubet*. Displacing 11,486 tons full load with a length of 599 feet, the *Chakri Nareubet* is a smaller version of the SCS design with a 12-degree ski-ramp. She was commissioned in August 1997. The Thai ship serves primarily as a flagship with a number of wartime missions as well as specific peacetime missions. The latter included a platform for disaster relief, search and rescue, law enforcement, and other civilian support activities.

The ship can operate either 10 Matador VSTOL aircraft or 15 Seahawk and Sea King helicopters or a composite group. The Thai Harriers are former Spanish AV-8S and TAV-8S aircraft, later supplemented by surplus U.S. AV-8A/C variants.

Funding problems severely limit operations of the *Chakri Nareubet*, reducing her effectiveness in almost any role, with or without aircraft. Still, the Thai carrier program brought to six the number of nations flying Harrier/Sea Harrier aircraft: Great Britain, India, Italy, Spain, Thailand, and the United States.

For a brief moment in the early 1960s Indonesia contemplated acquisition of an aircraft carrier. In 1962 the *Sverdlov*-class light cruiser *Ordzonikidze* was delivered as part of the major Soviet warship transfers

to Indonesia.[18] This 12,900-ton ship—armed with 12 6-inch guns—was the largest Soviet warship transferred to a foreign navy in the 20th Century. Subsequently, the Indonesian Navy inquired about the possibility of completing one of the unfinished *Sverdlov*s as a light carrier. No action followed on this inquiry.

Two other Asian nations periodically are reported to be considering the acquisition of aircraft carriers: Japan and China. The Japanese constitution of 1947 provides for military forces only for self-defense. To many Japanese of all political viewpoints the aircraft carrier is an offensive platform.

Recently built Japanese destroyers carry up to three SH-60J Seahawk ASW helicopters while a planned series of 13,500-ton "destroyers" are to carry three SH-60J and one MH-53E Sea Dragon helicopters. Two aircraft elevators will be fitted. Also, the new, 13,000-ton LSD-type amphibious ships of the *Osumi* class have a full-length main deck with a starboard-side island structure. While these ships can operate only helicopters on the after portion of the deck (with vehicle stowage forward), these LSDs and the new helicopter-carrying destroyers (DDH) are clearly the harbinger of more capable aviation ships.

The landing ships of the *Osumi* class have a full "flight deck," although only the after section is suitable for operating helicopters. The forward section can be used to stow vehicles or containers. This is the *Kunisaki*, one of four of these 13,000-ton ships completed in 1998–2005. The ships' large docking well, accessed by a stern gate, can accommodate two U.S. air cushion landing craft. (*Ships of the World*)

China is more enigmatic: Early in the communist regime the Chinese attitude toward aircraft carriers appears to have been similar to that of their Soviet mentors—such ships were aggressive weapons of Western imperialism. A major change to this attitude occurred in the early 1980s under the guidance of Admiral Liu Huaqing, the head of the Chinese Navy from 1982 to 1988 and the vice chairman of the powerful Central Military Commission from 1989 to 1997. Liu had studied at the Voroshilov Naval War College in Leningrad from 1954 to 1958, a period of great turmoil in the Soviet Navy.[19]

Admiral Liu wrote in *Zhongguo Haiyang Bao* (China's Maritime Paper) shortly before his retirement in 1997 that it was "extremely necessary" for China to possess aircraft carriers. According to Liu, aircraft carriers were needed to protect China's sovereignty and maritime resources, especially with regard to Taiwan and the South China Sea; to guard China's sea lanes of communications as the country industrialized and increasingly became a major trading power; to enable China to keep up with regional powers such as India and Japan; and to give China's Navy a decisive edge in future naval warfare.

In the early 1990s the Chinese Navy began a large-scale modernization program, acquiring advanced submarines, destroyers, anti-ship missiles, and aircraft,

The ex-Soviet carrier *Varyag* at the Chinese port of Darlian. The ship, riding high in the water, has been repainted and "cleaned up." But there is no evidence that the Chinese plan to rehabilitate the ship and place her in service. Rather, the ship, whose basic design dates to the 1960s, has provided Chinese naval architects with "hands-on" experience in carrier design. (John Rice)

primarily from Russia. Rumors of a carrier program began to abound when China acquired the unfinished Russian *Varyag* and the retired Russian carrier *Minsk* in the late 1990s. But both ships had been stripped of all useful military equipment, and their propulsion plants were inert; at best they could provide Chinese naval architects with hands-on design information.[20]

Still, as this volume went to press rumors abounded that China would either reactivate the *Varyag* or build a new carrier. The *Varyag*, moored at Dalian, has been painted in Chinese "naval colors" and has had cosmetic upgrades. For example, a South Korean newspaper stated,[21]

> A source close to Chinese military affairs said on March 27 that China has been promoting the construction of a 93,000-ton atomic-powered carrier under a plan titled "085 Project." The nation also has a plan to build a 48,000-ton non-nuclear-powered carrier under the so-called "089 Project," added the source.

And, "The non-nuclear-powered carrier is reported to be a revised version of Ukraine's *Varyag*, which China purchased in 1998." It seems highly unlikely that the Chinese could build a new ship or even rehabilitate the *Varyag* by 2010, a date sometimes referred to. A new-construction ship could certainly enter the fleet by 2020, although a 93,000-ton nuclear ship seems highly unlikely.

While Admiral Liu and other senior Chinese naval officers have expressed interest in the acquisition of aircraft carriers, the large naval expenditures of the 1990s and the early 21st Century, and the start-up effort to develop a fixed-wing carrier capability make it unlikely that China will acquire large-deck carriers in the near future.

(When this edition went to press there were reports that the ex-*Varyag* was to be renamed *Shilang* and placed in commission as a training ship. It was no clear, however, whether the ship would remain stationery or be towed, or eventually refitted with engines.)

South Korea is constructing two large docking well ships that have full flight decks. These are the 18,860-ton *Doko* and *Marado*. Resembling small carriers, they are designed to each operate ten EH.101 Merlin helicopters. A single deck-edge elevator connects the hangar and flight decks. In addition to a crew of some 300 men, the ships can carry 720 Marines plus vehicles and, in the docking well, two air cushion landing craft.

The *Doko* was completed in 2007 and the *Marado* was to be completed about 2010.

Finally, the Australian *Sydney*, employed as a fast transport since 1962, was paid off in 1973 and scrapped. The CVL *Melbourne* continued in service, suffering a major loss on December 5, 1976, when a hangar fire at the air station at Nowra destroyed 12 of the Navy's 13 S-2E Tracker ASW aircraft. The carrier underwent a major refit in 1978, but the VSTOL carrier *Invincible* was purchased from Britain in early 1982 to replace her. After the Falklands conflict the British government asked to retain the ship and Canberra agreed. The *Melbourne* was paid off in June 1982 and scrapped. Brief consideration was given to constructing an LPH-type ship for Australia in a U.S. shipyard, but Australia ceased carrier operations.

At the start of the 21st Century aircraft carriers of various types were operated by nine nations: Brazil, France, Great Britain, India, Italy, Russia, Spain, Thailand, and the United States. In many respects the most unusual carrier acquisition effort was that of the Soviet Union/Russia.

A Dassault Rafale M from Flottille 12.F aboard the *Charles de Gaulle* makes an arrested landing on a U.S. carrier in the Mediterranean in July 2007. The Rafale M and the similar, two-place Rafale N are Mach 1.8 aircraft with a ceiling of 50,000 feet and a radius of 700 n.miles carrying eight air-to-air missiles and four drop tanks. The aircraft has a loaded takeoff weight of 44,100 pounds and maximum weight of 54,000 pounds with almost 21,000 pounds of missiles, guided bombs, and drop tanks. (Octavio Ortiz, U.S. Navy)

22 THE RUSSIAN EXPERIENCE

The Russian-Soviet path to the development of aircraft carriers was long and torturous. The helicopter carrier-missile cruiser *Moskva* was the first aviation ship of the Soviet Navy. The *Moskva* and her sister ship *Leningrad* had a highly innovative design combining several weapon/sensor capabilities. While the ships were of limited success, they pioneered the development of aircraft carriers in the Soviet Navy. (J. T. Bullington, U.S. Navy)

For the first half of the 45-year Cold War the Soviet Union did not successfully develop aircraft carriers. To many Western naval analysts a Soviet Navy without carriers could be only a defensive force. Commander Robert W. Herrick, a leading U.S. naval analyst of the era wrote,

> Any navy which has been designed, constructed, and trained to contest for command of the sea has a single mission—that of destroying the enemy's naval forces; the Soviet Navy lacks mobile, sea-air power, thus cannot operate far at sea on a sustained basis because of the limited capabilities of its shore-based aircraft. . . .
>
> * * *
>
> Even though the Soviet Navy is second in tonnage only to the U.S. Navy, its complete lack of strike carrier forces constitutes a fundamental, qualitative difference that necessitates resorting to the defensive in naval strategy. It is in this area

of mobile naval air power that the Soviet Navy is so critically lacking.[1]

But the Soviet Navy did have the ability to carry out an offensive strategy with torpedo-attack, cruise missile, and ballistic missile submarines.[2] And, through skill and stealth, the Khrushchev regime was able to place more than 40,000 troops and military advisers and strategic and tactical ballistic missiles and to secretly deliver 158 nuclear warheads to Cuba—90 miles from Key West, Florida—in 1962.[3] The Soviet Union undertook these efforts without aircraft carriers.

Russia was an early leader in naval aviation. Russians cite Alexandr Fyodorovich Mozhaisky, a Navy captain, as the first man to build a successful flying machine. He initially built kites and flying models and in 1882 completed a full size monoplane.[4] Mozhaisky's monoplane, powered by two lightweight, British-built *steam* engines, weighed nearly a ton, too much for the available engine power, and it "flew" only a few feet.

By the start of the 20th Century several other aviation projects, including significant glider and balloon activity and efforts to build rotary wing and conventional airplanes, were under way in Russia. But not until 1909 was there a practical airplane flight in Russia, by a French-built Voisin biplane flown at Odessa on the Black Sea.

Soon several Russians were producing aircraft, some copies of foreign models and others highly innovative indigenous designs. The tsarist government officially recognized their military potential in 1910 by establishing the Imperial Russian Flying Corps with an Army Central Flying School at Gatchina, near St. Petersburg, and a Naval Flying School at Kronshtadt on St. Petersburg's Kotlin Island, with Navy flying being shifted during the winter months to Sevastopol on the Black Sea. A separate naval air arm has remained a part of the Navy up to the present.

When World War I began Russia had in service some 50 naval aircraft, mostly Curtiss flying boats. In comparison, in August 1914 the Royal Navy had 71 aircraft and 7 airships and the U.S. Navy had only 12 aircraft. The Russian Navy flew a variety of aircraft. In 1914 the Navy fitted one of the giant, four-engine Il'ya Mourometz bombers with floats to test the feasibility of water operations; this aircraft flew operational missions over the Baltic from a base at Libava (now Liepaja) during the war.[5] Naval aviators—among them noted air power intellect Alexandr P. de Seversky—test-fired rockets and an 82-millimeter recoilless cannon from aircraft.[6] At the time Russian Navy fighters were armed with 37-millimeter cannon in addition to the lighter machine guns common to other nations' aircraft. And, during the war the Russian Navy operated several seaplane carriers and tenders, mostly in the Black Sea.

The world war, revolution, civil war, and Allied intervention in Russia contributed to naval aviation's demise. By the early 1920s the Red Navy had 61 aircraft, mostly M-9 amphibians. However, the rebirth of the naval air forces was relatively swift, and by 1925 Soviet naval aviation had between 300 and 400 seaplanes. Five years later, in 1930, land-based naval aircraft began to appear in significant numbers. These aircraft soon began to predominate as they were more efficient and more versatile than seaplanes. In addition, much of the water on which seaplanes would operate was often icebound.

From the Revolution of 1917 until 1927 the relatively insecure Soviet leaders could afford neither the time nor money required to undertake warship construction. Vyacheslav I. Zof, the head of the Navy from December 1924 to August 1926, traveled to the Naval War College in Leningrad in early 1925 to, in Robert Herrick's words, "lay down the law":

> You speak of aircraft carriers and of the construction of new types of ships . . . at the same time completely ignoring the economic situation of our country and the corresponding condition of our technical means, completely ignoring the fact that perhaps tomorrow or the day after we will be called on to fight. And with what shall we fight? We will fight with those ships and personnel that we have already.[7]

But in the 1920s plans were quietly developed for completing the unfinished battle cruiser *Izmail* as an aircraft carrier that would operate 40 to 50 aircraft. No action was taken on this project.[8] Apparently some consideration was also given to rebuilding the dreadnought *Poltava*, completed in 1914, as a carrier. The *Poltava* displaced 23,000 tons standard and mounted a main battery of 12 12-inch guns. She never went to sea after the spring of 1918, was heavily damaged by fire in 1922, and then cannibalized for parts for other ships. No effort was undertaken to convert the battleship to a carrier.[9]

Post-revolution naval construction in Russia began in 1927. The first Soviet-built naval ships were submarines, part of the Soviet naval strategy referred to as the "young school" in which submarines and light surface warships, working with land-based aircraft, would be capable of controlling Soviet coastal waters. Kliment Voroshilov, the People's Commissar of Defense, articulated this defensive strategy to the 17th Party Congress in January 1934. Speaking about the newly established Northern and Pacific Fleets, Voroshilov explained,

> There we have not battleships and aircraft carriers, those means for the naval offensive. But, after all, as is well known, we do not intend to attack anyone at sea any more than on land. We only want to defend our shores and frontiers, and we are convinced that the light naval forces and coast defenses that we have there already, and above all our [land-based] naval air forces and submarines, will gravely cripple an attacking enemy.[10]

But this strategy was not compatible with external influences: Britain, with the Royal Navy the world's largest fleet, was considered to be a major threat to the Soviet regime; Japan, also a major naval power, was confronting Soviet interests in the Far East. Thus, while wanting to concentrate on light naval forces, the Soviet leadership was forced to consider the construction of major warships to confront its potential enemies.

Beginning in 1928 the three battleships originally completed in 1914 were extensively modernized. In 1934 the Soviets began to construct large destroyers and the following year the first Soviet-built cruisers of the *Kirov* class, designed as 8,500-ton ships with six 7.1-inch guns, were laid down. (Those ships that were completed were slightly heavier and armed with nine main battery guns.) The draft program of the period for

The seaplane carrier *Orlitza*, the former merchant ship *Imperatritza Aleksandra*, was one of several ships converted to that role for the Russian Navy during World War I. The *Orlitza* was modified in 1915 to carry seaplanes for the Baltic Fleet. Forward the ship had tent hangars that housed a pair of small seaplanes. (Boris V. Drashpil via U.S. Navy)

creating "a large maritime and oceanic navy" called for creating major battle fleets, including aircraft carriers. These programs reflected the convictions of Josef Stalin, who in the mid-1920s had become head of the Communist Party and de facto head of the Soviet State.

All major naval decisions required Stalin's personal approval or at least his acquiescence. The Soviet dictator would abide no question or opposition to his views. Admiral Nikolai G. Kuznetsov, Stalin's commander-in-chief of the Navy from 1939 to 1947 and again from 1951 to 1956, wrote in his memoirs,

> I well remember the occasion when Stalin replied to a request for more anti-aircraft [guns] on ships in the following words:
> "We are not going to fight off America's shores."[11]

The additional guns were not installed. Kuznetsov continued,

> On the other hand, Stalin had a special and curious passion for heavy cruisers. I got to know this gradually. At a conference in [A. A.] Zhdanov's office I made several critical remarks on the heavy cruiser project. Zhdanov said nothing, as if he had not heard what I said. When we left his office, one of the leading officials of the People's Commissariat for the Shipbuilding Industry, A. M. Redkin, warned me:
> "Watch your step, don't insist on your objection to these ships."
> He told me in confidence that Stalin had threatened to mete out strict punishment to anyone objecting to heavy cruisers. . . .[12]

Opposition to Stalin's views on naval matters was minimal. Indeed, in what would be known as the Great Purge, Stalin directed the execution and/or imprisonment of tens of thousands of government leaders and military officers whom he considered potential threats to his regime. Eight of the Navy's nine flagmen (admirals) were executed in 1938–1939.[13] Many lesser officers were also shot. In his frightening fictional account of the period, *Darkness at Noon*, Arthur Koestler tells how naval hero "Michael Bogrov" was shot because he differed with "No. 1" on whether to build large, long-range submarines or small, coastal submarines.[14]

In the midst of these purges, on January 17, 1938,

the lead articles in the newspapers *Pravda* and *Izvestiya*, reflecting Stalin's views, declared, "The mighty socialist industrial potential is capable of fulfilling any and every order of the People's Navy Commissariat. . . . The mighty specialized shipyards that are being rapidly completed at the present time will launch ships of all categories. . . ."

Building Major Warships

The Soviet ten-year shipbuilding program initiated in 1937–1938 included battleships and aircraft carriers. In the early 1930s designs for battleships were sought from Italy, which was assisting in other Soviet ship programs, and from the United States.[15] In 1936 the Soviet government began negotiations with American firms for the production of heavy armor for battleships and cruisers, followed by efforts to acquire heavy guns and ammunition. The American architectural firm Gibbs & Cox was approved in August 1937 to design a series of large warships for the Soviets. The U.S. Navy's leadership generally opposed cooperation with the Soviet regime. However, President Roosevelt encouraged cooperative efforts.

Gibbs & Cox accordingly produced battleship, destroyer, and fleet oiler designs as well as a massive combination battleship-carrier for the Soviets. Known as design "B," the last ship would have rivaled the Japanese *Yamato* in size and was slightly larger than the proposed U.S. *Montana* class (see table 22-1).

Variations of the Gibbs & Cox design provided—on smaller hulls—eight 18-inch guns (design "A") or ten 16-inch guns (design "C"). All three designs had a central flight deck served by two elevators with the main superstructure and funnel offset to starboard. The air-

Admiral Nikolai G. Kuznetsov. (U.S. Army)

Table 22-1
BATTLESHIP CHARACTERISTICS

	YAMATO CLASS[*]	DESIGN "B"	*IOWA* CLASS[**]	*MONTANA* CLASS[***]
Light displacement	—	58,800 tons	—	—
Standard displacement	65,000 tons	61,840 tons	45,000 tons	61,000 tons
Full load displacement	72,809 tons	74,000 tons	57,540 tons	73,000 tons
Length overall	862$\frac{2}{3}$ feet	1,005 feet	887¼ feet	903 feet
Main battery	9 18.1-inch	12 16-inch	9 16-inch	12 16-inch
Horsepower	153,553	300,000	212,000	212,000
Speed	27.5 knots	34 knots	35 knots[#]	29 knots

[*] Two ships completed 1941–1942.
[**] Four ships completed 1943–1944.
[***] Data was for the September 1940 design BB-67-1; there were two additional 1940 designs, both slightly smaller; no ships completed.
[#] Design speed was 33 knots; all four ships of the class achieved 35 knots in service.

craft capacity was to be 24 (design "C") to 36 carrier planes (designs "A" and "B") plus four floatplanes with two catapults in each ship.[16] In November 1938 the Gibbs & Cox design "B" was taken to Moscow for evaluation. It was rejected, and instead the Soviets asked Gibbs & Cox for a more conventional battleship design.[17] (The U.S. Navy's General Board secretly looked at design "B"—which it called "Battleship X"—but also rejected the design.[18])

The Soviets began construction of indigenously designed battleships of the *Sovetskiy Soyuz* (Soviet Union) class. The first ship was laid down in Leningrad (St. Petersburg) in 1938. A second ship was started at Nikolayev on the Black Sea, and two more at Molotovsk (Severodvinsk) in the Arctic. None of these ships was completed.[19] Also initiated were the *Kronshtadt*-class battle cruisers; the first two were laid down at the Admiralty yard in Leningrad and the Black Sea (formerly Marti) yard at Nikolayev.

Meanwhile, in February 1938 the head of the Main Navy Staff, Flagman 2nd Rank Lev M. Galler, approved the tactical-technical requirements for an aircraft carrier with the missions of reconnaissance, bombing, and anti-air warfare.[20] In 1939 the preliminary design of an aircraft carrier was undertaken as Project 71 at design bureau No. 45 (Nevskoye), with small (71a) and large (71b) variants with standard displacements of some 10,600 and 24,000 tons and carrying 30 and 70 aircraft, respectively. The smaller option was soon discarded.

(The same year Soviet engineers visited the carrier *Graf Zeppelin* then under construction in Germany.)

Delays followed. Revisions to the shipbuilding program continued in 1940 and the beginning of 1941: The number of battleships was decreased, but the number of cruisers was increased. Two aircraft carriers—one each for the Northern and Pacific Fleets—were approved. But on October 19, 1940, in response to the growing threat of attack by Germany, the Soviet government again reviewed the shipbuilding program. It was decreed that there would be no further battleship and heavy cruiser keel-layings. Work would be continued only on ships that could be completed in the near term. Also, the two Project 71 carriers were cancelled on the 19th. Thus ended the Soviet Navy's near term hopes for aircraft carrier construction.

In August 1939 Stalin had entered into a formal alliance with Adolf Hitler and became estranged from Western support. There had been major military cooperation between the two countries since the end of World War I, but with ship plans and an unfinished cruiser being provided by Germany to the Soviet Navy, Germany's carrier efforts were too rudimentary to be of help to the Soviets.

Germany invaded the Soviet Union in June 1941, and by the end of 1942 German troops had encircled the shipbuilding center of Leningrad and overrun the major shipyards on the Black Sea coast. Only the

The Soviet leadership, reflecting the Russian penchant for "bigness," commissioned an American ship design firm to produce plans for massive battleship-carrier hybrids. This was design "B," with triple turrets of 16-inch guns forward and aft, and a massive, starboard-side island structure alongside the ship's abbreviated flight deck. (Gibbs & Cox)

limited shipbuilding facilities at Molotovsk (Severodvinsk) in the Arctic, and Komsomol'sk and Vladivostok in the Far East remained intact. Warship construction came to almost a complete halt during the Great Patriotic War, as the war against Germany was known in the USSR.

The tide of war began to change in the winter of 1942–1943 with the savage battle for Stalingrad (now Volgagrad). During the next two years the relentless Soviet forces pushed the Germans back, finally forcing the capital of Berlin in April 1945 and bringing about Germany's capitulation. For the Soviet Navy the war at sea was fought primarily by land-based aircraft and submarines; coastal/riverine forces and naval infantry (marines) had a major role in the conflict.

At the outbreak of the German-Soviet War in June 1941, the Soviet naval air arm might have had as many as 1,000 aircraft, most of them land-based fighters and bombers. When the war ended in Europe, the naval air arm numbered some 2,500 aircraft, many of them supplied by the United States under the Lend-Lease program. All naval aircraft were shore based except for a few seaplanes on the larger warships.

After the war little prospect appeared for the near-term rebuilding of the Soviet Navy. The war had cost the Soviet Union the lives of more than 25 million men and women (a tenth of the population); millions more were crippled; other millions, in bad or indifferent health, were returning from German prison camps. Much of the nation's industry had been devastated, including the principal shipyards in Leningrad and Nikolayev.

Still, a new Soviet naval strategy was announced on July 28, 1945, when Stalin stated, "The Soviet People wish to see their fleet grow still stronger and more powerful. Our people are constructing new battleships and bases for the fleet." Priority was given to rehabilitating the shipbuilding industry. As soon as the major shipyards could resume work, the unfinished

hulls of the prewar and wartime programs were rushed to completion. These programs were principally the *Chapayev*-class light cruisers, destroyers, submarines, and lesser craft; the unfinished hulls of the battleships laid down in 1938–1940 were scrapped (although there were discussions about completing them as guided-missile ships).

Brief consideration was given after the war to completing the battle cruiser *Kronshtadt* at Leningrad and her sister ship *Sevastopol* at Nikolayev as aircraft carriers.[21] These would have been true fleet carriers, each embarking some 75 aircraft. No work was undertaken on the proposal.

Soviet engineers combed through German design offices and shipyards, collecting data and samples components for a future fleet. Several ex-German surface ships and submarines (as well as an Italian battleship) were taken over, as was the unfinished German aircraft carrier *Graf Zeppelin*, which had been scuttled in the Oder River. The carrier was carefully examined, refloated, and—never completed—sunk in weapon tests in August 1947 (see Appendix A).

Simultaneous with the postwar rejuvination of Soviet shipyards, the various ship design bureaus were rehabilitated and plans were prepared for a new generation of Soviet warships. The initial postwar ships were based largely on earlier designs, with some updating from captured German drawings, equipment, and ships, plus the assistance of former German technicians being used by the Soviets.

In the summer of 1945 the Soviet naval high command prepared the shipbuilding plan for 1946–1955 in accord with Stalin's pronouncement. Four aircraft carriers were included in the plan. But when Stalin reviewed the plan on September 27, 1945, Admiral Kuznetsov, CinC of the Navy, received the leader's reluctant approval for only two carriers. And even those two ships were deleted from the final iteration of the plan, dated November 27, 1945, on the insistence of the Peoples' Commissar of the Shipbuilding Industry, Ivan I. Nosenko, who did not consider his establishment ready to build them.[22]

Still, on December 12, 1945, Admiral Kuznetsov approved an operational-technical requirement (OTZ) for a small carrier with a light displacement 15,000 to 17,000 tons, a speed of 32 to 34 knots, and embarking 30 to 40 fighter aircraft. The ship was intended to provide fighter protection for the battle fleet. Kuznetsov was able to have the carrier included in the design plan approved by the government on October 16, 1946.

By the late 1940s the keels were being laid down for the first of the new surface warships and submarines. Work also began on the *only* postwar capital ships to be laid down by any nation—the *Stalingrad*-class battle cruisers. Stalin had direct input to their design and armament; he dictated their main armament of 12-inch guns and placed some of the 5.1-mm secondary guns on the centerline. The final (1951) design provided for a displacement of 36,500 tons standard and 42,300 tons full load and for carrying a principal armament of nine 12 inch guns.[23]

Stalin gave these ships high priority, and the *Stalingrad* was laid down in late 1951 at Nikolayev and a sister ship, probably to be named *Moskva*, at about the same time at the Ordzhonikidze yard in Leningrad. A third ship, probably to be named *Kronshtadt*, was laid down in early 1953 at Molotovsk. The third and later ships—at least seven were planned—were to be armed with anti-ship missiles as well as 12-inch guns.

Meanwhile, in January 1947, Stalin "fired" Admiral Kuznetsov as head of the Navy, making him chief of naval educational institutions in Leningrad. Kuznetsov—unlike several of his predecessors who were executed when fired by Stalin—was demoted to rear admiral in February 1949 and sent to the Far East to command one of the two numbered fleets in the Pacific. Admiral Ivan S. Yumashev, who had no interest in aircraft carriers, replaced him as head of the Navy. Stalin fired Yumashev, in turn, in July 1951, reportedly because of his heavy drinking. That same month Kuznetsov was returned to command of the Navy with the rank of admiral, probably because Stalin wanted his experience for rebuilding the fleet.[24]

A year later Kuznetsov presented a report to Stalin on the necessity of aircraft carriers. Stalin apparently approved the program, and an OTZ was issued. The head of the Aviation Industry gave his assurance that a turbojet-propelled fighter could be developed for carrier use. But the head of the shipbuilding industry, Vyacheslav A. Malyshev, declared that no resources were available for designing a carrier unless work was halted on one of the cruiser projects, which Stalin particularly favored. The carrier project was delayed again.

Stalin died on March 5, 1953. Six weeks later, on April 23, the construction of the large cruisers was ordered to be halted. The *Stalingrad*'s hull was launched in 1955 but never completed. She was used as an unmanned, self-propelled target ship for cruise missiles on the Black Sea's Feodosiya test range. The other unfinished battle cruiser hulls were scrapped. Soon

After a decade of plans and cancellations, the Soviet Union produced the *Moskva*, its first aviation ship, completed in 1967. Forward the ship had anti-submarine, anti-aircraft, and anti-ship weapons as well as an impressive array of electronic systems. A double hangar for Ka-25 Hormone helicopters was built into the superstructure, and two elevators connected the ship's flight and hangar decks. (U.S. Navy)

most other major warship programs were terminated or cut back, and several of the shipyards were shifted largely to merchant and fishing ship construction. Admiral Kuznetsov again raised the issue of aircraft carriers, and on May 18, 1953, he approved the OTZ for an aircraft carrier for fleet air defense. The OTZ did not mention displacement but cited:

Aircraft: Not less than 40 aircraft (approximately 12,000 pounds each) to be stowed in the hangar; aviation fuel and ammunition for ten sorties each.

Guns: The ship to have 16 5.1-inch dual-purpose guns in twin mounts with 250 rounds per barrel; also, no fewer than 32 45- or 57-mm anti-aircraft guns in quad mounts with 1,000 or 1,200 rounds per barrel; and at least 16 25-mm guns in quad mounts with 1,500 rounds per barrel.

Speed: Not less than 35 knots with a cruising range at 18 knots of at least 5,000 n.miles; an unreplenished endurance of 20 days.

The related scientific research institutes and TsKB-17 immediately encountered major difficulties with the proposal. Their experience with carriers was severely limited, being mainly *pre*-preliminary designs for aircraft carriers—Project 71 worked up in 1939 and Project 72 in 1944—and data from the *Graf Zeppelin* plus available public material on U.S. and British aircraft carriers.

By early 1954 a total of eight design options were developed for Project 85. These could meet all of the OTZ requirements, including operating 40 turbojet fighters, with standard displacements of 27,000 to 30,000 tons. Based on reviews by the Main Navy Staff,

The helicopter carrier-missile cruiser *Leningrad*, sister ship to the *Moskva*, shows the twin helicopter hangars for Ka-25 helicopters built into the after portion of the superstructure. Both flight deck elevators are lowered to the hangar deck. A net-like device on the helicopter spots retarded helicopters from rolling when on the flight deck. A towed-array sonar was fitted beneath the after end of the flight deck. (U.S. Navy)

the naval aviation staff, and other agencies, a reduction in displacements to 23,000 to 24,000 tons was made in July 1954. (At this stage the carrier design work was transferred from TsKB-17 to TsKB-16, but the latter's participation in the project was brief as that design bureau was being shifted to submarine projects. TsKB-17/Nevskoe then became the sole designer of major surface warships.)

In October 1954 Admiral Kuznetsov forwarded a report to the Minister of Defense, Nikolai A. Bulganin, and the Chairman of the Council of Ministers, Nikita S. Khrushchev, stating that aircraft carrier construction for the Northern and Pacific Fleets was provided for in the shipbuilding plan for 1956–1964. "This report only irritated Khrushchev and Bulganin," wrote aircraft carrier designer Arkadi B. Morin.[25]

Admiral Kuznetsov's time as CinC was again coming to an end. In May 1955 he suffered a heart attack and was incapacitated. His First Deputy CinC, Admiral Sergei G. Gorshkov, took command. In October the battleship *Novorossiysk* sank in the Black Sea port of Sevastopol, probably having struck an old mine; 630 men died in the disaster. Khrushchev and the new Minister of Defense, Marshal Georgi Zhukov, blamed Kuznetsov for the catastrophe, and he was demoted to vice admiral and retired in January 1956.[26] Kuznetsov had sought to continue the construction of large, conventional surface warships, but Khrushchev rejected them, wanting to counter Western naval forces with submarines and land-based aircraft, both carrying anti-ship missiles. Khrushchev, who had worked briefly with Gorshkov in the Black Sea during the war, described him as

a former submarine captain. He appreciated the role which German submarines had played in World War II by sinking so much English and American shipping, and he also appreciated the role which submarines could play for us in the event that we might have to go to war against Britain and the United States.[27]

Gorshkov was not a submarine officer. Rather, he had served in surface ships, had commanded mainly river flotillas during the war, and had become a rear admiral at age 32. He became CinC of the Navy and a Deputy Minister of Defense at 46. Gorshkov would have a major role in the development of aviation ships.

Under the Khrushchev regime, in the mid-1950s the Soviet Navy began a major warship construction program based on missile-armed destroyers and submarines, essentially a defensive naval strategy. Khrushchev even put forward his parameters for future warships:

- displacement limit of 5,000 tons standard
- gun armament of 5.1-inch or smaller weapons
- anti-ship cruise missiles to be provided

No aircraft carriers were in his shipbuilding plans. Khrushchev later wrote,

Aircraft carriers, of course, are the second most effective weapon in a modern navy [after submarines]. The Americans had a mighty carrier fleet—no one could deny that. I'll admit I felt a nagging desire to have some in our own navy, but we couldn't afford to build them. They were simply beyond our means. Besides, with a strong submarine force, we felt able to sink the American carriers if it came to war. In other words, submarines represented an effective defensive capability as well as reliable means of launching a missile counterattack.[28]

The *Moskva*'s island structure was inundated with electronic antennas: from left is the Top Sail 3-dimension air search radar; Head Net-C 3-dimension air search radar; and two Head Lights fire control radar/directors. The last supported anti-air and anti-submarine weapons. The four domes are Side Globe Electronic Warfare (EW) antennas. These are U.S.-NATO names for Soviet electronic equipment. (U.S. Navy)

But Admiral Gorshkov recalled that at a 1958 conference, "Khrushchev considered the possibility of designing and constructing a single carrier in order to work out the production technology and the experience of assimilating it into our Navy."[29] Both Khrushchev and Gorshkov—and their spokesmen—labeled Western aircraft carriers as "weapons of aggression," and the ships were of major concern to Soviet leaders.

In his landmark book *Voennaia Strategya* [Military Strategy] published in 1962, Marshal of the Soviet Union Vasiliy D. Sokolovsky declared,

> The most important task of our fleet from the very outset of the war will be to destroy enemy striking carrier-based units. The enemy will attempt to deploy these units in the most important theaters near the socialist countries and to deliver surprise nuclear attacks against important coastal objectives (naval bases, airfields, missile installations) and, possibly, against objectives quite far from the coast. . . . Such an attack will present a great danger if the [Soviet] fleet cannot cut it off and destroy the carrier-based striking units. This task can be fulfilled only with a high degree of combat readiness on the part of the fleet, their timely deployment, and skillful operations, taking into account the weak aspects of the enemy's assault carrier units.[30]

This was the first major book written on military strategy by senior Soviet officers since 1926. The Soviets described the late 1950s and 1960s as a "revolution in military affairs," as missiles, nuclear weapons, and other advanced technologies belatedly became a subject of discussion by the Soviet military leadership.[31] A principal target of the naval weapons developed in this period was Western aircraft carriers.

In the late 1950s there were major efforts to improve the air defenses of Soviet naval forces. Under the supervision of A. B. Morin at TsKB-17, the design of a "floating base for fighter aircraft" was initiated—"the term 'aircraft carrier' was strictly forbidden at that time."[32] The "floating base" was to carry out reconnaissance, destroy enemy reconnaissance aircraft, and detect low-flying aircraft *and missiles*. Such a ship would carry 36 aircraft—30 fighters, 4 radar picket aircraft, and 2 helicopters. The ship would have a standard displacement of about 30,000 tons.

Admiral Gorshkov did not support the carrier project. Rather, Gorshkov dutifully followed Khrushchev's dictum to dispose of conventional surface warships. Khrushchev had declared that, in Gorshkov's words, "we needed only a coastal Navy to protect our shores and that cruisers armed with guns were now needed 'only for visits,' and therefore he proposed not to build any more, but even to destroy those which were

A ship-based Kamov Ka-25 (NATO name Hormone-A) helicopter in a hover with her dipping sonar being lowered. Soviet designer N. I. Kamov produced a number of designs with contra-rotating rotors, which reduce the size of the helicopter and alleviate the need for a tail rotor. The Ka-25 has twin turboshaft engines that provide a maximum speed of 136 m.p.h. Two small ASW homing torpedoes or depth charges could be carried in an internal weapons bay. (National Air and Space Museum)

being built."[33] Gorshkov initiated a surface ship program centered on small ships armed with anti-ship and anti-submarine weapons as well as submarines and land-based aircraft. While the Soviet Navy's overall orientation during this period was strategically defensive, by the late 1950s the Soviet Navy led the world in the number of submarine-launched cruise and ballistic missiles for the land-attack role.

In this period there were some 850 naval aircraft, of which about 500 were "bomber types," land-based jet and turboprop attack and reconnaissance aircraft. Earlier the Soviet Navy had relinquished a large number of fighter aircraft, including some of the latest model MiGs, which had provided the Soviet naval air arm with a peak strength of some 4,000 aircraft in about 1957.

Anti-Submarine Cruisers

The appearance of U.S. Polaris missile submarines led to the Soviet decision to procure helicopter-carrying ships to provide long-range ASW search and attack. On February 8, 1957, the U.S. Chief of Naval Operations, Admiral Arleigh A. Burke, issued a requirement for a 1,500-n.mile missile launched from a submarine to be operational by 1965. This range would enable a submarine in the Norwegian Sea to target the Soviet capital of Moscow.[34] Information on this program—named Polaris—was soon available to Soviet officials.

In the summer of 1958 design bureau TsKB-17 made two proposals to the Ministry of Shipbuilding—one was for consideration of a "small anti-submarine defense ship–helicopter carrier"; the second was to complete some of the unfinished *Sverdlov* light cruisers as ASW helicopter carriers.[35] Defense Minister Marshal Rodion Ya. Malinovsky endorsed the concept, and a Central Committee resolution of December 3, 1958, addressed the necessity of designing and constructing such ships, to be operational by 1964. The project was given number 1123 and the cover name "Kondor." A. S. Savichev at TsKB-17 was named head of the design team.

The project went through considerable machinations before the lead ship, named *Moskva*, was laid down in December 1962.[36] Earlier designs were to be heavily armed, initially to embark four to six helicopters and to have a speed of 38 to 40 knots. The standard displacement was to be on the order of 4,000 tons, a remarkable design goal.

A Ka-25 Hormone-A at rest aboard an older Soviet cruiser. The contrarotating rotors are in the stowed position; the cockpit and left-side doors are open. There is a large search radar mounted in the "chin" position, with an antenna dome visible atop the after fuselage. The similar Hormone-B variant was employed for anti-ship missile guidance. (National Air and Space Museum)

The Main Navy Staff rationalized the requirements in a new OTZ, approved by Admiral Gorshkov in January 1959, that stipulated an around-the-clock ASW search by at least two helicopters during the period of the ship's unreplenished endurance, approximately 15 days. This required that at least eight helicopters be embarked. The requisite was subsequently refined: the proposed scenario was that as the helicopter carrier approach the intended search area to within a distance of about 31 miles—believed to be outside the sonar detection range of the submarine—two helicopters would be used to place 24-hour sonobuoys along the contour of the search area; after their return to the ship one airborne helicopter would provide a data link with the more distant buoys. Then a pair of attack helicopters would enter the search area to destroy the detected target. Given such a tactical model, the optimal, around-the-clock search 14 were required.[37] An air group of 10 to 14 helicopters was agreed to at a meeting of Navy and shipbuilding executives on August 18, 1959, and TsKB-17 undertook design of the ship.

The final design for Project 1123 was approved in January 1962. The ship was a missile cruiser forward; aft of the large superstructure was a clear, open flight deck. The superstructure was "stepped" forward to support missile launchers and radars and had a flat after face. New weapons, radars, sonars, and electronic warfare systems were introduced in the design. A small hangar was located between the stack uptakes in the superstructure to house two "ready" helicopters. Two elevators connected the flight deck to the hangar deck, which accommodated 12 Ka-25s, i.e., a total of 14 helicopters per ship. The stern was cut away for a variable-depth, passive sonar installation. The ship was also fitted with a large, retractable low-frequency sonar dome under the hull. The ship had a standard displacement of 11,300 tons, a full load displacement of 14,600 tons, and an overall length of 620¼ feet—the largest warship yet constructed by the Soviet regime.

In 1965 Project 1123 was designated *protivolodochnyy kreyser*—anti-submarine cruiser—reflecting its primary ASW role. Most Western naval analysts believed that the Soviets used that designation to avoid provisions of the Montreux Convention, a 1936 treaty governing the passage of warships through the Turkish Straits, between the Black Sea and the Mediterranean. However, a careful reading of the treaty shows that there are no restrictions on the passage of aircraft carriers belonging to Black Sea nations.[38]

Construction of the ships was undertaken at the Black Sea shipyard in Nikolayev. The lead ship, the *Moskva*, was launched on January 14, 1965, and delivered to the Fleet in December 1967; the second ship, the *Leningrad*, was launched on July 31, 1968, and entered the Fleet in June 1969. These ships established the practice of naming aviation ships for major cities. On their decks were Ka-25 ASW helicopters (NATO name Hormone) configured for ASW search with radar, dipping sonar, and sonobuoys, and for attack with homing torpedoes and nuclear as well as conventional depth bombs.[39]

A class of four such ships was initially planned. The third ship, to be named *Kiev*, was laid down in August 1966 as Project 1123.3.[40] She was of a modified design to provide improved survivability, seakeeping, and habitability, and—more important—an increase in the number of helicopters embarked with helicopter "spots" to be increased from four to six plus a spot for a "ready" plane guard helicopter. The modified design required an increase of 2,000 tons displacement and an addition of almost 40 feet in length. Russia naval historians V. P. Kuzin and V. I. Nikol'skiy observed,

> With a simple scale increase of the ship once again all of the designs previous shortcomings

"crept out," its fundamental rework was required. There was only one optimal way out: to locate seven takeoff and landing spots in one line, i.e. to create a "ribbon like" or, according to accepted terminology in the West, a "through" flight deck which, in the interest of economizing on the overall length of the ship, should be stuck at a small angle of 4–5 degrees onto the bow portion, taken up with weapons.[41]

The solution was a new design—Project 1143, the *Kiev* class.

The *Moskva* made her maiden deployment into the Mediterranean for 48 days in September–November 1968, joining the Soviet Navy's Fifth *Eskadra* (squadron).[42] Her longest at-sea deployment was from November 1977 to July 1978—222 days.

The *Leningrad* followed, and the two ships generally alternated operating in the central sea. Periodically they made forays into the North Atlantic and Baltic Sea for exercises. Both ships were at sea during the *Okean* multi-ocean exercise of 1970, the largest ever undertaken by the Soviet Navy.

The *Leningrad* operated two Mi-8 Hip helicopters in the mine clearance role at the southern entrance to the Suez Canal in 1973–1974.[43] That ship also operated for seven weeks in the Caribbean area in March–April 1984 as part of the periodic Soviet naval deployment to the Caribbean. The *Leningrad* was the largest Soviet warship ever to sail the Caribbean, conducting exercises and port visits with accompanying ships. The Soviets extensively used the *Moskva*s for political purposes, including port visits to a number of Eastern Bloc and Third World nations.

The *Moskva*'s flight deck was modified in 1972 for shipboard trials of the Yak-36M VSTOL demonstration aircraft with the first VSTOL landing taking place on November 18, 1972.[44] (The *Moskva* subsequently reverted to her original configuration.)

While the *Moskva* and *Leningrad* proved useful as missile cruisers and as helicopter carriers, their hull form was not completely successful. They were generally trimmed down by the bow and were reputed to be poor seaboats, an opinion confirmed by the changes planned for the third unit. Still, the *Moskva* design was the harbinger of the ambitious Soviet program for a carrier-led fleet.

23 SOVIET AIRCRAFT CARRIERS

The manifestation of an ocean-going fleet: the VSTOL carrier *Kiev* refuels at sea from the replenishment oiler *Genrikh Gasanov* in 1980. At the time of the demise of the Soviet Union in December 1991 the USSR had made major strides toward sending to sea a potent blue-water surface fleet. The Soviet undersea fleet had long been large and at times highly advanced in comparison with Western submarine forces. (U.S. Navy)

Leonid Brezhnev, a protegé of Nikita Khrushchev, succeeded him as head of the Communist Party and de facto head of the government in October 1964. Under Khrushchev, Admiral Sergei G. Gorshkov had gained approval to pursue the *Moskva*-class ASW ships, but Khrushchev was against building major surface warships. This was not the case with Brezhnev. Earlier, when Brezhnev was General Secretary of the Central Committee of the Communist Party and had the portfolio for military and defense issues, he said,

> We need an efficient and clear program for creating a new Navy which would take into consideration the economic capabilities of our nation, the trends in the development of the navies of the major imperialist powers, and also the experience of war. We are forced to build a large Navy—we are forced into this by the situation and by the aggressive intentions of the imperialist governments which are accelerating the growth of the strength of their own aircraft carriers, cruisers, submarines and landing ships in this connection, it is essential that we take into consideration the lessons of war.[1]

In 1970, after observing a major Soviet military exercise, Brezhnev declared, "No question of any importance in the world can be solved without our participation, without taking into account our economic and military might." Under Brezhnev the armed forces underwent a massive infusion of funds and the acceleration of the development and production of conventional as well as strategic weapons. For Admiral Gorshkov this meant new generations of aircraft, submarines, and surface ships.

351

In 1968 the TsKB-17/Nevskoye bureau began to revise the Project 1123.3 design of the third *Moskva* ASW cruiser, which transitioned into the workup of the preliminary design for Project 1143, given the project code name "Krechet." A key factor in the design was a government decision made in December 1967 to develop the Yak-38M (NATO code name Forger) shipboard attack aircraft based on the Yak 36 VSTOL technology demonstrator (NATO Freehand).[2]

The technical design of the third ASW carrier was completed in 1969 and approved in April 1970. A major anti-ship missile battery was provided with eight launchers for the Bazalt long-range missile (NATO SS-N-12 Sandbox) with eight below-deck reload missiles; in addition, improved anti-air and anti-submarine weapons were provided as were bow-mounted and variable-depth sonars, along with advanced radars and electronic warfare systems.[3] The ship's configuration provided for an angled fight deck 620-feet long with the bow section devoted to weapon installations. The large starboard island structure was inundated with weapons and electronic antennas. Two elevators were fitted to move aircraft between the hangar and flight decks.

The lead ship—the *Kiev*—was begun at Nikolayev's Black Sea Shipyard in 1970, launched on December 26, 1972, and completed in December 1975. She displaced 30,500 tons standard, 41,400 tons full load, and

The *Kiev* design evolved from the *Moskva*-class helicopter carrier-missile cruiser configuration. The *Kiev* featured a massive starboard island structure and angled flight deck with the weapons and sensors of a missile cruiser. In this view the *Kiev* had a dozen Ka-25 Hormone helicopters on her flight deck. The ship's two inboard elevators were sized for the Yak-38M Forger VSTOL aircraft and the Ka-25 Hormone. (U.S. Navy)

The forward section of carrier *Kiev*: from left are two RBU-6000 ASW rocket launchers; a twin-rail SA-N-3 Goblet surface-to-air missile launcher; and two sets of four SS-N-12 Sandbox anti-ship missile canisters (with a reloading hatch/elevator mounted between the sets). A twin 76.2-mm anti-aircraft gun mount and a second SA-N-3 missile launcher are mounted above the SS-N-12 (Soviet P.500) canisters, which elevate to fire. (Mitsuo Shibata via U.S. Department of Defense)

A massive array of electronic systems in the *Kiev* supported air operations and weapons: from left, a Head Lights fire control radar/director, the Top Sail 3-dimension air search radar; a tactical air navigation pod (atop the mast); Top Steer 3-D air search radar; and a second Head Lights system. The four domes are Side Globe EW antennas, topped with four Rum Tub EW antennas. These are U.S.-NATO names for Soviet electronic equipment. (U.S. Navy)

had a length of 895½ feet. Steam turbines turned four screws (compared to two shafts in the *Moskva*s) to provide a speed of about 30 knots. She was the largest warship yet constructed in the Soviet Union.

The *Kiev* was designed to embark 22 Yak-38M Forger VSTOL aircraft plus helicopters. However, in service the ship appears to have never operated more than 13 Yak-38s (one a two-seat trainer) plus a dozen or more ASW and search-and-rescue helicopters. The Forger became operational in 1976. The aircraft's development had been troublesome and lengthy. Further, the aircraft's lack of a search/navigation radar severely limited its range and effectiveness.

The decision to acquire the Yak-38 for shipboard service was difficult because from its initiation Admiral Gorshkov fully understood its limitations. At a conference of naval leaders at the Naval Academy in Leningrad he declared,[4] "Now we don't have a choice because the situation is desperate. We should begin construction of a carrier with such an aircraft and receive faster and better opportunities [for] . . . real full deck carriers in the near future." Gorshkov explained delaying the current program, that is, the *Kiev* and Yak-38, would only further delay development of more capable carriers.[5] All of the flag officers at the conference agreed with Gorshkov's views.

Developed by the design bureau of Aleksandr S. Yakovlev, the Yak-38 had a lift-plus-lift-cruise configuration using two forward lift engines that are mounted vertically and an aft-mounted, vectored-thrust engine for both vertical lift and propulsion. This configuration enhanced VTOL payload compared to the British-U.S. Harrier VSTOL aircraft, with the Yak-38 having a 64 percent VTOL payload advantage over the AV-8A and 25 percent over the AV-8B. The Soviet plane initially was seen flying only in the VTOL mode, but subsequently operated as a VSTOL aircraft as well. The Yak-38 had a swept-wing configuration with the outer panels folding upward for shipboard handling. The single seat A version was the standard variant, with one or two two-seat B variants normally embarked in carriers as an operational (combat) trainer.

The Yak-38's four wing pylons could accommodate approximately 6,600 pounds of bombs, missiles, or fuel tanks; in the interceptor role the aircraft generally carried two Aphid air-to-air missiles and two external fuel tanks. A small ranging radar was fitted.

(Shortly after the *Kiev* was begun, another large warship was started at the Baltic shipyard in Leningrad, which had not constructed warships since the *Sverdlov* cruiser program. After the *Sverdlov* cruisers, the yard had built the large nuclear-propelled icebreakers of the

The Yak-36 (NATO Freehand) was a technology demonstrator for the Yakovlev Yak-38M (NATO Forger), which became the fixed-wing aircraft flying from the *Kiev*-class carriers.

Arktika class. There was some speculation in the West that the new ship might be an aircraft carrier, possibly with nuclear propulsion. It was in fact the *Kirov*, a nuclear-propelled missile cruiser. Displacing 28,000 tons full load, the *Kirov* is the largest warship except for aircraft carriers built by any nation since World War II. The first of four ships in the class, the *Kirov* was laid down in 1973. Another class of smaller nuclear-propelled cruisers—intended for escorting nuclear-propelled aircraft carriers—was planned but not begun.)

The sister ships *Minsk* (Project 1143.2), completed in 1978, and the *Novorossiysk* (1143.3), completed in 1982, followed the *Kiev*. The third ship, with updated systems, was configured to operate the advanced Yak-141 VSTOL fighter as well as the Ka-27 Helix helicopter.[6] Also, the aviation fuel stowage was increased by 50 percent, which led to an increase of about 1,000 tons displacement. (In 1977 these ships were reclassified from ASW cruisers to heavy aviation carrying cruisers, which reflected the change in their combat capabilities.)

The Yak-141 (NATO Freestyle) was developed as a successor to the Yak-38. The later aircraft, which first flew in March 1989, was the world's first supersonic VSTOL aircraft. Like the Yak-38, the Yak-141 had three engines, one for forward flight and two for lift, with a complex fly-by-wire control system. The Yakovlev design bureau described the Mach 1.7 aircraft as being capable of air combat, close air support, and strike roles.

The aircraft was capable of both short-run and vertical takeoffs. Its features were a clean aerodynamic design with a relatively short span wing with four wing hardpoints and digital fly-by-wire flight controls (with mechanical backup). The airframe made extensive use of composite materials, with some 28 percent by weight being fabricated of carbon fibre, primarily in the tail assembly; the remainder of the structure was mainly aluminum lithium alloys. The aircraft's multi-mode radar was believed to be the same as in the MiG-29 Fulcrum, providing compatibility with a large number of advanced Soviet air-to-air and air-to-surface missiles. Like the MiG-29 the Yak-141 had a helmet-mounted sight for off-boresight targeting of air-to-air missiles. A two-place variant was planned. The wings folded for carrier stowage.

(Production of the Yak-141 was halted in August 1991. The first two flight test aircraft had flown about 200 flights logging some 150 hours from March 1989 through August 1991. Two additional aircraft served as ground test and system integration vehicles. The Yakovlev bureau began a new series of flight tests in September 1991. The bureau agreed to bear the costs of the flight tests with Yak-141s being offered for sale to both China and India. Neither country showed significant interest. In the event, the decision to discard

This Yak-38M is landing aboard the *Kiev* during 1976 operations in the Mediterranean. The hatch over the twin lift engines—behind the cockpit—is open. The Yak-38M was rated at a maximum speed of 625 m.p.h. at 36,000 feet (Mach 0.95). Its radius as a deck-launched interceptor was 115 miles with 75 minutes on station; its strike radius was 150 to 230 miles with approximately 6,600 pounds of external stores, the distance varying with the flight profile. (U.S. Navy)

the *Kiev*-class carriers led to complete termination of the Yak-141 program in 1992.)

A fourth *Kiev*-class carrier, Project 1143.4—subsequently named *Baku*—followed on the building ways at the Black Sea Shipyard. With the same basic hull form and propulsion machinery, the *Baku* had a greater displacement, 44,500 tons full load. She also was intended to operate the Yak-141 VSTOL fighter, although delay of that program meant that both the *Novorossiysk* and *Baku* went to sea with Yak-38s and Ka-27 Helix helicopters.[7]

The *Baku* carried more Bazalt missile launchers (12) but no reloads, that feature being found only in the *Kiev*. The later ship had improved surface-to-air missiles, an increased gun battery, and more advanced electronics, including a phased-array (fixed-antenna) search radar. The *Baku* was launched on March 31, 1982, and joined the Fleet in December 1987, the lengthy, 5½ year interval being required for her complex electronics suite. (The *Baku* would be renamed for Admiral Gorshkov after his death in 1988.)

Whereas the *Moskva* and *Leningrad* were based in the Black Sea, the *Kiev* and *Baku* were assigned to the Northern Fleet, deploying to the Atlantic and Mediterranean; the *Minsk* and *Novorossiysk* were assigned to the Pacific Fleet. These ships could not confront a

U.S. carrier force, as U.S. F-14 Tomcats and F/A-18 Hornets would easily sweep aside their VSTOL fighters. However, in the absence of a U.S. carrier, Soviet VSTOL aircraft could protect their ASW aircraft while attacking U.S. and NATO maritime patrol and reconnaissance aircraft.

The value of such VSTOL aircraft was also demonstrated in exercises, such as *Zapad-81* conducted in the Baltic during July and August 1981. There the *Kiev* and *Leningrad* participated in the war games, their aircraft joining land-based Soviet aircraft to support amphibious and ground operations.

And, the new carriers also had a political role. For example, when the *Minsk* transited from the Baltic to Vladivostok in 1979 to join the Pacific Fleet, she made port visits in Angola, East Africa, and South Yemen. Two modern cruisers, a large amphibious ship, and a replenishment oiler accompanied the *Minsk* on her transit.

In October 1978 the government decided to continue the construction of improved *Kiev*-class carriers with the next (fifth) ship to have catapults and arresting gear. In January 1979 the TsKB-17/Nevskoye bureau began to develop the Project 1143.5 design to operate an air group comprised of Su-27K/Su-33 Flanker fighters, Su-25UTG Frogfoot light attack and training aircraft,

The *Baku*, the fourth ship of the *Kiev* class, was completed with an extensively modified armament and electronics configuration. Her island structure has the flat faces of the Sky Watch phased-array radar (which may not have become operational); the Cylinder Blanc air navigation is housed in the circular antenna atop the island. There are 12 SS-N-12 Sandbox missile canisters forward, but without reloads. The ship was renamed for Admiral S. G. Gorshkov after his death in 1988. (U.S. Navy)

The *Tbilisi*, the Soviet Union's first—and final—full-deck aircraft carrier, at sea in late 1989. The ship's large island structure resembles those of the *Kiev*-class ships, but the forward portion of the ship is clear with a ski-ramp. With anti-ship, anti-air/missile, and anti-submarine weapons coupled with advanced electronics systems, the *Tbilisi* is a highly capable warship. She was later named for the late Admiral N. G. Kuznetsov. (Russian Navy)

Ka-27 Helix ASW helicopters, and the Ka-29RLD/Ka-31 variant of the Helix fitted for the airborne early warning role.[8]

The preliminary design of the ship was completed and approved at the end of 1979. The full load displacement was defined as 65,000 tons. However, at the beginning of 1980 the Minister of Defense, Dmitriy F. Ustinov, issued a directive to reduce the ship's displacement and orient its air group toward VSTOL aircraft. Instead of catapults for takeoff a bow ski-ramp was proposed. Accordingly, at the end of 1980 it was decided to complete the ship—given the project name "Nitka"—to support only VSTOL aircraft and to exclude the catapults. But the design was again revised to provide for the conventional Su-33, Su-25UTG, and MiG-29K Fulcrum-D aircraft as well as Yak-141s and Ka-27s. Also, development was under way on a radar picket/early warning aircraft for the ship. The total aircraft to be embarked was 52.

(As the Soviet Union was dissolved in 1991, so were many of its military programs: Neither the Yak-141 nor MiG-29K entered service—and only 24 Su-33 aircraft were built. The last, which entered naval service in 1996, never flew from a carrier deck.[9])

The new carrier would be significantly larger than the *Kiev* design, with a standard displacement of approximately 45,000 tons and some 55,000 tons at full load, with a length of 984 feet. The ship would have an angled flight deck, a striking 12-degree ski-ramp forward, and a large island structure to starboard mounting the Mars-Passat (NATO Sky Watch) phased-array radar. Another innovation to Soviet carriers with Project 1143.5 was the installation of two starboard-side, deck-edge elevators.

Recessed into the forward flight deck were 12 angled launch cells for the Granit long-range anti-ship missile (NATO SS-N-19 Shipwreck).[10] Surface-to-surface missiles were thus common to all classes of Soviet carriers.

Despite the efforts on Project 1143.5, in March 1980 the government directed the construction of two ASW helicopter carriers at the Black Sea Shipyard immediately after the fourth *Kiev*—in place of the fifth large carrier. The principal advocate of these ships was Deputy Chief of the Soviet General Staff, Admiral Nikolay N. Amel'ko, who was previously a deputy commander-in-chief of the Navy. Amel'ko was the principal opponent of large aircraft carriers within the Navy. On his initiative while he was Deputy CinC of the Navy a scientific research effort was begun to create an integrated ASW system, whose basic component would be the ASW helicopter carriers. The design of the carrier—initially based on a civilian container ship—began at TsKB Chernomorets. The design soon evolved into a completely new ship. The Nevskoye design bureau and the prestigious Krylov Central Scientific Research Institute of Naval Shipbuilding opposed this diversion to build two Project 1020 helicopter carriers. However, the ASW carrier venture was soon terminated.

The fifth carrier, Project 1143.5—initially named *Riga*—was laid down at the Black Sea Shipyard on September 1, 1982. However, little work was accomplished, and on February 22, 1983, the ship was "re-laid" and assigned the name *Leonid Brezhnev*, honoring the Soviet leader who had died in November 1982. The ship was launched on December 4, 1985.

Significantly, by the early 1980s there were indications of a "changing of the guard" in the Soviet naval leadership. A perceptive article by Dr. Robert C. Suggs, a civilian naval analyst, noted that the official journal *Morskoy sbornik* [Naval Digest] had increasingly published critiques of Admiral Gorshkov's views. In particular, a two-part article published in April–May 1981 brought "sharp, critical responses from a variety of participants in the Soviet naval hierarchy, including senior flag officers representing the operational, political, and educational communities."[11] *Krasnaya Zvezda* [Red Star], the official Ministry of Defense newspaper, continued the debate. In general, the critics claimed that the Gorshkov approach to naval theory was too narrow and independent of the study of military science. Indirectly, this was an attack on Gorshkov's programs and policies.

Admiral Gorshkov was retired in December 1985, as the *Brezhnev*, named for his late patron, was being launched. Admiral Vladimir N. Chernavin, a nuclear submariner succeeded Gorshkov as Commander-in-Chief of the Navy and Deputy Minister of Defense.[12] Chernavin continued the Soviet carrier program as the Soviet Union saw a continuing threat from the West during the Reagan administration's military buildup, the U.S. reaction to the Soviet shootdown of a Korean airliner in 1983, and the Soviet fear that a NATO command post exercise in 1983—code name Able Archer—was a prelude to a surprise attack on the USSR.

Work again slowed on the *Brezhnev*, and in August 1987, four and a half years after Brezhnev's death, the ship was renamed *Tbilisi*. The *Tbilisi* was the largest warship, except for U.S. aircraft carriers, constructed by any nation since World War II. The carrier went to sea in November 1989, "well ahead of our estimates," according to the U.S. Director of Naval Intelligence.[13] He speculated, "The fact that flight

There are **12** vertical-launch cells for the SS-N-19 Shipwreck (Soviet P.700) anti-ship missile "hidden" in the forward flight deck of the *Tbilisi* (now *Admiral Kuznetsov*). These are supersonic missiles with a range of some 300 n.miles, with over-the-horizon guidance provided by aircraft or satellites. The same missile is carried in the Project 949 (NATO Oscar) cruise missile submarines. (*Russia's Arms Catalog*)

operations were conducted so early in [the ship's] sea trials suggests the Soviet Navy felt the need to convince policymakers of the carrier's importance and viability during last fall's budget debate."

An Su-27K Flanker, piloted by Viktor Pugachev, a Hero of the Soviet Union and chief test pilot for the Sukhoi design bureau, on November 1, 1989, landed the first fixed-wing aircraft on the *Tbilisi*. A MiG-29K and Su-25UTG followed. The three aircraft made numerous arrested landings and ski-ramp takeoffs during the trials.

In this period the Navy had modified the Saki air base in the Crimea to support carrier development. A carrier deck outline was overlayed on a runway while work on arresting gear, ski-ramps, and catapults were evaluated at Saki. The base was also used to train fixed-wing carrier pilots.[14]

The ship, having recently been renamed *Admiral Flota Sovetskogo Soyuza Kuznetsov*, was delivered to the Navy on December 25, 1990. She was not yet operational and not until late 1991 did the *Kuznetsov* pass through the Turkish Straits, transit the Mediterranean, and then turn northward, dropping anchor at Severmorsk on the Kola Peninsula. The large carrier returned to the Mediterranean for a brief operational deployment in early 1996. Since then, the ship has spent little time at sea.

The second ship of this design, Project 1143.6, also carried the name *Riga*. She was launched on November 25, 1988, having a modified superstructure. In 1990,

Admiral S. G. Gorshkov. (Soviet Navy)

while still under construction, the ship was renamed *Varyag*, meaning "northman," a traditional name for Russian naval ships.[15] That ship was never completed, and the Ukraine sold it to a Chinese firm for use as a floating theme park.

Nuclear-Propelled Carriers

Shortly after the *Riga* (II) was launched in late 1988, construction of a nuclear-propelled aircraft carrier was begun in the Black Sea Shipyard's massive building dock, which had given birth to all previous Soviet aircraft carriers. Even while the pioneer carrier *Kiev* was still under construction, design efforts had been under way for a nuclear-propelled carrier.[16]

The Navy scientific research institutes developed a technical-tactical tasking for the creation of large aircraft carriers under the cover name "Orel." The TsKB-17/Nevskoye design team led by Arkadi B. Morin was directed to undertake the design of Project 1160. The

tasking envisioned a nuclear-propelled ship with a standard displacement of 75,000 to 80,000 tons embarking at least 70 aircraft. The ship was to have four steam catapults, with three elevators connecting the hangar and flight decks.

This ship would be similar to U.S. nuclear carriers. In the presentation of Project 1160 to the Minister of Defense, Marshal Andrei A. Grechko—reportedly the only one of all of the Ministers of Defense who supported the construction of aircraft carriers—stated, "What are you thinking about there! Make it just like the Americans, with the same air wing size."[17]

In 1973 the CinCs of the Navy and Air Forces and the ministers of the Shipbuilding and Aviation Industries approved the advanced design for Project 1160. But the Soviet bureaucracy then came into play: First came a directive by Secretary of the Central Committee Dmitriy F. Ustinov "to review the issue of the building of the third *Kiev* class ship in a modernized [updated] variant." A compromise was reached that recommended a new design for just 36 aircraft with catapult-launch capability but of the *Kiev*'s dimensions. Subsequently another agency—the Defense Industrial Commission under the Central Committee and the USSR Council of Ministers—agreed to the designing of a new, larger ship. A new design number—Project 1153—was assigned, and Admiral Gorshkov approved a tactical-technical tasking for the ship in June 1974.

But delays continued, and in April 1976 a resolution of the Central Committee and the Council of Ministers envisioned two nuclear carriers in the 1978–1985 period. In August 1976 Admiral Gorshkov approved new tasking for the ship because the first had become

Table 23-1
AIRCRAFT CARRIER NAMES

PROJECT	BUILT	RENAMED
1143	*Kiev*	—
1143.2	*Minsk*	—
1143.3	*Novorossiysk*	—
1143.4	*Baku*	*Admiral Flota Sovetskogo Soyuza Gorshkov* on Oct 4, 1990
1143.5	*Riga*	*Leonid Brezhnev* on Nov 26, 1982
		Tbilisi on Aug 11, 1987
		Admiral Flota Sovetskogo Soyuza Kuznetsov on Oct 4, 1990
1143.6	*Riga* (II)	*Varyag* on June 19, 1990
1143.7	*Ul'yanovsk*	—

Admiral Kuznetsov (formerly the *Tbilisi*) is the only aircraft carrier operated by the Russian Navy in the aftermath of the collapse of the Soviet Union. Shown here on one of the ship's periodic cruises to the North Atlantic and Mediterranean, there is a Ka-27 Helix helicopter on the angled deck; Su-33 Flanker aircraft are parked (with wings folded) next to the massive island structure. Note the Sky Watch phased-array radar antennas mounted above the ship's bridge. (Royal Air Force)

outdated: a new carrier of about 60,000 tons standard displacement with an air group of 50 aircraft with two catapults, propelled by a three-shaft nuclear propulsion plant. This was considered the smallest possible nuclear-propelled carrier and, consequently, the least effective design variant. The decision to make a smaller carrier was made because the construction of a large carrier was hindered by limitations on the building dock at Nikolayev.

A new attack on the ship next came from an unexpected direction: aircraft designer Aleksandr S. Yakovlev, who proposed refitting the *Novorossiysk* (the third *Kiev*-class ship) with a "gas ducting" system to improve VSTOL takeoff characteristics. Work on the system was begun but was quickly halted, and construction of the *Novorossiysk* to the original design resumed. As a result of this design diversion, delivery of the ship was delayed from 1979 to 1982.

This diversion further delayed the convoluted efforts to develop a nuclear carrier. In 1976 the prelimi-

nary design of the Project 1153 ship was completed when further design work on the ship was halted. "Who, specifically, took this decision, remains a mystery. . . . In this way was interdicted our independent line of creating nuclear-powered carriers, and it was decided to improve elements of the *Kiev* class ships under construction with the inclusion of catapult takeoff aviation on them. Thus, in 1977 we returned to that which we had passed through in 1973," according to historians V. P. Kuzin and V. I. Nikol'skiy.[18] Ustinov, a defense industrial specialist, who had little regard for aircraft carriers, succeeded Marshal Grechko as Minister of Defense.

At this stage *Kiev*-class carriers were in series production and major improvements were being made to each ship. Accordingly, Admiral Gorshkov approved the provision of catapults in the fifth ship (Project 1143.5) in January 1979. In comparison with the last approved design variant it was proposed to reduce the ship's displacement, to provide conventional propulsion, and to reduce the aircraft capacity to 42.

The Yakovlev Yak-44 was a twin-engine AEW aircraft developed for operation from the carrier *Admiral Kuznetsov* (formerly *Tbilisi*). The aircraft was to have twin turboprop engines and a rotating search radar antenna, similar to the Grumman E-2 Hawkeye. This was a mockup of the Yak-44; the demise of the carrier program with the demise of the Soviet Union led to the cancellation of this Yak-44 program before the prototype was completed.

The next effort to construct a nuclear-propelled carrier came in the mid-1980s when the government confirmed the 1986–1995 shipbuilding plan. In December 1984 the tactical-technical tasking was issued for the development of the seventh heavy aircraft carrying cruiser—a nuclear-propelled ship with greater displacement and a larger air group.

In 1986 the preliminary design for Project 1143.7 was completed and approved, and in 1987 the technical design was completed. The ship was to carry up to 70 aircraft—Su-33 and MiG-29K fighters, Yak-44 radar picket and targeting aircraft, and Ka-27/29 helicopters. The new Yak-44 would have been a twin-turboprop aircraft similar to the U.S. E-2 Hawkeye (it never progressed past the mock-up stage). The ship would have an angled flight deck with two waist catapults and a ski-ramp forward. The ship would have a large anti-air/missile battery and 12 vertically launched anti-ship missiles. She would have a standard displacement of about 66,000 tons, a full load displacement of more than 75,000 tons, with a length of some 1,065 feet. Propulsion would be nuclear, providing a speed of 30 knots.

The name *Ul'yanovsk* was assigned to honor V. I. Lenin's native city. Thus the tradition of naming carriers for cities continued. The ship was laid down in the massive building dock at the Black Sea Shipyard on November 25, 1988, immediately after the launching of the *Riga* (II). At the time the U.S. Navy had five nuclear-propelled aircraft carriers in service and two more under construction. About then U.S. naval intel-

ligence estimated that based on a 20-year projection of Soviet naval strength, the USSR could posses 15 aircraft carriers by 2010—a building rate of one ship every two years. "At the rate carrier-type ships have been built over the preceding 15 years, this was not an unreasonable projection," said Rear Admiral Thomas A. Brooks, the U.S. Director of Naval Intelligence in 1988–1991. "But," he added, "the crumbling of the Soviet Union had only just begun . . . and no one in the West predicted its extent and speed."[19]

Red Star Falling

Western intelligence sources—primarily satellite photography—indicated that work had been stopped on both the *Riga* (II) and the *Ul'yanovsk* in November 1991. The Ministry of Defense had halted the ships' financing. They were, respectively, 70 percent and 20 percent complete.

At the end of December 1991 the Soviet Union ceased to exist. The Soviet armed forces immediately entered a state of disarray. The Navy's problems were extremely complex as new, independent nations began to lay claim to naval ships in their waters. The Ukraine claimed not only the *Moskva* and *Leningrad* but also the unfinished *Varyag*. The Ukrainian government decided to scrap the *Ul'yanovsk* to provide space in the massive Nikolayev building dock for merchant ship construction. Her dismantling began on February 3, 1992.[20]

A Sukhoi Su-33 (NATO Flanker-D) from the *Admiral Kuznetsov* over the Mediterranean. The Su-33 was developed from the Su-27, with the first naval variant, the Su-27K (for *Korabelny* or "shipborne"), flying on August 17, 1987. The aircraft can carry a 410-gallon drop tank or a 9,920-pound Kh-41 Moskit (Mosquito) anti-ship missile on the centerline position. Twin turbofan engines provide a maximum speed of 1,430 m.p.h. at 32,780 feet (Mach 2.17), with an rate of climb of 45,235 feet per minute, and a ceiling of 55,720 feet. The Su-33KUB has side-by-side seating. (Royal Air Force)

Sukhoi's Su-25 (NATO Frogfoot) is a subsonic ground attack aircraft that has been adopted for carrier operation. It is similar in concept to the U.S. A-10 Thunderbolt close air support aircraft. The Frogfoot was used extensively in anti-guerrilla operations in Afghanistan during the 1980s. About 8,800 pounds ordnance and fuel tanks can be carried on eight wing pylons and two missile rails; the latter can hold air-to-air missiles for self-defense or for attacking helicopters. A rotary 23-mm anti-tank cannon is fitted in the fuselage. Twin turbojet engines provide a maximum speed of 605 miles per hour; ceiling is 22,960 feet; and radius is 340 miles with 4,000 pounds of ordnance and two drop tanks. (Richard Seaman)

After some negotiations, in 1994 the Russian government declined to resume the *Varyag*'s construction. The total cost of the ship was estimated at US$2.4 *billion*, and more than US$500 million was needed to complete her construction. Further complicating matters would be problems in acquiring some of the planned systems for the ships. The Ukraine decided in June 1994 to scrap the *Varyag* after unsuccessful attempts to sell the unfinished ship to Russia, China, or India. However, sale of the hulk for US$20 million was announced on March 17, 1998, to a Chinese company with the agreement that the ship would not be used for military purposes. Much of her equipment had never been installed or had been removed.

After the division of surviving Black Sea Fleet ships between Russia and the Ukraine, the *Moskva* and *Leningrad* undertook no operations. The *Moskva*, the first Soviet "carrier," was decommissioned in 1995 and served briefly as an accommodation ship before being stricken in 1996. The following year she was towed to India and scrapped. The *Leningrad* was stricken in 1991 and towed to Greece in 1995 for scrapping.

The Russian Federation retained control of the four *Kiev*-class ships. However, the retirement of the Yak-

38 from naval service in 1992 left these ships without fixed-wing aircraft. The *Kiev* was decommissioned in 1994 and in May 2000 began a long tow to India for scrapping. Her sister ships *Minsk* and *Novorossiysk* were both stricken in 1993. The *Minsk* was sold in 1995 to South Korea for scrap but was resold to a Chinese firm for use as a floating (immobile) gambling casino and amusement park near Hong Kong. That commercial firm went bankrupt, and the ship, crammed with carnival attractions, was abandoned in a harbor near Shenzhen. The *Novorossiysk* was also sold to South Korea for scrap but subsequently was towed to India to be cut up.

The *Baku* was renamed *Admiral Flota Sovetskogo Soyuza Gorshkov* on October 4, 1990, as the city of Baku would not be in the new Russian Federation. The *Gorshkov* ceased operations in 1991 and, while in reserve at the Rosta Shipyard near Murmansk, suffered a major fire in February 1994. After a decade of negotiations, the carrier was sold to India on January 20, 2004. She is being extensively reconstructed and was to be delivered in 2010 or later (see Chapter 21).

As the Soviet Union was breaking apart, the *Tbilisi* was renamed; she became the *Admiral Flota Sovetskogo Soyuza Kuznetsov* on October 4, 1990. The ship

The Kamov Ka-27PL (NATO Helix-A) is successor to the Ka-25 Hormone in the ship-based ASW role. It has twin turboshaft engines and the familiar contrarotating rotors of Kamov helicopters. The Helix-A has dipping sonar or magnetic detection gear, sonobuoys, and radar for submarine detection, and carries homing torpedoes for attack. Maximum speed is 167 m.p.h. Mission endurance is 4½ hours. The first flight of the Ka-27 was in December 1974. Variants of the helicopter are designated Ka-29 and Ka-31. The Helix is also flown by China, India, South Korea, Ukraine, and Vietnam.

The Kamov Ka-29RLD/Ka-31 is the ship-based AEW variant of the Helix. The helicopter's folding search antenna is evident. The concept is similar to the Royal Navy's innovative Sea King AEW/ASaC helicopter. This capability enables carriers to operate beyond the range of land-based AEW aircraft. (Richard Seaman)

is assigned to the Northern Fleet and periodically has deployed to the North Atlantic and the Mediterranean. On her rare deployments the ship has at times operated an air group consisting of

6 Su-33 Flanker-D fighters
2 Su-33 KUB Flanker fighter-trainers
2 Su-25UBP attack aircraft trainers
6 Ka-27PL Helix-A ASW helicopters
2 Ka-27PS Helix-C rescue helicopters
3 Ka-31 Helix AEW helicopters

Admiral Kuznetsov, fired by Stalin and fired by Khrushchev, was truly rehabilitated when his name was carried by the only operational Russian aircraft carrier at the start of the 21st Century. Thus, the ambitious Soviet carrier program cndcd with but one operational carrier with a severely limited aviation capability.

The Yak-141 was a supersonic VSTOL aircraft intended for operation from the *Kiev*-class carriers. The aircraft's maximum speed was 1,116 m.p.h at sea level (Mach 1.7), with a ceiling of more than 49,000 feet. Range in the interceptor role with vertical takeoff and internal fuel was estimated at 870 miles. Unlike the Yak-38, the Yak-141 had an internal 30-mm cannon. The four wing positions could carry up to 6,700 pounds of missiles, bombs, rocket pods, and external fuel, including laser-guided weapons. Like the Yak-38M, the later aircraft was intended primarily for rolling takeoffs. Yak-141 was the Yakovlev bureau designation; in service the aircraft would probably have been the Yak-41.

24 REHABILITATION AND RETALIATION

Looking like a "real ship," the aircraft carrier *John C. Stennis* (CVN 74) heels 14 degrees to starboard in a high-speed turn during her sea trials in October 1995. In the final years of the Cold War carrier construction in the United States confronted major cost issues; their vulnerabilities were rarely spoken of because of their continued contributions to crises and limited conflicts. (Thomas Hensley, U.S. Navy)

The end of the Vietnam War led to major reductions in U.S. military and naval forces. The Carter administration of the late 1970s severely cut U.S. defense spending. In the presidential campaign of 1980 Ronald Reagan ran on a political platform calling for the rebuilding of the U.S. military establishment and major increases in strategic and naval forces.

Following his inauguration in January 1981, President Reagan named John Lehman as the Secretary of the Navy.[1] Lehman, a 41-year-old Naval Reserve officer and longtime government executive, initiated a 600-ship program based largely on proposals of Admiral Thomas Hayward, Chief of Naval Operations from 1978 to 1982. This was part of a "Maritime Strategy," a "plan" for aggressive U.S. naval operations in conflict against the Soviet Union. The strategy was based in large part on the U.S. intelligence penetration of the Soviet high command and naval leadership in the late

1970s and early 1980s through communications intercepts and "human intelligence"—spies. This "deep penetration" provided unprecedented insight into Soviet strategic planning for several years.[2]

The Maritime Strategy called for carrier battle groups in time of war to steam north into Soviet operating areas to launch nuclear strike aircraft against the Soviet homeland. As part of his buildup under the aegis of the Maritime Strategy, Secretary Lehman sought to increase the Navy's carrier force to 15 ships from the 13 then in commission. During the previous Carter administration (1977–1981) proposals for a severe reduction in the number of carriers, possibly to as few as six ships, had been considered. When Congress added the CVN 71—the fourth *Nimitz*-class nuclear carrier—to the fiscal 1979 defense budget, President Carter vetoed the entire $36 *billion* defense authorization bill (the carrier cost was put at $2 *billion*). At his press conference, Carter said,

> The ultimate effect of this bill would also weaken our Navy by aggravating the dangerous trend away from a larger number of different kinds of ships which can maintain our military presence on the high seas, and toward a disturbingly small number of ships which are increasingly costly. What the Congress has done with the money being cut from these vital areas is to authorize a fifth nuclear-powered aircraft carrier, which we do not need. This would be the most expressive ship ever built. Its purchase price, even estimated now, would be a least $2 billion, and the aircraft it would carry and the extra ships required to escort and defend it would cost billions more in years to come.
>
> In order to use our dollars for their maximum effect, we must choose armor, artillery, aircraft, and support that will immediately bolster our strength, especially in NATO. By diverting funds away from more important defense needs in order to build a very expensive nuclear aircraft carrier, this bill would reduce our commitment to NATO, waste the resources available for defense, and weaken our Nation's military capabilities in the future.

Congress could not override President Carter's veto of the fiscal 1979 authorization bill. A new bill was passed without a carrier.

John F. Lehman, Jr. (Department of Defense)

The following year an enthusiastic Congress again voted for a nuclear carrier and Carter, now intimidated by Congress as well as by Soviet actions, signed the fiscal 1980 legislation funding the CVN 71. One of the Navy officers working "behind the scenes" on Capitol Hill to lobby for the carrier was Captain John McCain, a Navy liaison officer to the Senate. The ex-carrier pilot and ex–prisoner of war was highly effective in making the case for the CVN 71 as was John Lehman, then working for the Republican National Committee. As Lehman later wrote,

> As a kind of hobby, I spent a good deal of my time . . . working *pro bono* with Senators [Henry] Jackson and [John] Tower, and lobbying all sorts of other people in the House and Senate to kill the CVV and replace it with another *Nimitz* class carrier. I wrote a book called *Aircraft Carriers: The Real Choices* in preparation for the debate.[3]

In the subsequent Reagan administration, Secretary Lehman, working astutely with the powerful Virginia congressional delegation, obtained unprecedented funding for two super carriers in two separate years—the CVN 72 and 73 in fiscal 1983 and the CVN 74 and 75 in fiscal 1988.[4] Not since World War II had two first-line carriers been authorized in a single fiscal year. Lehman was able to sell his two-carrier buys to Congress because of better contracting arrangements with the Newport News Shipbuilding yard, which, reportedly, garnered significant cost savings.[5] With the older *Enterprise*, these four ships would give the Navy nine nuclear carriers by the end of the century:

SHIP		COMPLETED
CVN 65	*Enterprise*	1961
CVN 68	*Nimitz*	1975
CVN 69	*Dwight D. Eisenhower*	1977
CVN 70	*Carl Vinson*[6]	1982
CVN 71	*Theodore Roosevelt*	1986
CVN 72	*Abraham Lincoln*	1989
CVN 73	*George Washington*	1992
CVN 74	*John C. Stennis*	1995
CVN 75	*Harry S. Truman*	1998

For his more immediate goal of increasing the carrier force from 13 to 15 ships, Secretary Lehman sought to reactivate the mothballed carrier *Oriskany*, the last of the *Essex*-class ships. But, according to Lehman, she had been "ridden hard and put away wet at the end of the Vietnam War, without an overhaul or proper preservation," and was in no condition to be reactivated.[7] Thus, the carrier force remained at 13 ships through 1987, when, for three years 14 carriers were in commission. That number again dropped to 13 carriers in 1990 and then to 12 the following year, the number in service into the 21st Century.

In 1978 a new fighter-attack aircraft became operational, the carrier-based F/A-18 Hornet. The F/A-18 was developed in response to congressional pressure on the Navy to obtain a lightweight fighter to complement the F-14 Tomcat in carrier air wings. Congress directed the Navy to accept the winner of the Air Force's lightweight fighter competition of the mid-1970s between the General Dynamics YF-16 and Northrop YF-17 prototypes. The Air Force selected the F-16 for production; the Navy selected the YF-17 but made major modifications, which evolved the aircraft into the F/A-18, developed jointly by McDonnell Douglas and Northrop.[8]

The prototype YF-18 flew on November 18, 1978. The twin-engine Hornet could carry a variety of bombs, missiles, and rockets, including up to four 2,000-pound bombs; a 20-mm Gatling gun was installed. The aircraft's fire control system could shift from the air-to-surface to the air-to-air mode with the flip of a switch. However, the naval aircraft failed to fully achieve its range/payload goals in the attack role.

The F/A-18 entered service with both Navy and Marine fleet squadrons in 1983 with Navy strike-fighter squadron VFA-113 and Marine fighter-attack squadron VMFA-314. The F/A-18 eventually replaced the A-6E Intruder, A-7E Corsair, and F-14 Tomcat; subsequently the EA-18 Growler electronic countermeasures/attack variant was selected to replace the EA-6B Prowler in Navy service.[9] Thus, by the late 1990s the F/A-18 became the most numerous fixed-wing aircraft in naval aviation. (Eight other nations fly F/A-18 variants as land-based fighter-attack aircraft.)

Similarly, the Navy adopted the Army's UH-60 Black Hawk transport helicopter to become the next generation anti-submarine helicopter. Initially it was

The McDonnell Douglas/Northrop F/A-18 Hornet became the principal fighter/attack aircraft of the U.S. Navy and Marine Corps. The improved F/A-18C variant, which entered service in 1987, could exceed Mach 1.7 at 36,000 feet. It could carry two Sidewinder missiles on wingtips plus more than 13,000 pounds of bombs, missiles, targeting pods, and fuel tanks on six store stations; a 20-mm M61 Vulcan multi-barrel cannon is also fitted. With only air-to-air missiles, the aircraft can maintain a Combat Air Patrol (CAP) station 175 miles from the carrier for 1 hour, 45 minutes; its strike-missions radius is up to 330 miles with reduced payloads. The F/A-18B, D, and F variants are two-seat aircraft. This F/A-18C from VFA-143 is launching from the carrier *Dwight D. Eisenhower*. (Rafael Medina, U.S. Navy)

Sikorsky's H-60 series "Hawk" helicopters are flown by all U.S. military services. The SH-60F was developed specifically for carrier ASW operations. With twin turboshaft engines, the SH-60F has maximum cruise speed of 145 m.p.h. with a ceiling of 19,000 feet. It can carry two Mk 46 or Mk 50 ASW torpedoes; AN/AQS-13F dipping sonar, sonobuoys, and Magnetic Anomaly Detection (MAD) are fitted. Forward deployed SH-60s can be armed with M60 or M240 7.62-mm machine guns to fire from the door opening. This SH-60F is from helicopter ASW squadron HS-8 aboard the carrier *Stennis*. (Tina Lamb, U.S. Navy)

procured from Sikorsky as the SH-60B Light Airborne Multi-Purpose System (LAMPS) III for use aboard surface combatants. Becoming operational in 1980, the SH-60B could also be employed for surface surveillance and attack, using the Norwegian-developed Penguin anti-ship missile in the latter role. The success of the SH-60B—named the Seahawk—led to the SH-60F variant for carrier ASW operation, replacing the SH-3 Sea King. The SH-60F entered service in 1991; it had dipping sonar (in place of sonobuoys) and, like the SH-60B variant, could carry two Mk 46 or Mk 50 acoustic homing torpedoes.

The H-60 series eventually became the Navy's universal helicopter. The HH-60 flies in the combat rescue/special forces support role, and later the MH-60R succeeded both the SH-60B and -60F in the multisensor and multiweapon ASW/anti-surface roles and the MH-60S in the vertical replenishment, mine countermeasures, and utility roles. From the late 1990s, with the demise of the S-3 Viking as a carrier-based ASW aircraft, multipurpose squadrons flying the SH-60F and, later, the multi-role MH-60R became the only U.S. carrier-based ASW aircraft.

North . . . To the Kola Peninsula

The Reagan administration, by its actions and rhetoric, was of great concern to the Soviet leadership. Reacting to President Reagan entering the White House and to the U.S. deployment of new theater nuclear missiles to Europe, Soviet leader Leonid Brezhnev and KGB Chairman Yuri Andropov made a joint appearance before a closed session of senior KGB officers in May 1981.[10]

At this session Brezhnev took the podium and briefed the assembled intelligence officers on his concerns about U.S. policy under Reagan. Andropov then spoke, asserting that the United States was making preparations for a surprise nuclear attack on the Soviet Union. He declared that the KGB and Soviet military intelligence (GRU) would join forces to monitor indications and to provide early warning of U.S. war preparations. The intelligence effort was given the code name RYAN—an acronym for *Raketno-Yadernoye Napadenie* (nuclear missile attack).

Then, in August–September 1981, in an exercise in support of the Maritime Strategy, an armada of 83 U.S., British, Canadian, and Norwegian ships, led by the carrier *Eisenhower*, sailed from the Atlantic into the Norwegian Sea, undetected by Soviet forces, using a variety of carefully crafted and previously rehearsed concealment and deception measures. These included passive measures (maintaining radio silence, carefully controlling radar emissions, and flying aircraft below Soviet radar) and active measures (radar-jamming and transmission of false radar signals). The carrier group was able to elude a Soviet low-orbit, active-radar satellite launched specifically to locate the ships. The exercise—with the "Ike" carrying nuclear-capable strike aircraft—was of major concern to the Soviet leadership.

The concern continued, and on February 17, 1983, KGB headquarters notified senior intelligence officers in foreign embassies that RYAN had "acquired an especial degree of urgency" and was "now of particularly grave importance." Soviet concerns were raised another notch on March 23 when President Reagan announced his plan for a national missile defense system, which was promptly dubbed "Star Wars" by the press after the films produced by George Lucas. Four days after the president's announcement—and in direct response—Andropov lashed out. Having succeeded to head the Soviet leadership upon Brezhnev's death in November 1982, the career KGB officer accused the United States of preparing a first-strike attack on the Soviet Union and asserted that President Reagan was "inventing new plans on how to unleash a nuclear war in the best way, with the hope of winning it," reported the Soviet newspaper *Pravda* on March 27, 1983.

Subsequently, some 40 ships of the U.S. Pacific Fleet conducted a major exercise in April–May 1983 with a high degree of stealth. These ships came within 450 miles of the port of Petropavlovsk on the Kamchatka Peninsula, the major Soviet missile submarine base in the Pacific. The participating U.S. carriers *Midway* and *Enterprise* both had nuclear strike aircraft on board.

Finally, in November 1983 a North Atlantic Treaty Organization command post exercise called Able Archer included a practice drill that took NATO forces through a large-scale simulated release of nuclear weapons. In response, on November 8 or 9, KGB headquarters sent a flash cable to West European operatives advising them—incorrectly—that U.S. forces in Europe had gone on alert and that troops at some bases were being mobilized. The cable speculated that the (nonexistent) alert might have been ordered in response to the recent truck-bomb attack on the U.S. Marine barracks in Beirut that had killed 241 Americans or was related to impending U.S. Army maneuvers or was the beginning of a countdown to a surprise nuclear attack. Recipients were asked to confirm the U.S. alert and to evaluate these hypotheses. In the tense atmosphere generated by the crises and the rhetoric of the previous few months, some KGB officials concluded that American forces had been placed on alert—and might even have begun the countdown to war.

A short time later the Soviet alert dissipated, in part because President Reagan reduced his rhetoric against the Soviet Union in light of indications that the Soviets were reacting to U.S. stimuli. Also contributing to the resolution of the threat was the death of Andropov in February 1984.

Intelligence historians Christopher Andrew and Oleg Gordievsky wrote, "The world did not quite reach the edge of the nuclear abyss during Operation RYAN. But during Able Archer 83 it had, without realizing it, come frighteningly close—certainly closer than at any time since the Cuban missile crisis of 1962."[11]

Meanwhile, U.S. aircraft carriers were in action in this period.

Carriers vs. Iran

Iran—earlier known as Persia—had been an ally of the United States since the 1950s.[12] Mohammad Reza Shah Pahlevi, ruler of the country since 1941, was a key U.S. ally and encouraged strong U.S.-Iranian military and intelligence ties.[13] In 1978 a fundamentalist Muslim revolution erupted in Iran. As fighting flared in the streets of Iranian cities, the Shah fled the country on January 16, 1979. A month later armed Iranians broke into the U.S. embassy compound in the capital of Tehran. Two U.S. Marines were wounded in the incident. Tense relations between the two countries continued until November 4, 1979, when Iranian militants seized the U.S. embassy, taking 66 Americans as prisoners, including 14 Marines and 3 Navy personnel. The militants demanded the return of the deposed Shah, who was in a New York hospital, to Iran for trial.[14]

President Carter initially resisted proposals by U.S. military commanders (and the Israeli government) to assault the embassy and rescue the hostages. But public and congressional reaction to the situation caused Carter—who sought the hostage release through negotiations—to finally approve a military rescue attempt, Operation Eagle Claw.

An extremely complex operation was initiated to rescue the 53 American hostages still held in Tehran. Eight Navy RH-35D Sea Stallions from Helicopter Mine Countermeasures Squadron 16 were clandestinely loaded aboard the carrier *Nimitz*, having been flown in Air Force C-5 transports from Norfolk to an overseas staging base. They were flown by Marines instead of their normal Navy flight crews.

On April 24, 1980, as the *Nimitz* operated in the Arabian Sea, the eight helicopters were launched to a remote desert location in Iran where they were to load a U.S. commando team for the flight into Tehran. Six Air Force C-130 Hercules transports took off from Egypt carrying the commandos and fuel bladders for the helicopters. When the raiders assaulted the compound, AC-130 Hercules gunships were to circle overhead to provide fire support.

The *Nimitz* was the first of a ten-ship class of nuclear-propelled super carriers. These ships fought in the 1991 and 2003 conflicts in the Middle East, and the *Nimitz* launched the ill-fated RH-53D Sea Stallion helicopters for the aborted effort to rescue American hostages in Tehran in 1979. Here, during operations in the Atlantic in 1975, the *Nimitz* steams with the ammunition ship *Mount Baker*. Two of the carrier's deck-edge elevators are lowered to the hangar deck. (U.S. Navy)

The assault began to fall apart when a sandstorm forced two of the helicopters to land short of the transfer point—code name Desert One—and another helicopter developed mechanical problems. With only five helicopters available, the commander of the rescue mission cancelled the operation. Then, during the refueling at Desert One as the U.S. aircraft prepared to depart Iranian territory, a C-130 and one of the remaining RH-53Ds collided. Three Marines and five Air Force personnel were killed in the accident. The four remaining RH-53Ds were intentionally destroyed, and the surviving personnel flew out of the area in the C-130s.

Retired Navy Captain Paul Ryan observed,

The Joint Chiefs of Staff believed that the operation had a 60 to 70 percent chance of success, which meant also that it had a 30 to 40 percent chance of failure. These were not good odds when the lives of fifty-three American hostages were hanging in the balance. We know that, if necessary, [the U.S. commandos] were prepared to see many Iranians die. Once his men were inside the embassy compound, it was certain that the Iranian guards would have been met by

a stream of bullets. Hundreds of other Iranians might have been felled if [Colonel Charles] Beckwith had called in the C-130 gunships circling overhead.[15]

Following the Desert One disaster the U.S. government continued to build up naval forces in the Indian Ocean and Persian Gulf in a "show of force" that was, in fact, meaningless and now without impact on the hostage situation. On April 27, 1980, a nine-ship U.S. battle group led by the carrier *Constellation* entered the Indian Ocean. The "Connie" was to relieve the *Coral Sea* battle group, which was operating in company with the *Nimitz* battle group.

Two days later a three-ship battle group centered on the carrier *Eisenhower* entered the Indian Ocean, bringing to 37 ships the U.S. naval forces in the area. The "Ike" group was to relieve the *Nimitz* battle group. A major carrier force was kept in the area until January 1981, when, upon President Reagan entering the White House, the Tehran hostages were released.

The U.S. commando raid on the Son Tay prison in North Vietnam in 1970 had failed because of poor intelligence. The Tehran raid failed for several reasons:

it was too complex, in the interest of secrecy it was too compartmented, the forces were inadequately trained (for example, the Marine pilots flying Navy helicopters with minimal training), there was a lack of adequate weather reporting along the helicopter flight route, the participants failed to use appropriate communications systems, and they simply had bad luck.

Carriers versus Libya[16]

Difficult relations with another Muslim country led to open conflict in the 1980s. Libya was an early U.S. ally in the Cold War and home to a Strategic Air Command bomber base near Tripoli. However, U.S.-Libyan relations deteriorated after the September 1969 coup by Army officers that led to the dictatorship of Muammar Qaddafi, at the time a 27-year-old captain in the signal corps. In 1970 Qaddafi negotiated an arms agreement with the Soviet Union.

In 1974 the Libyan dictator declared that the portion of the Mediterranean Sea south of 32°30' North latitude—the entire Gulf of Sidra—"constitutes an integral part of the territory of the Libyan Arab Republic and is under its complete sovereignty." The 250-mile wide opening of the Gulf of Sidra far exceeded the 25-mile maximum allowed for a bay under international law.[17] The U.S. State Department declared that Libya's assertion of sovereignty over the gulf was a violation of international law.

In early December 1979—a month after Iranian militants captured the American embassy in Tehran—a Libyan mob overran, sacked, and burned the American embassy in Tripoli. By May 1980 the last U.S. government officials were withdrawn from the country.

The first direct confrontation with U.S. forces came on September 16, 1980, when two Libyan MiG-23 Flogger fighters attacked a U.S. Air Force RC-135 reconnaissance aircraft flying in international air space over the Mediterranean. The Carter administration, preoccupied with events in Iran, took no action against Libya. The Reagan administration, entering the White House in January 1981, approved a central Mediterranean exercise set for August 1981 with the carriers *Forrestal* and *Nimitz* participating. The carriers remained north of the 32°30' line, but on August 18 two destroyers steamed into the Gulf of Sidra while remaining in international waters.

Early the next morning an E-2C Hawkeye from the *Nimitz* detected two aircraft at a distance of 80 miles flying north from the Libyan airfield at Ghurdabiyah. The aircraft, soon identified as Libyan Su-22 Fitter-J fighters, approached two F-14s on patrol near the task force.[18] When some 60 miles north of the Libyan coast and closing with the F-14s, one of the Su-22s fired an AA-2 Atoll missile, which missed the U.S. aircraft.

The Tomcats attacked. One downed an Su-22 with a Sidewinder missile; the Libyan pilot ejected from the burning aircraft. The second F-14 struck the other Su-22 with a Sidewinder; the Libyan plane exploded, but its pilot was also able to eject. U.S. Navy historian Joseph T. Stanik observed, "The Fitter was considerably slower than the Tomcat and unable to turn as tightly. Moreover, its two internal 30-mm cannons and two AA-2 Atoll heat-seeking air-to-air missiles were no match for the weapons carried on the American planes."[19]

The U.S. aircraft recovered aboard the *Nimitz* without incident. These were the first aerial kills by any U.S. aircraft since the Vietnam War.

Two RH-5D Sea Stallion helicopters are brought up to the flight deck on the carrier *Nimitz* in preparation for Operation Eagle Claw (also known as Evening Light), the attempted rescue of American hostages in Tehran. These were the most capable helicopters in U.S. service at the time. Auxiliary fuel tanks are fitted on their sponsons; their rotor blades and tail sections are folded for carrier stowage. All Navy markings are deleted. (U.S. Navy)

As the central Mediterranean quieted down, violence erupted in the eastern Mediterranean. In 1983, in response to the civil war raging in Lebanon, as part of a United Nations effort the United States, Britain, and France sent troops into the country. The effectiveness of the intervention was questionable, and on October 23 an explosive-laden truck crashed into a U.S. Marine barracks at the Beirut airport; 241 Americans were killed and 60 injured, most of them Marines.[20] The same day an attack was made on French paratroopers encamped near Beirut; 58 troops were killed. Iranian-supported Hezbollah terrorists carried out the attacks.

U.S. leaders sought an immediate response by the two carriers then in the eastern Mediterranean, the *Independence* and *Kennedy*. National leaders in Washington discussed and delayed the response. Meanwhile, Syrian air defenses fired on carrier-based F-14 Tomcats flying reconnaissance missions over Lebanon.

Finally, approval was given for a strike against Syrian anti-aircraft positions near Hammana, Lebanon. Further, Washington and U.S. European Command headquarters in Stuttgart prescribed the specifics of the strike—time, flight path, and ordnance. The two carriers flew off a strike of aircraft on the morning of December 4. The flight profile brought the attack aircraft over Lebanon in conditions that made them easy targets for Syrian air defenses, which shot down an A-7E Corsair from the "Indy" and an A-6E Intruder from the "JFK." The Corsair and Intruder pilots were killed, and Syrian troops captured the A-6E bombardier-navigator. The strike temporarily knocked out a Syrian radar and destroyed two gun emplacements. (The Navy also used the battleship *New Jersey* to bombard "enemy" positions in Lebanon during December 1983.[21])

After negotiations, the captured *Kennedy* aviator was released.[22] Additional carrier strikes were flown against Syrian military positions in January without American losses. U.S. troops departed Lebanon in February 1984, ending a disagreeable episode.[23]

Subsequently, the carrier *Saratoga* was involved in a terrorist-pirate incident in the Mediterranean. In October 1985 four Palestinian terrorists armed with automatic weapons seized the Italian cruise ship *Achille Lauro*, which had just departed Alexandria, Egypt. After killing a crippled American passenger, the terrorists negotiated to ride a tug into Port Saïd and on October 10 boarded an Egypt Air Boeing 737 passenger plane at Al Maza air base northeast of Cairo.

Reportedly, Israeli intelligence, monitoring area communications, advised Washington of the terrorists' flight. President Reagan directed that the plane be intercepted and forced down. The *Saratoga* launched seven F-14 Tomcats plus radar E-2C surveillance and KA-6D tanker aircraft. Off the coast of Crete the Tomcats intercepted the airliner and signaled the 737 to follow them. One hour, 15 minutes later the 737 landed at the Sigonella naval air station in Italy, and the terrorists were taken into custody. The Tomcats recovered aboard their carrier without incident after their seven-hour mission, which required several air-to-air refuelings.

Libya continued to be the focus of U.S. attention in the region, and Qaddafi was linked to several terrorist acts in Europe. Also, on September 12, 1984, the British minehunter *Gavinton* recovered a seafloor mine detected about 15 n.miles south of the entrance to the Suez Canal. The mine was of Soviet manufacture, dated 1981. It was subsequently determined that the Libyan roll-on/roll-off freighter *Ghat*, which transited the Suez Canal and Gulf of Suez in early July 1984, had laid several mines. Several ships were damaged in the terrorist operation.

On January 24, 1986, two U.S. carrier battle groups centered on the *Coral Sea* and *Saratoga* began operations near the Gulf of Sidra to again demonstrate freedom of the seas. The exercise—Operation Attain Document—ran until January 31 and was followed by a second, Operation Attain Document II, from February 10 to 15, 1986. During this phase of naval operations more than 140 Libyan aircraft approached the U.S. carrier groups and were "politely" escorted out of the area by Navy fighters. The *Coral Sea* had four squadrons of the new F/A-18 Hornet—two of them Marine squadrons—as well as a squadron of A-6E Intruders.

On March 19 the carrier *America* passed through the Strait of Gibraltar, giving the Commander Sixth Fleet, Vice Admiral Frank B. Kelso II, three carriers. Kelso was to direct the third phase of Operation Attain Document, as planned by the White House in January 1986. This phase "was to increase pressure on the Libyan dictator by deploying surface and air elements of three carrier battle groups south of the 'line of death.' American leaders fully realized that the exercises might prompt hostilities."[24] Kelso, known as a meticulous and caring commander, visited each of the three carriers to emphasize the operation's importance and to review the rules of engagement.[25] He had some 250 aircraft on the decks of the three carriers and an armada of cruisers, destroyers, and frigates. Two nuclear attack submarines and land-based patrol and electronic surveillance aircraft were also available to Kelso.

In response to Libya's aggressive actions against U.S. ships operating in international waters, at midnight on March 24–25, the carriers began launching aircraft to operate over international waters south of the 32°30' line. Libyan coastal radars near Sirte locked onto the American aircraft, but no missiles were immediately fired. A pair of Libyan MiG-25s that flew out from the coast turned away as U.S. fighters approached. During the next few days no Libyan aircraft approached the U.S. ships.

At 1 P.M. on the 25th a three-ship Surface Action Group crossed the "line of death." There was no immediate reaction, but at 2:52 P.M. Libyan radars again locked onto carrier aircraft and SA-5 missiles were fired at them without effect. In response, Admiral Kelso ordered the fleet to engage any Libyan forces that threatened U.S. forces, but such actions were to take place after dark. "We operate very well at night. They don't," said Kelso.[26]

With darkness SA-5 and then SA-2 Guideline missiles were fired at U.S. aircraft over the gulf. Then, at 9 P.M., an E-2C Hawkeye detected a warship leaving the coast at 24 knots. This was the *Waheed*, a Libyan Combattante II–class missile craft armed with four Ottomat anti-ship missiles with a 40-mile range.

A pair of A-6E Intruders from the *America* attacked with Harpoon missiles, scoring two hits on the 260-ton warship. This marked the first combat use of the Harpoon missile.[27] A short time later two A-6Es from the *Saratoga* sank the ship with Rockeye cluster bombs. There were 16 survivors.

Next, at 10 P.M., as the Sirte radar again locked on U.S. aircraft, A-7E Corsairs from the *Saratoga* attacked

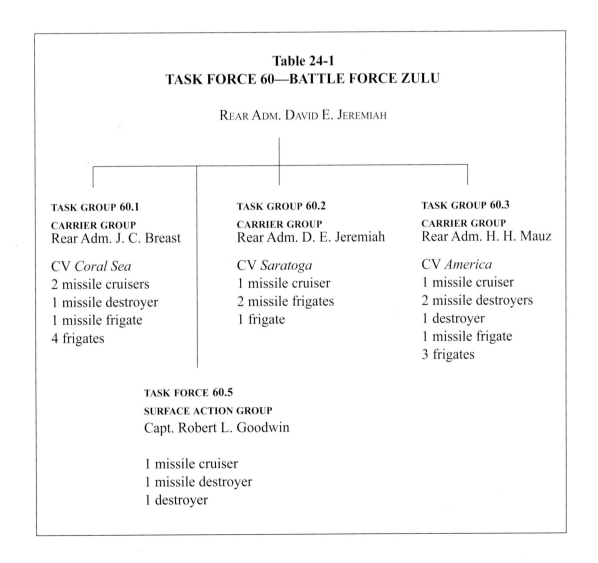

Table 24-1
TASK FORCE 60—BATTLE FORCE ZULU

REAR ADM. DAVID E. JEREMIAH

TASK GROUP 60.1
CARRIER GROUP
Rear Adm. J. C. Breast

CV *Coral Sea*
2 missile cruisers
1 missile destroyer
1 missile frigate
4 frigates

TASK GROUP 60.2
CARRIER GROUP
Rear Adm. D. E. Jeremiah

CV *Saratoga*
1 missile cruiser
2 missile frigates
1 frigate

TASK GROUP 60.3
CARRIER GROUP
Rear Adm. H. H. Mauz

CV *America*
1 missile cruiser
2 missile destroyers
1 destroyer
1 missile frigate
3 frigates

TASK FORCE 60.5
SURFACE ACTION GROUP
Capt. Robert L. Goodwin

1 missile cruiser
1 missile destroyer
1 destroyer

The F-14 Tomcat was prominent in the U.S.-Libyan crises. The F-14 was one of the world's most potent fighter aircraft during its 33 years in the fleet. It's total aerial kills in that period were four Libyan fighters during clashes in the 1980s, and an Iraqi helicopter in 1991. Left, an F-14 from VF-41 is carrying four Sidewinder and four larger Sparrow air-to-air missiles plus two 227-gallon fuel tanks; right, an F-14 from VF-74 is towed across the deck of the carrier *Saratoga* in March 1986. (Gerald B. Parsons, U.S. Navy; Mac M. Thurston, U.S. Navy)

with AGM-88 HARM anti-radar missiles.[28] One struck, knocking out the radar for four hours. Subsequently, more "Sara" A-7Es used HARMs to destroy the radar installation.

U.S. radars then detected another Libyan warship, a Nanuchka II–type missile ship with four improved Styx missiles having a range of 45 miles, departing the coast. Beginning at 11:35 P.M., A-6Es from the *America* attacked the ship with Rockeye cluster bombs and inflicted severe damage. The planes were unable to use Harpoon missiles because a neutral merchant ship was nearby. The damaged Soviet-built ship sought refuge alongside the merchant ship and returned to Benghazi under cover of darkness. During the night of March 24–25 two U.S. cruisers fired Harpoons at suspected Libyan ships, but no debris was found and intelligence sources found no Libyan ships missing.

With daylight on the 25th an E-2C detected another Nanuchka II, the *Ean Mira*, at sea. A-6Es from the *Coral Sea* stopped the 560-ton ship dead in the water with two Rockeye hits, after which *Saratoga* A-6Es hit the ship with a Harpoon and two more Rockeyes, sinking her.

This was the last combat action of Operation Attain Document. The engagement of Libyan forces was tagged Operation Prairie Fire. Two Libyan warships had been sunk and another heavily damaged. No U.S. ships, aircraft, or personnel were lost. The three carriers flew 1,546 sorties through March 27, of which 375 were south of the "line of death." Three U.S. surface ships had operated south of the line for 75 hours to enforce the concept of freedom of navigation in international waters.

El Dorado Canyon

On April 5, 1986, terrorists bombed a West Berlin discotheque, killing a U.S. soldier and a Turkish civilian and wounding 79 persons, several of them Americans. U.S. eavesdropping on Tripoli–East Berlin cable communications indicated that Libya had supported the terrorists. The Reagan administration quickly decided to retaliate against the Qaddafi government for the bombing. In the view of the White House, U.S. retaliation would both be a legitimate act of self-defense and send a clear message that those who supported terrorism would pay a heavy price.

Obviously a military operation in the Mediterranean would involve aircraft carriers. But this time the Air Force's 48th Tactical Fighter Wing in Britain with F-111 strike aircraft would participate. Further, after the aircraft losses in the December 4, 1983, raid on Syrian positions in the Bekaa Valley, the Libyan attack would be made at night.

Vice Admiral Kelso had the *America* at Livorno, Italy, while the *Coral Sea* was at Malaga, Spain, about to "chop" out of the Mediterranean. Kelso kept the *Coral Sea*, which, after an at-sea replenishment, rendezvoused with the *America* on April 12. The two ships and their escorts conducted exercises. The attack was planned for before dawn on April 15.

France and Spain denied permission for U.S. Air Force overflights, hence the 18 F-111F attack and 4

EF-111A electronic jamming aircraft taking off from Britain had to fly a circuitous route out over the Atlantic and through the Mediterranean. Their roundtrip flight was almost 6,000 n.miles, and several in-flight refuelings were required.

The 18 F-111Fs from Britain were to attack simultaneously with 12 Navy and Marine A-6E aircraft from the *America* and *Coral Sea*. Numerous other carrier-based aircraft provided air defense, electronic, and other support for the strike aircraft in Operation El Dorado Canyon, including EA-6B Prowlers, which, with the EF-111As, were to jam Libyan radars. A combination of laser-guided and free-fall bombs would be used against a variety of Libyan targets.

The F-111s flying from Britain required four in-flight refuelings during the six-and-a-half-hour flight to their targets. Their total flight necessitated a force of 30 Air Force tankers—17 KC-10 and 13 KC-135R aircraft—to make the night refuelings without radio communications. Equipment failures and pilot errors forced two F-111s to abort the mission, reducing the Air Force strike to 16 planes plus the jammers.

By 1:24 A.M. the two carriers had launched their strike and support aircraft. As the strike aircraft approached their targets at low levels, the EF-111A and EA-6B electronic aircraft attempted to jam Libyan radars, while carrier-based F/A-18 Hornets and A-7E Corsairs launched 30 HARM and 12 Shrike missiles against detected radar emissions. Secretary of the Navy Lehman called the Libyan air defenses "one of the thickest and most sophisticated air defense systems in the world."[29]

The attack force of 16 F-111s and 12 Intruders popped up from their low-level approach and released their weapons. Several MiG-23s and other aircraft were destroyed and damaged at the military airfields at Benia and Tripoli; army barracks were struck; and at al-Aziziyah, Qaddafi's headquarters-residence was bombed. One F-111 dropped its bombs in error, striking a residential neighborhood and damaging the French Embassy in Tripoli.

One F-111 was shot down while exiting the target area, its two-man crew lost. The surviving Air Force aircraft refueled from their tankers near Sicily and turned westward for the flight back to their British bases. They landed after a 15-hour flight. The *America* and *Coral Sea* safely recovered all their aircraft by 2:53 A.M.

President Reagan, in a televised speech on the night of April 15, revealed the attack, declaring, "Tonight we have done what we had to do. If necessary, we shall do it again." The carrier planes had been quickly refueled and rearmed and readied for another strike, if so ordered. The F-111s that touched down at their British bases could not fly another strike. They were grounded by British politics, their pilots' exhaustion, and the aircrafts' maintenance needs.

What was the final U.S. Navy–Libyan combat encounter occurred on January 4, 1989, when two Libyan MiG-23 Flogger fighters approached a pair of

A Libyan *Ean Mira*, a Nanuchka II–class missile corvette, erupts in flame and sinks after being attacked by U.S. carrier aircraft during U.S. combat operations against Libya. This was the largest Soviet-built warship to be sunk by U.S. forces; smaller torpedo boats were sunk by U.S. carrier aircraft at North Vietnamese ports in 1964. (U.S. Navy)

F-14s in a threatening manner. The F-14s from the carrier *Kennedy* were on patrol over the carrier force. Warned by an E-2C of the MiGs' takeoff and approach, the F-14s changed course several times. The Libyan fighters continued to approach the F-14s.

The combat information center in the "JFK" monitored the maneuvers, and the F-14s were given permission to engage. The F-14s fired two Sparrows and one Sidewinder as the MiGs closed on them. The MiG-23s were struck by one of the Sparrows and the Sidewinder. Both Libyan pilots successfully ejected but apparently were lost at sea.

Carriers versus Iraq

Iraq, suffering major financial problems following its war with Iran in the 1980s, on August 2, 1990, invaded the small, neighboring kingdom of Kuwait, claiming that the nation was illegally drilling in Iraqi oil fields. At the time Iraq had the largest and most heavily armed army in the Middle East with more than 800,000 troops, 4,700 tanks, 3,700 artillery tubes, and a highly advanced air defense system. Kuwait had 20,000 troops and 165 tanks. The invasion led to the largest U.S. military operation since the Vietnam War. Within one hour the carriers *Independence* in the Indian Ocean and the *Eisenhower* in the eastern Mediterranean were ordered into the Red Sea and the Gulf of Oman, respectively.

The Department of Defense report on the Gulf War notes that these carrier groups "were the only sustainable U.S. combat forces nearby when Iraq invaded Kuwait."[30] The two carriers—each with some 85 combat aircraft embarked—arrived in the area ready to fight. In comparison, the initial land-based tactical aircraft flown from the United States arrived in Saudi Arabia after a 15-hour flight with seven air-to-air refuelings from tanker aircraft; the combat readiness of these F-15 fighters and their pilots was seriously degraded after their transocean deployment. Simultaneously, the timely arrival of the 82nd Airborne Division, flown from the United States, provided a light infantry force to defend the Saudi bases being used by U.S. forces. The arrival a few days later of two groups of prepositioning ships with Marine weapons, vehicles, and equipment provided the first U.S. heavy forces in the area, which were "married up" with Marines flown into nearby bases.

At the same time, the U.S. Navy imposed a United Nations–declared blockade of shipping bound for Iraq. Several coalition warships joined that effort.

Meanwhile, the United States, with major contributions by Britain and France, was building up major combat forces in Saudi Arabia and the Persian Gulf emirates. The forces provided a screen to prevent further advances by the Iraqi Army into Saudi Arabia and to, eventually, liberate Kuwait. The *Independence* entered the Persian Gulf on October 1, 1990; it was the first time an aircraft carrier had entered that waterway since 1974. She was relieved in the gulf on November 1 by the *Midway*, which had recently celebrated her 45th year in commission—a world record. Thereafter carriers and battleships sailed regularly into the gulf, demonstrating the ability of the U.S. "blue-water" fleet to operate in relatively restricted waters.

During Operation Desert Shield—from August 1990 through mid-January 1991—the U.S. Navy and Air Force transported hundreds of thousands of U.S. troops and their equipment into the Gulf area, with munitions, fuels, and provisions to sustain the largest U.S. ground operation since the Vietnam War. The U.S. naval buildup included six aircraft carriers, with initially four operating in the Red Sea and two in the Persian Gulf:

RED SEA	PERSIAN GULF
America	*Midway*
John F. Kennedy	*Ranger*
Saratoga	
Theodore Roosevelt	

The coalition air campaign began on the night of January 16–17, 1991—the start of Operation Desert Storm. Led by Army AH-64A Apache attack helicopters that crossed the Saudi border into Iraq to destroy two radar installations, waves of coalition aircraft, land- and carrier-based, struck targets in Iraq. U.S. warships in the eastern Mediterranean and Persian Gulf fired 288 Tomahawk missiles to add to the destruction of Iraqi forces and installations.[31]

As the air campaign progressed, the carriers *America* and "TR" entered the gulf, to bring to four the number of carriers in that waterway. The six carriers in the area flew almost 20,000 sorties during the conflict, dropping more than 10,500 tons of ordnance on Iraqi targets. In addition, 20 Marine AV-8B Harriers flew from the assault ship *Nassau* (LHA 4), operating as a "Harrier carrier," and another six flew from the *Tarawa* (LHA 1). Additional Marine Harriers flew from shore bases, as did other Navy and Marine aircraft.

The coalition ground assault began on February 24. Four days later the ground war ended as did the 42-day air campaign. At its peak the coalition naval forces numbered some 150 ships—100 U.S. ships and 50 ships from 17 other nations. Included was the British VSTOL carrier *Ark Royal*, which operated off the coast of Libya in response to Libyan declarations of support for Iraq.

Despite the massive U.S. carrier force, carrier aircraft missions provided only 24 percent of the combat sorties flown in the air campaign and dropped 28 percent of the U.S. air weapons used during Desert Storm. They employed only 9 percent of the precision-guided air weapons. Naval aviation was still "dumb bomb" oriented. And, the carrier force could not receive the daily Air Tasking Order (ATO) from Riyadh, Saudi Arabia, electronically as could the land-based coalition air forces. Instead, an S-3B Viking had to fly the ATO out to the carriers every day, a cumbersome operation.

	Table 24-2	
	U.S. CARRIER FORCE, JANUARY 21, 1991	
	FIGHTER-STRIKE	SPECIAL MISSION
CV *America*	20 F-14 Tomcat 18 F/A-18 Hornet 14 A-6E Intruder	5 EA-6B Prowler 4 E-2C Hawkeye 8 S-3B Viking 4 KA-6D Intruder 6 SH-3H Sea King
CV *Kennedy*	20 F-14 Tomcat 24 A-7E Corsair 13 A-6E Intruder	5 EA-6B Prowler 5 E-2C Hawkeye 8 S-3B Viking 3 KA-6D Intruder 6 SH-3H Sea King
CV *Midway*	30 F/A-18 Hornet 14 A-6E Intruder	4 EA-6B Prowler 4 E-2C Hawkeye 4 KA-6D Intruder 6 SH-3H Sea King
CV *Ranger*	20 F-14 Tomcat 22 A-6E Intruder	4 EA-6B Prowler 4 E-2C Hawkeye 8 S-3B Viking 4 KA-6D Intruder 6 SH-3H Sea King
CV *Roosevelt*	20 F-14 Tomcat 19 F/A-18 Hornet 18 A-6E Intruder	5 EA-6B Prowler 4 E-2C Hawkeye 8 S-3B Viking 4 KA-6D Intruder 6 SH-3H Sea King
CV *Saratoga*	20 F-14 Tomcat 18 F/A-18 Hornet 14 A-6E Intruder	4 EA-6B Prowler 4 E-2C Hawkeye 8 S-3B Viking 4 KA-6D Intruder 6 SH-3H Sea King

Finally, the carriers were dependent upon U.S. and Royal Air Force tankers for long-range operations. And, even the existing force of KA-6D tankers would soon be given up, followed by the S-3B Vikings that were also being employed as tankers.[32]

In many respects the Navy's principal contribution to the air war were the 288 Tomahawk cruise missiles launched from battleships, cruisers, destroyers, and submarines.

Carrier aircraft downed only three Iraqi aircraft, the small number in part because of the Navy's operating area on the eastern flank of the conflict. Also, the Iraqi Air Force generally avoided aerial combat, and after a few days, most of the Iraqi aircraft fled to bases in Iran. On January 17, 1991, two Navy F/A-18C Hornets from the *Saratoga* shot down two Iraqi MiG-21 fighters using both Sparrow and Sidewinder missiles.[33] On February 6 an F-14A Tomcat from the *Ranger* shot down an Iraqi Mi-8 Hip helicopter with a Sidewinder missile. This helicopter and four Libyan fighters shot down in 1981 and 1989 were the only hostile aircraft to be shot down by F-14s during their 33-year career in the fleet.

A total of 40 Iraqi aircraft were shot down during the air campaign—3 by U.S. Navy fighters, 33 by U.S. Air Force F-15C fighters, 2 by Saudi F-15C fighters, and 2 by A-10 Thunderbolts. Twenty-six U.S. kills were made with radar-guided Sparrow missiles, 10 with heat-seeking Sidewinders, 2 by A-10s with 30-mm cannon (both helicopters).

In the air campaign the Navy suffered seven aircraft lost to hostile ground fire—1 F-14A Tomcat, 2 F/A-18 Hornets, and 4 A-6E Intruders; the Navy also suffered four operational losses.[34] The Marines lost 5 AV-8B Harriers and 2 OV-10 Broncos to ground fire and had 8 noncombat losses.

The carrier *Midway* was decommissioned a year after the Gulf War. She had been in service for 46½ years and was the last World War II–era carrier in commission. Her sister ships *Franklin D. Roosevelt* and *Coral Sea* had been decommissioned in 1977 and 1990, respectively. They were the only U.S. Navy carriers to have served with the designation CVB.[35]

The Gulf War also marked the end of the A-7 Corsair in the U.S. Navy service. The *Kennedy* had the last two Navy A-7E squadrons. The multi-role F/A-18 Hornet had taken the A-7E deck spots on other carriers. The A-7E proved to be a highly effective "light" attack aircraft and a suitable successor in that role to the A4D/A-4 Skyhawk. Both aircraft saw extensive combat in the Vietnam War. The last A-7 squadrons—VA-46 and VA-72—were disestablished in May 1991. Other nations flew the aircraft as a land-based attack aircraft. (The U.S. Marine Corps did not fly the A-7.)

All six carriers in the Gulf War had A-6E Intruder squadrons, each ship operating 13 to 22 aircraft. The Marines flew another 20 A-6Es from land bases. Shortly after the Gulf War the Navy began phasing out Intruder squadrons. The last Navy A-6E was retired from the fleet in December 1996 when VA-75 completed its last deployment aboard the carrier *Enterprise*. With the demise of the Intruder, the U.S. Navy's strike role was taken over by bomb- and missile-carrying variants of the F-14 Tomcat fighter and the F/A-18 Hornet strike-fighter. (The last Marine A-6E squadron was disbanded in 1993).

An improved A-6F, with new avionics, the AN/APQ-173 radar, more powerful engines, and composite material wings was being developed in the 1980s. That aircraft was cancelled, as was a proposed follow-on A-6G with other improvements. The A-12 Avenger, a carrier-based low-observable or "stealth" aircraft, was to have replaced the Intruder. Contractor overruns and Navy mismanagement killed that program. A proposed follow-on effort known as the AX also failed to produce an attack aircraft.

Of significance, with the phasing out of the A-6E, the KA-6D tankers were also discarded. This left ship-based tanking to the S-3B Viking, which had lost its ASW role in the late 1990s, and to buddy stores carried by F/A-18 Hornets. The Vikings were soon to be discarded, while the F/A-18s engaged in the tanker role took aircraft away from the fighter/strike role.[36]

Thus ended the dedicated attack aircraft (VA-VAH) in the U.S. Navy, which had its origins in the bomb and torpedo planes of the World War I era. The Electronic Countermeasures (ECM) variant, the EA-6B Prowler, continued in service into the 21st Century in Navy and Marine squadrons, with naval units also taking over the Air Force ECM mission.

Finally, in the Gulf War five carriers operated F-14 Tomcat fighters; four had the standard F-14A variant while the *Saratoga*'s two fighter squadrons, VF-74 and VF-103, had the improved F-14A+ (soon redesignated F-14B). The F-14A+ had improved engines and avionics and was fitted with racks for "iron bombs." Ironically, such an updated fighter-attack variant—also

A two-place F/A-18D Hornet from Marine all-weather fighter-attack squadron VMFA(AW)-121 over Kuwait City in 1991. Sidewinder air-to-air missiles are fitted to the wingtips; three drop tanks are carried. Several F/A-18 variants—in Navy as well as Marine Corps squadrons—fill the fighter and attack roles aboard U.S. carriers, replacing the F-14 Tomcat, A-6E Intruder, and A-7E Corsair. (McDonnell Douglas)

called F-14B—was proposed when the aircraft was developed in the late 1960s but was never pursued. The Tomcat was first used in the air-to-ground role in combat on September 5, 1995, when an F-14B from the carrier *Theodore Roosevelt* dropped two 2,000-pound bombs on Serb positions in Bosnia.

Beginning in 1996, all surviving F-14s were fitted with the AN/AAQ-14 LANTIRN (Low Altitude Navigation and Targeting Infrared for Night) targeting pod for aiming laser-guided munitions, making them what one wag called "bombcats." The subsequent F-14D, with the improved engines, was fitted with the AN/APG-71 radar, a digital version of the AN/AWG-9, capable of multi-mode operation, including ground attack. This enabled the F-14D to carry air-to-ground missiles as well as bombs.[37] The F-14A+/B and F-14D aircraft were both conversions of earlier types and new builds.

Carriers to the Balkans

Although a communist country, Yugoslavia had steered an independent course under the autocratic leadership of Josipy Broz—known as Tito—who had led anti-German guerrilla forces in the area during World War II. After Tito's death in 1980 his successors generally continued his policies. But when Soviet troops withdrew from Eastern Europe, the ethnic animosities in the region exploded.

On June 25, 1991, the provinces of Croatia and Slovenia declared their independence from Yugoslavia. Civil war erupted as the primarily Serb government of Yugoslavia attempted to reassert control over the breakaway provinces. Other areas declared independence from the central government and new alliances—republics—were formed. By early 1992 the capital of Belgrade controlled only two Yugoslav provinces, Montenegro and Serbia. The aspiration of independence and historic hatred between Croats, Muslims, and Serbs led to open combat, rape, murder, expulsion of whole towns, and genocide—euphemistically called "ethnic cleansing." Military historian Tim Ripley wrote, "The war was a conflict of shifting alliances that confused even the most learned students of Balkan history."[38]

A United Nations peacekeeping force of 23,000 personnel was sent into Bosnia to establish safe areas and to guard humanitarian relief convoy routes. That effort was unsuccessful and a NATO combat force was sent into the region. Complications immediately arose as the two organizations had different chains of command and, at times, competing missions. The civil war continued. Some NATO cargo aircraft bringing in relief supplies were struck by anti-aircraft fire, and an Italian transport was shot down.

As Serb aircraft attacked Muslim enclaves, NATO aircraft—mostly American—began to enforce "no fly" zones. U.S. and other NATO air forces began operations over Yugoslavia—a 78-day air war called Operation Allied Force. Most NATO aircraft flew from Aviano and Sigonella (Sicily) airfields in Italy.[39] The carrier *Theodore Roosevelt* and her battle group were hurried across the Atlantic and into the Mediterranean Sea to add more aircraft. The *Roosevelt* was joined by the helicopter carrier *Nassau*, which sent her AV-8B

The British VSTOL carriers *Invincible* (left) and *Ark Royal* operated in the Adriatic Sea in support of NATO operations in the Balkans. Sea Harriers and Sea Kings are on their decks. Both ships have the Sea Dart surface-to-air launcher forward (since removed). The *Invincible* has a U.S. Phalanx 20-mm multi-barrel gun mounted forward of the launcher; the *Ark Royal* has a 30-mm Goalkeeper multi-barrel gun forward. (Royal Navy)

Harriers into the aerial battle. Meanwhile, France and Britain each dispatched a carrier to the Adriatic Sea while more land-based aircraft were sent to NATO airfields in the region. In addition, Navy and Marine Corps EA-6B Prowler electronic attack aircraft also supported operations from Aviano.

In some respects the most important U.S. Navy-Marine contribution to Operation Allied Force were the EA-6B Prowlers. They provided protection for allied strike and other air missions, seeking out hostile radar emissions and, when detected, jamming them or launching HARM anti-radar missiles. Of 19 active and reserve Navy and Marine EA-6B squadrons—each with four aircraft—10½ squadrons were forward deployed overseas during the Kosovo campaign.[40] At the height of the campaign, six EA-6B squadrons were flying from Aviano. (After May 1998 the Prowler was the only fixed-wing electronic countermeasures/attack aircraft in the U.S. arsenal.[41] The last U.S. Air Force aircraft in this category, the EF-111A Raven, was phased out of service in 1998.)

There were frequent strikes by B-2 stealth bombers flying from the United States and B-52 Stratofortress bombers based in Britain and the United States, in addition to combat aircraft based mostly at Aviano and aboard ship. Tomahawk land-attack missiles were launched from several U.S. cruisers, destroyers, and submarines and the British submarine *Splendid* in 1995

and 1999. The latter marked the second time that year that U.S. naval forces struck targets in a land-locked target area.[42] The previous one was the Tomahawk strike against purported terrorist facilities in Afghanistan and Sudan (see Chapter 26).

During these operations, on June 2, 1995, an Air Force F-16C fighter was shot down over Bosnia by a surface-to-air missile. The pilot, Captain Scott O'Grady, parachuted to the ground in hostile territory. At dawn on June 8 the helicopter carrier *Kearsarge* (LHD 3), which had relieved the *Nassau*, launched a Marine-Navy team to rescue the pilot. With a covering force of NATO land-based aircraft, the rescue force consisted of two CH-53E Super Stallions carrying some 40 troops. Two AH-1W Cobra gunship helicopters and two AV-8B Harrier VSTOL aircraft flew close cover for the rescue effort. The rescue party was on the ground for eight minutes. The Marines came under fire as they pulled out and Bosnian Serb troops fired two surface-to-air missiles without effect. One helicopter was lightly damaged by automatic weapons fire. O'Grady was recovered without casualties to the rescue party. (An Air Force F-117A stealth attack aircraft was also shot down over hostile territory; the pilot died.)

The NATO combat involvement was primarily an air operation as the allies were reluctant to send in ground combat forces. Some 1,500 Russian troops joined the NATO peacekeepers on the ground, causing further command and political complications. By the end of 1995 a peace had been negotiated in the area, although U.S.-NATO involvement in the area has continued.

Beyond the Balkans conflicts, U.S. naval forces were heavily engaged after the 1991 assault on Iraq. The participation of aircraft carriers and VSTOL/helicopter carriers in significant political-military events during the few years after the Gulf War are shown in table 24-3.

There were also crises and confrontations in the Pacific region during this period, primarily related to the China-Taiwan relationship and the bellicose pronouncements of North Korea. But the focus of the U.S. government in this period—by the George H. W. Bush and Clinton administrations (1989–1993 and 1993–2001, respectively)—was the Middle East–Persian Gulf area.

Following the Gulf War of 1991 the United Nations placed severe economic sanctions and limitations on Iraqi military operations. "No-fly" zones, in which no fixed-wing military aircraft could operate, were established in the northern and southern areas of the country. These zones—above 36° North and below 32° South—were demarcated to inhibit government operations against Kurds and other ethnic groups.

Coalition aircraft, including U.S. carrier-based aircraft from ships operating in the Persian Gulf, enforced the no-fly zones. Periodically during the next 12 years U.S. and other coalition aircraft attacked Iraqi radars and missile launchers in the no-fly zones when the aircraft were "painted" by the radars. And, on two occasions U.S. Navy ships fired Tomahawk missiles into this area.

Thus, U.S. carriers continued air operations over and against Iraq up to the American invasion of March 2003.

A Marine AH-1W SeaCobra helicopter gunship takes off from the USS *Kearsarge* as the VSTOL/helicopter carrier launches a rescue mission on June 6, 1995, to recover Air Force pilot Scott O'Grady, shot down over Bosnia. During the Balkans campaign Allied aircraft faced major restrictions on operations from land bases in Italian territory. Carrier/LHA/LHD operations provided flexibility and secrecy. (Dave A. Garten, U.S. Marine Corps)

Table 24-3
MAJOR U.S. NAVAL RESPONSES, 1992–1994

DATE	FORCES*	ORIGINAL DEPLOYMENT	CRISIS LOCATION
Dec 1992	CV *Ranger* CVBG LPH *Tripoli* ARG	Persian Gulf	Somalia (humanitarian relief)
Jan 1993	CV *Kitty Hawk* CVBG	Somalia	Persian Gulf (support Tomahawk strike against Iraq)
Oct 1993	CV *America* CVBG	Mediterranean-Adriatic Sea	Somalia (response to increasing casualties ashore)
Apr 1994	LHA *Peleliu* ARG	Somalia	Rwanda (non-combat evacuation operations)
Aug 1994	LHA *Tripoli* ARG	Mombasa	Entebbe (humanitarian relief)
Oct 1994	CVN *George Washington* CVBG	Mediterranean-Adriatic Sea	Persian Gulf/Red Sea Adriatic Sea (Iraq confrontation)

* CVBG = Carrier Battle Group
ARG = Amphibious Ready Group

25 AMPHIBIOUS ASSAULT

The largest concentration of VSTOL/helicopter carriers ever assembled sailed the Persian Gulf in April 2003, participating in the war against Iraq. Led by the USS *Tarawa*, from left are the *Bonhomme Richard*, *Kearsarge*, *Bataan*, *Saipan*, and *Boxer*. They were part of the 32-ship amphibious force—Task Force 51—that did not conduct an amphibious landing during the conflict. All six ships have World War II-era carrier names, although the CV 31 was named *Bonhomme Richard*. (Larry S. Carison, U.S. Navy)

The great value of the U.S. LPH-type helicopter ships and the British commando ships in the amphibious assault and other "force projection" roles caused the U.S. Navy to develop a larger, more capable helicopter carrier—the amphibious assault ship (LHA). In addition to the eight "small" LPHs—the ex-CVE *Thetis Bay* and the seven *Iwo Jima*–class ships—the Navy operated four *Essex*-class carriers in the LPH role with their large size providing more flight deck and hangar space as well as troop berthing. However, their late 1930s-design steam propulsion plants and the general configuration of those ships required large crews and had high operating costs; the last were retired in 1970.[1]

As replacements for the LPHs, in 1971 the Navy began construction on the *Tarawa* (LHA 1), which combined the capabilities of several types of amphibious ships in a single, large hull.[2] The ship's principal "cargo" were 1,700 Marines and up to 30 large CH-46 Sea

Knight and CH-53 Sea Stallion helicopters. Later six AV-8 Harrier VSTOL aircraft were generally embarked. A large starboard island structure dominated the flight deck. In addition to a full-length flight deck and large hangar, connected by two deck-edge elevators as well as internal ramps, the *Tarawa* had a large docking well, 268 feet long and 78 feet wide. The well could be flooded to accommodate 4 large, *LCU 1610* landing craft or 17 LCM(6)s or 45 LVTP-7 amphibious assault vehicles or a single LCAC air-cushion landing craft plus some smaller craft.

The *Tarawa*, at 26,255 tons light displacement with a length of 820 feet, was approximately the size of an *Essex*-class carrier. Steam turbines gave the LHA a sustained speed of 24 knots, significantly slower than a true aircraft carrier.

The *Tarawa* was commissioned in May 1976, and four sister ships joined the fleet through 1980. Nine ships of this class were originally planned in the early 1960s. The Navy announced on January 20, 1971, that LHA 6–9 would not be constructed. They were casualties of the high cost of the Vietnam War. The five LHAs joined the seven LPHs of the *Iwo Jima* class to provide a full-deck helicopter carrier in each of 12 amphibious squadrons operated by the Navy from the 1960s onward. Each squadron embarked some 2,200 troops of a Marine Expeditionary Unit (MEU).[3]

The principal helicopters operated by the LPH/LHA amphibious ships in this period were the CH-46 Sea Knight and CH-53 Sea Stallion. The Sea Knight, replacing the HUS series, was the Marine Corps' principal assault helicopter, while the Navy flew CH-46/ HH-46/UH-46 variants in the vertical replenishment and search-and-rescue roles.

The Sikorsky H-53 variants are the largest operational helicopters flown in the West, the type having entered service during the Vietnam War. The CH-53 has served as a Marine assault helicopter and a Navy cargo helicopter,[3] the RH-53D and later MH-53E Sea Dragon were fitted for mine countermeasures. Also flown by the Air Force, Sikorsky delivered 384 CH-53A/D variants to the Marine Corps and Navy plus 30 RH-53D helicopters to the Navy.[4]

Subsequently, Sikorsky developed the CH-53E Super Stallion, employing an enlarged fuselage mounting three more powerful turboshaft engines. This he-

The *Tarawa* was lead ship for the LHA/LHD series of large VSTOL/helicopter carriers. These ships are about the size of World War II–era *Essex*-class carriers. The *Tarawa* has a large starboard island structure, with a port-side, deck-edge elevator and a second elevator cut into her stern, above the opening for her docking well. Two LCM landing craft are aft of the island in this view of the *Tarawa* during sea trials in 1976. (Litton/Ingalls Shipbuilding)

A Marine AV-8A Harrier approaches the VSTOL/helicopter carrier *Tarawa* during an exercise off Mindoro in the Philippine Islands in 1980. Harriers and CH-53 Sea Stallion and CH-46 Sea Knight helicopters are ranged on the *Tarawa*'s flight deck. The ship's docking well is open and she is ballasted down aft. In addition to the ship's large aviation and landing craft capabilities, there is berthing for 1,700 troops. (Ken George, U.S. Navy)

licopter could carry 55 troops and lift 16 tons by sling—more than any other helicopter in the West. Beginning in 1981 the CH-53E replaced the earlier CH-53A/D variants flown by the Marine Corps, and the Navy took delivery of MH-53E Sea Dragon variants for the mine countermeasures and replenishment-at-sea roles. The first CH-53E was delivered to the Marines in 1980, and 177 "E" models were produced for the U.S. Navy and Marine Corps. (In 2006 a contract was awarded to Sikorsky for development of a more-powerful CH-53K variant for the Marine Corps.)

Both the H-46 and H-53 helicopters became star performers, operating from LPH/LHA/LHDs as well as other amphibious ships as U.S. Navy-Marine amphibious forces participated in numerous conflicts and crises.

Meanwhile, as the seven *Iwo Jima*–class LPHs were beginning to reach the end of their service life they were succeeded by the LHD—the amphibious assault ship (multipurpose). The *Wasp* (LHD 1) was completed in July 1989, the first of a new class of large VSTOL/helicopter carriers. The *Wasp* was about the same size as the previous *Tarawa* (LHA) class—28,050 tons light, 41,000 tons full load, with a length of 844 feet. The basic LHA design was adopted with the principal differences of (1) improved Harrier VSTOL support capability; (2) movement of the stern elevator to the starboard side of the flight deck; (3) redesign of the docking well to accommodate three air-cushion LCACs with an LPD/LSD stern gate instead of the sectional, "split" gate of the LHA; and (4) changes in the ship's self-defense armament.

Six additional LHDs were completed through 2001 to provide 12 LHA/LHD-type carriers to form the core of 12 amphibious squadrons.

Like their LPH predecessors, these ships were periodically employed in humanitarian as well as military roles. For example, after Hurricane Katrina devastated the U.S. Gulf Coast in August 2005 the LHDs *Bataan* and *Iwo Jima* as well as other amphibious ships served as afloat medical facilities, berthing for emergency response personnel, and command centers. The ships' medical facilities, staffed by crewmen as additional Navy medical teams, provided on-board and ashore services.

And, in 2007 the LHA *Peleliu* undertook a three-month humanitarian and medical training mission to the Western Pacific area. Previously the U.S. Navy had sent the large hospital ships *Mercy* and *Comfort* on such humanitarian-training missions. Whereas the two Navy hospital ships are manned by relatively small civilian crews under the aegis of the Military Sealift Command (MSC), the *Peleliu* has a crew of some 1,100 officers and enlisted personnel. While the LHA's large flight and hangar decks facilitates handling helicopters bringing medical personnel, patients, and students to and from the ship, the *Peleliu*'s employment in this mission seems to be overkill and a waste of a large flight-deck ship that could be more profitably employed as the United States fought two wars and continued to have forward-deployment requirements in several areas of the world. (The two hospital ships do have limited helicopter facilities.)

American Harriers

Helicopters were joined aboard the LHA and later LHD amphibious ships by the Americanized version of the British-developed Sea Harrier. Following evaluation of the British Kestrel and Harrier VSTOL aircraft in the 1960s (see Chapter 19), the U.S. Marine Corps acquired the Harrier GR.50 produced by Hawker Siddeley with McDonnell Douglas as the American support contractor. The Marines took delivery of 102 single-seat AV-8A (GR.50) and 8 two-seat TAV-8A (T.4) aircraft from 1971 to 1976. These were assigned to land-based attack squadrons with VMA-231 taking the first deliveries.

Harriers had gone to sea aboard the helicopter carrier *Guam* in January 1972 when she evaluated the Sea Control Ship (SCS) concept (see Chapter 18). That ship continued in that role until June 1974, when she reverted to her amphibious role. That September the *Guam* departed Norfolk, Virginia, with a detachment of AV-8A Harriers in addition to her troop helicopters, the first U.S. ship to operationally deploy with the VSTOL aircraft. She participated in a NATO exercise in the North Atlantic and then deployed to the Mediterranean until March 1975.

In October 1976 the carrier *Franklin D. Roosevelt* took aboard 14 AV-8A Harriers of VMA-231 as part of Carrier Air Wing 19 for a Mediterranean deployment. The deployment continued into April 1977 (with the "FDR" being decommissioned shortly after returning to the United States). On a regular basis VMA detachments, usually with six Harriers, deployed aboard LHA/LHDs. During a 1981 deployment the *Nassau* evaluated the "sea control" configuration for these ships when she successfully operated 19 AV-8A Harrier aircraft; that same year the *Tarawa* made the first extended deployment of an LHA with Harriers on board, carrying six AV-8A aircraft during a deployment to the Western Pacific. Subsequent studies showed than an LHA in the sea control role could effectively operate 20 Harriers plus 4 to 6 SH-60B LAMPS III helicopters.

An advanced variant of the Harrier was proposed as a joint project of McDonnell Douglas and Hawker Siddeley. Begun in 1973 and designated AV-16 in the United States, the aircraft was to have a transonic speed with greater range than the Harrier, made possible by a supercritical wing design and an uprated engine. But the cost of the aircraft and engine development led to abandonment of the project.

Instead, the firms undertook a revision of the Harrier design with a composite-structure wing of super-

The AV-8A Harrier (equivalent of the British GR.50) was procured by the U.S. Marine Corps for use from land bases and amphibious ships. The AV-8A was capable of 737 m.p.h. at 1,000 feet, with a ceiling of over 50,000 feet. It could carry up to 5,000 pounds of external stores plus two gun pods under the fuselage. The larger AV-8B Harrier II is rated at 668 m.p.h. at sea level with a ceiling of 50,000 feet. The plane can lift up to 11,920 pounds of external stores, with a radius of 175 miles with 12 500-pound bombs with one hour loiter in the short-takeoff mode or 690 miles with 7 500-pound bombs in the short-takeoff mode. A multi-barrel 25-mm cannon is fitted. Above, an AV-8B hovering over the LHA *Saipan* in 1990; below, an AV-8A on the carrier *Franklin D. Roosevelt* in 1976. (Kip Burke, U.S. Navy; Greg Haas, U.S. Navy)

critical shape, larger trailing-edge flaps, drooped ailerons, redesigned engine intakes, strengthened landing gear, and a more powerful engine. This aircraft would have twice the payload of the AV-8A with up to 13,235 pounds of external stores—bombs, rockets, missiles, or 300-gallon fuel tanks on seven attachment points—plus a 25-mm gun. This was the U.S. AV-8B Harrier II.

The U.S. Marine Corps deemed the Harrier a success despite a high accident rate; several surviving AV-8A aircraft were upgraded to the AV-8C and two AV-8A Harriers were converted to YAV-8B prototypes, the first of which flew on November 9, 1978. These presaged American production of the AV-8B and TAV-8B. The first "new" AV-8B flew on November 5, 1981. McDonnell Douglas produced 274 AV-8B and 22 two-seat TAV-8B aircraft for the Marine Corps to replace the A-4M Skyhawks and AV-8A Harriers in VMA squadrons. The first squadron to receive the AV-8B was VMA-331 in January 1985.

With the success of the advanced Harrier designs, the aircraft's chief designer, John W. Fozard, proposed an airborne early warning variant of the Harrier. The aircraft would have had a large nose-mounted radar with electronic pods mounted atop the wing. The single-place aircraft would data-link information to surface ships for analysis and the direction of fighter aircraft.[5] The United States in fact developed a supersonic VSTOL aircraft—but it could not fly. Produced under a Navy contract by Rockwell International, the XFV-12A had a unique thrust-augmented wing system with the engine airflow ducted to the canards and wings. It was to be a Mach 2+ fighter.[6] But the lift scheme did not work and the single prototype flew in 1978—suspended by a cable.

One other fixed-wing aircraft, has periodically operated from U.S. helicopter/VSTOL carriers, the OV-10 Bronco. Developed by North American for Marine Corps use in the Counterinsurgency (COIN) role, the aircraft had twin turboprop engines with twin booms and a small center fuselage that housed the two-man crew. Up to 3,600 pounds of bombs, gun pods, rockets, or fuel tanks could be carried. Later variants were fitted with night-operating systems and an unmanned ventral 20-mm rapid-fire gun turret to complement the four fixed 7.62-mm machine guns.

Seven YOV-10A prototypes were produced with the first flying on July 10, 1965. The aircraft was ordered into production for the Marine Corps and Air Force, and the U.S. Navy later acquired OV-10A Broncos to support riverine forces in Vietnam. Several other nations also procured the aircraft.

Although not fitted with arresting hooks or suitable for catapult launch, its Short Takeoff and Landing (STOL) characteristics enabled the OV-10 to easily operate from VSTOL/helicopter carriers and, on occasion, from large-deck carriers. Its first carrier flights were reported to be from the *Saipan* (LHA 2) on September 13, 1980, during a NATO exercise off Scotland.

The Rockwell International OV-10 Bronco was a Counter Insurgency (COIN) aircraft flown by the U.S. Army, Air Force, Navy, and Marine Corps. Above, an OV-10A from Navy light attack squadron VAL-4 poses for the camera, and at left a Marine OV-10 lands aboard an *Essex*-class LPH. The Navy flew the OV-10A in Vietnam in 1969–1972; Marine OV-10s periodically operated aboard LPH/LHA helicopter carriers. The OV-10A had a maximum speed of 281 m.p.h. at sea level without stores and a ceiling of 26,000 feet. Later variants had infrared and laser equipment with a 20-mm ventral gun turret. (U.S. Navy)

Special Missions

Periodically U.S. Navy documents for LPH/LHA/LHD ships addressed the potential for use as platforms for Mine Countermeasures (MCM) and for Anti-Submarine Warfare (ASW) helicopters. These ships were employed frequently in the MCM role. Specialized RH-53D and later MH-53E MCM helicopters towed a variety of devices to detect and to detonate mines. The helicopters could be partially disassembled to be flown to overseas bases in C-5 Galaxy cargo aircraft. There, reassembled and flight tested, they would be joined by crews, support personnel, and equipment that were flown to the base and then loaded aboard the helicopter carrier.

The first major ship-based MCM effort came in early 1973 preceeding conclusion of the Vietnam War.[7] Beginning on May 8, 1972, three U.S. carriers began using A-6 Intruders, and A-7 Corsairs began mining North Vietnamese ports. The subsequent cease-fire agreement between the U.S. and North Vietnamese governments called for the United States to clear the mines. A large force of surface and helicopter MCM units, supported by amphibious ships, was assembled for the effort. These include the LPH *Inchon* serving as a base for MCM helicopters (as did other amphibious ships); the aviation component consisted of Marine squadrons HMH-463 and HMM-165 with 24 CH-53D Sea Stallions, and Navy HM-12 with 13 CH-53D helicopters.[8]

HM-12 helicopters made the initial sweep on February 27. With several starts and stops, the operation—named End Sweep—continued until early July 1973. Although carrier aircraft had sown several hundred mines off North Vietnamese ports, the air-surface sweep effort detonated only one mine, a Mk 52 on March 9, as a CH-53D towed a "sled" near the mine. The other mines had either self-detonated or, mostly, self-sterilized (i.e., they deactivated after a specific period).

The next major helicopter MCM effort was smaller but more complex. Following the October 1973 war between Israel and several Arab states, sunken ships, unexploded weapons, and mines blocked the Suez Canal. An international effort was undertaken to clear and reopen the canal. A U.S. Navy flag officer directed the overall effort.

The U.S. MCM component—named Nimbus Star—swept a track from Port Saïd to Port Suez. Now flying RH-53D Sea Stallions, squadron HM-12 operated

from the LPHs *Inchon* and *Iwo Jima* for a month in the spring of 1974. This was a more difficult operation than the North Vietnam operation because the squadron lacked knowledge of the number and types of mines and because sunken ships and other ordnance cluttered the canal. The LPH-based helicopters did not detonate any mines. The foreign forces involved in this effort included the Soviet helicopter carrier *Leningrad* operating two Mi-8 Hip helicopters with MCM equipment.

Mines again became a concern for the U.S. Navy in the 1980s as the Iraq-Iran conflict saw Iran laying mines in the Persian Gulf, and in 1991 when the Gulf War saw coalition forces confronted by Iraqi mines. The flagship of the U.S. air-surface MCM force was the LPH *Tripoli*, operating MH-53E Sea Dragon helicopters. On February 18 the *Tripoli* struck a moored contact mine 50 miles off Kuwait. The ship had been operating in an undetected minefield for 11 hours. The explosion blew a 16-by-25-foot hole in the ship. There were no fatalities, and the ship was never in danger of sinking. (A few hours later a mine severely damaged the Aegis missile cruiser *Princeton* about ten miles away.)

Mine warfare briefly and temporarily resurged in the U.S. Navy following the Gulf War. As part of this effort the *Inchon*, the last LPH in commission, was converted to an MCM support ship in 1995–1996 and was redesignated MCS 12.[9] There had long been a need for such a ship to enhance the effectiveness and on-station time of forward-deployed MCM forces, both surface ships and helicopters.

The ship was configured with a command center and to provide logistic and maintenance support as well as medical facilities for MCM forces, and to embark and sustain naval special forces (i.e., SEALs). An airborne MCM group of eight MH-53E and two CH-46 helicopters was normally embarked, the latter to provide mine spotting and search and rescue. A composite active-reserve crew manned the *Inchon* in her new role, and some 20 percent of her almost 700 officers and enlisted crew were female.[10]

The *Inchon*'s service in that role was brief. She made deployments to European waters in 1997 and again in 1999, the latter included providing support for refugees from the civil war raging in the Balkans. Her last deployment began in April 2001 when the ship—based at Ingleside, Texas—cruised the Pacific. Back at her home port, on October 19 the *Inchon* suffered a fire in her boiler spaces that killed one sailor and

The helicopter carrier *Inchon* while serving as a mine countermeasures support ship (MCS 12) at anchor in Mutsu Bay, Japan. She was the last LPH to be completed and the last to be decommissioned, in 2002. In this view four MH-53E Sea Dragons and a single CH-46 Sea Knight (forward) are on deck. The LPHs were versatile ships, being used in the MCS, MCM, SCS, evacuation, and disaster relief as well as amphibious assault roles. (Courtesy *Ships of the World*)

injured seven. She was taken out of service and decommissioned the following June. The lack of a dedicated MCM support ship was felt in the Fleet as the last of the U.S. Navy LPHs was stricken.

The capability remains for LHA/LHD-type ships to operate mine countermeasure helicopters, which have become the principal U.S. MCM force pending construction of the new littoral combat ship.

Crises and War in the Middle East

During Operation Desert Shield—the buildup of U.S. military forces during the latter half of 1990 for an assault on Iraq—a civil war in Somalia on the eastern coast of Africa led to a confused battle for control of the capital of Mogadishu. Americans and other foreign nationals in Somalia at the time sought refuge in the U.S. Embassy compound in Mogadishu. On January 1, 1991, the American ambassador to Somalia requested military assistance to evacuate the compound.

The next day Operation Eastern Exit was initiated: two Navy amphibious ships, the *Guam* and the docking-well ship *Trenton*, carrying several hundred Marines, were dispatched from the U.S. naval buildup in the North Arabian Sea, and Air Force C-130 Hercules were staged through nearby Kenya. It was initially planned that those C-130s would evacuate the endangered people. But as the situation in Mogadishu's

airport was unsafe, the LPH *Guam* became the key to evacuation.

At 2:45 A.M. on January 5, at a distance of 465 n.miles from Mogadishu, the *Guam* launched the two CH-53E Super Stallions she carried, lifting into the embassy compound a 60-man Marine-Navy security detachment. (The ships' other helicopters were CH-46 Sea Knights.) The flight required two in-flight refuelings by Marine KC-130 tankers; the first refueling ensured the two helicopters could safely reach the compound; the second provided fuel to begin the return flight with evacuees.

The CH-53Es landed at the embassy compound at 7:10 A.M. Shortly afterward an Air Force AC-130 gunship arrived from Kenya. Orbiting overhead, the "Herk" would provide fire support if needed. After unloading the security force, the two CH-53Es took off with 61 evacuees for the flight back to the *Guam*. Only one in-flight refueling was needed as the amphibious ships were now only 350–380 n.miles from the coast.

Meanwhile, a few stray bullets struck the compound, which was surrounded by Somalis. The Marine security force did not return fire. The amphibious ships reached the coast just after midnight on the night of January 5–6. The ships now used CH-46s to supplement the CH-53Es in the evacuation and to recover the security force. As the last helicopters lifted from the compound, armed looters scaled the embassy walls. The last CH-46 touched down on the *Guam* at 3:43 A.M. on January 6. The ships then turned north, heading for Oman with 281 evacuees from 30 countries, including 61 Americans.

Meanwhile, the air campaign against Iraq was continuing and the brief, 100-hour ground war erupted on January 16, 1991. A 31-ship naval amphibious force was assembled in the Persian Gulf with some 17,000 Marines on board in readiness for an amphibious assault into Kuwait or Iraq. The force did not conduct an amphibious assault, but their troops were landed in administrative (noncombat) landings to reinforce the 77,000 Marines already ashore.[11] The assault ship *Nassau* operated as a "Harrier carrier" during the conflict with 20 Marine AV-8B Harriers carrying out strikes ashore; another six Harriers flew from the LHA *Tarawa*. During the final week of Operation Desert Storm the *Nassau*'s Harriers flew up to 60 sorties per day.[12] After the conflict, General Norman Schwarzkopf, commander of the coalition forces, cited three aircraft in his list of weapons that made a significant contribution to a quick and decisive victory: the F-117 Nighthawk stealth attack aircraft, AH-64 Apache attack helicopter, and AV-8B Harrier.

At the same time, the *Tripoli* was operating in the gulf as a mine countermeasures support ship with a squadron of MH-53E Sea Dragon helicopters. The five helicopter/VSTOL carriers operating with the gulf amphibious force were

LHA	1	*Tarawa*
LHA	4	*Nassau*
LPH	3	*Okinawa*
LPH	10	*Tripoli*
LPH	11	*New Orleans*

Twelve years later the United States again assaulted Iraq, this time in search of weapons of mass destruction and to effect a regime change. Again, a large Navy amphibious force was assembled in the Persian Gulf, and again there was no plan for an amphibious assault against Iraq's small coastline.

The "amphibs" assembled in the gulf in the spring of 2003 numbered 32 with 6,500 Marines embarked. There were six helicopter/VSTOL carriers:

LHA	1	*Tarawa*
LHA	2	*Saipan*
LHD	3	*Kearsarge*
LHD	4	*Boxer*
LHD	5	*Bataan*
LHD	6	*Bonhomme Richard*[13]

The nominal "air group" assigned to each LHA/LHD consisted of

12 CH-46E Sea knight medium-lift helicopters
 4 CH-53E Super Stallion heavy-lift helicopters
 4 AH-1W SeaCobra gunship helicopters
 2 UH-1N Huey utility helicopters
 6 AV-8B Harrier fighter-attack aircraft

The Sikorsky CH-53E Super Stallion is the West's largest helicopter. With a gross weight of 73,500 pounds, the CH-53E has a top speed of 195 m.p.h. at sea level with a ceiling of 18,500 feet. The CH-53E's radius is rated at 57 miles with 16 tons of external (slung) cargo and 575 miles with 10 tons of external cargo. Fifty-five troops can be carried internally. These Marine CH-53Es are on the USS *Bataan* in the Persian Gulf in 2007. Note the in-flight refueling probes. (Ken J. Riley, U.S. Navy)

A Marine AV-8B Harrier makes a vertical landing on the helicopter/ VSTOL carrier *Bataan* as the ship operates in the Red Sea in April 2003 during Operation Iraqi Freedom. The *Bataan* and her sister ship *Bonhomme Richard* served as "Harrier carriers" during the assault on Iraq, again demonstrating the flexibility of LHA/LHD/LPH-type ships. (Jonathan Carmichael, U.S. Navy)

In the 2003 conflict the *Bataan* and *Bonhomme Richard* offloaded their helicopters to other ships and operated as "Harrier carriers," carrying 22 and 24 AV-8B Harriers, respectively.

Operating LHA/LHD ships as "Harrier carriers" imposed a considerable burden on amphibs. The requirements for pilot briefings, intelligence and communications staff augmentation, and the rate of consumption of fuel and bombs demanded great innovation. The LHA/LHD community had neither planned nor trained for Harrier carrier operation. Still, the officers and enlisted men and women of the ships and squadrons "made it work."

The helicopter/VSTOL carriers had operated almost exclusively as the core of amphibious squadrons since their debut in the U.S. Navy in the mid-1950s. In a move to increase the flexibility of fleet deployments, in August 2003 the Navy established Expeditionary Strike Group 1 consisting of what had been an amphibious squadron plus warships: the carrier *Peleliu* (LHA 5), two amphibious ships, an Aegis missile cruiser and destroyer, an anti-submarine frigate, and a nuclear-propelled attack submarine. This group, the forerunner of all amphibious squadrons being reformed as such groups, provided the capability of operating in relatively high-threat areas and carrying out a much broader range of operations than could amphibs alone.

Marines and Soldiers on Carriers

Marine aircraft had flown from U.S. aircraft carriers since the late 1920s, and Marine detachments had long served in carriers as well as cruisers and battleships.[14]

In 1992 the U.S. Atlantic Command began studying the feasibility of putting Marine *ground* combat units aboard large-deck carriers.

The rationale for the move was (1) to better justify large-deck carriers by giving them an assault capability, (2) to provide more fleet flexibility by allowing a Marine assault force to rapidly embark in a carrier, and (3) to provide an assault capability in an area without deploying an amphibious ready group of three to five amphibious ships embarking a Marine expeditionary unit.

Accordingly, in mid-January 1992, 538 Marines went aboard the large-deck carrier *Theodore Roosevelt* for a month of at-sea training and workup. Designated as a Special-Purpose Marine Air-Ground Task Force (SPMAGTF), the Marines consisted of a rifle company, a command staff, and various detachments, including a reconnaissance platoon and heavy helicopter squadron HMH-362 with a component from utility and attack helicopter squadron HMLA-167. Aviation personnel comprised about 230 of the 538 Marines.

Subsequently, on March 11, 1993, the *Roosevelt* battle group departed Norfolk, steaming for the Mediterranean and a six-month forward deployment as a component of the Sixth Fleet. Aboard the *Roosevelt*— in addition to the Marines—was Carrier Air Wing 8 minus Air ASW Squadron 24, the wing's S-3B Viking unit, which was left ashore to make room for the Marine helicopters. The Vikings were of particular concern to some Navy planners because of their ASW capability and also their effectiveness for general surveillance and their special value as tankers for extending the range of the F/A-18 Hornets. The

Marine helicopters in the carrier were: six CH-53D Sea Stallions and four UH-1N Hueys.

The *Roosevelt* deployment identified a number of problems with Marines aboard large-deck carriers. There were benefits to be gained and lessons to be learned by such experiments as placing the SPMAGTF aboard the "TR." However, the costs and disadvantages far outweighed the benefits, and the concept was not continued.

More than 300 soldiers and airmen went aboard the carrier *George Washington* in April 1994 for a joint exercise. The troops—Army Rangers and Green Berets and Air Force special operations units—brought their helicopters, including large Air Force HH-53J Pave Low aircraft, with them.

In September 1994, 1,800 troops of the Army's 10th Mountain Division and their 54 helicopters embarked in the USS *Dwight D. Eisenhower* for the invasion of Haiti as part of the multinational Operation Uphold Democracy. On the morning of September 19 the division's 1st Brigade made an air-assault landing on the island's Port-au-Prince airport.

Subsequently, following the terrorist attacks on the United States in September 2001, the Yokosuka-based carrier *Kitty Hawk* served for several months as a floating base for Special Operational Forces (SOF) during the U.S. assault on Afghanistan. She departed Yokosuka on September 30 carrying the Army's 160th Special Operations Aviation Regiment with MH-47, MH-53, and MH-60 helicopters, and a total of some 1,000 Army,

Navy, and Air Force SOF personnel. The ship operated south of Pakistan, carrying out intensive operations in support of the U.S. assault on Afghanistan.

The ship's Carrier Air Wing 5 provided several F/A-18C Hornet strike fighters and a small number of EA-6B Prowler and E-2C Hawkeye support aircraft; the remainder of the wing was left ashore in Japan. She departed the gulf area on December 8, 2001, and returned to Yokosuka on the 23rd.

Also participating in the assault on Afghanistan, the helicopter carriers *Bataan* and *Peleliu* sent more than 300 Marines into the airfield at Kandhar in Afghanistan by helicopter. More Marines followed, with the *Bonhomme Richard* also taking part in the "helicopter assault" of Operation Enduring Freedom. Following the *Kitty Hawk*'s successful employment, the Department of Defense examined the feasibility of a specialized SOF support ship, including converting the soon-to-be-decommissioned CV *Constellation* or a new-built LHA/LHD for that role. After assessment of the various platforms, in February 2002, Maersk Line Ltd. received the sole commercial award for the design of an Afloat Forward Staging Base (AFSB) conversion based on the firm's S-class container ships.

The Maersk S-class ships were the world's largest container ships. First completed in 1997, they are known as post-PANAMAX (Panama Maximum) ships because they are too large to transit the Panama Canal. More than a score of S-class ships, each with the capacity of 8,000 containers in an overload condition, were in worldwide service. Conversion of an S-class ship to the AFSB configuration would take 12 to 18 months.[15]

Marines take a break on the flight deck of the carrier *Theodore Roosevelt* during the ship's 1993 deployment to the Mediterranean. This effort to carry a Marine assault force and its helicopters in a fleet carrier was unsuccessful. More feasible has been embarking Harrier fighter-attack aircraft in LHA/LHD amphibious ships with Marines and their helicopters. (U.S. Navy)

Some 1,800 troops of the Army's 10th Mountain Division with their helicopters and equipment boarded the carrier *Dwight D. Eisenhower* at the Norfolk naval base in September 1994 as part of the multinational force taking control of Haiti. Like the *Kitty Hawk* in 2001, the "Ike" served effectively as a floating base for ground forces. A Navy SH-3 Sea King is in the foreground; behind are Army UH-60 Black Hawks. (Steve Enfield, U.S. Navy)

In the AFSB configuration, the ship would have a flight deck forward and aft of the amidships island structure. She would have a full hangar deck, with two internal elevators carrying aircraft between the enclosed hangar and flight decks. The Department of Defense requirement was for a flight deck capable of accommodating up to 15 large, H-53 series helicopters or 12 MV-22 Osprey aircraft in a ready-to-fly condition. The hangar deck was to support the AV-8B Harrier and F-35 Joint Strike Fighter (JSF). The AFSB was to have modular (containerized) berthing, messing, laundry, and toilet facilities for up to 6,000 troops and support personnel.

The original AFSB design provided for side ramps to provide a roll-on/roll-off capability for unloading vehicles into air cushion landing craft (LCAC) or conventional landing craft. However, in 2005 the Naval Research Advisory Committee (NRAC) recommend instead fitting the ship with traverse side-hull openings for LCACs to enter the ship and be loaded/unloaded in a stable environment during high sea states.[16]

In commercial service 14 mariners plus a small number of maintenance personnel man the S-class ships. In naval service the ship would be operated by the Military Sealift Command with an operating crew of about 40 civilian mariners plus 43 support personnel (cooks, cleaning and laundry workers) for every 1,000 troops and air crewmen embarked. But, as with the similar Arapaho concept two decades earlier, no action has been taken on the AFSB proposal.

Two U.S. ships had earlier operated ASW helicopters to evaluate new concepts. The first was the LPH *Guam*, which served as a test platform for the Sea Control Ship (SCS) concept in 1972–1974 (see Chapter 18). The second was the Arapaho concept, tested at sea in 1982–1984.

The Arapaho system was developed to provide rapidly installed ASW helicopter facilities in container ships.[17] The system provided for the entire helicopter support facility to be fitted in standard freight containers and container footprints: the flight deck, hangars, crew quarters, galley, aviation fuel, ordnance, power supply, maintenance shops, and even administrative offices.

The containerized helicopter facility could be installed at the loading port atop several hundred cargo-carrying containers. The exact number of containers in the Arapaho facility would depend upon the ship's configuration. The facility could support several SH-3H Sea King helicopters. Upon arrival at the overseas port, the Arapaho containers would be removed and then returned to the original ship after the new cargo containers were loaded or installed in another ship.

In October 1982 the Arapaho facility—59 containers—was loaded aboard the partially activated container ship *Export Leader* at Norfolk in under 12 hours by a standard stevedore team. Operating under tow, the *Export Leader* carried out extensive trials with Navy and Marine helicopters, recording 178 day and 45 night landings during a 40-hour period without significant

The carrier *Kitty Hawk* was employed as a floating base for Special Operations Forces (SOF) during the U.S. assault on Afghanistan in 2001. Operating mostly Army SOF helicopters, such as this MH-47 Chinook, the ship embarked about 1,000 troops for the operation. Most of the *Kitty Hawk*'s Carrier Air Wing 5 was left ashore in Japan. At left are S-3B Vikings and F/A-18 Hornets. (U.S. Navy)

problems. About 3,700 gallons of JP-5 aviation fuel was transferred to helicopters. Up to four Sea Kings were hangared aboard the ship at one time. Also participating in the Arapaho sea trials were UH-1N and HH-1K Huey, SH-2F LAMPS, and CH-46D/E Sea Knight helicopters. Later, a 30,000-pound CH-53 Sea Stallion flew from the Arapaho setup while installed at the Lakehurst naval air station in New Jersey.

The Royal Navy leased the Arapaho system, shipped it to England in 1983, and installed it in the Royal Fleet Auxiliary *Reliant*.[18] Fitted with the system, the *Reliant* operated the troop-carrying Sea King HC.4 helicopters of No. 846 Squadron and Chinook and other Army helicopters. The helicopters embarked British troops in an evacuation from Lebanon in 1984. The *Reliant* served as a base for Chinook helicopters that shuttled more than 500 civilians of several nationalities from Beirut to Cyprus. Subsequently, in 1984–1985 the *Reliant*—with Sea King helicopters of No. 826 Squadron—operated in the South Atlantic carrying out shipping surveillance, fisheries patrol, and other missions. British service modifications to the Arapaho system permitted five Sea King–type helicopters to be stowed in the hangar and three deck spots were provided.

Neither the U.S. nor Royal Navies pursued the concept. Despite the success of the Arapaho sea trials, the U.S. Navy's aviation leadership—wedded to the large-carrier concept—refused to support further funding for the program. If helicopter operations from merchant ships were continued, Harrier trials would have undoubtedly been launched from Arapaho-type ships.

Other Navies

Several nations have procured large amphibious ships with major aviation capabilities, albeit none as large as the U.S. Navy LHA/LHD classes.

The largest full-deck amphibious ships built outside of the United States are the French Navy's two *Mistral*-class helicopter carriers.[19] The lead ship, laid down in 2003, was completed in 2005 and her sister ship, the *Tonnerre*, in 2006. They have full flight decks with a starboard superstructure; their hangar deck is connected by an aircraft elevator and a vehicle elevator. Troops—normally 450, with 900 berthed for short voyages—and their vehicles and equipment can be accommodated. The ships have a small docking well for landing craft. Extensive command center and hospital spaces are also provided. The ships' maximum speed of 19 knots is their major limitation. These ships can each operate 20 or more troop helicopters.

The French Navy also operates several dock landing ships (LSD/LPD) that have large flight decks. These ships generally have more aviation capability than similar U.S. Navy ships.

The Royal Navy, a pioneer in development of the helicopter carrier concept, constructed HMS *Ocean*, an LPH-type ship originally referred to as an Aviation Support Ship (ASS). The *Ocean* has a carrier configuration but was built to merchant ship standards.

After several delays in her start, the *Ocean* was begun in 1995 and entered service in 1999. The ship has a hangar deck with two elevators to move aircraft. However, she has no aviation support facilities, thus

The French amphibious ships *Mistral* (right) and *Tonnerre* are large and capable ships. Their hangars have space for 16 large NH-90 helicopters; the docking well can accommodate two LCACs or four LCM(8) landing craft. Note the stern helicopter elevator and, aft of the island structure, a large cargo/vehicle elevator (adjacent to the crane). The NH-90 is a multi-role helicopter produced by a consortium of the Aérospatiale-MBB-Agusta Westland firms. (*Ships of the World*)

while the *Ocean* can transport helicopters and VSTOL aircraft as well as vehicles, she cannot effectively operate them. Military vehicles can be transported and four LCVP landing craft are carried; 500 troops can be accommodated, with emergency provisions for another 300. The ship's greatest handicap is her 18-knot sustained speed.

Despite the ship's limitations, during the invasion of Iraq in March 2003, the *Ocean*, embarking a main-

tenance team from the naval air station at Yeovilton, successfully operated No. 845 and No. 847 helicopter squadrons in the northern Persian Gulf. The former squadron had Sea King HC.4 "Commando" transports while the latter flew both Lynx attack and Gazelle reconnaissance helicopters.

Italy, a late arrival in constructing aviation ships, has built two LPDs with full flight decks and a starboard island structure. The *San Giorgio*, completed in

HMS *Ocean* is rated as an assault helicopter carrier (LPH). While there is a superficial resemblance to the *Invincible*-class carriers, the *Ocean* is diesel propelled (vice gas turbine) and does not have a ski-ramp. She differs from the French and U.S. VSTOL/ helicopter carriers in not having a docking well. Four Sea King HC.4 troop helicopters are on her fight deck. The ship can hangar 12 Merlin or Sea King helicopters. (Royal Navy)

The helicopter/VSTOL carrier *Wasp* was the lead LHD. Slightly larger than the previous LHA design, the *Wasp* has a modified docking well, different elevator arrangement, and improved VSTOL support capabilities. Here the *Wasp* refuels from the replenishment ship *Supply* during Middle East operations in July 2002. The *Wasp* had a Marine expeditionary unit embarked; 22 of the unit's helicopters and four AV-8B Harrier VSTOL aircraft are on the flight deck. (Teresa Ellison, U.S. Navy)

1988, and *San Marco*, completed a year later, are configured for disaster relief as well as military functions. A single elevator connects the hangar and flight decks. Although the troop capacity is only 345, the ships are relatively capable for their size. And, beyond their docking well, the ships carry a pair of LCVPs.

In some respects the most interesting of these aviation ships are the Japanese LSDs of the *Osumi* class, with four units completed from 1998 to 2005. Only part of the full-length flight deck is suitable for helicopter operations, in part because of the width of the starboard island structure. While the ship has two elevators connecting a hangar level to the flight deck, they are for vehicles and cannot handle helicopters. The *Osumi* and her sister ships can berth 330 troops, with possibly 1,000 being carried for brief periods.

The *Osumi*-class ships and the new helicopter-capable missile destroyers represent a major step in Japan's development of a true helicopter/VSTOL carrier.

At various times the Soviet Union had considered helicopter-carrying amphibious ships, and the Nevskoye bureau produced several designs. However, no ships were constructed.

The U.S. and British experiments with assault helicopters aboard ships, and the Royal Navy's operation of helicopter carriers in the Suez assault in 1956 have demonstrated the value of these ships in military operations. While large LHA/LHD ships are not affordable by any nation other than the United States, smaller aviation "amphibs"—primarily LSD/LPD-type ships with full flight decks—can be expected to be constructed in the coming years. Such ships, of course, like the larger carriers, are also well suited for humanitarian and rescue operations.

Table 25-1
FLIGHT-DECK AMPHIBIOUS SHIPS, 2007

NATION	SHIP	FULL LOAD DISPLACEMENT	COMPLETED	BUILT
France	*Mistral*	21,500 tons	2006–2007	2
Great Britain	*Ocean*	21,578 tons	1999	1
Italy	*San Giorgio*	7,665 tons	1988–1989	2
Japan	*Osumi*	13,000 tons	1998–2005	4
South Korea	*Doko*	18,860 tons	2007–	1***
USA	*Tarawa*	39,400 tons	1976–1980	5*
USA	*Wasp*	39,925 tons	1989–	7**

* Two of these ships were decommissioned, one in 2005 and one in 2007.
** The *Makin Island* (LHD 8) is under construction to be completed in 2008.
*** Second ship to be completed about 2010.

Beginning in 2007 the U.S. Marine Corps also flew the MV-22 Osprey from LHA/LHD-type ships. The MV-22 is a high-speed, rotary-wing aircraft being produced for the Marine assault role as a replacement for the CH-46E Sea Knight and CH-53D Sea Stallion.[20]

The V-22 design—developed from the XV-15A technology-demonstration aircraft—has twin rotor engine nacelles mounted on a connecting wing. The nacelles rotate to a horizontal position for conventional aircraft flight and are vertical for vertical takeoff and landing or hover. Conversion from the hovering mode to forward airplane flight takes 12 seconds. Rolling takeoffs and landings are the normal operating mode, although VTOL operations are feasible. Thus, the design has the advantages of both a conventional aircraft and helicopter. An in-flight refueling probe is provided.

The basic aircraft has an internal cargo capacity of 10,000 pounds and an external (sling) capacity of 15,000 pounds. Thus, the MV-22 can internally carry 24 troops or 12 litters, or a "Humvee" (High Mobility Multipurpose Wheeled Vehicle).

The availability of the MV-22, and the potential of specialized V-22 variants for anti-submarine and airborne early warning aircraft, offers the promise of a significant increase in capabilities for helicopter/ VSTOL carriers.

The MV-22 Osprey—shown landing aboard the USS *Wasp* in December 2006—is the replacement for the CH-46 Sea Knight and the CH-53D Sea Stallion flown by the Marine Corps. In flight the engine nacelles rotate to the horizontal position for high-speed flight and the wheels fully retract into the fuselage. The rear ramp is partially lowered. An inflight refueling probe can be fitted. The Osprey's top speed is 316 m.p.h. with a range of 500 miles with 24 troops or 6,000 pounds of cargo in the VTO mode or 250 miles with 8,300 pounds of external cargo in the VTO

26 INTO THE 21ST CENTURY

The old and the new: The Brazilian carrier *São Paulo*, formerly the French *Foch*, completed in 1963, steams with the USS *Ronald Reagan* completed in 2003. When the ships operated together in South American waters in June 2004 the only older flattop in service was the Indian *Viraat*, completed as HMS *Hermes* in 1959. The *Reagan* was the penultimate ship of the *Nimitz* class, followed by the *George H.W. Bush*, to complete in 2008. The *Sao Paulo* has an A-4 Skyhawk forward and an SH-3 Sea King aft. (John Lill, U.S. Navy)

By the beginning of the 21st Century the United States and other Western nations were engaged in fighting what has been labeled World War III—the conflict against terrorism spawned by Muslim fundamentalism. Unlike the previous "hot" wars fought by the United States—the Korean, Vietnam, and Gulf War conflicts—this war affects almost every country in the world.[1]

It is difficult to determine when and where World War III began: It may have been the abortive attempt to blow up the World Trade Center in 1993; the attack on the American barracks known as Khobar Towers in Saudi Arabia in 1996; the car-bombing of the U.S. embassies in Nairobi, Kenya, and Dar es Salaam, Tanzania, in 1998; the attack on the U.S. destroyer *Cole* at Aden in 2000; or the devastating assault on the World Trade Center and the Pentagon on September 11, 2001.[2]

On the morning of September 11, shortly after ter-rorists crashed passenger aircraft into the symbols of American economic and military power, at about 10 A.M. the carrier *John F. Kennedy* got under way from Mayport, Florida. The carrier steamed northward and was soon followed by the *George Washington*, which was already at sea. The two carriers divided the planes of Carrier Air Wing 7, ashore at Oceana, Virginia, at the time of the attacks, to provide combat air patrols, joining Air Force and Marine land-based aircraft to defend against the possibility of additional terrorist air attacks.[3] Aegis missile ships also added to the defense of key East Coast cities.

On the West Coast the carrier *John C. Stennis* sortied from San Diego and went to sea to add more aircraft to the West Coast fighter patrols.

For the U.S. Navy the war against terrorism raised questions such as, What were the roles for naval forces

Discarding KA-6D Intruder tankers and reduction in S-3B Viking squadrons forced carrier aircraft to increasingly refuel from Air Force tankers and to employ buddy stores on F/A-18 Hornets. Here an Air Force KC-10 Extender refuels an F/A-18C Hornet from VFA-147 aboard the *John C. Stennis* while a pair of French Super Étendard fighters from the *Charles de Gaulle* wait their turn. (Dan Cheever, U.S. Navy)

in this global conflict? What kinds of ships and aircraft, and how many are required to fulfill those roles? And, could they be funded within likely budget allocations?

Soon after the demise of the Soviet Union and the end of the Cold War, the U.S. Navy adopted a new strategy centered on the support of operations ashore. Subsequently, this strategy was refined to include U.S. naval "dominance" in the littoral or coastal waters, especially in those areas where U.S. forces were required to operate ashore. But the first challenge of the new conflict was against a land-locked country—Afghanistan.

Afghanistan[4]

The Soviet invasion of Afghanistan and its unsuccessful efforts to subjugate that country from 1979 to 1989 left the remote nation in chaos with civil war raging. The Taliban clan took control in 1996 and sought to create a pure, fundamentalist Islamic state.[5] The Taliban leadership opened the country to the al Qaeda terrorist organization led by Osama bin Laden.

In August 1998, in response to the bombings of two U.S. embassies in Africa, the Clinton administration ordered ship-launched Tomahawk missile strikes against six reported al Qaeda sites in Afghanistan as well as a pharmaceutical plant in the Sudanese capital of Khartoum. Thus, targets in two land-locked states were attacked from the sea. (The targets in Afghani-

stan were largely abandoned camps, while no proof that the Khartoum plant was involved in producing chemical-biological weapons has been reported.)

Following the September 11, 2001, attacks on the United States, the George W. Bush administration decided to remove the Taliban regime and with it the use of Afghanistan as a base for al Qaeda. The invasion forces would support anti-Taliban groups still fighting in the Afghan civil war. The lack of available airfields in Afghanistan became a critical factor for U.S. military planners looking into options for the assault. Thus, they opted to employ carrier-based aircraft. The southern border of Afghanistan is some 250 miles from the Arabian Sea, and Kabul is some 600 miles from the sea. Pakistan, which lies between Afghanistan and the sea, gave permission for U.S. overflights of its territory, although there was a severe restriction on the American use of bases in Pakistan.

Operation Enduring Freedom—the U.S. assault on Afghanistan—began late on the night of October 7, 2001. Some 15 U.S. land-based strategic bombers and 25 strike aircraft from the carriers *Carl Vinson* and *Enterprise*, operating in the Arabian Sea, carried out the initial strikes.[6] They were coordinated with the launch of some 50 Tomahawk land-attack missiles fired from four U.S. surface ships and a U.S. and a British submarine in the Arabian Sea.

The carrier strike consisted of F-14 Tomcat and F/A-18 Hornet strike aircraft. In addition to carrying guided bombs, the U.S. aircraft had air-to-air missiles in the event that they were challenged by the small number of Taliban MiG-21 and Su-22 fighters. There was no aerial opposition as the airfields and air defense sites were attacked, and the Taliban air force was destroyed.

A third U.S. carrier, the *Kitty Hawk*, participated in the assault on Afghanistan. U.S. Central Intelligence Agency and special operations troops had been in Afghanistan, working with anti-Taliban forces, prior to the U.S. assault. The *Kitty Hawk* carried special operations helicopters and troops, being employed as a "steel lily pad—a Forward Operating Base," according to

General Tommy Franks, the Commander-in-Chief U.S. Central Command.[7]

As the carriers provided the tactical air for operations in Afghanistan, U.S. officials carried out frantic negotiations to obtain the use of nearby airfields pending the seizure of bases in Afghanistan. The government of Kyrgyzstan finally permitted U.S. aircraft to use the former Soviet bomber base at the capital city of Bishkek. This base and the subsequent availability of airfields in Afghanistan eased the burden on the carriers.

In Operation Enduring Freedom the availability of carrier decks again enabled U.S. military action in a forward area, even though it was hundreds of miles from the sea. From October through the end of December 2001 the carriers flew the majority of the strike

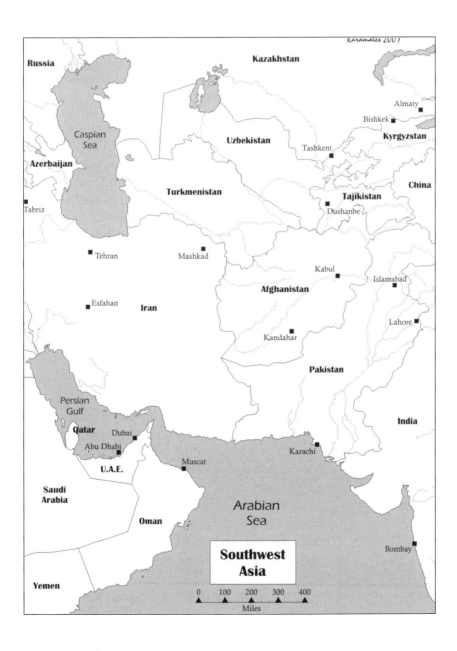

The F/A-18 Hornet was the predominant aircraft on U.S. carriers at the start of the 21st Century with each ship usually operating four strike-fighter squadrons (VFA or Marine VMFA) with an aggregate of 48 aircraft. Here two F/A-18C Hornets are over the *Ronald Reagan* during the carrier's deployment to the Western Pacific in March 2007. (Tam Pham, U.S. Navy)

sorties. Navy and Marine aircraft, operating from carriers and then from shore bases, flew 4,900 missions compared to 701 sorties by Air Force strategic bombers, 720 by Air Force fighters, and 225 by Air Force special operations aircraft (primarily AC-130 gunships). But Air Force strategic bombers dropped the most tonnage of bombs. Of the Navy and Marine aircraft munitions, 93 percent were precision-guided weapons, either GPS satellite or laser guided.[8] Only 7 percent were "dumb" or "iron" bombs.

The range of operations from carriers proved the value of ship-based tanker aircraft, primarily the S-3B Viking, which had lost its ASW gear several years earlier. After a brief period Air Force KC-135 and KC-10 tankers were available over Afghanistan to support the carrier aircraft. Also important to the campaign in Afghanistan were E-2C Hawkeyes, soon supplemented by Air Force E-3 Sentry aircraft; EA-6B Prowler electronic attack aircraft; and land-based P-3C Orion maritime patrol aircraft. The P-3s used their electro-optical and infrared sensors to identify targets and also served as communications relay aircraft.

Against Iraq—Round 2

As anti-Taliban and al Qaeda operations continued in Afghanistan, preparations were being made for an as-

sault against Saddam Hussein's regime in Iraq. The U.S. intelligence community believed—albeit based on faulty intelligence—that Iraq was developing chemical, biological, and possibly nuclear weapons. However, the exclusion of United Nations inspectors, the halt to U-2 spyplanes collecting intelligence for the United Nations, and other actions by the Iraqi government led both the international body and the U.S. Congress to approve military action against Iraq.

General Franks briefed President George W. Bush on a plan of operations for Iraq as early as December 2001. Franks wanted a much faster air campaign than that of the 1991 assault on Iraq, which was possible in part because of the steady reduction of air defenses as U.S. and British forces enforced no-fly zones for Iraqi military aircraft over northern and southern Iraq. Carriers had played a major role in that effort—as they would in the coming war—because of severe restrictions placed on U.S. military aircraft operating from Saudi Arabian bases.

Planning for operations against Iraq continued through 2002, with a steady increase in U.S. naval operations in the Persian Gulf and adjacent areas. Five large-deck carriers were available for the campaign—the *Abraham Lincoln*, *Harry S. Truman*, and *Theodore Roosevelt*, all *Nimitz*-class nuclear-propelled ships; and the oil-burning *Constellation* and *Kitty Hawk*. The *Roosevelt* and *Truman* were in the eastern Mediterranean to support the northern campaign against Iraq, which was originally to be launched through Turkey (which in the event denied permission for the U.S. troop transit but allowed air overflights). The *Lincoln* had been in Perth, Australia, over the Christmas holidays 2002, en route back to the United States. New orders sent the carrier back to the Persian Gulf for the coming war.

After last-minute ultimatums by the U.S. government, late on March 19 the Anglo-American air, ground, and naval forces assaulted Iraq in what was called Operation Iraqi Freedom. Special operations teams had been inserted beginning two days earlier. The carrier-based aircraft were supplemented by limited flight operations from Saudi Arabia as well as the Gulf states, with U.S. long-range bombers flying from Britain and Diego Garcia supplementing the strikes. Some 40 Tomahawk missiles from U.S. warships struck key targets in Baghdad, while a pair of F-117 stealth attack aircraft struck a compound where Saddam was believed to be ensconced.

In comparison with the Gulf War of 1991, Iraqi air defenses—fighters, surface-to-air missiles, and anti-aircraft artillery—were minimal in 2003. The carriers' F-14D "Bombcats" and F/A-18 Hornets carried out strike and close air support missions, while their S-3B Vikings served as tankers, the E-2C Hawkeyes provided air surveillance and control, and the EA-6B Prowlers sought out Iraqi radars and communications nodes. The Navy- and Marine-piloted Prowlers, as the all-service electronic jamming and attack aircraft, were integral to all air strikes, including those by B-2 and F-117 stealth aircraft.

Again, the overwhelming majority of the air-launched weapons were "smart," that is, either laser or GPS satellite guided. During the operation, the Iraqis used Russian-built jamming systems in an attempt to disrupt American use of GPS in the theater. The jamming efforts failed, and GPS-guided weapons destroyed the equipment.

The carriers' helicopters supported Navy special operations forces while providing combat search-and-rescue functions.

Baghdad fell to U.S. troops in early April. The "war" was over. The insurrection began soon afterward. Defense writer Rebecca Grant observed,

the carrier strike capacity was not pushed to the limit even by [Operation Iraqi Freedom]. Planners calculated that the sustained sorties rate was about 350 sorties per day, with surge rate near 428 sorties per day. It was only during the most intense period of destruction of the Republican Guards in early April that the carriers' combined strike totals got near the projected sustained sortie rate, topping off with a one-day total of 326.[9]

In addition to attack and close air support missions, some F/A-18s fitted with SHARP, a multifunction reconnaissance system with both electro-optical and infrared cameras with a datalink to surface ships or other aircraft, flew "road patrols." These flights sought to identify in specific areas over time the changes that could indicate the placement of Improvised Explosive Devices (IED). And, EA-6B Prowlers prowled the skies over Iraq, using their electronic warfare systems to detect and jam terrorist communications and electronic control of IED detonation devices.

In the wake of the assaults on Afghanistan and Iraq U.S. carrier air wings saw major changes. The F-14 Tomcat, in its ultimate F-14D multi-role configuration, was retired in 2006. The last two squadrons, VF-31 and VF-213 with a total of 22 aircraft, deployed to the Persian Gulf from October 2005 to February 2006 aboard the carrier *Roosevelt*. According to Lieutenant Commander

One of the last flights of a Tomcat: an F-14D "Bombcat" from fighter squadron VF-213 aboard the *Theodore Roosevelt* over Iraq in December 2005. The plane has a laser-guided bomb and a "dumb" bomb under its fuselage, with a Sidewinder missile under its right wing; two 267-gallon drop tanks are fitted. The Tomcat was still a highly capable and versatile aircraft when retired from the U.S. Navy in 2006. (Scott Timmester, U.S. Navy)

The Boeing/Northrop Grumman EA-18G Growler is the successor to the EA-6B Prowler in the electronic attack role. The two-seat Growler is derived from the F/A-18F Hornet and is to enter Navy squadrons in 2009. The aircraft is being fitted with an advanced jamming and information system. It will carry AMRAAM air-to-air and HARM anti-radar missiles; no gun is fitted. Four detection/jamming pods are carried as are wingtip antennas (preventing the carrying of Sidewinder launch rails). The name "Growler" is a combination of the G from EA-18G and *Prowler*. (U.S. Navy)

Robb Soderholm of VF-213, "We were flying between 14 and 18 sorties per day. . . . At least a third of these flights were six-hour marathons up into Iraq."[10]

The F-14D was still a highly capable fighter-attack aircraft. However, its high maintenance costs compared to the F/A-18 Hornet series caused the Tomcat's demise. Thus ended the 33-year career of the F-14, one of the world's most advanced fighter aircraft of its time. During that period Tomcats had downed only five enemy aircraft—four Soviet-built Libyan fighters and an Iraqi helicopter. (Significantly, the Tomcats flown by Iran continued in service. They were credited with numerous air-to-air kills against the Iraqi Air Force.[11])

Next to leave the carrier decks were the S-3B Vikings. They had lost their ASW capability in the 1990s but remained a valuable air wing component, being used for reconnaissance and, especially, tanker duties. The last Vikings were to be discarded by about 2010. This leaves the F/A-18s carrying "buddy" refueling stores as the only carrier-based aircraft with tanker capability.

And, shortly after the S-3B Vikings leave carriers, the last Navy EA-6B Prowler electric attack/counter-measures aircraft will be discarded. Their replacement will be the EA-18G Growler variant of the F/A-18 Hornet. Although a highly capable electronic aircraft, the EA-18 has but a single electronic countermeasures officer (in addition to the pilot) compared to three such officers in the EA-6B.

F/A-18 Hornets and the derivative EA-18G Growler will thus dominate the carrier flight decks pending arrival of the F-35 Joint Strike Fighter. The other fixed-wing aircraft on large-deck carriers will be the improved E-2D Hawkeye AEW aircraft and MH-60 Seahawk helicopters.

Beginning about 2012–2013 the Joint Strike Fighter (JSF) will replace the F/A-18 Hornet in U.S. carriers and, probably, the Harrier in British ships. Designated F-35 (based on the prototype X-35) and named Lightning II, the JSF is being developed in three basic configurations: F-35A conventional variant for the U.S. Air Force; F-35B STOVL variant for U.S. Marine Corps and Royal Navy; and F-35C carrier variant for U.S. Navy.

Developed by Lockheed Martin, the X-35/F-35 design won a competition with the Boeing X-32. All three versions of the F-35 have the same F135 turbofan engine and similar fuselage, two internal weapon bays, common outer mold lines, swept-back wings, and comparable tail assembly. The side-by-side weapon bays are an unusual feature in contemporary carrier-based aircraft; other naval fighters and light/medium attack aircraft carry their weapons on external pylons and attachment points. The F-35 will also have six wing pylons for weapons, sensors, and external fuel. Only the F-35A will have an internal gun, the GAU-12 25-mm rotary barrel weapon; the other variants can carry gun pods. The aircraft will have low-observable (stealth) features.

A Mach 1.8 aircraft, the F-35 will not be a low-level attack aircraft, but will operate above the kill zones of small arms and shoulder-launched missiles. This tactic requires that the plane employ stand-off tactical missiles and guided bombs. The availability of data links to off-board sensors (unmanned aerial vehicles, satellites, other aircraft, and ground forces) will provide the F-35 with precision targeting data for stand-off weapons.

When this volume went to press the F-35B variant was to enter U.S. Marine Corps and Royal Navy service in 2012, and the F-35A and F-35C variants were to enter service one year later with the U.S. Air Force and Navy, respectively. The total U.S.-British procurement is planned at almost 2,800 aircraft, with several other countries expressing interest in F-35 variants.

Five carriers participated in Operation Iraqi Freedom compared to six in Operation Desert Storm (1991). A sixth carrier arrived in mid-April 2003, when the *Nimitz*, which had departed San Diego on March 3, arrived in the area to replace the *Lincoln*. The latter carrier arrived back at San Diego on May 5, ending the longest U.S. carrier deployment since the Vietnam War—262 days.

And, six U.S. Navy LHA/LHD helicopter carriers participated in Operation Iraqi Freedom, two of them operating as "Harrier carriers." (See Chapter 25.)

Another carrier, the VSTOL carrier *Ark Royal*, the third ship of *Invincible* class, was part of the British force that participated in the assault on Iraq. She had departed Portsmouth on January 12, 2003, with amphibious ships embarking some 3,000 Royal Marines. Only helicopters populated the "Ark's" flight deck. In her LPH role she participated in the assault on Iraq's Al Faw Peninsula at the start of the campaign.

Following participation in the Iraqi assault, the *Ark Royal* returned to Britain and soon underwent an extensive refit that was completed in 2007. She emerged from the Babcock shipyard in Rosyth, Fife, as a commando ship with accommodations for 600 Marines in addition to her ship's company and all-helicopter air group. In the LPH role the *Ark Royal* was a substitute for HMS *Ocean*, which began a lengthy overhaul.

Royal Navy Conundrum

At the start of the 21st Century the Royal Navy's air arm was undergoing radical changes. The aircraft carrier–future (CVF) program seeks to provide the Royal Navy with two large, conventional ships to eventually replace the three *Invincible*-class VSTOL ships.

Royal Navy officer and analyst Gordon Wilson wrote,

> The Royal Navy's most important—and in some respects most controversial—program is the future aircraft carrier (CVF). The two-ship program . . . will produce the largest warships ever built by Britain. If they are not constructed, the future effectiveness of the Royal Navy will be reduced to coastal operations.[12]

Studies of replacement options for the three *Invincible*-class VSTOL carriers were begun in 1994. Beyond looking at the construction of larger ships to provide larger air wings, the studies considered converting merchant ship designs or carrying out service life extension of the *Invincible* class. Soon after the Labour Party came to power in May 1997, the new Secretary of State for Defence, George Robertson, launched

a review of Britain's armed forces. At the center of the debate was the issue of replacing the *Invincible* class. The report stated,

> We judge that there is therefore a continuing need for Britain to have the capability offered by aircraft carriers.

The *Invincible* Class carriers were designed for Cold War anti-submarine warfare operations with helicopters and a limited air defence capability provided by a small number of embarked Sea Harriers. This is no longer the main requirement. The emphasis is now on increased

A Lockheed Martin F-35A Lightning II, with wheels down, on a test flight, and a closeup of the lift fan and auxiliary air intake of the F-35B. The Joint Strike Fighter (JSF) is an effort to provide the U.S. and British air arms with a single aircraft for the fighter and attack roles. The U.S. Marine Corps is also considering an F-35 variant for the electronic attack role to replace the EA-6B Prowler. The F-35 is rated at 1,200 m.p.h. (Mach 1.8) with a 600-mile combat radius with internal fuel and weapons. (Lockheed Martin)

The planned CVF *Queen Elizabeth* will have an unconventional design, reflecting the continued British innovation in carrier aviation. The ship will have separate island structures with two starboard-side deck-edge elevators, and a ski-ramp forward; the second elevator is aft of the after island structure. The aircraft shown on the deck of this artist's representation appear to be F-35 Lightning II Joint Strike Fighters. (Thales)

offensive air power, and an ability to operate the largest possible range of aircraft in the widest possible range of roles.[13]

The Robertson review proposed that when the three *Invincible* carriers were retired they should be replaced by two larger ships, with "present thinking" suggesting ships of some 30,000 to 40,000 tons, each capable of operating up to 50 aircraft, fixed-wing and helicopters. While stating that no decision had been made on what aircraft would fly from the new ships, the report mentioned that the U.S. Joint Strike Fighter (F-35) "was a strong contender." Subsequently, Ministry of Defence officials noted that in addition to the JSF they were also studying a navalized Eurofighter 2000, an upgraded Sea Harrier, and other U.S. and French carrier aircraft.[14]

With respect to operational concepts, one *Invincible*-class ship is normally available and at sea, replacing another which returns to port for maintenance, re-equipping, crew rest, and training, while the third ship is in deep maintenance (including dry docking). The plan for the new ships—the *Queen Elizabeth*

class—is to have one of the two carriers available at all times and the other available part of the time by putting the ships into dry dock only once every six years or so; the rest of the below-waterline work would be accomplished by underwater methods without requiring the docking of the ship.

The new carriers will be some 950 feet in length, only about 130 feet shorter than the U.S. *Nimitz*-class carriers, although they are only half the displacement. The new carriers are so large that Britain no longer has a shipyard able to build them. Rather, the ships would be built in sections in various yards around Britain and assembled at one location. Even this plan is somewhat ambitious in view of the poor state of the British shipbuilding industry at the start of the 21st Century.

The CVF design provides for an unusual "split" starboard island structure with two starboard-side elevators connecting the hangar and flight decks. The ship will have a ski-ramp but not a true angled deck. Fast, efficient munitions handling—the ability to generate a very high aircraft sortie rate—is considered vital to the carriers. The designers are planning on 500 sorties over five days, consuming perhaps 800 metric tons of ordnance. The ships will have gas turbine engines with electric motors providing a maximum speed of 25 knots. The manning goal is for a carrier crew of some 600 plus up to 800 in the embarked squadrons and command staff, a total of about 1,400 men and women.

The CVF program proposed by the French-owned Thales UK firm was selected in January 2003. Subsequently, the Ministry of Defence directed that the losing competitor—BAE (British Aerospace)—would be the prime contractor. The two firms formed the Aircraft Carrier Alliance to produce the ships. And, following extensive discussions, in March 2006 the French and British governments reached an agreement to base the next French carrier, to complement the nuclear-propelled *Charles de Gaulle*, on a modified CVF design. The French Navy had hoped to have the new carrier—designated the PA2—operational before the beginning of the *de Gaulle*'s refueling and comprehensive overhaul scheduled to begin in 2015.[15] It is unlikely that the schedule can be met.

The British plan provides for the *Queen Elizabeth* to join the Fleet in 2014 and the second ship, the *Prince of Wales*, in 2016. The Royal Navy announced on July 25, 2007, that a contract for the two ships—£3.8 billion—had been awarded.

As the CVF program was being formulated, the Fleet Air Arm was undergoing major changes. The highly effective Sea Harrier FRS.1 aircraft, victor of the Falklands, was replaced from 1993 to 1999 by the Sea Harrier FA.2 variant.[16] Like its predecessor, the FA.2 was optimized for air-to-air combat with a limited attack capability. Thirty-four earlier Sea Harriers were upgraded to the FA.2 configuration and another 18 were built to that standard for a 52-aircraft program. The first FA.2 aerodynamic prototype (a conversion) flew on September 19, 1988. The four major improvements in the FA.2 were the improved Blue Vixen, look-down radar; improved cockpit displays; increased air-to-air weapons payload, including the U.S. AIM-120 AMRAAM missile; and increased range.

The 34 conversions, including two prototypes, were delivered from 1988 through 1997, and the new-build aircraft from 1995 through 1999. FAA No. 801 Squadron was the first to receive the Sea Harrier FA.2, and its first operational deployment was in April 1994 as part of the United Nations force in Bosnia. But the FA.2's service life was brief.

In 2002 the Ministry of Defence announced plans to retire all Sea Harriers by 2006 even though the successor, the F-35B Joint Strike Fighter, would not be available until 2012 at earliest. The decision was made to reduce maintenance and support costs by having both

A Sea Harrier T.10 (above) and a Sea Harrier FA.2 overfly the Royal Naval Air Station Yeovilton during the decommissioning ceremonies for No. 899 squadron. The premature retirement of the Sea Harrier—called "Shar" in the Fleet—left the British VSTOL carriers with only GR.7 and GR.9 "attack" Harriers in addition to their helicopters. These Harriers are flown by both FAA and RAF squadrons. (Royal Navy)

the FAA and Royal Air Force operate the same Harrier GR-series aircraft, abandoning fighter-type aircraft in the carriers until the JSF becomes available.

The last Sea Harrier squadron to stand down was No. 801, which disestablished promptly after retiring its last FA.2 aircraft in March 2006. It was reestablished on October 1, 2006, with Harriers GR.7 and GR.9 aircraft.

The need for additional attack aircraft had earlier led to the Ministry of Defence decision to place RAF GR.7 and GR.9 variants aboard the VSTOL carriers. This decision was caused, in part, by the continued withdrawal of British land and air forces from overseas bases. Thus, the RAF could project tactical air power into forward areas only from carriers. Accordingly, on April 1, 2000, the Joint Force Harrier (JFH) was established to combine the two FAA Sea Harrier squadrons with the two RAF Harrier squadrons under a new command, No. 3 Group within the RAF Strike Command.[17] A naval officer, Rear-Admiral Iain Henderson, was named the first commanding officer of No. 3 Group, which also operated the RAF Nimrod maritime patrol aircraft and Sea King search-and-rescue helicopters. Henderson additionally served as Flag Officer Maritime Aviation, in other words the head of the FAA.

The Harriers GR.7 and GR.9 are the only aircraft available for carrier operation in addition to helicopters. The British plan is to acquire the F-35B STOVL version of the U.S. JSF to replace Harriers aboard the CVF. When this volume went to press the British plan was to acquire 150 of the STOVL aircraft beginning in 2012 for both carrier- and land-based operation.

Similar to the JFH organization, the Joint Helicopter Command (JHC) was set up on October 1, 1999, to combine the Navy-Marine commando helicopter squadrons—44 helicopters, most of them Sea King HC.4 aircraft, plus spares—with RAF and Army Air Corps helicopters. This new force provided helicopters for amphibious operations from HMS *Ocean* and from other ships, including the *Invincible* class.

At the start of the century the three VSTOL carriers and the *Ocean* could also embark Sea King HAS.5 and HAS.6 helicopters for ASW. The Sea Kings were soon succeeded by the multi-role Merlin HM.1 helicopter. There were three squadrons of eight or nine Merlins plus No. 849 Squadron with eight Sea King AEW.2/ASaC.7 helicopters. The first two Mk 7 helicopters, which are upgraded AEW.2 variants, had

Searchwater 2000 radar and an advanced mission co-ordination system, leading to their redesignation as Airborne Surveillance and Area Control (ASaC) aircraft. Sea King ASaC.7 helicopters were first deployed aboard the *Ark Royal* for Operation Iraqi Freedom. Two of those helicopters were lost in a midair collision on March 22, 2003.[18] In 2006 the "standard" air group for the carriers *Invincible* and *Illustrious* consisted of 21 aircraft:

9 Harrier GR.7/9
9 Sea King HAS.6 or Merlin HMA.1
3 Sea King AEW.2/ASaC.7

Then There Were Eleven

The U.S. Navy operated 12 large-deck carriers from the mid-1990s until 2006. Despite the heavy commitment of carriers in the Gulf War as well as in Operations Enduring Freedom and Iraqi Freedom and in lesser conflicts and confrontations, various defense reviews postulated a future force of only 11 carriers would be suitable for U.S. interests. In reality, even fewer carriers have been available as since 1980 one large carrier has been undergoing modernization and (if nuclear) refueling, leaving a two- to three-year period during which the ship is unavailable. These upgrades add about 15 years to the nominal 30-year service life of a CV/CVN.

The penultimate oil-burning large carrier in service was the *John F. Kennedy*. The ship ceased air operations in 2006 because of the need to repair/upgrade her arresting gear and catapults. However, Congress demanded that the Navy retain the ship in commission, primarily because her homeport of Jacksonville, Florida, financially benefited from the ship's crew and dependents.

The "JFK" was finally retired in 2007 leaving the Yokosuka-based *Kitty Hawk* as the only conventional large-deck carrier in U.S. service. The *Kitty Hawk* was scheduled to be decommissioned in 2008 and replaced by the carrier *George Washington* as the U.S. Navy's only forward-based carrier.

Meanwhile, the construction of *Nimitz*-class super carriers continued: the *Ronald Reagan* was completed in 2003 and the *George H. W. Bush* was to be completed in 2008. As all previous nuclear carriers, they were built at the Newport News shipyard in Virginia. These bring to ten the number of ships in the *Nimitz* class, the last of which is to be completed 33 years after the first. This is the longest that any class of warships in any country has been in continuous construction. For at least a few years the number of U.S. carriers will number ten CVNs following the retirement of the *Enterprise* in 2013. The commissioning of the *Gerald R. Ford* (CVN 78) about 2016 should bring CVN strength back to 11 ships (with one of those carriers in longterm refueling-overhaul).

In the early 1990s the U.S. Navy initiated the CVX program—the designation for the next generation of aircraft carriers. This was to be a major departure from the *Nimitz* design, which had evolved directly from the oil-burning *United States* and *Forrestal* designs of the late 1940s. The CVX was to be funded in fiscal year 2006 and to join the Fleet in about 2013.

The CVX concept promised a more efficient warship, capable of handling advanced aircraft at a faster operating cycle; lower radar, acoustic, and infrared detection signatures (for enhanced survivability); a smaller crew; and significantly lower construction and operating costs. These and other advanced concepts were being studied at the Carrier Innovation Center of Newport News Shipbuilding in Virginia. The center was also examining non-nuclear propulsion concepts for the ship, primarily gas turbines.

The CVX, according to the Navy's Director of Air Warfare, was being designed on a "clean sheet of paper" and would "feature improved characteristics in selected areas, such as launch and recovery equipment, flight deck layout, C^{4}I [Command-Control-Communications-Computers/Intelligence] systems, information networks and propulsion systems . . . [and] features that will make them more affordable to operate."[19]

This "entirely new class" was cancelled because of funding shortfalls. Although the Navy never announced a total development and design cost for the CVX, the fiscal 1999 defense program indicated just over $1 *billion* in development costs. The Navy never adequately funded the CVX, but Navy leadership continued to promote the CVX concept. Indeed, the Navy continued to promote the CVX concept in public even after the Chief of Naval Operations, Admiral Jay L. Johnson, announced that the next carrier would definitely have nuclear propulsion, certainly a contradiction of the "clean sheet" concept. The Navy's powerful nuclear propulsion community, then led by Admiral Frank (Skip) Bowman, had already decided that nuclear power "is a given" for the CVX, according to a leading

The U.S. Navy had an all-big-deck carrier force following the retirement of the long-serving carrier *Midway* in 1992. This unusual photo shows four super carriers moored at adjacent piers at Norfolk, Virginia, in October 1985: from left are the USS *Nimitz, John F. Kennedy, America*, and *Dwight D. Eisenhower*. With the retirement of the *Kitty Hawk* in 2008 the U.S. Navy has an all-CVN carrier force—plus the large, versatile LHA/LHD-type amphibious ships. (Jeff Wooddell, U.S. Navy)

defense writer.[20] "Without this endurance and flexibility [provided by nuclear-propelled carriers], we would be hard put to do what we are doing today," continued Bowman.

Despite this acquiescence to the nuclear propulsion community, the CVX program continued to be underfunded by the Navy while it was still publicized as the Navy's future. The program received an infusion of support in early 2001 when Donald Rumsfeld became Secretary of Defense in the George W. Bush administration.[21]

Rumsfeld, who had served as Secretary of Defense from 1975 to 1977 in the Ford administration, sought "transformation" programs in the military services, a transition to joint operations and innovative uses of existing systems, and the development of advanced systems to counter emerging threats.[22] Embracing a revitalized CVX program as a transformational effort, Rumsfeld approved a two-step program, the CVX-1 as a "partial" transformational carrier from the *Nimitz* class and the "ultimate" CVX-2, the next-generation carrier.

The two ships were subsequently combined into the prototype for the next-generation carrier, initially designated CVN-21 (for 21st Century) and then assigned the hull number CVN 78. The new ship would have an improved *Nimitz* design, with a revised flight deck arrangement (with increased deck space) and a new design superstructure, located farther aft than in *Nimitz*-class ships. Aircraft operating features would include provision of three or four electro-magnetic catapults, which would replace the steam catapults used in U.S. aircraft carriers since the 1950s.[23] Three (rather than four) elevators would be fitted. The bridge structure will probably incorporate fixed-antenna, phased-array radars as well as phased-array communication antennas.

A new, two-reactor propulsion plant has been designed for the CVN 78. A large electrical generation plant is planned for introduction in the ship and all possible auxiliary steam equipment (e.g., galley and laundry equipment, hot water heaters, air heating systems) will be converted to electric. Of course, electric drive is necessary to permit the use of electro-magnetic catapults.[24]

The Chief of Naval Operations, Admiral Vern Clark, indicated that he hoped for personnel reductions on the order of 50 percent over the *Nimitz*-class manpower requirements. About one-half that number is the set goal for the CVN 78, a reduction of some 800 men and women, although, when this volume went to press, many observers said that half that number, about 400, would be a more realistic estimate.

Significantly, compared to the *Nimitz* class, the CVN 78 would (1) carry no more aircraft, (2) probably carry no more munitions, and (3) not have a greater speed. Number of aircraft and munitions and speed are the warfighting characteristics of an aircraft carrier.

Still, the CVN 78, named the *Gerald R. Ford* shortly before the death of the former president in 2007, would be costly. The previous nuclear carrier, the *George H. W. Bush*, cost an estimated $7 *billion*; the *Ford's* cost is estimated at between $8 and $12 *billion*, in addition to some several billion dollars for research and development efforts related to the design. (By comparison, the LHA/LHD carriers cost less than $2.5 *billion* per ship.) The *Ford* is expected to be completed in about 2015 with additional ships of the design to be constructed at four- or five-year intervals.[25]

In the first decade of the 21st Century other questions, beyond construction cost issues, were being raised about the viability of large, nuclear-propelled carriers:

Design: The CVX/CVN 78 continues the basic design concepts—with significant improvements—of the late 1940s. A large number of more innovative designs have been developed to varying degrees by Navy agencies but have invariably received quick dismissal.

Reconnaissance: Historically carriers have been effective platforms for high-performance reconnaissance aircraft. Long gone, however, are the specialized RA-3B Skywarriors, RA-5C Vigilantes, RF-4B Phantoms, and RF-8 Crusaders.[26] Today tactical reconnaissance from carriers is undertaken in their place by F/A-18 Hornets with the SHARP system. But SHARP is limited in capabilities and the F/A-18 pilots do not have the specialized training of "recce" pilots. Rather, unmanned aerial vehicles, satellites, and long-range, land-based aircraft—including the venerable U-2 spyplane—provide effective tactical, theater, and strategic reconnaissance.

Anti-submarine warfare: Aircraft carriers had long provided ASW aircraft for fleet defense, both in the context of specialized carriers and multi-mission carriers (CV/CVN). In the late 1990s the fixed-wing

Eight Marine MV-22 Osprey tiltrotor aircraft were aboard the LHD *Bataan* for carrier trials in June 2005. These troop/cargo aircraft were assigned to Marine test and evaluation squadron VMX-22. There have long been proposals to configure the V-22 for AEW and ASW roles. Ospreys in those roles—coupled with the F-35B Lightning II—could provide LHA/LHD-ships with significant capabilities for certain operations that now require CV/CVN-type ships. (Jeremy Grisham, U.S. Navy)

carrier ASW aircraft—the S-3B Viking—lost its anti-submarine role.

Subsequently, the MH-60R Seahawk multipurpose helicopter replaced the specialized SH-3 Sea King and SH-60F Seahawk ASW helicopters. The MH-60R has an ASW role but is also employed in surveillance, anti-ship, special operations, and other roles. Thus, the carrier-based ASW capabilities have been severely reduced.

Strike warfare: With the demise of the carrier-based A-6 Intruder the strike capability of U.S. carriers is limited to a couple of hundred miles with the F/A-18 Hornet. Today all Navy cruisers, destroyers, and attack submarines can launch Tomahawk land-attack missiles. These weapons can strike farther than carrier planes, are more accurate, and are less vulnerable to enemy defenses. The new TACTOM (Tactical Tomahawk) missile can be re-targeted while in flight.

Perhaps most significant, cruise missiles can be launched from about 135 surface ships and submarines, not just 11 aircraft carriers.

Fleet air defense: In the past carrier-based fighters have been the stalwarts of fleet air defense. The F-14 Tomcat was the "ultimate" fleet air defense fighter, a long-range aircraft fitted with the multi-target AN/AWG-9 radar and the Phoenix missile. The relatively short range of the F/A-18 Hornet precludes its use as an effective combat air patrol/air defense fighter. At the same time, all U.S. cruisers and destroyers have the Aegis air/missile defense system, with several ships being fitted with a ballistic missile defense system.

While the two defensive concepts—aircraft and ship-based—are not interchangeable, in the post–Cold War environment a major reevaluation of the carrier's role in the air/missile defense environment is warranted.

Future aircraft: The F-35B configuration of the Joint Strike Fighter will be a STOVL aircraft. Like its predecessor, the highly successful Harrier, the F-35B will be capable of operating from smaller ships, especially the U.S. LHA/LHD helicopter carriers. The F-35B will be a high-performance aircraft, comparable with advanced land-based fighter/attack aircraft.

Similarly, the V-22 Osprey VSTOL aircraft, which is now being employed by the U.S. Marine Corps for assault lift, has been proposed for the AEW and ASW roles from carriers. Studies conducted since the 1970s indicate the feasibility of these roles, again enabling LHA/LHD-type ships to operate relatively high-performance aircraft in those roles.

Nuclear propulsion: A final issue related to the U.S. large-deck carriers is nuclear propulsion. Two major studies, one by the Government Accounting Office (GAO) and one by a non-government organization, Greenpeace, objectively identify most of the issues related to nuclear propulsion.[27]

The GAO report (1998) noted that (1) analysis shows that conventional and nuclear carriers both have been effective in fulfilling U.S. forward presence, crisis response, and war-fighting requirements and share many characteristics and capabilities; (2) conventional and nuclear carriers both have the same standard air wing and train to the same mission requirements; (3) each type of carrier offers certain advantages; (4) for example, conventional carriers spend less time in extended maintenance and as a result they can provide more forward presence coverage; (5) nuclear carriers can store larger quantities of aviation fuel and munitions and are thus less dependent upon at-sea replenishment; (6) there was little difference in the operational effectiveness of nuclear and conventional carriers in the Gulf War (1991); (7) investment, operating and support, and inactivation and disposal costs are greater for nuclear carriers; and (8) life-cycle costs for conventional and nuclear carriers—for a national 50-year service life—are estimated at $14.1 *billion* and $22.2 *billion*, respectively (in fiscal year 1997 dollars).

The Greenpeace report (1994) concluded, in part,

> The cost of nuclear power is not justified in peacetime or in wartime, in terms of useful military capability. Nuclear ships are more expensive, less available, and only comparable in generating and sustaining air operations. They operate as part of integrated and increasingly joint military missions close to land, and nuclear-powered carriers are not used any differently than their conventional counterparts.[28]

Based on carrier operations of the Vietnam War and the 1991 conflict in the Persian Gulf, the period between the two conflicts, and the operation of carriers in crisis response as well as deployments in general, the Greenpeace report observes,

> Nuclear-powered carriers do not transit faster to a region, remain longer on-station, or drop significantly more ordnance or launch more aircraft sorties than do conventionally powered carriers. In fact the Navy itself does not appear to distinguish between nuclear and conventional carriers in its operational planning or crisis preparation.[29]

Three additional factors should be noted with respect to nuclear carriers: First is the greater cost of recruiting, training, and retaining nuclear-trained engineering personnel for nuclear carriers compared to oil-burning ships. Second, nuclear-propelled carriers were "sold" on the basis of their ability to rapidly deploy to trouble areas, accompanied by nuclear-propelled escorts. However, insufficient nuclear escorts were built, and the last of those nine ships was stricken in 1999. Third, oil costs had long been touted as justifying the need for nuclear surface ships. In 2005 U.S. national oil consumption was 16 million barrels per day, of which 330,000 barrels—less than 2 percent—was used by the Department of Defense. Within DOD the oil usage was:

Air	73%
Ground	15%
Sea[29]	8%
Installations	4%

Efforts to "save oil" would be expended better in reducing aircraft and ground vehicle use than in reducing naval usage.

The issue of large-deck nuclear carriers will be re-examined in the coming years, especially in view of the costs of the next-generation CVN 78 class.

Summing Up

The aircraft carrier can be addressed in the context of five historic roles:

First, from the Japanese intervention in China in the 1930s through the Anglo-American operations in Afghanistan and Iraq in the first decade of the 21st Century, carriers have been used to strike land targets and to support land operations. On several occasions during this period of more than 70 years, the carrier has provided the only effective means to project air strikes and air support to ground troops—by the Japanese in China (1930s), in the first major Allied landings of World War II at Guadalcanal (1942) and North Africa (1942), to counter the North Korean invasion of South Korea (1950), to support French forces in Indochina (early 1950s), in the Anglo-French invasion of Egypt (1956), in the U.S. assaults into Afghanistan (2002) and Iraq (2003), and in numerous other combat operations.

Second, and to some extent overlapping the support of land operations, the advent of ship-based helicopters in the 1940s led to the subsequent development of specialized carriers to operate helicopters and, later, VSTOL aircraft by the Royal Navy and the U.S. Marine Corps. Although such helicopter carriers have launched troop-laden helicopters into combat on only one occasion, HMS *Ocean* and *Theseus* at Suez in 1956, they have been extremely useful in a score of crises. These ships—intended primarily for the amphibious assault role—have grown in size until today the U.S. Navy's LHA/LHD-type ships are larger than many previous (and contemporary) ships that could be categorized as fleet carriers.

Third, as an extension of air strikes, from the early 1950s until 1976, U.S. aircraft carriers additionally

The Soviet Union had developed an ocean-going fleet based in part on carrier aviation when the regime fell in December 2001. The VSTOL carrier *Kiev*, shown here in August 1993, abandoned at Murmansk, symbolized the demise of the Red Navy and the end of its challenge to the U.S. Navy on the high seas. Some observers believe that the Chinese Navy will challenge U.S. naval interests in the near future.

provided a flexible contribution to the nation's nuclear attack plan, the Single Integrated Operational Plan (SIOP). Although no longer a part of the SIOP, nuclear weapons were kept aboard U.S. carriers until 1992 for tactical strike and ASW roles. British and French carriers also had nuclear strike capabilities during much of this period.

Fourth, from 1941 through 1945 the aircraft carrier was the capital ship for fleet-versus-fleet and lesser naval operations. Beginning with the Pearl Harbor attack in December 1941—in which Japanese carrier planes destroyed a fleet at anchor as well as the adjacent air bases—to the sinking of the massive battleship *Yamato* in April 1945, the carrier was the decisive warship of the Pacific theater.

Significantly, British carriers in the Mediterranean and the Atlantic in 1940–1943 had an important if not decisive role in stopping and then defeating the Axis naval forces, including the German battleship *Bismarck* and the Italian battle fleet. And, British and U.S. escort carriers were a key factor in defeating the U-boats.

Related to these operations, British carriers and the USS *Wasp* (CV 7), also influenced the Allied vic-tory in the Mediterranean in the war by providing hundreds of fighter aircraft to the island fortress of Malta. The survival of Malta as a British base for strike aircraft, surface ships, and submarines contributed to the Axis defeat in North Africa and Allied control of the Suez Canal.

Fifth, in the Cold War era—from 1946 to 1991—the aircraft carrier was relied upon for fleet air defense with missile-armed fighters as well as for anti-submarine operations. The latter role employed both fixed-wing aircraft and helicopters, which were armed with conventional and, in the U.S., British, and Dutch carriers, with nuclear ASW depth bombs. While available Soviet data is sparse, Soviet aircraft carriers were armed with various combinations of nuclear surface-to-air, anti-ship, and ASW weapons, and Soviet ship-based helicopters could deliver nuclear depth bombs.

Although fleets no longer fight against fleets in major surface actions, navies still play a vital role in the political-military policies of many nations. For those nations that can afford the ships and their embarked aircraft, aircraft carriers are important naval components and will continue to be for the foreseeable future.

APPENDIX A
WAR WITHOUT CARRIERS

The "neversail": The Italian carrier *Aquila* at Genoa in 1943, swathed in camouflage netting during a boiler test. Both the German and Italian Navies realized the value of aircraft carriers but the dogmatic attitudes of their air force commanders prevented their carriers from being sent to sea. The *Aquila* (Eagle) was converted from a passenger liner. (Collection of Aldo Fraccaroli)

In marked contrast to Japan's highly successful development and employment of aircraft carriers during World War II, neither European Axis power produced an operational carrier. The primary reason for this failure was the control of all military aviation by a single service in both Germany and Italy.

The commanders of the German and Italian air forces were adamant in their demand for total control of all military aviation, whether land or sea based. Both Hitler and Mussolini gave full support to their respective air forces because of the extravagant claims, made in the period between the wars, that aircraft could win battles and even wars quickly and cheaply. Also, the newborn air services had unquestioned loyalty to their creators, whereas the long-established armies and, especially, navies were centered on heritage and esprit de corps.

In Germany the first "naval aviator" was naval engineer Karl Loew, who earned his flying certificate in March 1911. Official interest in aviation by the German Admiralty led to the establishment of a naval air arm in May 1913. During World War I the German Navy stressed the development of airships, which not only supported fleet operations but, beginning on May 31, 1915, carried out the bombing attacks on London.

The German Navy also created a small seaplane force, and several so-called *Flugzeugmutterschiffe* (aircraft mother ships) were converted from merchantmen to provide afloat support for seaplanes. These ships were the *Answald* (of 5,401 gross tons), *Glyndwr* (2,425 gross tons), *Oswald* (5,401 gross tons), *Santa Elena* (7,415 gross tons), and *Adeline Hugo Stinnes III*. Each ship could accommodate three or four seaplanes in a hangar; the planes were hoisted out for water takeoffs. In addition, the light cruiser *Stuttgart* (3,470 tons, completed in 1908) was fitted to support seaplanes in 1918 and could carry three aircraft. There were also plans for converting a liner to an aircraft carrier, but no work was undertaken on that project.

After the war the Allied-imposed Versailles Treaty of 1919 denied Germany all military aviation. However, Germany kept several seaplanes in service until 1920 to spot mines in the North and Baltic Seas. Later, because the Versailles Treaty contained a clause that allowed the Navy the right to possess anti-aircraft guns, the Navy interpreted the clause as also giving it the right to conduct practice firing at targets towed by aircraft. Accordingly, an undercover air organization was begun under the name "Air Service, Incorporated." A nucleus of naval aviators who had served in World War I was assembled and potential naval cadets were given a year's training in aviation before they were sworn into the Navy. In addition, there was a great effort in Germany to develop commercial aviation, sport flying, and gliding. Germany's central location, technical skill, and enterprise soon excelled, and by 1926, the year that Germany joined the League of Nations, the country's airlines carried more passengers, mail, and cargo than all other European airlines combined. This effort, coupled with some clandestine military air activity, provided the basis for development of an air force—the Luftwaffe.

Although many contend that German actions in this period violated the "spirit" if not the letter of the Versailles Treaty, many Germans at the time believed that the treaty, having been imposed and not accepted, laid the vanquished under no moral obligation to observe its stipulations. Still, not until 1933, with the appointment of Adolf Hitler as chancellor and the open rebuilding of the German armed forces, did the German Navy consider the question of aircraft carriers. Such ships were viewed as a part of the balanced fleet that the Navy hoped to construct. There was practically no knowledge or detailed technical literature concerning aircraft carriers available in Germany. The best information available to the German Admiralty at the time were the specifications in the annuals *Jane's Fighting Ships* and Weyer's *Taschenbuch der Kriegsflotten*. From these publications the German Admiralty drew up the following specifications:

> For study purposes an aircraft carrier is to be designed to displace 25–30,000 tons; to carry 50 to 60 planes; to have a speed of 33 knots and an armament of eight 20.3 cm [8-inch] guns in four twin mounts. Strong anti-aircraft armament is to be provided.
>
> Armor protection is to be on the same scale as that on German cruisers.

These specifications were for preliminary planning. No Admiralty officials were certain if they were valid specifications. There was even some question as to whether the guns or aircraft were to be considered the ship's "main battery." The 15-year void in major naval and air operations had left the German Navy at a considerable disadvantage in comparison with the other maritime nations. With this limitation, planning was begun for a specific ship, Aircraft Carrier "A." The ship's name, in accord with German custom, would not be revealed until launching.[1]

Design of Aircraft Carrier "A" commenced under the supervision of Wilhelm Hadeler, a 1925 graduate of the Technical University in Berlin who had remained at the university for nine years as assistant to the chair for Warship Construction. Hadeler was appointed in April 1934 and immediately supervised the collection and organization of all data relating to aircraft carriers that could be found in books, magazines, newspapers, and even motion pictures. Of particular interest was a lecture titled "Some Experiences in Connection with the Design of Aircraft Carriers and Remarks on the *Lexington* and *Saratoga*," given by the then-chief of the U.S. Navy's Bureau of Construction and Repair, Rear Admiral George H. Rock, before the Society of Naval Architects and Marine Engineers in 1928. According to Hadeler, "I collected everything relating to aircraft carriers and at last the situation was that I had the most complete information on the British carriers *Courageous* and *Glorious*,"[2] a factor that greatly influenced the German design for an aircraft carrier. A fundamental influence on the carrier at this stage was the absence of any cooperation from aviation specialists. The Luftwaffe's small staff was unable to provide attention to carrier issues, and the small naval air arm that had been started was abolished as Hermann Göring, the Minister for Aviation, argued for an independent Luftwaffe uniting all aspects of military and naval aviation.

Some guidelines on aviation matters were required while the carrier was being designed. The Admiralty collected all available data on British, French, and U.S. carrier—based aircraft. When this material was assembled the highest possible numerical values were determined, 15 to 20 percent was added as a safety factor, and the "typical" carrier planes were derived for use in determining the characteristics of the ship's hangar, flight deck, and elevators. These figures were found to be reliable throughout the period in which the carrier was being considered in the German Navy.

It also became obvious that the armament originally planned—eight 8-inch guns in twin turrets—could not be mounted in a satisfactory manner. The big-gun advocates' objections were squelched by pointing out—incorrectly—that the U.S. and Japanese carriers armed with large-caliber guns were so armed for political rather than military reasons. At first there was agreement on installation of eight 5.9-inch guns, mounted in such a way to enable four to fire in any direction to provide protection against enemy destroyers. This arrangement was made possible by recessing the guns in the ship's sides. The design was soon modified to provide 16 of these guns in double casements, although in view of subsequent hangar space requirements it was impossible to provide sufficient ammunition or a complete crew for each gun in the hull casements.

The carrier's intended anti-aircraft armament would be 10 (and later 12) 4.1-inch guns, 22 37-mm guns, and several 20-mm guns. The heavy anti-aircraft guns were all arranged to starboard, forward and aft of the island structure, restricting their field of fire, especially against aircraft attacking from the port side if planes were on the deck.

The ship's speed requirement was increased to 35 knots soon after design work started. A steam turbine plant was decided upon as being the most feasible with the power output increased to the maximum possible (eventually 196,000 horsepower) in the event the ship's displacement increased in later stages because of the still-unknown requirements of aviation equipment such as elevators, arresting gear, and catapults.

In appearance the ship would have a conventional configuration with an island structure on the starboard side of the flight deck that incorporated control stations and funnel. "About" 40 aircraft were to be carried. The design was completed in the late summer of 1935, and the construction of Aircraft Carrier "A" was ordered at the Deutsche Werke shipyard in Kiel.

Also in 1935, formal cooperation with the Luftwaffe on the carrier program was established, and beginning in 1936 a Luftwaffe liaison officer who was an experienced shipbuilding engineer was appointed to work with the German Admiralty. This officer, Hauptmann der Luftwaffe [Captain] Friedrich Popp, had distinguished himself as a naval aviator in the Dardanelles campaign of World War I.

In the fall of 1935 a German naval engineer, a naval officer, and a Luftwaffe officer visited Japan and

The carrier *Graf Zeppelin* immediately after being launched on December 28, 1938. Adolf Hitler attended the christening, but the Führer never understood the use of navies in war. Similarly, his naval commander, Admiral Erich Raeder, sought to build a balanced fleet to challenge the Royal Navy. The island structure has not yet been installed; note the casement openings for two guns on each quarter. (Collection of Erich Gröner)

returned to Germany with a voluminous report and detailed blueprints of the carrier *Akagi*. However, the German carrier design was so far along that the influence of the "Japan Commission" was almost negligible. The most significant change made as a result of the information from Japan was the provision for a third, centerline elevator in the German carrier. The real significance of the report on Japanese carriers was its confirmation that German carrier design was correct. Significantly, although Japanese carriers did not have catapults, the decision was made to provide two in Aircraft Carrier "A," as in British and U.S. carriers.

The keel for Aircraft Carrier "A" was laid down at Kiel on December 28, 1936. Work progressed at a good pace, and the ship was launched on December 8, 1938, with Hitler, Marshal Göring, and numerous high-ranking Navy and Luftwaffe officers in attendance. On Hitler's orders Countess Hella von Brandenstein-Zeppelin, daughter of the famed airship builder, christened the carrier the *Graf Zeppelin*.

Shortly after launching, the *Graf Zeppelin*'s straight stem was replaced by a clipper-type bow, viewed as more suitable for operation in the Atlantic. (Superstitious yard workmen considered the change an omen of bad luck for the ship.) Thus modified, the *Graf Zeppelin* had an overall length of 862¾ feet and when completed would have a standard displacement of 23,200 tons.

Meanwhile, the Germana Werft, also at Kiel, was ordered to build a sister ship to the *Graf Zeppelin*. Progress on Aircraft Carrier "B" was slow, and only a few hundred tons of material had been assembled by the time the *Graf Zeppelin* was launched.[3] Because of the limited water outside of the shipyard where Aircraft Carrier "B" was under construction she was to be launched with her bow lacking a 98½-foot section that would be added later. In almost all respects this ship was to be identical to the *Graf Zeppelin*.

Within the German Admiralty plans were being prepared for a shipbuilding program that could provide a fleet capable of challenging the Royal Navy. On January 27, 1938, Hitler directed that this naval program—the "Z" Plan—was to take precedence over all other military projects, including army and air force expansion. While the German Navy had envisioned the building program being completed by 1948, Hitler gave a six-year deadline. As originally approved, the "Z" Plan called for a battle fleet consisting of

- 4 aircraft carriers (about 20,000 tons standard displacement)
- 10 large battleships (including the *Gneisenau* and *Scharnhorst* of 31,830 tons)
- 12 battleships (20,000 tons)
- 3 armored ships (so-called "pocket battleships" of 10,000 tons)
- 5 heavy cruisers (10,000 tons)
- 16 light cruisers (8,000 tons)
- 6 light cruisers (6,000 tons)
- 22 scout cruisers (5,000 tons)
- 68 destroyers
- 90 torpedo boats
- 27 long-range submarines
- 62 short-range submarines

This program included warships already in service and under construction, hence two more aircraft carriers were being proposed. However, within the program aircraft carriers were relegated a low priority, and when war came in September 1939, only the *Graf Zeppelin* had been launched. The ship was about 85 percent complete when the war began.

Commenting on the "Z" Plan, Vice Admiral Friedrich Ruge, a post–World War II head of the German Navy, wrote,

> From an operational standpoint the weakest feature of the Z-plan was the small number of aircraft carriers. It is perhaps understandable that the German Navy should have shown a predilection for battleships—of which it had previous experience—though the Treaty of Versailles did not allow it any such vessels. It is also possible that indifference to aircraft carriers was due to the lack of experience in this type. Had Germany possessed even one aircraft carrier in peacetime, exercises with the fleet would soon have shown the great value of such a ship.[4]

Also, in 1939 the Luftwaffe began preparations for training the first carrier squadrons. Earlier the Arado Flugzeugwerke had initiated design of a combination torpedo-bomber/reconnaissance airplane for shipboard use. Designated Ar 95, the aircraft was a trim-looking single-engine, two-place biplane that could be fitted with wheels or twin floats. The first prototype Ar 95V1, equipped with floats, flew in the fall of 1936. Trials

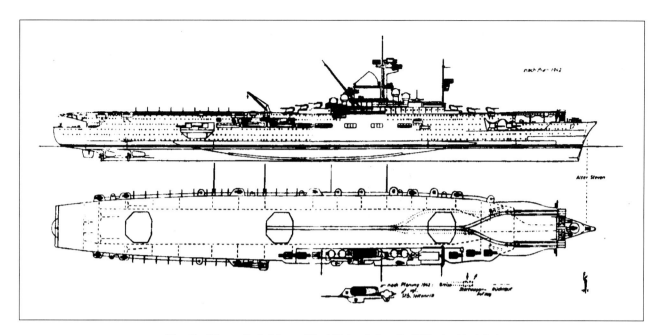

The *Graf Zeppelin* (with modified "Atlantic bow"). (Wilhelm Hadeler)

with several prototypes revealed that the aircraft fell short of the required performance.

Although other aircraft designs were proposed for development for shipboard use, notably the Arado Ar 195 and the Fieseler Fi 167, the Luftwaffe decided to instead modify aircraft already in production because of the short time available. The aircraft to be adopted for carrier operation were the Messerschmitt Bf 109E-3 fighter and the Junkers Ju 87B-1 (Stuka) dive bomber. The shipboard versions of these aircraft would be designated Bf 109T-0 and Ju 87T, respectively, the suffix "T" denoting their carrier role, *Träger* in German.

At the time the Bf 109E was the only operational fighter in the German arsenal, and it was superior in many ways to contemporary marks of the Spitfire and Hurricane. The Träger conversions had slightly longer wings than the land-based 109s, spoilers on their upper wing surfaces to obtain a steeper glide angle, manually folding wings, catapult attachment points, and an arresting hook.[5]

The gull-winged Ju 87 was ugly and awkward, slow and cumbersome, but proved remarkably successful during the German assaults on Poland, France, and the Low Countries, where air opposition was light. And, of course, Stukas had smashed British carriers in the Mediterranean battles. The Ju 87B-1 could reach 210 m.p.h. at 16,000 feet, had a ceiling of 24,500 feet, and could normally carry up to 2,200 pounds of bombs with a capacity of almost 4,000 pounds for short-range mis-sions. The 87B model had two wing-mounted 7.9-mm machine guns and one flexible 7.9-mm gun aft.

As part of the pilot-training program for the carrier squadrons, the Luftwaffe operated a small airfield on the Norwegian island of Drontheim, which resembled a carrier in size and shape. However, the short runway caused so many accidents that these operations were abandoned before arresting gear was installed. An arresting wire system was installed at Travemünde in northern Germany, and the first arrested landings were made by Bf 109s in February 1939. Subsequently, catapult tests were also conducted at Travemünde.

For service on the carrier *Graf Zeppelin* the Luftwaffe established Trägergeschwader (Carrier Air Group) 186 composed of I Gruppe with Ju 87s and II Gruppe with the Bf 109s. However, when the war began it was evident that the *Graf Zeppelin* would not be ready for sea in the immediate future, and the planes of T.G. 186 were allocated to air force assignments. Interestingly, the Bf 109s of II/T.G.186 were assigned to Jagdgeschwader 77, one of the fighter components of General Hans Geisler's Fliegerkorps X, which played a vital role in the attacks on British carriers in the Mediterranean.

Germany at War

The outbreak of war in September 1939 found the German Navy far short of the "Z" Plan goals, as it lacked even the fleet's first full-fledged battleships *Bismarck* and *Tirpitz*. The *Graf Zeppelin* had progressed only to the point where it was anticipated, with normal construction schedules, she could be commissioned by the end of 1940 and ready for service before the end of 1941. After discussions at the highest levels in the German Navy and in the government, construction was halted on all unfinished large warships except for the battleships *Bismarck* and *Tirpitz*, the heavy cruisers *Prinz Eugen* and *Seydlitz*, and the *Graf Zeppelin*. Work on Aircraft Carrier "B" was stopped on September 19, 1939, and the accumulated steel plates were scrapped.

The rapid German successes in the West and the emphasis on submarine warfare in the Atlantic further reduced the incentive to complete the *Graf Zeppelin*. And, on April 29, 1940, the Commander-in-Chief of the German Navy recorded, "The Führer is of the opinion that, considering the probable developments in aircraft, carriers with *planes with internal combustion engines* will not be usable anymore in this war" (emphasis added).[6] All work on the carrier had stopped. By the beginning of June 1940, to provide berthing space for other ships at Kiel and to remove her from the danger of British air attacks, the *Graf Zeppelin* was moved eastward to the Polish port of Gdynia. The ship's 5.9-inch guns were removed for use as shore batteries in Norway, and her cooking and sanitation equipment was taken out for use at the submarine school at Pilau. The anti-aircraft guns already installed in the carrier were retained. Some had already been fired in anger against British aircraft, and on one such occasion a 37-mm shell hit a radio mast attached to the ship's funnel, inflicting the first damage suffered by the carrier.

German interest in aircraft carriers oscillated. In July 1940, with France defeated and the capitulation of Britain seemingly imminent, the decision was made to complete the *Graf Zeppelin* and send her on sea trials. But increasing British bomber attacks on Germany led to the carrier being towed to Gotenhafen that month. There she served as a warehouse for lumber.

At about this time the German Admiralty drew up its "Views of the Naval Staff on Expansion of the Navy After the War," which noted,

> It appears necessary to develop a cruiser able to carry a sufficient number of planes for reconnaissance and escort duties essential to an independently operating group—possibly in place of the aircraft carrier. The Naval Staff visualizes a vessel similar to cruiser M [8,500 tons, 600¼ feet], carrying about fourteen planes. To allow for installations necessary for stowing and operating the planes, certain concessions could be made in speed and armament.

However, the Navy was involved with preparations for the planned invasion of England and other operations, and both the *Graf Zeppelin* and the proposals for building carrier-cruisers lay idle. As the war continued the Germans watched with interest the successes of British and Japanese carriers. The role of British carrier aircraft in sinking the *Bismarck*, the British carrier strike on Taranto, and the Japanese success at Pearl Harbor contributed to the March 1942 report of the Commander-in-Chief Navy to Hitler that declared, "The carrier is of decisive importance for the operation of our heavy ships." Hitler agreed that the aircraft carrier was urgently needed. Indeed, the report of Hitler's conference with his senior commanders on March 14, 1942, notes:

A Royal Air Force reconnaissance plane photographed the carrier *Graf Zeppelin* at the Polish port of Gdynia after the ship was moved eastward to escape possible British bombing. A British photo interpreter marked an arrow on the film to indicate the area where catapults were being installed. All large carriers built during the war period had catapults except for those of Japan. (Imperial War Museum)

The Füher believes that the aircraft carrier [*Graf Zeppelin*] is urgently needed and will direct the C.-in-C. accordingly. Everything must be done toward the early formation of a German task force composed of the [battleship] *Tirpitz*, the [battle cruiser] *Scharnhorst*, one aircraft carrier, two heavy cruisers and twelve to fourteen destroyers. It would be a serious threat to the enemy in the northern area and could be used very effectively.[7]

But the CinC Navy's report to the Führer on April 12, 1942, held little hope for having the *Graf Zeppelin* operational in the near future:

Completion of the aircraft carrier *Graf Zeppelin*:

A. It will take at least until the summer of 1943 to complete the hull and install the engines. There are the essential factors:

1. Delivery of auxiliary engines which either are missing entirely or have been removed and installed elsewhere.
2. Installation of a bulge as a counterbalance in case the ship lists after being damaged.
3. Increasing the fuel capacity, thus improving the cruising range by 25 percent at a speed of 19 knots.

B. The total time necessary to complete the carrier does not depend on completing the hull and engines but on changing the flight installations for use of planes adapted from the Ju 87D and Bf 109F.

About two years are required to develop, construct and test the catapults necessary for these planes. If it is possible to convert the existing catapults the time limit will be reduced by six months. New winches for the arresting Year are needed. The company producing these winches has not yet announced when they can be delivered.

The carrier cannot therefore be completed before the winter of 1943. . . .

E. Planes for the carrier.

1. Only a small number of the planes designed originally for this carrier is still available. They are sufficient only for test runs of the carrier, not for combat. The Air Force claims more of this type cannot be constructed.
2. If a new, special carrier plane is developed, mass production cannot start until 1946.
3. Thus the only types of carrier planes which the Air Force can deliver at present are converted combat models. The following two types are proposed for conversions:

    Bf 109F, a pursuit plane

    Ju 87D, a dive bomber and reconnaissance plane

The use of the above mentioned adaptations has serious disadvantages:

a. In addition to a maximum of ten pursuit planes there are only 21 to 23 Ju 87D; six of these are not ready for immediate use. (Original plans call for thirty-three bombers.) There are no torpedo planes.

Thus, the Navy estimated that the *Graf Zeppelin* could not be ready for combat operations until the winter of 1943–1944, and then with only 10 fighters and about 22 dive bomber/reconnaissance aircraft—32 planes if there were no operational losses and air attacks did not interrupt the carrier work.

At this time a plan was also proposed to convert the unfinished heavy cruiser *Seydlitz*, about 90 percent complete, and the passenger liners *Europa*, *Gneisenau*, and *Potsdam* to aircraft carriers. The *Seydlitz*, a sister ship to the highly successful *Prinz Eugen*, was to have mounted eight 8-inch guns on a hull 681¼ feet long and displacing 15,660 tons standard.

Of the liners, the *Europa* (completed 1930) was the largest at 49,746 tons, 936 feet overall, and capable of 28 knots. At one time she had been equipped with a catapult and carried a seaplane for providing her passengers with airmail service. The *Gneisenau* and *Potsdam* were smaller ships, the first being 18,160 tons and 652 feet overall, and the second 17,5l8 tons and 631 feet overall. Both ships were capable of 21 knots. (The Japanese acquired a third liner of this general design, the *Scharnhorst*, in 1942 and converted her to the carrier *Shinyo*.) As carriers the *Europa* would operate some 42 aircraft and the other ships about 24 each.

Further studies soon revealed that the passenger liners would not prove satisfactory as carriers because they lacked stability; their conversions never progressed beyond the proposal stage. The *Seydlitz* conversion was begun and workers started removing her superstructure, but this project also was abandoned. Even had the carrier conversions been completed there would not have been suitable aircraft available for them until at least 1946.

German interest in carrier aviation was sufficiently aroused that the *Graf Zeppelin*, since moved to Stettin on the Oder River in the summer of 1941, was towed back to Kiel, arriving there on December 3, 1942, for further work. The ship was immediately placed in a floating dry dock. During this period the ship was temporarily armed with three 37-mm twin mounts and six 20-mm quad mounts plus four searchlights to provide a minimal air-defense capability.

Hadeler, at the time a Fregattenkapitän (commander) in the Construction Corps, was ordered to Kiel to take charge of completing the *Graf Zeppelin*. Several changes were to be made in her design. Developments in radar, communications, and fire control equipment and the requirement for an armored conning station within the ship's island structure led to significant increases in the superstructure's size and weight. Simultaneously, the decision was made to install bulges on each side of the hull to carry additional fuel oil and enhance protection against torpedo attack (the bulges were weighted differently to compensate for the starboard island structure). Additional minor changes were made to the ship, and the planned number of 20-mm guns was increased from seven to 28. The *Graf Zeppelin* was scheduled for completion in the fall of 1943.

This period of intense activity on the *Graf Zeppelin* was brief. A month after British warships sank the battle cruiser *Scharnhorst* in Arctic waters in late December 1942, the Commander-in-Chief of the German Navy was dismissed, and on February 2, 1943, Hitler halted all big-ship construction. The surviving major warships were withdrawn from active service, and the *Graf Zeppelin* again lay idle. During March 1943 the carrier was once more moved eastward and moored in the Monne Channel at Stettin on the Oder River. There much of her remaining auxiliary machinery was removed for use in other ships and her condition deteriorated for lack of maintenance. Admiral Ruge visited the *Graf Zeppelin* at her mooring and declared her absolutely useless.

Early in 1945, as Soviet armies approached the Oder, orders were given to scuttle the carrier. The local naval commander had depth charges exploded in the ship's engine and boiler rooms, wrecking the power plant and sinking the carrier in shallow water. As Soviet forces neared the *Graf Zeppelin* in late April 1945 she was hit several times by artillery fire and sustained minor additional damage.

After the German surrender the Soviets stopped up the leaks, pumped out the carrier, and moved her to Swinemünde (now Swinoujœcie) at the mouth of the Oder. Soviet engineers and naval officers carefully examined the carrier—among other German naval projects. In this period the ship was designated as a "floating base"—PO-101—by the Soviets.

The Tripartite Commission, which allocated former Axis warships to the Allies, would not allow the Soviets to complete the *Graf Zeppelin*. Western officials believed that when the Soviet examination was completed the *Graf Zeppelin* was loaded with war booty, including heavy machinery and, reportedly, sections of unfinished U-boats. The heavily laden carrier departed under tow for Leningrad (now St. Petersburg). Most Western sources at the time believed that she sank in the Baltic from previous damage, coupled with a rough crossing, or that she had struck a mine.[8]

Rather, the ship was towed to the naval operating area off Swinemünde and anchored for use as a test ship for explosive damage and as a training target for

The *Graf Zeppelin*—redesignated as a floating base—after the war. Soviet engineers and naval officers minutely examined the carrier, after which she was expended in weapons tests. Most Western officials believed that, heavily laden with booty, the carrier had sunk in the Baltic, either in a storm or after striking a mine. (Soviet Navy)

The *Graf Zeppelin*, abandoned. Beyond constructing the *Graf Zeppelin* and laying the keel for a second carrier, the German Navy began the conversion of several other ships to carriers. However, as in Italy, these efforts were delayed too long by their respective air forces. And, even if completed, those ships would have been provided—after delays—with second-rate carrier aircraft.

dive bombers and torpedo craft. The tests began on August 16, 1947. First aerial bombs were placed on the flight and hangar decks and in the superstructure and detonated to determine the explosive effects on the ship. Subsequently the dive bombers used the ship as a target, and torpedo boats attacked her. Six bombs and two 21-inch torpedoes struck her before she sank.[9]

Thus, the *Graf Zeppelin* survived the Third Reich only briefly and had an equally inglorious ending. The German Navy had been unable to produce an adequate surface fleet before Hitler plunged the nation into war. Had the two carriers that were started or even the four planned ships been completed before Germany's surface warships had been driven from the sea, it is questionable if even the *Graf Zeppelin* could have become operational in view of the Navy's lack of experience with such ships and the Luftwaffe's tight control of the German "naval air arm"—Luftwaffe personnel and aircraft under *limited* naval operational control.

The Luftwaffe attitude toward the German Navy is perhaps best embodied in Grossadmiral Erich Raeder's plea to Hitler when he was relinquishing his position of Commander-in-Chief Navy in January 1943: "Please protect the Navy and my successor against Göring."[10]

The Italian Failure

The Italian Navy also made an effort to develop carrier aviation during World War II. The Italian Navy had taken an early interest in aviation. The nation's second military pilot was Lieutenant Mario Calderara of the Navy, who earned his license in 1909. Calderara had long been interested in aviation, and in 1907 he had flown a seaplane glider on a number of successful flights. The aircraft had been pulled into the air by the destroyer *Lanciere* during those flights.

The Italians looked to Britain, France, and the United States for their early seaplanes. Some naval aviators were trained in France before the Italian Navy established a flying school at Venice in 1912. When World War I began the Italian Navy had about 30 seaplanes; at the end of the war the Navy had approximately 500 aircraft, including numerous land planes.

The merchant ship *Quarto*, 8,800 tons and built in Scotland in 1895, was acquired in 1915 to serve as a seaplane tender. Renamed *Europa*, she was fitted with two hangars on her deck, forward and aft, that could accommodate eight seaplanes, which cranes handled over the side for launch and recovery. She was classified as a "hydroplanes and submarines support ship." Also, the protected cruiser *Elba* of 2,732 tons, also completed in 1895, was fitted in 1907 as a balloon ship. From 1914 she carried three seaplanes.

But even as Italian naval aviation was growing, the seeds for its destruction were being sown. In 1916 an ex-cavalry officer, who had embraced military aviation in the early 1900s, was being court-martialed for his extreme views. This officer was Giulio Douhet, who later wrote, "Consequently, I say: No aerial defense, because it is practically useless. No auxiliary [Army and Navy] aviation, because it is practically useless or superfluous. Instead, a single Independent Air Force, to include all the aerial resources available to the nation, none excepted. This is my thesis."[11]

This call for an independent air force became the creed of Britain's Hugh Trenchard, Germany's Hermann Göring, and America's "Billy" Mitchell, as well as others in those countries. But the experiences of aviation in World War I failed to support the thesis. Douhet was tried, found guilty by court-martial, and sentenced to one year's imprisonment. Then, in February 1918, following changes in the Italian government that culminated in Benito Mussolini's march on Rome, Douhet was recalled to military service and made head of the Central Aeronautical Bureau. The Italian Navy's air arm survived the collapse of Italy's war effort—on the Allied side—in late 1917 and the unstable period immediately after the war.

However, in 1923 the Mussolini government decided to unify all air forces into a single organization with the Navy forbidden by legislation from operating aircraft. The Navy strongly opposed this move, and in 1925 the Navy minister resigned his post in protest. Mussolini himself took the post of Navy minister and, concurrently, the Italian Air Force was formally established as an independent service. The Italian Navy's future was decided at a meeting of senior admirals, at which Mussolini acted as chairman, in December 1925. According to Admiral Romeo Bernotti, a senior Italian naval officer and historian,

> No discussion was allowed on the question of a naval air force, and the conference agreed that Italy should not build aircraft carriers—a decision that was peculiarly arrived at. This fundamental question was asked: "If the naval budget were to be increased to a certain extent, and additional millions of lire appropriated for the purpose, how could the funds be best exploited?" In answering, each officer was concerned with his own category, and there was, of course, no representative of naval aviation. The question in these terms was not suitable for an open-minded discussion. The various opinions were limited to practical details, and Mussolini's preconceptions were thus confirmed.[12]

General Italo Balbo—who would gain international fame for his mass trans-Atlantic seaplane flights of the early 1930s—became Secretary of State for Air in 1926 and Minister of the Air Force in 1929. He later told Admiral Bernotti, "You want carriers, but I shall not let you build them." Balbo declared that Italy itself—the peninsula, Sicily, and Sardinia—formed a natural carrier. From Italian bases Aeronautica could strike all vital points in the Mediterranean area.[13]

This reasoning was reasonable *if* the air force had developed effective reconnaissance and anti-ship aircraft and suitable tactics and had properly trained flight crews. But that was not done.

Still, the 1935 shipbuilding program, proposed by Admiral Domenico Cavagnari, the head of the Navy, called for the construction of three 22,000-ton aircraft carriers as components of a "break out fleet."[14] The fleet was intended to break out into the Atlantic through British forces controlling the Strait of Gibraltar. Economic constraints and changing priorities led to a scaling back by the end of 1935 to two 14,000-ton carriers—considered roughly equivalent to the USS *Ranger*, "the ideal platform as far as total dimensions and characteristics."[15] By the summer of 1936 this plan was reduced to a single unit and then to seaplane carriers with two stream catapults for float planes with a triple 6-inch gun turret forward.

The Navy's leadership, still desirous of a full-deck aircraft carrier, in 1935 had proposed an emergency alternative: conversion of the 32,583-ton, 705-foot passenger liner *Roma* (completed 1926) to a carrier. But all of these proposals and plans died because of economic limitations and the strong opposition from the Air Force. Naval officers made numerous other proposals for aviation ships. As early as 1921, Lieutenant G. Fioravanzo had proposed a hybrid "anti-aircraft cruiser," a 10,000-ton, 30-knot ship that would carry 16 fighter aircraft as well as a heavy gun battery. Subsequent cruiser-carrier designs were to carry guns up to 8-inch in caliber.

In 1937 legislation did establish a "naval air arm"—with an Air Force general as its commander. Air Force pilots and Navy navigators flew the planes. By the time of Italy's entry into the war this "naval" air arm had more than 280 flying boats and floatplanes, most of which were outdated and about one-third of which were not fully operational.

Thus, the Italian Navy entered World War II with a limited air arm and without even the remotest possibility of obtaining an aircraft carrier. This situation existed until the Battle of Matapan in March 1941. Off Cape Matapan, in the first major fleet battle since World

War I, the British Mediterranean Fleet sank three Italian heavy cruisers and two destroyers and damaged a battleship. The cost of the battle to the British was one aircraft and its three-man crew from HMS *Formidable*. No British warship was damaged in the operation. The complete failure of Italian and German aircraft support in the battle belatedly convinced Mussolini that the Navy could obtain proper air support only by having aircraft carriers.

The decision was immediately made to convert the passenger liner *Roma* into an aircraft carrier. The ship was already in a Genoa shipyard being converted to a troop transport. As an aircraft carrier she was to be fitted with new geared turbines to increase her speed from 21 knots to about 30 knots.[16] And her armament would consist of eight 5.3-inch dual-purpose guns and a powerful anti-aircraft battery of 12 65-mm and 62 20-mm guns. Two elevators would lift aircraft from her hangar to the flight deck with two aircraft catapults being planned. The ship was renamed *Aquila* or "Eagle" in 1943 following completion of the battleship *Roma* late the previous year.

The carrier planes—to be flown by the Air Force—would be the Reggiane Re.2001 fighter-bomber. The

The conversion of the passenger liner *Roma* to the carrier *Aquila* was almost completed when Italy surrendered to the Allies in September 1943. The rapid progress on the conversion was possible in part because of German assistance. This ship, like the never-finished *Graf Zeppelin*, was to have had two aircraft catapults forward. (U.S. Army)

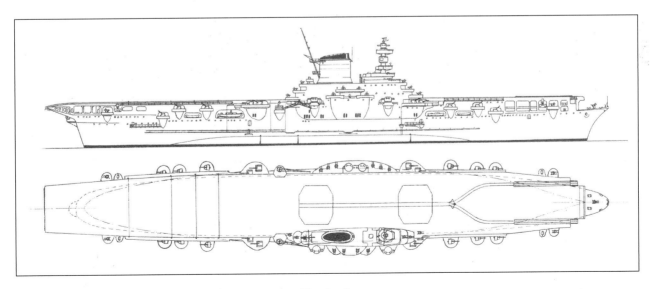

The *Aquila*.

The Reggiane Re.2001 fighter intended to operate from the *Aquila* was the basic Re.2000 fighter (shown here on a battleship catapult) with a different engine. The Re.2001 had a maximum speed of 393 m.p.h., a ceiling of 36,000 feet, and an armament of two 20-mm cannon in streamlined external pods. A 220-pound bomb could be carried under the fuselage and experiments were conducted to enable the plane to lift a 1,430-weapon. (Italian Navy)

Aquila was to operate 50 aircraft with 36 ready for action and another 14 suspended from the overhead of her hangar. (The earlier Re.2000 was modified for catapult launching from cruisers and battleships, trials having been carried out in 1941–1942.)

A short time after the decision was made to convert the *Roma*, her sister ship *Augustus* (completed 1927) was taken in hand for conversion to a carrier. The *Augustus* was rated at 19 knots compared to 21 knots for the *Roma*.[17] The ship was given the naval name *Falco* and then *Sparviero* in 1943.

Work on the liners progressed slowly, and all work on the *Augustus* was halted from December 1942 until March 1943. When Italy surrendered on September 8, 1943, the *Aquila* was about 80 percent complete as a carrier. She was that far along, in part, because of assistance from German engineers and the use of some aviation equipment obtained from the *Graf Zeppelin*.

Meanwhile, German industry provided Italy with carrier arresting gear, which was set up and tested at the Perugia research center. Beginning in March 1943 landing trials were carried out by both German and Italian pilots flying Ar 96B and Ju 87C aircraft as well as an Italian SAIMAN 200 biplane, Fiat G.50, and Reggiane Re.2001 fighters. Of the Italian planes, only the Re.2001 was considered suitable for carrier use.[18]

Both of the Italian carriers fell into German hands at Genoa. The Germans scuttled the *Augustus-Sparviero* on October 5, 1944. The *Roma-Aquila* was damaged in an Allied air attack on June 16, 1944, and was sunk by Italian guided torpedoes at Genoa on April 19, 1945, to prevent the Germans from scuttling her in a position to block the port. The ships were refloated after the war and broken up for scrap.

An operational aircraft carrier in either the German or Italian Navy would have been of some value to the Axis. At the very least, fleet exercises with a carrier

An Ardo 96B-1 training aircraft provided by Germany is "trapped" in the German-developed arresting gear at Perugia, Italy, early in 1943. The arresting gear was originally developed by the Demag firm for the German carrier *Graf Zeppelin*. It was provided to Italy when completion of the German ship was delayed. (*Aerofan*)

The carrier *Aquila* at Genoa, having been severely damaged by Allied air attacks of the Italian port. Neither Germany nor Italy could have changed the course of the war had their limited carrier programs been completed. However, those carriers could have been useful in specific operations.

would have exposed naval commanders to the potentials and threats of a seaborne air striking force.

With proper aircraft and personnel, and some operational experience, an aircraft carrier with an Axis battle fleet or raiding squadron could have provided invaluable reconnaissance, defense, and possibly offensive capabilities. It is unlikely—on the basis of carrier experience during the war—that Germany or Italy could have produced an effective carrier striking force. The requirements in men, ships, aircraft, weapons, and leadership in this field appear to have been beyond their competence. Still, even one carrier, with a few squadrons of good aircraft flown by naval aviators in the German or Italian fleet might have had an effect on a battle or two but certainly not on the outcome of the war.

The carrier *Aquila* is guarded by German soldiers in Genoa after Italy capitulated in September 1943. The *Aquila* survived until early 1945 when the ship was sunk by the Allies to prevent the Germans from using her to block the port. She subsequently was raised and scrapped. (German Army)

APPENDIX B
U.S. AIRCRAFT CARRIER DESIGNATIONS

Two very different kinds of aircraft carriers with two very different designations: the amphibious assault ship *Bonhomme Richard* (LHD 6) is in company with the nuclear-propelled aircraft carrier *John C. Stennis* (CVN 74) as they transit the Gulf of Oman in May 2007. Both ships are among the newest and largest of their categories. The *Stennis* has ancestry dating back to the USS *Langley* (CV 1) of 1922 and the *Bonhomme Richard* back to the USS *Thetis Bay* (LPH 6, ex-CVHA 1, ex-CVE 90) of 1956. (Denny Cantrell, U.S. Navy)

U.S. Navy ships and most small craft are classified by type and by sequence within that type. The list of classifications is issued periodically, updating a system that was established in 1920. In the following list boldfaced type indicates currently used ship designations.

ACV	Auxiliary aircraft carrier
AKV	Aircraft ferry and cargo ship
AVG	Aircraft escort ship (later CVE)
AVT	(1) Aircraft transport
	(2) Training aircraft carrier
	(3) **Auxiliary aircraft landing training ship**
BAVG	British aircraft escort ship
CV	**Aircraft carrier**
CVA	(1) Heavy aircraft carrier
	(2) Attack aircraft carrier
CVAN	Attack aircraft carrier (nuclear propulsion)

CVB	Large aircraft carrier
CVE	Escort aircraft carrier
CVEK	Escort aircraft carrier (hunter-killer)
CVL	Small aircraft carrier
CVLK	Small aircraft carrier (hunter-killer)
CVN	**Aircraft carrier (nuclear propulsion)**
CVS	(1) Anti-submarine support aircraft carrier
	(2) Anti-submarine aircraft carrier
CVT	Training aircraft carrier (later AVT)
CVU	Utility aircraft carrier
LHA	**Amphibious assault ship (general purpose)**
LHD	**Amphibious assault ship (multipurpose)**
LPH	Amphibious assault ship (helicopter)

Three nonofficial ship designations have been used extensively in official documents:

CVV	VSTOL support ship
SCS	Sea control ship
VSS	VSTOL support ship

Some carrier designations and the carriers themselves have disappeared: The USS *Independence* (CVL 22) was the first small or light carrier commissioned by the U.S. Navy. A total of 11 CVLs were placed in commission from 1943 to 1947. None survive. The *Independence* is shown here on January 29, 1951, as her hulk is about to be sunk in weapon tests. The World War II veteran was heavily damaged in the 1946 atomic bomb tests at Bikini, after which she was used as a radiological test bed at San Francisco. None of the other ten CVLs survive. (U.S. Navy/Leo van Ginderen Collection)

APPENDIX C
AIRCRAFT CARRIER CHARACTERISTICS

The USS *Ranger* (CV 4) at anchor astern of the USS *Lexington* (CV 2), *Yorktown* (CV 5), and *Enterprise* (CV 6) during exercises in the Caribbean in early 1939. At the time the U.S. Navy had five aircraft carriers—the USS *Saratoga* (CV 3) was in the Pacific. Seven years later, despite war losses, the U.S. Navy had 98 aircraft carriers in service with additional ships under construction. Other American-built escort carriers served in the British and French Navies. (U.S. Navy)

Dimensions and characteristics are for the lead ship of a class as completed as an aircraft carrier. It should be noted that even official documents do not always agree with respect to dimensions and details of ships.

Naval names are in capital letters; merchant names are in italics. Class numbers in headings are for ships completed.

Commission/completion dates are as aircraft carriers.

Displacements for U.S. ships are given in long tons, i.e., 2,240 pounds; all other navies use metric tons (*tonnes*), i.e., 1,000 kilograms or 2,204 pounds.

Guns less than 20-mm in size are not listed.

Complement numbers include aviation units and staffs embarked.

Abbreviations are listed at the end of this appendix.

ARGENTINA

TYPE	NAME			STATUS
CVL	INDEPENDENCIA	ex-British WARRIOR ex-Canadian WARRIOR	c. Jan 26, 1959	str. 1971 (scrapped)
CVL	25 DE MAYO	ex-Dutch KAREL DOORMAN ex-British VENERABLE	c. Mar 12, 1969	str. 1997 (scrapped)

These were near sister ships belonging to the COLOSSUS class

AUSTRALIA

TYPE	NAME			STATUS
CVL	SYDNEY	ex-British TERRIBLE	c. Feb 5, 1949	str. 1973 (scrapped)
CVL	VENGEANCE	ex-British VENGEANCE	c. Nov 13, 1952	to Brazil 1956
CVL	MELBOURNE	ex-British MAJESTIC	c. Oct 28, 1955	str. 1983 (scrapped)

The TERRIBLE and MAJESTIC belonged to the MAJESTIC class. The VENGEANCE was a unit of the COLOSSUS class.

BRAZIL

TYPE	NAME			STATUS
CVL	MINAS GERAIS	ex-Australian VENGEANCE ex-British VENGEANCE	c. Dec 6, 1960	str. 2001 (scrapped)
CV	SÃO PAULO	ex-French FOCH	c. Nov 15, 2000	**active**

The FOCH is the only French-built carrier to serve in another navy.

CANADA

TYPE	NAME			STATUS
CVL	WARRIOR	ex-British WARRIOR	c. Mar 14, 1946	to Argentina 1958
CVL	MAGNIFICENT	ex-British MAGNIFICENT	c. Apr 17, 1948	str. 1957 (scrapped)
CVL	BONAVENTURE	ex-British POWERFUL	c. Jan 17, 1957	str. 1970 (scrapped)

The BONAVENTURE was commissioned in the Canadian Navy upon completion. The WARRIOR was a COLOSSUS-class ship; the MAGNIFICENT and BONAVENTURE belonged to the MAJESTIC class.

CHINA

TYPE	NAME		STATUS
CV	VARYAG	ex-Soviet VARYAG	hulk

Chinese commercial firms previously purchased several aircraft carriers for scrap and for conversion to "recreation" activities. The never-completed VARYAG was sold to a Chinese company for US$20 million in 1998, with the agreement that the ship would not be used for military purposes. This was reflected by much of her equipment never having been installed or having been removed.

However, the ship has been moored at Darlian and, riding high in the water, has been repainted and "cleaned up." But there was no evidence when the volume went to press that the Chinese planned to rehabilitate the ship and place her in service.

FRANCE

TYPE	NAME			STATUS
CVE	DIXMUDE	ex-British BITER ex-U.S. BITER	c. Apr 9, 1945	decomm. 1956
CVL	ARROMANCHES	ex-British COLOSSUS	c. Aug 6, 1946	decomm. 1973 (scrapped)
CVL	LA FAYETTE	ex-U.S. LANGLEY (CVL 27)	c. June 6, 1951	str. 1963
CVL	BOIS DE BELLEAU	ex-U.S. BELLEAU WOOD (CVL 24)	c. Sep 5, 1953	str. 1960

HMS BITER was the American-built AVG/CVE 3. She was transferred to France after British service. The BITER was employed as an accommodation ship from 1956 to 1966, when she was returned to U.S. custody and scrapped.

The CVL 24 and 27 were transferred during the Indochina conflict. Along with the USS CABOT (CVL 28) transferred to Spain, they are the only U.S.-built carriers other than escort carriers to serve in another navy.

1 AIRCRAFT CARRIER: CONVERTED BATTLESHIP

TYPE	NAME	BUILDER		STATUS
CV	BÉARN	Mediterranean, La Seyne	l. Apr 1920 c. May 1927	str. 1966 (scrapped)

Displacement:	22,146 tonnes standard 28,854 tonnes full load
Dimensions:	599 ft oa (576 ft wl) x 89 ft x 30½ ft
Flight deck:	115½ ft
Propulsion:	2 steam turbines + 2 reciprocating engines; 37,200 shp; 4 shafts
Boilers:	12
Speed:	21.5 knots
Gun battery:	8 6.1-inch (8 single) 6 3.9-inch AA (6 single) 8 3-pounder AA (8 single)
Torpedo tubes:	4 21.7-inch (above water)
Aircraft:	40
Catapults:	none
Elevators:	3 centerline
Complement:	875

The BÉARN was converted while under construction as a battleship. She never launched aircraft in combat, but was employed primarily as a transport. She became a submarine depot ship alongside the quay at Missiessy (Toulon) in 1948; she was paid off in 1966 and subsequently scrapped.

AIRCRAFT CARRIERS: "JOFFRE" CLASS

TYPE	NAME	BUILDER	STATUS
CV	JOFFRE	Ateliers, St. Nazaire-Penhoët	cancelled
CV	PAINLEVÉ	Ateliers, St. Nazaire-Penhoët	cancelled

Displacement:	18,288 tonnes standard
	20,320 tonnes full load
Dimensions:	774¼ ft oa (748 ft wl) x 82 ft x 21⅔ ft
Flight deck:	91⅚ ft
Propulsion:	steam turbines; 120,000 shp; 4 shafts
Boilers:	8
Speed:	32 knots
Gun battery:	8 5.1-inch DP (4 twin)
	8 37-mm AA (4 twin)
Aircraft:	40
Catapults:	none
Elevators:	2 centerline
Complement:	1,250

These ships were laid down in 1938 and 1939, respectively. All work on these ships stopped when Germany invaded France in 1940. Their hulls were scrapped on the building ways. A third ship was reportedly planned.

2 AIRCRAFT CARRIERS: "CLEMENCEAU" CLASS

TYPE	NAME	BUILDER		STATUS
CV	CLEMENCEAU	Brest Arsenal	l. Dec 21, 1957 c. Nov 22, 1961	str. 1997
CV	FOCH	Atlantique, St. Nazaire	l. July 28, 1960 c. July 15, 1963	to Brazil 2000

Displacement:	22,000 tonnes standard
	32,780 tonnes full load
Dimensions:	869 ft oa (780 ft wl) x 104 ft x 28¼ ft
Flight deck:	168 ft
Propulsion:	steam turbines; 126,000 shp; 2 shafts
Boilers:	6
Speed:	32 knots
Gun battery:	8 3.9-inch AA (8 single)
Aircraft:	40
Catapults:	2 steam catapults
Elevators:	1 centerline, 1 deck edge
Complement:	2,240

These were France's first built-for-the-purpose aircraft carriers. The FOCH was completed at the Brest yard.

1 AIRCRAFT CARRIER: "CHARLES DE GAULLE"

TYPE	NAME	BUILDER		STATUS
CVN	CHARLES DE GAULLE	Brest Arsenal	l. May 15, 1994 c. May 18, 2001	**active**

Displacement:	37,085 tonnes standard
	40,000 tonnes full load
Dimensions:	$857^3/_4$ ft oa ($760^2/_3$ ft wl) x $103^1/_3$ ft x $27^{11}/_{12}$ ft
Flight deck:	
Propulsion:	steam turbines; 83,000 shp; 2 shafts
Reactors:	2 K15 pressurized-water
Speed:	25 knots
Missile launchers:	32 Aster AA missiles in vertical launchers
	2 Sadral point-defense missile systems
Gun battery:	8 20-mm AA (8 single)
Aircraft:	40
Catapults:	2 steam
Elevators:	2 deck edge
Complement:	1,850

France is the second nation to operate a nuclear-propelled aircraft carrier after the United States. Although the Soviet Union initiated nuclear carrier construction, none was completed.

2 HELICOPTER CARRIERS: "MISTRAL" CLASS

TYPE	NAME	BUILDER		STATUS
LHD	MISTRAL	Brest Arsenal and Alstrom, St. Nazaire	l. Oct 6, 2004 c. Dec 2005	**active**
LHD	TONNERRE	Brest Arsenal and Alstrom, St. Nazaire	l. July 26, 2005 c. Dec 2006	**active**

Displacement:	16,500 tonnes standard
	21,500 tonnes full load
Dimensions:	$688^2/_3$ ft oa ($652^3/_4$ ft wl) x $91^5/_6$ ft x $20^1/_3$ ft
Flight deck:	105 ft
Propulsion:	4 diesel generators with electric drive; 19,040 bhp; 2 podded thrusters
Speed:	19 knots
Missile launchers:	2 6-cell Simbad AA missile launchers
Gun battery:	2 30-mm multibarrel CIWS
Aircraft:	20+ helicopters
Catapults:	none
Elevators:	2 deck edge
Complement:	310 + 450 troops

These are the largest amphibious ships built outside of the United States. They have full flight decks with a starboard superstructure. The ships have a small docking well for landing craft.Extensive command center and hospital spaces are also provided.

They can accommodate 16 large (NH-90) helicopters or 35 light helicopters.

These ships are officially designated *Bâtiment de Projection et de Commandement*.

The nuclear-propelled carrier *Charles de Gaulle* is a large and graceful ship. However, the ship has been plagued by cost overruns, engineering problems, and the need for a flight deck extension to enable the operation of E-2C Hawkeye AEW aircraft. French plans to construct a second CVN has been dropped in favor of joining the British in developing a variation of the CVF (aircraft carrier—future), which is now on order for the Royal Navy. (Leo Van Ginderen collection)

GERMANY

AIRCRAFT CARRIERS: "GRAF ZEPPELIN" CLASS

TYPE	NAME	BUILDER		STATUS
GRAF ZEPPELIN		Deutsche-Kiel	l. Dec 8, 1938	cancelled to USSR 1945 sunk 1947
Aircraft Carrier "B"		Germania-Kiel		cancelled

Displacement:	23,200 tonnes standard (approx. 24,500 tonnes with bulges)
	29,700 tonnes full load (approx. 33,550 tonnes with bulges)
Dimensions:	844 ft oa original; 861 ft oa with "Atlantic bow" x 88$^{7}/_{12}$ ft x 24$^{11}/_{12}$ ft
Flight deck:	98$^{5}/_{12}$ ft
Propulsion:	steam turbines; 200,000 shp; 4 shafts
Boilers:	16
Speed:	35 knots
Gun battery:	16 5.9-inch/55-cal (8 twin)
	12 4.1-inch AA (6 twin)
	22 37-mm AA (11 twin)
	28 20-mm AA
Aircraft:	40
Catapults:	2 hydraulic
Elevators:	3 centerline
Complement:	1,760

These were the only aircraft carriers begun by Germany. The "Z" plan of 1937 called for four such ships.

The GRAF ZEPPELIN was laid down on December 28, 1936. The ship's bow was changed during construction to a longer "Atlantic bow." Similarly, during construction the decision was made to add bulges to increase fuel capacity and to enhance anti-torpedo protection.

The ship was scuttled on April 25, 1945; subsequently salvaged by the USSR and later sunk in explosive tests and as a target for dive bombers and torpedo boats.

Unofficial statements indicate that the second ship was to have been named PETER STRASSER.

GREAT BRITAIN

1 AIRCRAFT CARRIER: CONVERTED LARGE LIGHT CRUISER

TYPE	NAME	BUILDER		STATUS
CV	FURIOUS	Armstrong-Newcastle	l. Aug 15, 1916 c. July 4, 1917	reserve 1944 str. 1948 (scrapped)

Displacement:	19,100 tonnes light
	22,890 tonnes full load
Dimensions:	786½ ft oa (750 ft wl) x 88 ft x 24 ft
Flight deck:	
Propulsion:	steam turbines; 94,000 shp; 4 shafts
Boilers:	18
Speed:	31.5 knots
Gun battery:	1 18-inch
	11 5.5-inch (11 single)
	2 3-inch AA (2 single)
	4 3-pounder
Torpedo tubes:	6 21-inch (4 above water; 2 submerged)
Aircraft:	10
Catapults:	none
Elevators:	none
Complement:	880

The FURIOUS was converted during construction from a large light cruiser (two 18-inch guns). The ship's 18-inch gun (deleted in late 1917) was the largest ever mounted in a warship except for the 18.1-inch guns of the Japanese battleships YAMATO and MUSASHI.

The British large light cruisers COURAGEOUS and GLORIOUS were similar; both were converted to aircraft carriers after service as cruisers.

The above data are as completed. She underwent three major reconstructions: in 1917-1918 her after 18-inch gun was removed and a landing-on deck was provided. Subsequently, she emerged from a major conversion in 1932 with a flush deck and a flying-off deck at the hangar level. A later modification deleted the lower flying-off deck. A small starboard island structure was added in 1939.

1 AIRCRAFT CARRIER: CONVERTED MERCHANT SHIP

TYPE	NAME	BUILDER		STATUS
CV	ARGUS ex-*Conte Rosso*	Beardmore	l. Dec 2, 1917 c. Sep 14, 1918	decomm. 1944 (scrapped)

Displacement:	14,000 tonnes standard
	16,500 tonnes full load
Dimensions:	550 ft oa (535½ ft wl) x 68½ ft x 24¾ ft
Flight deck:	69 ft
Propulsion:	steam turbines; 20,000 shp; 4 shafts
Boilers:	12
Speed:	20.2 knots
Gun battery:	6 4-inch guns (6 single)
	4 3-pounder (40-mm) guns (4 single)
Aircraft:	20

Catapults:	none (1 hydraulic fitted 1936-1938)
Elevators:	2 centerline (after lift deleted 1936-1938)
Complement:	760

The ARGUS was converted during construction from a merchant ship. She was the world's first ship completed as a full-deck aircraft carrier. After being decommissioned she was used as an accommodation ship at Chatham until she was discarded in 1947.

1 AIRCRAFT CARRIER: CONVERTED BATTLESHIP

TYPE	NAME	BUILDER		STATUS
CV	EAGLE ex-ALMIRANTE COCHRANE ex-SANTIAGO	Armstrong-Clydebank	l. June 8, 1918 c. Feb 20, 1924	sunk Aug 11, 1942

Displacement:	22,200 tonnes standard
	27,229 tonnes full load
Dimensions:	$667\frac{1}{2}$ ft oa ($627\frac{1}{12}$ ft wl) x $105\frac{1}{6}$ ft x $26\frac{2}{3}$ ft
Flight deck:	95 ft
Propulsion:	steam turbines; 50,000 shp; 4 shafts
Boilers:	32
Speed:	24 knots
Gun battery:	9 6-inch/50-cal (9 single)
	5 4-inch/45-cal AA (5 single)
Aircraft:	24
Catapults:	none
Elevators:	2 centerline

The EAGLE was converted while under construction as a battleship ordered by Chile.

1 AIRCRAFT CARRIER: "HERMES"

TYPE	NAME	BUILDER		STATUS
CV	HERMES	Armstrong-Newcastle	l. Sep 11, 1919 c. Feb 18, 1924	sunk Apr 9, 1942

Displacement:	11,024 tonnes standard
	13,208 tonnes full load
Dimensions:	600 ft oa (548 ft wl) x $70\frac{1}{4}$ ft x $21\frac{1}{2}$ ft
Flight deck:	65 ft
Propulsion:	steam turbines; 40,000 shp; 2 shafts
Boilers:	6
Speed:	25 knots
Gun battery:	6 5.5-inch AA (6 single)
	3 4-inch AA (3 single)
Aircraft:	20
Catapults:	none
Elevators:	2 centerline
Complement:	700

The HERMES was the world's first ship designed from the outset to be aircraft carrier. (The Japanese HOSHO was the first purpose-built ship to be completed.) The HERMES— the world's first aircraft carrier to be sunk—was destroyed by Japanese carrier-based aircraft.

2 AIRCRAFT CARRIERS: CONVERTED LARGE LIGHT CRUISERS

TYPE	NAME	BUILDER		STATUS
CV	COURAGEOUS	Armstrong-Parsons	l. Feb 5, 1916 c. May 5, 1928	sunk Sep 17, 1939
CV	GLORIOUS	Harland & Wolff	l. Apr 20, 1916 c. Mar 10, 1930	sunk June 8, 1940

Displacement:	22,352 tonnes standard 26,518 tonnes full load
Dimensions:	786½ ft oa (735 ft wl) x 90½ ft x 27¼ ft
Flight deck:	84½ ft
Propulsion:	steam turbines; 90,670 shp; 4 shafts
Boilers:	18
Speed:	30 knots
Gun battery:	16 4.7-inch AA (16 single)
Aircraft:	48
Catapults:	2 hydraulic (installed in 1936)
Elevators:	2 centerline
Complement:	1,260

These ships were completed in 1916 as light battle cruisers (four 15-inch guns); both were converted in 1924-1930 to aircraft carriers.

The COURAGEOUS was sunk by a U-boat; the GLORIOUS was sunk by gunfire from German surface ships.

1 AIRCRAFT CARRIER: "ARK ROYAL"

TYPE	NAME	BUILDER		STATUS
CV	ARK ROYAL	Cammell Laird	l. Apr 13, 1937 c. Nov 16, 1938	sunk Nov 14, 1941

Displacement:	22,352 tonnes standard 28,143 tonnes full load
Dimensions:	800 ft oa (685 ft wl) x 94³/₄ ft x 27³/₄ ft
Flight deck:	96 ft
Propulsion:	steam turbines; 102,000 shp; 3 shafts
Boilers:	6
Speed:	31 knots
Gun battery:	16 4.5-inch AA (8 twin) 32 2-pounder (40-mm) pom-pom AA (4 octuple)
Aircraft:	60
Catapults:	2 hydraulic
Elevators:	3 offset centerline
Complement:	1,580

The ARK ROYAL was Britain's first "modern" carrier. She was sunk by a U-boat.

TYPE	NAME	BUILDER		STATUS
CV	ILLUSTRIOUS	VA-Barrow	l. Apr 5, 1939 c. May 25, 1940	decomm. 1954 str. 1956 (scrapped)
CV	FORMIDABLE	Harland & Wolff	l. Aug 17, 1939 c. Nov 24, 1940	str. 1947 (scrapped)
CV	VICTORIOUS	VA-Newcastle	l. Sep 14, 1939 c. May 15, 1941	str. 1967 (scrapped)
CV	INDOMITABLE	VA-Barrow	l. Mar 26, 1940 c. Oct 10, 1941	str. 1953 (scrapped)
CV	IMPLACABLE*	Fairfield	l. Dec 10, 1942 c. Aug 28, 1944	str. 1954 (scrapped)
CV	INDEFATIGABLE*	Clydebank	l. Dec 8, 1944 c. May 3, 1944	decomm. 1954 (scrapped)

Displacement:	23,368 tonnes; 23,825 tonnes* 28,661 tonnes; 32,624 tonnes*
Dimensions:	743³/₄ ft oa (673 ft wl) x 95³/₄ ft x 28 ft
Flight deck:	80 ft
Propulsion:	steam turbines; 111,000 shp; 3 shafts
Boilers:	6
Speed:	30.5 knots
Gun battery:	16 4.5-inch/45 cal AA (8 twin) 40 2-pounder (40-mm) pom-pom AA (5 octuple) 3 40-mm Bofors/56-cal AA (3 single) 52 20-mm Oerlikon AA (19 twin, 14 single)
Aircraft:	36 (72*)
Catapults:	1 hydraulic
Elevators:	2 centerline
Complement:	1,200

These were the world's first armored-deck carriers. Although they fall into sub-classes, the six ships are invariably referred to as the ILLUSTRIOUS class. The early ships could accommodate 36 aircraft in their hangar.

The VICTORIOUS and INDOMITABLE were redesigned early in construction and fitted with two-level hangars and increased aviation gasoline capacity at the cost of ship's fuel stowage. The INDEFATIGABLE and IMPLACABLE had less side armor than other ships of the class (1½-inch side instead of 4½ inches), were one knot faster, and could accommodate twice the aircraft in their hangars as could the earlier ships (72 instead of 36).

2 AIRCRAFT CARRIERS: "AUDACIOUS" CLASS

TYPE	NAME	BUILDER		STATUS
CV	EAGLE ex-AUDACIOUS	Harland & Wolff	l. Mar 19, 1946 c. Oct 1, 1951	decomm. 1972 (scrapped)
CV	AFRICA	Fairfield		cancelled
CV	EAGLE	VA-Tyne		cancelled
CV	ARK ROYAL ex-IRRESISTIBLE	Cammell Laird	l. May 3, 1950 c. Feb 25, 1955	str. 1978 (scrapped)

Displacement:	36,800 tonnes standard 46,452 tonnes full load

Dimensions:	803³⁄₄ ft oa (750 ft) x 119³⁄₄ ft x 36 ft
Flight deck:	105 ft
Propulsion:	steam turbines; 152,000 shp; 4 shafts
Boilers:	8
Speed:	31.5 knots
Gun battery:	16 4.5-inch DP (8 twin)
	58 40-mm Bofors/56-cal AA (sextuple and single)
Aircraft:	80
Catapults:	2 steam
Elevators:	3 (2 centerline, 1 deck edge)
Complement:	2,755

These were the largest aircraft carriers constructed in Britain prior to the CVF program. The AFRICA and EAGLE were cancelled, the latter laid down in April 1944.

The EAGLE was modified to a "limited" angled deck configuration (5.5°) in 1954-1955; provided with a "full" angled deck (8°) in 1959-1964. She was retained for six years after decommissioning to be cannibalized for spare parts to support the ARK ROYAL.

The ARK ROYAL was converted to a "full" angled deck (8°) in 1966-1970. She was the first British carrier to be fitted with a deck-edge lift.

LARGE AIRCRAFT CARRIERS: "GIBRALTAR" CLASS

TYPE	NAME	BUILDER	STATUS
CVB	GIBRALTAR	VA-Tyne	cancelled 1945
CVB	MALTA	Clydebank	cancelled 1945
CVB	NEW ZEALAND	Cammell Laird	cancelled 1945

Displacement:	47,650 tonnes standard
	57,709 tonnes full load
Dimensions:	916¹⁄₂ ft oa (820 ft wl) x 115³⁄₄ ft x 34¹⁄₂ ft
Flight deck:	136 ft
Propulsion:	steam turbines; 200,000 shp; 4 shafts
Boilers:	8
Speed:	33 knots
Gun battery:	16 4.5-inch DP (8 twin)
	55 40-mm Bofors/56-cal AA (8 sextuple, 7 single)
Aircraft:	100+
Catapults:	
Elevators:	
Complement:	

These ships were similar in concept and many features to the large carriers of the U.S. MIDWAY class. Only the MALTA *may* have been laid down.

1 MAINTENANCE/LIGHT AIRCRAFT CARRIER: "UNICORN"

TYPE	NAME	BUILDER		STATUS
CVM	UNICORN	Harland & Wolff	l. Nov 20, 1941	scrapped 1959
			c. Mar 12, 1943	

Displacement:	16,794 tonnes standard
	20,625 tonnes full load

Dimensions:	640 ft oa (575 ft wl) x 90 ft x 24 ft	
Flight deck:	80 ft	
Propulsion:	steam turbines; 40,000 shp; 2 shafts	
Boilers:	4	
Speed:	24 knots	
Gun battery:	8 4-inch/45-cal AA (4 twin)	
	16 2-pounder (40-mm) pom-pom AA (4 quad)	
	10 20-mm Oerlikon AA (5 twin)	
Aircraft:	35 (as operational carrier)	
Catapults:	1 hydraulic	
Elevators:	2 centerline	
Complement:	1,200	

The UNICORN was built as an aviation maintenance carrier, but also served as an operational carrier. The UNICORN's design formed the basis for the 1942 light carrier COLOSSUS class.

10 LIGHT AIRCRAFT CARRIERS: "COLOSSUS" CLASS

TYPE	NAME	BUILDER		STATUS
CVL	COLOSSUS	VA-Parsons	l. Sep 30, 1943	to France 1946
			c. Dec 16, 1944	
CVM	PERSEUS ex-EDGAR	VA-Newcastle	l. Mar 26, 1943 c. Oct 10, 1945	str. 1957 (scrapped)
CVL	GLORY	Harland & Wolff	l. Nov 27, 1943 c. Apr 2, 1945	reserve 1956 str. 1957 (scrapped)
CVM	PIONEER ex-MARS	VA-Barrow	l. May 20, 1944 c. Feb 8, 1945	decomm. 1946 str. 1954 (scrapped)
CVL	OCEAN	Stephen	l. July 8, 1944 c. Aug 8, 1945	decomm. 1957; str. 1958 (scrapped)
CVL	THESEUS	Fairfield	l. July 6, 1944 c. Feb 9, 1946	decomm. 1956; str. 1958 (scrapped)
CVL	TRIUMPH	Hawthorn	l. Oct 2, 1944 c. May 9, 1946	decomm. 1975; str. 1981 (scrapped)
CVL	VENERABLE	Cammell Laird	l. Dec 30, 1943 c. Jan 17, 1945	to Netherlands 1948 to Argentina 1968
CVL	VENGEANCE	Swan Hunter	l. Feb 23, 1944 c. Jan 15, 1945	to Australia 1952 to Brazil 1956
CVL	WARRIOR	Harland & Wolff	l. May 20, 1944	to Canada 1946 to Argentina 1958

Displacement:	13,401 tonnes standard	
	18,329 tonnes full load	
Dimensions:	695 ft oa (650 ft wl) x 80 ft x 23½ ft	
Flight deck:	80 ft	
Propulsion:	steam turbines; 40,000 shp; 2 shafts	
Boilers:	4	
Speed:	25 knots	
Gun battery:	24 2-pounder (40-mm) pom-pom AA (6 quad)	
	32 20-mm Oerlikon AA (11 twin, 10 single)	
Aircraft:	42	
Catapults:	1 hydraulic	
Elevators:	2 centerline	
Complement:	1,300	

Four ships of this class were transferred to other navies.

The PERSEUS and PIONEER were completed as maintenance carriers. The PERSEUS began conversion to a submarine tender in 1955, but worked ceased in 1957 and she was placed on the disposal list. The TRIUMPH was converted to a heavy repair ship in 1957-1965.

The WARRIOR was the only unit of the class that did not serve in the Royal Navy, being commissioned on January 24, 1946, as HMCS WARRIOR.

6 LIGHT AIRCRAFT CARRIERS: "MAJESTIC" CLASS

TYPE	NAME	BUILDER		STATUS
CVL	HERCULES	VA-Parsons	l. Sep 22, 1945	to India 1957
CVL	LEVIATHAN	Swan Hunter	l. June 7, 1945	suspended 1946 (scrapped)
CVL	MAGNIFICENT	Harland & Wolff	l. Nov 16, 1944	to Canada 1946
CVL	MAJESTIC	VA-Barrow	l. Feb 28, 1945	to Australia 1955
CVL	POWERFUL	Harland & Wolff	l. Feb 27, 1945	to Canada 1952
CVL	TERRIBLE	Davenport-Parsons	l. Sep 30, 1944	to Australia 1948

Displacement:	14,224 tonnes standard
	18,085 tonnes full load
Dimensions:	695 ft oa (650 ft wl) x 80 ft x 23½ ft
Flight deck:	75 ft
Propulsion:	steam turbines; 40,000 shp; 2 shafts
Boilers:	4
Speed:	24.5 knots
Gun battery:	24 2-pounder (40-mm) pom-pom AA (6 quad)
	25 40-mm Bofors/56-cal AA (8 twin, 9 single)
Aircraft:	37
Catapults:	1 hydraulic
Elevators:	2 centerline
Complement:	1,200

These ships were similar to the COLOSSUS class but with flight deck and (larger) lifts strengthened to operate larger aircraft (up to 24,000 pounds vice 15,000 pounds in the earlier ships). The above data are nominal characteristics for the original design.

None of these ships served in the Royal Navy. Construction of all six ships was halted after World War II. Five were transferred upon completion to other navies; the LEVIATHAN was not completed. In 1966 the LEVIATHAN's boilers and turbines were removed for sale and installation in the Dutch carrier KAREL DOORMAN (ex-HMS VENERABLE) in preparation for her service in the Argentine Navy (renamed 25 DE MAYO).

4 LIGHT AIRCRAFT CARRIERS: "HERMES" CLASS

TYPE	NAME	BUILDER		STATUS
CVL	ALBION	Swan Hunter-Wallsend	l. May 6, 1947	str. 1973
			c. May 26, 1954	(scrapped)
CVL	ARROGANT	Swan Hunter		cancelled
CVL	BULWARK	Harland & Wolff	l. June 22, 1948	str. 1981
			c. Nov 4, 1954	(scrapped)
CVL	CENTAUR	Harland & Wolff	l. Apr 22, 1947	decomm. 1965
			c. Sep 1, 1953	(scrapped)
CVL	HERMES ex-ELEPHANT	VA-Barrow	l. Feb 16, 1953	to India 1987
			c. Nov 18, 1959	

CVL	HERMES	Cammell Laird	cancelled
CVL	MONMOUTH	Fairfield	cancelled
CVL	POLYPHEMUS	Davenport	cancelled

Displacement:	18,593 tonnes standard
	24,892 tonnes full load
Dimensions:	737³/₄ ft oa (686 ft wl) x 90 ft x 27 ft
Flight deck:	100 ft
Propulsion:	steam turbines; 78,000 shp; 2 shafts
Boilers:	4
Speed:	28 knots
Gun battery:	32 40-mm Bofors/56-cal AA (2 sextuple, 8 twin, 4 single)
Aircraft:	42
Catapults:	2 hydraulic
Elevators:	2 centerline
Complement:	1,600

The ALBION was laid up immediately after launch; she was the first British carrier to be completed with an angled flight deck. The ship was converted to a commando ship in 1961-1962.

The CENTAUR served as an accommodations ship from 1965 to 1972.

The HERMES was converted to a commando ship in 1971-1973; she was modified and recommissioned as an ASW carrier in 1976; in 1980 she was converted to a VSTOL (Harrier) carrier. The HERMES—which saw action in the Falklands War (1982)—was the last British carrier of the World War II programs in active service. She was transferred to India in 1987 (renamed VIRAAT).

AIRCRAFT CARRIERS: "QUEEN ELIZABETH" CLASS

TYPE	NAME	STATUS
CVA	QUEEN ELIZABETH	cancelled 1966
CVA	PRINCE OF WALES	cancelled 1966

Displacement:	50,800 tonnes standard
	55,372 tonnes full load
Dimensions:	963 ft oa (890 ft wl) x 122 ft x 32 ft
Flight deck:	191 ft
Propulsion:	steam turbines; 135,000 shp; 3 shafts
Speed:	30 knots
Missile launchers:	2 Sea Dart GWS.30 twin launcher AA
Aircraft:	45
Catapults:	2 steam
Elevators:	2 deck edge
Complement:	3,230

These ships were intended to replace the surviving World War II-built carriers in British service. In the event the Defence White Paper of 1966 called for their cancellation and the end of fixed-wing aircraft carriers in the Royal Navy.

The ships were designated CVA.01 and CVA.02, respectively. Their characteristics varied as the design evolved.

3 VSTOL AIRCRAFT CARRIERS: "INVINCIBLE" CLASS

TYPE	NAME	BUILDER		STATUS
CV	INVINCIBLE	Vickers SB Barrow	l. May 3, 1977 c. July 11, 1980	**active**
CV	ILLUSTRIOUS	Swan Hunter-Wallsend	l. Dec 1, 1978 c. June 18, 1982	**active**
CV	ARK ROYAL	Swan Hunter-Wallsend	l. June 2, 1981 c. July 1, 1985	**active**

Displacement:	16,256 tonnes standard
	19,812 tonnes full load
Dimensions:	677 3/4 ft oa (632 ft wl) x 90 ft x 29 ft
Flight deck:	115 ft
Propulsion:	4 gas turbines; 112,000 shp (94,000 shp max continuous); 2 shafts
Speed:	28 knots
Missile launchers:	1 Sea Dart GWS.30 twin launcher AA
Guns:	3 30-mm Goalkeeper CIWS
Aircraft:	approx. 20 (see Chapters 19 and 20)
Catapults:	none
Elevators:	2 centerline
Complement:	1,100

These ships had a convoluted development, being originally thought of as "through-deck cruisers." They have a ski-ramp forward for launching of Harrier VSTOL aircraft.

The ILLUSTRIOUS was the first Royal Navy ship to be placed in commission while at sea.

(2) AIRCRAFT CARRIERS: "QUEEN ELIZABETH" CLASS

TYPE	NAME	BUILDER			STATUS
CV	QUEEN ELIZABETH	BAE Systems	l. c.	 2014	building
CV	PRINCE OF WALES	BAE Systems	l. c.	 2016	building

Displacement:	65,000 tonnes full load
Dimensions:	$928^{1}/_{4}$ ft oa x $127^{11}/_{12}$ ft x $39^{1}/_{3}$ ft
Flight deck:	$259^{1}/_{6}$ ft
Propulsion:	2 gas turbines with electric motors; 100,000 shp; 2 shafts
Speed:	25 knots
Missile launchers:	
Gun battery:	
Aircraft:	40
Catapults:	none
Elevators:	2 deck edge
Complement:	1,400

These ships are designated CVF for aircraft carriers—future. The contract to construct these ships was awarded in July 2007. These will be the largest ships built in Britain. The work will be shared among a number of companies, including BAE Systems' Govan and Scotstoun yards in Glasgow; the ships will be built in sections and then assembled at the Rosyth dockyard in Fife.

The ships will have an ski-jump and an unusual "split-island" superstructure.

The French Navy plans to construct a similar ship.

1 COMMANDO SHIP: "OCEAN"

TYPE	NAME	BUILDER		STATUS
LPH	OCEAN	Kvaerner Govan, Clyde	l. Oct 11, 1995 c. Sep 30, 1998	**active**

Displacement:	21,578 tonnes full load
Dimensions:	667$^{1}/_{6}$ ft oa (663 ft wl) x 93$^{1}/_{2}$ ft x 21$^{5}/_{6}$ ft
Flight deck:	106$^{11}/_{12}$ ft
Propulsion:	diesel; 18,360 bhp; 2 shafts
Speed:	18 knots
Gun battery:	3 20-mm Phalanx CIWS
	5 20-mm AA (5 single)
Aircraft:	18 helicopters
Catapults:	none
Elevators:	2 centerline
Complement:	500 + 500 troops

The OCEAN was designed as an Aviation Support Ship (ASS), but in reality operates as a commando ship (LPH). The ship has a carrier configuration but was built to commercial (merchant) ship standards to reduce costs.

Although the ship has a hangar deck with two elevators to move aircraft, she has no aviation support facilities. Thus, while the OCEAN can transport helicopters and VSTOL aircraft as well as vehicles, she cannot effectively operate them.

Four LCVP Mk 5 landing craft are normally carried.

ESCORT CARRIER NOTES

The Royal Navy built four escort carriers on merchant hulls. Thirty-eight additional escort carriers were built in the United States for the Royal Navy during World War II. Former U.S. hull numbers are shown in parentheses for these 38 ships; for those ships the "c" date is first commissioning, in either U.S. Navy or Royal Navy.

1 ESCORT CARRIER: CONVERTED MERCHANT SHIP

TYPE	NAME	BUILDER		STATUS
CVE	AUDACITY ex-*Empire Audacity,* ex-*Hannover*	Vulkan-Bremen	l. Mar 29, 1939 c. June 20, 1941	sunk Dec 21, 1941

Displacement:	10,395 tonnes full load
Tonnage:	5,537 tons gross
Dimensions:	467$^{1}/_{4}$ ft x (435$^{1}/_{2}$ ft wl) 56$^{1}/_{4}$ ft x 27$^{7}/_{12}$ ft
Fight deck:	60 ft
Propulsion:	diesel; 5,200 bhp; 1 shaft
Speed:	14.5 knots
Gun battery:	1 4-inch/45-cal AA gun
	4 2-pounder (40-mm) pom-pom AA (4 single)
	4 20-mm Oerlikon AA guns (4 single)
Aircraft:	8
Complement:	210

A captured German passenger-cargo ship, the AUDACITY was Britain's first escort carrier and the world's first escort carrier to see combat.

The ship was completed as the *Hannover* on May 10, 1939; she was captured by British ships on March 7, 1940, and placed in British service as the *Sinbad.* Her conversion to an armed boarding vessel to be named *Empire Audacity* began in November 1940, but she was instead completed as an escort carrier. She was renamed AUDACITY in July 1941.

No catapult, hangar, or elevator were fitted.

1 ESCORT CARRIER: "PRETORIA CASTLE"

TYPE	NAME	BUILDER		STATUS
CVE	PRETORIA CASTLE ex-*Pretoria Castle*	Harland & Wolff	l. Oct 12, 1938 c. July 29, 1943	str. 1946

Displacement:	19,964 tonnes standard
	23,825 tonnes full load
Tonnage:	17,392 tons gross
Dimensions:	594^{7}/$_{12}$ ft oa (560 ft wl) x 76^{1}/$_{2}$ ft x 28 ft
Flight deck:	75 ft
Propulsion:	diesel; 16,000 bhp; 2 shafts
Speed:	18 knots
Gun battery:	4 4-inch/45-cal AA (2 twin)
	16 2-pdr pom-pom (40-mm) AA (4 quad)
	20 20-mm Oerlikon AA (10 twin)
Aircraft:	21
Catapults:	1 hydraulic
Elevators:	1 centerline
Complement:	580

The PRETORIA CASTLE was built as a passenger liner; she was acquired for use as an armed merchant cruiser and commissioned for that role in November 1939. She was converted to an escort carrier from June to August 1943, and was employed for training and deck landing trials.

4 ESCORT CARRIERS: AVENGER CLASS (AMERICAN C3 TYPE)

TYPE	NAME	BUILDER		STATUS
CVE (BAVG 1)	ARCHER ex-*Mormacland*	Sun SB	l. Dec 14, 1939 c. Nov 17, 1941	returned USA 1946 (merchant)
CVE (BAVG 2)	AVENGER ex-*Rio Hudson*	Sun SB	l. Nov 17, 1940 c. Mar 2, 1942	sunk Nov 15, 1942
CVE (BAVG 3)	BITER ex-*Rio Parana*	Sun SB	l. Dec 18, 1940 c. Apr 6, 1942	to France 1945
CVE (BAVG 5)	DASHER ex-*Rio de Janiero*	Sun SB	l. Apr 12, 1941 c. July 2, 1942	sunk Mar 27, 1943

Displacement:	10,384 tonnes standard
	13,066 tonnes full load
Dimensions:	492 ft oa (465 ft wl) x 70 ft x 26¼ ft
Flight deck:	70 ft
Propulsion:	diesel; 8,500 bhp; 1 shaft
Speed:	17 knots
Gun battery:	3 4-inch AA guns (3 single)
	10 to 19 20-mm Oerlikon AA guns (twin and single)
Aircraft:	15
Catapults:	1 hydraulic
Elevators:	1 centerline
Complement:	550

These were the first of 38 escort carriers built in the United States on C3 cargo hulls for service in the Royal Navy. The CHARGER (BAVG 4) of this series was retained by the U.S. Navy as the CVE 30.

The DASHER was lost in an accidental, aviation gas-related explosion. The AVENGER was sunk by a U-boat. The ARCHER was converted for merchant service after the war. The BITER was transferred to the French Navy (DIXMUDE).

TYPE	NAME	BUILDER		STATUS
CVE (BAVG 6)	TRACKER ex-*Mormacmail*	Seattle-Tacoma	l. Mar 7, 1942 c. Jan 31, 1943	returned USA 1945 (merchant)
CVE (6)	BATTLER ex-ALTAMAHA (USN) ex-*Mormacmail*	Ingalls	l. Apr 4, 1942 c. Oct 31, 1942	returned USA 1946 (scrapped)
CVE (7)	ATTACKER ex-BARNES (USN) ex-*Steel Artisan*	Western Pipe	l. Sep 27, 1941 c. Sep 30, 1942	returned USA 1946 (merchant)
CVE (8)	HUNTER ex-TRAILER (RN) ex-BLOCK ISLAND (USN) ex-*Mormacpen*	Ingalls	l. May 22, 1942 c. Jan 9, 1943	returned USA 1945 (merchant)
CVE (10)	CHASER ex-BRETON (USN) ex-*Mormacgulf*	Ingalls	l. June 15, 1942 c. Apr 9, 1943	returned USA 1946 (merchant)
CVE (14)	FENCER ex-CROATAN (USN)	Western Pipe	l. May 4, 1942 c. Feb 20, 1943	returned USA 1946 (merchant)
CVE (15)	STALKER ex-HAMLIN (USN)	Western Pipe	l. Mar 5, 1942 c. Dec 21, 1942	returned USA 1945 (merchant)
CVE (17)	PURSUER ex-ST. GEORGE (USN) ex-*Mormacland*	Ingalls	l. July 18, 1942 c. June 14, 1943	returned USA 1946 (scrapped)
CVE (19)	STRIKER ex-PRINCE WILLIAM (USN)	Western Pipe	l. May 7, 1942 c. Apr 29, 1943	returned USA 1946 (scrapped)
CVE (22)	SEARCHER	Seattle-Tacoma	l. June 20, 1942 c. Apr 7, 1943	returned USA 1945 (merchant)
CVE (24)	RAVAGER ex-CHARGER (USN)	Seattle-Tacoma	l. July 16, 1942 c. Apr 25, 1943	returned USA 1946 (merchant)
CVE (32)	SLINGER* ex-CHATHAM (USN)	Seattle-Tacoma	l. Dec 15, 1942 c. Aug 11, 1943	returned USA 1946 (merchant)
CVE (33)	ATHELING* ex-GLACIER (USN)	Seattle-Tacoma	l. Sep 7, 1942 c. July 3, 1943	returned USA 1946 (merchant)
CVE (34)	EMPEROR* ex-STINGER ex-*Pybus*	Seattle-Tacoma	l. Oct 7, 1942 c. Aug 6, 1943	returned USA 1946 (scrapped)
CVE (35)	AMEER* ex-UPRAIDER (RN) ex-BAFFINS (USN)	Seattle-Tacoma	l. Oct 18, 1942 c. June 28, 1943	returned USA 1946 (merchant)
CVE (36)	BEGUM* ex-BALINAS (USN)	Seattle-Tacoma	l. Nov 11, 1942 c. Aug 2, 1942	returned USA 1946 (merchant)
CVE (37)	TRUMPETER* ex-BASTIAN (USN) ex-LUCIFER (USN)	Seattle-Tacoma	l. Dec 15, 1942 c. Aug 4, 1943	returned USA 1946 (merchant)
CVE (38)	EMPRESS* ex-CARNEGIE (USN)	Seattle-Tacoma	l. Dec 30, 1942 c. Aug 12, 1943	returned USA 1946 (scrapped)
CVE (39)	KHEDIVE* ex-CARDOVA (USN)	Seattle-Tacoma	l. Jan 30, 1943 c. Aug 25, 1943	returned USA 1946 (merchant)
CVE (40)	SPEAKER* ex-DELGADA (USN)	Seattle-Tacoma	l. Feb 20, 1943 c. Nov 20, 1943	returned USA 1946 (merchant)

TYPE	NAME	BUILDER		STATUS
CVE (41)	NABOB* (USN) ex-EDISTO	Seattle-Tacoma	l. Mar 9, 1943 c. Sep 7, 1943	returned to USA (merchant)
CVE (42)	PREMIER* ex-ESTERO (USN)	Seattle-Tacoma	l. Mar 22, 1943 c. Nov 3, 1943	returned USA 1946 (merchant)
CVE (43)	SHAH* ex-JAMAICA (USN)	Seattle-Tacoma	l. Apr 21, 1943 c. Sep 27, 1943	returned USA 1945 (merchant)
CVE (44)	PATROLLER* ex-KEEWEENAW (USN)	Seattle-Tacoma	l. May 6, 1943 c. Oct 22, 1943	returned USA 1946 (merchant)
CVE (45)	RAJAH* ex-PRINCE ex-McCLURE	Seattle-Tacoma	l. May 18, 1943 c. Jan 17, 1944	returned USA 1946 (merchant)
CVE (46)	RANEE* ex-NIANTIC (USN)	Seattle-Tacoma	l. June 2, 1943 c. Nov 8, 1943	returned USA 1946 (merchant)
CVE (47)	TROUNCER* ex-Perdito	Seattle-Tacoma	l. June 16, 1943 c. Jan 31, 1944	returned USA 1946 (merchant)
CVE (48)	THANE* ex-SUNSET (USN)	Seattle-Tacoma	l. July 15, 1943 c. Nov 19, 1943	returned USA 1945 (scrapped)
CVE (49)	QUEEN* ex-ST. ANDREWS (USN)	Seattle-Tacoma	l. Aug 2, 1943 c. Dec 7, 1943	returned USA 1946 (merchant)
CVE (50)	RULER* ex-ST. JOSEPH (USN)	Seattle-Tacoma	l. Aug 21, 1943 c. Dec 22, 1943	returned USA 1946 (scrapped)
CVE (51)	ARBITER* ex-ST. SIMON (USN)	Seattle-Tacoma	l. Sep 9, 1943 c. Dec 31, 1943	returned USA 1946 (merchant)
CVE (52)	SMITER* ex-VERMILLION (USN)	Seattle-Tacoma	l. Sep 27, 1943 c. Jan 20, 1944	returned USA 1946 (merchant)
CVE (53)	PUNCHER* ex-WILLAPA (USN)	Seattle-Tacoma	l. Nov 8, 1943 c. Feb 5, 1944	returned USA 1946 (merchant)
CVE (54)	REAPER* ex-WINJAH (USN)	Seattle-Tacoma	l. Nov 22, 1943 c. Feb 18, 1944	returned USA 1946 (merchant)

Displacement:	11,363 tonnes standard
	14,630 tonnes standard
Dimensions:	492 ft oa (465 ft wl) x 69½ ft x 26 ft
Flight deck:	82 ft
Propulsion:	steam turbines; 8,500 shp; 1 shaft
Boilers:	2
Speed:	18.5 knots
Gun battery:	2 or 3 4-inch AA (2 or 3 single)
	or 2 5-inch/38-cal DP (2 single)*
	16 40-mm Bofors/56-cal AA (8 twin)
	20 to 35 20-mm Oerlikon AA (twin and single)
Aircraft:	30
Catapults:	1 hydraulic
Elevators:	2 centerline
Complement:	650

These 34 escort carriers were built in the United States on C3 cargo hulls. All were transferred upon completion to the Royal Navy. Some ships were commissioned in the U.S. Navy prior to transfer to the Royal Navy. These ships were referred to as both the ATTACKER and RULER class, more often the latter.

Eleven additional ships of this type served in the U.S. Navy as the BOGUE (CVE 9) class.

Eleven ships were laid down as merchant hulls and 23 as aircraft carriers. (*) The latter ships were armed with U.S. 5-inch weapons.

Twenty-seven of these ships were converted for merchant service after the war.

The NABOB and PUNCHER were manned by the Canadian Navy. The NABOB, severely damaged by a German U-boat on August 22, 1944, was able to limp into port and was considered a total loss (see Volume I, page 348). She was decommissioned on September 30, 1944, and, retained in nominal reserve, was cannibalized for spare parts for sister ships. On March 16, 1946, the NABOB was returned to the U.S. Navy and stricken; she was sold for scrap in March 1947, but was resold to a German firm, rehabilitated and reengined. and from 1952 was used as a civilian training ship for the German merchant service, retaining the name NABOB. In 1968 the ship was renamed *Glory* and registered in Panama. In December 1977 the ship was sold for scrap.

1 ESCORT CARRIER: CONVERTED MERCHANT SHIP

TYPE	NAME	BUILDER		STATUS
CVE	ACTIVITY ex-*Telemachus*	Caledon-Dundee	l. May 30, 1942 c. Sep 29, 1942	str. 1946 (merchant)

Displacement:	11,989 tonnes standard 14,529 tonnes full load
Dimensions:	512³/₄ ft oa (475 ft wl) x 66¹/₂ ft x 26¹/₁₂ ft
Flight deck:	66 ft
Propulsion:	diesel; 12,000 bhp; 2 shafts
Speed:	18 knots
Gun battery:	2 4-inch AA (1 twin) 20 20-mm Oerlikon AA (6 twin, 8 single)
Aircraft:	15
Catapults:	none
Elevators:	1 centerline
Complement:	700

The *Telemachus* was a fast refrigerated cargo ship, converted during construction to an escort carrier.

1 ESCORT CARRIER: CONVERTED MERCHANT SHIP

TYPE	NAME	BUILDER		STATUS
CVE	CAMPANIA	Harland & Wolff	l. June 17, 1943 c. Mar 7, 1944	str. 1955 (scrapped)

Displacement:	12,649 tonnes standard 16,226 tonnes full load
Dimensions:	540 ft oa (510 ft wl) x 70 ft x 22⁵/₆ ft
Flight deck:	70 ft
Propulsion:	diesel; 13,250 bhp; 2 shafts
Speed:	18 knots
Gun battery:	2 4-inch AA (1 twin) 16 2-pdr (40-mm) pom-pom AA guns (4 quad) 16 20-mm Oerlikon AA guns (8 twin)
Aircraft:	20
Catapults:	none
Elevators:	1 centerline
Complement:	640

The CAMPANIA was laid down as a merchant ship; she was taken over by the Navy for conversion to a carrier in July 1942.

2 ESCORT CARRIERS: CONVERTED MERCHANT SHIPS

TYPE	NAME	BUILDER	STATUS	
CVE	VINDEX	Swan Hunter	l. May 4, 1943 c. Dec 3, 1943	str. 1947 (scrapped)
CVE	NAIRANA	John Brown	l. May 20, 1943 c. Dec 12, 1943	to Netherlands 1946

Displacement:	14,046 tonnes standard 17,252 tonnes full load
Dimensions:	528½ ft oa (498¼ ft wl) 68 ft x 25⅔ ft
Flight deck:	65 ft
Propulsion:	diesel; 10,700 bhp; 2 shafts
Speed:	17 knots
Gun battery:	2 4-inch/45-cal AA guns (1 twin) 16 2-pdr pom-pom (40-mm) AA guns (4 quad) 16 20-mm Oerlikon AA guns (8 twin)
Aircraft:	20
Catapults:	none
Elevators:	1 centerline
Complement:	640

These ships were laid down as refrigerated cargo ships; they were taken over during construction for conversion to aircraft carriers.

The NAIRANA was loaned to the Netherlands in 1946 (becoming the KAREL DOORMAN). She was returned to Britain in 1948 and sold for merchant service.

1 HELICOPTER TRAINING/TRANSPORT SHIP: CONVERTED MERCHANT SHIP

TYPE	NAME	BUILDER	STATUS	
—	ARGUS *ex-Contender Bezant*	CNR Breda, Venice	l. 1981 c. June 1, 1988	**active**

Displacement:	22,256 tonnes standard 28,480 tonnes full load
Dimensions:	574½ ft oa x 99¾ ft x 27 ft
Flight deck:	92 ft
Propulsion:	diesel; 23,400 bhp; 2 shafts
Speed:	22 knots
Gun battery:	4 30-mm AA guns
Aircraft:	12 helicopters
Catapults:	none
Elevators:	2 offset centerline
Complement:	250

Built as a combination roll-on/roll-off-container ship with a superstructure forward configuration. When the merchant ship *Contender Bezant* the ship was employed-with the *Atlantic Conveyor-as* a Harrier/helicopter transport during the Falklands conflict of 1982. Subsequently this ship was converted from 1984-1988 to a combination helicopter training/transport ship for naval operation.

The complement consists of 80 merchant mariners, 35 permanent Royal navy personnel, and the remainder aviation personnel embarked with helicopters.

The hangar is service by an elevator amidships, abaft the ship starboard-side funnel.

The Royal Fleet Auxiliary *Argus* enters Mayport, Florida, with several containers on her helicopter deck. Note the ship's unusual starboard-side amidships funnel. The helicopter training/transport ship was converted from a merchant ship that served as a Harrier/helicopter transport in the Falklands War. Below, several HM.1 Merlin helicopters operate from the *Argus*. Her after elevator is visible below the forward helicopter. Note the ship's unusual funnel arrangement. (Jared D. Wilson, U.S. Navy; Royal Navy)

INDIA

TYPE	NAME			STATUS
CVL	VIKRANT	ex-British HERCULES	c. Mar 4, 1961	str. 1997
CVL	VIRAAT	ex-British HERMES	c. May 12, 1987	**active**
CV	VIKRAMADITYA	ex-Russian ADMIRAL GORSHKOV	c. ~2013	conversion

The VIKRANT, decommissioned on January 31, 1997, is planned as a museum at Mumbai. She would be the only carrier serving as a museum outside of the United States.

Completion of the conversion of the ADMIRAL GORSHKOV/ VIKRAMADITYA at Russia's Sevmash shipyard has been delayed several years.

(1) AIRCRAFT CARRIER: "VIKRANT"

TYPE	NAME	BUILDER			STATUS
CV	VIKRANT	Cochin Shipyard, Kochi	l. `		building
			c.	~2013	

Displacement:	37,500 tonnes full load
Dimensions:	827½ ft oa x ...... x 27½ ft
Flight deck:	190¼ ft
Propulsion:	4 gas turbines; 108,000 shp; 2 shafts
Speed:	28 knots
Missile launchers:	Barak surface-to-air missiles in vertical launchers
Gun battery:	4 76-mm OTO Melara AA (4 single)
Aircraft:	approx. 30
Catapults:	none
Elevators:	2 deck edge
Complement:	approx. 1,800

The VIKRANT is designated as an Air Defense Ship (ADS). She will be the largest ship built in India. A ski-ramp will be fitted.

A second ship of this class is planned.

ITALY

AIRCRAFT CARRIER: CONVERTED LINER

TYPE	NAME	BUILDER	STATUS	
CV	AQUILA ex-*Roma*	Societa Anonima Ansaldo	l. Feb 26, 1926	sunk Apr 19, 1945 (scrapped)

Displacement:	23,350 tonnes standard
	27,600 tonnes full load
Tonnage:	32,583 tons gross
Dimensions:	680 ft oa x 96⁵/₁₂ ft x 24 ft
Flight deck:	83 ft
Propulsion:	steam turbines; 140,000 shp; 4 shafts
Boilers:	
Speed:	approx. 30 knots
Gun battery:	8 6—inch/55 cal DP (4 twin)
	12 3.5-inch/50 cal AA
	104 37-mm AA
Aircraft:	50
Catapults:	2 hydraulic
Elevators:	2 centerline
Complement:	1,400

In World War II the passenger liner *Roma* was taken in hand for conversion to a troop transport, but in March 1941 orders were given to complete her as an aircraft carrier. She was about 80 percent complete as a carrier at the time of the Italian capitulation in September 1943.

She was damaged by Allied bombings on June 16, 1944, and was sunk at Genoa by "human torpedoes" manned by Italian frogmen in 1945 to prevent the Germans from sinking her in the harbor channel. She was salvaged in 1946 and scrapped.

During her conversion to a carrier the AQUILA was re-fitted with the turbines of two unfinished light cruisers.

TYPE	NAME	BUILDER		STATUS
CV	SPARVIERO ex-FALCO ex-*Augustus*	Societa Anonima Ansaldo	l. Dec 13, 1926	scuttled Oct 5, 1944 (scrapped)

Displacement:
Tonnage: 32,650 tons gross
Dimensions: 664 ft oa x 82³/₄ ft x 30¹/₆ ft
Flight deck:
Propulsion: diesel engines; 28,000 bhp; 4 shafts
Speed: 19 knots
Gun battery: 6 6-inch/55 cal (3 twin)
                          4 4-inch AA (4 single)
Aircraft:
Catapults:
Elevators:
Complement:

The *Augustus* was a near sister of the *Roma* and was taken in hand in November 1942 for conversion to a carrier. She was incomplete when Italy surrendered in September 1943. The ship was scuttled by German troops at Genoa in September 1944, refloated in 1946, and scrapped.

Unlike the AQUILA, the SPARVIERO was not to have an island structure.

1 VSTOL AIRCRAFT CARRIER:

TYPE	NAME	BUILDER		STATUS
CVV	GIUSEPPE GARIBALDI	Fincantieri, Monfaleone	l. June 4, 1983 c. Sep 30, 1985	**active**

Displacement: 10,100 tonnes standard
                         13,850 tonnes full load
Dimensions: 591 ft oa (570 ft wl) x 78 ft x 26¹¹/₁₂ ft
Flight deck: 99³/₄ ft
Propulsion: 4 gas turbines; 80,000 shp; 2 shafts
Speed: 29.5 knots
Missile launchers: 2 Aspide launchers with 48 AA missiles
Gun battery: 6 40-mm/70-cal OTO Melara Dardo AA (3 twin)
Torpedo tubes: 6 12.75 inch (2 triple) for Mk 46 torpedoes
Aircraft: 18
Catapults: none
Elevators: 2 centerline
Complement: 825

The GARIBALDI is fitted with a ski-ramp forward; she has hull-mounted sonar.

1 VSTOL AIRCRAFT CARRIER: "CAVOUR"

TYPE	NAME	BUILDER		STATUS
CVV	CAVOUR	Fincantieri, La Spezia	l. July 20, 2004 c. 2007	**active**

Displacement:	22,130 tonnes standard
	26,500 tonnes full load
Dimensions:	768⅚ ft oa (707¹⁄₆ ft wl) x 96¾ ft x 26½ ft
Flight deck:	127¹¹⁄₁₂ ft
Propulsion:	4 gas turbines; 118,000 shp; 2 shafts
Speed:	28+ knots
Missile launchers:	4 Aster-15 launchers with 132 AA missiles
Gun battery:	2 40-mm/62-cal OTO Melara AA (2 single)
	3 25-mm/87-cal OTO Melara AA (3 single)
Torpedo tubes:	4 12.75-inch (fixed) for MU-90 torpedoes
Aircraft:	12
Catapults:	none
Elevators:	1 centerline, 1 deck edge
Complement:	850 + 360 troops

The CAVOUR has a ski-ramp; she is fitted with hull-mounted sonar.

2 HELICOPTER CARRIERS: "SAN GIORGIO" CLASS

TYPE	NAME	BUILDER		STATUS
LPD	SAN GIORGIO	Fincantieri, Riva Trigoso	l. Feb 25, 1987 c. Feb 13, 1988	**active**
LPD	SAN MARCO	Fincantieri, Riva Trigoso	l. Oct 21, 1987 c. May 6, 1989	**active**

Displacement:	6,687 tonnes standard
	7,665 tonnes full load
Dimensions:	437¼ ft oa (387 ft wl) x 67¼ ft x 17¼ ft
Flight deck:	
Propulsion:	2 diesel engines; 16,800 bhp; 2 shafts
Speed:	21 knots
Gun battery:	2 20-mm/70-cal Oerlikon AA (2 single)
Aircraft:	5 helicopters
Catapults:	none
Elevators:	1 centerline
Complement:	160 + 345 troops

These are large docking-well amphibious ships wuith a full flight deck and starboard island structure. The ships are configured for disaster relief as well as military functions.

They can accommodate three large (CH-47/SH-3D) or five light helicopters on their flight decks; the hangar deck is not normally used for aircraft.

1 AIRCRAFT CARRIER: "HOSHO"

TYPE	NAME	BUILDER		STATUS
CV	HOSHO	Asano SB	l. Nov 13, 1921 c. Dec 27, 1922	scrapped 1947

Displacement:	7,590 tonnes standard
	10,160 tonnes full load
Dimensions:	551½ ft oa (541⅓ ft wl) x 59¹/₁₂ x 20¼ ft
Flight deck:	70 ft
Propulsion:	steam turbines; 30,000 shp; 2 shafts
Boilers:	8
Speed:	25 knots
Gun battery:	4 5.5-inch guns (4 single)
Aircraft:	21
Catapults:	none
Elevators:	2 centerline
Complement:	550

The HOSHO was Japan's first aircraft carrier and after HMS HERMES the world's second ship designed from the outset for that role. A second ship of this design, to be named SHOKAKU, was proposed but not built.

The ship was constructed with a small starboard bridge structure; removed in 1923.

1 AIRCRAFT CARRIER: CONVERTED BATTLE CRUISER

TYPE	NAME	BUILDER		STATUS
CV	AKAGI	Kure NYd	l. Apr 22, 1925 c. Mar 25, 1927	sunk June 4, 1942

Displacement:	30,074 tonnes standard
	36,500 tonnes full load
Dimensions:	857 ft oa (816¾ ft wl) x 95 ft x 28½ ft
Flight deck:	100 ft
Propulsion:	steam turbines; 133,000 shp; 4 shafts
Boilers:	19
Speed:	32.5 knots
Gun battery:	10 8-inch (2 twin, 6 single)
	12 4.7-inch AA (6 twin)
	28 25-mm AA
Aircraft:	60
Catapults:	none
Elevators:	3 centerline
Complement:	1,600

This AKAGI was begun as a battle cruiser (ten 16-inch guns). As completed she had three flying-off decks forward. She was rebuilt in 1935-1936 and provided a full, flush-deck configuration. Her displacement was increased to 36,500 tonnes/42,700 tonnes.

She was sunk by U.S. carrier aircraft.

1 AIRCRAFT CARRIER: CONVERTED BATTLESHIP

TYPE	NAME	BUILDER		STATUS
CV	KAGA	Kawasaki-Kobe	l. Nov 17, 1921 c. Mar 31, 1928	sunk June 4, 1942

Displacement:	30,074 tonnes standard
	38,200 tonnes full load
Dimensions:	$812^{1}/_{3}$ ft ($754^{7}/_{12}$ ft wl) x 97 ft x 26 ft
Flight deck:	100 ft
Propulsion:	steam turbines; 91,000 shp; 4 shafts
Boilers:	12
Speed:	27.5 knots
Gun battery:	10 8-inch (2 single, 6 single)
	12 4.7-inch AA (6 twin)
Aircraft:	90
Catapults:	none
Elevators:	2 centerline
Complement:	1,340

The KAGA replaced the AMAGI for conversion to an aircraft carrier after the latter ship was severely damaged in the earthquake of 1923. The KAGA was begun as a battleship (ten 16-inch guns); conversion to a carrier began in 1924. She became operational in 1930 with three flying-off decks, as the AKAGI. The KAGA was extensively rebuilt in 1935, being fitted with a full, flush-deck configuration. Her displacement was increased to 38,200 tonnes/43,650 tonnes.

She was sunk by U.S. carrier aircraft.

1 AIRCRAFT CARRIER: "RYUJO"

TYPE	NAME	BUILDER		STATUS
CV	RYUJO	Yokosuka NYd	l. Apr 2, 1931 c. May 9, 1933	sunk Aug 24, 1942

Displacement:	8,128 tonnes standard
	10,600 tonnes full load
Dimensions:	$590^{1}/_{4}$ ft oa ($575^{5}/_{12}$ ft wl) x $66^{2}/_{3}$ ft x $18^{1}/_{4}$ ft
Fight deck:	$75^{1}/_{2}$ ft
Propulsion:	steam turbines; 66,269 shp; 2 shafts
Boilers:	6
Speed:	29 knots
Gun battery:	12 5-inch AA (6 twin)
Aircraft:	48
Catapults:	none
Elevators:	2 centerline
Complement:	600

The RYUJO was sunk by U.S. carrier aircraft.

2 AIRCRAFT CARRIERS: "SORYU" CLASS

TYPE	NAME	BUILDER		STATUS
CV	SORYU	Kure NYd	l. Dec 23, 1935 c. Jan 29, 1937	sunk June 4, 1942
CV	HIRYU	Yokosuka NYd	l. Nov 16, 1937 c. July 5, 1939	sunk June 5, 1942

Displacement:	16,154 tonnes standard
	20,117 tonnes full load
Dimensions:	746^5/$_{12}$ ft oa (728^1/$_3$ ft wl) x 69^{11}/$_{12}$ ft x 25 ft
Flight deck:	85^1/$_2$ ft
Propulsion:	steam turbines; 152,000 shp; 4 shafts
Boilers:	8
Speed:	34.5 knots
Gun battery:	12 5-inch DP (6 twin)
	several 25-mm AA (triple and twin)
Aircraft:	70
Catapults:	none
Elevators:	3 centerline
Complement:	1,100

Both ships were sunk by U.S. carrier aircraft.

2 AIRCRAFT CARRIERS: "SHOKAKU" CLASS

TYPE	NAME	BUILDER		STATUS
CV	SHOKAKU	Yokosuka NYd	l. June 1, 1939 c. Aug 8, 1941	sunk June 19, 1944
CV	ZUIKAKU	Kawasaki-Kobe	l. Nov 27, 1939 c. Sep 25, 1941	sunk Oct 25, 1944

Displacement:	25,675 tonnes standard
	32,619 tonnes full load
Dimensions:	844^5/$_6$ ft oa (820^1/$_4$ ft wl) x 85^1/$_3$ ft x 29 ft
Flight deck:	95 ft
Propulsion:	steam turbines; 160,000 shp; 4 shafts
Boilers:	8
Speed:	34.25 knots
Gun battery:	16 5-inch/40-cal DP (8 twin)
	36 or 48 25-mm AA (12 or 16 triple)
Aircraft:	84
Catapults:	none
Elevators:	3 centerline
Complement:	1,660

These ships were the equivalent of the U.S. ESSEX (CV 9) class. The SHOKAKU was sunk by a U.S. submarine and the ZUIKAKU by U.S. carrier aircraft.

1 LIGHT AIRCRAFT CARRIER: CONVERTED SUBMARINE TENDER

TYPE	NAME	BUILDER		STATUS
CVL	RYUHO ex-TAIGEI	Yokosuka NYd	l. Nov 16, 1933 c. Nov 28, 1942	scrapped 1946

Displacement:	13,574 tonnes standard 16,764 tonnes full load
Dimensions:	$707^1/_3$ ft oa (689 ft wl) x $64^1/_4$ ft x $21^3/_4$ ft
Flight deck:	$75^1/_2$ ft
Propulsion:	steam turbines; 52,000 shp; 2 shafts
Boilers:	4
Speed:	26.5 knots
Gun battery:	8 5-inch/40-cal DP (4 twin) 38 25-mm AA (12 triple, 2 single)
Aircraft:	31
Catapults:	none
Elevators:	2 centerline
Complement:	990

The TAIGEI was similar to the later submarine tenders converted to the carriers SHOHO and ZUIHO. All of these ships were designed from the outset for conversion to fast oilers or aircraft carriers.

The TAIGEI was completed as a submarine tender in 1934; she was taken in hand in December 1941 for conversion to an aircraft carrier, being renamed RYUHO. As built the ship had diesel engines; they were replaced by steam turbines during her conversion to a CVL.

The RYUHO was severely damaged by U.S. bombing at Kure on March 19, 1945. Most of her upper decks were burned out and she was inoperational.

2 LIGHT AIRCRAFT CARRIERS: CONVERTED SUBMARINE TENDERS

TYPE	NAME	BUILDER		STATUS
CVL	SHOHO ex-TSURUGIZAKI	Yokosuka NYd	l. June 1, 1935 c. Jan 26, 1942	sunk May 8, 1942
CVL	ZUIHO ex-TAKASAKI	Yokosuka NYd	l. June 19, 1936 c. Dec 27, 1940	sunk Oct 25, 1944

Displacement:	11,442 tonnes standard 14,427 tonnes full load
Dimensions:	$674^1/_4$ ft oa ($660^{11}/_{12}$ ft wl) x $59^3/_4$ ft x $21^7/_{12}$ ft
Flight deck:	$75^1/_2$ ft
Propulsion:	steam turbines; 52,000 shp; 2 shafts
Boilers:	4
Speed:	28 knots
Gun battery:	8 5-inch DP (4 twin) 61 25-mm AA (10 triple, 4 twin, 23 single)
Aircraft:	30
Catapults:	none
Elevators:	2 centerline
Complement:	785

The TSURUGIZAKI was completed in 1939 as a submarine tender. In January 1941 she began conversion to an aircraft carrier, being renamed SHOHO.

The TAKASAKI was under construction when the decision as made in January 1940 to complete her as a carrier.

As built these ships had diesel engines; they were replaced by steam turbines during their conversion to CVLs. Both of these carriers were sunk by U.S. carrier aircraft.

2 LIGHT AIRCRAFT CARRIERS: CONVERTED MERCHANT SHIPS

TYPE	NAME	BUILDER		STATUS
CVL	HIYO ex-*Izumo Maru*	Kawasaki-Kobe	l. June 24, 1941 c. July 31, 1942	sunk June 20, 1944
CVL	JUNYO ex-*Kashiwara Maru*	Mitsubishi-Nagasaki	l. June 26, 1941 c. May 5, 1942	scrapped 1947

Displacement:	24,526 tonnes standard 29,464 tonnes full load
Dimensions:	719$^{1}/_{2}$ ft oa (706$^{1}/_{3}$ ft wl) x 87$^{7}/_{12}$ x 26$^{3}/_{4}$ ft
Flight deck:	89$^{1}/_{2}$ ft
Propulsion:	steam turbines; 56,250 shp; 2 shafts
Boilers:	6
Speed:	25.5 knots
Gun battery:	12 5-inch DP (6 twin) 76 20-mm AA (15 triple, 2 twin, 27 single) 6 120-mm multiple AA rocket launchers
Aircraft:	53
Catapults:	none
Elevators:	2 centerline
Complement:	1,200

These ships were taken over by the Navy while under construction as passenger liners and were completed as aircraft carriers.

The HIYO was sunk by U.S. carrier aircraft.

2 LIGHT AIRCRAFT CARRIERS: CONVERTED SEAPLANE TENDERS

TYPE	NAME	BUILDER		STATUS
CVL	CHITOSE	Kure NYd	l. Nov 29, 1936 c. Jan 1, 1944	sunk Oct 25, 1944
CVL	CHIYODA	Kure NYd	l. Nov 19, 1937 c. Oct 31, 1943	sunk Oct 25, 1944

Displacement:	11,190 tonnes standard 15,300 tonnes full load
Dimensions:	631$^{7}/_{12}$ ft oa (610 ft wl) x 61$^{2}/_{3}$ ft x 24$^{2}/_{3}$ ft
Flight deck:	75 ft
Propulsion:	steam turbines/diesels; 44,000 shp/12,800 bhp; 2 shafts
Boilers:	4
Speed:	29 knots
Gun battery:	8 5-inch/40-cal DP (4 twin) 30 25-mm AA (10 triple)
Aircraft:	30
Catapults:	none
Elevators:	2 centerline
Complement:	800

These ships were built as seaplane tenders, both being completed in 1938. They had a hybrid turbine-diesel propulsion plant.

In 1941 they were modified to additionally carry and launch midget submarines with a stern ramp being fitted (12 midgets carried). Like the SHOHO-class CVLs, these ships were designed from the outset for conversion to aircraft carriers. The conversion of the CHIYODA began in December 1942 and on the CHITOSE in January 1943.

Both ships were sunk by U.S. carrier-based aircraft.

1 AIRCRAFT CARRIER: "TAIHO"

TYPE	NAME	BUILDER		STATUS
CV	TAIHO	Kaswasaki-Kobe	l. Apr 7, 1943 c. Mar 7, 1944	sunk June 19, 1944

Displacement:	29,769 tonnes standard
	37,866 tonnes full load
Dimensions:	855 ft oa (830$^1/_{12}$ ft wl) x 90$^{11}/_{12}$ ft x 31$^1/_2$ ft
Flight deck:	98$^1/_2$ ft
Propulsion:	steam turbines; 160,000 shp; 4 shafts
Boilers:	8
Speed:	33.33 knots
Gun battery:	12 3.9-inch AA (6 twin)
	51 25-mm AA (17 triple)
Aircraft:	60
Catapults:	none
Elevators:	2 centerline
Complement:	1,750

This was the largest built-for-the-purpose carrier constructed in Japan and represented a relatively advanced design. The TAIHO was to have been the lead ship of a class of at least six carriers; five others were ordered under the 1942 modified shipbuilding program. The later ships were to have been completed in 1947-1948, but were cancelled (see Volume I, page 264).

A U.S. submarine sank the TAIHO.

1 LARGE AIRCRAFT CARRIER: CONVERTED BATTLESHIP

TYPE	NAME	BUILDER		STATUS
CVB	SHINANO	Yokosuka NYd	l. Oct 8, 1944 c. Nov 1944	sunk Nov 29, 1944

Displacement:	62,000 tonnes standard
	73,040 tonnes full load
Dimensions:	872$^2/_3$ ft oa (839$^{11}/_{12}$ ft wl) x 119$^1/_{12}$ ft x 33$^5/_6$ ft
Flight deck:	131 ft
Propulsion:	steam turbines; 150,000 shp; 4 shafts
Boilers:	12
Speed:	27 knots
Gun battery:	16 5-inch/430-cal DP (8 twin)
	145 25-mm AA (35 triple, 40 single)
	12 120-mm multiple AA rocket launchers
Aircraft:	47
Catapults:	none
Elevators:	2 centerline
Complement:	2,400

The SHINANO was the world's largest aircraft carrier to be completed until completion of the USS FORRESTAL (CVA 59) in 1955. The SHINANO had been laid down on April 7, 1940, as the third ship of the YAMATO class.

Following the Battle of Midway she was ordered to be completed as an aircraft carrier.

The ship was intended to rearm, refuel, and repair aircraft flying from land bases and other carriers, hence her small assignment. She could have accommodated some 120 aircraft based on her hangar size.

The SHINANO was sunk by a U.S. submarine before becoming operational.

2 AIRCRAFT CARRIERS: "UNRYU" CLASS

TYPE	NAME	BUILDER		STATUS
CV	UNRYU	Yokosuka NYd	l. Sep 25, 1943 c. Aug 6, 1944	sunk Dec 19, 1944
CV	AMAGI	Mitsubishi-Nagasaki	l. Oct 15, 1943 c. Aug 10, 1944	sunk July 24,1945
CV	KATSURAGI*	Kure NYd	l. Jan 19, 1944	cancelled
CV	KASAGI	Mitsubishi-Nagasaki	l. Oct 19, 1944	cancelled
CV	ASO*	Kure NYd	l. Nov 1, 1944	cancelled
CV	IKOMA	Kawasaki-Kobe	l. Nov 17, 1944	cancelled

Displacement:	17,424 tonnes standard 22,860 tonnes full load
Dimensions:	$745^{11}/_{12}$ ft oa ($731^2/_3$ ft wl) x $72^1/_6$ ft x $25^3/_4$ ft
Propulsion:	steam turbines; 152,000 ship (* 104,000 shp); 4 shafts
Boilers:	8
Speed:	34 knots (* 32 knots)
Gun battery:	12 5-inch/40-cal DP (6 twin) 51 25-mm AA (17 triple) 6 120-mm multiple AA rocket launchers
Aircraft:	65
Catapults:	none
Elevators:	2 centerline
Complement:	1,600

This design was a modification of the SORYU class. A total of 16 ships of this class were planned; 11 additional ships were to be completed from 1945 to 1948. Those ships, ordered under the 1942 modified program, were never laid down and were cancelled (see Volume I, page 264).

The ASO and KATSURAGI had destroyer-type turbines.

The AMAGI was sunk by U.S. aircraft while at Kure and the UNRYU by a U.S. submarine.

LIGHT AIRCRAFT CARRIER: CONVERTED HEAVY CRUISER

TYPE	NAME	BUILDER		STATUS
CVL	IBUKI	Kure NYd	l. May 25, 1943	scrapped 1947

Displacement:	14,800 tonnes standard
Dimensions:	($650^7/_8$ ft wl) x $69^1/_2$ ft x $20^2/_3$ ft
Propulsion:	steam turbines; 72,000 shp; 2 shafts
Boilers:	4
Speed:	29 knots
Gun battery:	4 3.9-inch AA (2 twin) 48 20-mm AA (16 triple) 4 120-mm multiple AA rocket launchers
Aircraft:	27
Catapults:	none
Elevators:	2 centerline
Complement:	1,015

The IBUKI was laid down on April 24, 1942, as a SUZUYA-class heavy cruiser (ten 8-inch guns). Her planned role was changed several times during construction as build-ing programs and shipyard priorities were con-tinually being revised. At one point consideration was given to completing her as a high-speed replenish-ment tanker.

Her unfinished hull was moored at Kure until the decision was made in October 1943 to complete her as a CVL. The IBUKI was towed to Sasebo late in November and work continued on her until March 1945. She was about 80 percent complete when construction was halted because of priorities being given to small submarines.

3 ESCORT CARRIERS: CONVERTED MERCHANT SHIPS

TYPE	NAME	BUILDER		STATUS
CVE	CHUYO ex-*Nitta Maru*	Mitsubishi-Nagasaki	l. May 20, 1939 c. Nov 25, 1942	sunk Dec 4, 1943
CVE	UNYO ex-*Yawata Maru*	Mitsubishi-Nagasaki	l. Oct 31, 1939 c. May 31, 1942	sunk Sep 16, 1944
CVE	TAIYO ex-*Kasuga Maru*	Mitsubishi-Nagasaki	l. Sep 19, 1940 c. Sep 15, 1941	sunk Aug 18, 1944

Displacement:	18,115 tonnes standard
Dimensions:	$591^1/_3$ ft oa ($569^{11}/_{12}$ ft wl) x $73^5/_6$ ft x $25^5/_{12}$ ft
Flight deck:	$75^1/_2$ ft
Propulsion:	steam turbines; 25,200 shp; 2 shafts
Boilers:	4
Speed:	21 knots
Gun battery:	6 4.7-inch AA (2 twin, 2 single) 8 25-mm AA (4 twin)
Aircraft:	27
Catapults:	none
Elevators:	2 centerline
Complement:	750

These were the first Japanese aircraft carriers converted from passenger liners. The conversions took about six months per ship.

All three carriers of this class were sunk by U.S. submarines.

1 ESCORT CARRIER: CONVERTED MERCHANT SHIP

TYPE	NAME	BUILDER		STATUS
CVE	KAIYO ex-*Argentina Maru*	Mitsubishi-Nagasaki	l. Dec 9, 1938 c. Nov 23, 1943	scrapped 1946

Displacement:	13,818 tonnes standard 16,748 tonnes full load
Dimensions:	$546^5/_{12}$ ft oa ($523^7/_{12}$ ft wl) x $71^5/_6$ ft x 27 ft
Flight deck:	72 ft
Propulsion:	steam turbines; 52,510 shp; 2 shafts
Boilers:	4
Speed:	23.8 knots
Gun battery:	8 5-inch/40-cal DP (4 twin) 24 20-mm AA (8 triple)
Aircraft:	24
Catapults:	none
Elevators:	2 centerline
Complement:	830

The *Argentina Maru* was completed as a luxury passenger liner; she was converted to an escort carrier beginning in December 1942. During conversion her diesel engines were replaced by destroyer-type steam turbines. She was severely damaged by U.S. aircraft while at Beppu and sank in shallow water on July 24, 1945.

Her sister ship *Brazil Maru* was planned for a similar conversion, but was sunk while being used as a transport.

1 ESCORT CARRIER: CONVERTED MERCHANT SHIP

TYPE	NAME	BUILDER		STATUS
CVE	SHINYO ex-*Scharnhorst*	A.G. Weser-Bremen	l. Dec 14, 1934 c. Dec 15, 1943	sunk Nov 17, 1944

Displacement:	17,780 tonnes standard
Dimensions:	621$^1/_4$ ft oa (606$^{11}/_{12}$ ft) x 84 ft x 26$^3/_4$ ft
Flight deck:	80 ft
Propulsion:	steam turbines; 26,000 shp; 2 shafts
Boilers:	4
Speed:	22 knots
Gun battery:	8 5-inch/40-cal DP (4 twin)
	30 25-mm AA (10 triple)
Aircraft:	33
Catapults:	none
Elevators:	2 centerline
Complement:	940

The SHINYO was a former German passenger liner, taken in hand in September 1942 at the Kure Navy Yard for conversion to a carrier. The steel used in her conversion was from unfinished hull No. 111, the fourth battleship of the YAMATO class.

She was sunk by a U.S. submarine.

2 ESCORT CARRIERS: CONVERTED NAVAL OILERS

TYPE	NAME	BUILDER		STATUS
CVE	SHIMANE MARU	Kawasaki-Kobe	l. Dec 17, 1944 c. Feb 28, 1945	sunk July 24,1945
CVE	OTAKISAN MARU	Kawasaki-Kobe	l. Jan 14, 1945	sunk Aug 25, 1945

Displacement:	11,989 tonnes standard
Dimensions:	526$^7/_{12}$ ft oa (502 ft wl) x 65$^7/_{12}$ ft x 29$^5/_6$ ft
Flight deck:	75$^1/_2$ ft
Propulsion:	steam turbines; 8,600 shp; 1 shaft
Boilers:	2
Speed:	18.5 knots
Gun battery:	2 4.7-inch AA (2 single)
	52 25-mm AA (8 triple, 28 single)
Aircraft:	12
Catapults:	none
Elevators:	1 centerline
Complement:	

Two additional naval oilers were scheduled to have been converted to escort carriers, but the conversions were not begun and the project was cancelled in early 1945. Depth charges were carried.

The SHIMANE MARU was sunk by U.S. carrier aircraft at Kure; the OTAKISAN MARU was sunk by a mine off Kobe harbor.

ESCORT CARRIERS: CONVERTED OILERS

TYPE	NAME	BUILDER		STATUS
CVE	YAMASHIO MARU	Mitsubishi-Yokohama	l. Nov 14, 1944 Feb 17, 1945	unfinished; sunk (scrapped)
CVE	CHIGUSA MARU	Yokohama Dock	l. Dec 29, 1944	completed as cargo ship 1949

Displacement:	22,048 tonnes full load
Dimensions:	$516^{1}/_{3}$ ft oa ($485^{1}/_{3}$ ft wl) x $66^{11}/_{12}$ ft x $29^{1}/_{2}$ ft
Flight deck:	$75^{1}/_{2}$ ft
Propulsion:	steam turbine; 5,000 shp; 1 shaft
Boilers:	2
Speed:	15 knots
Gun battery:	16 25-mm AA (8 twin)
Aircraft:	8
Catapults:	none
Elevators:	none
Complement:	220

These ships were under construction as tankers when they were chartered by the Japanese Army for conversion to aircraft carriers similar to the SHIMANE MARU. They were not fitted with hangars or elevators.

Work on the CHIGUSA MARU ceased in the spring of 1945. Work was resumed after the war and she was completed as a cargo ship.

When the YAMASHIO was almost completed the decision was made to convert her to a coal-burning cargo ship. She was sunk before completion in an air raid on Yokohama and scrapped after the war.

HELICOPTER—MISSILE DESTROYERS: "HUYGA" CLASS

NO.	NAME	BUILDER		STATUS
DDH 16	HUYGA	Marine United	l. Aug 23, 2007 c. 2009	building
DDH 17	......	Marine United	l. c. 2011	building

Displacement:	13,500 tonnes standard 18,000 tonnes full load
Dimensions:	$639^{7}/_{12}$ ft oa x 105 ft x 23 ft
Flight deck:	105 ft
Propulsion:	4 gas turbines; 120,000 shp; 2 shafts
Speed:	30 knots
Missile Launchers:	64 vertical launch cells for Enhanced Sea Sparrow AA missiles
Gun battery:	2 20-mm Phalanx multibarrel CIWS (2 single)
Torpedo tubes:	6 12.75 inch (2 triple) for Type 73 or Mk 46 torpedoes
Aircraft:	11 helicopters
Catapults:	none
Elevators:	2 centerline
Complement:	345

The HUYGA is a helicopter-carrying destroyer, combining an extensive helicopter capability with an Aegis-type air defense system and other weapon capabilities. The vertical-launch cells can also fire the ASROC anti-submarine weapon (but not the U.S. Standard or Tomahawk missiles). A sonar is installed for the ASW role.

The initial "air group" for these ships is three SH-60J Seahawk and one MH-53E Super Stallion helicopters. Eleven H-60 series helicopters can be stowed in the hangar deck.

A class of four ships was planned when this volume went to press.

NETHERLANDS

TYPE	NAME		STATUS
CVE	KAREL DOORMAN (I) ex-British NAIRANA	c. 1946	str. 1948 (merchant)
CVL	KAREL DOORMAN (II) ex-British VENERABLE	c. May 28, 1948	to Argentina 1969

SPAIN

TYPE	NAME		STATUS
CVL	DÉDALO ex-U.S. CABOT (CVL 28)	c. Aug 30, 1967	str. 1989 (scrapped)

The CABOT was converted during construction from a light cruiser, originally commissioned as an aircraft carrier in July 1943.

1 AIRCRAFT CARRIER: SEA CONTROL SHIP

TYPE	NAME	BUILDER		STATUS
SCS	PRINCIPE DE ASTURIAS ex-CANARIAS ex-ALMIRANTE CARRERO	Bazán shipyard, Ferrol	l. May 25, 1982 c. May 30, 1988	**active**

Displacement:	15,912 tonnes standard
	17,188 tonnes full load
Dimensions:	$639^{11}/_{12}$ ft oa (615 ft wl) x 80 ft x 22 ft
Flight deck:	$98^5/_{12}$ ft
Propulsion:	2 gas turbines; 46,400 shp; 1 shaft
Speed:	26 knots
Gun battery:	4 20-mm Meroka multibarrel CIWS
Aircraft:	24
Catapults:	none
Elevators:	1 offset centerline, 1 deck edge
Complement:	755

The PRINCIPE DE ASTURIAS design is based on the U.S. Navy's Sea Control Ship (SCS). The ship has a ski-jump forward. She normally carries two LCVP-type landing craft.

1 AMPHIBIOUS ASSAULT SHIP: "JUAN CARLOS I"

TYPE	NAME	BUILDER		STATUS
LHD	JUAN CARLOS I	Navantia, Ferrol	l. 2007 c. 2009	building

Displacement:	27,000 tonnes full load
Dimensions:	757 ft oa x 105 ft x 25¼ ft
Flight deck:	
Propulsion:	2 gas turbines + diesel-electric; 2 shafts
Speed:	21.5 knots
Missile launchers:	point-defense system
Gun battery:	4 20-mm Oerlikon multibarrel CIWS
Aircraft:	12
Catapults:	none
Elevators:	1 deck edge, 1 stern
Complement:	

Designated as a "strategic projection ship," the JUAN CARLOS I will have a starboard-side island structure and a ski-jump. The ship will have a docking well for one LCAC-type air cushion vehicle or four LCM(8) landing craft.

She will be the largest warship to be constructed in Spain.

THAILAND

1 AIRCRAFT CARRIER: SEA CONTROL SHIP

TYPE	NAME	BUILDER		STATUS
SCS	CHAKRI NARUEBET	Izar (Bazan), Ferrol	l. Jan 20, 1996 c. Aug 10, 1997	**active**

Displacement:	11,486 tonnes full load
Dimensions:	599$^1/_{12}$ ft oa (538$^1/_4$ ft wl) x 73$^5/_6$ ft x 20$^1/_{12}$ ft
Flight deck:	100 ft
Propulsion:	2 gas turbines + diesels; 44,250 shp/11,200 bhp; 2 shafts
Speed:	27.5 knots (17 knots on diesels)
Missile launchers:	3 Sadral launchers with 18 AA missiles
Gun battery:	2 20-mm AA (2 single)
Aircraft:	18
Catapults:	none
Elevators:	1 offset centerline, 1 deck edge
Complement:	600 + 675 troops

The CHAKRI NARUEBET is a multi-purpose ship, based on the U.S. Navy's Sea Control Ship (SCS). She has a ski-jump forward.

UNITED STATES

World War II-built carriers have their maximum approved armament listed; some ships were completed with only partial armament in the early years of the conflict.

1 AIRCRAFT CARRIER: CONVERTED COLLIER

TYPE	NAME	BUILDER		STATUS
CV 1	LANGLEY ex-AC 3 JUPITER	Mare Island NYd	l. Aug 24, 1912 c. Mar 20, 1922	to AV 3 1937

Displacement:	12,700 tons standard
Dimensions:	542 ft oa (520 ft wl) x 65 ft x 18⁵/₆ ft
Flight deck:	64 ft
Propulsion:	turbo-electric drive; 7,150 hp; 2 shafts
Boilers:	3
Speed:	15 knots
Gun battery:	4 5-inch/51-cal (4 single)
Aircraft:	42
Catapults:	1 flywheel
Elevators:	1 centerline
Complement:	468

The LANGLEY was converted in 1920-1922 from the naval collier JUPITER, which was originally commissioned in 1913. She was converted to a seaplane tender (AV 3) in 1937, and was sunk in that configuration by Japanese land-based aircraft on February 27, 1942.

2 AIRCRAFT CARRIERS: CONVERTED BATTLE CRUISERS

TYPE	NAME	BUILDER		STATUS
CV 2	LEXINGTON ex-CC 1	Fore River	l. Oct 3, 1925 c. Dec 14, 1927	sunk May 8, 1942
CV 3	SARATOGA ex-CC 3	New York SB	l. Apr 7, 1925 c. Nov 16, 1927	sunk July 25, 1946

Displacement:	33,000 tons standard 41,000 tons full load
Dimensions:	888 ft oa (850 ft wl) x 106 ft x 24¹/₆ ft
Flight deck:	90 ft
Propulsion:	steam turbines; 180,000 shp; 4 shafts
Boilers:	16
Speed:	33.9 knots
Gun battery:	8 8-inch/55-cal (4 twin) 12 5-inch/25-cal AA (12 single)
Aircraft:	80+ (space for 120)
Catapults:	1 flywheel
Elevators:	2 centerline
Complement:	2,120

These were the world's largest aircraft carriers until the U.S. MIDWAY-class large carriers completed 1945-1947 except for the Japanese SHINANO. Under the terms of the Washington Naval Treaty (1922) the "Lex" and "Sara" were converted during construction as battle cruisers (to be armed with eight 16-inch guns); their conversion to carriers was authorized on July 1, 1922. They had been laid down as battle cruisers in 1921 and 1920, respectively. Four unfinished sister ships were scrapped on the building ways.

The LEXINGTON and SARATOGA were technically in violation of the Washington Naval Treaty provision that carriers be restricted to no more than 33,000 tons. Both ships displaced 36,000 tons standard, but a technical loophole in the treaty allowed for an additional 3,000 ton of weight for armor to protect against air attack.

The LEXINGTON achieved 34.5 knots in service (with 210,000 shp) and the SARATOGA reached 33.91 knots.

The 8-inch guns were removed in 1942 and installed as coastal defense guns on Oahu. The SARATOGA had eight 5-inch/38 guns in twin mounts installed in their place.

The LEXINGTON was sunk by Japanese carrier aircraft; the SARATOGA was sunk in the Bikini atomic bomb tests.

1 AIRCRAFT CARRIER: "RANGER"

NO.	NAME	BUILDER		STATUS
CV 4	RANGER	Newport News	l. Feb 25, 1933 c. June 4, 1934	decomm. 1946; str. 1947 (scrapped)

Displacement:	14,500 tons standard 20,500 tons full load
Dimensions:	769 ft (730 ft wl) x 80$^{1}/_{12}$ ft x 19$^{2}/_{3}$ ft
Flight deck:	86 ft
Propulsion:	steam turbines; 53,500 shp; 2 shafts
Boilers:	6
Speed:	29.25 knots
Gun battery:	8 5-inch/25-cal AA (8 single)
Aircraft:	80+
Catapults:	none
Elevators:	3 centerline
Complement:	1,435

The RANGER was the U.S. Navy's first built-for-the-purpose aircraft carrier.

3 AIRCRAFT CARRIERS: "YORKTOWN" CLASS

NO.	NAME	BUILDER		STATUS
CV 5	YORKTOWN	Newport News	1. Apr 4, 1936 c. Sep 30, 1937	sunk June 7, 1942
CV 6	ENTERPRISE	Newport News	1. Oct 3, 1936 c. May 12, 1938	to CVA 1952 to CVS 1953 decomm. 1947; str. 1958 (scrapped)
CV 8	HORNET	Newport News	1. Dec 14, 1940 c. Oct 20, 1941	sunk Oct 26, 1942

Displacement:	19,900 tons standard 25,500 tons full load
Dimensions:	809$^{1}/_{2}$ ft (770 ft wl) x 83$^{1}/_{4}$ ft x 21$^{2}/_{3}$ ft
Flight deck:	86 ft
Propulsion:	steam turbines; 120,000 shp; 4 shafts
Boilers:	9
Speed:	33.6 knots

Gun battery:		8 5-inch/38-cal DP (8 single)		
Aircraft:		80+		
Catapults:		2 hydraulic		
Elevators:		3 centerline		
Complement:		1,800		

The HORNET was completed to a slightly modified design. These ships had a hangar-deck catapult; removed from all ships in 1942.

The YORKTOWN, heavy damaged by Japanese carrier aircraft at the Battle of Midway, was then sunk by a Japanese submarine. The HORNET was sunk by Japanese carrier aircraft.

1 AIRCRAFT CARRIER: "WASP"

NO.	NAME	BUILDER		STATUS
CV 7	WASP	Bethlehem-Quincy	l. Apr 4, 1939 c. Apr 25, 1940	sunk Sep 15, 1942

Displacement:	14,700 tons standard
	18,500 tons full load
Dimensions:	769 ft (688 ft wl) x 80¾ ft x 20 ft
Flight deck:	93 ft
Propulsion:	steam turbines; 75,000 shp; 2 shafts
Boilers:	6
Speed:	29.5 knots
Gun battery:	8 5-inch/38 DP (8 single)
Aircraft:	80+
Catapults:	2 hydraulic
Elevators:	2 centerline (see text)
Complement:	1,890

The ship was built with a hangar-deck catapult; removed in 1942. The WASP also had a deck-edge aircraft lift device (see Volume I, pages 75–76). The WASP was sunk by a Japanese submarine.

23 AIRCRAFT CARRIERS: "ESSEX" CLASS

NO.		NAME	BUILDER		STATUS
CV	9	ESSEX	Newport News	l. July 31, 1942 c. Dec 31, 1942	to CVA 1952 to CVS 1960 decomm. 1969; str. 1973 (scrapped)
CV	10	YORKTOWN ex-BON HOMME RICHARD	Newport News	l. Jan 21, 1943 c. Apr 15, 1943	to CVA 1952 to CVS 1957 decomm. 1970; str. 1973 (museum)
CV	11	INTREPID	Newport News	l. Apr 26, 1943 c. Aug 16, 1943	to CVA 1952 to CVS 1962 decomm. 1974; str. 1982 (museum)
CV	12	HORNET ex-KEARSARGE	Newport News	l. Aug 30, 1943 c. Nov 29, 1943	to CVA 1952 to CVS 1958 decomm. 1970; str. 1989 (scrapped)

NO.		NAME	BUILDER		STATUS
CV	13	FRANKLIN	Newport News	l. Oct 14, 1943 c. Jan 31, 1944	to CVA 1952 to CVS 1953 decomm. 1947; str. 1964 (scrapped)
CV	14	TICONDEROGA ex-HANCOCK	Newport News	l. Feb 7, 1944 c. May 8, 1944	to CVA 1952 to CVS 1969 decomm. 1973; str. 1973 (scrapped)
CV	15	RANDOLPH	Newport News	l. June 29, 1944 c. Oct 9, 1944	to CVA 1952 to CVS 1959 decomm. 1969; str. 1973 (scrapped)
CV	16	LEXINGTON ex-CABOT	Beth-Quincy	l. Sep 26, 1942 c. Mar 17, 1943	to CVA 1952 to CVS 1962 to CVT 1969 to AVT 1978 decomm./str. 1991 (scrapped)
CV	17	BUNKER HILL	Beth-Quincy	l. Dec 7, 1942 c. May 24, 1943	to CVA 1952 to CVS 1953 decomm. 1947; str. 1966 (scrapped)
CV	18	WASP ex-ORISKANY	Beth-Quincy	l. Aug 17, 1943 c. Nov 24, 1943	to CVA 1952 to CVS 1956 decomm./str. 1972 (scrapped)
CV	19	HANCOCK ex-TICONDEROGA	Beth-Quincy	l. Jan 24, 1944 c. Apr 15, 1944	to CVA 1952 to CV 1975 decomm./str. 1976 (scrapped)
CV	20	BENNINGTON	New York NYd	l. Feb 26, 1944 c. Aug 6, 1944	to CVA 1952 to CVS 1959 decomm. 1970; str. 1989 (scrapped)
CV	21	BOXER	New York SB	l. Dec 14, 1944 c. Apr 16, 1945	to CVA 1952 to CVS 1956 to LPH 4 1959
CV	31	BON HOMME RICHARD	New York NYd	l. Apr 29, 1944 c. Nov 26, 1944	to CVA 1952 decomm. 1971; str. 1989 (scrapped)
CV	32	LEYTE ex-CROWN POINT	Newport News	l. Aug 23, 1945 c. Apr 11, 1946	to CVA 1952 to CVS 1953 decomm. 1959 to AVT 10 1959 str. 1969 (scrapped)
CV	33	KEARSARGE	New York NYd	l. May 5, 1945 c. Mar 2, 1946	to CVA 1952 to CVS 1958 decomm. 1970; str. 1973 (scrapped)
CV	35	REPRISAL	New York NYd	l. Feb 1946	cancelled (scrapped)

NO.		NAME	BUILDER		STATUS
CV	36	ANTIETAM	Philadelphia NYd	l. Aug 20, 1944 c. Jan 28, 1945	to CVA 1952 to CVS 1953 decomm. 1963; str. 1973 (scrapped)
CV	37	PRINCETON cx-VALLEY FORGE	Philadelphia NYd	l. July 8, 1945 c. Nov 18, 1945	to CVA 1952 to CVS 1954 to LPH 5 1959
CV	38	SHANGRI-LA	Norfolk NYd	l. Feb 24, 1944 c. Sep 15, 1944	to CVA 1952 to CVS 1969 str. 1971; str. 1982 (scrapped)
CV	39	LAKE CHAMPLAIN	Norfolk NYd	l. Nov 2, 1944 c. June 3, 1945	to CVA 1952 to CVS 1957 decomm. 1966; str. 1969 (scrapped)
CV	40	TARAWA	Norfolk NYd	l. May 12, 1944 c. Dec 8, 1945	to CVA 1952 to CVS 1955 to AVT 12 1961 decomm. 1960; str. 1967 (scrapped)
CV	45	VALLEY FORGE	Philadelphia NYd	l. Nov 18, 1944 c. Nov 3, 1946	to CVA 1952 to CVS 1954 to LPH 8 1961
CV	46	IWO JIMA	Newport News	—	cancelled (scrapped)
CV	47	PHILIPPINE SEA	Beth-Quincy	l. Sep 5, 1945 c. May 11, 1946	to CVA 1952 to CVS 1955 to AVT 11 1959 decomm. 1958; str. 1969 (scrapped)

Displacement:	27,100 tons standard 33,000 tons full load
Dimensions:	872 ft oa (820 ft wl) x 93 ft x $28^{7}/_{12}$ ft (see text)
Flight deck:	96 ft
Propulsion:	steam turbines; 150,000 shp; 4 shafts
Boilers:	8
Speed:	32.7 knots
Gun battery:	12 5-inch/38 cal DP (4 twin; 4 single) 68 or 72 40-mm/56-cal Bofors AA (17 or 18 quad) 40 20-mm/70-cal Oerikon AA (20 twin)
Aircraft:	100+
Catapults:	2 hydraulic
Elevators:	2 centerline, 1 deck edge
Complement:	3,450

This was the largest class of fleet carriers to be constructed by any nation. Thirteen of these ships were 888 feet in length, sometimes referred to as the "long-hull" ESSEX class (CV 14, 15, 19, 21, 32, 33, 36—40, 45, 47). They were incorrectly listed in some documents as the TICONDEROGA class.

The heavily damaged BUNKER HILL and FRANKLIN were completely rebuilt at the end of World War II, but were not returned to service. After being stricken, the BUNKER HILL served as a stationary electronics test ship, moored at San Diego, California, until 1972.

The REPRISAL and IWO JIMA were cancelled on

August 11, 1945: The REPRISAL (laid down July 1, 1944 and 52.3% complete) was launched and used in underwater weapon tests in 1946-1948; she was sold for scrap in 1949. The unfinished IWO JIMA (laid down on January 29, 1945) was scrapped on the building ways.

Some early ships were initially fitted with one flight-deck catapult; later increased two two. Six early ships were also fitted with a hangar-deck catapult, all of which were removed within a year of completion.

Most of these ships were extensively modernized; see Appendix D. The ORISKANY was completed to a modified design and is listed separately.

1 AIRCRAFT CARRIER: MODIFIED "ESSEX" CLASS

NO.	NAME	BUILDER		STATUS
CV 34	ORISKANY	New York NYd	l. Aug 24, 1945 c. Sep 25, 1950	to CVA 1952 to CV 1975 decomm. 1976, str. 1989 (scuttled)

Displacement:	33,100 tons standard 41,900 tons full load
Dimensions:	888 ft oa (820 ft wl) x 102 ft x 31 ft
Flight deck:	152 ft
Propulsion:	steam turbines; 150,000 shp; 4 shafts
Boilers:	8
Speed:	32 knots
Gun battery:	8 5-inch/38-cal DP (8 single) 28 3-inch/50-cal AA (14 twin) 14 20-mm/70-cal Oerlikon AA (14 single)
Aircraft:	70+
Catapults:	2 hydraulic
Elevators:	2 centerline, 1 deck edge
Complement:	2,500+

Construction of the "long-hull" ORISKANY was suspended at the end of World War II. She was completed to a modified design to operate jet-propelled aircraft, the world's first carrier to be completed with that capability.

She was scuttled for use as an artifical reef in the Gulf of Mexico in 2006.

9 LIGHT AIRCRAFT CARRIERS: CONVERTED LIGHT CRUISERS

NO.	NAME	BUILDER		STATUS
CVL 22	INDEPENDENCE ex-CL 59 AMSTERDAM	New York SB	l. Aug 22, 1942 c. Jan 14, 1943	sunk June 29, 1951
CVL 23	PRINCETON ex-CL 61 TALLAHASSEE	New York SB	l. Oct 18, 1942 c. Feb 25, 1943	sunk Oct 24, 1944
CVL 24	BELLEAU WOOD ex-CL 76 NEW HAVEN	New York SB	l. Dec 6, 1942 c. Mar 31, 1943	decomm. 1947; to France 1953-1960; str. 1960 (scrapped)
CVL 25	COWPENS ex-CL 77 HUNTINGTON	New York SB	l. Jan 27, 1943 c. May 28, 1943	decomm 1947 to AVT 1 1959 str. 1959 (scrapped)
CVL 26	MONTEREY ex-CL 78 DAYTON	New York SB	l. Feb 28, 1943 c. June 17, 1943	decomm. 1956 to AVT 2 1959 str. 1970 (scrapped)
CVL 27	LANGLEY ex-CL 85 FARGO	New York SB	l. May 22, 1943 c. Aug 31, 1943	decomm. 1947; to France 1951-1963 (scrapped)

NO.	NAME	BUILDER		STATUS
CVL 28	CABOT ex-CL 79 WILMINGTON	New York SB	l. Apr 4, 1943 c. July 24, 1943	decomm. 1955 to AVT 3 1959 to Spin 1967-1989 (scrapped)
CVL 29	BATAAN ex-CL 99 BUFFALO	New York SB	l. Aug 1, 1943 c. Nov 17, 1943	decomm. 1954 to AVT 4 1959 str. 1959 (scrapped)
CVL 30	SAN JACINTO ex-CL 100 NEWARK	New York SB	l. Sep 26, 1943 c. Dec 15, 1943	decomm. 1947 to AVT 5 1959 str. 1970 (scrapped)

Displacement:	11,000 tons standard 15,100 tons full load
Dimensions:	622½ ft oa (600 ft wl) x 71½ ft x 26 ft
Flight deck:	73 ft
Propulsion:	steam turbines; 100,000 shp; 4 shafts
Boilers:	4
Speed:	31.6 knots
Gun battery:	26 40-mm/56-cal Bofors AA (2 quad, 9 twin) 10 20-mm/70-cal Oerlikon AA (10 single)
Aircraft:	30+
Catapults:	2 hydraulic
Elevators:	2 centerline
Complement:	1,570

These ships were ordered as light cruisers of the CLEVELAND (CL 55) class and converted during construction to CVLs. See Volume I, page 266 for dates reordered as carriers.

Their original design provided for four 5-inch/38 dual-purpose guns; none was installed except that the lead ship, the INDEPENDENCE, was completed with a single 5-inch gun on her bow, subsequently replaced by a quad 40-mm mount.

The INDEPENDENCE was a target ship at the Bikini atomic bomb tests in 1946; her badly damaged hulk was then used as a radiological research platform until she was sunk in weapon tests in 1951. The PRINCETON was sunk by a Japanese land-based bomber in the Leyte Gulf battles.

3 LARGE AIRCRAFT CARRIERS: "MIDWAY" CLASS

NO.	NAME	BUILDER		STATUS
CVB 41	MIDWAY	Newport News	l. Mar 20, 1945 c. Sep 10, 1945	to CVA 1952 to CV 1975 decomm. 1992; str. 1997 (museum)
CVB 42	FRANKLIN D. ROOSEVELT ex-CORAL SEA	New York NYd	l. Apr 29, 1945 c. Oct 27, 1945	to CVA 1952 to CV 1975 decomm. 1992; str. 1997 (scrapped)
CVB 43	CORAL SEA	Newport News	l. Apr 2, 1946 c. Oct 1, 1947	to CVA 1952 to CV 1975 decomm./str. 1990 (scrapped)

Displacement:	45,000 tons standard		
	55,000 tons full load		
Dimensions:	968 ft oa (900 ft wl) x 113 ft x 35 ft		
Flight deck:	136 ft		
Propulsion:	steam turbines; 212,000 shp; 4 shafts		
Boilers:	12		
Speed:	33 knots		
Gun battery:	18 5-inch/54-cal DP (18 single)		
	84 40-mm/56-cal Bofors AA (21 quad)		
	several 20-mm/70-cal Oerlikon AA		
Aircraft:	144		
Catapults:	2 hydraulic		
Elevators:	2 centerline, 1 deck edge		
Complement:	4,100		

These were the largest aircraft carriers constructed during World War II except for the short-lived Japanese SHINANO, which was converted during construction from a YAMATO-class battleship.

Three additional ship of this class were planned but not laid down: The CVB 44 was cancelled on January 11, 1943, and the CVB 56 and 57 on March 27, 1945; all were to be built at the the Newport News shipyard.

Only the MIDWAY and ROOSEVELT were completed with 18 5-inch guns; the CORAL SEA with 14 5-inch guns. All three ships were extensively modernized during their service lives; see Appendix D.

The CVB 42 was renamed immediately after the death of President Roosevelt on April 12, 1945.

2 LIGHT AIRCRAFT CARRIERS: "SAIPAN" CLASS

NO.	NAME	BUILDER		STATUS
CVL 48	SAIPAN	New York SB	l. July 8, 1945 c. July 14, 1946	decomm. 1957 to AVT 6 1959 to AGMR 2 1956 decomm. 1970; str. 1975 (scrapped)
CVL 49	WRIGHT	New York SB	l. Sep 1, 1945 c. Feb 9, 1947	decomm. 1956 to AVT 7 1959 to CC 2 1963 decomm. 1970; str. 1977 (scrapped)

Displacement:	14,500 tons standard
	20,000 tons full load
Dimensions:	683$^{7}/_{12}$ ft oa (664 ft wl) x 78$^{2}/_{3}$ ft x 27 ft
Flight deck:	108 ft
Propulsion:	steam turbines; 120,000 shp; 4 shafts
Boilers:	4
Speed:	33 knots
Gun battery:	40 40-mm/56-cal Bofors AA (5 quad, 10 twin)
	32 20-mm/70-cal Oerlikon AA
Aircraft:	50
Catapults:	2 hydraulic
Elevators:	2 centerline
Complement:	1,820

These were built-for-the-purpose light carriers; their hulls and propulsion machinery were similar to heavy cruisers of the BALTIMORE (CA 68) class.

The SAIPAN began conversion to a command ship (CC 3) in 1963; she was completed as a communications relay ship (AGMR 2) in 1966, renamed ARLINGTON.

The WRIGHT was converted to a command ship (CC 2) in 1962-1963 (name retained).

HEAVY AIRCRAFT CARRIER: "UNITED STATES"

NO.	NAME	BUILDER	STATUS
CVA 58	UNITED STATES	Newport News	cancelled

Displacement:	61,569 tons light
	66,850 tons standard
	83,200 tons full load
Dimensions:	1,090 ft oa (1,030 ft wl) x 125 ft x 34½ ft
Flight deck:	190 ft
Propulsion:	steam turbines; 280,000 shp; 4 shafts
Boilers:	8
Speed:	30+ knots
Gun battery:	8 5-inch/54-cal DP (single)
	12 3-inch/50-cal AA (twin)
	20 20-mm/70-cal Oerlikon AA
Aircraft:	(see text)
Catapults:	4 hydraulic
Elevators:	4 deck edge
Complement:	4,127

Construction of the UNITED STATES was cancelled on April 23, 1949, five days after her keel was laid down. She was to have been the first "super carrier," designed specially to operate heavy attack aircraft—at one point 12 aircraft and later 24 (approximately 100,000 pounds). She could have operated 70+ contemporary carrier aircraft.

Navy long-range planning called for four carriers of this type, each to operate in a task group with a MIDWAY-class carrier and one or more ESSEX-class ships.

4 AIRCRAFT CARRIERS: "FORRESTAL" CLASS

NO.	NAME	BUILDER		STATUS
CVA 59	FORRESTAL	Newport News	l. Dec 11, 1954 c. Oct 1, 1955	to CV 1975 to AVT 1992 decomm./str. 1993
CVA 60	SARATOGA	New York NSYd	l. Oct 8, 1955 c. Apr 14, 1956	to CV 1972 decomm./str. 1994
CVA 61	RANGER	Newport News	l. Sep 29, 1956 c. Aug 10, 1957	to CV 1972 decomm. 1993; str. 2004
CVA 62	INDEPENDENCE	New York NSYd	l. June 6, 1958 c. Jan 10, 1959	to CV 1973 decomm. 1998; str. 2004

Displacement:	55,524 tons light
	60,000 tons standard
	76,600 tons full load
Dimensions:	1,039 ft oa (990 ft wl) x 129⅓ ft x 33¾ ft
Flight deck:	252 ft
Propulsion:	steam turbines; 260,000 shp; 4 shafts
Boilers:	8
Speed:	33 knots
Gun battery:	8 5-inch/54-cal DP (8 single)
Aircraft:	75+
Catapults:	4 steam
Elevators:	4 deck edge
Complement:	5,300+

These were the first super carriers to be completed. The FORRESTAL was redesigned during construction to an angled-deck configuration (the original design was similar to the UNITED STATES). These ships were completed with only 5-inch dual-purpose guns; subsequently 20-mm Gatling guns and Sea Sparrow launchers were installed for close-in defense.

The FORRESTAL was redesignated as a training ship (AVT 59), but never served in that role.

The FORRESTAL and SARATOGA are moored near Newport, R.I., and the RANGER at Bremerton, Wash., their fate not yet decided when this edition went to press in 2007. The INDEPENDENCE was expected to be scrapped.

1 AIRCRAFT CARRIER: "ENTERPRISE"

NO.	NAME	BUILDER		STATUS
CVAN 65	ENTERPRISE	Newport News	l. Sep 24, 1960 c. Nov 25, 1961	to CVN 1975 **active**

Displacement:	75,700 tons standard 89,600 tons full load
Dimensions:	1,123 ft oa (1,040 ft wl) x 133 ft x 35¼ ft
Flight deck:	257 ft
Propulsion:	steam turbines; approx. 280,000 shp; 4 shafts
Reactors:	8 A2W pressurized-water
Speed:	30+ knots
Gun battery:	none
Aircraft:	100+
Catapults:	4 steam
Elevators:	4 deck edge
Complement:	5,600+

This was the world's second nuclear-propelled surface warship; the first was the missile cruiser LONG BEACH (CGN 9), completed a few months earlier. The ship was completed without guns or missile launchers; subsequently 20-mm Gatling guns and Sea Sparrow launchers were installed for close-in defense.

All U.S. nuclear-propelled carriers (CVAN 65, CVN 68—) have been constructed at the Newport News yard (which also builds nuclear-propelled submarines).

The ENTERPRISE was scheduled to be decommissioned in 2013 after 52 years of service.

4 AIRCRAFT CARRIERS: "KITTY HAWK" CLASS AND "KENNEDY"

NO.	NAME	BUILDER		STATUS
CVA 63	KITTY HAWK	Newport News	l. May 21, 1960 c. Apr 29, 1961	to CV 1973 decomm. 2008
CVA 64	CONSTELLATION	New York SB	l. Oct 8, 1960 c. Oct 27, 1961	to CV 1975 decomm./str. 2003
CVA 66	AMERICA	Newport News	l. Feb 1, 1964 c. Jan 23, 1965	to CV 1975 decomm./str. 1996 (scuttled)
CVA 67	JOHN F. KENNEDY	Newport News	l. May 27, 1967 c. Sep 7, 1968	to CV 1973 decomm. 2007

Displacement:	60,100 tons standard 80,800 tons full load
Dimensions:	1,062½ ft oa (990 ft wl) x 129½ ft x 36 ft
Flight deck:	249 ft

Propulsion:	steam turbines; 260,000 shp; 4 shafts			
Boilers:	8			
Speed:	30+ knots			
Missile launchers:	2 Terrier Mk 10 twin launcher AA in CVA 63, 64, 66 (see text)			
Aircraft:	75+			
Catapults:	4 steam			
Elevators:	4 deck edge			
Complement:	5,400+			

These ships were improved FORRESTAL-class carriers with an improved flight deck and elevator arrangement. Three ships were built with surface-to-air missile launchers; they were subsequently removed and all four ships were fitted with Sea Sparrow launchers and 20-mm Gatling guns for close-in defense.

The AMERICA was built with AN/SQS-23 sonar, the only U.S. aircraft carrier to be built with sonar. The set was removed in 1981.

The AMERICA was scuttled in weapon tests on May 14, 2005, the world's largest warship to be sunk at sea.

The KENNEDY ceased air operations in 2006 because of catapult and arresting gear problems. The Navy's leadership sought to dispose of the ship, but congressional edict required that the ship be retained until 2009 in a "ready" condition although not operational. She was formally decommissioned on March 24, 2007.

10 AIRCRAFT CARRIERS: "NIMITZ" CLASS

NO.		NAME	BUILDER		STATUS
CVN	68	NIMITZ	Newport News	l. May 13, 1972 c. May 3, 1975	active
CVN	69	DWIGHT D. EISENHOWER	Newport News	l. Oct 11, 1975 c. Oct 18, 1977	active
CVN	70	CARL VINSON	Newport News	l. Mar 15, 1980 c. Mar 13, 1982	active
CVN	71	THEODORE ROOSEVELT	Newport News	l. Oct 27, 1984 c. Oct 25, 1986	active
CVN	72	ABRAHAM LINCOLN	Newport News	l. Feb 13, 1988 c. Nov 11, 1989	active
CVN	73	GEORGE WASHINGTON	Newport News	l. July 21, 1990 c. July 4, 1992	active
CVN	74	JOHN C. STENNIS	Newport News	l. Nov 13, 1993 c. Dec 2, 1995	active
CVN	75	HARRY S. TRUMAN	Newport News	l. Sep 7, 1996 c. July 25, 1998	active
CVN	76	RONALD REAGAN	Newport News	l. Mar 10, 2001 c. July 12, 2003	active
CVN	77	GEORGE H.W. BUSH	Newport News	l. Oct 7, 2006 c. 2009	building

Displacement:	81,600 tons standard 91,400 tons full load
Dimensions:	1,092 ft oa (1,040 ft wl) x 134 ft x 37 ft
Flight deck:	252 ft
Propulsion:	steam turbines; approx. 260,000 shp; 4 shafts
Reactors:	2 A4W pressurized-water
Speed:	30+ knots
Gun battery:	(see text)
Aircraft:	85+
Catapults:	4 steam
Elevators:	4 deck edge
Complement:	5,700+

The NIMITZ-class ships were constructed over a longer period than any other warship design (i.e., 34 years from the launching of the NIMITZ to the launching of the BUSH). There were a succession of modifications and improvements to these ships, most causing an increase in the displacement of subsequent ships. The BUSH has a full load displacement of 102,000 tons.

These ships were completed with various combinations of Sea Sparrow misisle launchers (later RAM missile launchers) and 20-mm gatling guns for close-in defense.

(1) AIRCRAFT CARRIER: "GERALD R. FORD" CLASS

NO.		NAME	BUILDER		STATUS
CVN	78	GERALD R. FORD	Newport News	l. c. 2015	building

Displacement:	100,000+ tons full load
Dimensions:	1,092 ft oa x 134$^1/_2$ ft x 38$^2/_3$ ft
Flight deck	aprox. 250 ft
Propulsion:	steam turbines; approx. 280,000 shp; 4 shafts
Reactors:	2 A1B pressurized-water
Speed:	33 knots
Missile battery:	(see text)
Aircraft:	70+
Catapults:	4 electro-magnetic
Elevators:	3 deck edge
Complement:	approx. 4,600

The FORD is an improved NIMITZ-class ship with a new reactor plant, electric propulsion (drive), electro-magnetic catapults, and modified flight-deck and island structure arrangements. The first hull plate for the ship was laid down on August 11, 2005.

The Navy plans to build additional ships of this design at four- to five-year intervals.

ESCORT CARRIER NOTES

U.S. escort carriers were originally designated aircraft escort vessel (AVG with BAVG for ships orders for Britain). On August 20, 1942, they were reclassified as auxiliary aircraft carrier (ACV) until July 15, 1943, when they were changed to escort aircraft carrier (CVE). For clarity the designation CVE is used throughout this appendix.

The hull numbers CVE 2—5 were not assigned.

The escort carriers reclassified as CVHE and CVU retained their CVE hull numbers; those changed to AKV were renumbered.

The U.S. Maritime Commission's design type is shown in parenthesis after the class or type name in the headings. The first letter indicated type (C = Cargo; S = Special); the second the type of propulsion (M = Motorship/diesel; S = Steam/turbine); and the third the modification of the basic type.

1 ESCORT CARRIER: "LONG ISLAND" (C3 TYPE)

NO.		NAME	BUILDER		STATUS
CVE	1	LONG ISLAND ex-*Mormacmail*	Sun SB	l. Jan 11, 1940 c. June 2, 1941	decomm./str. 1946

Displacement:	7,886 tons standard 15,400 tons full load
Dimensions:	492 ft oa (465 ft wl) x 69$^1/_2$ ft x 25$^1/_2$ ft
Flight deck:	102 ft
Propulsion:	diesel; 8,500 bhp; 1 shaft
Speed:	17.6 knots
Gun battery:	1 5-inch/38-cal DP 2 3-inch/50-cal AA (2 single)
Aircraft:	20
Catapults:	1 hydraulic
Elevators:	1 centerline
Complement:	970

The LONG ISLAND entered merchant service as the *Mormacmail* in 1940. She was acquired by the Navy in 1941 for conversion to an aircraft escort vessel(AVG 1).

11 ESCORT CARRIERS: "BOGUE" CLASS (C3-S-A1 TYPE)

NO.		NAME	BUILDER		STATUS
CVE	9	BOGUE ex-*Steel Advocate*	Seattle-Tacoma	l. Jan 15, 1942 c. Sep 26, 1942	to CVHE 9 1955 decomm. 1946; str. 1959
CVE	11	CARD	Seattle-Tacoma	l. Feb 21, 1942 c. Nov 8, 1942	to CVHE 1955 to CVU 1958 to AKV 40 1959 decomm. 1959; str. 1970
CVE	12	COPAHEE ex-*Steel Architect*	Seattle-Tacoma	l. Oct 21, 1941 c. June 15, 1942	to CVHE 1955 decomm. 1946; str. 1959
CVE	13	CORE	Seattle-Tacoma	l. May 15, 1942 c. Dec 10, 1942	to CVHE 1955 to CVU 1958 to AKV 41 1959 decomm. 1946; str. 1970
CVE	16	NASSAU	Seattle-Tacoma	l. Apr 4, 1942 c. Aug 20, 1942	to CVHE 1955 decomm. 1946; str. 1959
CVE	18	ALTAMAHA	Seattle-Tacoma	l. May 22, 1942 c. Sep 15, 1942	to CVHE 1955 decomm. 1946; str. 1959
CVE	20	BARNES	Seattle-Tacoma	l. May 22, 1942 c. Feb 20, 1943	to CVHE 1955 decomm. 1946; str. 1959
CVE	21	BLOCK ISLAND	Seattle-Tacoma	l. June 6, 1942 c. Mar 8, 1943	sunk May 29, 1944
CVE	23	BRETON	Seattle-Tacoma	l. June 27, 1942 c. Apr 12, 1943	to CVHE 1955 to CVU 1958 to AKV 42 1959 decomm. 1946; str. 1971
CVE	25	CROATAN	Seattle-Tacoma	l. Aug 3, 1942 c. Apr 28, 1943	to CVHE 1955 to CVU 1958 to AKV 43 1959 decomm. 1946; str. 1970
CVE	31	PRINCE WILLIAM	Seattle-Tacoma	l. Aug 23, 1942 c. Apr 9, 1943	to CVHE 1955 decomm. 1946; str. 1959

Displacement:	7,800 tons standard 15,700 tons full load
Dimensions:	$495^2/_3$ ft (465 ft wl) x $69^1/_2$ ft x 26 ft
Flight deck:	$111^1/_2$ feet
Propulsion:	steam turbine; 8,500 shp; 1 shaft
Boilers:	4

Speed:	17.6 knots	
Gun battery:	2 5-inch/38-cal DP (2 single)	
	20 40-mm/56-cal Bofors AA (10 twin)	
	27 20-mm/70-cal Oerlikon AA (27 single)	
Aircraft:	20+	
Catapults:	1 hydraulic	
Elevators:	2 centerline	
Complement:	890	

Twenty-six additional ships of this type were transferred to the Royal Navy upon completion; their U.S. Navy hull numbers were BAVG 6 and AVG/CVE 6—8, 10, 14, 15, 17, 19, 22, 24, 32—54. All were returned to U.S. custody.

The BLOCK ISLAND was the only U.S. escort carrier sunk in the Atlantic, by a German U-boat.

1 ESCORT CARRIER: "CHARGER" (C3 TYPE)

NO.	NAME	BUILDER		STATUS
CVE 30	CHARGER ex-*Rio De La Plata*	Sun SB	l. Mar 1, 1941 c. Mar 3, 1942	decomm./str. 1946

Displacement:	8,000 tons standard
	15,900 tons full load
Dimensions:	492 ft oa (465 ft wl) x 69½ ft x 26¼ ft
Flight deck:	111¹/₆ ft
Propulsion:	diesel; 8,500 bhp; 1 shaft
Speed:	17.6 knots
Gun battery:	1 5-inch/51-cal
	4 4-inch/50 AA (4 single)
	16 40-mm/56-cal Bofors AA (4 quad)
	several 20-mm/70-cal Oerlikon AA
Aircraft:	15
Catapults:	1 hydraulic
Elevators:	1 centerline
Complement:	856

The CHARGER was converted while under construction as merchant ship to an escort carrier for the Royal Navy (designated BAVG 4). She was retained by the U.S. Navy after the United states entered the war in December 1941; she retained her British name. Four sister ships went to the Royal Navy as the AVENGER class (BAVG 2—4, 5).

4 ESCORT CARRIERS: CONVERTED FLEET OILERS (T3-S2-A1 TYPE)

NO.		NAME	BUILDER		STATUS
CVE	26	SANGAMON ex-AO 28 ex-*Esso Trenton*	Federal-Kearney	l. Nov 4, 1939 c. Aug 25, 1942	decomm./str. 1945
CVE	27	SUWANNEE ex-AO 33 ex-*Markay*	Federal-Kearney	l. Mar 4, 1939 c. Sep 24, 1942	to CVHE 1955 decomm. 1947; str. 1959
CVE	28	CHENANGO ex-AO 31 ex-*Esso New Orleans*	Sun SB	l. Apr 1, 1939 c. Sep 19, 1942	to CVHE 1955 decomm. 1946; str. 1959
CVE	29	SANTEE ex-AO 29 ex-*Seakay*	Sun SB	l. Mar 4, 1939 c. Aug 24, 1942	to CVHE 1955 decomm. 1946; str. 1959

Displacement:		12,000 tons standard		
		24,275 tons full load		
Dimensions:		553 ft oa (525 ft wl) x 75 ft x 32 ft		
Flight deck:		114¼ ft		
Propulsion:		steam turbines; 13,500 shp; 2 shafts		
Boilers:		4		
Speed:		18 knots		
Gun battery:		2 5-inch/38-cal DP (2 single)		
		28 40-mm/56-cal Bofors AA (2 quad, 10 twin)		
		several 20-mm/70-cal Oerlikon AA		
Aircraft:		30+		
Catapults:		2 hydraulic		
Elevators:		2 centerline		
Complement:		1,080		

These four ships were among 12 National Defense tankers ordered in 1938 that were acquired by the U.S. Navy shortly after their completion and used as fleet oilers (AO 22—33). Subsequently these four ships, originally completed in 1940-1941, were converted to escort carriers.

They were highly successful as CVEs and served as model for the later COMMENCEMENT BAY class. Part of their attraction was retention of a large liquid cargo capacity and their twin screws. (Their fuel oil capacity was 37,500 barrels, significantly more than other CVL/CVE-type carriers, and compared to 44,000 to 45,000 barrels in ESSEX-class CVs.)

50 ESCORT CARRIERS: "CASABLANCA" CLASS (S4-S2-BB3)

NO.		NAME	BUILDER		STATUS
CVE	55	CASABLANCA ex-ALAZON BAY ex-AMEER (RN)	Kaiser SB	l. Apr 5, 1943 c. July 8, 1943	decomm./str. 1946
CVE	56	LISCOME BAY	Kaiser SB	l. Apr 19, 1943 c. Aug 7, 1943	sunk Nov 24, 1943
CVE	57	ANZIO ex-CORAL SEA ex-ALIKULA BAY	Kaiser SB	l. May 1, 1943 c. Aug 27, 1943	to CVHE 1955 decomm. 1946; str. 1959
CVE	58	CORREGIDOR ex-ANGUILLA BAY	Kaiser SB	l. May 12, 1943 c. Aug 31, 1943	to CVU 1955 decomm./str. 1958
CVE	59	MISSION BAY ex-ATHELING	Kaiser SB	l. May 26, 1943 c. Sep 12, 1943	to CVU 1955 decomm. 1947/ str. 1958
CVE	60	GUADALCANAL ex-ASTROLABE BAY	Kaiser SB	l. June 5, 1943 c. Sep 25, 1943	to CVU 1955 decomm. 1946; str. 1958
CVE	61	MANILA BAY ex-BUCARELI BAY	Kaiser SB	l. July 10, 1943 c. Oct 5, 1943	to CVU 1955 decomm. 1946; str. 1958
CVE	62	NATOMA BAY ex-BEGUM (RN)	Kaiser SB	l. July 20, 1943 c. Oct 14, 1943	to CVU 1955 decomm. 1946; str. 1958
CVE	63	ST. Lô ex-MIDWAY ex-CHAPIN BAY	Kaiser SB	l. Aug 17, 1943 c. Oct 23, 1943	sunk Oct 25, 1944
CVE	64	TRIPOLI ex-DIDRICKSON BAY	Kaiser SB	l. Sep 2, 1943 c. Oct 31, 1943	to CVU 1955 decomm. 1958; str. 1959

NO.		NAME	BUILDER		STATUS
CVE	65	WAKE ISLAND ex-DOLOMI BAY	Kaiser SB	l. Sep 15, 1943 c. Nov 7, 1943	decomm./str. 1946
CVE	66	WHITE PLAINS ex-ELBOUR BAY	Kaiser SB	l. Sep 27, 1943 c. Nov 15, 1943	to CVU 1955 decomm. 1946; str. 1958
CVE	67	SOLOMONS ex-NASSUK BAY ex-EMPEROR (RN)	Kaiser SB	l. Oct 6, 1943 c. Nov 21, 1943	decomm./str. 1946
CVE	68	KALININ BAY	Kaiser SB	l. Oct 15, 1943 c. Nov 27, 1943	decomm./str. 1946
CVE	69	KASAAN BAY	Kaiser SB	l. Oct 24, 1943 c. Dec 4, 1943	to CVHE decomm. 1946; str. 1959
CVE	70	FANSHAW BAY	Kaiser SB	l. Nov 1, 1943 c. Dec 9, 1943	to CVHE decomm. 1946; str. 1959
CVE	71	KITKUN BAY	Kaiser SB	l. Nov 8, 1943 c. Dec 15, 1943	decomm./str. 1946
CVE	72	TULAGI ex-FORTAZELA BAY	Kaiser SB	l. Nov 15, 1943 c. Dec 21, 1943	decomm./str. 1946
CVE	73	GAMBIER BAY	Kaiser SB	l. Nov 22, 1943 c. Dec 28, 1943	sunk Oct 25, 1944
CVE	74	NEHENTA BAY ex-KHEDIVE (RN)	Kaiser SB	l. Nov 28, 1943 c. Jan 3, 1944	to CVU 1955 to AKV 24 1959 decomm. 1946; str. 1959
CVE	75	HOGGATT BAY	Kaiser SB	l. Dec 4, 1943 c. Jan 11, 1944	to CVHE 1955 to AKV 25 1959 decomm. 1946; str. 1959
CVE	76	KADASHAN BAY	Kaiser SB	l. Dec 11, 1943 c. Jan 18, 1944	to CVU 1955 to AKV 26 1959 decomm. 1946; str. 1959
CVE	77	MARCUS ISLAND ex-KANALKU BAY	Kaiser SB	l. Dec 16, 1943 c. Jan 26, 1944	to CVHE 1955 to AKV 27 1959 decomm. 1946; str. 1959
CVE	78	SAVO ISLAND ex-KAITA BAY	Kaiser SB	l. Dec 22, 1943 c. Feb 3, 1944	to CVHE 1955 to AKV 28 1959 decomm. 1946; str. 1959
CVE	79	OMMANEY BAY	Kaiser SB	l. Dec 29, 1943 c. Feb 11, 1944	sunk Jan 4, 1945
CVE	80	PETROF BAY	Kaiser SB	l. Jan 5, 1944 c. Feb 18, 1944	to CVU 1955 decomm. 1946; str. 1958
CVE	81	RUDYERD BAY	Kaiser SB	l. Jan 12, 1944 c. Feb 25, 1944	to CVU 1955 to AKV 29 1959 decomm. 1946; str. 1959

NO.		NAME	BUILDER	STATUS
CVE	82	SAGINAW BAY	Kaiser SB	l. Jan 19, 1944 c. Mar 2, 1944	to CVHE 1955 decomm. 1946l str. 1959
CVE	83	SARGENT BAY	Kaiser SB	l. Jan 31, 1944 c. Mar 9, 1944	to CVU 1955 decomm. 1946; str. 1958
CVE	84	SHAMROCK BAY	Kaiser SB	l. Feb 4, 1944 c. Mar 15, 1944	to CVU 1955 decomm. 1946; str. 1958
CVE	85	SHIPLEY BAY	Kaiser SB	l. Feb 12, 1944 c. Mar 21, 1944	to CVHE 1955 decomm. 1946; str. 1959
CVE	86	SITKOH BAY	Kaiser SB	l. Feb 19, 1944 c. Mar 28, 1944	to CVU 1955 to AKV 30 1959 decomm. 1954; str. 1960
CVE	87	STEAMER BAY	Kaiser SB	l. Feb 26, 1944 c. Apr 4, 1944	to CVHE 1955 decomm. 1946; str. 1959
CVE	88	CAPE ESPERANCE ex-TANANEK BAY	Kaiser SB	l. Mar 3, 1944 c. Apr 9, 1944	to CVU 1955 decomm./str. 1959
CVE	89	TAKANIS BAY Kaiser SB		l. Mar 10, 1944 c. Apr 15, 1944	to CVU 1955 to AKV 31 1959 decomm. 1946/ str. 1959
CVE	90	THETIS BAY	Kaiser SB	l. Mar 16, 1944 c. Apr 21, 1944	to CVHA 1 1955 to LPH 6 1959
CVE	91	MAKASSAR STRAIT ex-ULITAKA BAY	Kaiser SB	l. Mar 22, 1944 c. Apr 27, 1944	to CVU 1955 decomm. 1946; str. 1958
CVE	92	WINDHAM BAY	Kaiser SB	l. Mar 29, 1944 c. May 3, 1944	to CVU 1955 decomm./str. 1959
CVE	93	MAKIN ISLAND ex-WOODCLIFF BAY	Kaiser SB	l. Apr 5, 1944 c. May 9, 1944	decomm./str. 1946
CVE	94	LUNGA POINT ex-ALAZON BAY	Kaiser SB	l. Apr 11, 1944 c. May 14, 1944	to CVU 1955 to AKV 32 1959 decomm. 1946; str. 1960
CVE	95	BISMARCK SEA ex-ALIKULA BAY	Kaiser SB	l. Apr 17, 1944 c. May 20, 1944	sunk Feb 21, 1945
CVE	96	SALAMAUA ex-ANGUILLA BAY	Kaiser SB	l. Apr 22, 1944 c. May 26, 1944	decomm./str. 1946
CVE	97	HOLLANDIA ex-ASTROLABE BAY	Kaiser SB	l. Apr 28, 1944 c. June 1, 1944	to CVU 1955 to AKV 33 1959 decomm. 1947; str. 1960
CVE	98	KWAJALEIN ex-BUCARELI BAY	Kaiser SB	l. May 4, 1944 c. June 7, 1944	to CVU 1955 to AKV 34 1959 decomm. 1946; str. 1960
CVE	99	ADMIRALTY ISLANDS Kaiser SB ex-CHAPIN BAY		l. May 10, 1944 c. June 13, 1944	decomm./str. 1946

NO.		NAME	BUILDER		STATUS
CVE	100	BOUGAINVILLE ex-DIDRICKSON BAY	Kaiser SB	l. May 16, 1944 c. June 18, 1944	to CVU 1955 to AKV 35 1959 decomm. 1946; str. 1960
CVE	101	MATANIKAU ex-DOLOMI BAY	Kaiser SB	l. May 22, 1944 c. June 24, 1944	to CVU 1955 to AKV 36 1959 decomm. 1946; str. 1960
CVE	102	ATTU ex-ELBOUR BAY	Kaiser SB	l. May 27, 1944 c. June 30, 1944	decomm./str. 1946
CVE	103	ROI ex-ALAVA BAY	Kaiser SB	l. June 2, 1944 c. July 6, 1944	decomm./str. 1946
CVE	104	MUNDA ex-TONOWEK BAY	Kaiser SB	l. June 8, 1944 c. July 8, 1944	to CVU 1955 decomm. 1946; str. 1958

Displacement:	6,730 tons standard 10,400 tons full load
Dimensions:	$512\frac{1}{4}$ ft oa (490 ft wl) x $65\frac{1}{6}$ ft x $22\frac{1}{2}$ ft
Flight deck:	$108\frac{1}{12}$ ft
Propulsion:	reciprocating engines; 9,000 shp; 2 shafts
Boilers:	4
Speed:	19 knots
Gun battery:	1 5-inch/38-cal DP 16 40-mm/56-cal Bofors AA (8 twin) several 20-mm/70-cal Oerlikon AA
Aircraft:	30+
Catapults:	1 hydraulic
Elevators:	2 centerline
Complement:	860

This was the largest class of aircraft carriers ever built with all 50 ships constructed at the Kiaser shipyard in Vancouver, Washington; the last ship was commissioned one year after the first. These were also the first U.S. escort carrier built specifically for that role.

The CVE 55, 62, 67, and 74 were to have gone to Britain under Lend Lease (see Royal Navy names above); they were retained by the U.S. Navy and the CVE 34—36 and 39, respectively, were transferred in their place.

Many ships were renamed during construction to honor World War II battles. The CVE 57 and CVE 63 were renamed to make names of the hsitoric 1942 carrier battles available for the Navy's large carriers (CVB).

Five ships were lost during World War II: The LISCOME BAY to a Japanese submarine; the GAMBIER BAY to Japanese surface ships; and the ST Lô, OMMANEY BAY, and BISMARCK SEA to Japanese kamikazes.

19 ESCORT CARRIERS: "COMMENCEMENT BAY" CLASS

NO.		NAME	BUILDER		STATUS
CVE	105	COMMENCEMENT BAY ex-ST. JOSEPH BAY	Todd-Tacoma	l. May 9, 1944 c. Nov 27, 1944	to CVHE 1955 to AKV 37 1959 decomm. 1946; str. 1971
CVE	106	BLOCK ISLAND ex-SUNSET BAY	Todd-Tacoma	l. June 10, 1944 c. Dec 30, 1944	to LPH 1 1957 to CVE 1959 to AKV 38 1959 decomm. 1954; str. 1959

NO.	NAME	BUILDER		STATUS
CVE 107	GILBERT ISLANDS ex-ANDREWS BAY	Todd-Tacoma	l. July 20, 1944 c. Feb 5, 1945	to AKV 39 1959 decomm. 1955; str. 1961 (became AGMR 1; see text)
CVE 108	KULA GULF ex-VERMILION BAY	Todd-Tacoma	l. Aug 15, 1944 c. May 12, 1945	to AKV 8 1959 decomm. 1955; str. 1970
CVE 109	CAPE GLOUCESTER ex-WILLAPA BAY	Todd-Tacoma	l. Sep 12, 1944 c. Mar 5, 1945	to CVHE 1955 to AKV 9 1959 decomm. 1946; str. 1971
CVE 110	SALERNO BAY ex-WINJAH BAY	Todd-Tacoma	l. Sep 26, 1945 c. May 19, 1945	to AKV 10 1959 decomm. 1954; str. 1960
CVE 111	VELLA GULF ex-TOTEM BAY	Todd-Tacoma	l. Oct 19, 1944 c. Apr 9, 1945	to CVHE1955 to AKV 11 1959 decomm. 1946; str. 1960
CVE 112	SIBONEY ex-FROSTY BAY	Todd-Tacoma	l. Nov 9, 1944 c. May 14, 1945	to AKV 12 1959 decomm. 1956; str. 1970
CVE 113	PUGET SOUND ex-HOBART BAY	Todd-Tacoma	l. Nov 30, 1944 c. June 18, 1945	to CVHE 1955 to AKV 13 1959 decomm. 1946; str. 1960
CVE 114	RENDOVA ex-MOSSER BAY	Todd-Tacoma	l. Dec 28, 1944 c. Oct 22, 1945	to AKV 14 1959 decomm. 1955; str. 1971
CVE 115	BAIROKO ex-PORTAGE BAY	Todd-Tacoma	l. Jan 25, 1945 c. July 16, 1945	to AKV 15 1959 decomm. 1955; str. 1960
CVE 116	BADOENG STRAIT ex-SAN ALBERTO BAY	Todd-Tacoma	l. Feb 15, 1945 c. Nov 14, 1945	to CVHE 1955 to AKV 16 1959 decomm. 1957; str. 1970
CVE 117	SAIDOR ex-SALTERY	Todd-Tacoma BAY	l. Mar 17, 1945 c. Sep 4, 1945	to CVHE 1955 to AKV 17 1959 decomm. 1947; str. 1970
CVE 118	SICILY ex-SANDY BAY	Todd-Tacoma	l. Apr 14, 1945 c. Feb 27, 1946	to AKV 18 1959 decomm. 1954; str. 1960
CVE 119	POINT CRUZ ex-TROCADERO BAY	Todd-Tacoma	l. May 18, 1945 c. Oct 16, 1945	to AKV 19 1959 decomm. 1956; str. 1970
CVE 120	MINDORO	Todd-Tacoma	l. June 27, 1945 c. Dec 4, 1945	to AKV 20 1959 decomm. 1955; str. 1959
CVE 121	RABAUL	Todd-Tacoma	l. June 14, 1945	to CVHE 1955 to AKV 21 1959 str. 1971

NO.	NAME	BUILDER		STATUS
CVE 122	PALAU	Todd-Tacoma	l. Aug 6, 1945 c. Jan 15, 1945	to AKV 22 1959 decomm. 1954; str. 1960
CVE 123	TINIAN	Todd-Tacoma	l. Sep 15, 1945	to CVHE 1955 to AKV 23 1959 str. 1970
CVE 124	BASTOGNE	Todd-Tacoma		cancelled
CVE 125	ENIWETOK	Todd-Tacoma		cancelled
CVE 126	LINGAYEN	Todd-Tacoma		cancelled
CVE 127	OKINAWA	Todd-Tacoma		cancelled

Displacement:	10,900 tons standard
	24,275 tons full load
Dimensions:	$557^{1}/_{12}$ ft oa (525 ft wl) x 75 ft x 32 ft
Flight deck:	$105^{1}/_{6}$ ft
Propulsion:	steam turbines; 16,000 shp; 2 shafts
Boilers:	4
Speed:	19 knots
Gun battery:	2 5-inch/38-cal DP (2 single)
	36 40-mm/57-cal Bofors AA (3 quad, 12 twin)
	several 20-mm/70-cal Oerlikon AA
Aircraft:	50
Catapults:	2 hydraulic
Elevators:	2 centerline
Complement:	1,065

These ships are based on the SANGAMON-class CVEs with similar dimensions and displacement, albeit with a smaller fuel capacity. The CVE 121 was delivered on to the Navy on August 30, 1945, and the CVE 123 on July 30, 1946, but neither ship was placed in commission. Sixteen ships of this class were cancelled on August 11, 1945: the CVE 124—139; the CVE 128—139 were unnamed. The CVE 124—131 were to be built at Todd-Tacoma; the CVE 132—139 at Kaiser, Vancouver, i.e., follow-on ships to the CASABLANCA class. The CVE 124—127 were laid down in 1945.

The CVE 106 and 116 were completed by Commercial Iron Works, and the CVE 108 and 114 by Willamette.

The GILBERT ISLANDS was stricken on June 1, 1961; she was reinstated on the Navy List on June 1, 1963, and converted to a major communications relay ship (AGMR 1), being renamed ANNAPOLIS and placed in commission on March 7, 1964. She was again decommissioned in 1969 and stricken in 1976.

TRAINING CARRIER NOTES

The U.S. Navy acquired two paddle-wheel steamers in World War II for conversion to training carriers. Operating on the Great Lakes, the SABLE and WOLVERINE alleviated the need for front-line carriers to be employed for carrier qualification training. In the post-World War II era several CVLs were employed in this role, followed by two ESSEX-class carriers, the ANTIETAM (CVS 36) from 1957 to 1962, and the LEXINGTON (CVS/CVT/AVT 16) from 1963 to 1991. The large FORRESTAL was reclassified as a training carrier (AVT 59) in 1992 but never served in that role and was decommissioned and stricken the following year.

From 1942 to 1945 the two carriers qualified 17,820 pilots with 65,000 landings on the WOLVERINE and 51,000 landings on the SABLE.

1 TRAINING CARRIER: "WOLVERINE"

NO.	NAME	BUILDER		STATUS
IX 64	WOLVERINE	American SB-	l. 1913	decomm./str. 1945
	ex-*Seeandbee*	Wyandotte	c. Aug 12, 1942	

Displacement:	7,200 tons full load
Dimensions:	500 ft oa (484½ ft wl) x 58 ft x 15½ ft
Flight deck:	58 ft
Propulsion:	reciprocating engine; 11,000 shp; 2 sidewheels
Boilers:	4
Speed:	18 knots
Gun battery:	none
Aircraft:	none assigned
Catapults:	none
Elevators:	none
Complement:	325

The ship was acquired by the Navy on March 12, 1942; her conversion to a training carrier began in May 1942. No hangar, catapult, or elevators were provided in these ships.

Both the SABLE and WOLVERINE were decommissioned on November 7, 1945, and stricken later that same month; both were scrapped.

The designation IX indicated "miscellaneous unclassified."

1 TRAINING CARRIER: "SABLE"

NO.	NAME	BUILDER		STATUS
IX 81	SABLE	American SB-Lorain	l. 1924	decomm./str. 1945
	ex-*Greater Buffalo*		c. Apr 8, 1943	

Displacement:	8,000 tons standard
Dimensions:	550 ft oa (519 ft wl) x 58 ft x 15½ ft
Flight deck:	58 ft
Propulsion:	reciprocating engines; 10,500 shp; 2 sidewheels
Boilers:	4
Speed:	18 knots
Gun battery:	none
Aircraft:	none assigned
Catapults:	none
Elevators:	none
Complement:	300

The ship was acquired by the Navy on August 7, 1942. her hull length was 535 foot; the flght deck had a 15 foot overhang,

AMPHIBIOUS ASSAULT SHIPS

NO.	NAME		LPH COMM.	STAUS
LPH 1	BLOCK ISLAND (ex-CVE 106)		—	conversion cancelled
LPH 4	BOXER (ex-CV 21)		1959	str. 1969
LPH 5	PRINCETON (ex-CV 37)		1959	str. 1970
LPH 6	THETIS BAY (ex-CVE 90)		1956	str. 1964
LPH 8	VALLEY FORGE (ex-CV 45)		1961	str. 1970

The LPH classification for amphibious assault ship was established in the U.S. Navy in 1955. (The U.S. Navy designation LPH *never* signified "Landing Platform Helicopter," as has appeared in some publications.)

The World War II-era escort carrier BLOCK ISLAND was to have been LPH 1, but her conversion was cancelled in 1958. Three large aircraft carriers of the ESSEX (CV 9) class subsequently were modified to LPHs as was the escort carrier THETIS BAY. The THETIS BAY was reclassified as CVHA 1 in 1955 and was changed to LPH 6 in 1959.

The TARAWA (CVS 40) operated extensively with Marine helicopters in the late 1950s but was not recassified.

The THETIS BAY underwent extensive conversion in 1955-1956 for the LPH role. She was initially designated CVHA 1, but changed to LPH in 1959 to avoid confusion and budget competition with CV-type aircraft carriers.

The LPH/LHA/LHD carriers have "battle" names or are named for earlier warships, most of which were named for battles.

7 HELICOPTER/VSTOL CARRIERS: "IWO JIMA" CLASS

NO.	NAME	BUILDER		STATUS
LPH 2	IWO JIMA	Puget Sound NSYd	l. Sep 17, 1960 c. Aug 26, 1961	decomm./str. 1993 (scrapped)
LPH 3	OKINAWA	Philadelphia NSYd	l. Aug 14, 1961 c. Apr 14, 1992	decomm./str. 1992 (target)
LPH 7	GUADALCANAL	Philadelphia NSYd	l. Mar 16, 1963 c. July 20, 1963	decomm./str. 1994 (target)
LPH 9	GUAM	Philadelphia NSYd	l. Aug 22, 1964 c. Jan 16, 1965	decomm./str. 1998 (target)
LPH 10	TRIPOLI	Ingalls SB	l. July 31, 1965 c. Aug 6, 1966	decomm./str. 1995 (scrapped)
LPH 11	NEW ORLEANS	Philadelphia NSYd	l. Feb 3, 1968 c. Nov 16, 1968	decomm. 1997; str. 1998 (target)
LPH 12	INCHON	Ingalls SB	l. May 24, 1969 c. June 20, 1970	to MCS 12 1995 decomm. 2002; str. 2004 (target)

Displacement:	13,465 tons light 19,395 tons full load
Dimensions:	592 ft oa x 84 ft x 26 ft
Flight deck:	104 ft
Propulsion:	steam turbine; 22,000 shp; 1 shaft
Boilers:	2
Speed:	20 knots
Gun battery:	8 3-inch/50-cal AA (4 twin)
Aircraft:	24 helicopters/VSTOL
Catapults:	none
Elevators:	2 deck edge
Complement:	530 + 2,090 troops

The IWO JIMA class represented an improved World War II type escort carrier design with accommodations for a Marine battalion and a helicopter squadron. Some ships later operated Harrier VSTOL aircraft on a limited basis. Unlike the Royal Navy's commando carriers and the later TARAWA/WASP classes, the LPHs did not carry landing craft except that LCVP davits were provided in the INCHON. The GUAM served as an interim Sea Control Ship (SCS) in 1971-1972. Several of these ships have been employed in the mine countermeasures role, operating CH-53/MH-53/RH-53 helicopters.

The INCHON was converted to a mine countermeasures support ship (MCS 12) in 1995-1996. She was prematurely decommissioned and stricken on June 20, 2002, following a fire that caused extensive damage while undergoing an overhaul.

Several ships were sunk as targets in weapon trials.

5 HELICOPTER/VSTOL CARRIERS: "TARAWA" CLASS

NO.	NAME	BUILDER		STATUS
LHA 1	TARAWA	Litton/Ingalls	l. Dec 1, 1973 c. May 29, 1976	**active**
LHA 2	SAIPAN	Litton/Ingalls	l. July 18, 1974 c. Oct 15, 1977	decomm./str. 2007
LHA 3	BELLEAU WOOD	Litton/Ingalls	l. Apr 11, 1977 c. Sep 23, 1978	decomm./str. 2005 (target)
LHA 4	NASSAU	Litton/Ingalls	l. Jan 21, 1978 c. July 28, 1979	**active**
LHA 5	PELELIU ex-DA NANG ex-KHE SANH	Litton/Ingalls	l. Nov 25, 1978 c. May 3, 1980	**active**

Displacement:	26,255 tons light 39,925 tons full load
Dimensions:	820 ft oa (778 ft wl) x $106^2/_3$ ft x $27^1/_2$ ft
Flight deck:	132 ft
Propulsion:	steam turbines; 70,000 shp; 2 shafts
Boilers:	2
Speed:	24 knots
Missile launchers:	2 Sea Sparrow AA launchers (2 octuple)
Gun battery:	3 5-inch/54-cal DP (3 single) 6 20-mm AA (6 single)
Aircraft:	approx. 30 helicopters/VSTOL
Catapults:	none
Elevators:	1 deck edge, 1 stern
Complement:	730 + 1,900 troops

These are large helicopter carriers with a limited VSTOL capability. They are larger in some dimensions than World War II-era ESSEX-class carriers. Their design includes a large docking well and elaborate troop accommodations and vehicle and equipment stowage.

Nine ships of this class were originally planned in the early 1960s. The LHA 6- 9 were cancelled on February 9, 1971.

The BELLEAU WOOD was sunk as a target in weapon tests in 2006.

(1) HELICOPTER/VSTOL CARRIERS: IMPROVED "TARAWA" CLASS

NO.	NAME	BUILDER		STATUS
LHD 6	......	NGSS Ingalls	l. c. 2012	building

Displacement:	48,775 tons full load
Dimensions:	$920^2/_3$ ft oa x 106 ft x 26 ft
Flight deck:	$149^{11}/_{12}$ ft
Propulsion:	2 gas turbines; 72,000 shp; 2 shafts
Speed:	24 knots
Missile launchers:	1 28-cell Enhanced Sea Sparrow AA launcher
	2 21-cell RAM AA launchers
Gun battery:	3 20-mm Phalanx multibarrel CIWS
Aircraft:	30 helicopters/VSTOL
Catapults:	none
Elevators:	2 deck edge
Complement:	.... + 1,680 troops

The Navy plans to construct several of these ships as replacements for the TARAWA class. The contract for the lead ship was awarded on June 1, 2007.

This ship differs from the TARAWA class in having a "dry" well deck and an enlarged hangar deck to accommodate VSTOL aircraft, including the F-35B Joint Strike Fighter/ Lightning II. The dry well deck can accommodate air cusion landing craft (LCAC) as well as tracked amphibious assault vehicles (LVT/AAV/EFV).

7 HELICOPTER/VSTOL CARRIERS: "WASP" CLASS

NO.	NAME	BUILDER		STATUS
LHD 1	WASP	Litton/Ingalls	l. Aug 4, 1987 c. July 29, 1989	active
LHD 2	ESSEX	Litton/Ingalls	l. Feb 23, 1991 c. Oct 17, 1992	active
LHD 3	KEARSARGE	Litton/Ingalls	l. Mar 26, 1992 c. Oct 16, 1993	active
LHD 4	BOXER	Litton/Ingalls	l. Aug 7, 1993 c. Feb 11, 1995	active
LHD 5	BATAAN	Litton/Ingalls	l. Mar 15, 1996 c. Sep 20, 1997	active
LHD 6	BONHOMME RICHARD	Litton/Ingalls	l. Mar 14, 1997 c. Aug 15, 1998	active
LHD 7	IWO JIMA	NGSS Ingalls	l. Mar 25, 2001 c. June 30, 2001	active

Displacement:	28,050 tons light
	41,000 tons full load
Dimensions:	844 ft oa ($777^2/_3$ ft wl) x 106 ft x $26^2/_3$ ft
Flight deck:	140 ft
Propulsion:	steam turbines; 70,000 shp; 2 shafts
Boilers:	2
Speed:	24 knots
Missile launchers:	2 Sea Sparrow AA launchers (2 octuple)
Gun battery:	3 20-mm Phalanx multibarrel CIWS
Aircraft:	30 helicopters/VSTOL
Catapults:	none
Elevators:	2 deck edge
Complement:	1,080 + 1,900 troops

These are improved TARAWA-class amphibious assault ships with improved docking wells and enhanced facilities for supporting VSTOL aircraft.

Note that the BONHOMME RICHARD carries the name of the ship commanded by John Paul Jones in 1779; the earlier carrier was the BON HOMME RICHARD (CV 31)

1 HELICOPTER/VSTOL CARRIER: IMPROVED "WASP"

NO.	NAME	BUILDER		STATUS
LHD 8	MAKIN ISLAND	NGSS Ingalls	l. Sep 22, 2006 c. 2008	building

Displacement:	28,333 tons light 41,335 tons full load
Dimensions:	844 ft oa (777²/₃ ft wl) x 106 ft x 28 ft
Flight deck:	140 ft
Propulsion:	2 gas turbines; 72,000 shp; 2 shafts
Speed:	24 knots
Missile launchers:	2 Sea Sparrow AA launchers (2 octuple) 2 21-cell RAM AA launchers
Gun battery:	2 20-mm Phalanx multibarrel CIWS 3 25-mm/75-cal Bushmaster AA (3 single)
Aircraft:	30 helicopters/VSTOL
Catapults:	none
Elevators:	2 deck edge
Complement:	.... + 1,900 troops

The one-of-a-kind MAKIN ISLAND differs from the WASP-class LHDs primarily in having gas turbine propulsion with electric auxiliary power; the latter is capable of providing a speed of 13 knots.

An American-built carrier and American-built aircraft: HMS *Ruler* in the Western Pacific in 1945 with a deckload of Avengers, Corsairs, and Hellcats. Laid down in the United States on March 25, 1943, as the *St. Joseph* (CVE 50), she was transferred to the Royal Navy upon completion. During 1945 she served in British Pacific Fleet as an aircraft transport and as a combat carrier, in the latter role providing air cover for replenishment groups. (Leo Van Ginderen collection)

UNION OF SOVIET SOCIALIST REPUBLICS

Soviet-era naval ships were assigned project numbers during the design stage, beginning with Project No. 1, the LENINGRAD-class large destroyers, first completed in 1936. (This scheme was similar to the U.S. Navy's Ship Characteristics Board numbers assigned from 1947 onward.)

All Soviet-era aviation ships were constructed at Shipyard No. 444—referred to as the Nikolayev south yard—located south of the city of Nikolayev, at the mouth of the Southern Bug River, near the Black Sea.

U.S.-NATO designations are used in this section for missile systems (Soviet designations in parens).

2 HELICOPTER CARRIER—MISSILE CRUISERS: "MOSKVA" CLASS

PROJECT	NAME	BUILDER		STATUS
1123.1	MOSKVA	Nikolayev	l. Jan 14, 1965 c. Dec 25, 1967	str. Nov 7, 1996
1123.2	LENINGRAD	Nikolayev	l. July 31, 1968 c. June 2, 1969	str. June 24, 1991

Displacement:	11,300 tonnes standard 14,600 tonnes full load
Dimensions:	$620\frac{1}{4}$ ft oa (587 ft wl) x $75\frac{5}{12}$ ft x $25\frac{1}{4}$ ft
Flight deck:	$111\frac{1}{2}$ ft
Propulsion:	steam turbines; 90,000 shp; 2 shafts
Boilers:	4
Speed:	29 knots
Missile launchers:	2 SA-N-3 Goa twin launchers AA
Gun battery:	4 57-mm/80-cal AA (2 twin)
Torpedo tubes:	10 21-inch torpedo tubes (2 x quintuple)
Aircraft:	14 helicopters
Catapults:	none
Elevators:	2 offset centerline
Complement:	540

These ships were highly innovative combination helicopter carrier—missile cruisers developed for the ASW role. They were the first specialized aviation ships to be built by the Soviet Union. In addition to the hangar deck beneath the flight deck, two hangars for Ka-25 Hormone helicopters were built into the after face of the superstructure.

The MOSKVA ceased operations in 1992 and served as an accommodation ship until stricken.

The ships were fitted with MG-342 low-frequency, hull-mounted sonar and MG-325 medium-frequency, variable depth sonar. Two ASW weapon systems were installed in addition to the torpedo tubes: two RBU-6000 rocket launchers (2 x 12 tubes) and one SUW-N-1 twin rocket launcher.

The SA-N-3 missile system had an anti-air and anti-surface capability.

3 VSTOL CARRIERS: "KIEV" CLASS

PROJECT	NAME	BUILDER		STATUS
1143.1	KIEV	Nikolayev	l. Dec 26, 1972 c. Dec 28, 1975	str. 1993
1143.2	MINSK	Nikoyavev	l. Sep 30, 1975 c. Sep 27, 1978	str. 1993
1143.3	NOVOROSSIYSK	Nikolavev	l. Dec 26, 1978 c. Aug 14, 1982	str. 1993

Displacement:	30,500 tonnes standard
	41,400 tonnes full load
Dimensions:	895$^{1}/_{2}$ ft oa (818$^{1}/_{3}$ ft wl) x 107$^{1}/_{4}$ ft x 29$^{1}/_{2}$ ft
Flight deck:	164 ft
Propulsion:	steam turbines; 180,000 shp; 4 shafts
Boilers:	8
Speed:	30 knots
Missile launchers:	8 SS-N-12 Sandbox anti-ship (4 twin)
	2 SA-N-3 Goa twin AA launchers
Gun battery:	4 76.2-mm/59-cal DP (2 twin)
	8 30-mm multibarrel CIWS
Aircraft:	36 helicopters/VSTOL
Catapults:	none
Elevators:	1 centerline, 1 off center
Complement:	1,300

These ships were an enlarged development of the MOSKVA class, combining the features of a VSTOL carrier and a missile cruiser. The lengthy design and construction period led to significant differences among these ships. The fourth unit, the BAKU, was significantly different and is addressed separately.

The ships had bow-mounted, hull-mounted, and towed-array sonars. Two RBU-6000 rocket launchers were fitted (2 x 12 tubes) as were ten 21-inch torpedo tubes (2 quintuple). Eight reload missiles were carried for the SS-N-12 launchers.

1 VSTOL CARRIER: IMPROVED "KIEV" CLASS

PROJECT	NAME	BUILDER		STATUS
1143.4	ADMIRAL FLOTA SOVETSKOGO SOYUZA GORSHKOV ex-BAKU	Nikolavev	l. Mar 31, 1982 c. Dec 11, 1987	to India 2004

Displacement:	34,500 tonnes standard
	44,500 tonnes full load
Dimensions:	895$^{1}/_{2}$ ft oa (818$^{1}/_{3}$ ft wl) x 107$^{1}/_{4}$ ft x 31$^{1}/_{6}$ ft
Flight deck:	173$^{5}/_{6}$ ft
Propulsion:	steam turbines; 180,000 shp; 4 shafts
Boilers:	8
Speed:	30 knots
Missile launchers:	12 SS-N-12 Sandbox anti-ship (2 sextuple)
	8 24-cell SA-N-9 Gopher rotary AA launchers
Gun battery:	2 100-mm/70-cal DP (2 single)
	8 30-mm multibarrel CIWS
Aircraft:	36 helicopters/VSTOL
Catapults:	none
Elevators:	1 centerline, 1 off center
Complement:	1,600

The ship was renamed for Admiral of the Fleet of the Soviet Union Gorshkov in 1990. No reloads were carried for the SS-N-12 launchers. As built, two RBU-6000 ASW rocket launchers were provided.

The ship is being extensively modified for service in the Indian Navy.

1 AIRCRAFT CARRIER: "RIGA" CLASS

PROJECT	NAME	BUILDER		STATUS
1143.5	ADMIRAL FLOTA SOVETSKOGO SOYUZA KUZNETSOV ex-TBILISI ex-LEONID BREZHNEV ex-RIGA	Nikolayev	l. Dec 5, 1985 c. Dec 25, 1990	**active**
1143.6	VARYAG ex-RIGA	Nikolayev	l. Nov 25, 1988	cancelled

Displacement:	45,000 tonnes standard
	55,000 tonnes full load
Dimensions:	984 ft oa x 130$^{1}/_{4}$. ft x 32$^{5}/_{6}$ ft
Flight deck:	213$^{1}/_{6}$ ft
Propulsion:	steam turbines; 200,000 shp; 4 shafts
Boilers:	8
Speed:	29 knots
Missile launchers:	16 SS-N-19 Shipwreck anti-ship (16 single)
	8 24-cell SA-N-9 Gopher rotary AA launchers
	8 combination SA-N-11 close-in defense missile/
	2 30-mm multibarrel CIWS mountings
Gun battery:	6 30-mm multibarrel CIWS
Aircraft:	50
Catapults:	none
Elevators:	2 outboard
Complement:	1,500

The long-range Shipwreck missiles are "buried" in the forward flight deck. The ship is fitted with an angled flight deck and ski-jump forward.

The ship was renamed for Leonid Brezhnev in 1982, then Tbilisi in 1987, and for Admiral of the Fleet of the Soviet Union Kuznetsov in 1990. The second ship was renamed VARYAG in 1990.

AIRCRAFT CARRIERS "UL'YANOVSK" CLASS

PROJECT	NAME	BUILDER	STATUS
1143.7	UL'YANOVSK	Nikolayev	cancelled

Displacement:	66,000 tonnes standard
	75,000 tonnes full load
Dimensions:	1,049$^{7}/_{12}$ ft oa x .... ft x 34$^{5}/_{12}$ ft
Flight deck:	259 ft
Propulsion:	steam turbines; 280,000 shp; 4 shafts
Reactors:	2 pressurized-water
Speed:	30 knots
Missile launchers:	
Gun battery:	
Aircraft:	70
Catapults:	2 steam
Elevators:	3 deck edge
Complement:	

The UL'YANOVSK was to have been the Soviet Union's first nuclear-propelled aircraft carrier. A second ship was planned and, although not authorized, components and material were being assembled for her at Nikolayev when the program was cancelled following the demise of the Soviet Union. The UL'YANOVSK was laid down in 1988 and, when 20 percent complete, was scrapped in the building dock beginning in 1992.

The two catapults were to be fitted on the angled deck; a ski-jump was to be installed forward.

A Yak-38M—NATO code-name Forger—VSTOL aircraft rides an elevator in a *Kiev*-class aircraft carrier. The Soviet Navy's carrier program evolved very differently than did West carrier efforts. Beginning with the *Moskva*-class helicopter ships, the Soviet program was oriented toward the ASW role and combined missile cruiser capabilities with the carrier configuration. The demise of the Soviet Union at the end of 1991 also terminated the highly innovative carrier effort.

ABBREVIATIONS:

AA	anti-aircraft	mm	millimeter
bhp	brake horsepower (diesel engines)	NYd	Navy Yard
c.	commissioned	NYSd	Naval Shipyard
cal	caliber	oa	overall
CIWS	Close-In Weapon System	SB	shipbuilding
decomm.	decommissioned	shp	shaft horsepower
DP	dual-purpose	str.	stricken (from the Navy List)
ft	feet	wl	waterline
l.	launched	x	length x beam x draft

BUILDERS:

France
Alstrom, St. Nazaire
Ateliers, St. Nazaire-Penhoët
Atlantique, St. Nazaire
Brest Arsenal
Mediteranean Shipyard, La Seyne

Germany
A.G. Weser, Bremen
Deutsche, Kiel
Germania, Kiel
Vulkan, Bremen

Great Britain *
Alexander Stephen & Sons, Govan
Armstrong, Clydebank
Armstrong, Newcastle
Armstrong, Wallsend

BAE Systems (formerly Royal Dockyard Rosyth)

Beadmore, Glasgow

Caledon SB & Engineering, Dundee

Cammell Laird, Birkenhead

Davenport Dock Yard

Fairfield SB & Engineering, Clydeside

Harland & Wolff, Belfast

Hawthorn Leslie, Heburn-on-Tyne

John Brown SB & Engineering, Clydebank

Kvaerner Govan, Clyde

Sir W.G. Armstrong Whitworth, Newcastle-on-Tyne

Stephen & Sons, Glasgow

Swan Hunter & Wigham Richardson, Wallsend-on-Tyne

Vickers Armstrong, Barrow-in-Furness

Vickers Armstrong, Newcastle-on-Tyne

India

Cochin Shipyard, Kochi

Italy

Cantier; Navali Bveda

Fincantieri, La Spezia

Fincantieri, Monfaleone

Fincantieri, Riva Trigoso

Societa Anonima Ansaldo, Genoa

Societa Anonima Ansaldo, Ponente

Japan

Asano SB, Tsurumi

Kawasaki, Kobe

Kure Navy Yard

Marine United, Yokohama

Mitsubishi, Nagasaki

Yokohama Dock

Yokosuka Navy Yard

Spain

Bazán shipyard, Ferrol (later Izar Shipyard)

Navantia, Ferrol

United States **

American SB, Lorain, Ohio

American SB, Wyandotte, Mich.

Bethlehem Steel, Quincy, Mass. (formerly Fore River SB)

Ingalls SB, Pascagoula, Miss. (Acquired by Northrop Grumman Ship Systems in 2001)

Kaiser SB, Vancouver, Wash.

Mare Island Naval Shipyard, Vallejo, Calif.

Newport News Shipbuilding & Dry Dock, Va. (Acquired by Northrop Grumman in 2001)

New York Naval Shipyard, Brooklyn, N.Y.

New York SB, Camden, N.J.

Norfolk Naval shipyard, Va.

Philadelphia Naval Shipyard, Pa.

Puget Sound Naval Shipyard, Bremerton, Wash.
Seattle-Tacoma SB, Tacoma, Wash.
Sun SB & Dry Dock, Chester, Pa.
Todd-Pacific Shipyards, Tacoma, Wash.
Western Pipe & Steel, San Francisco, Calif.

USSR
Black Sea (Shipyard No. 444), Nikolayev (South) (After December 1991 the shipyard was in Ukraine.)

* In 1928 Armstrong, Whitworth merged with Vickers of Barrow-in-Furness to form Vickers-Armstrong.
** U.S. Navy Yards were redesignated Naval Shipyards on November 30, 1945.

A U.S. Navy MH-60S Seahawk helicopter lands aboard the recently completed South Korean amphibious ship *Doko* during operations in the Sea of Japan in November 2007. Placed in commission the previous July, the 18,860-ton *Doko* and the later *Maradao* resemble small aircraft carriers. They have a docking well that can accommodate air cushion landing craft. Note the *Doko*'s carrier-type starboard island structure. In the future such "amphibs" that can operate the F-35B VSTOL variant of the U.S. Joint Strike Fighter as well as helicopters will provide a significant naval capability. (Christian Lemus, U.S. Navy)

CV 18 *Wasp**
    SCB-27A   Sep 1948—Sep 1951   New York NSYd
    SCB-125   May 1955—Dec 1955 San Francisco NSYd

CV 19 *Hancock*
    SCB-27C   July 1951—Mar 1954 Puget Sound NSYd
    SCB-125   Aug 1955—Nov 1956 San Francisco NSYd

CV 20 *Bennington**
    SCB-27A   Oct 1950—Nov 1952 New York NSYd
    SCB-125   July 1954—Apr 1955 New York NSYd

CV 31 *Bon Homme Richard*
    SCB-27C   and
    SCB-125   July 1952—Nov 1955 San Francisco NSYd

CV 33 *Kearsarge**
    SCB-27A   Jan 1950—Mar 1952 Puget Sound NSYd
    SCB-125   Jan 1956—Jan 1957 Puget Sound NSYd

CV 34 *Oriskany*
completed as SCB-27A
    SCB-27C and
    SCB-125   July 1956—Mar 1959 San Francisco NSYd

CV 36 *Antietam*
    angled deck   Sep 1952—Dec 1952 New York NSYd

CV 38 *Shangri-La*
    SCB-27C and
    SCB-125   July 1952—Feb 1955 Puget Sound NSYd

CV 39 *Lake Champlain*
    SCB-27A   Aug 1950—Sep 1952 Newport News Shipbuilding

CVB 41 *Midway*
    SCB-110 and
    angled deck   July 1954—Nov 1957 Puget Sound NSYd

CVB 42 *Franklin D. Roosevelt*
    SCB-110 and
    angled deck   Oct 1953—May 1956 Puget Sound NSYd

CVB 43 *Coral Sea*
    SCB-110 and
    angled deck   July 1956—Mar 1960 Puget Sound NSY

APPENDIX E
HARRIER AIRCRAFT PRODUCTION

The British-developed Harrier was the first VSTOL aircraft to become operational and has served in six military air arms as well as in the Tripartite Squadron formed by Great Britain, West Germany, and the United States. This is a Spanish Navy AV-8B Harrier II operating from the carrier *Principe de Asturias* during a NATO exercise in the Balearic Sea in 2007. The Spanish carrier is a variant of the planned U.S. Sea Control Ship (SCS), developed in the early 1970s but never built. (Leonardo Carrillo, U.S. Navy)

MODEL	PROCURED	CREW	INITIAL USER
P.1127	6	1	Prototypes
Kestrel FGA.1/GR.1	9	1	Tripartite Squadron*
Harrier GR.1/GR.1A	84	1	Royal Air Force
Harrier T.2	12	2	Royal Air Force
Harrier T.2A	2	2	Royal Air Force
Harrier GR.3	40	1	Royal Air Force
Harrier T.4/T.4A	14	2	Royal Air Force
Harrier T.4N	3	2	Fleet Air Arm
Harrier Mk 52	1	2	Hawker Siddeley/British Aerospace**
Harrier GR.5	43	1	Royal Air Force

Harrier GR.5A	19	1	Royal Air Force
Harrier GR.7	34	1	Royal Air Force
Harrier T.10	13	2	Royal Air Force
Sea Harrier FRS.1	57	1	Fleet Air Arm
Sea Harrier FRS.51	23	1	Indian Navy
Sea Harrier FA.2	18	1	Fleet Air Arm
Harrier T.60	4	2	Indian Navy
AV-8A Harrier	102	1	U.S. Marine Corps
TAV-8A Harrier	8	2	U.S. Marine Corps
AV-8S Matador	11	1	Spanish Navy
TAV-8S Matador	2	2	Spanish Navy
AV-8B Harrier II	232	1	U.S. Marine Corps
EAV-8B Harrier II	12	1	Spanish Navy
AV-8B+ Harrier II	30	1	U.S. Marine Corps
	16	1	Italian Navy
EAV-8B+ Harrier II	9	1	Spanish Navy
TAV-8B Harrier II	21	2	U.S. Marine Corps
	2	2	Italian Navy
	1	2	Spanish Navy

Total 828

* Established to evaluate the Kestrel by Great Britain, West Germany, and the United States.

** The Mk 52 was the privately funded Hawker Siddeley two-seat demonstration aircraft, given the commercial registration G-VTOL and the military registration ZA250. The latter was assigned to permit the aircraft to carry weapons.

NOTES

Chapter 1: The "Peaceful" Years

1 Gen. James H. Doolittle, *I Could Never Be So Lucky Again* (New York: Bantam Books, 1991), pp. 466–468. Mitscher had been the commanding officer of the carrier *Hornet* (CV 8) that launched the Doolittle-led B-25B bombers on the 1942 surprise raid against the Japanese home islands.

2 Adapted from David A. Rosenberg and Floyd D. Kennedy, Jr., "Supporting Study: US Aircraft Carriers in the Strategic Role," October 1975, prepared for the Deputy Chief of Naval Operations (Plans and Policy), Department of the Navy, p. I-11. This was part of the Department of Defense–directed study "History of the Strategic Arms Competition, 1945–1972"; the Navy portion of the study was performed by the Lulejian Corp. under the direction of the principal author of this book.

3 Joint Chiefs of Staff, January 11, 1946; reprinted in W. A. Shurcliff, *Bombs at Bikini: The Official Report of Operation Crossroads* (New York: William H. Wise, 1947), p. 14.

4 Shurcliff, *Bombs at Bikini*, p. 6.

5 The target ships included the German heavy cruiser *Prinz Eugen*, the Japanese battleship *Nagato*, and a Japanese light cruiser.

6 The Navy had wanted to detonate this air-burst bomb from a tethered balloon. The Army Air Forces insisted on a B-29 air drop to provide practice for the bomber crew and to demonstrate the accuracy of the bombing system. The bomb missed the aim point by two miles, thus damaging much of the sensitive monitoring equipment and reducing the scientific usefulness of the detonation.

7 The atomic bomb tests and, especially, the damage to the carriers are well described in James P. Delgado, Daniel J. Lenihan, and Larry Murphy, *The Archeology of the Atomic Bomb* (Santa Fe, N.M.: Southwest Cultural Resources Center, 1991).

8 Most sources list the *Midway* air group at 130+ aircraft, e.g., Friedman, *U.S. Aircraft Carriers*, p. 395, lists 64 F4U-4 Corsairs, 64 SB2C-5 Helldivers, and 4 F6F-5N and 4 F6F-5P Hellcats. The 144 aircraft is based on Memorandum from Op 03-5 to Informal Advisory Board, subj.: Design of New Aircraft Carrier, June 30, 1946, p. 2.

9 Nine fast battleships, five old battleships (with 16-inch guns), and the two *Alaska*-class battle cruisers were mothballed for possible future service. Of those 16 ships, only the three mothballed *Iowa*-class dreadnoughts would ever be reactivated. In addition, to these 16 capital ships, the old battleship *Mississippi* (BB 41) was converted to a gunnery-missile test ship (AG 128); she remained in commission in that role until 1956.

10 Iran (Persia) had been jointly occupied by Soviet and British troops during the war, dividing the country in half.

11 The principal difference between the F4U-4 and F4U-4B was their respective armament of six .50-cal machine guns and four 20-mm cannon.

On September 1, 1948, all carrier air groups were designated CVG regardless of the type of carrier in which they were embarked.

12 Following the establishment of the North Atlantic Treaty Organization on April 4, 1949, the Sixth Fleet additionally became the Striking and Support Forces, Southern Europe. Initially the U.S. chain of command for the Sixth Fleet was through the CinC U.S. Naval Forces Eastern Atlantic and Mediterranean (NELM) and subsequently CinC U.S. Naval Forces Europe (NavEur), who reported to the U.S. CinC Europe (CinCEur). As a NATO command, the fleet reported to the NATO CinC Southern Europe (a U.S. admiral) and through him to the Supreme Allied Commander Europe (SACEur), who also served as the U.S. CinCEur.

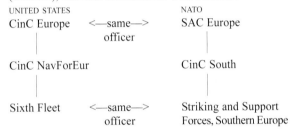

13 JATO = Jet Assisted Takeoff—a misnomer for the rocket boosters.

14 In October 1945 the British fired three captured V-2 missiles from Cuxhaven on the North Sea in Operation Backfire. Subsequently, in both the United States and USSR the Germans helped to assemble and test V-2 missiles. Sixty-eight were test fired in the United States and 11 in the Soviet Union over the next few years.

15 Office of the Chief of Naval Operations, Navy Department, *Report of Operation Sandy: The Launching of a V-2 Rocket from the Deck of the Carrier U.S.S. Midway at Sea* (Summer 1947).

16 Max Rosenberg, *The Air Force and the National Guided Missile Program* (Washington, D.C.: U.S. Air Force Historical Division Liaison Office, June 1964), p. 9.

17 Orville Wright had sent the Wright Flyer to the Science Museum in South Kensington, London, in 1928 after the Smithsonian Institution claimed that the Langley Aerodrome had been the first successful powered aircraft. That statement was not publicly retracted until 1942.

18 The Wright Flyer is now on display in the National Air and Space Museum on The Mall in Washington, D.C.

19 Adm. John was the son of noted artist Augustus Edwin John. The younger John was First Sea Lord from May 1960 to August 1963.

20 After a strenuous 27 years of service, the *Furious* was taken out of service in September 1944; she was then offered to the British Pacific Fleet, but instead of becoming an accommodation ship, was placed in reserve. From 1945 to 1948,

berthed at Loch Striven, near Rothesay, she was used as a trials ship, mainly as a target for aircraft weapons. She was sold off for scrapping in 1948.

21 The *Campania* was completed in March 1944; her aircraft were credited with sinking two U-boats and shooting down two German reconnaissance aircraft.

22 The British government had asked the U.S. government for permission to detonate the first British A-bomb at the Nevada test site. The two governments could not reach agreement on using a U.S. test site. Also, the British government wanted to test the bomb in a simulated harbor environment.

23 Operational configurations of the Blue Danube were tested beginning October 14, 1953; a limited Valiant bomber/Blue Danube operational capability was achieved from July 1955.

24 Capt. Eric M. Brown, RN, *Wings of the Navy* (London: Jane's, 1980), p. 157.

25 The Netherlands Navy operated several aircraft squadrons on British carriers during World War II and the MAC-ships *Gadila* and *Macoma* were under the Dutch flag, the first aircraft-carrying ships to operate under those colors.

26 Schout-bij-Nacht (Rear Adm.) Doorman commanded an Allied naval force that engaged superior Japanese ships in the Java Sea on February 28, 1942. He died when his flagship, the light cruiser *de Ruyter*, was sunk.

Chapter 2: Jets and Whirlybirds

1 The Bell XP-59 was a piston-engine aircraft; the jet-propelled Airacomet was given the same designation with suffix letters to confuse enemy intelligence.

2 The world's first operational jet-propelled combat aircraft was the Messerschmitt Me 262 *Sturmvogel* (Stormbird); it made its first jet flight on July 18, 1941, and was operational in the Luftwaffe in 1944–1945.

3 The twin-boom configuration resulted from the need to keep the jet "pipe" short to limit the loss of thrust from the Goblin engine, which was installed immediately behind the pilot with the air intakes in the wing roots. The booms were used to lift the tail control surfaces clear of the exhaust. This de Havilland configuration was carried on to the firm's Venom and Vixen series.

4 No. 800 Squadron was formed on August 22, 1951, with eight aircraft, later increased to 12.

5 In 1947 the aircraft was changed to FH-1 when the McDonnell designator was changed from D to H to avoid confusion with Douglas aircraft.

Fighter squadron VF-17A became VF-171 on September 1, 1948.

6 FH-1s equipped one Navy and two Marine fighter squadrons. The aircraft served in Naval Air Reserve units for jet pilot introduction from 1949 to 1953.

7 The Air Force two-seat aircraft initially was designated P-80C; the designation was changed to T-33 in 1949.

8 The last Hellcats in U.S. Navy service were F6F-5Ns, retired in 1953 from Composite Squadron 4.

9 See Edward H. Heinemann and Capt. Rosario Rausa, USNR (Ret.), *Ed Heinemann: Combat Aircraft Designer* (Annapolis, Md.: Naval Institute Press, 1980), pp. 96–100 and 125–140, for a discussion of the development of the AD Skyraider. This is an excellent biography of the aircraft designer.

10 The Pratt & Whitney R-4360 engine was also used in the B-36 Peacemaker and B-50 Superfortress strategic bombers.

11 Heinemann and Rausa, *Ed Heinemann*, p. 126. The best journal article on the aircraft is Hill Goodspeed, "Douglas AD/A-1 Skyraider," *International Air Power Review* (vol. 17, 2005), pp. 128–157.

12 One of Heinemann's key engineers at this time was R. G. Smith, who would achieve international fame as an aviation artist.

13 These 25 aircraft were completed as:
19 XBT2D-1
2 XBT2D-1N
1 XBT2D-1P
1 XBT2D-1Q
1 XBT2D-1W
1 XAD-2

14 Squadron VA-19A was changed to VA-194 in August 1948 and was disestablished on December 1, 1949.

15 The ambulance was the AD-5 variant, which had fuselage space for additional electronic equipment or four stretchers. Takeoff and landing trails were conducted with volunteers on stretchers at Naval Air Station Patuxent River, Maryland. However, the scheme was apparently never used in the fleet.

One stretcher patient was quoted as saying, "if the carrier was sinking and he had two broken arms and two broken legs, he would take his chances swimming for it rather than take another flight on a stretcher in the belly of an AD." (Bill Campbell, "Mail Call," *Warbirds* [April 2006], p. 46.)

16 Low-level training exercises for these missions were called "Sandblower" operations because the planes' propwash often blew up sand as they crossed a beach.

17 A first-person account by a pilot of the Skyraider nuclear strike mission whose target was Sevastopol in the USSR is Daniel Ford, "Able Dog," *Foundation* [Naval Aviation Museum] (Fall 1999), pp. 46–53.

18 BOAR was in service from 1956 to 1963. BOAR stood for Bureau of Ordnance Atomic Rocket.

19 Vice Adm. Jerry Miller, USN (Ret.), *Nuclear Weapons and Aircraft Carriers: How the Bomb Saved Naval Aviation* (Washington, D.C.: Smithsonian Institution Press, 2001), pp. 214–215.

20 The U.S. Marine Corps flew the Skyraider in 13 squadrons, from 1951 to 1958.

21 The original Grumman XF9F-1 design was for a two-seat night fighter with four wing-mounted turbojet engines, a competitive design to the Douglas F3D Skyknight.

22 The U.S. pilot was Lt. Comdr. (later Vice Adm.) Donald D. Engen. He described the rubber-deck trials in *Wings and Warriors: My Life as a Naval Aviator* (Washington, D.C.: Smithsonian Institution Press, 1997), pp. 150–152. Brown described the trials in *Wings on my Sleeve* (London: Arthur Baker, 1961), pp. 140–143.

23 The trials and tribulations of the Patuxent River experiments are told by Navy test pilot Comdr. John Moore, USN (Ret.), *The Wrong Stuff: Flying on the Edge of Disaster* (North Branch, Minn.: Specialty Press, 1997), pp. 142–160.

24 Capt. R. N. Liptrot, RN, *Rotating Wing Activities in Germany during the Period 1939–1945* (London: Her Majesty's Stationery Office, 1948), p. 28.

25 Among the ships was the ex-Yugoslav seaplane tender *Zmaj*, which, like the German *Drache*, carried out trials of the Fl 282 in 1942–1943 in the Aegean Sea.

26 The Coast Guard, nominally under the Treasury Department, was transferred to the Navy from November 1, 1941, to December 28, 1945, by directive of President Roosevelt.

27 Sikorsky, a Russian immigrant, had designed and built the world's first four-engine aircraft, *The Grand*, in 1913, as well as the world's first four-engine bombers of the Il'ya Mourometz type, of which 79 were produced from 1914 to 1917. He came to the United States in 1919 and quickly achieved prominence as a flying boat designer.

28 During the war the Army also flew R-4s in combat rescue operations in Burma.

29 HMX-1 began providing helicopter transportation for U.S. presidents in September 1957, when an HUS-1 (UH-34) from HMX-1 carried President Dwight D. Eisenhower from Newport, R.I., to NAS Quonset Point, Conn. In 1976 the Marine Corps was given sole responsibility for the helicopter transport of the president, having previously shared the presidential helicopter-transport role with the Army.

Chapter 3: Atomic Bombs Aboard Ship

1 Sullivan, who served as Assistant Secretary of the Treasury from January 1940 to November 1944, became Assistant Secretary of the Navy for Air in July 1945, the Under Secretary of the Navy in June 1946, and served as secretary of the Navy from September 1947 to May 1949.

2 John L. Sullivan, Acting Secretary of the Navy, letter to President Truman, July 22, 1946, OP-602 ser. 0014P602 (SC)A-23, Operational Archives, NHC, Washington, D.C.

3 Rear Adm. Daniel V. Gallery, USN, memorandum to the DCNO (Air), December 17, 1947, ser. 00124P57. The memo was reprinted in the *Army-Navy-Air Force Register*, December 11, 1954. The Gallery documents are located in the OP-00 (Chief of Naval Operations) and OP-23 records in the Operational Archives, NHC.

4 Walter Millis (ed.), *The Forrestal Diaries* (New York: Viking, 1951), p. 467.

5 Dr. Jeffrey Barlow, Naval Historical Center, "Comments on Draft Chapter 31," memorandum to N. Polmar, October 7, 2005.

6 Millis, *The Forrestal Diaries*, p. 467.

7 See Al Christman, *Target Hiroshima: Deak Parsons and the Creation of the Atomic Bomb* (Annapolis, Md.: Naval Institute Press, 1998).

8 The Mk III was the production version of the Fat Man bomb dropped on Nagasaki; it weighed 10,300 pounds and had an explosive force of approximately 21 kilotons. The weapon was in service from August 1945 to 1950. The Mk IV was an improved Fat Man–type implosion bomb, weighing 10,800 pounds and having a yield of 1 to 31 kilotons, depending upon the nuclear capsule inserted into the casing. It was in service from March 1949 to 1953.

9 The Neptune's takeoff weight for the record flight was 85,000 pounds. The plane's distance record was broken by an Air Force B-52H Stratofortress that flew 12,532 miles in 1962. It broke the record 16 years after it was set.

10 Under a secret contract, Lockheed modified one P2V-2 and 11 P2V-3 aircraft. See Wayne Mutza, *Lockheed P2V Neptune: An Illustrated History* (Atglen, Pa.: Schiffer, 1996), pp. 52–57; and Chuck Hansen, "Nuclear Neptunes: Early Days of Composite Squadrons 5 & 6," *American Aviation Historical Society Journal* (Winter 1979), pp. 262–268.

11 Both were uranium gun-type weapons. The Little Boy weighed 8,400 pounds and at Hiroshima detonated with a yield of 15 KT. It was in the inventory from August 1945 to January 1951. The improved Mk VIII weighed almost 3,300

pounds and was rated at 15 to 20 KT. It was in service from December 1951 to August 1957. The latter weapon was developed for naval use against hardened targets (e.g., submarine pens), being the first U.S. nuclear bomb fused to detonate after striking the ground rather than in an air burst.

12 The Atomic Energy Commission was established on January 1, 1947, to control all U.S. nuclear efforts, taking over military programs from the Army's Manhattan Project (officially the Manhattan Engineering District).

13 Adm. Sherman would serve as Chief of Naval Operations from November 1949 to July 1951. Adm. Radford would serve as Chairman of the Joint Chiefs of Staff from June 1953 to August 1957. His career was unusual as he was a line officer who reached four-star rank without having commanded a ship.

14 During World War II the Navy's composite squadrons consisted of fighter and bomber aircraft operating from escort carriers. Ironically, the Army Air Forces nuclear bomber unit established in December 1944 was designated the 509th *Composite* Bomb Group.

15 This takeoff was a remarkable achievement considering this was almost 20,000 pounds above the gross design weight of the P2V-3.

16 The strengthening of the flight decks added weight relatively high in the *Midway*s; as compensation several of their 5-inch gun mounts were removed.

17 Vice Adm. Hayward letter to N. Polmar, March 15, 1966. There were at least two "hard landings" during the Patuxent River trials.

18 The Air Force nuclear strike capability at this time was also limited. In January 1949 the Air Force had 66 "Silverplate" B-29s fitted to deliver atomic bombs; in January 1950 the number was 95.

19 The P2V-3C aircraft were operational from 1949 until early 1952, after which a few were flown in the training role.

20 Hayward letter, March 15, 1966.

21 Five composite squadrons (VC) were redesignated as heavy attack squadrons in 1955–1956 as were 4 patrol squadrons (VP). A total of 11 deployable heavy attack squadrons (VAH) were formed, plus 2 transition training squadrons (designated as RAG—for Replacement Air Group—squadrons):

SQUADRON	ESTABLISHED	NOTES
VAH-1	Nov. 1, 1955	formerly VP-3
VAH-2	Nov. 1, 1955	formerly VP-29
VAH-3	June 15, 1956	formerly VP-34; RAG squadron
VAH-4	July 1, 1956	formerly VP-57
VAH-5	Feb. 3, 1956	formerly VC-5
VAH-6	July 1, 1956	formerly VC-6
VAH-7	July 1, 1955	formerly VC-7
VAH-8	May 1, 1957	new
VAH-9	Nov. 1, 1955	formerly VC-9
VAH-10	May 1, 1961	new
VAH-11	Nov. 1, 1955	formerly VC-8
VAH-13	Jan. 3, 1961	new
VAH-123	June 15, 1957	est. as training unit; to VAH RAG squadron June 29, 1959

22 Details of these flights are found in R. Cargill Hall and Clayton D. Laurie, eds., *Early Cold War Overflights 1950–1956* (Washington, D.C.: National Reconnaissance Office, 2003), vol. I *Memoirs* and vol. II *Appendixes*.

23 The Canberra became operational in the RAF in the bomber variant in 1951. Subsequently specialized reconnaissance

variants were developed. The Canberra was also produced in the United States by Martin as the B-57 and was flown in the bomber and tactical and strategic reconnaissance roles. The strategic photo-reconnaissance variant flew in RAF service until 2006.

24 Capt. William C. Chapman, USN (Ret.), "Steve Brody and the Banshee," *Foundation* [Museum of Naval Aviation] (Spring 1993), pp. 44–48; and author's discussions with Chapman. Steve Brody was a New York saloon keeper who, in 1886, jumped off the Brooklyn Bridge to win a wager. "To pull a Brody" instantly became a term for doing a dangerous stunt.

25 See Maj. Gen. Marion Carl, USMC (Ret.), and Barrett Tillman, *Pushing the Envelope: The Career of Fighter Ace and Test Pilot Marion Carl* (Annapolis, Md.: Naval Institute Press, 1994), pp. 81–85.

26 The U-2 piloted by Francis Gary Powers that was shot down on May 1, 1960.

27 Vice Adm. Forrest Sherman, USN, memorandum from DCNO (Operations) OP-03 to DCNO (Logistics) OP-04, June 12, 1946.

28 Dr. David A. Rosenberg, "American Postwar Air Doctrine and Organization: The Navy Experience," in *Air Power and Warfare*, Proceedings of the Eighth Military History Symposium, U.S. Air Force Academy (Washington, D.C.: Office of Air Force History, 1979), p. 252; the paper was presented on October 20, 1978.

29 The debate is described in two excellent studies: Paul Y. Hammond, "Super Carriers and B-36 Bombers: Appropriations, Strategy and Politics," in Harold Steiner, ed., *American Civil-Military Decisions: A Book of Case Studies* (Tuscaloosa: University of Alabama Press, 1963), pp. 465–568; and Dr. Jeffery G. Barlow, *Revolt of the Admirals: The Fight for Naval Aviation, 1945–1950* (Washington, D.C.: Naval Historical Center, 1994). The latter account benefits from 30 years of additional memoirs and document declassification.

30 Fleet Adm. William D. Leahy, USN, had served as de facto Chairman JCS from July 20, 1942, to March 21, 1949. Gen. Omar N. Bradley, USA, became Chairman JCS on August 16, 1949.

31 Walter Millis, *Arms and Men: A Study of American Military History* (New York: G. P. Putnam's Sons, 1956), p. 325.

32 The NATO code-name scheme for Soviet aircraft:
    B-series names for bombers
    F-series names to fighters
    H-series names for helicopters
    M-series names for maritime patrol, training,
       and miscellaneous aircraft

33 Barlow, "Comments on Draft Chapter 31," p. 3.

34 Gen. Kenney was the first commander of the Strategic Air Command, from March 1946 to October 1948.

35 U.S. Congress, House, Committee on Armed Services, hearings on *The National Defense Program—Unification and Strategy*, 81st Cong., 1st sess. (1949).

36 Ibid., p. 57 (testimony of October 7, 1949).

37 Memorandum from Secretary Matthews, presented at meeting with officials of the Navy League on January 11, 1950, Washington, D.C. The memo was made available to the author by the secretary's son, Frank Matthews. Although Secretary Matthews had been given a copy of the Bogan letter, he had not had an opportunity to read it.

38 Matthews memo, p. 9.

39 A total of 264 B-36 bombers and 121 RB-36 reconnaissance aircraft plus one aircraft in a cargo configuration—the XC-99—were produced through 1954. Some B-36s subsequently were converted to a combination reconnaissance-bomber configuration. None ever dropped a bomb in anger, either conventional or nuclear.

40 Matthews memo, p. 9.

41 Matthews was then appointed U.S. Ambassador to Ireland. He suffered a heat attack and died on October 19, 1952. Adm. Sherman died from a heart attack on July 22, 1951, while visiting Naples. Sherman was succeeded as CNO by Adm. William D. Fechteler. He had served early in World War II in the Bureau of Naval Personnel, subsequently commanded a fast battleship, and then command amphibious forces. He was Commander-in-Chief Atlantic Fleet when named CNO.

42 Barlow, *Revolt of the Admirals*, p. 294.

Chapter 4: "The Wrong War"

1 Official records (including pilot log books) differ as to whether these were F9F-2 or F9F-2B aircraft; in fact they were the latter. A large number of early production F9F-2s were modified to F9F-2B fighter-bombers with four pylons under each wing; beginning with the 365th F9F-2 the pylons were factory installed. The inboard pylons could carry a 150-gallon drop tank or bombs up to 1,000 pounds; the three outboard racks could carry 250-pound bombs or 5-inch rockets. Maximum external payload, however, was 3,000 pounds.

2 Dr. Robert Frank Futrell, *The United States Air Force In Korea 1950–1953* (New York: Duell, Sloan and Pearce, 1961), p. 83.

3 The Douglas-built Invader had entered the U.S. Army Air Forces in 1944 as the A-26; in June 1948 the Air Force changed the designation to B-26, leading to endless confusion with the Martin B-26 Marauder of World War II fame.

4 On June 27—the day U.S. forces entered the conflict—three North Korean Yak-9 piston-engine fighters were shot down by F-82s, the first U.S. aerial victories in the conflict.

5 Yak and Il indicated the aircraft designed by bureaus named for Aleksandr S. Yakovlev and Sergei V. Ilyushin, respectively.

6 Furtell, *The United States Air Force In Korea*, p. 27.

7 The story of British carriers in the conflict is recounted by John R. P. Lansdown in his excellent *With the Carriers in the Korean War: Sea and Air War in SE Asia, 1950–1953* (Winslow, Cheshire: Crécy Publishing, 1997).

8 The Seafire Mk 47 was the first of that aircraft type with folding wings; it had a greater range than previous marks—940 miles with external tanks.

9 Vice Adm. Donald D. Engen, USN (Ret), *Wings and Warriors: My Life as a Naval Aviator* (Washington, D.C.: Smithsonian Institution Press, 1997), p. 112.

10 The Marine fighter squadron was VMF-214, the "Black Sheep" squadron renowned for its air-to-air combat under the command of Maj. Gregory (Pappy) Boyington during World War II.

11 Tu indicated a design of the bureau named for Andrei N. Tupolev.

12 The body of the Russian flier was transferred to the *Valley Forge* and placed in a meat locker; it subsequently was put ashore at the Navy facility at Sasebo, Japan, but its ultimate disposition is unknown.

Chapter 5: "An Entirely New War"

1. A comprehensive description of Soviet and Chinese air force participation in the Korean air war is Xiaoming Zhang, *Red Wings Over the Yalu: China, the Soviet Union, and the Air War in Korea* (College Station: Texas A&M University Press, 2002). Also see John R. Bruning, *Crimson Sky: The Air Battle for Korea* (Washington, D.C.: Brassey's, Inc., 1999). Also relevant are the personal memoirs of several senior Soviet fighter commanders who fought in Korea that are found in Yefim Gordon and Vladimir Rigmant, *MiG-15: Design, Development and Korean War Combat History* (Osceola, Wisc.: Motorbooks International, 1993), pp.120–139.

2. MiG indicated the aircraft design bureau named for Artem I. Mikoyan and Mikhail I. Gurevich. The MiG-15 was produced in greater numbers than any other jet aircraft in history with more than 15,000 built in the USSR, China, Czechoslovakia, and Poland.

3. A popular U.S. Air Force ditty at the time, recorded as "The Prettiest Ship" by folk singer Oscar Brand, went:
   The prettiest ship out on the line,
   The MiG-15 flies fast and fine.

   When we go up and fly at noon,
   The MiG-15s jump off the moon.
   Then they come down and pretty soon
   They start to play a noisy tune.

   Ten planes race by; here's what it means:
   One F-86 . . . nine MiG-15s.
   The moral of this song is clear:
   When you start home, just check your rear.

   'Cause if you don't, you're sure to find,
   A MiG-15 tucked in behind.

4. Zhang, *Red Wings Over the Yalu*, p. 88.

5. Bruning, *Crimson Sky*, p. 126.

6. Soviet fighter units had been stationed in China—initially to defend against Nationalist air attack from Formosa (Taiwan)—beginning in early 1950. Soviet-piloted MiG-15s made their combat debut over China on April 28, 1950.

7. U.S. intercept stations had first heard Russian-speaking MiG-15 pilots on December 7, 1950; by early April 1951, a U.S. Air Force intercept station outside Tokyo was able to break into the Soviet PVO ground control communications for MiG-15s operating over Manchuria and North Korea.

8. The naval fighter regiment was in combat from August 1952 to April 1953 with the 133rd Fighter Air Division.

9. Zhang, *Red Wings Over the Yalu*, p. 106.

10. Zhang, *Red Wings Over the Yalu*, pp. 189–192.

11. The *Princeton* had been decommissioned on June 20, 1948.

12. Brown was long believed to be the first black pilot in the U.S. Navy. He was the first to complete Navy flight training and to be designated as a naval aviator, on October 21, 1948. However, another black, Oscar Holmes, entered the Navy as a qualified civilian pilot; on June 30, 1943, he completed Navy flight instructor training as an ensign, but was qualified only for special flying duty, i.e, training activities.

13. The *Boxer* embarked Carrier Air Group 101 consisting of:

SQUADRON	AIRCRAFT
VF-721*	F9F-2B
VF-791*	F4U-4
VF-884*	F4U-4
VA-702*	AD-2/4Q
VC-3 det.	F4U-5NL
VC-11 det.	AD-4W
VC-35 det.	AD-4N
VC-61 det.	F9F-2P
HU-1 det.	HO3S-1

    * Naval Air Reserve squadron.

14. Attack Squadron 195 provided the five AD-4 aircraft and Composite Squadron (VC) 35 provided the three AD-4N aircraft; the latter were included because only three VC-35 pilots had experience dropping torpedoes among the Skyraider pilots aboard the *Princeton*. See Barrett Tillman and Joseph G. Handleman, "The Hwachon Dam and Carlson's Canyon: Air Group 19's *Princeton* Deployment of 1950–51," *The Hook* (Spring 1984), p. 36. Also see Rear Adm. William H. Langenberg, USNR (Ret), "Aerial Torpedoes Reincarnated!" *Foundation* [Naval Aviation Museum] (Spring 1993), pp. 50-57.

15. VF-23 flew the F9F-2 Panther and VA-55 flew the AD-4 Skyraider. The two reserve squadrons in CVG-19X were VF-821 and VF-871, both flying the F4U-4 Corsair.

16. The best published account of Armstrong's adventure is James Hansen, *First Man: The Life of Neil A. Armstrong* (New York: Simon & Schuster, 2005), pp. 91–96.

17. The 300-gallon napalm bombs weighed about 2,000 pounds. They would engulf an area of about 50 by 200 yards with burning jellied gasoline. VF-53 flew F4U-4 and 4B Corsairs; VF-54 flew AD-2, 3, and 4 Skyraiders. The *Essex* also carried VF-51 with F9F-2 Panthers and VF-172 with F2H-2 Banshees, plus various special-mission detachments.

18. After World War II several turbojet night fighter projects were started in the United States: the Air Force initiated the Curtiss F-87 Black Hawk and the Northrop F-89 Scorpion; the Navy's night fighter projects were the Grumman F9F and Douglas F3D. The F9F-1 was to be a four-turbojet aircraft; it was cancelled and instead Grumman pursued the project as the F9F-2 Panther, the first of a long line of turbojet fighters from the "Grumman Iron Works." The Curtiss F-87 flew on March 5, 1948, but did not enter production.

19. Technically the F3D-2 could carry two bombs of up to 2,000 pounds each or lesser weapons or two 300-gallon drop tanks on two wing pylons. So far as known, bombs were never carried by F3Ds in combat. Later several F3Ds were modified to carry the Sparrow air-to-air, radar-guided missile (F3D-1M and -2M variants); another 35 were modified for the electronic countermeasures role (F3D-2Q, later EF 10B). The Marines employed the latter aircraft to ferret out North Vietnamese radars in the 1960s. Those aircraft were retired in 1969; other F3Ds served in research roles into the 1980s.

20. Capt. G. G. O'Rourke, USN (Ret.), *Night Fighters over Korea* (Annapolis, Md.: Naval Institute Press, 1998), p. 85. This is an excellent history of carrier night fighter development and operations.

21. Earlier the two Marine night fighter squadrons in Korea flying the F7F Tigercat—VMF(N)-513 and VMF(N)-542—had attempted to fly night escort for the B-29s.

22. The Air Force also struck these and other industrial targets during a four-day campaign with 730 fighter-bomber sorties and 238 counter-air sorties. Some 250 MiG fighters on nearby Manchurian airfields made no attempt to interfere with the strikes.

23. Po indicated a design of the bureau named for Nikolai N. Polikarpov.

24 During the winter of 1951 novelist James Michener embarked in the carriers *Essex* and then *Valley Forge*. His time aboard the carriers provided him with material for his article "The Forgotten Heroes of Korea" in *The Saturday Evening Post* (May 10, 1952), his novel *The Bridges at Toko-Ri* (1954), and the film of the same name (1955).

Chapter 6: Concluding a Conflict

1 British carrier operations in Korea are described in Lansdown, *With the Carriers in Korea*.

2 Lansdown, *With the Carriers in Korea*, pp. 226–228. An additional sortie by a Firefly was launched, but the plane aborted with a rough-running engine.

3 Comdr. David Hobbs, RN, *Aircraft Carriers*, p. 190. In July 1953, after the war ended, the *Unicorn* chased off pirates attempting to seize a merchant ship.

4 The *Philippine Sea* set a Korean War combat cruise record of ten months in 1950–1951.

5 Zhang, *Red Wings Over the Yalu*, p. 204.

6 See Jon Halliday, "A Secret War," *Far Eastern Economic Review* (April 22, 1993), pp. 32, 33, 36. The article includes an interview with Lt. Gen. Ageyevich Lobov, who commanded the Soviet fighter force based in Manchuria.

7 Zhang, *Red Wings Over the Yalu*, pp. 201–202.

8 Zhang, *Red Wings Over the Yalu*, p. 203.

9 See Maj. Jesse G. Folmar, USMC (Ret.), "MiG Kill," *Foundation* [Naval Aviation Museum] (Spring 2003), pp. 52–55, and Lt. Col. Jack Lewis, USMCR (Ret.), "Air Kill," *Leatherneck* (May 2004), pp. 26–29.

10 Future astronauts Lt. Walter Schirra, USN, on exchange duty with the Air Force, shot down a MiG-15, and Maj. John G. Glenn, USMC, also on Air Force exchange duty, shot down three MiG-15s.

11 Comdr. Malcolm W. Cagle, USN, and Comdr. Frank A. Manson, USN, *The Sea War in Korea* (Annapolis, Md.: U.S. Naval Institute, 1957), p. 270.

12 James A. Field, Jr., *History of United States Naval Operations—Korea* (Washington, D.C.: Naval History Division, 1962), p. vi.

Chapter 7: The Cold War Navy

1 The light cruiser was the *Worcester*, one of a two-ship class. These ships were actually large anti-aircraft cruisers with a main battery of 12 6-inch/47-caliber dual-purpose guns mounted in twin turrets.

2 The *Cabot*, *Monterey*, and *Saipan* served in turn as pilot-qualification training carriers, operating in the Gulf of Mexico, until the mid-1950s, when the *Antietam* was assigned to that role on a permanent basis.

3 The letter *T* was used as a prefix for ships assigned to the Military Sea Transportation Service (changed in 1970 to Military Sealift Command).

4 Other hunter-killer designations used in this period were:

CVLK	light carrier
CLK	cruiser
DDK	destroyer
SSK	submarine
SSKN	submarine (nuclear propulsion)

5 Deputy Chief of Naval Operations (Operations) memorandum to Chief of Naval Operations, May 3, 1951, enclosure (1), p. 20.

6 The TB2F was a Grumman response to a Navy proposal for a torpedo variant of the twin-engine F7F-2 Tigercat fighter; the designation was later changed to TSF-1. Development of the TB2F/TSF-1 was not pursued. (The F7F could carry a Mk 13 torpedo.) The TB3F was to carry two torpedoes in an internal bomb bay. The TB3F/AF Guardian is well described in Robert J. Kowalski, "Grumman AF-2 Guardian," *The Hook* (Fall 1985), pp. 34–49.

7 The AF total does not include two TB3F prototypes. In 1956 the U.S. Navy discarded its last TBM-3W2, the final Avenger in U.S. Navy markings; the aircraft continued in service with other nations.

8 Capt. A. Jay Cristol, USNR (Ret.), telephone conversation with N. Polmar, February 21, 2006.

9 The *Forrestal* was ordered as CVB 59 and changed to CVA 59 on October 1, 1952. James V. Forrestal served as a Navy pilot in World War I and was Secretary of the Navy from May 1944 until September 1947, when he became the first Secretary of Defense. He left that post in March 1949 because of mental and physical exhaustion. He committed suicide in May 1949. Only two previous aircraft carriers were named directly for people, the *Langley* (CV 1) and *Franklin D. Roosevelt* (CVB 42).

10 Early documentation for the *Saratoga* referred to CVB 60; however, she was ordered as the CVA 60. Only carriers No. 41–43, 56, 57, and 59 were designated CVB.

11 By the end of 1949 all floatplanes were removed from U.S. cruisers and the battleship *Missouri* (the only active dreadnought) with helicopters embarked in their place.

12 See Lt. Col. Eugene W. Rawlins, USMC, *Marines and Helicopters 1946–1962* (Washington, D.C.: History and Museum Division, 1976).

Chapter 8: French and British Carriers at War

1 The term *Viet Minh* was a Vietnamese abbreviation for League for the Revolution and Independence of Viet-Nam. The movement was abolished in 1951, but the name continued to be associated with communist regime and forces.

2 Arriving back in France in July 1946, the *Béarn* became a submarine depot ship alongside the quay at Missiessy (Toulon) in 1948; she was decommissioned in November 1966 and scrapped soon after, ending a long albeit undistinguished career.

3 The C-119 (Navy R4Q) was officially named Packet, but the twin-boom, highly efficient cargo aircraft was invariably called the Flying Boxcar.

4 Twenty-four of the 29 French C-119s were flown by American civilian pilots on loan from Civil Air Transport (CAT). That firm was an "air proprietary," sponsored by the U.S. Central Intelligence Agency. One C-119 was shot down by Viet Minh gunfire, crashing in a violent explosion with its cargo of six tons of ammunition blowing up. The two American pilots were killed—the only known U.S. combat fatalities in the French war in Indochina—as were two French crew members.

Some B-26 Invader twin-engine bombers of the French Air Force were also flown by Americans.

5 The A-26 Invader was the U.S. Army Air Forces most advanced medium bomber of World War II, entering combat in early 1944. It was redesignated B-26 in 1948 and was used extensively in the Korean War with a few surviving to serve in Vietnam in the 1960s.

The Privateer was developed from the B-24 Liberator. The French Privateers subsequently were used as bombers in Tunisia, and a few flew missions against the Egyptians during the Anglo-French Suez campaign of 1956. The last Privateers were retired from the French Navy in 1961 and were replaced by Lockheed P2V-6 Neptunes.

6 Jules Roy, *The Battle of Dienbienphu* (New York: Harper & Row, 1965), p. 243.

7 Bernard B. Fall, *Hell in a Very Small Place: The Siege of Dien Bien Phu* (Philadelphia: J. B. Lippincott, 1967), p. 337.

8 The 111 F4U-6/AU-1 aircraft were produced specifically for U.S. Marine Corps use in Korea.

9 The machinations over U.S. political and military intervention in Indochina are well described in John Prados, *The Sky Would Fall: Operation Vulture—the Secret U.S. Bombing Mission to Vietnam, 1954* (New York: Dial Press, 1983).

Radford, a World War II carrier task force commander, served as Chairman of the Joint Chiefs of Staff from August 1953 to August 1957. He was the second flag officer to hold that post, after Fleet Adm. William D. Leahy, who was chief of staff to the president and de facto chairman from July 1942 until March 1949.

10 Key documents related to these operations are cited in Vice Adm. Edwin Bickford Hooper, USN (Ret.), Dean C. Allard, and Oscar Fitzgerald, *The Setting of the Stage to 1959*, vol. I in *The United States Navy and the Vietnam Conflict* (Washington, D.C.: Naval Historical Division, 1976), pp. 234–255.

11 Rear Adm. Blick was nominally Commander Carrier Division 3; he was relieved in April 1954 by Rear Adm. Harry D. Felt.

12 Adm. Radford, interview with N. Polmar, May 3, 1966, Annapolis, Maryland. Also see Stephen Jurika, Jr., (ed.) *From Pearl Harbor to Vietnam: The Memoirs of Admiral Arthur W. Radford* (Stanford, Calif.: Hoover Institution Press, 1980), pp. 339 ff.

13 U.S. Joint Chiefs of Staff, Historical Division, *The Joint Chiefs of Staff and the War in Vietnam: History of the Indochina Incident, 1940–1954*, in *The History of the Joint Chiefs of Staff* (manuscript, February 1, 1955), p. 372.

14 U.S. Joint Chiefs of Staff, *The Joint Chiefs of Staff and the War in Vietnam*, p. 372.

15 The aviation casualties in the battle consisted of:

	KILLED	WOUNDED	MISSING	TOTAL
French Air Force	15	6	94	115
French Naval Aviation	21	4	7	32
American civilians	2	1	—	3

16 There are reports that the Chinese government believed that the Cathy aircraft was actually a plane flown by Civil Air Transport (CAT), an airline operated by the U.S. Central Intelligence Agency.

17 La = Lavochkin. These Soviet-built piston-engine fighters resembled the U.S. P-51 Mustang.

18 The "fighter" squadron flew the AD Skyraider from 1949 to 1957 in the attack role; it was redesignated from VF-54 to Attack Squadron (VA) 54 on June 15, 1956.

19 The English Electric Canberra was an outstanding strike and reconnaissance aircraft. It continued in RAF service as a strategic reconnaissance aircraft until 2006, having had more than a half-century of service.

20 At the time the terms "angled" and "canted" were used interchangeably. On February 24, 1955, the U.S. Chief of Naval Operations directed that the term "angled" be used in lieu of "canted" and other terms in describing carrier flight-deck configuration.

21 The *Bennington*'s commanding officer was Capt. William F. (Red) Raborn, USN. Shortly after commanding the *Bennington*, Raborn was named head of the Navy's Special Projects (Polaris) office, a position he held from 1955 to 1962; he was Director of Central Intelligence in 1965–1966.

22 The *Albion* was the first British carrier to have an angled flight deck installed while under construction.

23 Corsair production included aircraft built by Brewster (F3A) and Goodyear (FG/F2G), with 2,486 of the 15,056 Corsairs produced going directly to foreign services.

24 F4Us were also flown by the Argentine Navy until 1965—25 years after the XF4U-1 made its maiden flight. They were blown from shore bases by Central American navies for a few more years.

25 TF = Torpedo-strike Fighter. The single TF.3 aircraft was a two-seat variant.

26 Lt.-Comdr. David Hobbs, RN, *Aircraft of the Royal Navy Since 1945* (Liskeard, Cornwall: Maritime Books, 1982), p. 48.

Chapter 9: The Suez Operation

1 The last British troops in the canal zone departed on June 13, 1956.

2 No. 845 was the Royal Navy's first helicopter ASW squadron, established in March 1954.
HAR = Helicopter Air Rescue
HAS = Helicopter Anti-Submarine

3 At the time no Arab navies possessed submarines and Soviet submarines rarely appeared in the Mediterranean Sea.

4 Quoted in Brian Cull, *Wings Over Suez* (London: Grub Street, 1996), 229. This outstanding work addresses all participating air forces and their operations during the Suez conflict.

5 The Czech-built MiG-15s were supplemented just before the Suez conflict by MiG-17 fighters; MiG-15s provided to the Syrian Air Force were also delivered to Egypt for assembly and pilot training. The instructors were Czech and Russian, the latter including combat pilots who had flown in World War II and the Korean War. Few of the MiGs were operational when the war began. See David Nicolle, "Suez: The Egyptian Air Force in 1956 Campaign—The Other Side," *Air Enthusiast* (May/June 2004), pp. 56–65, and (July/August 2004), pp. 48–57; and, especially, Cull, *Wings Over Suez*.

6 See, for example, Chiam Herzog, *The Arab-Israeli Wars: War and Peace in the Middle East* (London: Arms and Armour Press, 1982), pp. 111–115 and 138–140. Herzog commanded the Jerusalem Brigade in 1956; he twice served as head of Israeli military intelligence and was the president of Israel from 1983 to 1993.

7 Randolph S. Churchill, *The Rise and Fall of Sir Anthony Eden* (London: MacGibbon and Kee, 1959), p. 279.

8 The MiG-17 was flown by some 40 nations, the world's most widely flown combat aircraft of the late 1950s and 1960s. The definitive MiG-17F was an all-weather intercepter fitted with three 20-mm cannon and could carry rocket pods or bombs. It could reach 635 m.p.h. at 39,370 feet (Mach 0.96) and 692 m.p.h. at sea level.

9 Cull, *Wings Over Suez*, p. 273.

10 Reportedly, the French pilot, Lieutenant de Vaisseau Lancrenon, was captured by the Egyptians, placed in a cage, and later stoned to death.

Chapter 10: The Super Carriers

1 The *Forrestal* was built at the Newport News Shipbuilding and Dry Dock Company (Virginia); the New York Naval Shipyard was a major carrier maintenance and construction yard.

2 Burke had served in the flag rank of commodore from October 1944 to October 1945, after which he reverted to the rank of captain. He was again promoted to commodore from March 1946 to March 1947, while serving as chief of staff to Adm. Mitscher, after which he reverted to captain. He subsequently was promoted to rear admiral. He was named CNO by President Eisenhower and promoted to admiral (bypassing the rank of vice admiral); he served an unprecedented six years as CNO, from August 1955 to August 1961.

   During World War II, Vice Adm. Mitscher twice recommended that Burke be promoted to rear admiral, at least four years ahead of his contemporaries. Burke responded, "I can't think of any way the Navy could get any more out of me if I wore two stars." (*Sources*: Burke, letter to Roberta Burke, August 18, 1944, and Burke, letter to Rear Adm. J. L. Kaufmann, August 12, 1944, both in Personal File, Burke Papers, NHC.)

3 A squadron of F9F-8 Cougars armed with Sidewinder missiles sailed from Norfolk in the carrier *Randolph* for operations with the Sixth Fleet in the Mediterranean in mid-July 1956; a month later a squadron of FJ-3 Fury aircraft aboard the *Bon Homme Richard* left the U.S. West Coast in the first Sidewinder deployment to the Seventh Fleet in the Western Pacific.

4 The F11F was flown by the Navy's Blue Angels flight demonstration team for 11 years.

5 Chance Vought, which produced the F4U Corsair, F6U Pirate, and F7U Cutlass fighters, merged in 1961 with Ling-Temco Electronics to form Ling-Temco-Vought (LTV). Although the LTV aircraft/aerospace group underwent several name changes, the term LTV is used on subsequent pages.

6 Glenn subsequently became the first American astronaut to orbit the earth and later served as a U.S. senator.

7 The aborted carrier *United States* (CVA 58) was intended to operate nuclear-armed strike aircraft with a takeoff weight up to 100,000 pounds.

8 Heinemann and Rausa, *Ed Heinemann*, p. 202.

9 The Air Force procured 209 B-66s, most electronic (EB-66) and reconnaissance (RB-66) variants.

10 Betty was the first Western nuclear depth bomb. The Naval Ordnance Test Station also developed a conventional version of the BOAR, a 30½-inch-diameter, air-to-surface weapon sans nuclear warhead, confusingly referred to as the "Bombardment Aircraft Rocket" (also BOAR).

11 Of these, 294 Skyhawks were foreign orders; numerous ex-U.S. aircraft subsequently were transferred to other nations.

12 A firsthand account of A4D nuclear tactics, readiness, and training is provided in Jim Walters, "Training for the A-4 Nuclear Delivery Mission," *Skyhawk Association Quarterly* (Winter 2006), pp. 4–6.

13 George Fielding Eliot, *Victory Without War, 1958–1961* (Annapolis, Md.: U.S. Naval Institute, 1958), pp. 66–67.

14 Col. Albert P. Sights, Jr., USAF, "Lessons of Lebanon," *Air University Review* (July–August 1965), p. 41.

15 Sights, "Lessons of Lebanon," p. 42.

16 There are numerous versions of this story. This account is based on Lt. Col. Uri Yarom, Israel Air Force (Ret), telephone discussion with N. Polmar and e-mail of November 10, 2006, and Yarom, *Knaf Renanim* [Goodly Wings] (Tel Aviv: Ministry of Defence, 2001), pp. 219-221

Chapter 11: New Carrier Concepts

1 The Navy consistently used *Alpha*; Thach preferred *Alfa*, the first letter of the Greek alphabet, as his task force was the first of its kind.

2 The *Lexington* served as a training carrier with the designation CVS 16 until January 1, 1969, when the designation changed to CVT 16; on July 1, 1978, she became AVT 16. She was decommissioned on November 8, 1991, without replacement by a dedicated training carrier.

3 U.S. Commander-in-Chief Pacific, "Interim Evaluation Report No. 4 (January 1, 1952, to June 30, 1952)," p. 5–41.

4 U.S. Commander-in-Chief Pacific, "Interim Evaluation Report No. 5 (July 1, 1952, to January 31, 1953)," p. 5–83.

5 WS = Weapon System.

6 Brig. Gen. Andrew J. Goodpaster, USA, Memorandum for the Record, June 25, 1958. Goodpaster was military secretary to President Eisenhower.

7 For dates and location of launches and types of balloons, see Curtis Peebles, *The Moby Dick Project: Reconnaissance Balloons Over Russia* (Washington, D.C.: Smithsonian Institution Press, 1991), pp. 206–211.

8 Brig. Gen. Goodpaster, USA, Memorandum for the Record, July 29, 1958.

9 See Donald E. Welzenbach, "Observation Balloons and Weather Satellites," *Studies in Intelligence* (Spring 1986), pp. 26–28.

10 The AKV 1 and AKV 2 were World War II–era aircraft cargo ships operated by the Navy (formerly APV 1 and APV 2); the AKV 3–7 were World War II–built ships operated by the Army and transferred to the Navy's Military Sea Transportation Service in 1950.

11 LPH indicated amphibious assault ship, *not* landing platform helicopter, as sometimes reported. The L-series for large amphibious ships (e.g., LCC-LKA-LPA-LPR) was established on August 14, 1968; previously they had A-series designations (AGC-AKA-APA-APD).

12 The Terrier-series missiles had a conventional or, in the BTN variant, a W45 nuclear warhead; BTN = Beam-riding Terrier, Nuclear. The missile was also fitted in a large number of cruisers and destroyers-type ships.

13 This and statements by other U.S. officials discussing carrier programs in subsequent pages of this volume are taken from the officials' congressional testimony.

14 U.S. Navy, Office of the Chief of Naval Operations, "The Navy of the 1970 Era" (January 1958), p. 1.

15 The Navy ship designation system added the letter *N* in parenthesis for nuclear-propelled ships on October 25, 1951; the parenthesis were deleted on October 3, 1967.

16 Nikita Khrushchev, speech to Communist Party activists, Moscow, January 6, 1961. President Kennedy believed that this was one of Khrushchev's most important speeches; he memorized portions of it and urged his cabinet members to read and study the speech. See "Paste This in Your Hat," *Time* (February 2, 1962).

Chapter 12: Carrier Proliferation

1 This section is based, in part, on the excellent collection of essays in Thomas J. Hirschfeld and Peter Hore (eds.), *Maritime Aviation: Light and Medium Aircraft Carriers into the Twenty First Century* (Hull [England]: University of Hull Press, 1999).

2   In all, the Brazilian Navy procured 12 Westland WS-55 Whirlwind Mk 1 and Mk 3 helicopters and one Sikorsky S-55 in the 1960s. Apparently none was used in the ASW role, but—called *Vacas* (cows)—they were employed in the VIP, transport, and rescue roles.

3   The Indian procurement of Sea Hawks totaled 45 FGA.6 and 28 FGA.100 variants. The latter had originally been in West German service.

4   Commo. C. Uday Bhaskar, Indian Navy, "The Indian Naval Carrier Experience: A Conceptual Reappraisal" in Hirschfield and Hore, *Maritime Aviation*, p. 32. Also see Bhaskar, "Indian Naval Air," U.S. Naval Institute *Proceedings* (March 1987), pp. 106–108.

5   Several countries other than those that operated aircraft carriers flew F4U Corsairs. In July 1969 El Salvador flew 6 FG-1D variants and Honduras operated 10 F4U-5/5N and 9 F4U-4 aircraft when they fought the 100-hour "Soccer War." In an aerial encounter on July 17 a Honduran F4U-5N piloted by Maj. Soto Henriquez shot down two Salvadoran Corsairs in history's only Corsair-versus-Corsair battle. Henriquez also shot down a Salvadoran Mustang the same day. See Mario E. Overall, "The 100 Hour War: Honduras versus El Salvador," *Air Enthusiast* (July/August 2005), pp. 8–27.

6   A 3-D radar simultaneously provides information on a target's altitude, distance, and bearing.

7   AOP = Air Observation Post. See David Willis, "Military Auster A to Z," Part 2, *Air Enthusiast* (March/April 2006), pp. 47, 51.

8   Hawker Siddeley acquired the Blackburn firm in 1960.

9   Beyond the Scimitar and Buccaneer, the only British naval aircraft to carry nuclear weapons have been the Sea Harrier and ASW helicopters. All carried variants of the WE177 nuclear weapon, by the Sea Harrier as a free-fall bomb and by the Sea King as a nuclear depth bomb. The WE177 came in several versions; see Chapter 20, fn 30.

10 The F-4K Phantom was intended to carry nuclear weapons; however, the planes were not wired for them. Similarly, no operational U.S. Navy or Marine Corps Phantoms were wired to carry nuclear weapons.

11 Beyond the AS and AEW variants of the Gannet, the Royal Navy also operated a few Aircraft configured for carrier on-board delivery (COD.4) and for electronic countermeasures training (ECM.21, later Mk 22).

12 The term commando carrier was officially changed to commando ship in January 1962.

13 Lt.-Comdr. A. A. Hensher, RN, "The Navy Flies Over Sabah," *Navy* [British Navy League] (December 1964), p. 371.

14 Lt.-Col. T. M. P. Stevens, Royal Marines, "A Joint Operation in Tanganyika," *The Royal United Service Institution Journal* (February 1965), p. 52.

15 In addition to various Ministry of Defence and Royal Navy fact sheets, the best account of the CVA.01 is Capt. Eric M. Brown, RN, "Phantom Carrier," U.S. Naval Institute *Proceedings* (February 1967), pp. 138-142; the article is reprinted (with additional comments) in Brown, *Wings on My Sleeve* (London: Weidenfeld & Nicolson, 2006), pp. 269-273. Capt. Brown was Deputy Director, Naval Air Warfare in 1961—1964 and responsible for many operational features of the CVA.01. For a comprehensive data base see the web site www.navy-matters.beedall.com/cva01.htm.

Chapter 13: New Ships and Planes

1   The AN/SPS-32/SPS-33 radars were mounted in only one other warship, the nuclear-propelled missile cruiser *Long Beach* (CGN 9), also completed in 1961. The SPS-32/SPS-33 radars subsequently were removed from both ships as they were very difficult to maintain.

2   Brig. Gen. S. L. A. Marshall, USA (Ret.), "Naval Power as Understood by a Soldier," in *Naval Review 1962–1963* (Annapolis, Md.: U.S. Naval Institute, 1962), p. 14.

3   The CVA 66—subsequently named *America*—was constructed of "thin steel" to reduce building costs; this eventually reduced her service life in comparison to other super carriers.

4   The early F8Us were named Crusader; the improved F8U-2 (later F-8C) was unofficially referred to as the Crusader II. Chance Vought initially considered asking the Navy to designate its enlarged variant the XF9U-1; instead, the aircraft became the XF8U-3 and was generally known as the Crusader III. During this period Chance Vought became LTV (Ling-Temco-Vought).

5   The competition between the two fighters is described in Engen, *Wings and Warriors*, pp. 209–214.

6   The British carrier-based F-4K Phantom was to have been nuclear-capable but was never wired for nor deployed with nuclear weapons. The RAF F-4M was nuclear capable.

7   The McDonnell and Douglas firms merged in 1967. U.S. production consisted of 1,244 Phantoms for the Navy and Marine Corps, 2,870 for the U.S. Air Force, and 936 for foreign users, with some Air Force planes being subsequently transferred to other nations.

8   Although the B27 was the standard weapon carried in the linear bomb bay, the aircraft also could carry a B28 or B43 bomb internally. Alternatively up to four of these weapons could be carried on wing pylons.

9   The drop tanks were never carried on operational missions as the additional weight/drag of the four tanks meant a useful benefit of less than 20 percent of the additional fuel.

10 Nine operational RVAH squadrons flew the RA-5C. The RA-5C was retired in 1979, the first and last deployments being aboard the USS *Ranger*.

11 Anti-submarine air groups retained the group designation (CVSG).

12 The Hercules has been in continuous production from 1954 to the present for military and civilian use. The standard military transport version can carry 90 combat troops.

13 Flatley became the first U.S. carrier aviator to achieve 1,000 arrested landings. He retired as a rear admiral in 1987.

14 The C-142 was derived from the Hiller X-18, a combination twin-turboprop/single-turbojet VSTOL transport that first flew in 1959. Five prototype XC-142 aircraft were produced. That aircraft was to carry 32 combat troops or 8,000 pounds of cargo.

15 Lightweight ASW torpedoes were originally developed during World War II for use by Navy airships (blimps). They were approximately 7½ feet long and 12¾ inches in diameter; three lightweight torpedoes with several variants were in use during the Cold War—the Mk 43, Mk 44, and Mk 46. These were carried by aircraft and surface ships.

16 The VSF program is discussed in detail in the excellent article by Comdr. Robert R. Powell, USN (Ret.), "Vee Ess Eff— Very Small Fighters," *The Hook* (Spring 2006), pp. 26–37.

17 Two reserve Skyhawk units, VSF-76 and VSF-86, each made one CVS deployment in 1971.

Chapter 14: Carriers to Cuban Waters

1 "What the public knows as the Bay of Pigs, the White House knew as Operation Zapata, the CIA gave birth to it as Operation Crosspatch, and the Navy renamed Bumpy Road. The anti-Castro Expeditionary Force went ashore under the code name Pluto, god of the underworld."—Capt. William C. Chapman, USN (Ret), "A View from PriFly," U.S. Naval Institute *Proceedings* (October 1962), p. 45. The best public sources for this operation are Peter Wyden, *Bay of Pigs: The Untold Story* (New York: Simon and Schuster, 1979), and Chapman's paper presented at the Ninth Naval History Seminar, U.S. Naval Academy, Annapolis, Md., October 1989. Chapman was air officer of the USS *Essex* at the time of the Bay of Pigs fiasco. Key documents concerning the Navy's role in the Bay of Pigs fiasco are found in Louis J. Smith (ed.), *Cuba 1961–1962*, vol. X in *Foreign Relations of the United States, 1961–1963* (Washington, D.C.: Department of State, 1997).

2 Some sources cite these as A4D-4 Skyhawks; however, VA-34 flew the A4D-2 until July 1962, when the squadron converted to the A4D-2N (redesignated A-4C on October 1, 1962).

3 Four Americans—CIA contract fliers—were killed in these B-26 shootdowns. One of them, Maj. Thomas Ray from the Alabama Air National Guard, survived the crash of his plane, but was killed by Cuban soldiers.

4 Message from Commander Special task Group 81.8 to CinC Atlantic, April 18, 1961, 4:42 P.M., reproduced in Smith, *Cuba 1961–1962*, p. 278.

5 Wyden, *Bay of Pigs*, p. 270.

6 Wyden, *Bay of Pigs*, p. 270. Another account, which does not precisely reflect Adm. Burke's view but is nonetheless of interest is Elias P. Demetracopoulos, "Muzzling Admiral Burke," U.S. Naval Institute *Proceedings* (January 2000), pp. 64–68.

Also see Comdr. Mitchell, "Transcript of Conversation in Chief of Naval Operations Office," Bumpy Road files, Adm. Arleigh A. Burke Papers, NHC.

7 Smith, *Cuba 1961–1962*, p. 405.

8 These land-based reconnaissance flights by F8U-1P aircraft are detailed in Dino A. Brugioni, *Eyeball to Eyeball: The Inside Story of the Cuban Missile Crisis* (New York: Random House, 1990), and in his "Chalk Up Another Chicken!" U.S. Naval Institute *Proceedings* (October 1992), pp. 96–101.

9 At the time of the Cuban Missile Crisis the F-101s were fitted with KA-1 and KA-2 cameras, which were unsuitable for high-speed, low-level photography. Only after KA-45 cameras produced by Chicago Aero Industries for the Navy were installed could the F-101s undertake the low-level photo missions.

10 Six of the Il-28s sent to Cuba were nuclear capable and six 407N nuclear bombs (12-kiloton yield) were sent to Cuba for those aircraft.

11 Those nuclear warheads ashore had arrived on the freighter *Indigiirka* on October 4. They consisted of 36 warheads for SS-4 ballistic missiles, 80 for coastal defense missiles, 12 for short-range Luna (Frog) artillery rockets, and 6 bombs for Il-28 bombers. Offshore was the freighter *Alexandrovsk* with 24 warheads for SS-5 ballistic missiles. See Lt. Gen. Anatoli I. Gribkov and Gen. William Y. Smith, USAF (Ret.), *Operation Anadyr: U.S. and Soviet Generals Recount the Cuban Missile Crisis* (Chicago: Edition "q," 1994), pp. 62–63.

12 Gregory W. Pedlow and Donald E. Welzenbach, *The CIA and the U-2 Program, 1954–1974* (Washington, D.C.: Central Intelligence Agency, 1992), p. 248.

13 Park interview in Bob Lawson, "ET TU, U-2?" *The Hook* (Summer 1992), p. 10.

14 Pedlow and Welzenbach, *The CIA and the U-2 Program*, p. 251. In a separate program, in 1973–1974 two Lockheed U-2R aircraft were modified to the U-2EPX configuration for evaluation by the U.S. Navy in the ocean surveillance role. The aircraft did not enter naval service. At the same time, Boeing proposed a much larger aircraft of this type (i.e., powered glider with a 200-foot wingspan) for the ocean surveillance role; it was not built. (EPX = Electronic Patrol, Xperimental.)

15 The Bear-D was a four-turboprop reconnaissance and missile-targeting aircraft with an unrefueled range of more than 7,700 miles; it was fitted for in-flight refueling. It could not carry bombs or missiles.

16 The Badger was a four-turbojet bomber/missile-launching aircraft that was also flown in the reconnaissance role as the Tu-16R and Tu-16RM; those variants were given the NATO code name Badger-D/E/F/K/L. They had a range of about 4,000 miles and were fitted for in-flight refueling; no bombs or missiles were carried by reconnaissance variants.

17 Vice Adm. G. E. Miller, USN (Ret.), "Some Thoughts about Soviet Aircraft Over Flights of U.S. Aircraft Carriers during the Cold War," working paper, November 20, 2003. Adm. Miller commanded the U.S. Second Fleet in the Atlantic and, subsequently, the Sixth Fleet in the Mediterranean.

Chapter 15: Wings Over Southeast Asia . . . Again

1 Chapters 15–18 covering the Vietnam War are based in large part on Peter B. Mersky and Norman Polmar, *The Naval Air War in Vietnam* (Annapolis, Md.: Nautical & Aviation, 1981).

2 Lt. Gen. John J. Tolson, USA (Ret.), *Airmobility 1961–1971* (Washington, D.C.: Department of the Army, 1989), p. 3. The *Core* was civilian manned and operated by the Navy's Military Sea Transportation Service (changed in 1970 to the Military Sealift Command).

3 The Piasecki H-21 was similar to the Navy's HRP-2. The Army called the H-21 the Shawnee, keeping with its practice of naming helicopters for Indian tribes. The Air Force H-21s were named Workhorse, which was soon used for all H-21s in Southeast Asia.

4 Robert S. McNamara, *In Retrospect: The Tragedy and Lessons of Vietnam* (New York: Random House, 1995), p. 130.

5 Of the three Soviet-built P-4 MTBs that made the attack on the *Maddox*, the *T 333*, the command unit, was undamaged; the *T 336* was slightly damaged with her commander killed; and the *T 339* was damaged and dead in the water with her engines stopped (but later restarted). The two damaged boats were beached to prevent them from sinking; both were repaired and returned to service.

Stockdale, flying from the carrier *Oriskany* in an A-4 Skyhawk on September 9, 1965, was shot down over North Vietnam and made a prisoner. He was incarcerated for seven and a half years. Returning to active duty upon being freed in early 1973, he later reached the rank of vice admiral.

6 Quoted in McNamara, *In Retrospect*, p. 133.

7   See Edwin E. Moïse, *Tonkin Gulf and the Escalation of the Vietnam War* (Chapel Hill: University of North Carolina Press, 1996); also see Capt. Dick McDonald, USN (Ret.), "A Footnote to the Gulf of Tonkin Affair," Naval Intelligence Professionals *Journal* (April 1998), pp. 1–5, and (Summer 1998), pp. 1–4. McDonald, a naval intelligence officer, was involved in the analyses of the August 2, 1964, and July 1, 1966, attacks by the same three North Vietnamese MTBs.

8   Throughout the Vietnam conflict the U.S. government was concerned about the possibility of overt Chinese or Soviet participation in the war, especially with air forces as in the Korean War. Relevant U.S. intelligence estimates are reproduced in National Intelligence Council, *Estimative Products on Vietnam 1948–1975* (Washington, D.C.: Government Printing Office, April 2005).

9   At the time the *Constellation* also had embarked detachments of RF-8A and RA-3B Skywarrior photo planes from Light Photographic Squadron (VFP) 63 and Heavy Photographic Squadron (VAP) 61, respectively.

10 SA-2 Guideline was the U.S.-NATO designation; the Soviet designation was V-75 Dvina. The missile entered service in 1957–1958 at sites around the cities of Baku, Leningrad, and Moscow.

    SA-2 missiles shot down the U-2 piloted by Francis Gary Powers over the Soviet Union on May 1, 1960, and the U-2 flown by Maj. Rudolph Anderson, Jr., USAF, over Cuba on October 27, 1962. SA-2s also shot down four CIA U-2 aircraft piloted by Taiwanese pilots over China.

11 The Air Force eschewed the term "attack." The F-105 carried no air-to-air armament except for a 20-mm Vulcan (multibarrel) cannon. The aircraft was intended primarily for nuclear weapons delivery, it had a small internal bomb bay for a single nuclear weapon, and it carried conventional bombs and missiles on wing and fuselage pylons. The later F-111 and F-117 were similarly specialized attack aircraft despite their fighter designation.

12 Details of U.S. air losses are described in Chris Hobson, *Vietnam Air Losses: United States Air Force, Navy, and Marine Corps Fixed-Wing Aircraft Losses in Southeast Asia 1961–1973* (Hinckley [England]: Midland Publishing, 2001). This excellent volume lists the following Navy aircraft shot down by Chinese MiGs:
    1 F-4B Phantom
    1 A-1H Skyraider
    1 KA-3B Skywarrior
    2 A-6A Intruder
    The Air Force aircraft were an F-4C and an F-104C.

13 Johnson described the shootdown in "Skyraider vs. MiG-17," *Foundation* [Naval Aviation Museum] (Spring 1995), pp. 48–55.

14 Later versions of the Skyraider flown by the Air Force were called "Sandys" because of their camouflage scheme.

15 All Air Force F-4 and RF-4 Phantoms were nuclear capable.

16 Miller, *Nuclear Weapons and Aircraft Carriers*, p. 223.

17 Miller, *Nuclear Weapons and Aircraft Carriers*, pp. 203, 204.

18 Nuclear-depth bombs—under U.S. control—were also provided for use by British, Canadian, Dutch, and Italian ASW aircraft; the Canadian and Dutch aircraft included modified carrier-based S2F Trackers.

19 Adm. U.S. Grant Sharp, USN (Ret.), *Strategy for Defeat: Vietnam in Retrospect* (San Rafael, Calif.: Presidio Press, 1978), p. 111.

Chapter 16: Escalation to Escalaton

1   William Green, *The World Guide to Combat Planes*, vol. 1 (Garden City, N.Y.: Doubleday, 1967), p. 136.

2   The "other side" of the MiG-21 operations in Vietnam is found in István Toperczer, *MiG-21 Units of the Vietnam War* (Botley: Oxford, 2001).

3   Lt. Comdr. White of VA-46 died in the *Forrestal* fire.

4   The destroyed aircraft cost another $44.5 million, and damaged aircraft cost another $10 million to repair.

5   Probably the best article describing the fire is James M. Caiella, "1051 Hell," *Foundation* [Naval Aviation Museum] (Fall 2003), pp. 48–57. Also see U.S. Navy, Judge Advocate General, *Final Investigative Report Concerning the Fire on Board the USS FORRESTAL (CVA 59)*, 1967.

6   Lt. Comdr. McCain was released in March 1973. He suffered severe privation; he had both of his arms and his right knee broken when his plane was shot down and never received proper medical treatment while a POW. His grandfather, Adm. John S. McCain, commanded Task Force 38/58 in the Pacific in 1944–1945; his father, Adm. John S. McCain, Jr., became Commander-in-Chief U.S. Pacific Command on July 31, 1968. See Lt. Comdr. McCain's autobiographic *Faith of My Fathers* (New York: Random House, 1999).

7   Adm. Sharp's message of January 14, 1967, to the Joint Chiefs of Staff is reprinted in his *Strategy for Defeat*, pp. 280–284.

8   McNamara, *In Retrospect*, pp. 169, ff.

9   In addition, four ASW carriers made eight deployments to Southeast Asia from August 1964 to the end of 1996. For details of all carrier deployments to Vietnam (and their air wings/groups) see Roy A. Grossnick, *United States Naval Aviation 1910–1995* (Washington, D.C.: Naval Historical Center, 1997), pp. 705–717.

10 An Israeli A-4H Skyhawk pilot, Lt. Col. Ezra Dotan, shot down two Syrian MiG-17s over southern Lebanon on May 12, 1970, one with 2.75-mm rockets and the second with the aircraft's 30-mm cannon. (The Israeli Skyhawks were fitted with two 30-mm cannon in place of the standard 20-mm weapons.)

11 The Navy's term Topgun became two words in 1986 when Hollywood released the blockbuster film *Top Gun* starring Tom Cruise.

12 This was more than twice the bombload normally carried by a B-17 Flying Fortress in World War II. The A-6A could carry a maximum of 18,000 pounds of conventional ordnance or one Mk 28 nuclear weapon plus four 300-gallon drop tanks.

13 The story of the Intruder in Vietnam is dramatically told in the novel by Stephen Coonts, *Flight of the Intruder* (Annapolis, Md.: Naval Institute Press, 1986). It subsequently was made into a movie with the same title.

14 The enlarged Walleye II had a 2,000-pound warhead and a range of 35 miles; the Air Force also had a nuclear variant of the Walleye.

15 The Corsair was produced for the Air Force in the A-7D variant.

16 In particular, see Lt. Col. William R. Fails, USMC, *Marines and Helicopters 1962–1973* (Washington, D.C.: Headquarters, U.S. Marine Corps, 1978).

17 HMM = Marine medium helicopter squadron.

18 HMH = Marine heavy helicopter squadron.

19 Prior to 1962, the EF-10B was designated F3D-2Q and the TF-9J was the F9F-8T.

20 The best published account of the *Pueblo* incident is Richard A. Mobley, *Flash Point North Korea: The* Pueblo *and EC-*

121 Crises (Annapolis, Md.: Naval Institute Press, 2003). Also see Lloyd Bucher, *Bucher: My Story* (Garden City, N.Y.: Doubleday, 1970); Trevor Armbrister, *A Matter of Accountability: The Story of the* Pueblo *Affair* (New York: Coward-McCann, 1969); Mobley, "*Pueblo*: A Retrospective," Naval War College *Review* (Spring 2001), pp. 98–117; and "The *Pueblo* Incident: Commander Bucher Replies," *Naval History* (Winter 1989), pp. 44–50. Bucher was commanding officer of the *Pueblo*.

21 The *Pueblo* was armed with two .50-caliber machine guns, which were not used during the North Korean assault, as well as small arms. The Navy had directed that a 3-inch/50-cal gun be installed, but the ship could not accommodate a weapon of that size and weight.

22 U.S. Congress, House Armed Services Committee, Special Subcommittee on the USS *Pueblo*, *Inquiry into the USS* Pueblo *and EC-121 Plane Incident*, HASC 91-12 (Washington, D.C.: 1969), p. 1620.

23 The very last Skyraider in Navy service, an NA-1E research aircraft assigned to the Naval Air Test Center Patuxent River, Md., was retired on July 7, 1971. The remarkable career of the "Spad" is well documented in Capt. Rosario Rausa, USNR (Ret), *Skyraider: The Douglas A-1 "Flying Dump Truck"* (Baltimore, Md.: Nautical & Aviation Publishing, 1982), and in B. R. Jackson, *Douglas Skyraider* (Fallbrook, Calif.: Aero Publishers, 1969).

Chapter 17: A War Lost

1 Skyhawks served in Marine squadrons until 1994. The two-seat TA-4J Skyhawk was in service as a naval training aircraft until 2003—a half-century after the first flight of the YA-4D prototype.

2 The French Navy flew the F8U-2NE Crusader from carriers until December 1999, and the Philippine Air Force flew the aircraft, for a brief period, from land bases.

3 The SA-2 battery that hit the plane was equipped with the Fan Song-E fire control radar, which could not be detected by the Phantom's radar warning receiver.

4 Navy carrier-based Phantoms normally carried four Sidewinders and two Sparrows; the Marines of VMFA-333 carried two additional Sparrows. Apparently North Vietnamese ground controllers and the MiG pilots counted the missiles fired by the Phantom and told the MiG when it was "safe" to counterattack.

5 Henry Kissinger, *White House Years* (Boston: Little, Brown, 1979), p. 1180.

6 The mines laid by the carrier planes were 1,000-pound Mk 52 mines and 500-pound Mk 82 bombs converted to mines with Mk 36 "Destructor" kits.

7 See Toperczer, *MiG-21 Units of the Vietnam War*, p. 66.

8 The SA-2 missiles shot down between 150 and 160 U.S. aircraft—including 81 Navy carrier aircraft—from 1965 to 1973. More than 9,000 missiles were fired for a kill rate of 1.7 percent. Despite the low aircraft loss rate, the vast number of SAMs caused many aircraft to jettison their bombs short of their targets, required numerous missions by anti-SAM and jamming aircraft, and often forced attacking planes to adopt tactics that made them more vulnerable to anti-aircraft guns.

9 This was also the last of 26 RA-5C Vigilantes lost in the Vietnam conflict. Most were downed by anti-aircraft gunfire, with four shot down by SA-2 missiles and one by a MiG-21. Significantly, North Vietnamese records do not show an RA-5C shot down by a MiG on that date.

10 The 11 days of Linebacker II strikes by B-52s were December 18–24 and 26–29; the B-52s were based at Guam and at Utapao airfield in Thailand.

11 Here, again, North Vietnamese records differ. The last MiG-21 loss listed by Hanoi was shot down on January 7, 1973, by an Air Force F-4C.

12 Seven additional MiGs are believed to have been shot down by U.S. ship-launched missiles. The Navy–Marine Corps air-to-air kills were credited as

    39 MiG-17
     2 MiG-19
    18 MiG-21

13 James Zumwalt, "Responding to *Pueblo*" [letter], *Navy Times* (February 20, 2006), p. 53.

14 See Toperczer, *MiG-21 Units of the Vietnam War*, pp. 77–78.

15 The U.S. Marine Corps transferred 15 CH-53A helicopters, strengthened with tow points, to the Navy and also accepted a secondary Mine Countermeasures (MCM) mission for its own CH-53A pilots and aircraft. Thirteen of the transferred Marine Corps helicopters (all redesignated RH-53A) were used to establish the world's first operational MCM squadron, Helicopter Mine Countermeasures Squadron (HM) 12, at Norfolk. HM-12 embarked 13 RH-53A helicopters in the *New Orleans* for Operation End Sweep. The Navy received its first of 30 specialized RH-53D MCM helicopters in 1973.

    See Tamara Moser Melia, *"Damn the Torpedoes": A Short History of U.S. Naval Mine Countermeasures, 1777–1991* (Washington, D.C.: Naval Historical Center, 1991), p. 99; also see Dr. Edward J. Marolda, (ed) *Operation End Sweep: A History of Minesweeping Operations in North Vietnam* (Washington, D.C.: Naval Historical Center, 1993).

16 See Capt. Charles Ellis, Jr., USN (Ret), "Operation Frequent Wind," *Foundation* [Naval Aviation Museum] (Spring 2003), pp. 42–51.

17 Grossnick, *United States Naval Aviation 1910–1995*, pp. 705–717.

18 The Cambodians had recently seized a Panamanian- and a Philippine-flag merchant ship, which were quickly released.

19 Minutes, National Security Council, May 12, 1975, enclosure to Memorandum "NSC Meeting of May 12, 1975," for Secretary Kissinger from W. R. Smyser. President Ford was present at the meeting.

20 Minutes, National Security Council, May 12, 1975.

Chapter 18: Carrier Controversies

1 Unless otherwise indicated, all statements by Department of Defense officials are from congressional testimony before the Senate and House armed services and appropriations committees for the year indicated.

2 The CVA 59–64, 66, and 67 were considered to be of the *Forrestal* "type" although technically they comprised two classes and a single-ship type.

3 The *Nimitz* was named for Fleet Adm. Chester W. Nimitz, CinC Pacific Fleet and Pacific Ocean Areas during World War II, and CNO from December 1945 to December 1947. The three other U.S. Navy fleet admirals—William D. Leahy, Ernest J. King, and William F. Halsey—were honored with large destroyer-type ships (DLG) being named for them. By naming a carrier for Nimitz the Navy itself initiated the practice of naming aircraft carriers for "people"—with the shambles in carrier naming that has followed. Three previous carriers were named for people—the *Franklin D. Roosevelt*

(CVB 42) and *Forrestal* (CV 59) honoring men of national stature who died in office and immediately after leaving office, respectively; and the *Langley* (CV 1) honored aviation pioneer Samuel P. Langley. The *Franklin* (CV 13) was named for a Revolutionary War ship of that name.

4   The first phase of the air attacks—Operation Moked—called for attacks on the key Arab airfields with a new (1966) runway demolition bomb. Details are found in Col. Eliezer Cohen, Israel Air Force, *Israel's Best Defense: The First Full Story of the Israeli Air Force* (New York: Orion Books, 1993), p. 195.

5   The most complete descriptions of the *Liberty* affair are Capt. A. Jay Cristol, USNR (Ret), *The Liberty Incident* (Washington, D.C.: Brassey's, 2002), and Harriet Dashiell Schwar and Edward C. Keefer (eds.), *Arab Israeli Crisis and War, 1967*, vol. XIX in *Foreign Relations of the United States, 1964–1968* (Washington, D.C.: Department of State, 2004). The latter is an official Department of State volume on the events of 1967.

6   The *America* had several aircraft aloft at the time carrying nuclear bomb "shapes."

7   An example of the erroneous statements: "Two nuclear armed F-4 Phantom jets left *America*'s catapults and headed almost straight up, afterburners roaring. Then two more became airborne to rendezvous with the first two, and together the four powerful jets turned toward *Liberty*, making a noise like thunder"; James M. Ennis, Jr., *Assault on the Liberty: The True Story of the Israeli Attack on an American Intelligence Ship* (New York: Random House, 1979), p. 77; Ennis was a lieutenant in the *Liberty* at the time of the attack.

The Navy did test the compatibility of the Phantom with the B28, B43, B57, and B61 nuclear bombs; see Naval Air Warfare Center, *History of the Naval Weapons Evaluation Facility, Albuquerque, New Mexico, 1948–1993* (March 1993), p. 13. However, no Navy or Marine Corps Phantoms were ever deployed with a nuclear weapons capability.

8   Vice Adm. Donald D. Engen, USN (Ret), discussion with N. Polmar, Washington, D.C., June 17, 1998; also see Engen, *Wings and Warriors*, pp. 320–322.

9   Quoted in Cristol, *The Liberty Incident*, p. 100.

10 Anthony R. Wells, "*Liberty* Victims Did Not Die in Vain," U.S. Naval Institute *Proceedings* (March 2005), p. 89.

11 For space launches and recovery ships see Don Blair, *Splashdown! NASA and the Navy* (Paducah, Ky.: Turner Publishing, 2004). The manned spacecraft that were recovered at sea were:

PROGRAM	PERIOD	NUMBER
Mercury	1961–1963	6
Gemini	1965–1966	10
Apollo	1968–1972	11
Skylab	1973–1974	3
Apollo-Soyuz	1975	1

12 All Soviet submarines deployed to the Mediterranean during the Cold War came from the Northern Fleet; the Montreux Convention of 1936 governing transits of the Turkish Straits prohibited the deployment of submarines from the Black Sea Fleet.

13 Quoted in Adm. Elmo R. Zumwalt, Jr., USN (Ret), *On Watch* (New York: New York Times Book Co., 1976), p. 447. Zumwalt provides a detailed description of the naval confrontation.

14 The *Lexington* (CV 16) was designated as a training carrier in December 1962; she became CVT 16 on January 1, 1969, and was changed to AVT 16—auxiliary aircraft landing training ship—on July 1, 1976.

15 These carrier concepts are described in detail in R. F. Cross Associates, *Sea-based Airborne Antisubmarine Warfare 1940–1977*, vol. II (Arlington, Va.: Office of Naval Research, 1978), pp. 139–226.

16 Zumwalt, *On Watch*, p. 77.

17 The additional ASW aircraft were flown aboard from the CVS *Wasp*.

18 Rear Adm. M. Staser Holcomb, USN (Ret), note to N. Polmar, August 9, 2001. Then-Captain Holcomb commanded a portion of the *Guam* SCS evaluation.

19 Adm. Zumwalt's predecessors were George W. Anderson (1961–1963), David L. McDonald (1963–1967), and Thomas H. Moorer (1967–1970). Zumwalt served as CNO from 1970 to 1974.

20 Zumwalt, *On Watch*, pp. 75–76.

21 The Sea Kings were from Navy Helicopter Squadron 15 and the Harriers from Marine Attack Squadron 513.

22 General Accounting Office, *Staff Study on Sea Control Ship* (Washington, D.C.: March 1974), p. 8. GAO was changed to Government Accountability Office on July 7, 2004.

23 Ingalls Shipbuilding, *Preliminary Design Study of an Air Capable DD 963: DD 963-V* (September 1, 1977) and Ingalls Shipbuilding, *The Value of an Air Capable Light Combatant DD 963-F: A Conceptual Design Developed as a Variant of the DD 963* (November 18, 1977).

24 The similar *Kidd*-class missile destroyers (4 ships) and *Ticonderoga*-class missile cruisers (27 ships) were built based on the *Spruance* hull, propulsion plant, and other components.

25 The DLG/DLGNs were redesignated as destroyers or cruisers in 1975.

26 Public Law 93-365, Title VIII, August 5, 1974; the provision was repealed by Public Law 94-485, Title VIII, October 20, 1978.

The 1974 legislation stipulated that all major combat ships of the strike forces of the Navy had to be nuclear-powered. This made the creation of an all-nuclear navy a matter of law, which said there could be only one way a non-nuclear major warship could be built: The president would have to advise Congress and say that a certain ship had to be powered by something other than a Rickover reactor because such a non-nuclear ship was "in the national inte-rest." On February 13, 1976—less than two years after the all-nuclear legislation—President Gerald R. Ford—formally made a finding that constructing an all-nuclear surface combatant force was not in the national interest. It was the Secretary of Defense's assessment that the military value of an all nuclear powered warship program did not warrant the increased costs or, alternatively, the reduced force levels. After that date only one more nuclear DLGN/cruiser was built (authorized in 1975), although nuclear-propelled carrier construction continued in addition to an all-nuclear sub-marine force.

27 The *Spruance* class was the Navy's first large warship propelled by aircraft-type gas turbine engines. Adm. Rickover had strongly opposed that type of propulsion because of the "threat" to nuclear-propelled surface ships. See Norman Polmar and Thomas B. Allen, *Rickover: Controversy and Genius* (New York: Simon & Schuster, 1982), pp. 232–236.

28 Subsequently, 27 highly effective Aegis "cruisers" were built based on the *Spruance* design. This was the *Ticonderoga* (CG 47) class.

29 In 2007 several members of Congress called for nuclear propulsion to be provided in a proposed class of guided missile

cruisers—designated CG(X) at the time—that would have the primary role of theater/homeland ballistic missile defense.

30 "Small CV Construction Is Urged by Stennis," *Navy Times* (March 10, 1980), p. 4. The CVN 74 was later named for Senator Stennis.

31 Secretary of Defense Donald H. Rumsfeld, *Annual Defense Department Report FY 1977* (Washington, D.C.: January 27, 1976), p. 164. Rumsfeld succeeded Schlesinger as Secretary of Defense in November 1975 and served until January 1977 and again served in that office from January 2001 until December 2006.

32 Adm. James L. Holloway III, USN, "The Transition to V/STOL," U.S. Naval Institute *Proceedings* (September 1977), p. 21.

33 Harold Brown, *Department of Defense Annual Report Fiscal Year 1980* (Washington, D.C.: January 25, 1979), p. 163. An excellent comparison of the CVV alternatives is found in Dr. Scott C. Truver, "The 1978 Carrier Controversy: Why Not the *Kennedy*?" *Naval War College Review* (February 1979), pp. 59–67.

34 Much of the wing technology evolved from Bell's "pot-bellied" X-5, the first U.S. swing-wing aircraft, and the Navy-Grumman XF10F Jaguar. The latter was a fighter aircraft, with the lone aircraft flying on May 19, 1952.

35 The Navy and contractors flew the seven F-111Bs until early 1971 as research and development aircraft. Two were lost in accidents.

36 Miller, *Nuclear Weapons and Aircraft Carriers*, p. 226.

Chapter 19: New Directions

1 The decision to procure the F-111K from the United States followed cancellation of the British-developed TSR.2 on April 6, 1965. The TSR.2 tactical strike-reconnaissance aircraft was to have been a Mach 2+ nuclear attack aircraft. Procurement of the F-111K by the RAF was cancelled.

2 Eric J. Grove, *Vanguard to Trident: British Naval Policy since World War II* (Annapolis, Md.: Naval Institute Press, 1987), p. 280.

3 The *Northampton*, begun as a heavy cruiser (CA 125), was cancelled in 1945 when 56.2 percent complete; she was reordered in 1948, completed as a tactical command ship (CLC 1) in 1953, and modified in 1962 to a national command ship (CC 1). She was stricken in 1977.

4 An attempt was made to preserve the *Bunker Hill*, the last straight-deck U.S. carrier afloat, as a museum-memorial ship. However, it was not to be; all World War II–era aircraft carriers that have been preserved in the United States are angled-deck ships.

5 In World War II the U.S. Army operated six Liberty-type ships configured as aircraft repair ships; see Volume I, page 498.

6 See Royal Navy, Naval Historical Branch, "Escort Cruiser to CVS(G): The 1962–1979 Design Process" (London: February 1997). In 1959 and 1961 the Royal Navy took delivery of two 9,500-ton cruisers, the *Tiger* and *Blake*. These ships each mounted a twin 6-inch gun turret forward and had a hangar and flight deck aft with accommodations for four Sea King helicopters. The ships were launched in 1945, but construction was suspended until they were taken in hand for conversion to helicopter cruisers.

7 These program machinations are described in Grove, *Vanguard to Trident*, pp. 317–320.

8 The XFV-1 and XFY-1 were pre-1962 designations; the XFV-12 was the 12th aircraft in the post-1962 *V* for Vertical series.

The YF-12 of the post-1962 fighter series was the fighter version of the SR-71 Blackbird, Mach 3 reconnaissance aircraft.

9 GR = Ground support/Reconnaissance.

In U.S. designations the letter *V* of XV-6A is one of six vehicle type letters listed in Department of Defense, *Model Designation of Military Aerospace Vehicles,* DOD 4120 (Washington, D.C.: various editions). The others are
G Glider
H Helicopter
Q Unmanned Aerial Vehicle (UAV)
S Spacecraft
Z Lighter-Than-Air (LTA)
The prefix letter *X* indicates an experimental vehicle.

10 The first Sea Harriers went to the Trials Unit, subsequently changed to No. 700A Naval Air Squadron; it was renamed No. 899 Squadron in March 1980. This was a shore-based training unit that periodically embarked in VSTOL carriers. Beginning in March 1980 Sea Harriers were assigned to operational squadrons—No. 800 and No. 801. A fourth squadron, No. 809, was established from April to December 1982 to provide replacement aircraft and pilots for the Falklands conflict. In addition to 34 Sea Harriers, the Navy initially acquired one two-seat Harrier T.4 and three two-seat T.8 aircraft for training and development; they had the Sea Harrier's Blue Fox radar.

FRS = Fighter Reconnaissance Strike.

11 A total of 57 Sea Harrier FRS.1 aircraft were produced for the Royal Navy. Because of the importance of the Harrier to several navies and to the U.S. Marine Corps, total Harrier production is provided in Appendix E of this volume.

12 Upon leaving the ski-jump the Harrier is *not* actually flying as there is a deficiency in wing lift. But due to the high thrust-to-weight ratio of the aircraft, there is sufficient thrust to accelerate the Harrier along its upward-inclined flight path. After a part-ballistic trajectory of about ten seconds, the Harrier picks up about 34.5 m.p.h. of additional airspeed and is then fully supported in flight. Significantly, before World War II the carriers *Courageous*, *Furious*, and *Glorious* had launching ramps at various times.

Chapter 20: Carrier War in the South Atlantic

1 The route from Britain to Ascension Island is 3,700 n.miles by the sea/air around Europe and Africa; from Ascension to the Falklands is more than 3,000 n.miles for a total distance of about 7,000 n.miles.

2 Dr. Robert L. Scheina, *Latin America's Wars: The Age of the Professional Soldier, 1900–2001,* vol. 2 (Washington, D.C.: Brassey's, 2003), p. 307. Anaya was Commander-in-Chief of the Argentine Navy and a member of the ruling junta.

3 The patrol ship *Endurance* was due to be retired in the near future without replacement. Some observers feel that action was a clear signal of the British government's lack of interest in the Falklands. The *Endurance*, a 3,600-ton ship, was armed with two 20-mm Oerlikon cannon.

4 GUPPY = Greater Underwater Propulsive Power (the *Y* being added for phonetic purposes). Fifty-two U.S. World War II–era submarines were modified to provide higher underwater speed and quieter operation.

5 The 25th of May is a national holiday in Argentina celebrating the 1810 revolution when the first autonomous government was formed.

6   See Capt. de Fragata Jorge Luis Colombo, ARA, "Falklands Operations: Super Étendard Naval Aircraft Operations during the Malvinas War," U.S. Naval War College *Review* (May–June 1984), pp. 12–22. To carry an Exocet, the Super Étendard's 30-mm gun pack was removed and other modifications were made to the aircraft. Several Argentine and British surface ships carried ship-launched Exocets.

7   The Argentine efforts to acquire additional Exocet missiles and British countermoves are well described in Nigel West (Rupert Allason), *The Secret War for the Falklands* (London: Little, Brown, 1997). Jack Higgins' *Exocet* (1983) is an exciting, fictionalized account of the Argentine attempts to obtain Exocets.

   By mid-1982 the French firm Aerospatiale had sold more than 1,800 air-launched AM-39 Exocets to Argentina, Britain, Brazil, Chile, Ecuador, and Peru, plus the French Navy. The ship/submarine-launched variants had been sold to additional countries.

8   The transports included seven C-130E/H Hercules. At least one flew a *bombing mission* on May 31, when bombs were rolled off of its rear ramp with one bomb reported to have bounced off of a ship without detonating. A second mission, on June 1, perhaps by the same aircraft, ended with the aircraft being shot down by a Sidewinder launched by a Sea Harrier and 240 rounds fired by the VSTOL's 30-mm cannon. See Roy Braybrook, *Battle for the Falklands: Air Forces* (London: Osprey, 1982), p. 11.

9   Eric J. Grove, *Vanguard to Trident*, p. 357. Beyond Professor Grove's fine work, the reader is directed to the official British report *The Falklands Campaign: The Lessons*; the U.S. Navy's *Lessons of the Falklands: Summary Report*; David Brown's *The Royal Navy and the Falklands War*; Nicholas van der Biji, *Nine Battles to Stanley*; and Max Hastings and Simon Jenkins, *The Battle for the Falklands*. See bibliography for full citations.

10 Adm. Sandy Woodward, RN, and Patrick Robinson, *One Hundred Days: The Memoirs of the Falklands Battle Group Commander* (Annapolis, Md.: Naval Institute Press, 1992), p. 66. Emphasis in the original.

11 The *Hermes* was laid down as a light fleet carrier in 1944 and launched in 1953.

12 Among the pilots flying Sea Kings in No. 820 Squadron in the *Invincible* was HRH Prince Andrew, second son of Prince Philip and Queen Elizabeth. Sub-Lt. Andrew served with distinction in the conflict.

13 Braybrook, *Battle for the Falklands*, pp. 11, 15.

14 The *Santa Fé*'s commander chose to remain on the surface where his submarine would be invulnerable to Mk 46 ASW torpedoes; his submarine was severely damaged by helicopter-launched missiles and depth charges.

15 The Vulcan required only one refueling on the flight back to Ascension, a total flight of 7,860 miles. It required 11 Victor tanker aircraft to undertake a single-bomber mission. This tanker requirement prevented multi-Vulcan operations. Five Vulcan aircraft formed the pool from which the strike aircraft were drawn. These aircraft were fitted with advanced navigation equipment.

16 Sometime during this period the British nuclear-propelled submarine *Splendid* made contact with the carrier *25 de Mayo*, but lost the contact before an attack could be carried out.

17 These were known as Black Buck missions and were numbered 1 through 5. A highly laudatory but comprehensive description of the Vulcan operations is "The Five Black Bucks," *Air International* (December 1982), pp. 291–298.

18 U.S. Navy, *Lessons of the Falklands*, p. 6.

19 Details of the British schemes are in West, *The Secret War for the Falklands*, pp. 72–89, 136–152.

20 The *Atlantic Conveyor* also carried 600 cluster bombs and the steel matting for building a Harrier airstrip ashore. The single Chinook that had been flown ashore, without spares or ground support, flew 109 hours in combat conditions, carrying up to 80 armed troops in a single lift.

21 The land-launched Exocets were from truck-mounted launchers flown into the Falklands from Argentina. The missiles had been removed from destroyers and jury-rigged for land launch. One was fired and missed the target a few days before the successful (but not fatal) hit on the British destroyer *Glamorgan*.

22 Secretary of State for Defence, *The Falklands Campaign: The Lessons*, p. 19.

23 Total British personnel losses in the Falklands were 255 killed from all services; Argentine losses were more than 700 killed and more than 15,000 taken prisoner (later repatriated).

24 British Aerospace, *V/STOL in the Roaring Forties* (Kingston Upon Thames, Surrey: October 1982), p. 16.

25 Secretary of State for Defence, *The Falklands Campaign: The Lessons*, p. 21.

26 Ministry of Defence, *Operation CORPORATE 1982: The carriage of nuclear weapons by the Task Force assembled for the Falklands Campaign* [n.d.], p. 4. Also see Robert S. Norris and Hans M. Kristensen, "British Nuclear Forces, 2005," *The Bulletin of the Atomic Scientists* (November/December 2005), pp. 77–79.

   In addition to the four ships that had nuclear weapons on board, several ships in the British force carried WE177 "training rounds" and "surveillance rounds," none of which contained nuclear material.

27 See Sir Lawrence Feedman, *The Official History of the Falklands Campaign* (London: Routledge, 2005).

28 Ministry of Defence, *Operation CORPORATE 1982*, p. 5.

29 During the Falklands campaign, the frigates *Brilliant* and *Broadsword*—after they had transferred their nuclear weapons—were both slightly damaged by 30-mm cannon fire from Dagger fighters (on May 21); the *Broadsword* was slightly damaged and her Lynx helicopter was destroyed in a bombing attack (May 29).

30 The WE177 came in three models: the A and B were strike weapons; the C model was an ASW weapon.

WEAPON	WEIGHT	YIELD	OPERATIONAL
WE177A	600 lb	200 KT	1972–1992
WE177B	950 lb	400 KT	1966–1995
WE177C	600 lb	10 KT	1966–1998

Chapter 21: Lessons and Finances

1   See Hirschfeld and Hore, *Maritime Aviation*.

2   One hundred Super Étendards were planned for the French Navy, but the number was reduced to 71 because of budget cuts.

3   The five Super Étendards on loan to Iran from 1983 to 1985, pending the delivery of Dassault Mirage F1 aircraft, were used in the war against Iraq. They were armed with Exocet anti-ship missiles.

4   The Super Frelon was designed by Sud-Aviation with technical assistance from Sikorsky. The SA 321 series posses several typical Sikorsky features such as a watertight hull for water

operations, float-type sponsons housing the main landing gear, and a Sikorsky-designed rotor system. External tanks hold fuel and contribute to the large size of the helicopter's troop-cargo area. The fuselage has a rear-loading ramp and the aft section of SA 321G variant's tail boom folds forward for carrier stowage, as does the six-blade main rotor.

5 Charles de Gaulle, a French Army officer and the author of several books on military subjects, commanded the Free French Forces, with headquarters initially in London, from June 1940, when the French government capitulated to Germany, until the end of World War II. He served as president of France from 1958 to 1967.

6 The Brest yard is operated by the state-owned *Directions des Constructions Navales* (DCN).

7 The ship is named for Count Camillo Bensodi Cavour, an 18th Century statesman. The previous *Cavour* was an Italian battleship that served in World War I and the beginning of World War II; British carrier-launched Swordfish aircraft sank that ship at Taranto on the night of November 11–12, 1940. (See Volume I, Chapter 7.) During construction the new ship was briefly assigned the name *Andrea Doria*.

8 EH indicated *Elicottero* Helicopter, the Italian and English words for the aircraft.

9 HM = Helicopter Maritime. The use of HM indicates an anti-surface and sea control role as well as ASW.

An Americanized version—the VH-71A—was selected in 2005 as the presidential transport helicopter. Operated by the U.S. Marine Corps, the VH-71A replaces the VH-3D Sea King in that role.

10 The Matadors are American-built AV-8B Harriers. Spain procured 11 AV-8S and 2 TAV-8S Matadors, and 12 EAV-8B, 9 EAV-8B+, and 1 TAV-8B Harrier II aircraft.

11 Viraat means supreme being (person) in Sanskrit.

12 India procured a total of 23 FR.51 and 8 two-seat T.60 aircraft through 2003. Two ex-RAF Harrier T.4 aircraft were also purchased.

13 Commo. Bhaskar, "The Indian Naval Carrier Experience . . . ," p. 34.

14 Originally named *Baku*; renamed *Admiral Flota Sovetskogo Soyuza Gorshkov* in 1990.

15 The Sevmash shipyard is the former Shipyard No. 402 at Severodvinsk (formerly Molotovsk) on the White Sea. Sevmash = Severodvinsk Machine Building Enterprise.

16 Vikramaditya is Sanskrit for "Almighty," the literal translation being "Sun of Strength." It was the name of a famous king in Indian mythology and a name used for King Chandragupta II, who ruled India from 375 to about 415 A.D.

17 In 2004 the Indian government ordered 16 MiG-29K aircraft for operation from the *Vikramaditya*. The Ka-27RLD was subsequently changed to Ka-31. RLD = *Radio-Lokatsionnogo Dozora* (early warning radar).

18 The *Ordzonikidze*, completed in 1951, was one of 14 ships of this class completed from 1951 to 1955.

19 This section is based partially on Ian Storey and You Ji, "China's Aircraft Carrier Ambitions: Seeking Truth from Rumors," *Naval War College Review* (Winter 2004), pp. 77–93. Liu's views are also described in Bernard D. Cole, *The Great Wall at Sea: China's Navy Enters the Twenty-First Century* (Annapolis, Md.: Naval Institute Press, 2001), pp. 165–172. Both of these sources cite Adm. S. G. Gorshkov as being an instructor at the Voroshilov college when Liu attended and as having influenced him. Gorshkov was never an instructor; in that period he was, successively, CinC Black Sea Fleet, First Deputy CinC of the Navy, and then CinC. However, he may have spoken at the institution. Liu was an Army officer and held Army rank until he was appointed to head the Navy. His position as Vice Chairman of the Central Military Commission was roughly equivalent to the U.S. Chairman of the Joint Chiefs of Staff.

20 A Chinese ship breaker had purchased the discarded CVL *Melbourne* in 1985. That provided an opportunity for Chinese naval architects to closely examine a carrier. The *Melbourne* was launched in 1945 as the British *Majestic*; she was not completed until 1955, hence her design was very dated.

21 University of California San Diego, blog by Blake Hounshell, "Is China building an aircraft carrier?" March 28, 2007.

Chapter 22: The Russian Experience

1 Comdr. Robert Waring Herrick, USN (Ret), *Soviet Naval Strategy: Fifty Years of Theory and Practice* (Annapolis, Md.: U.S. Naval Institute, 1968), pp. 145, 149.

2 The Soviet Navy developed both land-attack strategic and anti-ship cruise missiles and ballistic missiles for submarine launch.

3 The merchant ship *Indigrika* landed 128 tactical and strategic missile warheads and six nuclear bombs in Cuba; the merchant ship *Alekandrov* reached the Cuban port of La Isabela carrying another 24 missile warheads that were not unloaded.

4 Mozhaisky retired from the Navy that year with the rank of rear admiral.

5 The Il'ya Mourometz, designed by Igor Sikorsky, was the world's first four-engine military aircraft; his earlier *Grand* was the world's first four-engine aircraft (1913). Sikorsky immigrated to the United States in 1919 and became known for his outstanding flying boat and, subsequently, helicopter designs.

6 De Seversky soloed in the Russian Navy's Flying Service after a total flight time of 6 minutes, 28 seconds. He was credited with shooting down 13 German aircraft during World War I. After coming to the United States late in 1917 as Russian naval attaché, de Seversky left the service to become an aircraft designer and spokesman for air power; he wrote the seminal *Victory Through Air Power* (1943; subsequently made into an animated Walt Disney film).

7 V. I. Zof, "The International Situation and the Maritime Defense Missions for the Naval Defense of the USSR," *Morskoy sbornik* [Naval Journal], May 1925. Zof was head of the Navy from December 1924 to August 1926; he then held senior positions in the merchant marine, ministry of communications, and inland waterway transport.

Comdr. Herrick extensively examines Soviet naval policy and strategy in this period in his *Soviet Naval Strategy* and other works.

8 The *Izmail* was one of four ships of the *Borodino* class that were laid down in 1913. None was completed; three were scrapped in 1923, and the *Izmail*, considered for carrier conversion, was retained until 1931 and then scrapped. As battle cruisers the ships were to displace 32,500 tons normal and 38,000 tons full load and to mount 12 14-inch guns.

9 The *Poltava* (later renamed *Mikhail Frunze*) was the lead ship of a class of four dreadnoughts completed 1914–1915. Her hulk was towed to Kronstadt in 1941 for use as a blockship. She was scrapped in 1956. Two ships of the class remained in Soviet service until 1956–1957. As built the *Poltava* had a normal displacement of 23,300 tons and carried 12 12-inch guns.

10 *Stenograficheskiy otchet XXVII S'ezd KPSS* [Stenographic Record, 27th Congress of the CPSU] (Moscow: Political Press, 1934), p. 166.

11 Adm. N. G. Kuznetsov, "Naval Preparedness," in Seweryn Bailer (ed.), *Stalin and His Generals* (London: Souvenir Press, 1969), p. 173. This essay first appeared as "Pered voinoy" [On the Eve of War], *Oktiabr*` (No. 11, 1965), pp. 141–144. However, in his posthumously published memoirs, Kuznetsov wrote that "somebody" made the comment about fighting close to American shores (*Memoirs of Wartime Minister of the Navy* [Moscow: Progress Publishers, 1990; in English], p. 126).

12 Kuznetsov, "Naval Preparedness," p. 173, and Kuznetsov, *Memoirs*, p. 126. These ships were the *Stalingrad*-class battle cruisers mounting nine 12-inch guns.

13 The lone flag survivor was Lev Mikhailovich Galler, who served as vice commissar of the Navy during World War II; he was arrested on Stalin's order in February 1948 and died in prison in July 1950.

14 Arthur Koestler, *Darkness at Noon* (New York: Macmillan, 1941), pp. 150–151.

15 Descriptions of Soviet-era ships are based on I. D. Spassky (ed.), *Istoriya Otechestvennogo Sudostroeniya* [History of Indigenous Shipbuilding], vol. IV *1925–1945* and vol. V *1946–1991* (St. Petersburg: Sudostroenie, 1996); V. P. Kuzin and V. I. Nikol'skiy, *Voyenno-morskoy Flot SSSR, 1945–1991* [The Navy of the USSR, 1945–1991] (St. Petersburg: Historical Oceanic Society, 1996); and Jürgen Rohwer and Mikhail S. Monakov, *Stalin's Ocean-Going Fleet: Soviet Naval Strategy and Shipbuilding Programmes, 1935–1953* (London: Frank Cass, 2001).

16 Characteristics of the Gibbs & Cox designs are found in William H. Garzke, Jr., and Robert O. Dulin, Jr., *Battleships: Allied Battleships in World War II* (Annapolis, Md.: Naval Institute Press, 1980), pp. 308–313.

17 Gibbs & Cox designed light cruisers, destroyers, destroyer escorts, escort carriers, and landing ships for the U.S. Navy during World War II; the firm did not design capital ships other than the Soviet projects.

18 Mr. William Francis Gibbs, statement to the General Board of the Navy, December 5, 1939 (*Hearings of the Navy General Board*, 1939, vol. II, pp. 416–437); and letter from Chairman, General Board, to Secretary of the Navy, subject: Battleship Design—Ship X, December 27, 1939 (G.B. No. 420-6, serial No. 1911), Operational Archives, NHC.

19 The *Sovetskiy Soyuz* was to have had a standard displacement of 59,150 tons and full load displacement of 64,121 tons on a length of 889 feet; she was to have mounted a main battery of nine 16-inch guns with a maximum speed of 29 knots.

20 Admiral grades fell into disuse at the start of the Soviet regime. Position titles were used for senior naval officers until late 1935, when the ranks of flagman (flag-officer) 1st and 2nd rank were introduced. The various grades of admiral were reintroduced in the Soviet Navy on May 7, 1940, with initially seven officers given admiral ranks: N. G. Kuznetsov, the naval commissar, and I. S. Isakov and L. M. Galler, both at naval headquarters, were made full admirals; the commanders of the Baltic and Pacific Fleets became vice admirals; and the commanders of the Northern and Black Sea Fleets became rear admirals. The head of naval aviation became a lieutenant general.

21 K. P. Zagorodny, deputy director general, Nevskoye design bureau, discussion with N. Polmar, St. Petersburg, May 12, 1994. The *Khronstadt*-class battle cruisers were to have had a standard displacement of 36,420 tons and mount six 15-inch guns. At one point (1938) a total of 16 of these ships was planned.

22 A. M. Vasil'ev, "The First National Design of an Aircraft Carrier With Jet Aircraft," *Gangut* (No. 12-*bis*, 1991), p. 62.

23 The secondary armament was 12 5.1-inch dual-purpose guns in twin mounts; also provided were 24 45-mm anti-aircraft guns and 40 25-mm anti-aircraft guns, all in quadruple mounts.

24 In his memoirs Khrushchev took credit for returning Kuznetsov to the post of CinC; see *Khrushchev Remembers: The Last Testament* (Boston: Little, Brown, 1974), p. 21. But Stalin was still alive in 1951.

25 Arkadi B. Morin, "The Heavy Aircraft Carrying Cruiser *Admiral of the Fleet of the Soviet Union Kuznetsov*," *Gangut* (No. 11, 1991), p. 14.

26 Kuznetsov died in 1974; in 1988 he was posthumously returned to the rank of Admiral of the Fleet of the Soviet Union, which he had originally received in 1955. Khrushchev's memoirs discuss "The Fall of Admiral Kuznetsov," *Khrushchev Remembers: The Last Testament*, pp. 19–28.

27 Ibid., p. 31. "The Rise of Admiral Gorshkov" is addressed on pp. 28–34.

28 Ibid., p. 31.

29 Adm. of the Fleet Soviet Union. Sergei G. Gorshkov, *Vo Flotskom Stroyu* [Military Memoirs], (St. Petersburg: Logos, 1996), p. 178.

30 Marshal Soviet Union. V. D. Sokolovsky, *Military Strategy* (Moscow: Voyenizdat, 1962); Stanford Research Institute trans. January 1971, p. 345. Sokolovsky's credentials include having served as First Deputy Minister of Defense from 1949 to 1952, when he became Chief of the General Staff, a position that he held until 1960. From 1960 until his death in 1968 he was Inspector-General in the Ministry of Defense.

31 The U.S. defense establishment adopted the term "revolution in military affairs" in the 1990s but a few years later switched to the term "transformation."

32 Morin, "The Heavy Aircraft Carrying Cruiser," p. 15.

33 Gorshkov, *Vo Flotskom Stroyu*, p. 175.

34 The Polaris operational goal of 1965 was followed by a series of revisions and accelerations in the program. The first Polaris submarine, the USS *George Washington*, began the first missile patrol on November 15, 1960, with 16 missiles with a 1,200-n.mile range.

35 Twenty-four *Sverdlov* light cruisers were originally planned of which 19 were launched and 14 were completed in 1951–1955.

36 These machinations are detailed in D. Yu. Litinsky, "Pre-History of the 'Kondor,'" *Tayfun* (No. 6, 1997), pp. 27–34. Also see I. D. Spassky (ed.), *Shipbuilding in the Postwar Period 1946–1991*, vol. V in *The History of Indigenous Shipbuilding* (St. Petersburg: Sudostroenie, 1996), pp. 312–316. A useful and detailed, English-language appraisal of Soviet carriers is John Jordan, *Soviet Warships 1945 to the Present*, Rev. Ed. (London: Arms & Armour, 1992), pp. 51–68, 111–139.

37 Litinsky, "Pre-History of the 'Kondor,'" p. 33.

38 The treaty does restrict aircraft carriers to be escorted by no more than two destroyers and they are not to operate aircraft while in passage.

39 Ka indicted the design bureau named for Nikolai I. Kamov.

40 About this time a five-digit system of numbering designs, in which the fifth digit indicated the number of the sequential adjustment or modification of the basic design, was instituted.

Before the name *Kiev* was known, NATO assigned the code name Kurile to this class.

41 Kuzin and Nikol'skiy, *Voyenno-morskoy Flot SSSR, 1945–1991*, p. 98.

42 Recalling that the *Moskva*s were developed as anti-Polaris platforms, it is interesting to note that the first U.S. Polaris submarine entered the Mediterranean in March 1963 and two additional Polaris submarines entered in April 1963.

43 Mi indicated the design bureau named for Mikhail L. Mil'. The *Leningrad* had made a high-speed run from the Black Sea; she was accompanied by a guided missile destroyer and a replenishment oiler. In addition to the two large Mi-8 helicopters, the ship carried four Ka-25 helicopters.

44 Yak indicated the design bureau named for Aleksandr S. Yakovlev.

Chapter 23: Soviet Aircraft Carriers

1 Gorshkov, *Vo Flotskom Stroyu*, p. 172.

2 Four Yak-36 aircraft were built, with two used for test flights. Tethered flights began in 1963, and the first full VTOL flight occurred on March 24, 1966.

3 The P-500 Bazalt was the successor to the SS-N-3 Shaddock missile; the newer missile had a range of 300 n.miles, a high subsonic speed, with a conventional or 350-kiloton nuclear warhead. Targeting was done by aircraft or satellite.

The *Kiev* was the first aircraft carrier of any nation to be provided with significant anti-ship weapons since the U.S. carriers *Lexington* (CV 2) and *Saratoga* (CV 3) beached their 8-inch guns in early 1942.

4 The Soviet/Russian Naval Academy is the equivalent of the U.S. Naval War College in Newport, R.I. The undergraduate naval schools are referred to as Higher Naval Schools.

5 Adm. Igor Kuznetsov, *The Navy Came on the Ocean* (Moscow: Andreevsky Flag, 1996), p. 58.

6 This aircraft had the bureau designation Yak-41; the later military designation Yak-141 is used in this volume.

7 Yak-41/141 development began in 1975. Delayed because of a lack of funding and lengthy engine development, the first prototype did not fly until March 9, 1987. VSTOL aircraft are inherently complex.

8 Su indicated the design bureau named for Pavel O. Sukhoi. Su-27K was the bureau designation; Su-33 was the military designation.

UTG = *Uchesno-Trenirovochnyi Gakom* (training with hook).

9 Two of the four Yak-141s were flight test aircraft; reportedly both crashed during tests. One flew at the Paris air show of 1991 and at the Farnborough air show of 1992.

10 The P-700 Granit anti-ship missile had a range of 300 n.miles and a speed of Mach 2.5; it carried a conventional or nuclear 500-kiloton warhead.

11 Dr. Robert C. Suggs, "The Soviet Navy: Changing the Guard?" U.S. Naval Institute *Proceedings* (April 1983), p. 36.

12 Adm. Gorshkov had served as CinC of the Navy for almost 30 years; during that period the U.S. Navy had 13 Secretaries of the Navy and 9 Chiefs of Naval Operations, the equivalent positions of Gorshkov.

13 Rear Adm. Thomas A. Brooks, USN, Director of Naval Intelligence, testimony before the House Armed Services Committee, March 14, 1990. Brooks served as DNI from July 1988 to August 1991.

14 Saki came to the attention of the U.S. military establishment in February 1945, when President Roosevelt and Prime Minister Churchill met with Soviet leader Stalin at Yalta in the Crimea. The U.S. and British parties flew into Saki, 90 miles by mountain roads from Yalta. The parties flew out of Sevastopol.

15 This was the fourth Russian-Soviet cruiser named *Varyag*, the first having been built by the Cramp shipyard in Philadelphia and completed in 1901. Several pre–20th Century warships also carried that name.

16 A detailed discussion appears in Kuzin and Nikol'sky, *Voyenno-morskoy Flot SSSR, 1945–1991*, pp. 101–102.

17 Ibid., p. 101. Marshal Grechko was a First Deputy Minister of Defense and CinC of Ground Forces from 1957; he became CinC of Warsaw pact Forces and a First Deputy MOD from 1960 and Minister of Defense April 1967 until his death in April 1976.

18 Kozin and Nikol'skiy, *Voyenno-morskoy Flot SSSR, 1945–1991*, p. 102.

19 Rear Adm. Brooks discussion with N. Polmar, Springfield, Va., November 25, 2005.

20 U.S. Office of Naval Intelligence, Fact Sheet, "The Black Sea Fleet," July 7, 1992, p. 1.

Chapter 24: Rehabilitation and Retaliation

1 At the time Comdr. Lehman was a bombardier-navigator in a Naval Reserve A-6 Intruder squadron.

2 The only major published accounts of this effort when this volume went to press was by Dr. Christopher Ford and Dr. David A. Rosenberg, both naval reserve officers, who developed a classified account of the U.S. intelligence penetration; their published account is *The Admirals' Advantage: U.S. Navy Operational Intelligence in World War II and the Cold War* (Annapolis, Md.: Naval Institute Press, 2005); also see Rear Adm. Tom Brooks, USN (Ret), and Capt. Bill Manthorpe, USN (Ret), "Setting the Record Straight—A Critical Review of *Fall From Glory*," *The Submarine Review* (July 2007), pp. 147-152. Greg Vistica's *Fall From Glory* (1995) was an attempt-to defame the tenure of John F. Lehman, Jr., the Secretary of the Navy from 1981 to 1987. Brooks and Manthorpe, both professional intelligence officers, were deeply involved in exploiting the special intelligence sources of the late 1970s and early 1980s.

The U.S. penetration of the Soviet high command ended in 1985–1986 when Aldrich H. Ames, a CIA officer, revealed the American success to the KGB. Ames was arrested in 1994, tried, and sentenced to life imprisonment.

3 John F. Lehman, Jr., *Command of the Seas: Building the 600 Ship Navy* (New York: Charles Scribner's Sons, 1988), p. 173.

4 After 1961, the Newport News Shipbuilding yard in Virginia built all U.S. large carriers. The previous yards that built super carriers were New York Shipbuilding in Camden, N.J., and the New York Naval Shipyard in Brooklyn; both completed their last carriers, the *Kitty Hawk* and *Constellation*, respectively, in 1961. The Northrop Grumman Corporation acquired the Newport News yard in 2001.

5 Lehman, *Command of the Seas*, pp. 174–175.

6 Carl Vinson is believed to have been the second living American to have a naval ship named in his honor. The colonial schooner *Franklin* was placed in service in 1775, while Benjamin Franklin was living. Rep. Vinson (Democrat-Ga.)

served for 50 years in the House of Representatives, the longest tenure of any person in that body; he was a principal sponsor of the massive World War II–era shipbuilding programs. He died in 1981 at age 97.

7   Lehman, *Command of the Seas*, pp. 174–175.

8   In 1975—three years before the first Hornet flew—Vice Adm. William D. Houser, then Deputy Chief of Naval Operations (Air), determined that the designation F-18 would be used for the fighter variant and A-18 for the attack variant. However, on September 5, 1978, shortly before the first Hornet flight, Houser's successor, Vice Adm. Frederick C. Turner, wrote to the Commander, Naval Air Systems Command, stating his preference for the designation F/A-18, which did not follow the official aircraft designation guidance. The initial Navy order for 11 development aircraft used the designation YF-18. The designation F/A-18A was used for initial single-seat aircraft and F/A-18B for those with tandem seating.

A full discussion of the designation issue is found in James P. Stevenson, *The Pentagon Paradox: The Development of the F-18 Hornet* (Annapolis, Md: Naval Institute Press, 1993). This book is a program history of the F/A-18.

9   When this volume went to press the U.S. Marine Corps had declined to adopt the EA-18G and declared that it would continue to fly the EA-6B. The service was considering an electronic attack variant of the Joint Strike Fighter (JSF), the F-35 Lightning II.

10   These missiles were the Army MGM-31 Pershing II ballistic missile and the Air Force BGM-109G Gryphon, a ground-launched version of the Navy's Tomahawk cruise missile; deployments of the Pershing II began but not the Gryphon.

11   Christopher Andrew and Oleg Gordievsky, *KGB: The Inside Story of its Foreign Operations from Lenin to Gorbachev* (London: Hodder and Stoughton, 1990), p. 605. This work contains a comprehensive account of Operation RYAN, pp. 584–605.

12   The Baghdad Pact, signed in 1955 with American support, was intended to oppose Soviet influence in the Middle East. Iran was a principal participant. In 1959 it became the Central Treaty Organization (CENTO); the full members were Iran, Iraq, Pakistan, Turkey, and the United Kingdom with the United States as an associate member. CENTO was dissolved in 1979 because of changing Middle East politics.

13   For example, in the 1970s the United States agreed to sell 80 F-14A Tomcat fighters and Phoenix missiles as well as Aegis destroyers and submarines to Iran. Seventy-nine of the F-14s were delivered but none of the warships.

14   On November 19, 1979, Iranian militants freed three American hostages—one female staffer and two black Marines. Another ten Americans were released the following day. All but one of the 53 remaining hostages were held in captivity for more than a year.

15   Capt. Paul B. Ryan, USN (Ret), *The Iranian Rescue Mission: Why It Failed* (Annapolis, Md.: Naval Institute Press, 1985), p. 125. Also see Department of Defense, "Rescue Mission Report," August 1980 (Holloway Report); Gen. David C. Jones, USAF, press conference, Pentagon, April 29, 1980; and Col. Charlie Beckwith, USA, press conference, Pentagon, May 1, 1980; and Maj. Robert L. Earl, USMC, "A Matter of Principle," U.S. Naval Institute Proceedings (September 1983), pp. 29–36.

16   See Lt. Comdr. Joseph T. Stanik, USN, "*Swift and Effective Retribution*" (Washington, D.C.: Naval Historical Center,

1996), and *El Dorado Canyon Reagan's Undeclared War with Qaddafi* (Annapolis, Md.: Naval Institute Press, 2003).

17   Geneva Convention on the Territorial Sea and Contiguous Zone, 1958.

18   The carriers *Forrestal* and *Nimitz* had launched six F-14 Tomcats and 4 F-4 Phantoms on combat air patrol.

19   Stanik, "*Swift and Effective Retribution*," p. 10. The F-14s had a 20-mm internal Vulcan multi-barrel gun and carried AIM-7F Sparrow and AIM-9L Sidewinder missiles.

20   The Americans killed were 220 Marines, 18 sailors, and 3 soldiers. Others were wounded.

21   The *New Jersey* was the first of the four mothballed battleships of the *Iowa* class that were reactivated during the Reagan-Lehman naval buildup of the 1980s.

22   The captured aviator was returned to U.S. custody in January 1984. The body of the A-6E pilot, who died from injuries received when he ejected, was returned to the American embassy in Beirut. A Lebanese fisherman rescued the pilot of the downed A-7E.

23   About 100 U.S. soldiers remained in Beirut to guard American diplomats who were at the British Embassy. The American Embassy had been severely damaged in a terrorist attack on September 20, 1984.

24   Stanik, "*Swift and Effective Retribution*," p. 23. Vice Adm. Kelso was at sea in his flagship *Coronado*, a converted amphibious ship, but allowed his carrier force commander, Rear Adm. David E. Jeremiah, to direct the tactical operations. Neither Kelso nor Jeremiah were naval aviators; they were submarine and surface warfare officers, respectively.

25   Adm. Kelso served as Chief of Naval Operations from June 1990 to April 1994.

26   Stanik, "*Swift and Effective Retribution*," p. 25.

27   The AGM-84A Harpoon missile was originally an air-launched weapon developed to attack Soviet cruise missile submarines while on the surface. Such submarines were invulnerable to ASW torpedoes, which had a near-surface cutoff.

28   HARM is the AGM-88 High-speed Anti-Radiation Missile.

29   Stanik, "*Swift and Effective Retribution*," p. 40.

30   Department of Defense, *Conduct of the Persian Gulf War—Final Report to Congress* (Washington, D.C.: April 1992), p. 250. This is the most comprehensive unclassified report available on the conflict.

31   The air campaign is described in Dr. Richard P. Hallion, *Storm over Iraq: Air Power and the Gulf War* (Washington, D.C.: Smithsonian Institution Press, 1992); also see Rear Adm. Riley D. Mixson, USN, "Where We Must Do Better," U.S. Naval Institute *Proceedings* (August 1991), pp. 38–39; and Strike Fighter Squadron 87, "Aircraft—Yes! Tactics—Yes! WEAPONS—NO!" U.S. Naval Institute *Proceedings* (September 1991), pp. 55–57.

32   See Capt. Marc E. Liebman, USNR, "Navy Tankers Are Needed Now!" U.S. Naval Institute *Proceedings* (September 1991), pp. 82–84.

33   The two F/A-18C Hornets, each carrying four 2,000-pound bombs, were on a bombing mission when they engaged the two Iraqi fighters. The F/A-18s were able to continue their bombing mission not having had to jettison their bombs to engage the enemy aircraft.

34   Shot down by a Soviet-supplied SA-2 missile, this was the only combat loss of an F-14. The pilot and radar intercept officer ejected. U.S. forces rescued the pilot; the "backseater" was captured by Iraqi forces and released after the brief war.

35 The *Midway* had been homeported in Yokosuka, Japan, from 1973 to 1991. She was succeeded by the *Independence* from 1991 to 1998 and the *Kitty Hawk* from 1998, with the nuclear-propelled *George Washington* planned as her replacement in 2008. These were the only U.S. carriers to be forward based.

36 In addition, in 1992–1993 the Navy took delivery of 16 S-3A Vikings that had been converted to ES-3A electronic surveillance aircraft for carrier operation, replacing the EA-3B/EKA-3B Skywarrior in that role. Despite high praise from the Navy, the ES-3A Shadow aircraft were retired in 1999—without replacement—to save operating funds.

37 The F-14D was the only variant that could carry the AMRAAM (Advanced Medium-Range Air-to-Air Missile, successor to Sparrow missile), and HARM anti-radar missiles, and the Harpoon and SLAM (Standoff Land-Attack Missile, a modified Harpoon) air-to-surface missiles.

38 Tim Ripley, *Air War Bosnia: UN and NATO Airpower* (Shrewsbury: Airlife, 1996), p. 7. The author continued,

> Initially the Muslim-led Army of Bosnia-Herzegovina was locked in battle with the Bosnian Serb Army, backed occasionally by elements of the old Yugoslav Federal Army. Croatians living in Bosnia formed their own militia, the Croatian Defence Council, which allied itself with the [Bosnia-Herzegovina] and were on occasions supported by regular troops from Croatia proper. By 1993 the Croats were at war with the Bosnians and some Muslims in northwest Bosnia changed sides to fight with the Serbs against the Sarajevo government. In early 1994 the Croats and Muslims had patched up their differences and again started joint operations against the Serbs. After the success of the Croatian offensives against the Serb-held Krajina and western Slavonia regions, the Croatian Army pushed into Bosnia to engage Bosnian-Serb troops.

39 The Sigonella base is a U.S. naval air facility established in 1959 to support NATO operations in the Mediterranean.

40 The half-squadron was a two-plane detachment from Naval Air Reserve squadron VAQ-209.

41 The Navy designation VAQ indicated tactical electronic warfare squadron until March 30, 1998, when it was changed to electronic attack squadron.

42 HMS *Splendid* was the first British warship to be armed with Tomahawks.

Chapter 25: Amphibious Assault

1 Four *Essex*-class carriers were employed in the amphibious assault role:

SHIP	TO "AMPHIB"	DECOMM.	STRICKEN
CV 21 *Boxer*	LPH 4 1959	1969	1969
CV 37 *Princeton*	LPH 5 1959	1970	1970
CV 40 *Tarawa*	—	1961	1967
CV 45 *Valley Forge*	LPH 8 1961	1970	1970

Details are provided in Appendix C. The *Tarawa* was not reclassified as an LPH; after being decommissioned she was classified as an aircraft transport (AVT 12) in 1965.

2 The name *Tarawa* was previously assigned to the *Essex*-class carrier CV 40. This initiated the scheme of primarily using World War II–era CV/CVL names for amphibious assault ships.

3 A MEU nominally consisted of a Marine rifle battalion, composite helicopter (and later composite helicopter/Harrier VSTOL) squadron with artillery, engineer, tank, and support detachments plus a command element.

4 An additional six RH-53D mine countermeasures helicopters were provided to the Iranian Navy prior to the 1979 Islamic revolution.

5 John W. Fozard discussion with N. Polmar, Kingston Upon Thames [England], February 15, 1984.

6 To reduce costs, 35 percent of the FV-12A structure came from F-4 Phantom and A-4 Skyhawk aircraft.

7 See Edward J. Marolda (ed.), *Operation End Sweep: A History of Minesweeping Operations in North Vietnam* (Washington, D.C.: Naval Historical Center, 1993); and Tamara Moser Melia, *"Damn the Torpedoes": A Short History of U.S. Naval Mine Countermeasures, 1777–1991* (Washington, D.C.: Naval Historical Center, 1991).

8 HM = helicopter mine countermeasures squadron.

9 MCS = mine warfare command and support ship. The *Inchon* should have been designated MCS 8, after previous support ships designated MCS 1–7. However, the Navy's disregard for classification procedures was shown by retaining her LPH number with her MCS designation. See N. Polmar, *Ships and Aircraft of the U.S. Fleet* (Annapolis, Md.: Naval Institute Press, various editions).

10 The Navy listed the *Inchon*'s complement as 505 active and 177 reserve personnel, plus accommodations for approximately 150 aviation personnel and 75 explosive ordnance disposal personnel.

11 Marines were landed by helicopter from the *Okinawa* to capture the small island of Umm al Maradim, 12 miles off the Kuwaiti coast, on January 29, 1961.

12 Lt. Comdr. Cindy Rodriguez, USN, Maj. Michael Manzer, Jr., USMC, Comdr. Shawn Lobree, USN, and Comdr. Jon Dachos, USN, "Harrier Carriers Perform in Iraqi Freedom," U.S. Naval Institute *Proceedings* (February 2004), pp. 32–35; and William F. Morgan, *USS Nassau (LHA 4) and VMA-331 Strike Operations during Operation Desert Storm* CRM 91-140 (Alexandria, Va.: Center for Naval Analyses, June 1992).

13 The carrier CV 31 was named *Bon Homme Richard*. The first ship of that name, acquired by the U.S. government in France in early 1779, was named *Bonhomme Richard* by her captain, John Paul Jones. She sank on September 25, 1779, after a dramatic victory over a British warship.

14 Marine detachments were removed from U.S. aircraft carriers in 1992 with the removal of nuclear weapons from those ships. They were the last U.S. warships to regularly have Marine detachments assigned.

15 See Stephen M. Carmel, "A Commercial Approach to Sea Basing—Afloat Forward Staging Bases," U.S. Naval Institute *Proceedings* (January 2004), pp. 78–80, and "Adaptability in Sea-Base Platform Design," *RUSI Defense Systems* (Summer 2004), pp. 54–55; also N. Polmar, "Sea Base Ships for the Future," U.S. Naval Institute *Proceedings* (March 2005), pp. 104–105.

16 Naval Research Advisory Committee, *Sea Basing* (Arlington, Va.: 2005); the report is available at www.onr.navy.mil/nrac.

17 Lt. James J. Mulquin, USNR, "Arapaho Goes to Sea," *Naval Aviation News* (February 1983), pp. 30–33; and Warren Baker, "A Ping-Pong Program Pings Back to U.S.," *Sea Power* [Navy League] (April 1986), pp. 133–137. Mulquin was the Naval Air Systems Command's project manager for Arapaho.

18 Lt. James J. Mulquin, USNR, "Merchant Ship TacAir," U.S. Naval Institute *Proceedings* (March 1985), pp. 168–170.

19 These ships are officially designated *Bâtiment de Projection et de Commandement*.

20 The Air Force is procuring the CV-22 variant as a special operations aircraft. The Navy had planned to procure the HV-22 for the search-and-rescue role, but procurement of that variant had not been initiated when this volume went to press.

Chapter 26: Into the 21st Century

1 Former Secretary of the Navy John Lehman presented an excellent exposition on this subject at the U.S. Naval Institute's naval history symposium at Annapolis, Md., March 31, 2004. His remarks were published as "Our Enemy Is Not Terrorism," U.S. Naval Institute *Proceedings* (May 2004), pp. 52–54. Mr. Lehman was a member of the National Commission on Terrorist Attacks Upon the United States (the "9/11 Commission").

2 Similarly, it was difficult to determine precisely when World War II began—with the Japanese assaults on China in the 1930s? Or Hitler's invasion of Poland in 1939? Or Japan's attack on Pearl Harbor and American bases in the Philippines in December 1941?

3 The carrier-based aircraft were "folded" into the North American Air Defense (NORAD) command and control system.

4 The best published work on the carrier aspects of this operation as well as the 2003 invasion of Iraq is Rebecca Grant, *Battle-Tested: Carrier Aviation in Afghanistan and Iraq* (Washington, D.C.: IRIS Press, 2005). The book was based in large part on Ms. Grant's articles in *Air Force* magazine.

5 The Taliban's ruthless rule soon drove some two million refuges into neighboring Pakistan.

6 The land-based aircraft were two B-2 stealth bombers flying from Whiteman Air Force Base in Missouri, and B-1 and B-52 bombers flying from the British airfield on Diego Garcia in the Indian Ocean. The B-2s, after bombing targets in Afghanistan, flew on to Diego Garcia for an "engine-running" crew change and returned to Whiteman. Their flight, of about 36 hours, required numerous in-flight refuelings. Diego Garcia is some 2,500 miles from Afghanistan.

7 Grant, *Battle-Tested*, p. 36.

8 Satellite guidance was by the Global Positioning System (GPS).

9 Grant, *Battle-Tested*, p. 171.

10 Tony Holmes, "The Last Catfight," U.S. Naval Institute *Proceedings* (September 2006), p. 37. These were the Navy's last two fighter (VF) squadrons.

11 Little authoritative information has been written about the Iranian F-14 Tomcats. Apparently several F-14 pilots did become aces by scoring five or more kills against Iraqi aircraft in the 1980s conflict. See Tom Cooper, *Iranian F-14 Tomcat Units in Combat* (London: Osprey, 2004).

12 Capt. Gordon A. S. C. Wilson, RN (Ret.), "Whither the Flattops?" U.S. Naval Institute *Proceedings* (March 2006), p. 68. Wilson, who commanded several warships, served as head of Defence Studies (Royal Navy) from November 1986 to December 1992.

13 Secretary of State for Defence, *Strategic Defence Review* (July 1998), paragraphs 26, 27. (Published on July 8, 1998, as Command 3999.)

14 House of Commons, *Strategic Defence Review* (October 15, 1998), p. 36. (Research Paper RP 98/91.)

15 PA = *Porte–Avions*.

16 The aircraft was originally designated FRS.2; it was changed to FA.2 in May 1994 to reflect the conventional *A*ttack role rather than the nuclear *S*trike role because of the retirement of nuclear bombs from the British arsenal.

17 This was the 82nd anniversary of the establishment of the Royal Air Force and the demise of the Royal Naval Air Service (RNAS).

18 One of the Sea Kings was departing the *Ark Royal* and the other was approaching the carrier when they collided about 4:25 A.M. on March 22, 2003. Six British naval crew members and one U.S. Navy officer were killed in the collision of the two helicopters from No. 849 Squadron.

19 Director, Naval Air Warfare, Office of the Chief of Naval Operations, *Naval Aviation: Forward Air Power . . . From the Sea* (1998), p. 30. Also see N. Polmar, "Carrier Questions—and Some Answers," U.S. Naval Institute *Proceedings* (April 1998), pp. 103–104, and "The Sinking of a Carrier," *Proceedings* (July 1998), p. 88.

20 Tom Philpott, "Bowman Sees a Smaller Fleet More Reliant on Nuclear Power" (syndicated column Military Update), November 6, 1997.

21 Rumsfeld was a naval aviator from 1954 to 1957 and served in the House of Representatives from 1962 to 1969.

22 See Gen. Richard B. Myers, USA, "Understanding Transformation," U.S. Naval Institute *Proceedings* (February 2003), pp. 38–41. At the time Gen. Myers was Chairman of the Joint Chiefs of Staff.

23 The catapults are designated Electo-Magnetic Aircraft Launching System (EMALS).

24 For the current carrier controversy see N. Polmar, "Carrier Aviation on the Move: But Going Where?" U.S. Naval Institute *Proceedings* (June 2007), pp. 86-87, and subsequent articles and comments (letters) from various parties in the July through November 2007 issues of the *Proceedings*. Also see, Government Accountability Office, *Navy faces Challenges Constructing the Aircraft Carrier* Gerald R. Ford *Within Budget*, GAO-07-866 (Washington, D.C.: August 2007).

25 The carrier-capable RF-4B (former F4H-1P) variant of the Phantom was flown only by the Marine Corps, with 46 aircraft produced. However, Marine RF-4B detachments periodically flew from carriers and the Yokosuka-based carrier *Midway* had a detachment assigned to her air wing.

26 Government Accounting Office, *Navy Aircraft Carriers: Cost-Effectiveness of Conventionally and Nuclear-Powered Carriers*, NSIAD-98-1 (Washington, D.C., August 1, 1998); and Hans M. Kristensen, William M. Arkin, and Joshua Handler, *Aircraft Carriers: The Limits of Nuclear Power* (Washington, D.C.: Greenpeace, June 1994).

27 Kristensen, et. al., *Aircraft Carriers*, p. 2.

28 Ibid., p. 3.

29 Navy and Coast Guard.

Appendix A: War Without Carriers

1 See Wilhelm Hadeler, *Graf Zeppelin* (Freiburg: Militärgeschichtliches Forschungsamt, 1966); Hadeler, "The Aircraft Carrier in the German Navy 1934–1945, *American Society of Naval Engineers Journal* (August 1956), pp. 431–440; Hadeler, "Projektskizzen von Flugzeugschiffen der Kreigsmarine aus dem zweiten Weltkriege," *Marine-Rundschau* (January 1972), pp. 1–40; and Siegfried Breyer, *The German Aircraft Carrier* Graf Zeppelin (West Chester, Pa.: Schiffer Publishing, 1989).

2 Wilhelm Hadeler, letter to N. Polmar, February 23, 1996.

3 The name Peter Strasser for Aircraft Carrier "B," honoring the commander of the German Navy's Zeppelin force in World

War I, has been mentioned in literature about German carriers, but this name is purely speculative. Strasser, who joined the Navy at age 15, personally led Zeppelin raids on Britain and died when the *Z.70* was shot down over the Norfolk coast on August 6, 1918.

4 Vice Adm. Friedrich Ruge, FGN, *Der Seekrieg* (Annapolis, Md.: U.S. Naval Institute, 1957), pp. 37-38.

5 See Francis L. Marshall, *Sea Eagles: The operational history of the Messerschmitt Bf 109T* (Surrey: Air Research Publications, 1994).

6 German Navy [Kriegsmarine], *Fuehrer Conferences on Naval Affairs 1939–1945* (Annapolis, Md.: Naval Institute Press, 1990), p. 101.

7 German Navy, *Fuehrer Conferences . . .* , p. 266.

8 For example, H. T. Lenton, *German Warships of the Second World War* (London: Macdonald and Jane's, 1975), p. 53, cites the *Graf Zeppelin* having struck a mine and sunk off the island of Rügen in the Baltic Sea on August 15, 1947.

9 The Polish Navy located the wreckage of the *Graf Zeppelin* in July 2006.

10 Grand Adm. Karl Doenitz, German Navy, *Memoirs: Ten Years and Twenty Days* (Cleveland: World Publishing, 1959), p. 312.

11 Brig. Gen. Giulio Douhet, Italian Army, *The Command of the Air* (Washington, D.C.: Office of Air Force History, 1983), p. 194. Douhet (1869–1930) assumed command of the Italian aviation battalion in 1912. His major work, *The Command of the Air*, was originally published in 1921. This cited work is a reprint of the 1942 English-language translation of Douhet's works; while titled *The Command of the Air*, it actually consists of five separate works by Douhet with this citation from his lengthy article "Probable Aspects of the Future War" (1929).

12 Adm. Romeo Bernotti, Italian Navy, "Italian Naval Policy Under Fascism," U.S. Naval Institute *Proceedings* (July 1956), p. 725.

13 Claudio G. Sergé, *Italo Balbo: A Fascist Life* (Berkley: University of California Press, 1987), p. 189. The term "Balbo" entered common usage in the 1930s for any large flight of aircraft. Balbo Drive in Chicago and Balbo Avenue in New York City were named for the fascist aviator, who at one point was considered to be Mussolini's successor.

14 Adm. Cavagnari was head of the Italian Navy from 1933 to 1940. See Enrico Cernuschi and Vincent P. O'Hara, "The Breakout Fleet: The Oceanic Programmes of the Regia Marina, 1934–1940," in *Warship 2006* (London: Conway Maritime Press, 2006), pp. 86–101.

15 Cernuschi and O'Hara, "The Breakout Fleet," p. 93.

16 The *Roma* was being refitted with steam turbines from the light cruisers *Paolo Emilio* and *Cornelio Silla*, whose construction had been halted in 1940 and 1941, respectively, to provide the higher speed. The cruisers were of the *Capitani Romani* class, which, on a light displacement of 3,747 tons, had a maximum speed of 43 knots.

17 The *Roma* was propelled by four steam turbines, the *Augustus* by diesel engines; the latter was the world's largest "motor ship" at the time she was built.

18 See Giancario Garello, "Esperimentgi a Perugia per il caccia navale" [Experiments at Perugia for Naval Aviation], *Aerofan* (October-December 1981), pp. 18–21.

The Italian VSTOL carrier *Cavour* at sea prior to her commissioning in 2008. The *Cavour* is significantly larger, more heavily armed, and more capable as an aviation platform than her predecessor, the *Giuseppe Garibaldi,* completed more than two decades earlier. Note the *Cavour*'s large island structure and angled exhaust stack for the ship's four gas turbine engines. (*Ships of the World*)

SELECTED BIBLIOGRAPHY

This book is based in large part on personal correspondence and conversations (see Acknowledgments in Volumes I and II), official action reports, ship and unit logs and histories, hear-ings of committees of the U.S. Congress, and contemporary periodicals.

In addition to the books and reports listed below, the reader is referred to the two major naval histories of World War II: *The War at Sea* by Capt. S. W. Roskill (RN), and the *History of United States Naval Operations in World War II* by Rear Adm. Samuel Eliot Morison (USNR). Both works devote considerable coverage to aircraft carrier operations during the war. Roskill's three-volume history (1954–1961) is an official British military history; as such it is more accurate and more objective than the quasi-official, 15-volume work (1947–1962) by Morison. Another work addressing British carrier operations is the Ministry of Defence's *War With Japan* in six volumes (1995).

Considerable material on U.S. aircraft carrier development is in contained in the hearings of the General Board of the U.S. Navy, published periodically during the first half of the 20th Century.

Also of value are the operational monographs prepared by the U.S. Marine Corps and the *History of U.S. Marine Corps Operations in World War II* (in five volumes, 1958–1968)

The Army Air Forces in World War II (in six volumes, 1948–1955), by Wesley Frank Craven and James Lea Cate, has provided an important perspective on World War II's air campaigns.

Also, an outstanding collection of articles dealing with virtually all aspects of air power may be found in *The Impact of Air Power* (1959), edited by Eugene M. Emme; the authors include: Henry H. (Hap) Arnold, Alexander Graham Bell, Arleigh Burke, Bernard Brodie, Winston Churchill, Giulio Douliet, Hermann Göring, Adolf Galland, James H. Doolittle, Alexander de Seversky, Curtis LeMay, Viscount Montgomery, Franklin D. Roosevelt, George C. Kenney, Sir Robert Saundby, Carl A. Spaatz, Viscount Trencliard, Lord Tedder, Arthur W. Radford, and G. K. Zbukov.

A significant anthology is *American Civil-Military Decisions* edited by Harold Stein (1963). It contains the studies "The United States Fleet: Diplomacy, Strategy and the Allocation of Ships (1940–1941)," by Robert J. Quinlan, and "Super Carriers and B-36 Bombers: Appropriations, Strategy and Politics," by Paul Y. Hammond.

The following bibliography contains primarily English-language works. Several additional foreign-language works will be found in this book's footnotes. Also important to this work has been *Senshi Sosho*, the official Japanese history series of World War II.

Books

British and Commonwealth Carrier Aviation

Apps, Lt. Comdr. Michael, RN (Ret). *Send Her Victorious*. London: William Kimber, 1971.

Beaver, Paul. *The British Aircraft Carrier*. Wellingborough, Northamptonshire: Patrick Stephens, 1982.

Bell Davies, Vice-Adm. Richard, RN. *Sailor in the Air*. London: Peter Davies, 1967.

Braybrook, Roy. *Battle for the Falklands: Air Forces*. London: Osprey, 1982.

British Aerospace. *V/STOL in the Roaring Forties*. Kingston Upon Thames, Surrey: October 1982. [The Harrier in the Falklands War.]

Brown, David. *The Royal Navy and the Falklands War*. London: Leo Cooper, 1987.

Brown, Capt. Eric M., RN. *Wings on My Sleeve*. London: Arthur Barker, 1961; revised and expanded edition, London: Weidenfeld & Nicolson, 2006.

Cameron, Ian. *Wings of the Morning: The British Fleet Air Arm in World War II*. New York: William Morrow, 1963.

Churchill, Winston S. *The Second World War*, 6 vols. Boston: Houghton, Mifflin, 1948-1953.

Cunningham, Adm. of the Fleet A.B., RN. *A Sailor's Odyssey*, 2 vols. London: Hutchinson, 1951.

Cull, Brian. *Wings Over Suez*. London: Grub Street, 1996.

Freedman, Lawrence. *Britain and the Flaklands War*. Oxford: Basil Blackwell, 1988.

Grove, Eric J. *Vanguard to Trident: British Naval Policy Since World War Two*. Annapolis, Md.: Naval Institute Press, 1987.

Heckstall-Smith, Anthony. *The Fleet That Faced Both Ways*. London: Anthony Blond, 1963. [A prejudiced but valuable study of British operations against the French Navy in World War II.]

Jameson, Rear-Adm. William, RN. *Ark Royal*. London: Rupert Hart-Davis, 1957. [Biography of Britain's most famous carrier.]

Kemp, Lt.-Comdr. Peter K., RN. *Fleet Air Arm*. London: Herbert Jenkins, 1954.

Lansdown, John R.P. *With the Carriers in Korea: The Sea and Air War in SE Asia, 1950–1953*. Winslow, Cheshire: Crécy, 1997.

Macintyre, Capt. Donald, RN. *Battle for the Mediterranean*. London: B. T. Batsford, 1964.

Moore, Maj. W. Geoffrey, RAF. *Early Bird*. London: Putnam, 1963. [Autobiography of an early British naval aviator.]

Pack, Capt. S.W.C., RN. *The Battle of Matapan*. New York: Macmillan, 1961.

Poolman, Kenneth. *Ark Royal*. London: William Kimber, 1956.

———. *The Sea Hunters: Escort Carriers v. U-Boats, 1941–1945*. London: Arms and Armour, 1982.

Roskill, Capt. S.W. *Documents Relating to the Naval Air Service, vol. I, 1908–1918*. London: Naval Records Society, 1969.

———. *Naval Policy between the Wars*, 2 vol. London: Collins, 1968, 1976.

Samson, Air-Commo. Charles Rumney, RAF. *Fights and Flights*. London: Ernest Berm, 1930. [A candid and enjoyable autobiography of Samson's exploits in World War I.]

Schofield, Vice-Adm. B.B., RN. *The Russian Convoys*. Philadelphia: Dufour, 1964.

Seth, Ronald. *Two Fleets Surprised*. London: G. Bles, 1960. [The Battle of Matapan.]

Speed, Keith. *Sea Change: The Battle for the Falklands and the Future of the British Navy*. Bath: Ashgrove Press, 1982. [Mr. Speed was Under Secretary of State for Defence for the Royal Navy from May 1979 to May 1981.]

Sueter, Rear-Adm. Murray. F., RN. *Airmen or Noahs*. London: Sir Isaac Pitman and Sons, 1928. [A disorganized but interesting and useful study of the first two decades of aviation in the Royal Navy; Sueter was Director of the Air Department in Admiralty from 1912 to 1915.]

Young, Desmond. *Rutland of Jutland*. London: Cassell [nd]. [Biography of a pioneer British naval aviator.]

French Carrier Aviation

Auphan, Rear Adm. Paul, French Navy, and Jacques Mordal. *The French Navy in World II*. Annapolis, Md.: U.S. Naval Institute, 1959.

Fall, Bernard B. *Hell in a Very Small Place*. Philadelphia: J.B. Lippincott, 1966.

Roy, Jules. *The Battle of Dienbienphu*. New York: Harper and Row, 1965.

Sheldon-Duplaix, Alexandre. *Historie mondiale des Porte-Avions*. Cedex: E-T-A-I, 2006.

German Carrier Aviation

Breyer, Siegfried. *The German Aircraft Carrier Graf Zeppelin*. West Chester, Pa.: Schiffer Publishing, 1989.

Doenitz, GrossAdm. Karl, German Navy. *Memoirs: Ten Years and Twenty Days*. Cleveland, Ohio: World, 1959.

German Navy. *Fueher Conferences on Naval Affairs, 1939–1945*. Annapolis, Md.: Naval Institute Press, 1990.

Hadeler, Wilhelm. *Graf Zeppelin*. Freiburg: Militärgeschichtliches Forschungsamt, 1966.

Isby, David (ed.). *The Luftwaffe and the War at Sea 1939–1945: As Seen by Officers of the Kriegsmarine and Luftwaffe*. London: Chatham, 2005.

Ruge, Vice Adm. Friedrich, German Navy. *Der See-krieg*. Annapolis, Md.: U.S. Naval Institute, 1957.

Italian Carrier Aviation

Bragadin, Comdr. Marc' Antonio, Italian Navy. *The Italian Navy in World War II*. Annapolis, Md.: U.S. Naval Institute, 1957.

Japanese Carrier Aviation

Enright, Capt. Joseph F., USN. *Shinano! The Sinking of Japan's Secret Supership*. New York: St. Martin's Press, 1987.

Evans, David C., and Mark R. Peattie. *Kaigun: Strategy, Tactics, and Technology in the Imperial Japanese Navy, 1887–1941*. Annapolis, Md.: Naval Institute Press, 1997.

Fuchida, Capt. Mitsuo, IJN, and Comdr. Masatake Okumiya, IJN. *Midway*. Annapolis, Md.: U.S. Naval Institute, 1955. [An important but early account that contains several erroneous impressions.]

Goldstein, Donald M., and Katherine V. Dillon (ed.). *Fading Victory: The Diary of Admiral Matome Ugaki 1941–1945*. Pittsburgh, Pa.: University of Pittsburgh Press, 1991.

———. (eds.) *The Pearl Harbor Papers: Inside the Japanese Plans*. Washington, D.C.: Brassey's, 1993.

Ito, Masanori. *The End of the Imperial Japanese Navy*. New York: W.W. Norton, 1956.

Kohri, Katsu; Ikuo Komoro; and Ichiro Naito. *Aireview's the Fifty Years of Japanese Aviation 1910–1960*. Tokyo: Kantosha, 1961. [Pictorial coverage.]

Okumiya, Masatake, and Jiro Horikoshi. *Zero: The Inside Story of Japan's Air War in the Pacific*. New York: Ballantine, 1956.

Parshall, Jonathan, and Anthony Tully. *Shattered Sword: The Untold Story of the Battle of Midway*. Washington, D.C.: Potomac Books, 2005.

Peattie, Mark R. *Sunburst: The Rise of Japanese Naval Air Power, 1909–1941*. Annapolis, Md.: Naval Institute Press, 2001.

Prange, Gordon W. *God's Samurai: Lead Pilot at Pearl Harbor*. Washington, D.C.: Brassey's, 1990.

Russian-Soviet Carrier Aviation

Herrick, Comdr. Robert Waring, USN. *Soviet Naval Strategy: Fifty Years of Theory and Practice*. Annapolis, Md.: U.S. Naval Institute, 1968.

Khrushchev, Nikita. *Khrushchev Remembers: The Last Testament*. Boston: Little, Brown, 1974.

Kuzin, V.P., and V.I. Nikol'skiy. *Voyenno-morskoy Flot SSSR, 1945–1991* [The Navy of the USSR, 1945–1991]. St. Petersburg: Historical Oceanic Society, 1996.

Kuznetsov, Adm. N.G., Soviet Navy. *Memoirs of Wartime Minister of the Navy*. Moscow: Progress Publishers, 1990.

———. *Nakanune* [On the Eve]. Moscow: Voenizdat, 1966.

Morin, A., and N. Walujew. *Sowjetische Flugzeugträger: geheim 1910–1995*. Berlin: Brandenburgisches Verlagshaus, 1996.

Rohwer, Jürgen, and Mikhail S. Monakov. *Stalin's Ocean-Going Fleet: Soviet Naval Strategy and Shipbuilding Programmes, 1935–1953*. London: Frank Cass, 2001.

Sokolovsky, Marshal of the Soviet Union V.D. *Voennaia Strategya* [Military Strategy]. Moscow: Voenizdat, 1962.

U.S. Carrier Aviation

Baldwin, Hanson W. *Sea Fights and Shipwrecks*. Garden City, N.Y.: Doubleday, 1955. [Excellent essay on "The Sho Plan—The Battle for Leyte Gulf," with commentary by Adm. Halsey and Adm. Kinkaid.]

Barlow, Dr. Jeffrey. *Revolt of the Admirals: The Fight for Naval Aviation, 1945–1950*. Washington, D.C.: Naval Historical Center 1994.

Buchanan, Lt. A.R., USNR. *The Navy's Air War*. New York: Harper and Bros. 1946. [Official report of U.S. naval aviation in World War II.]

Burns, Eugene. *Then There Was One*. New York: Harcourt, Brace, 1944. [The USS *Enterprise* and the first year of the war.]

Cagle, Comdr. Malcolm W., USN, and Comdr. Frank A. Manson, USN. *The Sea War in Korea*. Annapolis, Md.: U.S. Naval Institute, 1957.

Carter, Rear Adm. Worrall Reed, USN. *Beans, Bullets, and Black Oil*. Washington, D.C.: Government Printing Office, 1952. [U.S. Navy logistics in the Pacific during World War II.]

Clark, Adm. J. J., USN (Ret). *Carrier Admiral*. New York: David McKay, 1967.

Condon, John Pomeroy. *Corsairs and Flattops: Marine Air Warfare, 1944–1945*. Annapolis, Md.: Naval Institute Press, 1998.

Cristol, A. Jay. *The Liberty Incident: The 1967 Israeli Attack on the U.S. Navy Spy Ship*. Washington, D.C.: Brassey's, 2002.

Davis, Vincent. *The Admirals Lobby*. Chapel Hill, N.C.: University of North Carolina Press, 1967.

———. *Postwar Defense Policy and the U.S. Navy, 1943–1946*. Chapel Hill, N.C.: University of North Carolina Press, 1966.

Doolittle, Gen. James H., USAF (Ret). *I Could Never Be So Lucky Again*. New York: Bantam, 1991.

Dyer, Vice Adm. George C., USN (Ret). *On the Treadmill to Pearl Harbor: The Memoirs of Admiral James O. Richardson, USN (Retired)*. Washington, D.C.: Naval History Division, 1973.

Field, James A., Jr. *History of United States Naval Operations Korea*. Washington, D.C.: Naval History Division, 1962.

Futrell, Robert F. *The United States Air Force in Korea, 1950–1953*. New York: Duell, Sloan and Pearce, 1961.

Gay, George. *Sole Survivor*. Naples, Fla.: Midway Publishers, 1980.

Grant, Rebecca. *Battle-Tested: Carrier Aviation in Afghanistan and Iraq*. Washington, D.C.: IRIS Press, 2005.

Hallion, Richard P. *The Naval Air War in Korea*. Baltimore, Md.: Nautical & Aviation, 1986.

———. *Storm Over Iraq: Air Power and the Gulf War*. Washington, D.C.: Smithsonian Institution Press, 1992.

Halsey, Fleet Adm. William F., USN, and J. Bryan III. *Admiral Halsey's Story*. New York: McGraw-Hill, 1947.

Holloway, Adm. James L., III. *Aircraft Carriers At War: A Personal Perspective of Korea, Vietnam, and the Soviet Confrontation*. Annapolis, Md.: Naval Institute Press, 2007. [Despite factual errors, a useful memoir.]

Hone, Thomas C., and Trent Hone. *Battle Line: The United States Navy, 1919–1939*. Annapolis, Md.: Naval Institute Press, 2006.

Hooper, Edwin B., Dean C. Allard, and Oscar P. Fitzgerald. *The United States Navy and the Vietnam Conflict, vol. I, The Setting of the Stage to 1959*. Washington, D.C.: Naval History Division, 1976.

Hooper, Edwin B., and Oscar P. Fitzgerald. *The United States Navy and the Vietnam Conflict, vol. II, From Military Assistance to Combat 1959–1965*. Washington, D.C.: Naval Historical Center, 1986.

Johnston, Stanley. *Queen of the Flat-Tops: The U.S.S. Lexington and the Coral Sea Battle*. New York: E.P. Dutton, 1942.

King, Fleet Adm. Ernest J., USN, and Comdr. Walter Muir Whitehill, USNR. *Fleet Admiral King*. New York: W.W. Norton, 1952.

Lawson, Capt. Ted W., USA. *Thirty Seconds Over Tokyo*. New York: Random House, 1943.

Lord, Walter. *Incredible Victory*. New York: Harper & Row, 1967. [Account of the Battle of Midway.]

Lundstrom, John B. *Black Shoe Admiral: Frank Jack Fletcher at Coral Sea, Midway, and Guadalcanal*. Annapolis, Md.: Naval Institute Press, 2006.

———. *The First Team: Pacific Naval Air Combat from Pearl Harbor to Midway*. Annapolis, Md.: Naval Institute Press, 1984.

———. *The First Team and the Guadalcanal Campaign: Naval Fighter Combat from August to November 1942*. Annapolis, Md.: Naval Institute Press, 1994.

MacDonald, Chief Journalist Scott, USN. *Evolution of Aircraft Carriers*. Washington, D.C.: Government Printing Office, 1964. [Combined reprint of 14 basic but useful articles that originally appeared in the official magazine *Naval Aviation News* during 1962 and 1963.]

Miller, Vice Adm. Gerald E., USN (Ret). *Nuclear Weapons and Aircraft Carriers: How the Bomb Saved Naval Aviation*. Washington, D.C.: Smithsonian Institution Press, 2001.

Millis, Walter. *The Forrestal Diaries*. New York: Viking Press, 1951.

Mitchell, Brig. Gen. William, USA. *Winged Defense*. New York: G.P. Putnam's Sons, 1925.

Moore, Comdr. John, USN (Ret). *The Wrong Stuff: Flying on the Edge of Disaster*. North Branch, Minn.: Specialty Press, 1997.

Nichols, Comdr. John B., and Barrett Tillman. *On Yankee Station: The Naval Air War over Vietnam*. Annapolis, Md.: Naval Institute Press, 1987.

Nordeen, Lon O. *Air Warfare in the Missile Age*. Washington, D.C.: Smithsonian Institution Press, 2002 (2nd ed.).

Prados, John. *Combined Fleet Decoded: The Secret History of American Intelligence and the Japanese Navy in World War II*. New York: Random House, 1995.

———. *The Sky Would Fall. Operation Vulture: The Secret U.S. Bombing Mission to Vietnam, 1954*. New York: Dial Press, 1983.

Reynolds, Dr. Clark G *The Fast Carriers: The Forging of an Air Navy*. New York: McGraw-Hill, 1968.

Ryan, Capt. Paul B., USN (Ret). *The Iranian Rescue Mission: Why It Failed*. Annapolis, Md.: Naval Institute Press, 1985.

Sharp, Adm. Ulysses S. Grant, USN (Ret). *Strategy For Defeat: Vietnam in Retrospect*. San Rafael, Calif.: Presidio Press, 1978.

Sherman, Adm. Frederick C., USN. *Combat Command*. New York: E.P. Dutton, 1950. [History of carrier operations in the Pacific War by an outstanding carrier commander.]

Sherrod, Robert. *History of Marine Corps Aviation in World War II*. Washington, D.C.: Combat Forces Press, 1952.

Stafford, Comdr. Edward P., USN (Ret). *The Big E*. New York: Random House, 1962. [Biography of the most famous U.S. aircraft carrier.]

Taylor, Theodore. *The Magnificent Mitscher*. New York: W.W. Norton, 1954. [Biography of the senior U.S. fast carrier task force commander in World War II.]

Tillman, Barrett. *Clash of the Carriers: The True Story of the Marianas Turkey Shoot of World War II*. New York: Penguin, 2005.

Turnbull, Capt. Archibald D., USNR, and Lt. Comdr. Clifford L. Lord, USNR. *History of United States Naval Aviation*. New Haven, Conn.: Yale University Press, 1949.

Van Deurs, Rear Adm. George, USN (Ret). *Wings for the Fleet*. Annapolis, Md.: U.S. Naval Institute, 1966.

Wheeler, Gerald E. *Prelude to Pearl Harbor: The United States Navy and the Far East, 1921–1931*. Columbia, Mo.: University of Missouri Press, 1963.

Wildenberg, Thomas. *All the Factors of Victory: Adm. Joseph Mason Reeves and the Origins of Carrier Air Power*. Dulles, Va.: Brassey's, 2003.

———. *Destined for Glory: Dive Bombing, Midway, and the Evolution of Carrier Airpower*. Annapolis, Md.: Naval Institute Press, 1998.

———. *Gray Steel and Black Oil: Fast Tankers and Replenishment at Sea in the U.S. Navy, 1912–1992*. Annapolis, Md.: Naval Institute Press, 1996.

Wilson, Comdr. Eugene E., USN. *Slipstream: The Autobiography of an Air Craftsman*. New York: McGraw-Hill, 1950. [Autobiography of the chief of staff of the first U.S. carrier division.]

Wohlstetter, Roberta. *Pearl Harbor: Warning and Decision*. Stanford, Calif.: Stanford University Press, 1962.

Woodward, C. Vann. *The Battle for Leyte Gulf*. New York: Macmillan, 1947.

Wordell, Lt. M. T., USN, and Lt. E. N. Seiler, USN. *"Wildcats" Over Casablanca: U.S. Navy Fighters in Operation Torch*. Dulles, Va.: Potomac Books, 2006. [Reprint of 1943 classic.]

Wyden, Peter. *Bay of Pigs: The Untold Story*. New York: Simon and Schuster, 1979.

Y'Blood, William T. *Hunter-Killer: U.S. Escort Carriers in the Battle of the Atlantic*. Annapolis, Md.: Naval Institute Press, 1983.

———. *The Little Giants: U.S. Escort Carriers Against Japan*. Annapolis, Md.: Naval Institute Press, 1987.

General Carrier Aviation

De Belot, Rear Adm. Raymond, FN. *The Struggle for the Mediterranean 1939–1945*. Princeton, N.J.: Princeton University Press, 1951.

Flower, Stephen. *A Hell of a Bomb: How the Bombs of Barnes Wallis helped win the Second World War*. Stroud, Gloucester: Tempus, 2002.

Guerlac, Henry E. *Radar in World War II*. Woodbury, N.Y.: American Institute of Physics, 1987.

Hagedorn, Dan. *Latin American Air Wars and Aircraft 1912–1969*. Osceola, Wisc.: Motorbooks, 2006.

Hezlet, Vice-Adm. Arthur, RN. *Aircraft and Sea Power*. New York: Stein and Day, 1970.

———. *Electronics and Sea Power*. New York: Stein & Day, 1973.

Hirschfield, Thomas J., and Peter Hore. *Maritime Aviation: Light and Medium Aircraft Carriers into the Twenty First Century*. Hull: University of Hull Press, 1999.

Hone, Thomas C., Norman Friedman, and Mark D. Mandeles. *American & British Aircraft Carrier Development 1919–1941*. Annapolis, Md.: Naval Institute Press, 1999.

Howse, Derek. *Radar at Sea: The Royal Navy in World War 2*. London: Macmillan, 1993.

Layman, R.D., and Stephen McLaughlin. *The Hybrid Warship: The Amalgamation of Big Guns and Aircraft*. London: Conway Maritime Press, 1991.

Macintyre, Capt. Donald, RN. *Wings of Neptune*. New York, W.W. Norton, 1964.

Muir, Malcolm, Jr. *Black Shoes and Blue Water: Surface Warfare in the United States Navy, 1945–1975*. Washington, D.C.: Naval Historical Center, 1996.

Ripley, Tim. *Air War Bosnia: UN and NATO Airpower*. Shrewsbury: Airlife, 1996.

Aircraft Carrier Characteristics

Breyer, Siegfried. *The German Aircraft Carrier Graf Zeppelin*. West Chester, Pa.: Schiffer, 1989.

Brown, David K. *Nelson to Vanguard: Warship Design and Development 1923–1945*. London: Chatham, 2000.

Chesneau, Roger. *Aircraft Carriers of the World, 1914 to the Present: An Illustrated Encyclopedia*. Annapolis, Md.: Naval Institute Press, 1984.

Cressman, Robert J. *USS RANGER: The Navy's First Flattop from Keel to Mast, 1934–46*. Washington, D.C.: Brassey's, 2003.

Fahey, James C. *The Ships and Aircraft of the U.S. Fleet*. Published by the author: 1st Ed., 1939 through 7th Ed., 1958; published by the U.S. Naval Institute, 8th Ed., 1965.

Faltum, Andrew. *The Essex Aircraft Carriers*. Baltimore, Md.: Nautical & Aviation, 1996.

———. *The Independence Light Aircraft Carriers*. Charleston, S.C. Nautical & Aviation, 2002.

Friedman, Norman. *British Carrier Aviation: The Evolution of the Ships and their Aircraft*. Annapolis, Md.: Naval Institute Press, 1988.

———. *U.S. Aircraft Carriers: An Illustrated Design History*. Annapolis, Md.: Naval Institute Press, 1983.

Fukui, Constructor Lt. Comdr. Shizuo, IJN. *Japanese Naval Vessels at the End of War*. Report of the Second Demobilization Bureau, Tokyo, April 25, 1947; published as *The Japanese Navy at the End of War*, Old Greenwich, Conn.: We [n.d.]; reprinted by Naval Institute Press, 1991.

Hobbs, Comdr. David, RN. *Aircraft Carriers of the Royal and Commonwealth Navies*. London: Greenhill Books, 1996.

Monsarrat, John. *Angel on the Yardarm: The Beginnings of Fleet Radar Defense and the Kamikaze Threat*. Newport, R.I.: Naval War College Press, 1985.

Polmar, Norman. *The Ships and Aircraft of the U.S. Fleet*. Annapolis, Md.: Naval Institute Press, 11th Ed., 1975 through 18th Ed., 2005.

Raven, Alan. *Essex-Class Carriers*. Annapolis, Md.: Naval Institute Press, 1988.

Silverstone, Paul H. *U.S. Warships of World War II*. London: Ian Allan, 1965.

Spassky, I. D. (ed.). *Istoriya Otechestvennogo Sudostroeniya* [The History of Indigenous Shipbuilding], vol. V *1946–1991*. St. Petersburg: Sudostroenie, 1996.

Stern, Robert C. *The Lexington Class Carriers*. Annapolis, Md.: Naval Institute Press, 1993.

Carrier Aircraft and Units

Andrews. C.F., and E.B. Morgan. *Supermarine Aircraft since 1914*. London: Putnam, 1987.

Barnes, C.H. *Shorts Aircraft since 1900*. London: Putnam, 1989.

Bowers, Peter M. *Boeing Aircraft since 1916*. Annapolis, Md.: Naval Institute Press, 1989.

———. *Curtiss Aircraft 1907–1947*. Annapolis, Md.: Naval Institute Press, 1979

Brown, Charles H. *Dark Sky, Black Sea: Aircraft Carrier Night and All-Weather Operations*. Annapolis, Md.: Naval Institute Press, 1999.

Brown, Eric M. *Duels in the Sky: World War II Naval Aircraft in Combat*. Annapolis, Md.: Naval Institute Press, 1988.

———. *Wings of the Navy: Flying Allied Carrier Aircraft of World War II*. London: Jane's, 1980.

Davies, Peter E., and Anthony M. Thornborough. *The Harrier Story*. Annapolis, Md.: Naval Institute Press, 1996.

Dorr, Robert F. *F-86 Sabre: History of the Sabre and FJ Fury*. Osceola, Wisc.: Motorbooks, 1993.

Fails, William R. *Marines and Helicopters, 1962–1973*. Washington, D.C.: Headquarters, U.S. Marine Corps, 1978.

Francillon, René J. *Douglas A-3 Skywarrior*. Arlington, Texas: Aerofax, 1987.

———. *Grumman Aircraft since 1929*. London: Putnam, 1989.

———. *Japanese Aircraft of the Pacific War*. London: Putnam, 1970.

———. *McDonnell Douglas Aircraft since 1920*. London: Putnam, 1979.

Green, William. *The World Guide to Combat Planes*, 2 vol. Garden City, N.Y.: Doubleday, 1967.

Hata, Ikuhiko, and Yasuho Izawa. *Japanese Naval Aces and Fighter Units in World War II*. Annapolis, Md.: Naval Institute Press, 1989.

Heinemann, Edward H., and Capt. Rosario Rausa, USNR (Ret). *Ed Heinemann: Combat Aircraft Designer*. Annapolis, Md.: Naval Institute Press, 1980.

Hobbs, Lt. Comdr. David, RN. *Aircraft of the Royal Navy since 1945*. Liskeard, Cornwall: Maritime Books [nd].

Horikoshi, Jiro. *Eagles of Mitsubishi: The Story of the Zero Fighter*. Seattle, Wash.: University of Washington Press, 1981.

Jackson, A.J. *De Havilland Aircraft since 1909*. London: Putnam, 1987.

King, H.F. *Sopwith Aircraft 1912–1920*. London: Putnam, 1980.

Lord Kilbracken. *Bring Back My Stringbag: Swordfish Pilot at War 1940–1945*. London: Peter Davies, 1979.

Mason, Francis K. *Harrier*. London: Patrick Stephens, 1981.

———. *Hawker Aircraft since 1920*. London: Putnam, 1991.

———. *The Hawker Hurricane*. Garden City, N.Y.: Doubleday, 1962.

Mersky, Peter B. *F-8 Crusader Units of the Vietnam War*. London: Osprey, 1998.

———. *RF-8 Crusader Units Over Cuba and Vietnam*. Oxford: Osprey, 1999.

———. *U.S. Marine Corps Aviation: 1921 to the Present*. Annapolis, Md.: Nautical & Aviation, 1983.

———. *US Navy and Marine Corps A-4 Skyhawk Units of the Vietnam War*. Oxford: Osprey, 2007.

———. *US Navy A-7 Corsair II Units of the Vietnam War*. Oxford: Osprey, 2004.

Mikesh, Robert C., and Shorzoe Abe. *Japanese Aircraft 1910-1941*. Annapolis, Md.: Naval Institute Press, 1990.

Nordeen, Lon O. *Harrier II: Validating V/STOL*. Annapolis, Md.: Naval Institute Press, 2006.

O'Rourke, G G *Night Fighters over Korea*. Annapolis, Md.: Naval Institute Press, 1998.

Polmar, Norman, and Floyd D. Kennedy. *Military Helicopters of the World: Military Rotary-Wing Aircraft Since 1917*. Annapolis, Md.: Naval Institute Press, 1981.

Powell, Robert R. *RA-5C Vigilante Units in Combat*. Oxford: Osprey, 2004.

Rausa, Capt. Rosario, USNR (Ret). *Skyraider: The Douglas A-1 "Flying Dump Truck."* Baltimore, Md.: Nautical & Aviation, 1982.

Rawlins, Lt. Col. Eugene W., USMC. *Marines and Helicopters 1946–1962*. Washington, D.C.: Headquarters, U.S. Marine Corps, 1976.

Smith, Peter C. *Aichi D3A1/2 Val*. Wilshire: Crowood Press, 1999.

———. *Skua! The Royal Navy's Dive-Bomber*. Barnsely, South Yorkshire: Pen & Sword, 2006.

Styling, Mark. *Corsair Aces of World War 2*. London: Osprey, 1995.

Swanborough, Gordon, and Peter M. Bowers. *United States Naval Aircraft since 1911*. Annapolis, Md.: Naval Institute Press, 1976.

Taylor, H.A. *Fairey Aircraft since 1915*. London: Putnam, 1988.

Taylor, John W.R. *Jane's All the World's Aircraft*. London: Jane's (various editions).

Thetford, Owen. *British Naval Aircraft since 1912*. London: Putnam, 1982.

Tillman, Barrett. *Avenger at War*. Annapolis, Md.: Naval Institute Press, 1990

———. *Corsair: The F4U in World War II and Korea*. Annapolis, Md.: Naval Institute Press, 1979.

———. *The Dauntless Dive Bomber of World War Two*. Annapolis, Md.: Naval Institute Press, 1976.

———. *Hellcat: The F6F in World War II*. Annapolis, Md.: Naval Institute Press, 1979.

———. *Hellcat Aces of World War 2*. London: Osprey, 1996.

———. *SBD Dauntless Units of World War II*. London: Osprey, 1998.

———. *TBD Devastator Units of the US Navy*. Oxford: Osprey, 2000.

———. *TBF/TBM Avenger Units of World War II*. Oxford: Osprey, 1999.

———. *U.S. Navy Fighter Squadrons in World War II*. North Branch, Minn.: Speciality Press, 1997.

———. *Wildcat Aces of World War 2*. London: Osprey, 1995.

Ward, Comdr. 'Sharkey,' RN. *Sea Harrier Over the Falklands: A Maverick At War*. Annapolis, Md.: Naval Institute Press, 1992.

Wilson, Stewart. *BAe/McDonnell Douglas Harrier*. Bungendore [Australia]: Notebook Publications, 2000.

Papers and Documents

This book has made extensive use of the three essays and several enclosures comprising "Deputy Chief of Naval Operations (Air)—Carrier Warfare" in the monograph series United States Naval Administra-tion in World War II. These essays were written shortly after World War II under the direction of Lt. Comdr. H.M. Dater, Head, Aviation History Unit, Deputy Chief of Naval Operations (Air). The individual essay titles are "Remarks on the Development of the Fast Carrier Task Force," by Lt. Andrew R. Hilen, Jr.; "Functional Development of the Small Carrier," by Lt. William G. Land; and "Fighter Direction," by Lts. William C. Bryant and Keith Hermans. All of these officers were U.S. Naval Reserve.

Chapman, J. H. B. "The Development of the Aircraft Carrier," paper presented to the Royal Institution of Naval Architects, London: March 23, 1960.

Fozard, John W. *The British Aerospace Harrier: Case Study in Aircraft Design*. AAIA Professional Study Series, July 1978.

Government Accountability Office. *Navy Faces Challenges Constructing the Aircraft Carrier* Gerald R. Ford *within Budget*. GAO-07-866. Washington, D.C.: August 2007.

Government Accounting Office. *Navy Aircraft Carriers: Cost-Effectiveness of Conventionally and Nuclear-Powered Carriers*, NSIAD-98-1. Washington, D.C.: August 1, 1998,

Hadeler, Wilhelm. "The Aircraft Carrier in the German Navy 1934–1945." *American Society of Naval Engineers Journal* (August 1956), 431–440.

Kristensen, Hans M., William M. Arkin, and Joshua Handler. *Aircraft Carriers: The Limits Of Nuclear Power.* Washington, D.C.: Greenpeace, June 1994.

United Kingdom, House of Commons. *Strategic Defense Review.* London: HMSO, October 15, 1998. (Research Paper RP 98/91.)

———, Secretary of State for Defence. *The Falklands Campaign: The Lessons.* London: HMSO, December 1982.

———, Secretary of State for Defence. *Strategic Defense Review.* London: HMSO, July 1998.

U.S. Army Forces Far East, Military History Section, *Japanese Monographs* [n.d.]. [Prepared by Japanese officers, these numerous monographs address all aspects of Japanese preparations for and operations in World War II.]

U.S. Joint Task Force One. *Operation Crossroads.* New York: William E. Wise, 1946.

U.S. Marine Corps, History and Museums Division. *Marine Corps Aviation: The Early Years 1912–1940.* Washington, D.C.: 1977.

U.S. Navy. Air Task Organization in the Pacific Ocean Areas: Ship-Based Aircraft in *United States Naval Administration in World War II.* Washington, D.C.: Deputy Chief of Naval Operations (Air) [n.d.].

———. *Allowances and Location of Navy Aircraft.* Washington, D.C.: Deputy Chief of Naval Operations (Air), various editions.

———. *Dictionary of American Naval Fighting Ships*, 8 vol. Washington, D.C.: Naval Historical Center, 1959 through 1981.

———. *Fleet Air Wings and Fleet Airship Wings: Historical Data World War II.* Washington, D.C.: Chief of Naval Operations, May 1, 1951.

———. *Fuehrer Con-ferences on Matters Dealing with the German Navy*, 9 vols. Washington, D.C.: Office of Naval Intelligence, 1947.

———. *The Japanese Story of the Battle of Midway.* Washington, D.C.: Office of Naval Intelligence, June 1947. [Translations of key Japanese documents.]

———. *Lessons of the Falklands: Summary Report.* Washington, D.C.: February 1983.

———. *Ships' Data U.S. Naval Vessels*, vol. I, Washington, D.C.: Bureau of Ships, April 15, 1945.

———. *U.S. Naval Administration in World War II: Air Task Organization in the Pacific Ocean Areas, Ship-Based Aircraft.* Washington, D.C.: Deputy Chief of Naval Operations (Air), [n.d.].

———. *U.S. Naval Aviation in the Pacific, A Critical Review.* Washington, D.C.: Office of the Chief of Naval Operations, 1947.

———. *U.S. Naval Chronology, World War II.* Washington, D.C.: Naval History Division, 1955.

U.S. Strategic Bombing Survey (Pacific). *Air Campaigns of the Pacific War.* Washington, D.C.: Government Printing Office, July 1947.

———. *The Campaigns of the Pacific War.* Washington, D.C.: Government Printing Office, 1946.

———. *Interrogations of Japanese Officials*, 2 vols. Washington, D.C.: Government Printing Office, 1946.

———. *The Japanese Aircraft Industry.* Washington, D.C.: Government Printing Office, May 1947.

———. *Japan's Struggle to End the War.* Washington, D.C.: Government Printing Office, July 1, 1946.

———. *Summary Report (Pacific War).* Washington, D.C.: Government Printing Office, July 1, 1946.

Articles

A wealth of information on carrier aviation has been found regularly in the pages of several English-language periodicals:

> *Aeroplane* (U.K.)
> *Air Enthusiast* (U.K.)
> *Air International* (U.K.)
> *Flight Deck* (U.K.)
> *Foundation* [Naval Aviation Museum](U.S.)
> *The Hook* (U.S.)
> *International Air Power Review* (U.K.)
> *American Aviation Historical Society Journal* (U.S.)
> *Naval Aviation News* (U.S.)
> *Naval Forces* (U.K.)
> *The O.N.I. Weekly* [Office of Naval Intelligence] (U.S.)
> *U.S. Naval Institute Proceedings* (U.S.)
> *World Air Power Journal* (U.K.)

Non-English language periodicals that were consulted include:

> *Gangut* (Russia)
> *Marine Rundschau* (Germany)
> *Morsky Sbornik* (Russia)
> *Revue Maritime* (France)
> *Ships of the World* (Japan)
> Sudostroeniye (Russia)

The reader is referred to the end notes of Volumes I and II for specific article citations. Several excellent essays on carrier-related subjects are found in the annual volume *Warship* (Conway Maritime Press, published since 1977), edited by the late Anthony Preston and by his successor, John Jordan.

The Japanese helicopter-carrying destroyer *Huyga*, shortly after being launched in August 2007. With the size and configuration of a small aircraft carrier, the *Huyga* must be considered a major step in Japanese carrier development. The U.S. Navy considered—and rejected—a similar albeit smaller concept based on the *Spruance*-class destroyers. Note the *Huyga*'s large starboard island structure and the "faces" of the Aegis phased-array radar antennas on the after structure. (*Ships of the World*)

INDEX

Squadrons (air)

Abbreviations

AE	ammunition ship	CVE	escort aircraft carrier
AG	miscellaneous auxiliary	CVH	VSTOL carrier
AGB	icebreaker*	CVHG	VSTOL carrier-missile cruiser
AGER	environmental research ship**	CVL	small (light) aircraft carrier
AGI	intelligence collection ship	CVM	maintenance aircraft carrier
AGMR	communications relay ship	CVS	ASW aircraft carrier
AGTR	technical research ship**	CVV	VSTOL carrier
AH	hospital ship	DD	destroyer
AO	oiler	DDG	guided missile dsetroyer
AOE	replenishment ship	DE	destroyer escort/frigate
AR	repair ship	DLG	guided missile frigate*
ARVH	helicopter repair ship	DMS	high-speed minesweeper (converted destroyer)
AV	seaplane tender	FF	frigate
AVT	training carrier	LCC	amphibious command ship
BB	battleship	LHA	amphibious assault ship (helicopter carrier)
CA	heavy cruiser	LHD	amphibious assault ship (helicopter carrier)
CB	battle cruiser	LPD	amphibious transport dock
CC	national command ship	LPH	amphibious assault ship (helicopter carrier)
CG	guided missile cruiser*	LSD	dock landing ship
CL	light cruiser	LST	tank landing ship
CLG	guided missile light cruiser	MS	minesweeper
CNO	Chief of Naval Operations	SCS	sea control ship
CV	aircraft carrier*	SS	attack submarine*
CVA	(1) heavy aircraft carrier	TS	training ship
	(2) attack aircraft carrier*	VSS	VSTOL support ship
CVB	large aircraft carrier	WPG	Coast Guard gunboat

* The suffix letter N indicates nuclear propulsion.
** Spy ship.

THE AUTHORS

NORMAN POLMAR is an analyst, author, and historian in the naval, aviation, and intelligence fields. He graduated from the American University in Washington, D.C. in 1965.

Mr. Polmar served as a reporter, columnist, and editor for various newspapers and magazines specializing in naval issues. From 1967 to 1970, he was with the Northrop Corporation, involved in several deep-ocean research and engineering projects, including the SEALAB seafloor habitation program and submarine escape and rescue. Also, from 1967 to 1977, he was editor of the U.S. section and several others of the annual *Jane's Fighting Ships.* The first American ever to hold an editorship with that publication, he was totally responsible for almost one-third of the volume in that period.

From 1970 to 1980, Mr. Polmar was an analyst and then executive with research firms specializing in naval, aviation, and intelligence issues. Since 1980 Mr. Polmar has been a consultant to several senior officials in the Navy and Department of Defense and has directed studies for U.S. and foreign shipbuilding and aerospace firms. From 1982 to 1986 he was a member of the Secretary of the Navy's Research Advisory Committee (NRAC) and has again been a member of NRAC since 2002. He has been named to the Secretary of the Navy's history advisory subcommittee. He was also a consultant to the Director of the Los Alamos National Laboratory and a panel member of the Naval Studies Board of the National Academy of Sciences.

Mr. Polmar has served as a consultant to three U.S. Senators and one member of the House of Representatives, and as a consultant or advisor to three Secretaries of the Navy and two Chiefs of Naval Operations. In 1997–1998 he held the Ramsey Chair of Naval Aviation History at the National Air and Space Museum in Washington, D.C., at which time he began preparing this second edition of *Aircraft Carriers.*

He has written more than 40 books and numerous articles on naval, aviation, and intelligence subjects. He is the author of the reference books *Ships and Aircraft of the U.S. Fleet* and *Guide to the Soviet Navy,* which are published at three-year intervals by the U.S. Naval Institute. These books are recognized internationally as the leading references in their fields.

Mr. Polmar is a columnist for the Naval Institute *Proceedings,* the Navy's professional journal. His articles have been published in numerous newspapers and magazines, among them *The New York Times, The Washington Post, Los Angeles Times, Miami Herald,* and *Saturday Evening Post.*

GENERAL MINORU GENDA, Japanese Air Self-Defense Force, graduated from the Imperial Naval Academy in 1924. He served in two cruisers before being commissioned an ensign in December 1925. After serving a year in the battleship *Ise,* Genda attended the Gunnery School and the Torpedo and Mine School, both at Yokosuka. In July 1927 he returned to the cruiser *Izumo* as assistant navigation officer.

He underwent pilot training in 1929, after which he reported to the aircraft carrier *Akagi* as a fighter pilot. In December 1931 he returned to shore duty as a flight instructor, at which time he organized and led a Navy aerial acrobatic team that was popularly called "Genda's Circus." Genda entered the Imperial Naval Staff College in November 1935 and graduated in July 1937. After brief duty as an air staff officer and as a flight instructor, from December 1938 until late 1940, he was assistant naval attaché in London. In November 1940, he became air operations officer for the First Carrier Division. While in this position he was one of two officers charged with developing the attack plan for the Pearl Harbor strike.

In April 1941, he also became air operations officer for the First Air Fleet, the Japanese carrier striking force (flagship *Akagi*). He saw action in the battles of Pearl Harbor, Indian Ocean, Midway, and the Solomons (flagship *Shokaku* in the last). Late in 1942 he became air operations officer for the 11th Air Fleet based at Rabaul, New Britain. In December 1942, Genda assumed staff duties with the Naval General Staff and Imperial Headquarters in Tokyo. Two years later—with the rank of captain—he took command of the 343rd Navy Air Corps charged with the air defense of the Japanese home islands.

After the war Genda was interrogated by U.S. officers who described him as "an aviator of broad experience, intelligent and alert. He was of the younger school of officers, inclined to criticize freely and perhaps associated with the earlier radical groups." Genda was demobilized in November 1945. He was recalled to active duty in July of 1954 as a Major General in the Japanese Air Self-Defense Force and appointed Deputy Chief of Staff for Material in that service. Late in 1955 he took command of the First Fighter Wing, flying F 86 Sabre aircraft. In July 1957 he became head of the Air Defense Command, and in July 1959 he became head of the Air Self-Defense Force with the rank of General. He retired from active duty in April of 1962 and was selected as a member of Japan's House of Councilors, serving until 1986.

He died in 1989.

CAPTAIN ERIC M. BROWN, Royal Navy, graduated from Edinburgh University in 1939 and was teaching in Germany when war broke out that fall. After being interrogated by the state police for three days he was released, made his way back to Britain, and joined the Royal Navy. After flight instruction he was posted to the first British shipboard squadron to fly the F4F Martlet fighter. The squadron—No. 802—was assigned to HMS *Audacity*, the first British escort carrier, in September 1941. Brown flew from the carrier until she was sunk by a German U-boat on the night of December 21–22, 1941.

From 1942 until the end of 1943 he was engaged in training, experimental, and acceptance flights with almost all of the 39 escort carriers that the United States transferred to Britain during the war plus a few other carriers. Late in 1943, Brown began experimental flight work. During this period he made the first carrier landing with a twin–engine Mosquito and flew a variety of aircraft including the German Fw 190, the U.S. P-51 Mustang and Sikorsky R-4B helicopter, multiengine bombers, and the jet-propelled Meteor and Vampire (making the first jet carrier landings and takeoffs in the last). Immediately after the war Brown traveled to Germany to recover and test enemy aircraft. During June 1945 he flew 30 different types of German aircraft.

His postwar experimental work included testing the concept of landing a wheelless aircraft on a flexible "carpet," including landings on the rubber deck installed in the carrier *Warrior*. From 1951 to 1953 he served at the U.S. Naval Air Test Center as a project officer for jet fighters. At that time he also worked on the development of the angled flight deck and U.S. tests of the British-developed steam catapult. Upon his return to Britain he served briefly in the frigate Rocket, then in several aircraft squadrons, and commanded No. 804 Squadron flying the Seahawk jet fighter-bomber.

From 1958 to 1960 he helped to activate the German naval air arm. Captain Brown then served three years as Deputy Director of the Naval Air Division in Admiralty before returning to Germany as Naval Attaché in Bonn. In October 1967, he became commanding officer of HMS Fulmar, the Royal Naval Air Station at Lossiemouth, Scotland.

Captain Brown has made more carrier landings than anyone else in history and has possibly flown more aircraft types than any other pilot.

PROFESSOR ROBERT M. LANGDON received his B.A. in history from Hamilton College in 1940 and his M.A. in history from the University of North Carolina in 1942. Between 1943 and 1947 he taught history at Cornell and Stanford Universities.

He was an instructor in the Department of English, History, and Government at the U.S. Naval Academy from 1947 until his death in a commercial air disaster in June 1967. In addition to his faculty duties at the Naval Academy, from 1951 to 1957, Professor Langdon was an associate editor of the U.S. Naval Institute *Proceedings;* from 1954 to 1967, he also prepared the annual column "Notable Naval Books" in the *Proceedings;* and from 1961 to 1967 he wrote the monthly column "Professional Reading" for the journal. He was also a member of the Secretary of the Navy's Naval Reading Program Committee and director of the Naval Institute's Distinguished Visitor Program.

COMMANDER PETER B. MERSKY, U.S. Naval Reserve, graduated from the Rhode Island School of design in 1967 with a degree in fine arts. He was commissioned through the Navy's Aviation Officer Candidate School in May 1968 and served for 23 years on active duty and in the reserves, mostly in intelligence assignments.

He worked as a visual information specialist from 1971 to 1984 in the Central Intelligence Agency prior to joining the staff of the Naval Safety Center in Norfolk, Virginia. He was assistant editor and then editor of *Approach,* the Navy and Marine Corps aviation safety magazine from 1984 to 2000. Mr. Mersky has written several books and numerous magazine articles on aviation subjects. The former include *U.S. Marine Corps Aviation: 1921 to the Present, The Grim Reapers: Fighting Squadron Ten in World War II, F-8 Crusaders Units in Vietnam, 1964–1975,* and *The Naval Air War in Vietnam* (with Norman Polmar). He is also book review editor for *Naval Aviation News,* the official journal of U.S. naval aviation.

U.S. *Midway* **(CVB 41) 1945   968 feet**

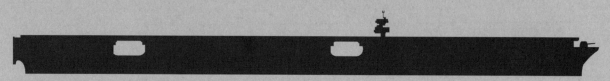

U.S. *United States* **(CVA 58) 1949   1,090 feet**

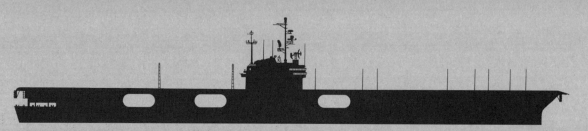

U.S. *Forrestal* **(CVA 59) 1955   1,039 feet**

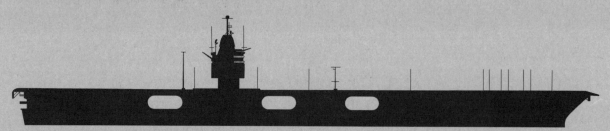

U.S. *Enterprise* **(CVAN 65) 1961   1,123 feet**

Soviet Union *Moskva* **1967   620¼ feet**

U.S. *Nimitz* **(CVAN 68) 1975   1,092 feet**